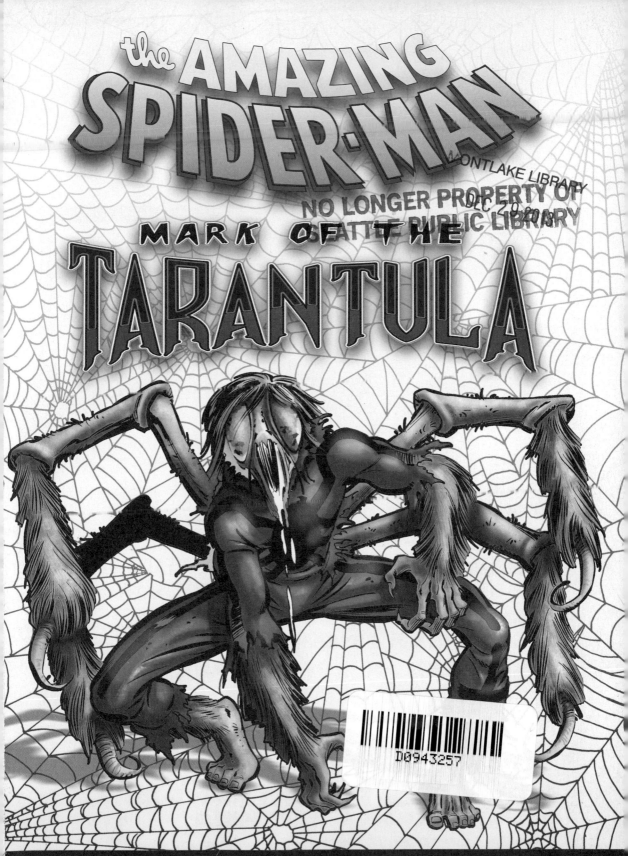

the AMAZING SPIDER-MAN

MARK OF THE TARANTULA

D0943257

SPIDER-MAN: MARK OF THE TARANTULA. Contains material originally published in magazine form as AMAZING SPIDER-MAN (1963) #231-237 and ANNUAL #16. First printing 2013. ISBN# 978-0-7851-8510-9. Published by MARVEL WORLDWIDE, INC., a subsidiary of MARVEL ENTERTAINMENT, LLC. OFFICE OF PUBLICATION: 135 West 50th Street, New York, NY 10020. Copyright © 1982, 1983 and 2013 Marvel Characters, Inc. All rights reserved. All characters featured in this issue and the distinctive names and likenesses thereof, and all related indicia are trademarks of Marvel Characters, Inc. No similarity between any of the names, characters, persons, and/or institutions in this magazine with those of any living or dead person or institution is intended, and any such similarity which may exist is purely coincidental. **Printed in the U.S.A.** ALAN FINE, EVP - Office of the President, Marvel Worldwide, Inc. and EVP & CMO Marvel Characters B.V.; DAN BUCKLEY, Publisher & President - Print, Animation & Digital Divisions; JOE QUESADA, Chief Creative Officer; TOM BREVOORT, SVP of Publishing; DAVID BOGART, SVP of Operations & Procurement, Publishing; C.B. CEBULSKI, SVP of Creator & Content Development; DAVID GABRIEL, SVP of Print & Digital Publishing Sales; JIM O'KEEFE, VP of Operations & Logistics; DAN CARR, Executive Director of Publishing Technology; SUSAN CRESPI, Editorial Operations Manager; ALEX MORALES, Publishing Operations Manager; STAN LEE, Chairman Emeritus. For information regarding advertising in Marvel Comics or on Marvel.com, please contact Niza Disla, Director of Marvel Partnerships, at ndisla@marvel.com. For Marvel subscription inquiries, please call 800-217-9158. **Manufactured between 10/4/2013 and 11/11/2013** by R.R. DONNELLEY, INC., SALEM, VA, USA.

10 9 8 7 6 5 4 3 2 1

MARK OF THE TARANTULA

WRITERS: ROGER STERN WITH BILL MANTLO

PENCILERS: JOHN ROMITA JR. & BOB HALL

INKERS: JIM MOONEY, DAN GREEN, FRANK GIACOIA & JOHN ROMITA SR.

COLORISTS: BOB SHAREN, GLYNIS WEIN & STAN GOLDBERG

LETTERERS: JOE ROSEN, DIANA ALBERS, RICK PARKER & JIM NOVAK

ASSISTANT EDITOR: LINDA GRANT

EDITOR: TOM DEFALCO

FRONT COVER ARTISTS: JOHN ROMITA JR., AL MILGROM & MATT MILLA

BACK COVER ARTISTS: JOHN ROMITA JR., FRANK GIACOIA & TOM SMITH

the AMAZING SPIDER-MAN

RESEARCH: DANA PERKINS
LAYOUT: JEPH YORK
COLOR RECONSTRUCTION: MICHAEL KELLEHER &
KELLUSTRATION
MASTERWORKS EDITOR: CORY SEDLEMEIER

COLLECTION EDITOR & DESIGN: NELSON RIBEIRO
ASSISTANT EDITOR: ALEX STARBUCK
EDITORS, SPECIAL PROJECTS:
MARK D. BEAZLEY & JENNIFER GRÜNWALD
SENIOR EDITOR, SPECIAL PROJECTS:
JEFF YOUNGQUIST
SVP OF PRINT & DIGITAL PUBLISHING SALES:
DAVID GABRIEL

EDITOR IN CHIEF: AXEL ALONSO
CHIEF CREATIVE OFFICER: JOE QUESADA
PUBLISHER: DAN BUCKLEY
EXECUTIVE PRODUCER: ALAN FINE

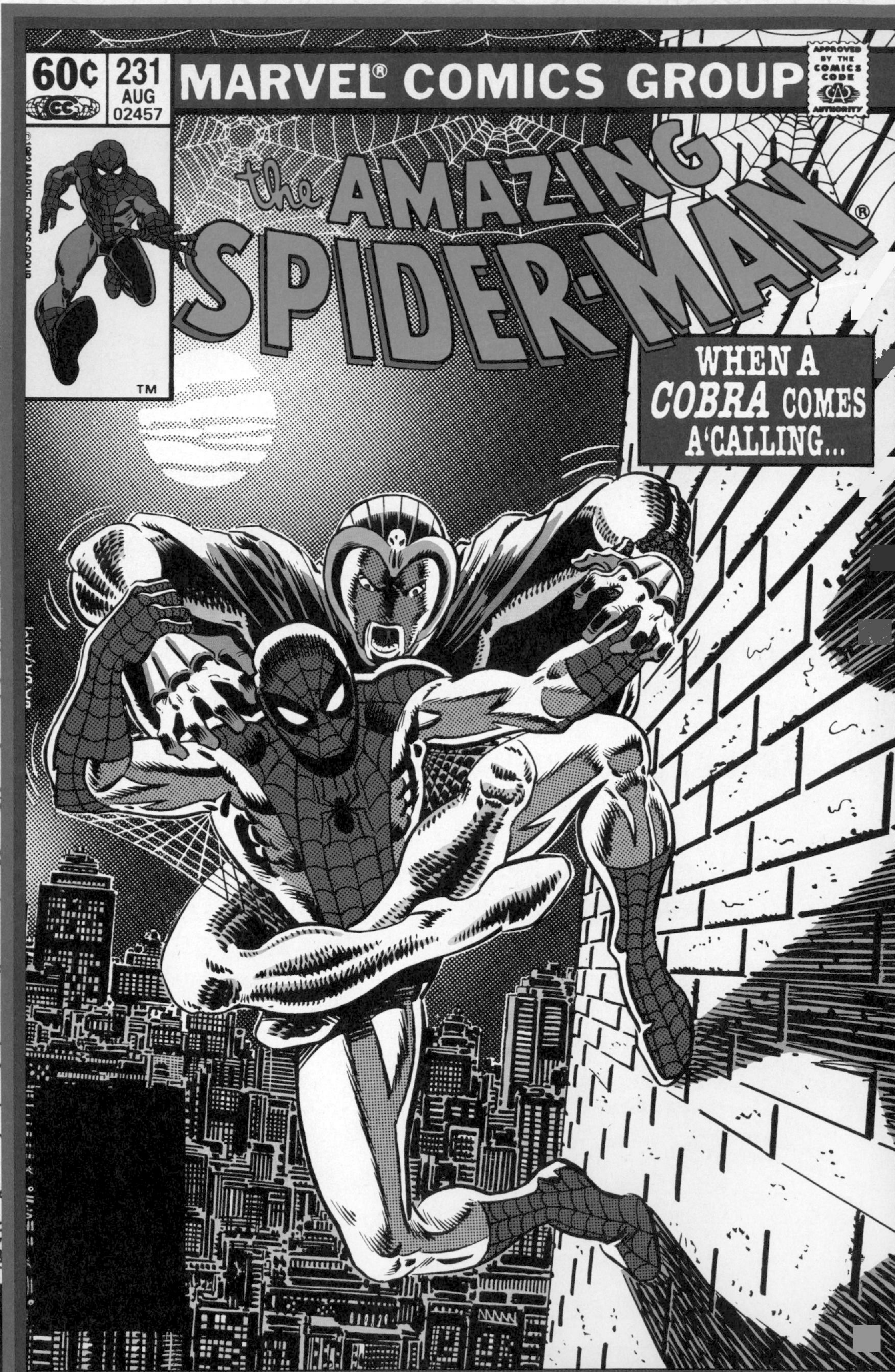
60¢
231
AUG
02457
MARVEL® COMICS GROUP
APPROVED BY THE COMICS CODE AUTHORITY
the AMAZING SPIDER-MAN®
TM
WHEN A COBRA COMES A'CALLING...

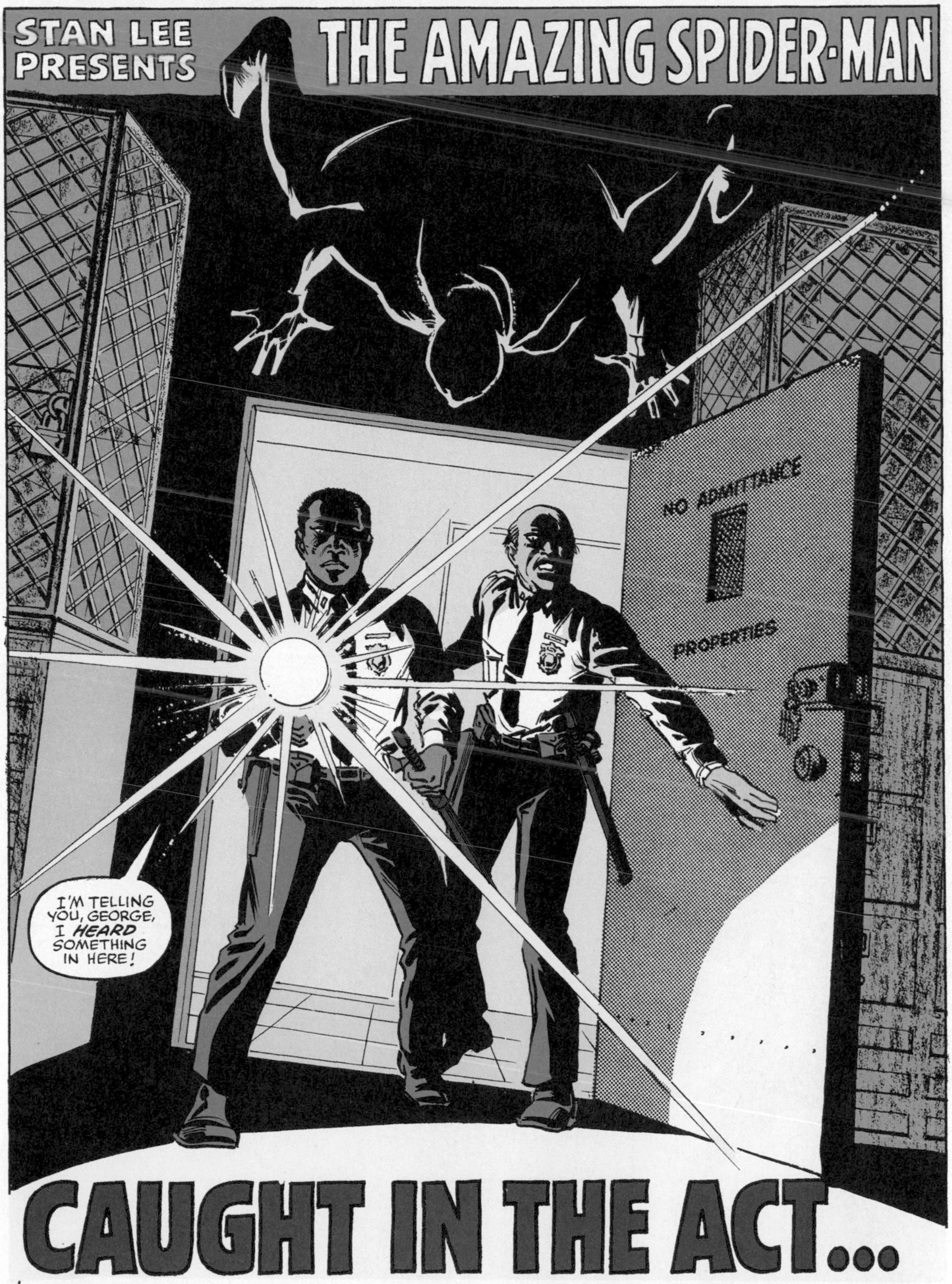
STAN LEE PRESENTS
THE AMAZING SPIDER-MAN
NO ADMITTANCE
PROPERTIES
I'M TELLING YOU, GEORGE, I *HEARD* SOMETHING IN HERE!
CAUGHT IN THE ACT...

by ROGER STERN SCRIPTER . JOHN ROMITA JR. & JIM MOONEY ARTISTS . JOE ROSEN LETTERER . BOB SHAREN COLORIST . TOM DeFALCO EDITOR . JIM SHOOTER PRECINCT CAPTAIN

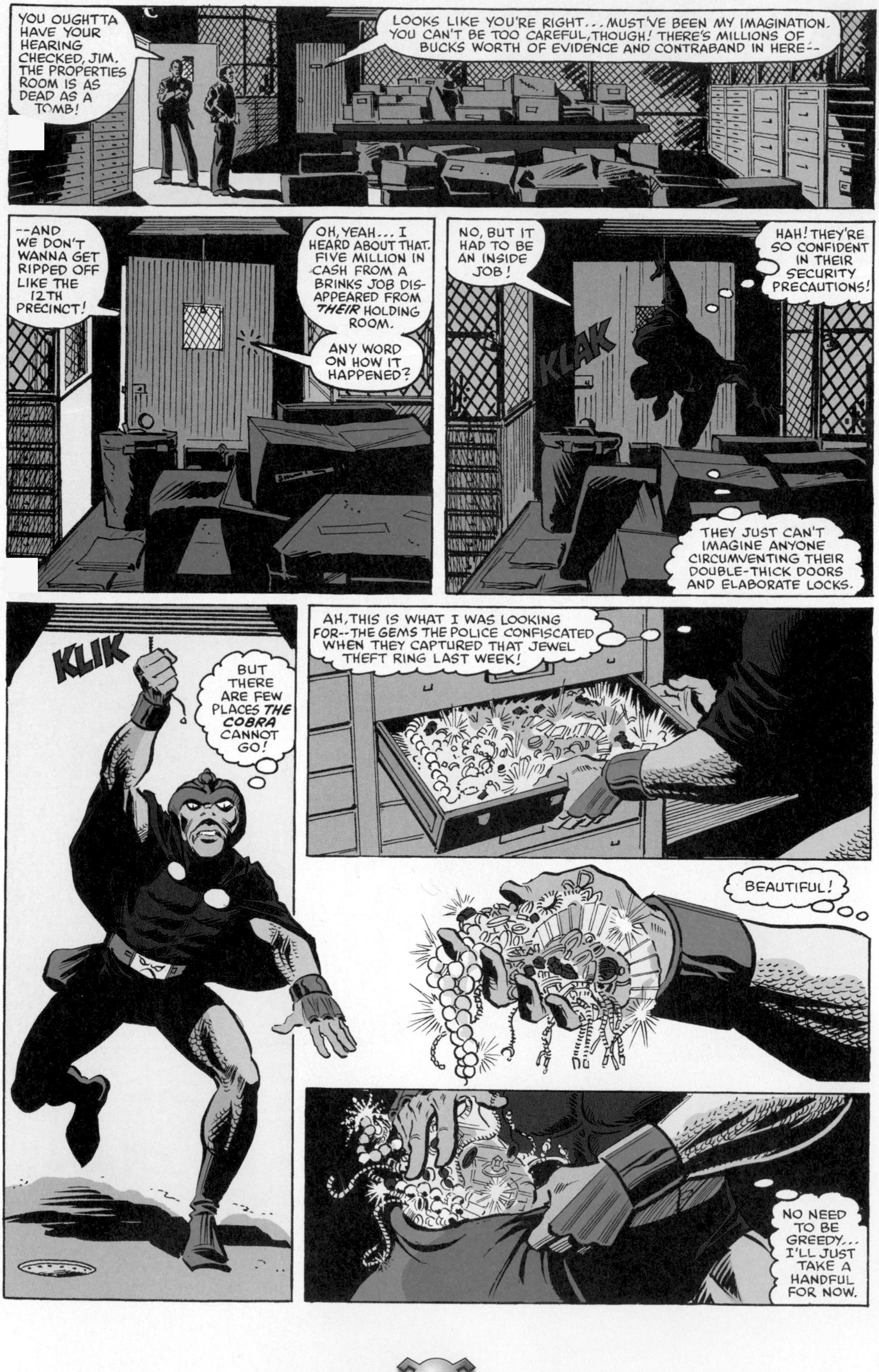

YOU OUGHTTA HAVE YOUR HEARING CHECKED, JIM. THE PROPERTIES ROOM IS AS DEAD AS A TOMB!
LOOKS LIKE YOU'RE RIGHT... MUST'VE BEEN MY IMAGINATION. YOU CAN'T BE TOO CAREFUL, THOUGH! THERE'S MILLIONS OF BUCKS WORTH OF EVIDENCE AND CONTRABAND IN HERE--
--AND WE DON'T WANNA GET RIPPED OFF LIKE THE 12TH PRECINCT!
OH, YEAH... I HEARD ABOUT THAT. FIVE MILLION IN CASH FROM A BRINKS JOB DISAPPEARED FROM THEIR HOLDING ROOM.
ANY WORD ON HOW IT HAPPENED?
NO, BUT IT HAD TO BE AN INSIDE JOB!
HAH! THEY'RE SO CONFIDENT IN THEIR SECURITY PRECAUTIONS!
KLAK
THEY JUST CAN'T IMAGINE ANYONE CIRCUMVENTING THEIR DOUBLE-THICK DOORS AND ELABORATE LOCKS.
KLIK
BUT THERE ARE FEW PLACES THE COBRA CANNOT GO!
AH, THIS IS WHAT I WAS LOOKING FOR--THE GEMS THE POLICE CONFISCATED WHEN THEY CAPTURED THAT JEWEL THEFT RING LAST WEEK!
BEAUTIFUL!
NO NEED TO BE GREEDY... I'LL JUST TAKE A HANDFUL FOR NOW.

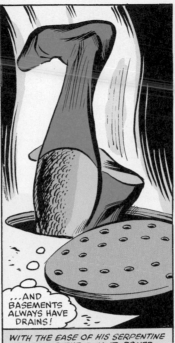

AFTER ALL, I CAN ALWAYS COME BACK FOR MORE!

HOW AMUSING! THIS IS THE MOST WELL-GUARDED ROOM IN THE ENTIRE PRECINCT HOUSE... BUT IT *IS* IN THE BASEMENT...

...AND BASEMENTS ALWAYS HAVE DRAINS!

WITH THE EASE OF HIS SERPENTINE NAMESAKE, THE PLIANT-BONED COBRA SLITHERS THROUGH AN OPENING TOO SMALL FOR ANY NORMAL MAN.

ONCE I REPLACE THE DRAIN COVER, NOT A CLUE WILL REMAIN OF MY ENTRY... SAVE FOR THE BURNING LIGHT.

THAT SHOULD GIVE THOSE TWO COPS SOMETHING TO WONDER ABOUT! HAH-HA!

BENEATH THE CITY STREETS, NEW YORK IS A LABYRINTH OF UNTOLD MILES OF PIPES AND CONDUITS.

FOR THE COBRA, IT IS CHILD'S PLAY TO TRAVEL THAT MAZE-LIKE NETWORK FROM THE LOWLY POLICE PROPERTIES ROOM TO A PLUSH PENTHOUSE ON CENTRAL PARK WEST.

AH...HOME!

I NEVER KNEW A WORD COULD SOUND SO SWEET!

AFTER SPENDING HALF MY LIFE IN WRETCHED PRISON CELLS, IT FEELS GOOD TO COME HOME AND RELAX AFTER A NIGHT'S WORK!

AND A GOOD NIGHT'S WORK IT'S BEEN! I SHOULD HAVE THOUGHT OF THIS SCHEME YEARS AGO. THERE'RE FEW RISKS, PRACTICALLY NO THREAT OF CAPTURE--

--AND THE POLICE COLLECT ALL MY LOOT FOR ME! WHO SAID CRIME DOESN'T PAY?

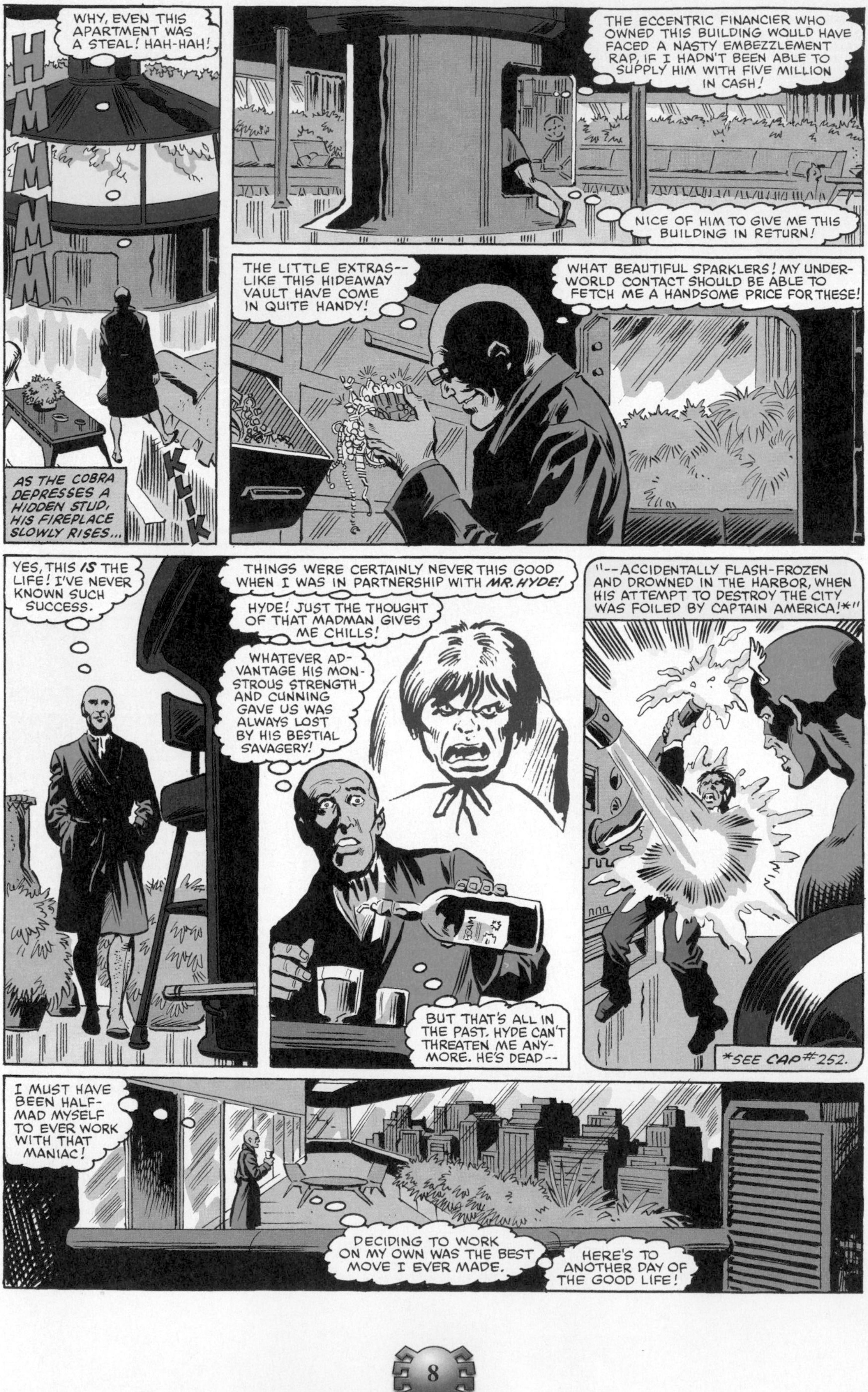
WHY, EVEN THIS APARTMENT WAS A STEAL! HAH-HAH!
HMMMMMM
THE ECCENTRIC FINANCIER WHO OWNED THIS BUILDING WOULD HAVE FACED A NASTY EMBEZZLEMENT RAP, IF I HADN'T BEEN ABLE TO SUPPLY HIM WITH FIVE MILLION IN CASH!
NICE OF HIM TO GIVE ME THIS BUILDING IN RETURN!
AS THE COBRA DEPRESSES A HIDDEN STUD, HIS FIREPLACE SLOWLY RISES...
KLIK
THE LITTLE EXTRAS-- LIKE THIS HIDEAWAY VAULT HAVE COME IN QUITE HANDY!
WHAT BEAUTIFUL SPARKLERS! MY UNDER-WORLD CONTACT SHOULD BE ABLE TO FETCH ME A HANDSOME PRICE FOR THESE!
YES, THIS IS THE LIFE! I'VE NEVER KNOWN SUCH SUCCESS.
THINGS WERE CERTAINLY NEVER THIS GOOD WHEN I WAS IN PARTNERSHIP WITH MR. HYDE!
HYDE! JUST THE THOUGHT OF THAT MADMAN GIVES ME CHILLS!
WHATEVER AD-VANTAGE HIS MON-STROUS STRENGTH AND CUNNING GAVE US WAS ALWAYS LOST BY HIS BESTIAL SAVAGERY!
BUT THAT'S ALL IN THE PAST. HYDE CAN'T THREATEN ME ANY-MORE. HE'S DEAD--
"--ACCIDENTALLY FLASH-FROZEN AND DROWNED IN THE HARBOR, WHEN HIS ATTEMPT TO DESTROY THE CITY WAS FOILED BY CAPTAIN AMERICA!*"
*SEE CAP #252.
I MUST HAVE BEEN HALF-MAD MYSELF TO EVER WORK WITH THAT MANIAC!
DECIDING TO WORK ON MY OWN WAS THE BEST MOVE I EVER MADE.
HERE'S TO ANOTHER DAY OF THE GOOD LIFE!

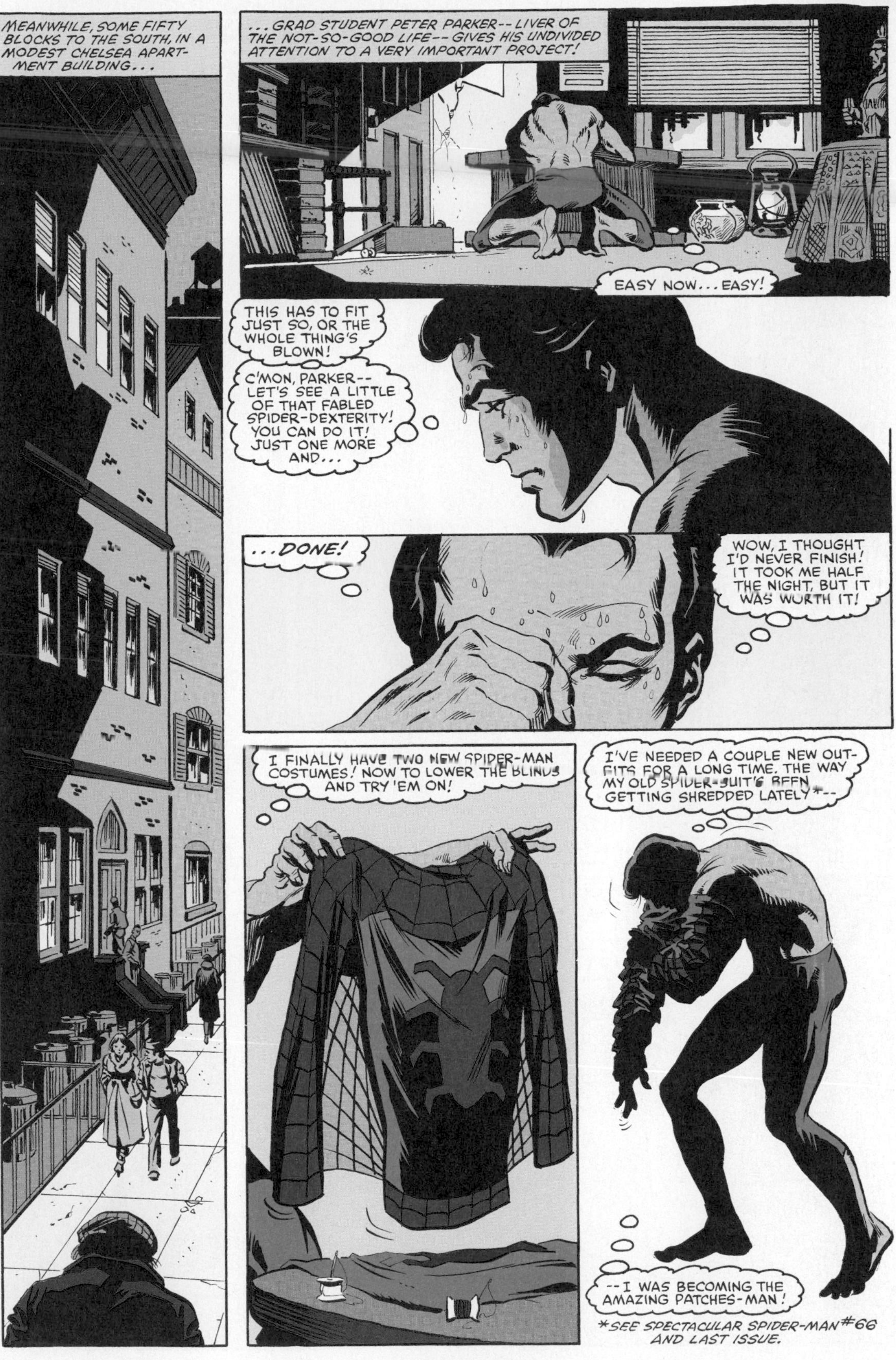
MEANWHILE, SOME FIFTY BLOCKS TO THE SOUTH, IN A MODEST CHELSEA APARTMENT BUILDING...
...GRAD STUDENT PETER PARKER--LIVER OF THE NOT-SO-GOOD LIFE--GIVES HIS UNDIVIDED ATTENTION TO A VERY IMPORTANT PROJECT!
EASY NOW...EASY!
THIS HAS TO FIT JUST SO, OR THE WHOLE THING'S BLOWN!
C'MON, PARKER--LET'S SEE A LITTLE OF THAT FABLED SPIDER-DEXTERITY! YOU CAN DO IT! JUST ONE MORE AND...
...DONE!
WOW, I THOUGHT I'D NEVER FINISH! IT TOOK ME HALF THE NIGHT, BUT IT WAS WORTH IT!
I FINALLY HAVE TWO NEW SPIDER-MAN COSTUMES! NOW TO LOWER THE BLINDS AND TRY 'EM ON!
I'VE NEEDED A COUPLE NEW OUTFITS FOR A LONG TIME. THE WAY MY OLD SPIDER-SUIT'S BEEN GETTING SHREDDED LATELY*--
--I WAS BECOMING THE AMAZING PATCHES-MAN!
*SEE SPECTACULAR SPIDER-MAN #66 AND LAST ISSUE.

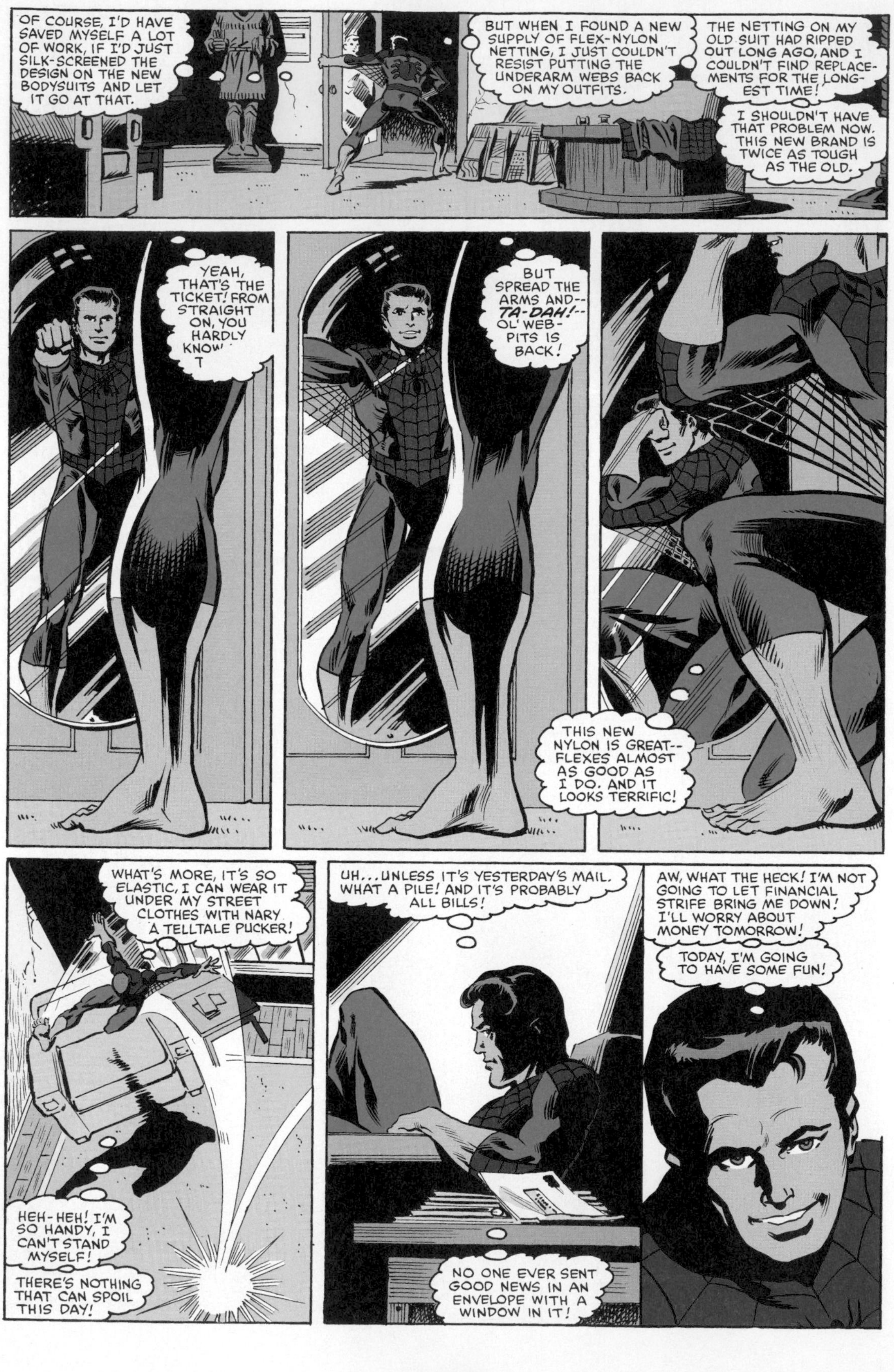
OF COURSE, I'D HAVE SAVED MYSELF A LOT OF WORK, IF I'D JUST SILK-SCREENED THE DESIGN ON THE NEW BODYSUITS AND LET IT GO AT THAT.
BUT WHEN I FOUND A NEW SUPPLY OF FLEX-NYLON NETTING, I JUST COULDN'T RESIST PUTTING THE UNDERARM WEBS BACK ON MY OUTFITS.
THE NETTING ON MY OLD SUIT HAD RIPPED OUT LONG AGO, AND I COULDN'T FIND REPLACEMENTS FOR THE LONGEST TIME!
I SHOULDN'T HAVE THAT PROBLEM NOW. THIS NEW BRAND IS TWICE AS TOUGH AS THE OLD.
YEAH, THAT'S THE TICKET! FROM STRAIGHT ON, YOU HARDLY KNOW IT
BUT SPREAD THE ARMS AND-- TA-DAH!-- OL' WEB-PITS IS BACK!
THIS NEW NYLON IS GREAT-- FLEXES ALMOST AS GOOD AS I DO. AND IT LOOKS TERRIFIC!
WHAT'S MORE, IT'S SO ELASTIC, I CAN WEAR IT UNDER MY STREET CLOTHES WITH NARY A TELLTALE PUCKER!
HEH-HEH! I'M SO HANDY, I CAN'T STAND MYSELF!
THERE'S NOTHING THAT CAN SPOIL THIS DAY!
UH...UNLESS IT'S YESTERDAY'S MAIL. WHAT A PILE! AND IT'S PROBABLY ALL BILLS!
NO ONE EVER SENT GOOD NEWS IN AN ENVELOPE WITH A WINDOW IN IT!
AW, WHAT THE HECK! I'M NOT GOING TO LET FINANCIAL STRIFE BRING ME DOWN! I'LL WORRY ABOUT MONEY TOMORROW!
TODAY, I'M GOING TO HAVE SOME FUN!

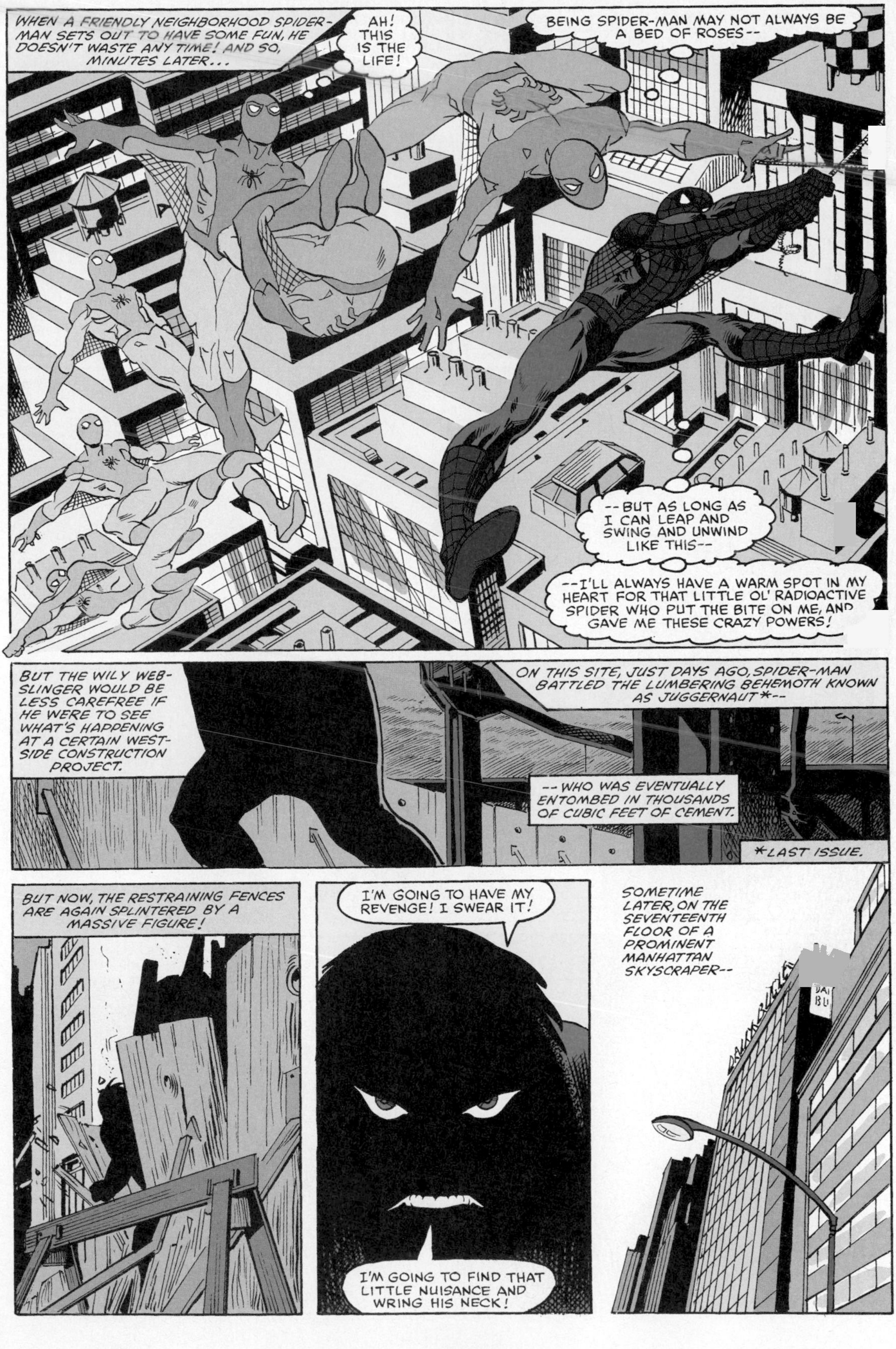
WHEN A FRIENDLY NEIGHBORHOOD SPIDER-MAN SETS OUT TO HAVE SOME FUN, HE DOESN'T WASTE ANY TIME! AND SO, MINUTES LATER...
AH! THIS IS THE LIFE!
BEING SPIDER-MAN MAY NOT ALWAYS BE A BED OF ROSES--
--BUT AS LONG AS I CAN LEAP AND SWING AND UNWIND LIKE THIS--
--I'LL ALWAYS HAVE A WARM SPOT IN MY HEART FOR THAT LITTLE OL' RADIOACTIVE SPIDER WHO PUT THE BITE ON ME, AND GAVE ME THESE CRAZY POWERS!
BUT THE WILY WEB-SLINGER WOULD BE LESS CAREFREE IF HE WERE TO SEE WHAT'S HAPPENING AT A CERTAIN WEST-SIDE CONSTRUCTION PROJECT.
ON THIS SITE, JUST DAYS AGO, SPIDER-MAN BATTLED THE LUMBERING BEHEMOTH KNOWN AS JUGGERNAUT*--
--WHO WAS EVENTUALLY ENTOMBED IN THOUSANDS OF CUBIC FEET OF CEMENT.
*LAST ISSUE.
BUT NOW, THE RESTRAINING FENCES ARE AGAIN SPLINTERED BY A MASSIVE FIGURE!
I'M GOING TO HAVE MY REVENGE! I SWEAR IT!
I'M GOING TO FIND THAT LITTLE NUISANCE AND WRING HIS NECK!
SOMETIME LATER, ON THE SEVENTEENTH FLOOR OF A PROMINENT MANHATTAN SKYSCRAPER--

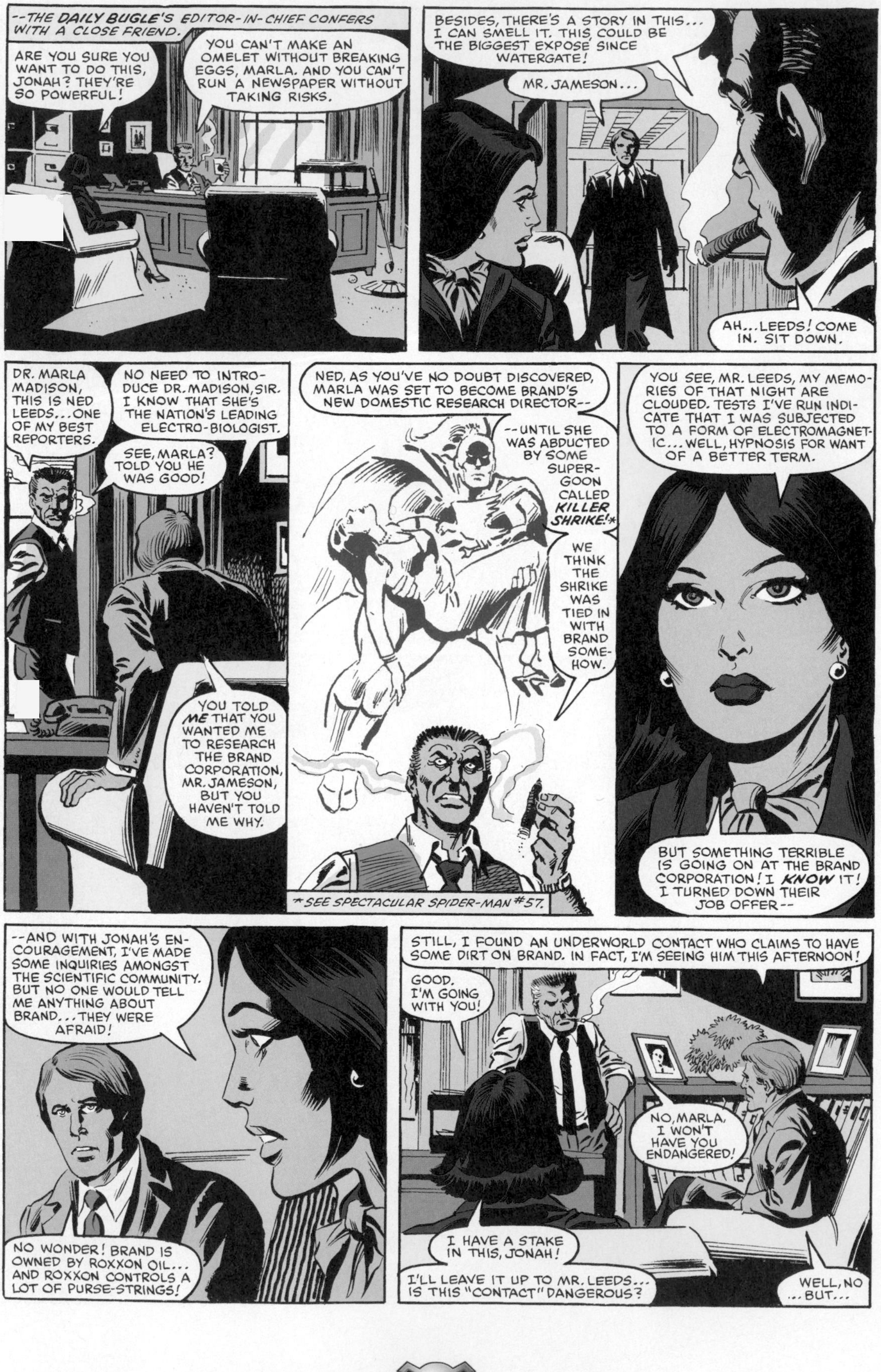
--THE DAILY BUGLE'S EDITOR-IN-CHIEF CONFERS WITH A CLOSE FRIEND.
ARE YOU SURE YOU WANT TO DO THIS, JONAH? THEY'RE SO POWERFUL!
YOU CAN'T MAKE AN OMELET WITHOUT BREAKING EGGS, MARLA. AND YOU CAN'T RUN A NEWSPAPER WITHOUT TAKING RISKS.
BESIDES, THERE'S A STORY IN THIS... I CAN SMELL IT. THIS COULD BE THE BIGGEST EXPOSÉ SINCE WATERGATE!
MR. JAMESON...
AH...LEEDS! COME IN. SIT DOWN.
DR. MARLA MADISON, THIS IS NED LEEDS...ONE OF MY BEST REPORTERS.
NO NEED TO INTRODUCE DR. MADISON, SIR. I KNOW THAT SHE'S THE NATION'S LEADING ELECTRO-BIOLOGIST.
SEE, MARLA? TOLD YOU HE WAS GOOD!
YOU TOLD ME THAT YOU WANTED ME TO RESEARCH THE BRAND CORPORATION, MR. JAMESON, BUT YOU HAVEN'T TOLD ME WHY.
NED, AS YOU'VE NO DOUBT DISCOVERED, MARLA WAS SET TO BECOME BRAND'S NEW DOMESTIC RESEARCH DIRECTOR--
--UNTIL SHE WAS ABDUCTED BY SOME SUPER-GOON CALLED KILLER SHRIKE!*
WE THINK THE SHRIKE WAS TIED IN WITH BRAND SOMEHOW.
*SEE SPECTACULAR SPIDER-MAN #57.
YOU SEE, MR. LEEDS, MY MEMORIES OF THAT NIGHT ARE CLOUDED. TESTS I'VE RUN INDICATE THAT I WAS SUBJECTED TO A FORM OF ELECTROMAGNETIC... WELL, HYPNOSIS FOR WANT OF A BETTER TERM.
BUT SOMETHING TERRIBLE IS GOING ON AT THE BRAND CORPORATION! I KNOW IT! I TURNED DOWN THEIR JOB OFFER--
--AND WITH JONAH'S ENCOURAGEMENT, I'VE MADE SOME INQUIRIES AMONGST THE SCIENTIFIC COMMUNITY. BUT NO ONE WOULD TELL ME ANYTHING ABOUT BRAND... THEY WERE AFRAID!
NO WONDER! BRAND IS OWNED BY ROXXON OIL... AND ROXXON CONTROLS A LOT OF PURSE-STRINGS!
STILL, I FOUND AN UNDERWORLD CONTACT WHO CLAIMS TO HAVE SOME DIRT ON BRAND. IN FACT, I'M SEEING HIM THIS AFTERNOON!
GOOD. I'M GOING WITH YOU!
NO, MARLA, I WON'T HAVE YOU ENDANGERED!
I HAVE A STAKE IN THIS, JONAH!
I'LL LEAVE IT UP TO MR. LEEDS... IS THIS "CONTACT" DANGEROUS?
WELL, NO ...BUT...

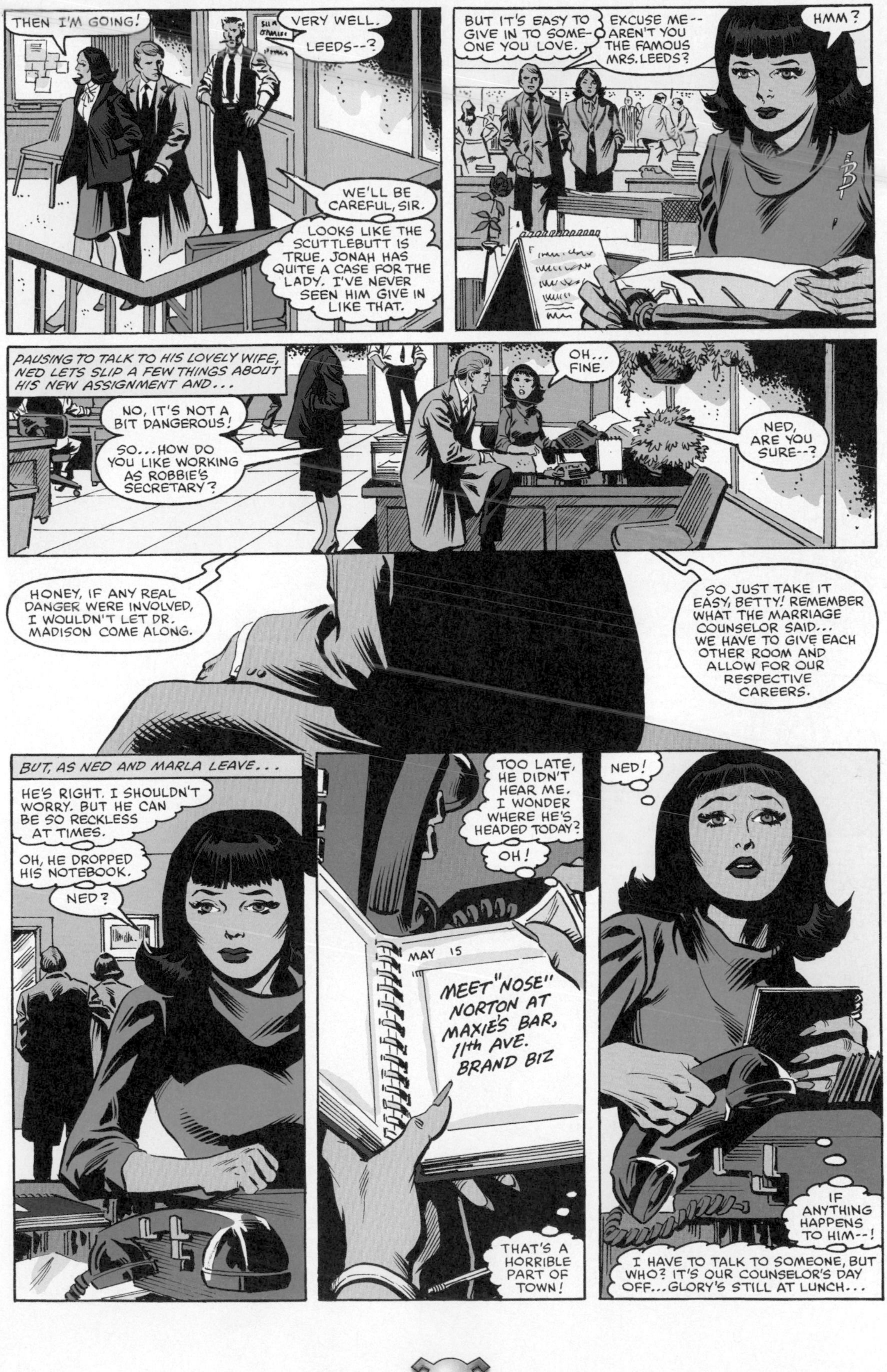
THEN I'M GOING!
VERY WELL.
LEEDS--?
WE'LL BE CAREFUL, SIR.
LOOKS LIKE THE SCUTTLEBUTT IS TRUE. JONAH HAS QUITE A CASE FOR THE LADY. I'VE NEVER SEEN HIM GIVE IN LIKE THAT.
BUT IT'S EASY TO GIVE IN TO SOME-ONE YOU LOVE.
EXCUSE ME-- AREN'T YOU THE FAMOUS MRS. LEEDS?
HMM?
PAUSING TO TALK TO HIS LOVELY WIFE, NED LETS SLIP A FEW THINGS ABOUT HIS NEW ASSIGNMENT AND...
NO, IT'S NOT A BIT DANGEROUS!
SO...HOW DO YOU LIKE WORKING AS ROBBIE'S SECRETARY?
OH... FINE.
NED, ARE YOU SURE--?
HONEY, IF ANY REAL DANGER WERE INVOLVED, I WOULDN'T LET DR. MADISON COME ALONG.
SO JUST TAKE IT EASY, BETTY! REMEMBER WHAT THE MARRIAGE COUNSELOR SAID... WE HAVE TO GIVE EACH OTHER ROOM AND ALLOW FOR OUR RESPECTIVE CAREERS.
BUT, AS NED AND MARLA LEAVE...
HE'S RIGHT. I SHOULDN'T WORRY. BUT HE CAN BE SO RECKLESS AT TIMES.
OH, HE DROPPED HIS NOTEBOOK.
NED?
TOO LATE, HE DIDN'T HEAR ME. I WONDER WHERE HE'S HEADED TODAY?
OH!
MAY 15
MEET "NOSE" NORTON AT MAXIE'S BAR, 11th AVE. BRAND BIZ
THAT'S A HORRIBLE PART OF TOWN!
NED!
IF ANYTHING HAPPENS TO HIM--!
I HAVE TO TALK TO SOMEONE, BUT WHO? IT'S OUR COUNSELOR'S DAY OFF...GLORY'S STILL AT LUNCH...

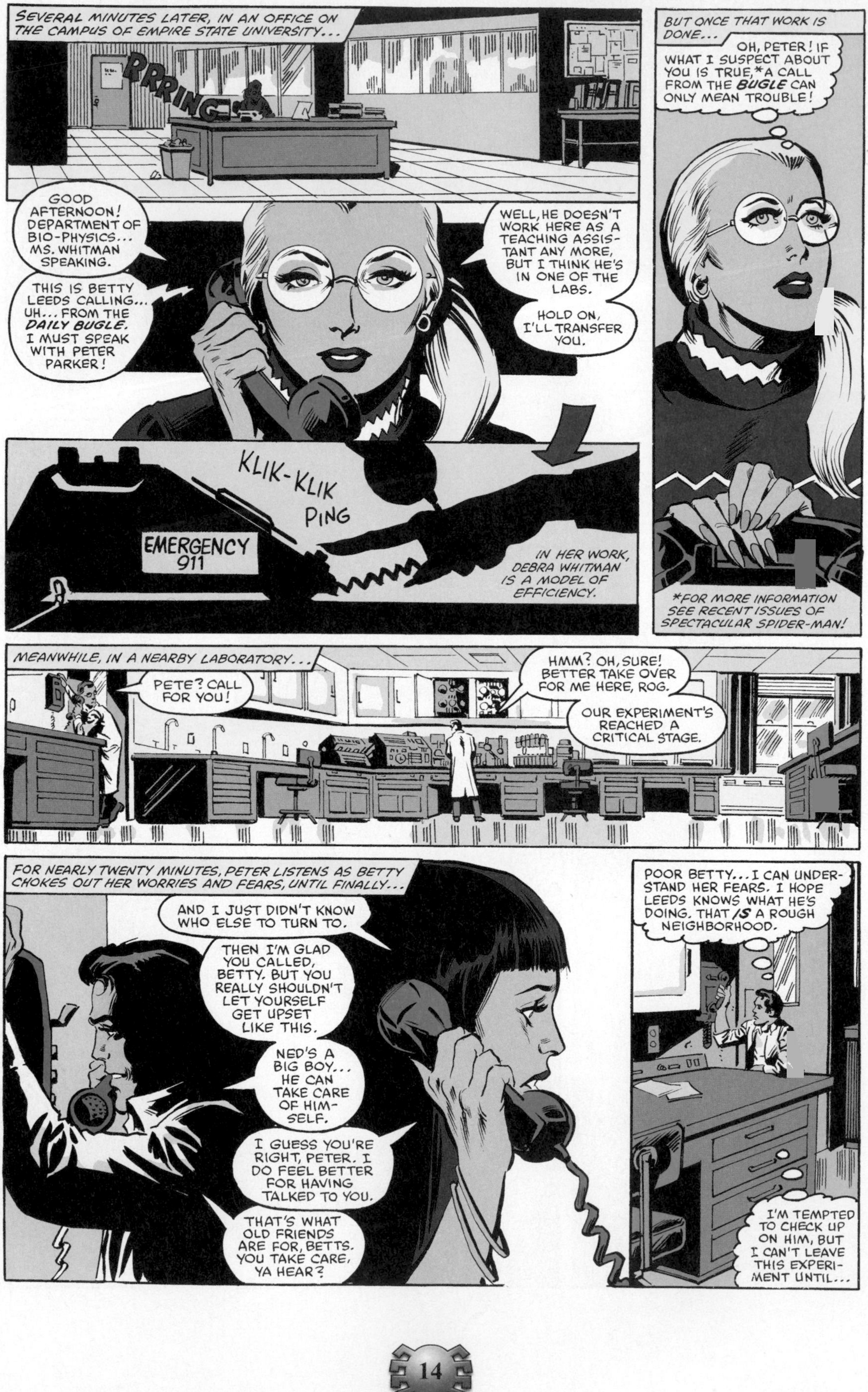

SEVERAL MINUTES LATER, IN AN OFFICE ON THE CAMPUS OF EMPIRE STATE UNIVERSITY...
RRRING
GOOD AFTERNOON! DEPARTMENT OF BIO-PHYSICS... MS. WHITMAN SPEAKING.
THIS IS BETTY LEEDS CALLING... UH... FROM THE DAILY BUGLE. I MUST SPEAK WITH PETER PARKER!
WELL, HE DOESN'T WORK HERE AS A TEACHING ASSISTANT ANY MORE, BUT I THINK HE'S IN ONE OF THE LABS.
HOLD ON, I'LL TRANSFER YOU.
KLIK-KLIK
PING
EMERGENCY 911
IN HER WORK, DEBRA WHITMAN IS A MODEL OF EFFICIENCY.
BUT ONCE THAT WORK IS DONE...
OH, PETER! IF WHAT I SUSPECT ABOUT YOU IS TRUE,* A CALL FROM THE BUGLE CAN ONLY MEAN TROUBLE!
*FOR MORE INFORMATION SEE RECENT ISSUES OF SPECTACULAR SPIDER-MAN!
MEANWHILE, IN A NEARBY LABORATORY...
PETE? CALL FOR YOU!
HMM? OH, SURE! BETTER TAKE OVER FOR ME HERE, ROG.
OUR EXPERIMENT'S REACHED A CRITICAL STAGE.
FOR NEARLY TWENTY MINUTES, PETER LISTENS AS BETTY CHOKES OUT HER WORRIES AND FEARS, UNTIL FINALLY...
AND I JUST DIDN'T KNOW WHO ELSE TO TURN TO.
THEN I'M GLAD YOU CALLED, BETTY. BUT YOU REALLY SHOULDN'T LET YOURSELF GET UPSET LIKE THIS.
NED'S A BIG BOY... HE CAN TAKE CARE OF HIMSELF.
I GUESS YOU'RE RIGHT, PETER. I DO FEEL BETTER FOR HAVING TALKED TO YOU.
THAT'S WHAT OLD FRIENDS ARE FOR, BETTS. YOU TAKE CARE, YA HEAR?
POOR BETTY... I CAN UNDERSTAND HER FEARS. I HOPE LEEDS KNOWS WHAT HE'S DOING. THAT IS A ROUGH NEIGHBORHOOD.
I'M TEMPTED TO CHECK UP ON HIM, BUT I CAN'T LEAVE THIS EXPERIMENT UNTIL...

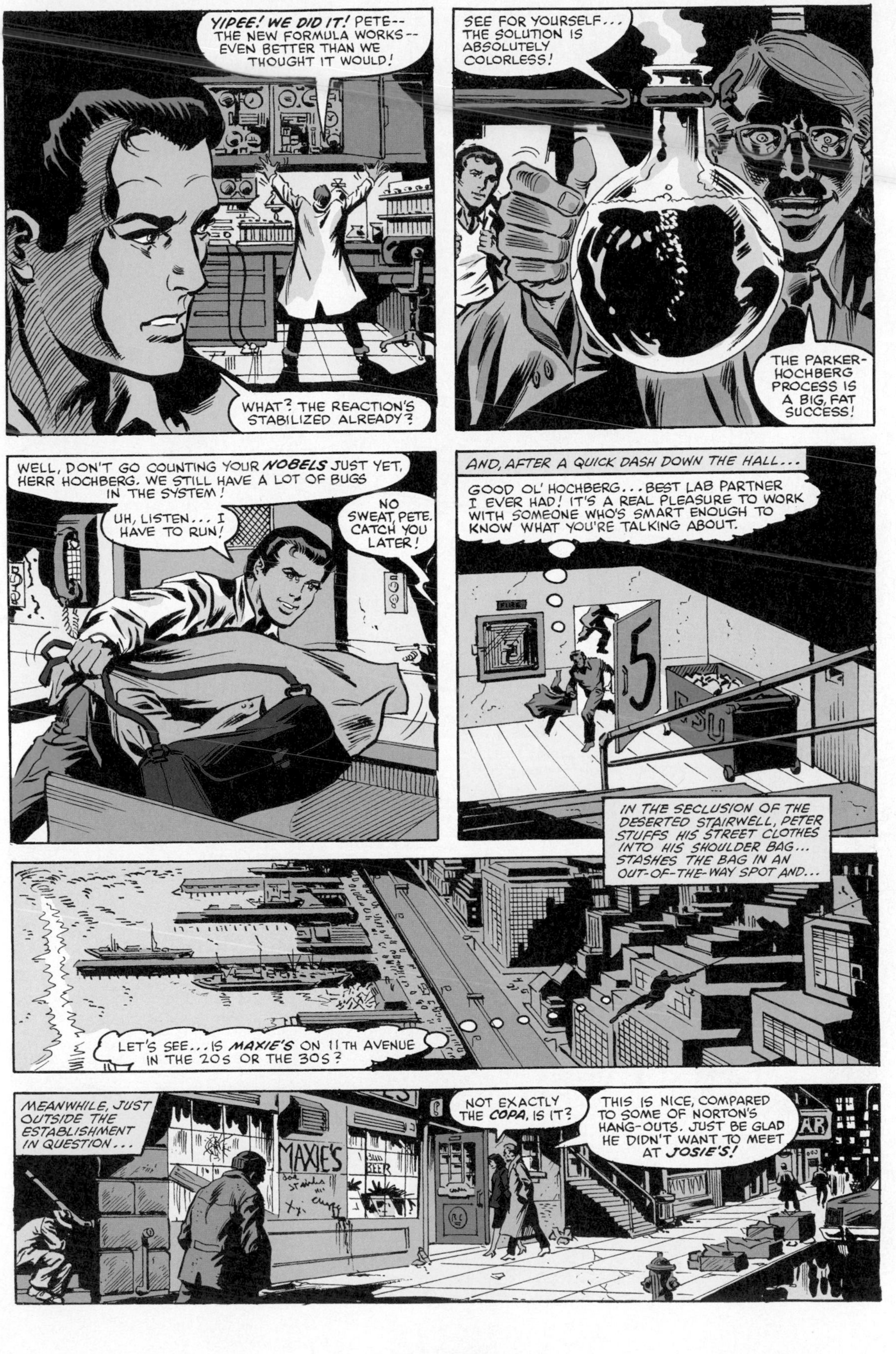
YIPEE! WE DID IT! PETE-- THE NEW FORMULA WORKS-- EVEN BETTER THAN WE THOUGHT IT WOULD!
WHAT? THE REACTION'S STABILIZED ALREADY?
SEE FOR YOURSELF... THE SOLUTION IS ABSOLUTELY COLORLESS!
THE PARKER-HOCHBERG PROCESS IS A BIG, FAT SUCCESS!
WELL, DON'T GO COUNTING YOUR NOBELS JUST YET, HERR HOCHBERG. WE STILL HAVE A LOT OF BUGS IN THE SYSTEM!
UH, LISTEN... I HAVE TO RUN!
NO SWEAT, PETE. CATCH YOU LATER!
AND, AFTER A QUICK DASH DOWN THE HALL...
GOOD OL' HOCHBERG... BEST LAB PARTNER I EVER HAD! IT'S A REAL PLEASURE TO WORK WITH SOMEONE WHO'S SMART ENOUGH TO KNOW WHAT YOU'RE TALKING ABOUT.
FIRE
5
ESU
IN THE SECLUSION OF THE DESERTED STAIRWELL, PETER STUFFS HIS STREET CLOTHES INTO HIS SHOULDER BAG... STASHES THE BAG IN AN OUT-OF-THE-WAY SPOT AND...
LET'S SEE... IS MAXIE'S ON 11TH AVENUE IN THE 20S OR THE 30S?
MEANWHILE, JUST OUTSIDE THE ESTABLISHMENT IN QUESTION...
MAXIE'S
BEER
NOT EXACTLY THE COPA, IS IT?
THIS IS NICE, COMPARED TO SOME OF NORTON'S HANG-OUTS. JUST BE GLAD HE DIDN'T WANT TO MEET AT JOSIE'S!

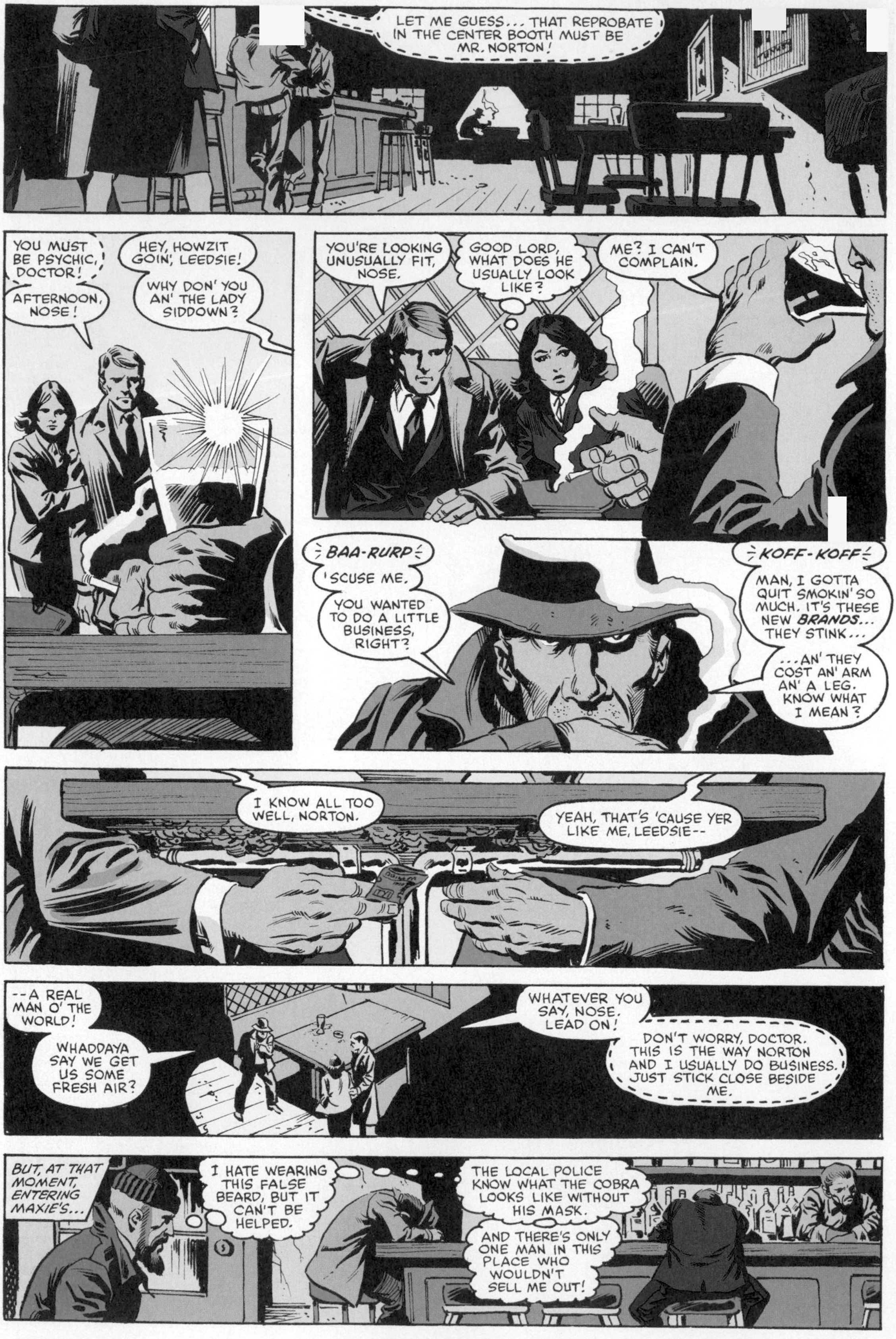
LET ME GUESS... THAT REPROBATE IN THE CENTER BOOTH MUST BE MR. NORTON!
YOU MUST BE PSYCHIC, DOCTOR!
AFTERNOON, NOSE!
HEY, HOWZIT GOIN', LEEDSIE!
WHY DON' YOU AN' THE LADY SIDDOWN?
YOU'RE LOOKING UNUSUALLY FIT, NOSE.
GOOD LORD, WHAT DOES HE USUALLY LOOK LIKE?
ME? I CAN'T COMPLAIN.
BAA-RURP
'SCUSE ME.
YOU WANTED TO DO A LITTLE BUSINESS, RIGHT?
KOFF-KOFF
MAN, I GOTTA QUIT SMOKIN' SO MUCH. IT'S THESE NEW BRANDS... THEY STINK...
...AN' THEY COST AN' ARM AN' A LEG. KNOW WHAT I MEAN?
I KNOW ALL TOO WELL, NORTON.
YEAH, THAT'S 'CAUSE YER LIKE ME, LEEDSIE--
--A REAL MAN O' THE WORLD!
WHADDAYA SAY WE GET US SOME FRESH AIR?
WHATEVER YOU SAY, NOSE. LEAD ON!
DON'T WORRY, DOCTOR. THIS IS THE WAY NORTON AND I USUALLY DO BUSINESS. JUST STICK CLOSE BESIDE ME.
BUT, AT THAT MOMENT, ENTERING MAXIE'S...
I HATE WEARING THIS FALSE BEARD, BUT IT CAN'T BE HELPED.
THE LOCAL POLICE KNOW WHAT THE COBRA LOOKS LIKE WITHOUT HIS MASK.
AND THERE'S ONLY ONE MAN IN THIS PLACE WHO WOULDN'T SELL ME OUT!

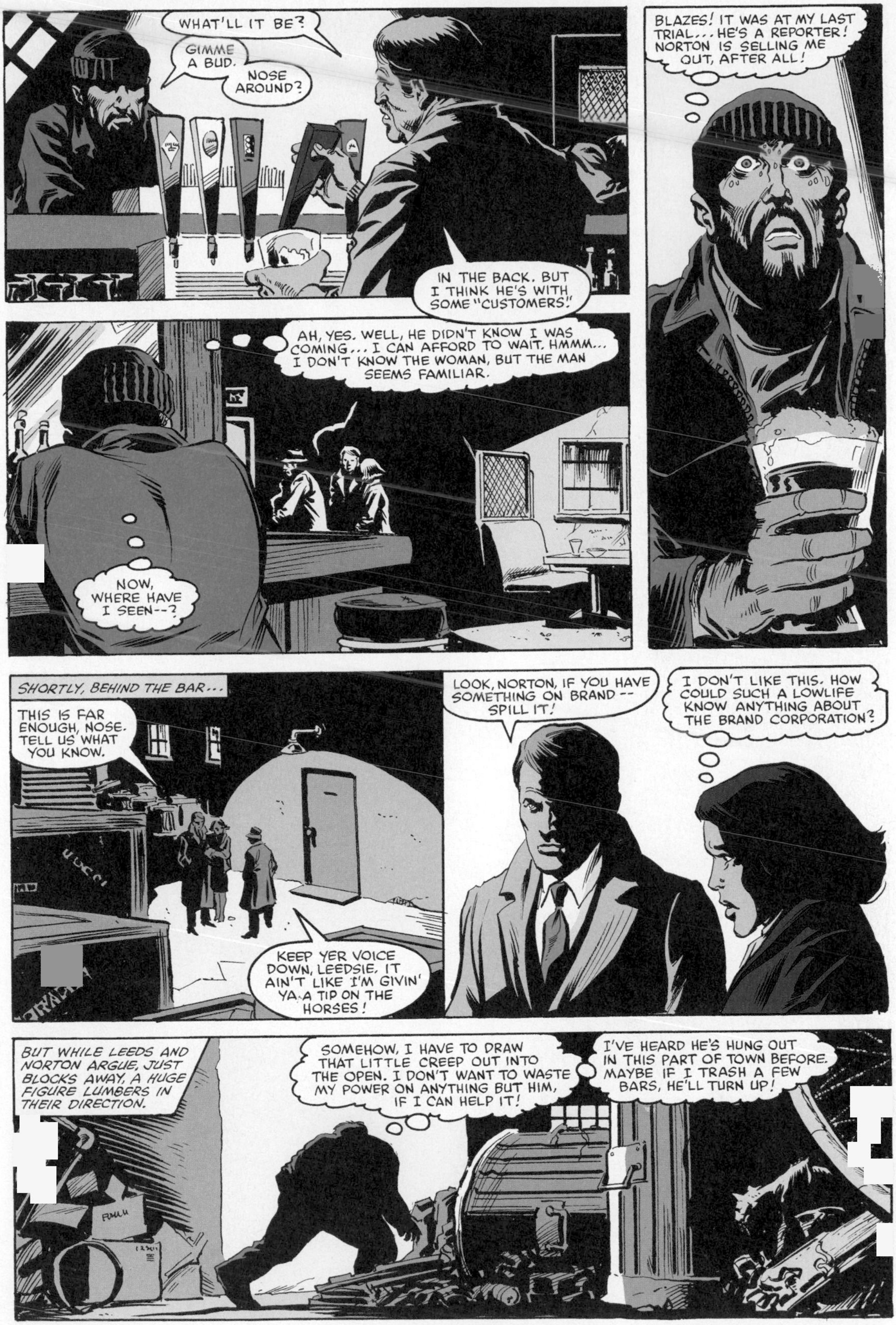
WHAT'LL IT BE?
GIMME A BUD.
NOSE AROUND?
IN THE BACK. BUT I THINK HE'S WITH SOME "CUSTOMERS."
AH, YES. WELL, HE DIDN'T KNOW I WAS COMING... I CAN AFFORD TO WAIT. HMMM... I DON'T KNOW THE WOMAN, BUT THE MAN SEEMS FAMILIAR.
NOW, WHERE HAVE I SEEN--?
BLAZES! IT WAS AT MY LAST TRIAL... HE'S A REPORTER! NORTON IS SELLING ME OUT, AFTER ALL!
SHORTLY, BEHIND THE BAR...
THIS IS FAR ENOUGH, NOSE. TELL US WHAT YOU KNOW.
KEEP YER VOICE DOWN, LEEDSIE. IT AIN'T LIKE I'M GIVIN' YA A TIP ON THE HORSES!
LOOK, NORTON, IF YOU HAVE SOMETHING ON BRAND -- SPILL IT!
I DON'T LIKE THIS. HOW COULD SUCH A LOWLIFE KNOW ANYTHING ABOUT THE BRAND CORPORATION?
BUT WHILE LEEDS AND NORTON ARGUE, JUST BLOCKS AWAY, A HUGE FIGURE LUMBERS IN THEIR DIRECTION.
SOMEHOW, I HAVE TO DRAW THAT LITTLE CREEP OUT INTO THE OPEN. I DON'T WANT TO WASTE MY POWER ON ANYTHING BUT HIM, IF I CAN HELP IT!
I'VE HEARD HE'S HUNG OUT IN THIS PART OF TOWN BEFORE. MAYBE IF I TRASH A FEW BARS, HE'LL TURN UP!

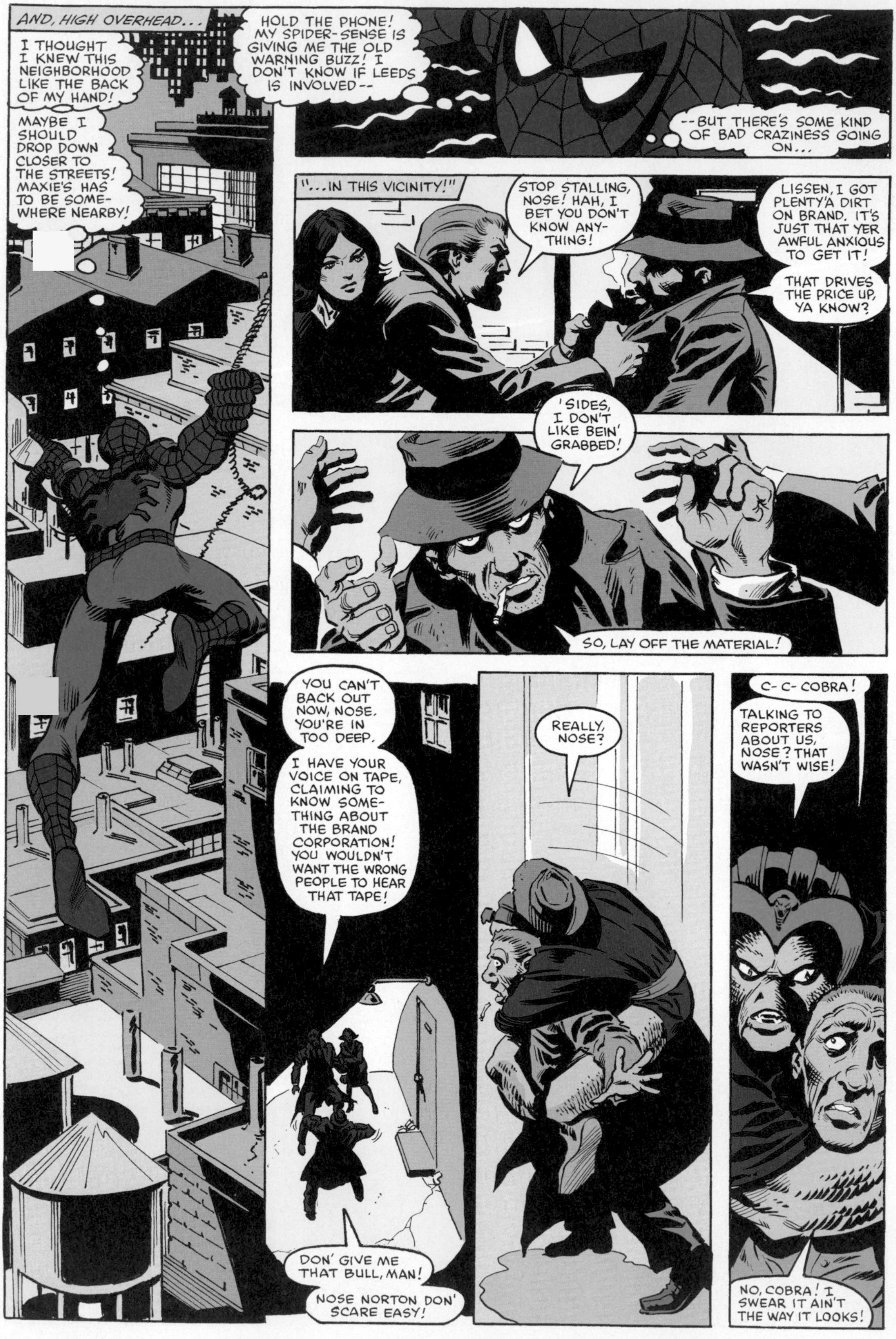
AND, HIGH OVERHEAD...
I THOUGHT I KNEW THIS NEIGHBORHOOD LIKE THE BACK OF MY HAND!
MAYBE I SHOULD DROP DOWN CLOSER TO THE STREETS! MAXIE'S HAS TO BE SOMEWHERE NEARBY!
HOLD THE PHONE! MY SPIDER-SENSE IS GIVING ME THE OLD WARNING BUZZ! I DON'T KNOW IF LEEDS IS INVOLVED--
--BUT THERE'S SOME KIND OF BAD CRAZINESS GOING ON...
"...IN THIS VICINITY!"
STOP STALLING, NOSE! HAH, I BET YOU DON'T KNOW ANYTHING!
LISSEN, I GOT PLENTY'A DIRT ON BRAND. IT'S JUST THAT YER AWFUL ANXIOUS TO GET IT!
THAT DRIVES THE PRICE UP, YA KNOW?
'SIDES, I DON'T LIKE BEIN' GRABBED!
SO, LAY OFF THE MATERIAL!
YOU CAN'T BACK OUT NOW, NOSE. YOU'RE IN TOO DEEP.
I HAVE YOUR VOICE ON TAPE, CLAIMING TO KNOW SOMETHING ABOUT THE BRAND CORPORATION! YOU WOULDN'T WANT THE WRONG PEOPLE TO HEAR THAT TAPE!
DON' GIVE ME THAT BULL, MAN!
NOSE NORTON DON' SCARE EASY!
REALLY, NOSE?
C-C-COBRA!
TALKING TO REPORTERS ABOUT US, NOSE? THAT WASN'T WISE!
NO, COBRA! I SWEAR IT AIN'T THE WAY IT LOOKS!

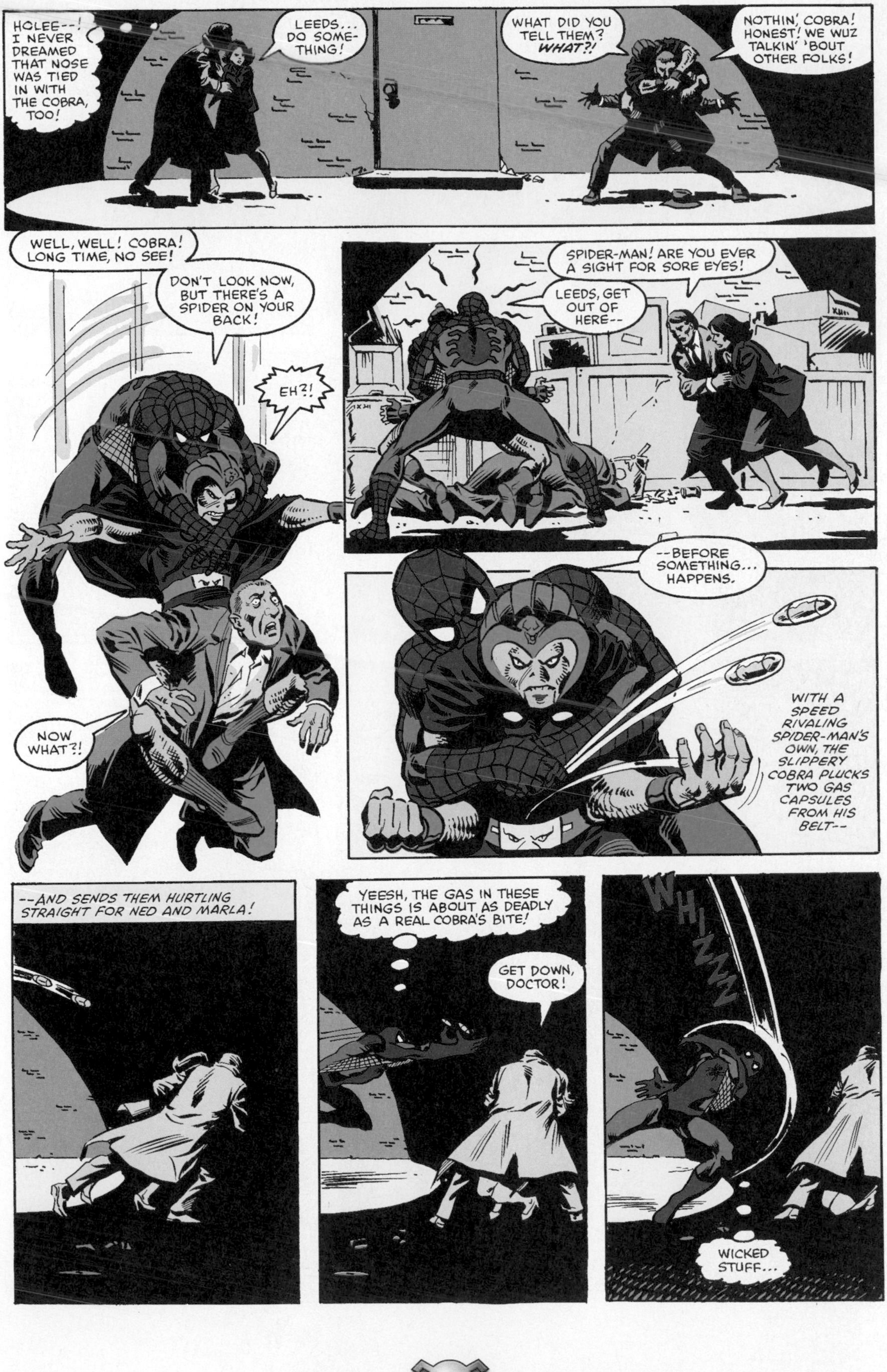
HOLEE--! I NEVER DREAMED THAT NOSE WAS TIED IN WITH THE COBRA, TOO!
LEEDS... DO SOME-THING!
WHAT DID YOU TELL THEM? WHAT?!
NOTHIN', COBRA! HONEST! WE WUZ TALKIN' 'BOUT OTHER FOLKS!
WELL, WELL! COBRA! LONG TIME, NO SEE!
DON'T LOOK NOW, BUT THERE'S A SPIDER ON YOUR BACK!
EH?!
NOW WHAT?!
SPIDER-MAN! ARE YOU EVER A SIGHT FOR SORE EYES!
LEEDS, GET OUT OF HERE--
--BEFORE SOMETHING... HAPPENS.
WITH A SPEED RIVALING SPIDER-MAN'S OWN, THE SLIPPERY COBRA PLUCKS TWO GAS CAPSULES FROM HIS BELT--
--AND SENDS THEM HURTLING STRAIGHT FOR NED AND MARLA!
YEESH, THE GAS IN THESE THINGS IS ABOUT AS DEADLY AS A REAL COBRA'S BITE!
GET DOWN, DOCTOR!
WHIZZZ
WICKED STUFF...

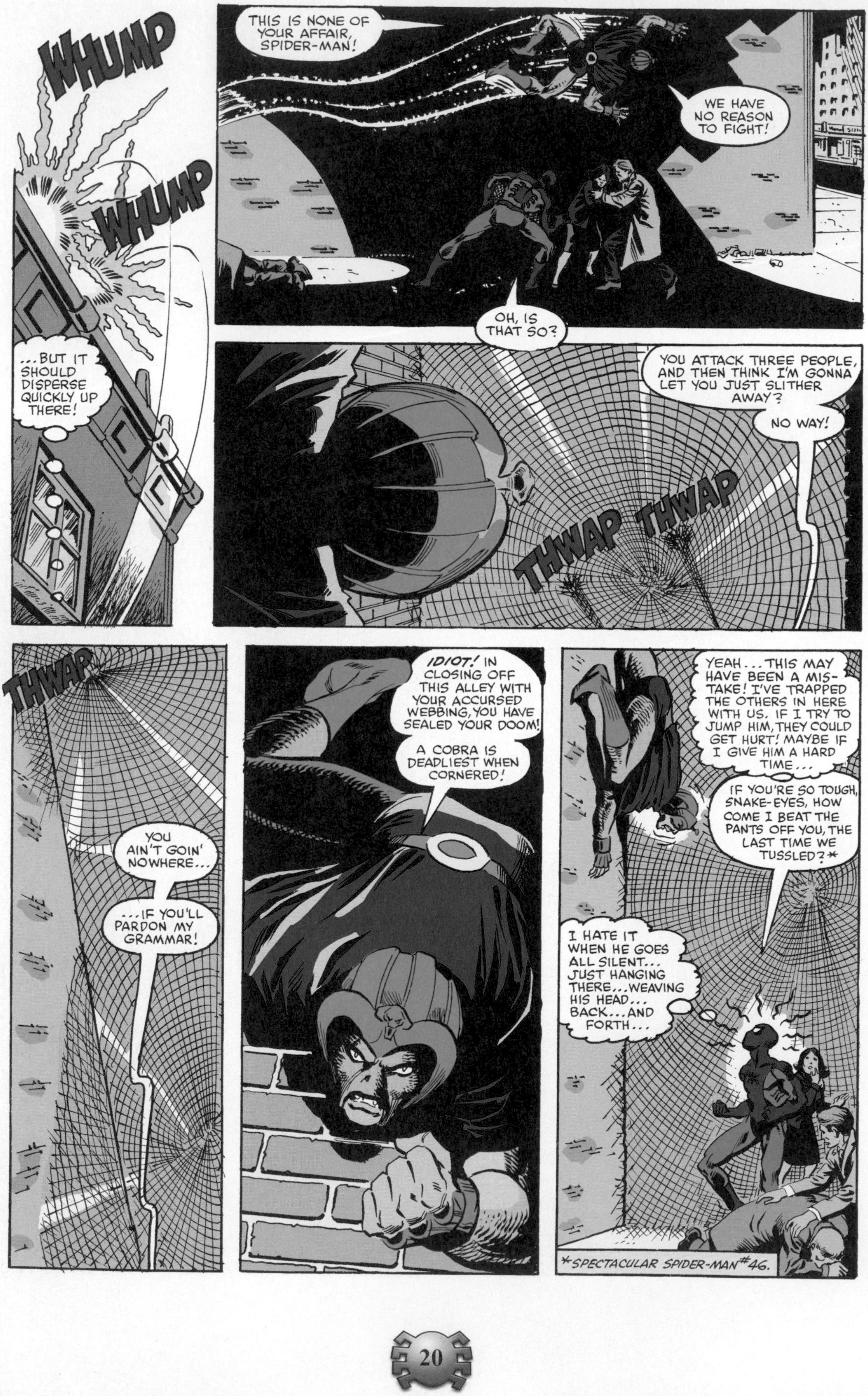
WHUMP
WHUMP
...BUT IT SHOULD DISPERSE QUICKLY UP THERE!
THIS IS NONE OF YOUR AFFAIR, SPIDER-MAN!
WE HAVE NO REASON TO FIGHT!
OH, IS THAT SO?
YOU ATTACK THREE PEOPLE, AND THEN THINK I'M GONNA LET YOU JUST SLITHER AWAY?
NO WAY!
THWAP THWAP
THWAP
YOU AIN'T GOIN' NOWHERE...
...IF YOU'LL PARDON MY GRAMMAR!
IDIOT! IN CLOSING OFF THIS ALLEY WITH YOUR ACCURSED WEBBING, YOU HAVE SEALED YOUR DOOM!
A COBRA IS DEADLIEST WHEN CORNERED!
YEAH... THIS MAY HAVE BEEN A MISTAKE! I'VE TRAPPED THE OTHERS IN HERE WITH US. IF I TRY TO JUMP HIM, THEY COULD GET HURT! MAYBE IF I GIVE HIM A HARD TIME...
IF YOU'RE SO TOUGH, SNAKE-EYES, HOW COME I BEAT THE PANTS OFF YOU, THE LAST TIME WE TUSSLED?*
I HATE IT WHEN HE GOES ALL SILENT... JUST HANGING THERE... WEAVING HIS HEAD... BACK... AND FORTH...
*SPECTACULAR SPIDER-MAN #46.

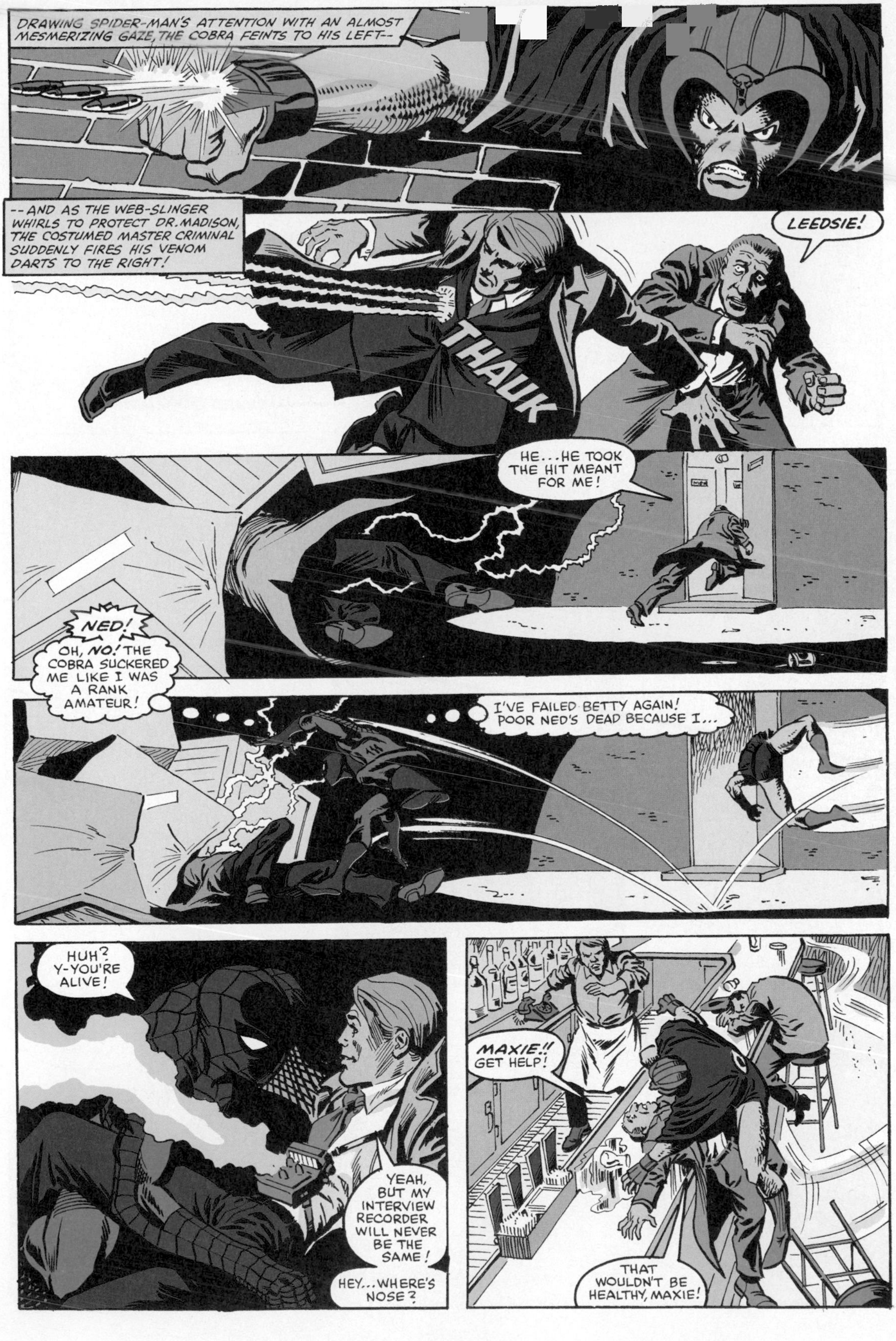
DRAWING SPIDER-MAN'S ATTENTION WITH AN ALMOST MESMERIZING GAZE, THE COBRA FEINTS TO HIS LEFT--
--AND AS THE WEB-SLINGER WHIRLS TO PROTECT DR. MADISON, THE COSTUMED MASTER CRIMINAL SUDDENLY FIRES HIS VENOM DARTS TO THE RIGHT!
LEEDSIE!
THAUK
HE...HE TOOK THE HIT MEANT FOR ME!
NED!
OH, NO! THE COBRA SUCKERED ME LIKE I WAS A RANK AMATEUR!
I'VE FAILED BETTY AGAIN! POOR NED'S DEAD BECAUSE I...
HUH? Y-YOU'RE ALIVE!
YEAH, BUT MY INTERVIEW RECORDER WILL NEVER BE THE SAME!
HEY...WHERE'S NOSE?
MAXIE!! GET HELP!
THAT WOULDN'T BE HEALTHY, MAXIE!

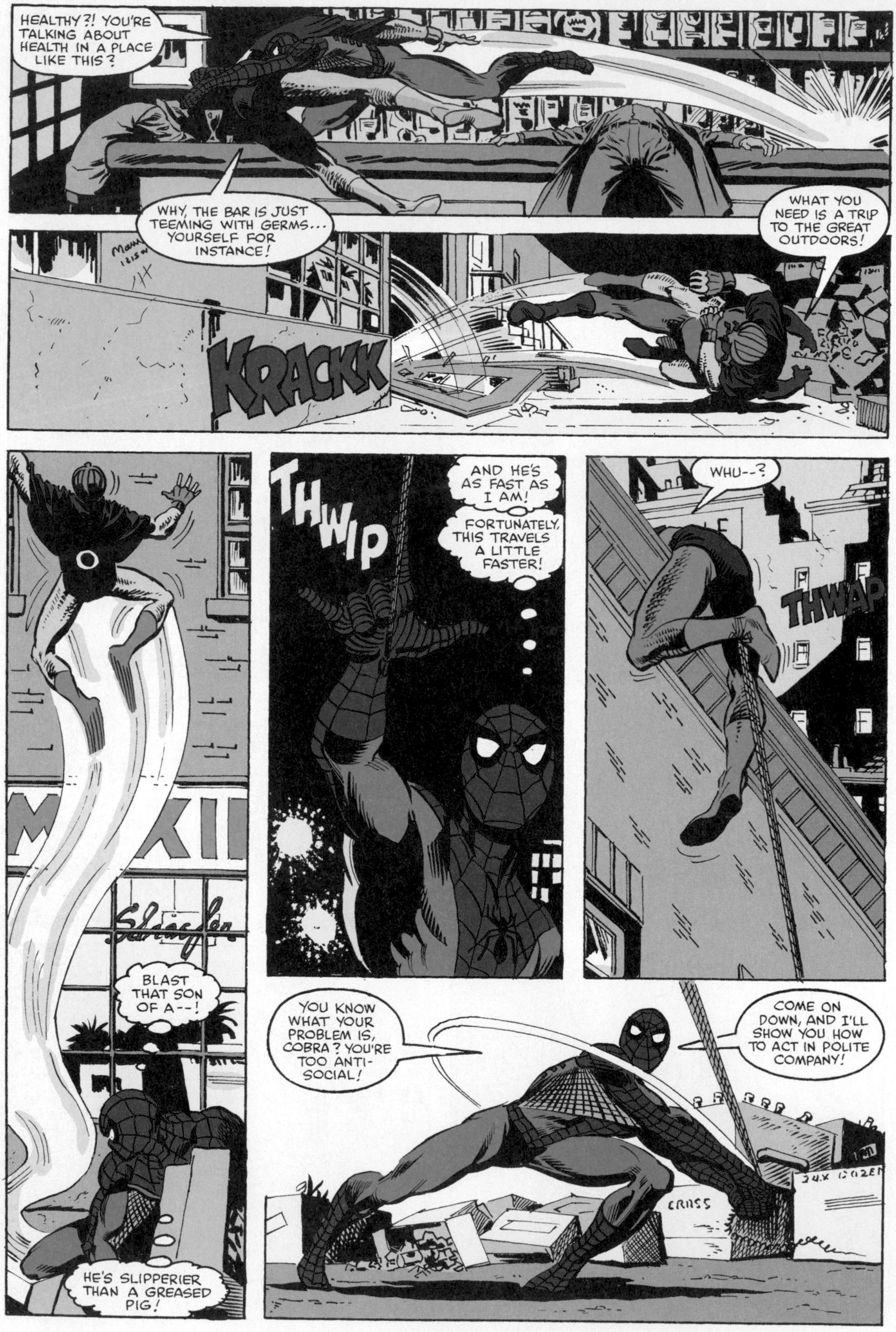
HEALTHY?! YOU'RE TALKING ABOUT HEALTH IN A PLACE LIKE THIS?
WHY, THE BAR IS JUST TEEMING WITH GERMS... YOURSELF FOR INSTANCE!
WHAT YOU NEED IS A TRIP TO THE GREAT OUTDOORS!
KRACKK
AND HE'S AS FAST AS I AM!
FORTUNATELY, THIS TRAVELS A LITTLE FASTER!
THWIP
WHU--?
THWAP
BLAST THAT SON OF A--!
HE'S SLIPPERIER THAN A GREASED PIG!
YOU KNOW WHAT YOUR PROBLEM IS, COBRA? YOU'RE TOO ANTI-SOCIAL!
COME ON DOWN, AND I'LL SHOW YOU HOW TO ACT IN POLITE COMPANY!

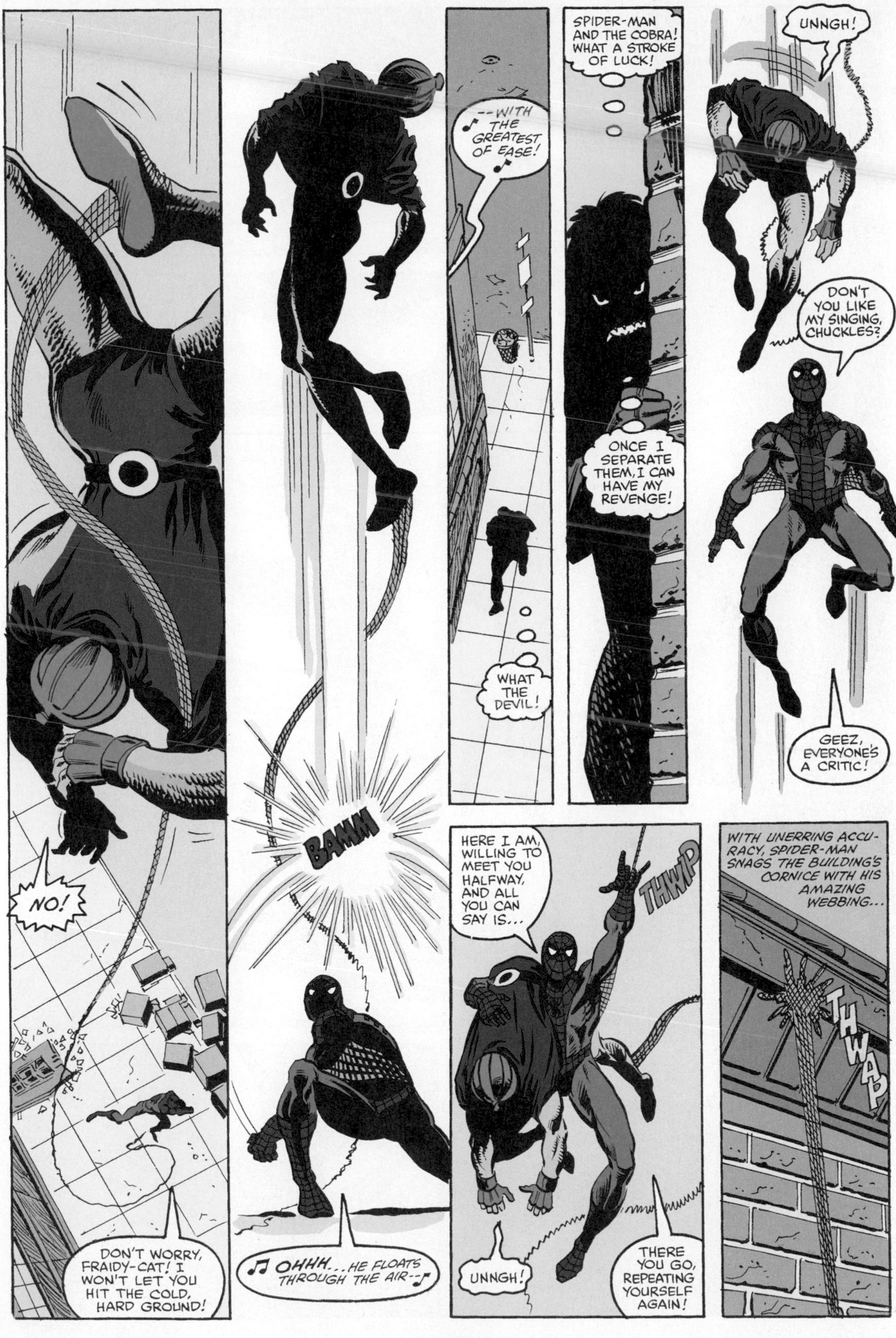
NO!
DON'T WORRY, FRAIDY-CAT! I WON'T LET YOU HIT THE COLD, HARD GROUND!
BAMM
OHHH...HE FLOATS THROUGH THE AIR--
--WITH THE GREATEST OF EASE!
WHAT THE DEVIL!
SPIDER-MAN AND THE COBRA! WHAT A STROKE OF LUCK!
ONCE I SEPARATE THEM, I CAN HAVE MY REVENGE!
UNNGH!
DON'T YOU LIKE MY SINGING, CHUCKLES?
GEEZ, EVERYONE'S A CRITIC!
HERE I AM, WILLING TO MEET YOU HALFWAY, AND ALL YOU CAN SAY IS...
THWIP
UNNGH!
THERE YOU GO, REPEATING YOURSELF AGAIN!
WITH UNERRING ACCURACY, SPIDER-MAN SNAGS THE BUILDING'S CORNICE WITH HIS AMAZING WEBBING...
THWAP

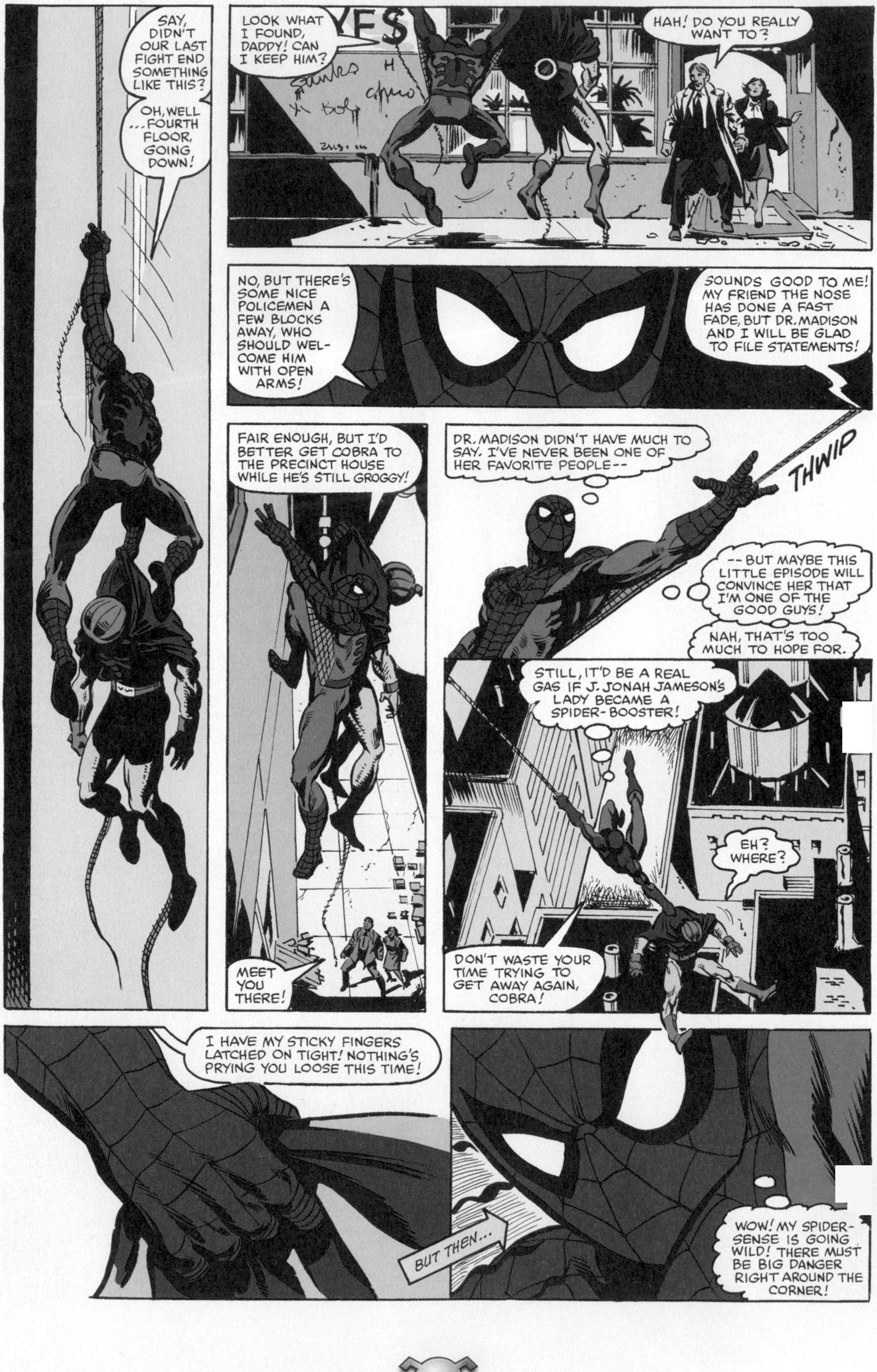

SAY, DIDN'T OUR LAST FIGHT END SOMETHING LIKE THIS?
OH, WELL ...FOURTH FLOOR, GOING DOWN!
LOOK WHAT I FOUND, DADDY! CAN I KEEP HIM?
HAH! DO YOU REALLY WANT TO?
NO, BUT THERE'S SOME NICE POLICEMEN A FEW BLOCKS AWAY, WHO SHOULD WEL-COME HIM WITH OPEN ARMS!
SOUNDS GOOD TO ME! MY FRIEND THE NOSE HAS DONE A FAST FADE, BUT DR. MADISON AND I WILL BE GLAD TO FILE STATEMENTS!
FAIR ENOUGH, BUT I'D BETTER GET COBRA TO THE PRECINCT HOUSE WHILE HE'S STILL GROGGY!
MEET YOU THERE!
DR. MADISON DIDN'T HAVE MUCH TO SAY. I'VE NEVER BEEN ONE OF HER FAVORITE PEOPLE--
THWIP
-- BUT MAYBE THIS LITTLE EPISODE WILL CONVINCE HER THAT I'M ONE OF THE GOOD GUYS!
NAH, THAT'S TOO MUCH TO HOPE FOR.
STILL, IT'D BE A REAL GAS IF J. JONAH JAMESON'S LADY BECAME A SPIDER-BOOSTER!
EH? WHERE?
DON'T WASTE YOUR TIME TRYING TO GET AWAY AGAIN, COBRA!
I HAVE MY STICKY FINGERS LATCHED ON TIGHT! NOTHING'S PRYING YOU LOOSE THIS TIME!
BUT THEN...
WOW! MY SPIDER-SENSE IS GOING WILD! THERE MUST BE BIG DANGER RIGHT AROUND THE CORNER!

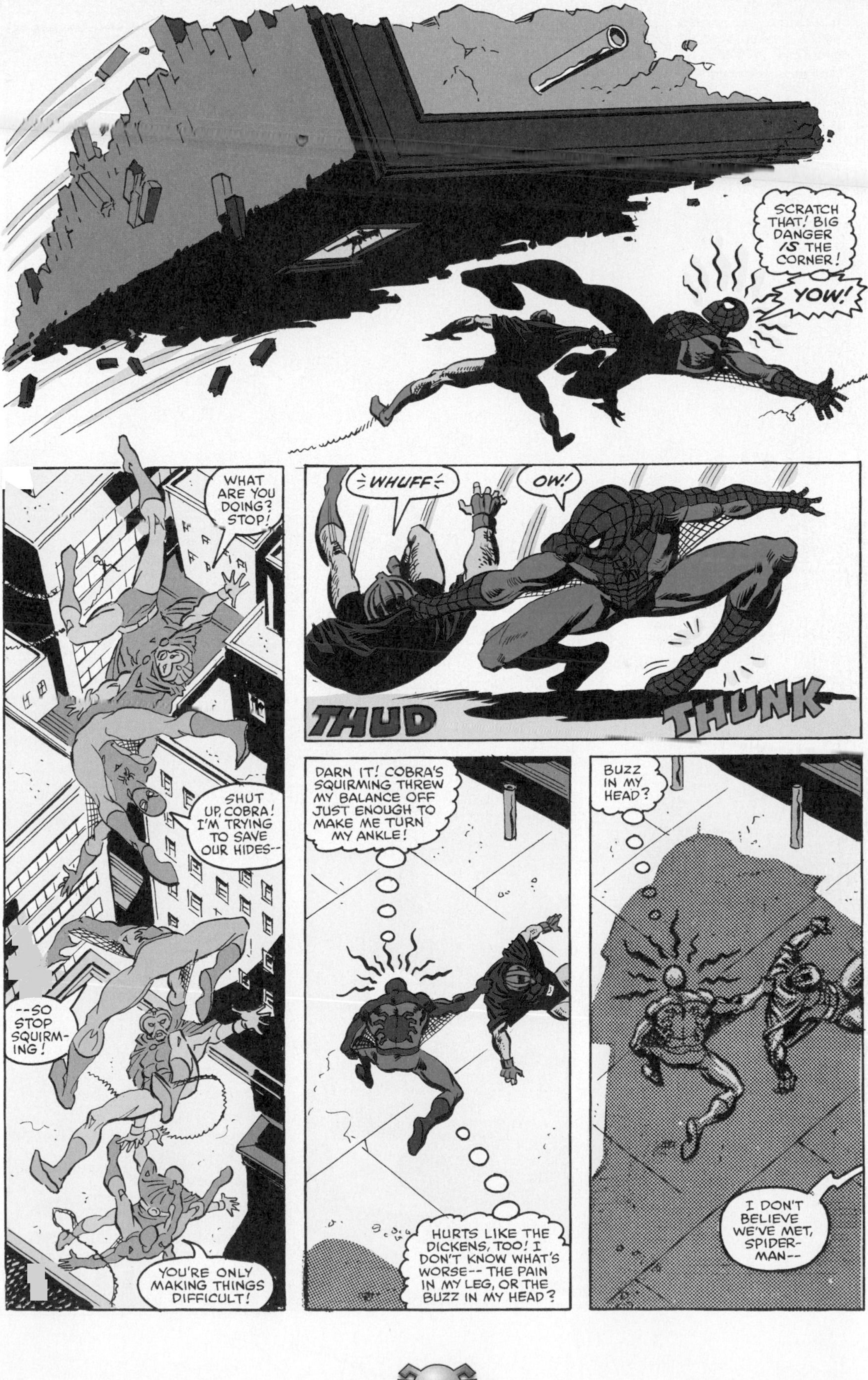
SCRATCH THAT! BIG DANGER IS THE CORNER!
YOW!
WHAT ARE YOU DOING? STOP!
SHUT UP, COBRA! I'M TRYING TO SAVE OUR HIDES--
--SO STOP SQUIRM-ING!
YOU'RE ONLY MAKING THINGS DIFFICULT!
WHUFF
OW!
THUD
THUNK
DARN IT! COBRA'S SQUIRMING THREW MY BALANCE OFF JUST ENOUGH TO MAKE ME TURN MY ANKLE!
HURTS LIKE THE DICKENS, TOO! I DON'T KNOW WHAT'S WORSE-- THE PAIN IN MY LEG, OR THE BUZZ IN MY HEAD?
BUZZ IN MY HEAD?
I DON'T BELIEVE WE'VE MET, SPIDER-MAN--

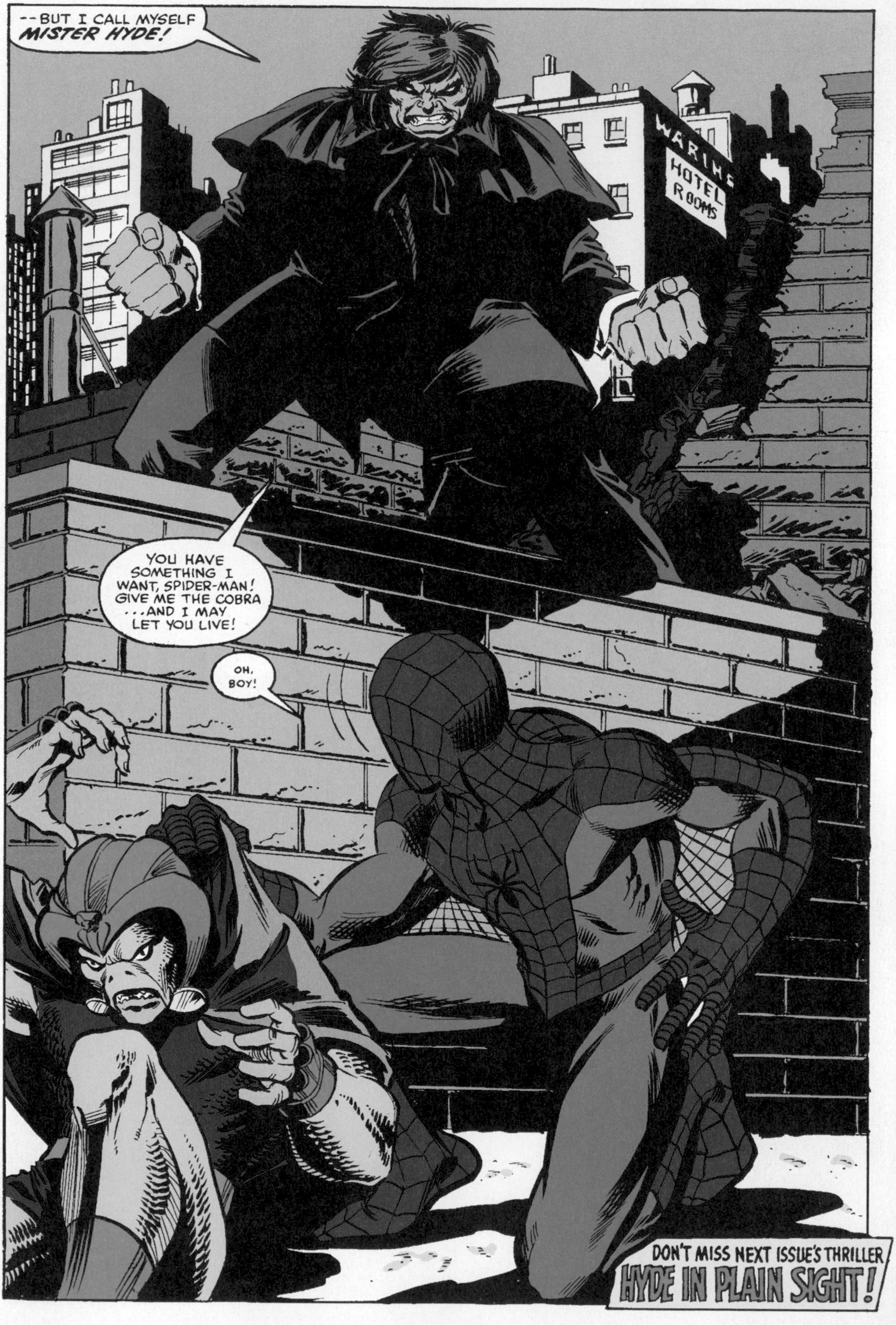
--BUT I CALL MYSELF MISTER HYDE!
YOU HAVE SOMETHING I WANT, SPIDER-MAN! GIVE ME THE COBRA ...AND I MAY LET YOU LIVE!
OH, BOY!
HOTEL ROOMS
DON'T MISS NEXT ISSUE'S THRILLER
HYDE IN PLAIN SIGHT!

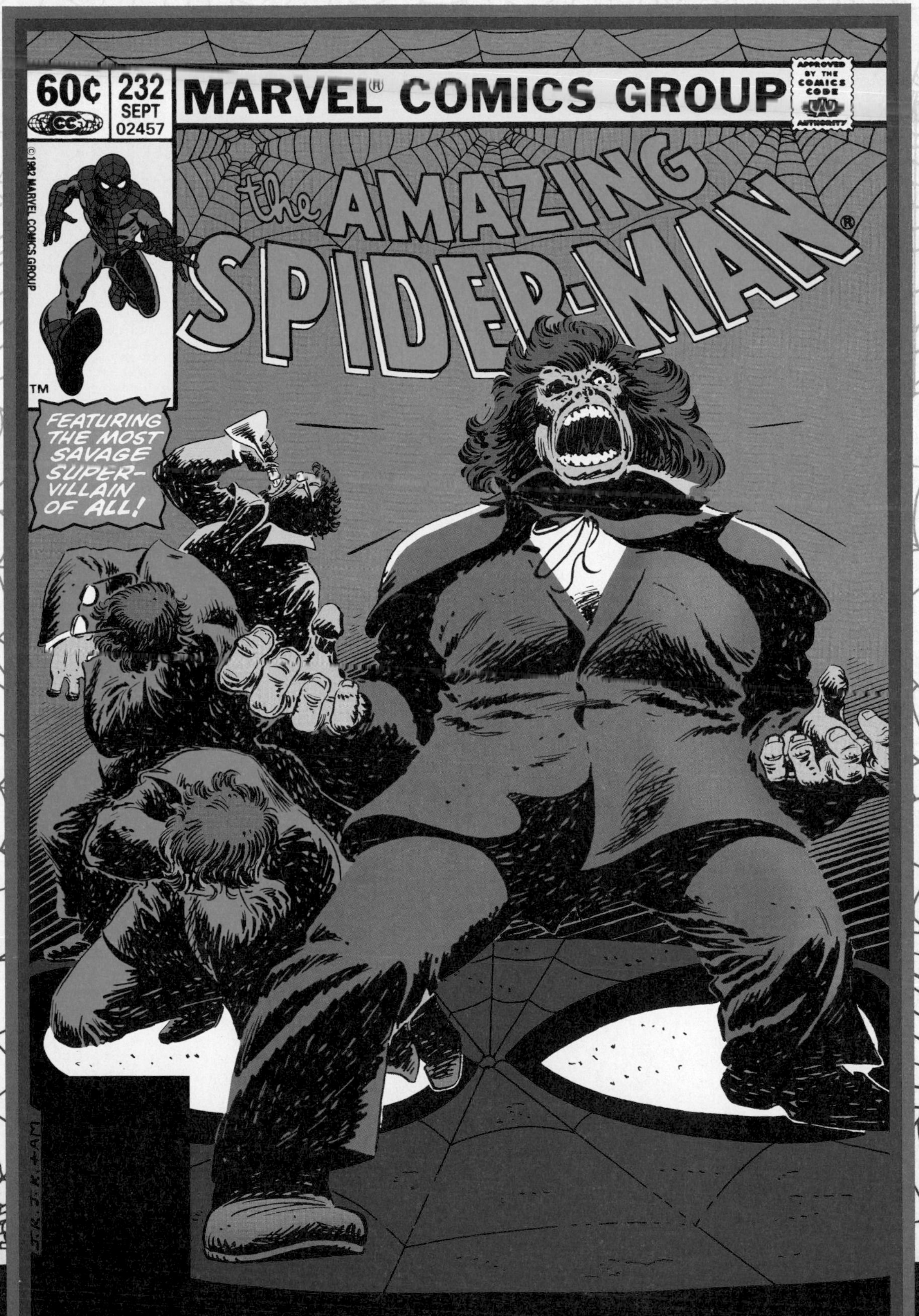
60¢
232
SEPT
02457
MARVEL® COMICS GROUP
APPROVED BY THE COMICS CODE AUTHORITY
©1982 MARVEL COMICS GROUP
the AMAZING SPIDER-MAN®
TM
FEATURING THE MOST SAVAGE SUPER-VILLAIN OF ALL!

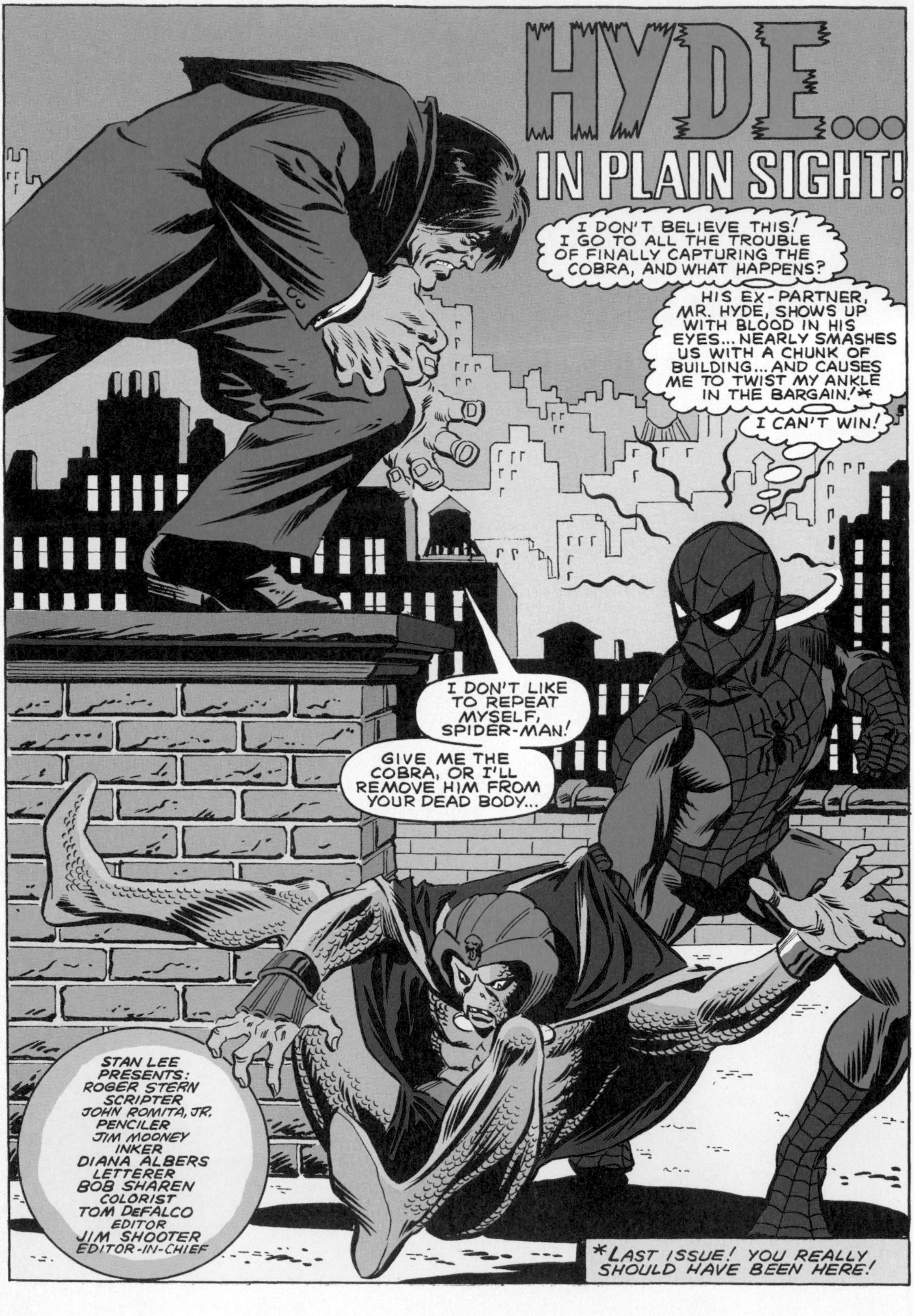
HYDE... IN PLAIN SIGHT!
I DON'T BELIEVE THIS! I GO TO ALL THE TROUBLE OF FINALLY CAPTURING THE COBRA, AND WHAT HAPPENS?
HIS EX-PARTNER, MR. HYDE, SHOWS UP WITH BLOOD IN HIS EYES... NEARLY SMASHES US WITH A CHUNK OF BUILDING... AND CAUSES ME TO TWIST MY ANKLE IN THE BARGAIN!*
I CAN'T WIN!
I DON'T LIKE TO REPEAT MYSELF, SPIDER-MAN!
GIVE ME THE COBRA, OR I'LL REMOVE HIM FROM YOUR DEAD BODY...
STAN LEE PRESENTS: ROGER STERN SCRIPTER JOHN ROMITA, JR. PENCILER JIM MOONEY INKER DIANA ALBERS LETTERER BOB SHAREN COLORIST TOM DEFALCO EDITOR JIM SHOOTER EDITOR-IN-CHIEF
*LAST ISSUE! YOU REALLY SHOULD HAVE BEEN HERE!

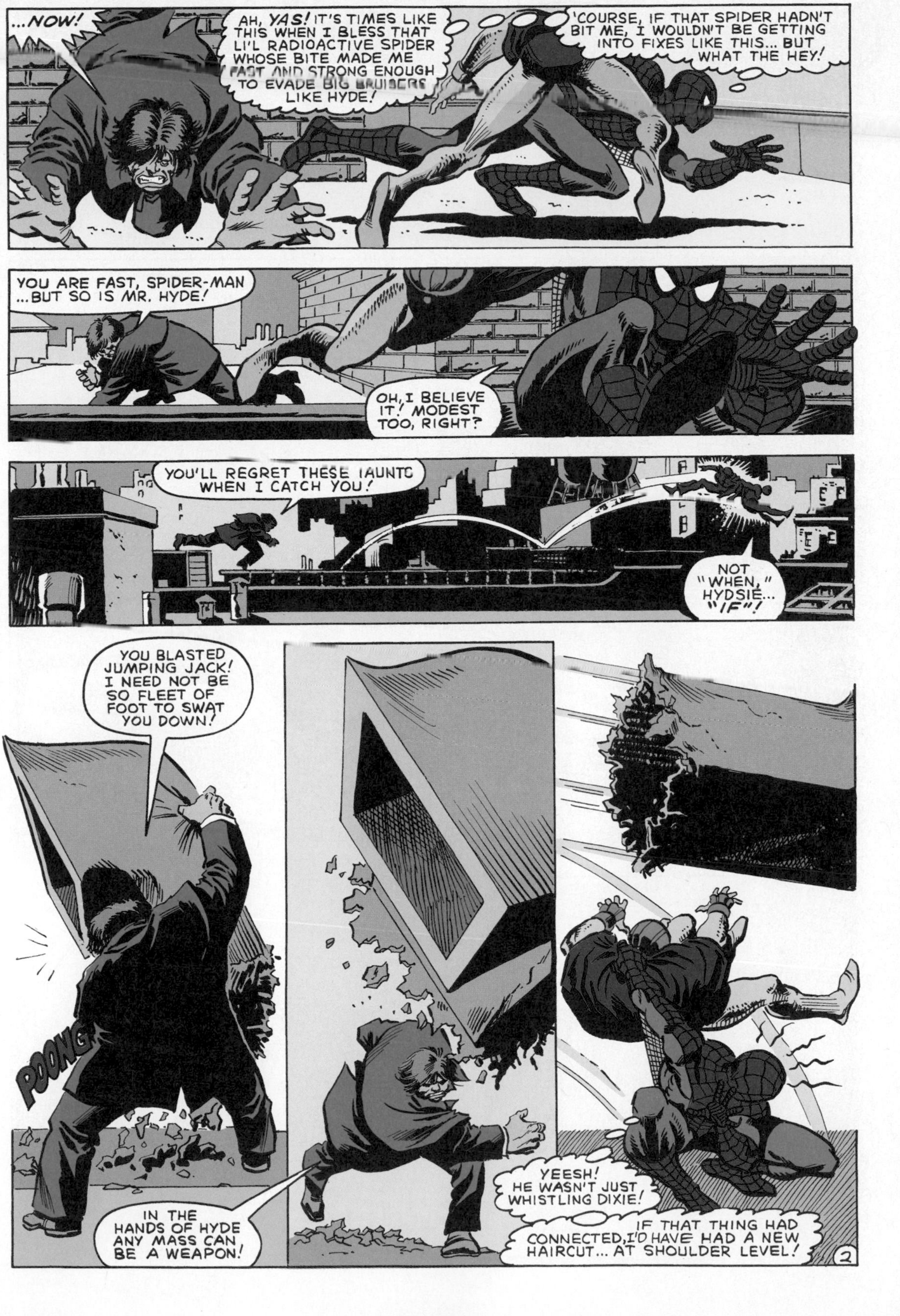
...NOW!
AH, YAS! IT'S TIMES LIKE THIS WHEN I BLESS THAT LI'L RADIOACTIVE SPIDER WHOSE BITE MADE ME FAST AND STRONG ENOUGH TO EVADE BIG BRUISERS LIKE HYDE!
'COURSE, IF THAT SPIDER HADN'T BIT ME, I WOULDN'T BE GETTING INTO FIXES LIKE THIS... BUT WHAT THE HEY!
YOU ARE FAST, SPIDER-MAN ...BUT SO IS MR. HYDE!
OH, I BELIEVE IT! MODEST TOO, RIGHT?
YOU'LL REGRET THESE TAUNTS WHEN I CATCH YOU!
NOT "WHEN," HYDSIE... "IF"!
YOU BLASTED JUMPING JACK! I NEED NOT BE SO FLEET OF FOOT TO SWAT YOU DOWN!
POONG
IN THE HANDS OF HYDE ANY MASS CAN BE A WEAPON!
YEESH! HE WASN'T JUST WHISTLING DIXIE!
IF THAT THING HAD CONNECTED, I'D HAVE HAD A NEW HAIRCUT... AT SHOULDER LEVEL!
2

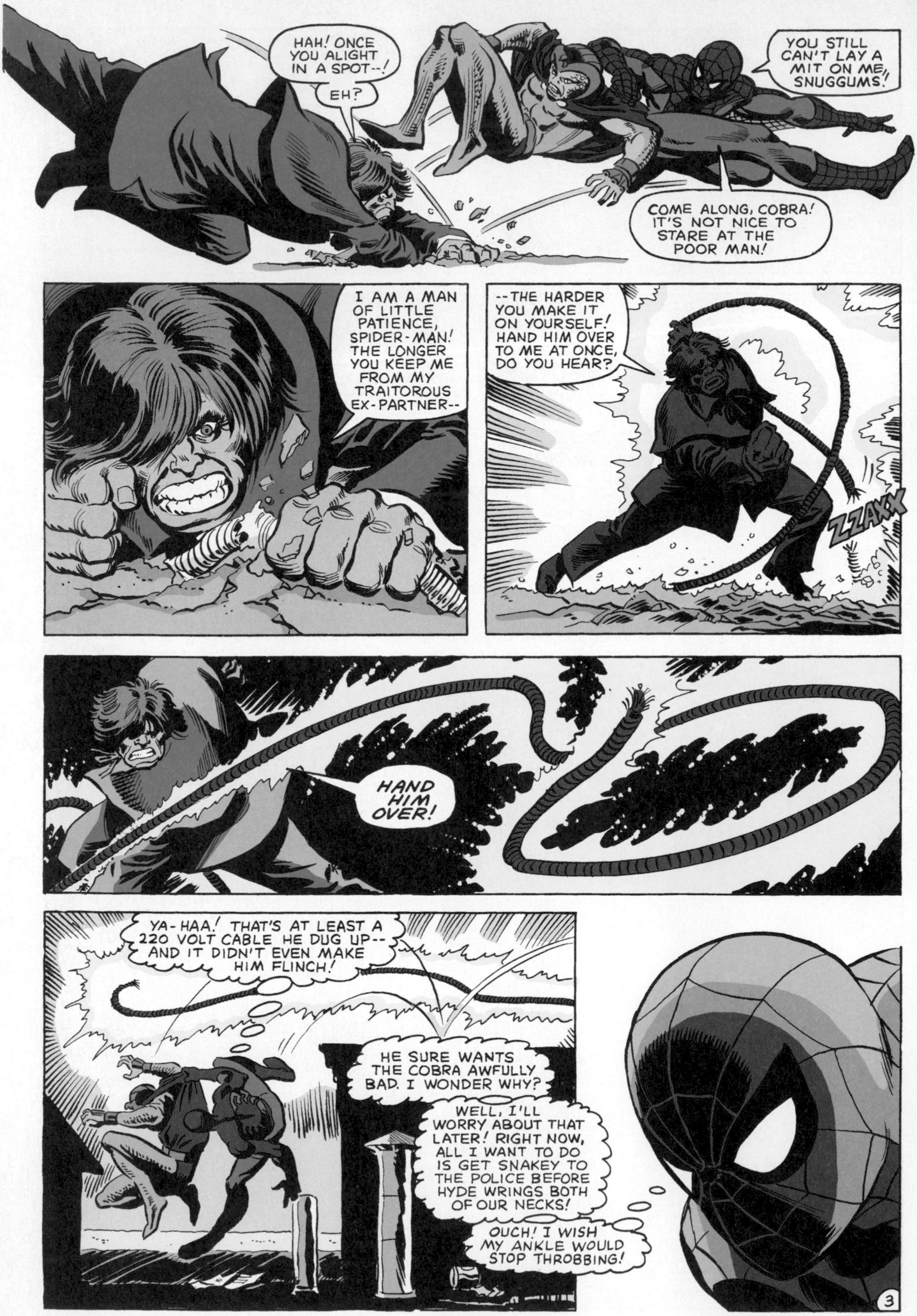
HAH! ONCE YOU ALIGHT IN A SPOT--!
EH?
YOU STILL CAN'T LAY A MIT ON ME, SNUGGUMS!
COME ALONG, COBRA! IT'S NOT NICE TO STARE AT THE POOR MAN!
I AM A MAN OF LITTLE PATIENCE, SPIDER-MAN! THE LONGER YOU KEEP ME FROM MY TRAITOROUS EX-PARTNER--
--THE HARDER YOU MAKE IT ON YOURSELF! HAND HIM OVER TO ME AT ONCE, DO YOU HEAR?
ZZAKK
HAND HIM OVER!
YA-HAA! THAT'S AT LEAST A 220 VOLT CABLE HE DUG UP-- AND IT DIDN'T EVEN MAKE HIM FLINCH!
HE SURE WANTS THE COBRA AWFULLY BAD. I WONDER WHY?
WELL, I'LL WORRY ABOUT THAT LATER! RIGHT NOW, ALL I WANT TO DO IS GET SNAKEY TO THE POLICE BEFORE HYDE WRINGS BOTH OF OUR NECKS!
OUCH! I WISH MY ANKLE WOULD STOP THROBBING!
3

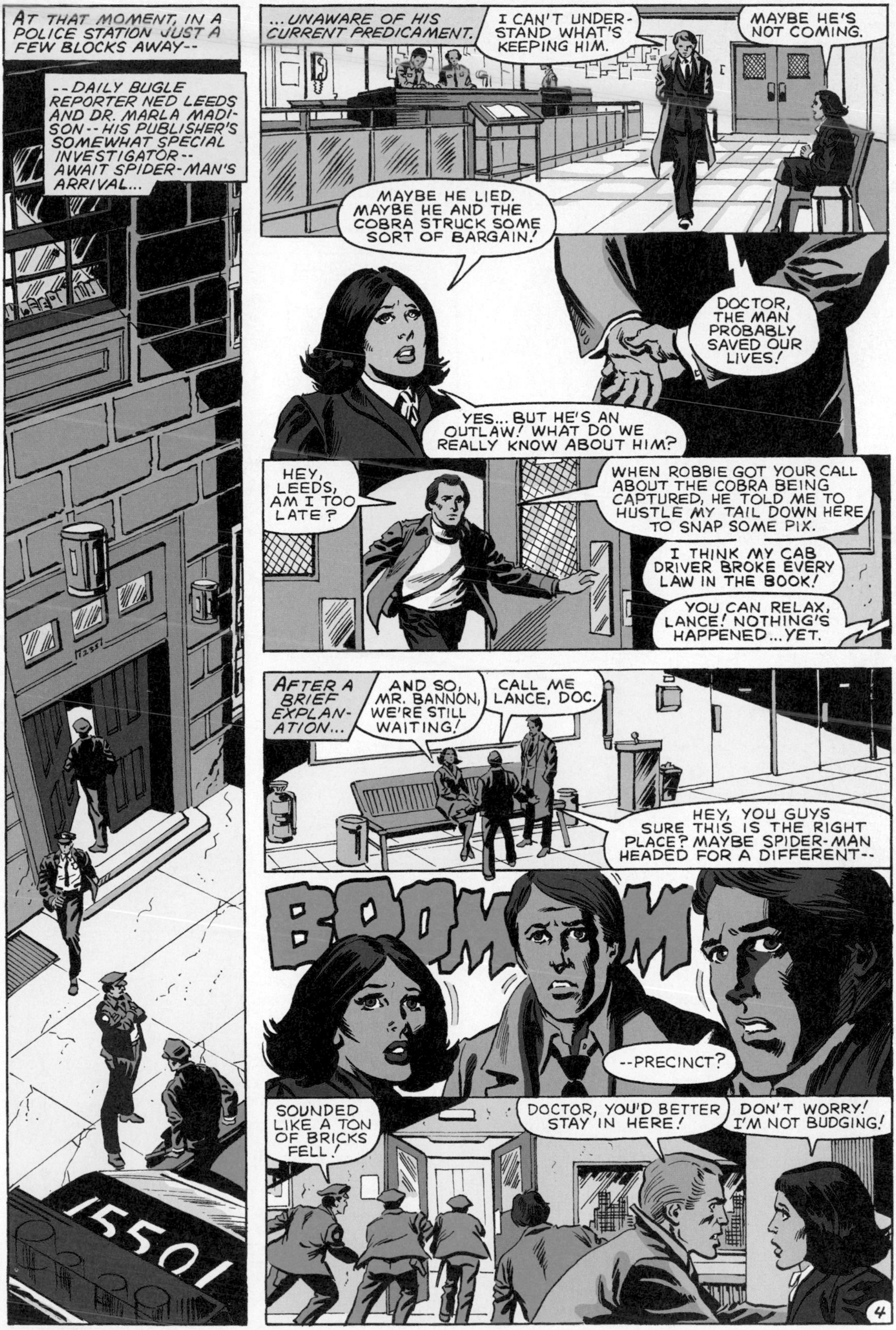

AT THAT MOMENT, IN A POLICE STATION JUST A FEW BLOCKS AWAY--
--DAILY BUGLE REPORTER NED LEEDS AND DR. MARLA MADISON--HIS PUBLISHER'S SOMEWHAT SPECIAL INVESTIGATOR--AWAIT SPIDER-MAN'S ARRIVAL...
...UNAWARE OF HIS CURRENT PREDICAMENT.
I CAN'T UNDERSTAND WHAT'S KEEPING HIM.
MAYBE HE'S NOT COMING.
MAYBE HE LIED. MAYBE HE AND THE COBRA STRUCK SOME SORT OF BARGAIN!
DOCTOR, THE MAN PROBABLY SAVED OUR LIVES!
YES... BUT HE'S AN OUTLAW! WHAT DO WE REALLY KNOW ABOUT HIM?
HEY, LEEDS, AM I TOO LATE?
WHEN ROBBIE GOT YOUR CALL ABOUT THE COBRA BEING CAPTURED, HE TOLD ME TO HUSTLE MY TAIL DOWN HERE TO SNAP SOME PIX.
I THINK MY CAB DRIVER BROKE EVERY LAW IN THE BOOK!
YOU CAN RELAX, LANCE! NOTHING'S HAPPENED...YET.
AFTER A BRIEF EXPLANATION...
AND SO, MR. BANNON, WE'RE STILL WAITING!
CALL ME LANCE, DOC.
HEY, YOU GUYS SURE THIS IS THE RIGHT PLACE? MAYBE SPIDER-MAN HEADED FOR A DIFFERENT--
BOOM
--PRECINCT?
SOUNDED LIKE A TON OF BRICKS FELL!
DOCTOR, YOU'D BETTER STAY IN HERE!
DON'T WORRY! I'M NOT BUDGING!
4

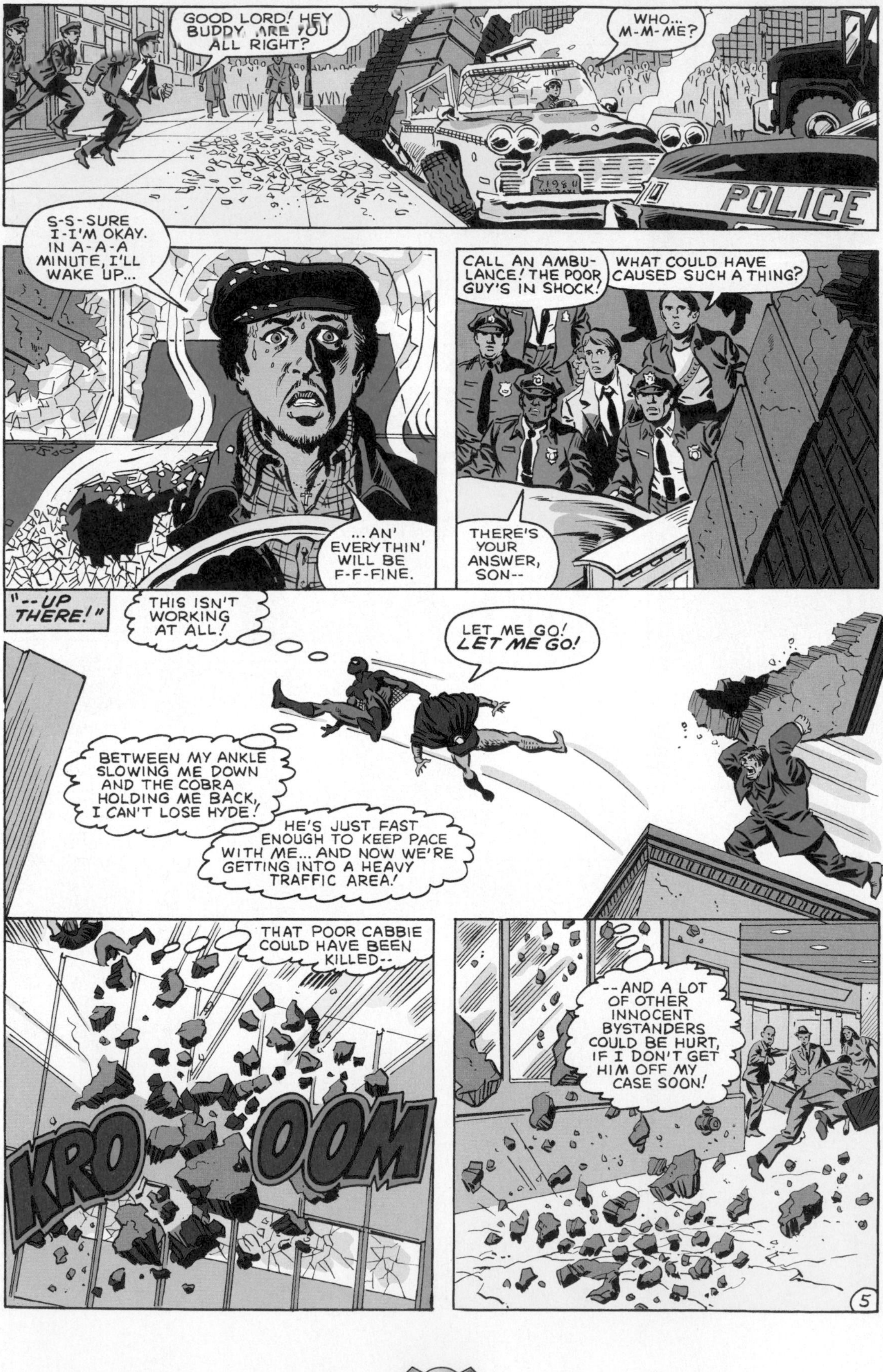
GOOD LORD! HEY BUDDY, ARE YOU ALL RIGHT?
WHO... M-M-ME?
POLICE
S-S-SURE I-I'M OKAY. IN A-A-A MINUTE, I'LL WAKE UP...
...AN' EVERYTHIN' WILL BE F-F-FINE.
CALL AN AMBULANCE! THE POOR GUY'S IN SHOCK!
WHAT COULD HAVE CAUSED SUCH A THING?
THERE'S YOUR ANSWER, SON--
"--UP THERE!"
THIS ISN'T WORKING AT ALL!
LET ME GO! LET ME GO!
BETWEEN MY ANKLE SLOWING ME DOWN AND THE COBRA HOLDING ME BACK, I CAN'T LOSE HYDE!
HE'S JUST FAST ENOUGH TO KEEP PACE WITH ME... AND NOW WE'RE GETTING INTO A HEAVY TRAFFIC AREA!
THAT POOR CABBIE COULD HAVE BEEN KILLED--
KROOOM
--AND A LOT OF OTHER INNOCENT BYSTANDERS COULD BE HURT, IF I DON'T GET HIM OFF MY CASE SOON!
5

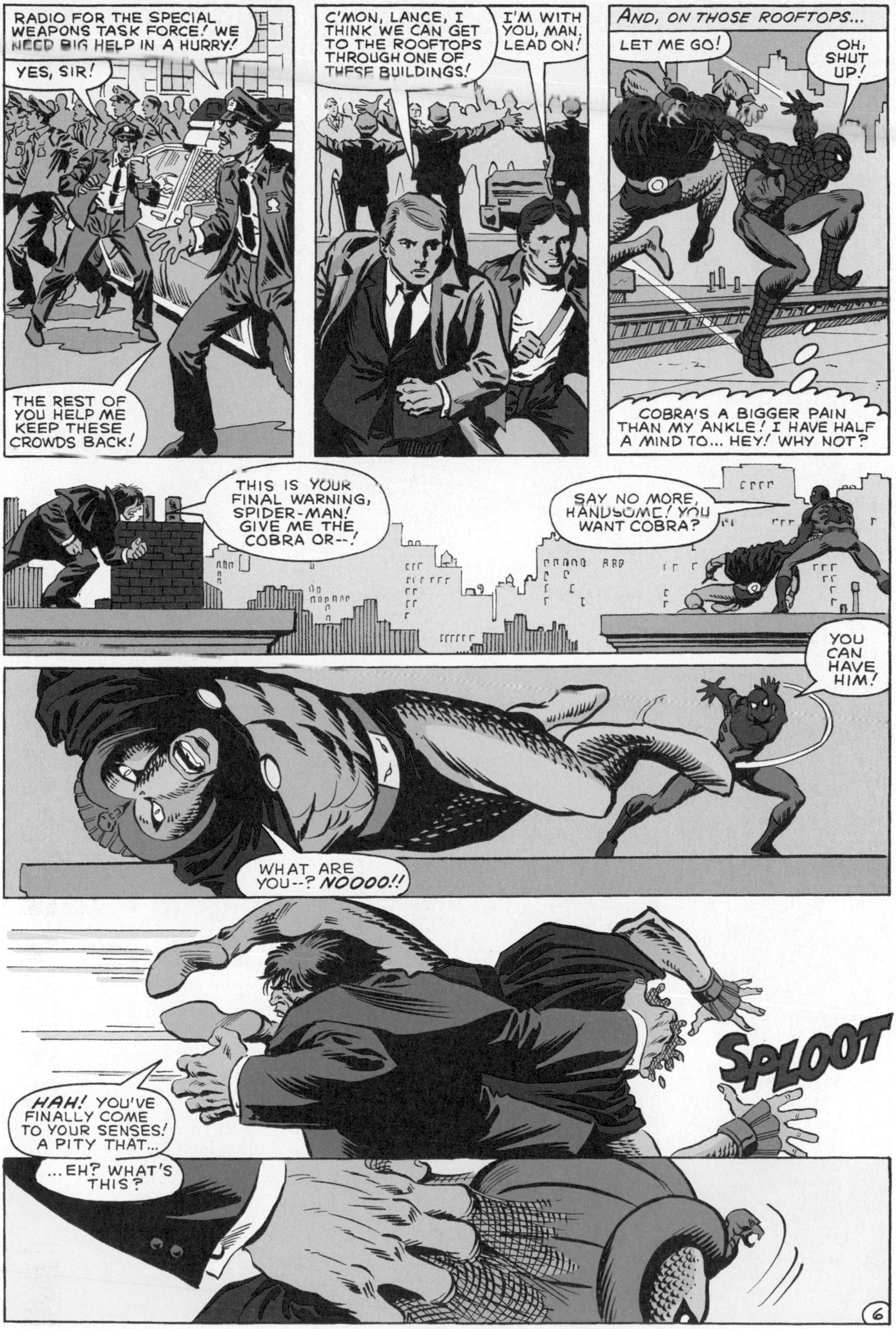
RADIO FOR THE SPECIAL WEAPONS TASK FORCE! WE NEED BIG HELP IN A HURRY!
YES, SIR!
THE REST OF YOU HELP ME KEEP THESE CROWDS BACK!
C'MON, LANCE, I THINK WE CAN GET TO THE ROOFTOPS THROUGH ONE OF THESE BUILDINGS!
I'M WITH YOU, MAN. LEAD ON!
AND, ON THOSE ROOFTOPS...
LET ME GO!
OH, SHUT UP!
COBRA'S A BIGGER PAIN THAN MY ANKLE! I HAVE HALF A MIND TO... HEY! WHY NOT?
THIS IS YOUR FINAL WARNING, SPIDER-MAN! GIVE ME THE COBRA OR--!
SAY NO MORE, HANDSOME! YOU WANT COBRA?
YOU CAN HAVE HIM!
WHAT ARE YOU--? NOOOO!!
SPLOOT
HAH! YOU'VE FINALLY COME TO YOUR SENSES! A PITY THAT...
...EH? WHAT'S THIS?
6

YOU COATED THE BACK OF HIS HELMET WITH YOUR INFERNAL WEB-BING! I'M STUCK TIGHT TO HIM!

FIGURE THAT OUT BY YOURSELF, OR DID YOU HAVE HELP?

I WAS STUCK WITH COBRA LONG ENOUGH... NOW, IT'S YOUR TURN!

WOW! WHAT A GREAT VANTAGE POINT FOR PHOTOS!

YOU THINK YOU CAN HOBBLE ME THIS WAY? *BAH!!*

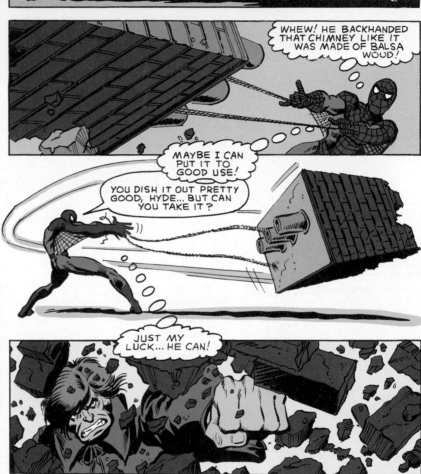

WHEW! HE BACKHANDED THAT CHIMNEY LIKE IT WAS MADE OF BALSA WOOD!

MAYBE I CAN PUT IT TO GOOD USE!

YOU DISH IT OUT PRETTY GOOD, HYDE... BUT CAN YOU TAKE IT?

JUST MY LUCK... HE CAN!

INCREDIBLE!

BE CAREFUL GETTING OUT ON THAT LEDGE, LANCE!

AW, DON'T BE AN OLD LADY, LEEDS! YA GOTTA TAKE RISKS TO GET GOOD SHOTS! EVER SEE PARKER'S PHOTOS?

LOUSY COMPOSITION, BUT GREAT ANGLES! YOU CAN BET HE TAKES RISKS!

BUT THESE SHOTS... THEY'RE GONNA MAKE HIS STUFF LOOK SICK!

7

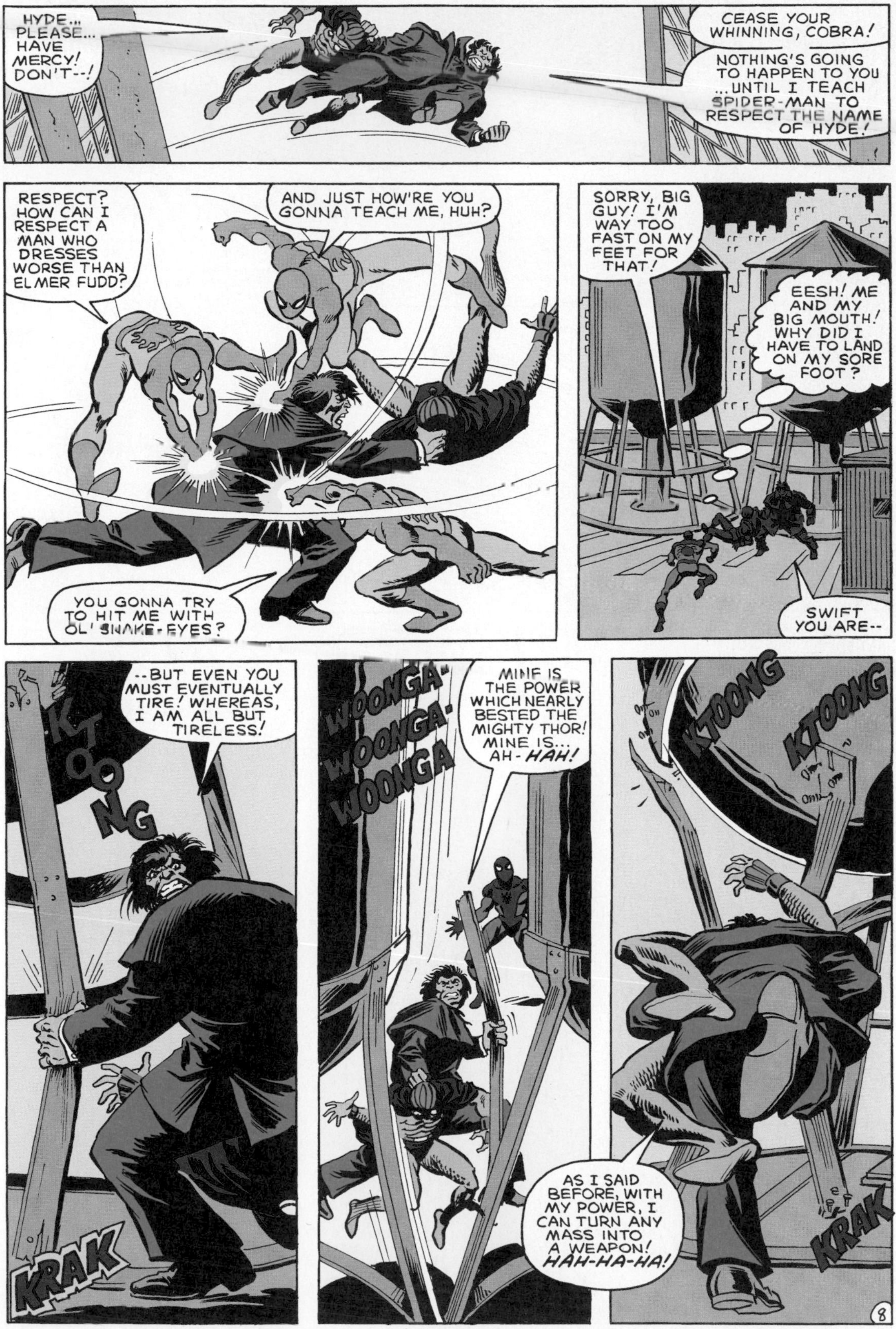
HYDE... PLEASE... HAVE MERCY! DON'T--!
CEASE YOUR WHINNING, COBRA!
NOTHING'S GOING TO HAPPEN TO YOU ...UNTIL I TEACH SPIDER-MAN TO RESPECT THE NAME OF HYDE!
RESPECT? HOW CAN I RESPECT A MAN WHO DRESSES WORSE THAN ELMER FUDD?
AND JUST HOW'RE YOU GONNA TEACH ME, HUH?
YOU GONNA TRY TO HIT ME WITH OL' SNAKE-EYES?
SORRY, BIG GUY! I'M WAY TOO FAST ON MY FEET FOR THAT!
EESH! ME AND MY BIG MOUTH! WHY DID I HAVE TO LAND ON MY SORE FOOT?
SWIFT YOU ARE--
--BUT EVEN YOU MUST EVENTUALLY TIRE! WHEREAS, I AM ALL BUT TIRELESS!
KTOONG
KRAK
WOONGA- WOONGA- WOONGA
MINE IS THE POWER WHICH NEARLY BESTED THE MIGHTY THOR! MINE IS... AH-HAH!
KTOONG
KTOONG
AS I SAID BEFORE, WITH MY POWER, I CAN TURN ANY MASS INTO A WEAPON! HAH-HA-HA!
KRAK
8

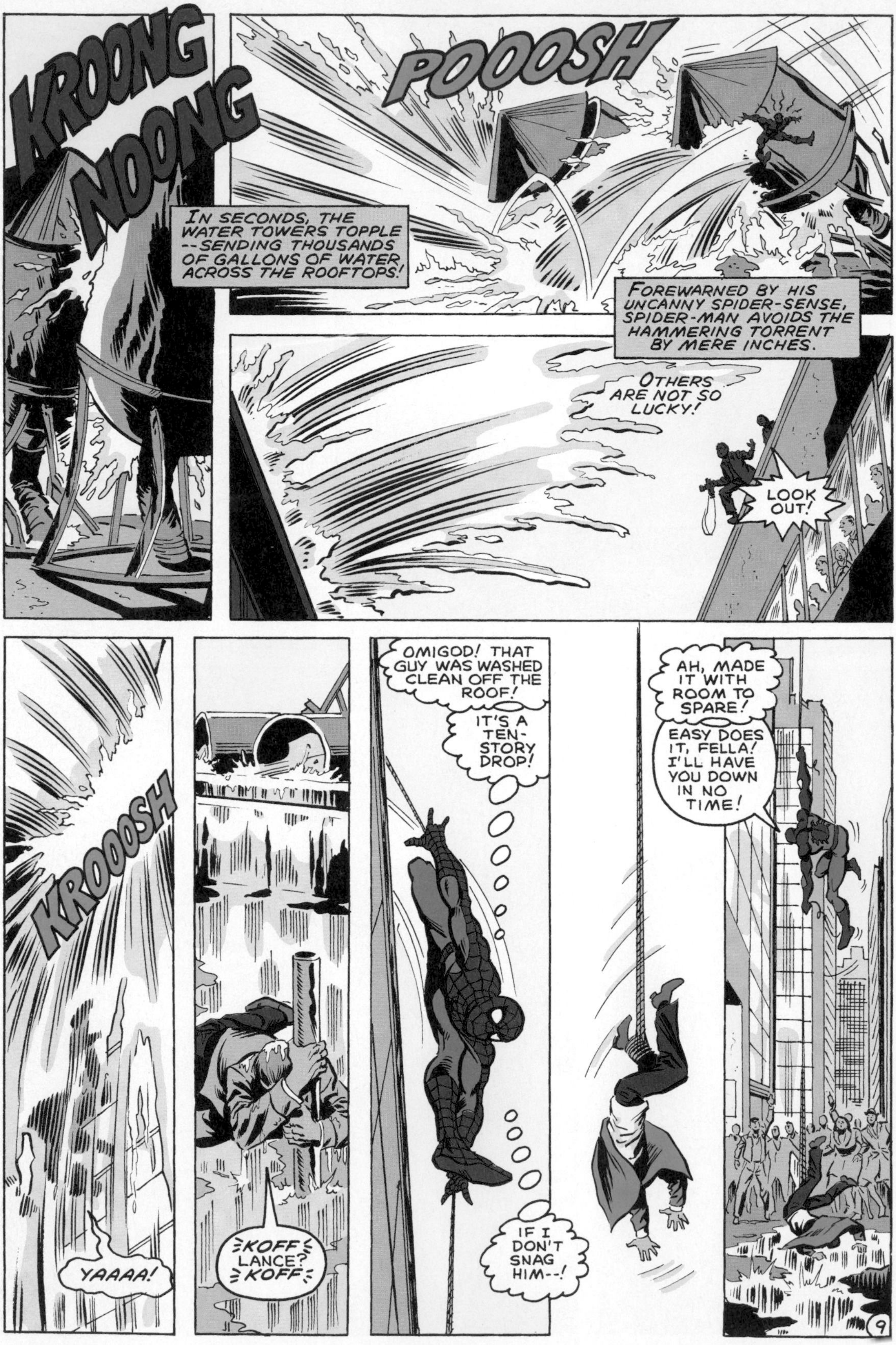
KROONG NOONG
POOOSH
IN SECONDS, THE WATER TOWERS TOPPLE --SENDING THOUSANDS OF GALLONS OF WATER ACROSS THE ROOFTOPS!
FOREWARNED BY HIS UNCANNY SPIDER-SENSE, SPIDER-MAN AVOIDS THE HAMMERING TORRENT BY MERE INCHES.
OTHERS ARE NOT SO LUCKY!
LOOK OUT!
KROOOSH
YAAAA!
KOFF LANCE? KOFF
OMIGOD! THAT GUY WAS WASHED CLEAN OFF THE ROOF!
IT'S A TEN-STORY DROP!
IF I DON'T SNAG HIM--!
AH, MADE IT WITH ROOM TO SPARE!
EASY DOES IT, FELLA! I'LL HAVE YOU DOWN IN NO TIME!
9

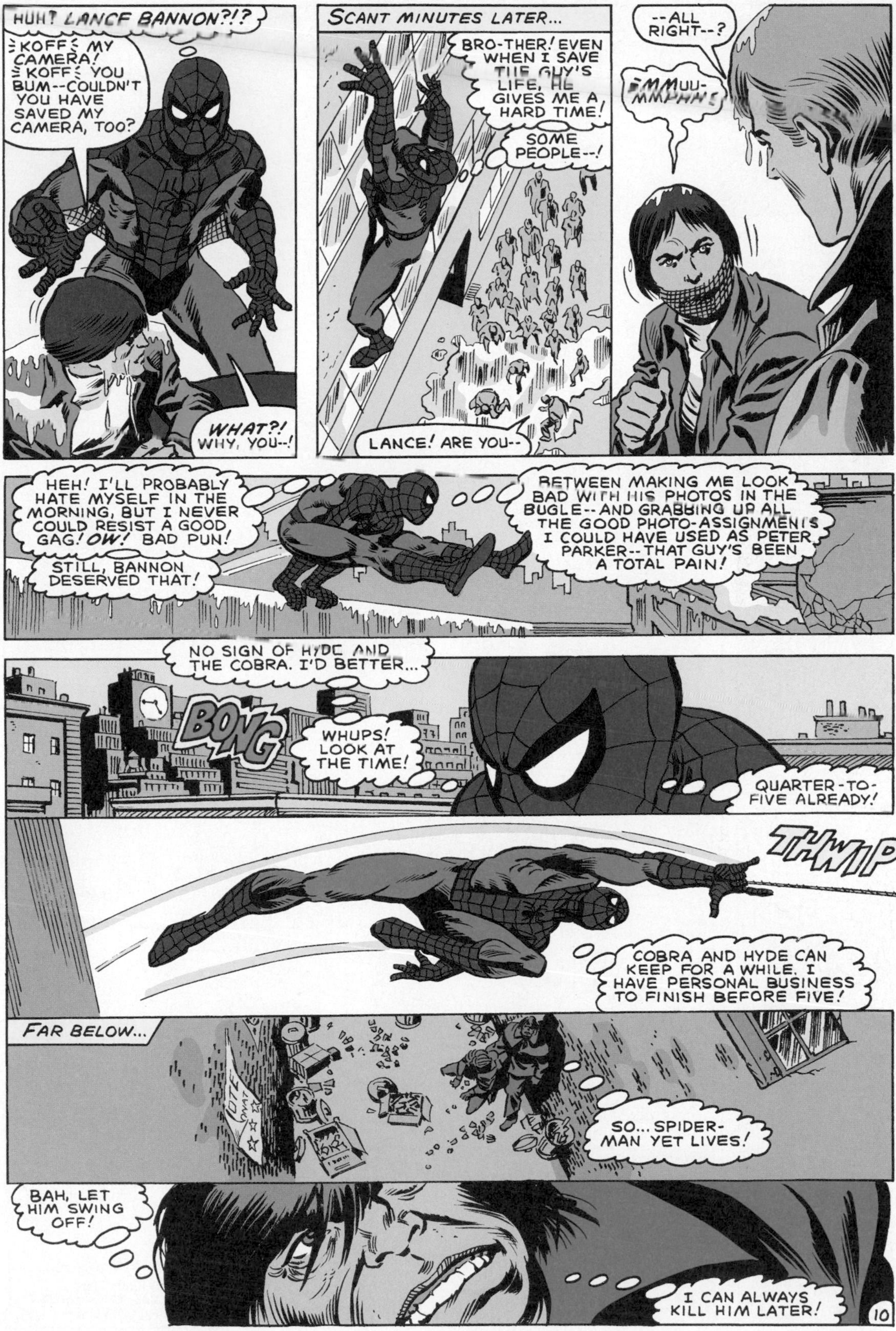
HUH? LANCE BANNON?!?
KOFF MY CAMERA! KOFF YOU BUM--COULDN'T YOU HAVE SAVED MY CAMERA, TOO?
WHAT?! WHY, YOU--!
SCANT MINUTES LATER...
BRO-THER! EVEN WHEN I SAVE THE GUY'S LIFE, HE GIVES ME A HARD TIME!
SOME PEOPLE--!
LANCE! ARE YOU--
--ALL RIGHT--?
MMMUU-MMPHN!
HEH! I'LL PROBABLY HATE MYSELF IN THE MORNING, BUT I NEVER COULD RESIST A GOOD GAG! OW! BAD PUN!
STILL, BANNON DESERVED THAT!
BETWEEN MAKING ME LOOK BAD WITH HIS PHOTOS IN THE BUGLE--AND GRABBING UP ALL THE GOOD PHOTO-ASSIGNMENTS I COULD HAVE USED AS PETER PARKER--THAT GUY'S BEEN A TOTAL PAIN!
NO SIGN OF HYDE AND THE COBRA. I'D BETTER...
BONG
WHUPS! LOOK AT THE TIME!
QUARTER-TO-FIVE ALREADY!
THWIP
COBRA AND HYDE CAN KEEP FOR A WHILE. I HAVE PERSONAL BUSINESS TO FINISH BEFORE FIVE!
FAR BELOW...
SO...SPIDER-MAN YET LIVES!
BAH, LET HIM SWING OFF!
I CAN ALWAYS KILL HIM LATER!
10

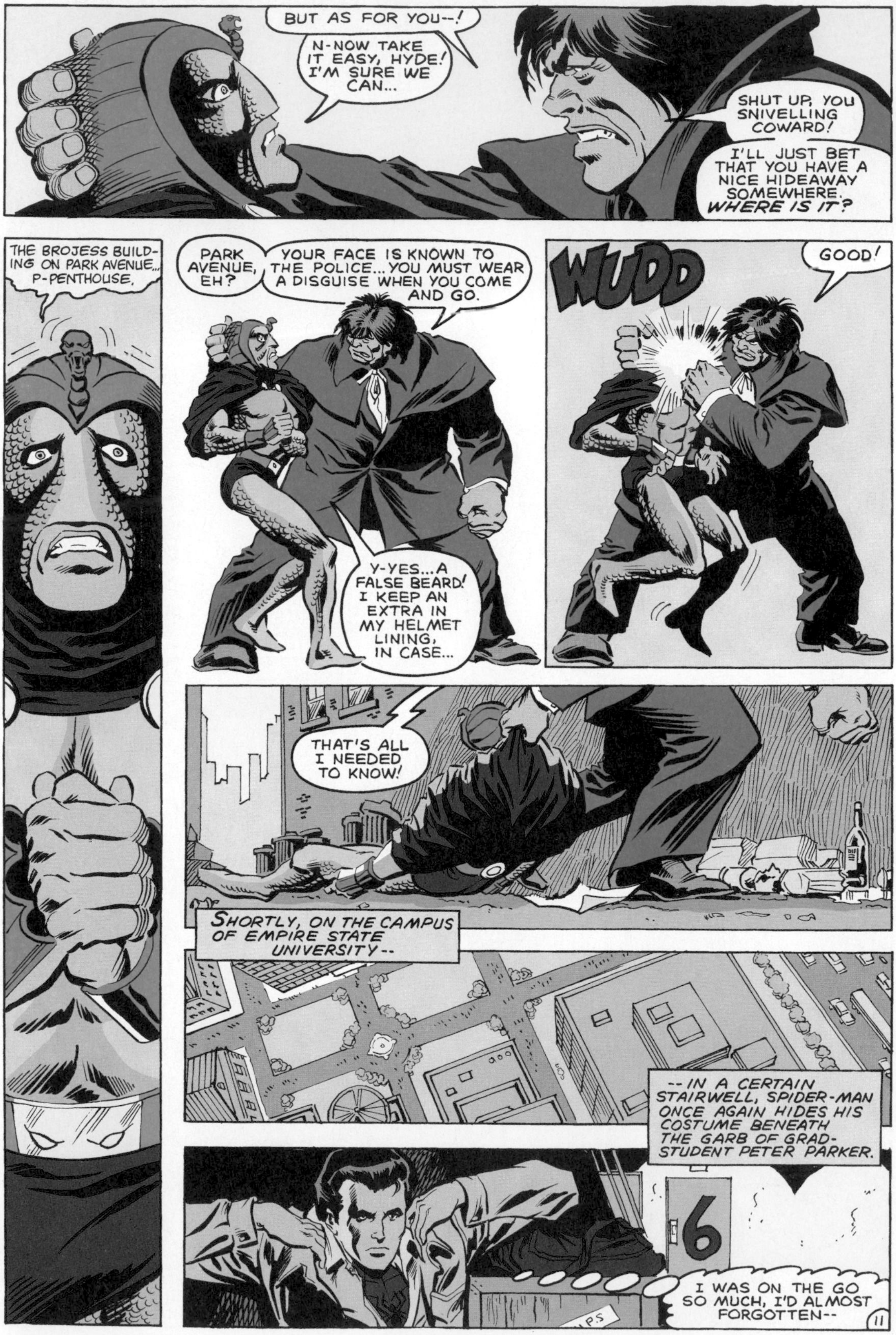
BUT AS FOR YOU--!
N-NOW TAKE IT EASY, HYDE! I'M SURE WE CAN...
SHUT UP, YOU SNIVELLING COWARD!
I'LL JUST BET THAT YOU HAVE A NICE HIDEAWAY SOMEWHERE. WHERE IS IT?
THE BROJESS BUILDING ON PARK AVENUE... P-PENTHOUSE.
PARK AVENUE, EH?
YOUR FACE IS KNOWN TO THE POLICE... YOU MUST WEAR A DISGUISE WHEN YOU COME AND GO.
Y-YES... A FALSE BEARD! I KEEP AN EXTRA IN MY HELMET LINING, IN CASE...
WUDD
GOOD!
THAT'S ALL I NEEDED TO KNOW!
SHORTLY, ON THE CAMPUS OF EMPIRE STATE UNIVERSITY--
--IN A CERTAIN STAIRWELL, SPIDER-MAN ONCE AGAIN HIDES HIS COSTUME BENEATH THE GARB OF GRAD-STUDENT PETER PARKER.
6
I WAS ON THE GO SO MUCH, I'D ALMOST FORGOTTEN--
11

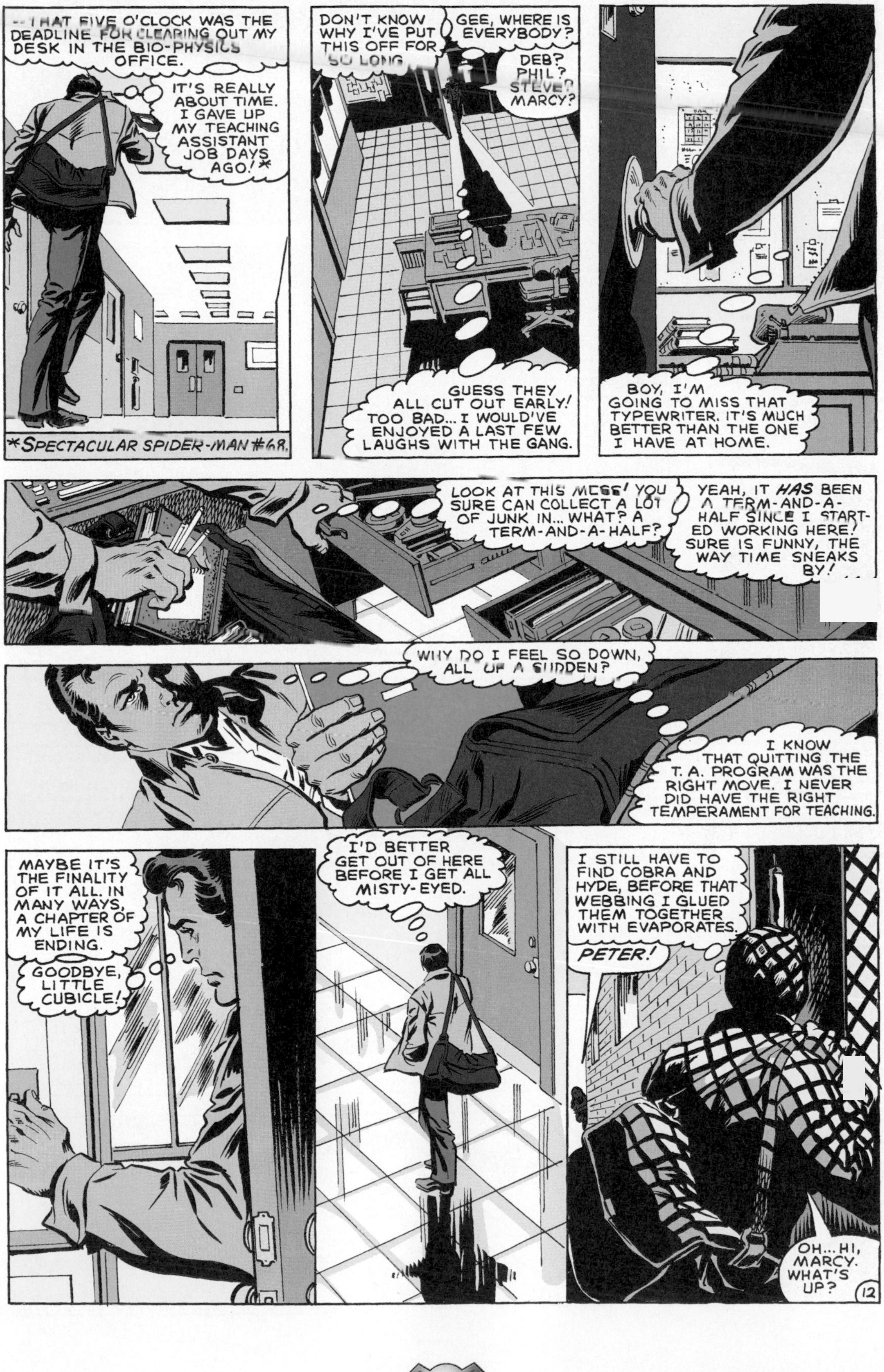
--THAT FIVE O'CLOCK WAS THE DEADLINE FOR CLEARING OUT MY DESK IN THE BIO-PHYSICS OFFICE.
IT'S REALLY ABOUT TIME. I GAVE UP MY TEACHING ASSISTANT JOB DAYS AGO!*
*SPECTACULAR SPIDER-MAN #68.
DON'T KNOW WHY I'VE PUT THIS OFF FOR SO LONG.
GEE, WHERE IS EVERYBODY?
DEB? PHIL? STEVE? MARCY?
GUESS THEY ALL CUT OUT EARLY! TOO BAD... I WOULD'VE ENJOYED A LAST FEW LAUGHS WITH THE GANG.
BOY, I'M GOING TO MISS THAT TYPEWRITER. IT'S MUCH BETTER THAN THE ONE I HAVE AT HOME.
LOOK AT THIS MESS! YOU SURE CAN COLLECT A LOT OF JUNK IN... WHAT? A TERM-AND-A-HALF?
YEAH, IT HAS BEEN A TERM-AND-A-HALF SINCE I STARTED WORKING HERE! SURE IS FUNNY, THE WAY TIME SNEAKS BY!
WHY DO I FEEL SO DOWN, ALL OF A SUDDEN?
I KNOW THAT QUITTING THE T. A. PROGRAM WAS THE RIGHT MOVE. I NEVER DID HAVE THE RIGHT TEMPERAMENT FOR TEACHING.
MAYBE IT'S THE FINALITY OF IT ALL. IN MANY WAYS, A CHAPTER OF MY LIFE IS ENDING.
GOODBYE, LITTLE CUBICLE!
I'D BETTER GET OUT OF HERE BEFORE I GET ALL MISTY-EYED.
I STILL HAVE TO FIND COBRA AND HYDE, BEFORE THAT WEBBING I GLUED THEM TOGETHER WITH EVAPORATES.
PETER!
OH... HI, MARCY. WHAT'S UP?
12

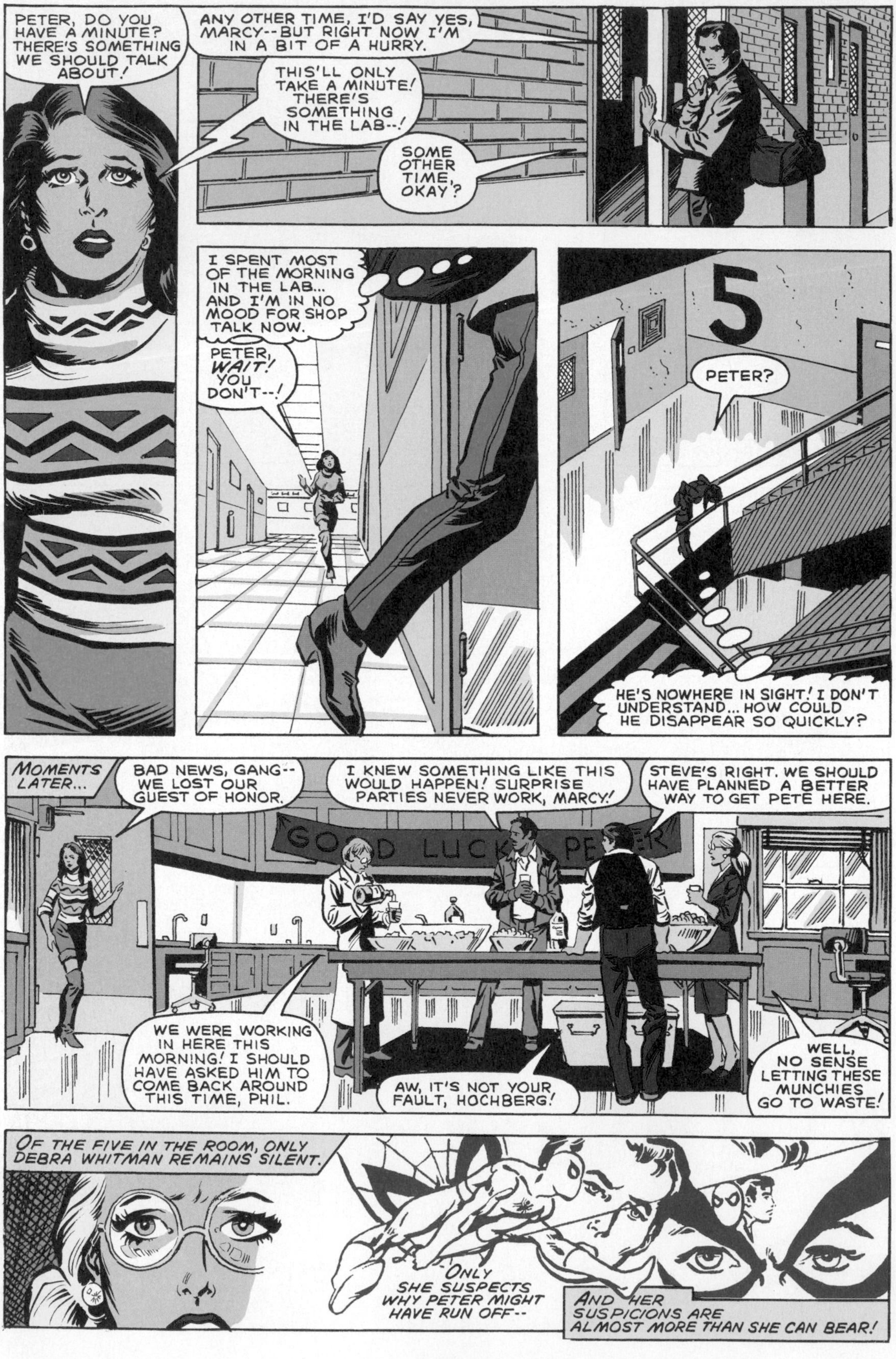
PETER, DO YOU HAVE A MINUTE? THERE'S SOMETHING WE SHOULD TALK ABOUT!
ANY OTHER TIME, I'D SAY YES, MARCY-- BUT RIGHT NOW I'M IN A BIT OF A HURRY.
THIS'LL ONLY TAKE A MINUTE! THERE'S SOMETHING IN THE LAB--!
SOME OTHER TIME, OKAY?
I SPENT MOST OF THE MORNING IN THE LAB... AND I'M IN NO MOOD FOR SHOP TALK NOW.
PETER, WAIT! YOU DON'T--!
5
PETER?
HE'S NOWHERE IN SIGHT! I DON'T UNDERSTAND... HOW COULD HE DISAPPEAR SO QUICKLY?
MOMENTS LATER...
BAD NEWS, GANG-- WE LOST OUR GUEST OF HONOR.
I KNEW SOMETHING LIKE THIS WOULD HAPPEN! SURPRISE PARTIES NEVER WORK, MARCY!
STEVE'S RIGHT. WE SHOULD HAVE PLANNED A BETTER WAY TO GET PETE HERE.
WE WERE WORKING IN HERE THIS MORNING! I SHOULD HAVE ASKED HIM TO COME BACK AROUND THIS TIME, PHIL.
AW, IT'S NOT YOUR FAULT, HOCHBERG!
WELL, NO SENSE LETTING THESE MUNCHIES GO TO WASTE!
OF THE FIVE IN THE ROOM, ONLY DEBRA WHITMAN REMAINS SILENT.
ONLY SHE SUSPECTS WHY PETER MIGHT HAVE RUN OFF--
AND HER SUSPICIONS ARE ALMOST MORE THAN SHE CAN BEAR!

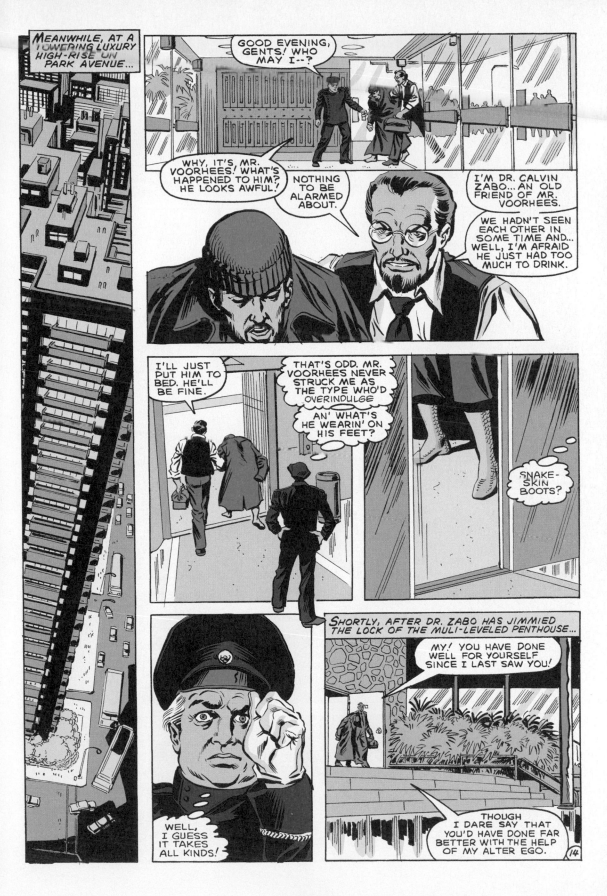

MEANWHILE, AT A TOWERING LUXURY HIGH-RISE ON PARK AVENUE...

GOOD EVENING, GENTS! WHO MAY I--?

WHY, IT'S MR. VOORHEES! WHAT'S HAPPENED TO HIM? HE LOOKS AWFUL!

NOTHING TO BE ALARMED ABOUT.

I'M DR. CALVIN ZABO... AN OLD FRIEND OF MR. VOORHEES.

WE HADN'T SEEN EACH OTHER IN SOME TIME AND... WELL, I'M AFRAID HE JUST HAD TOO MUCH TO DRINK.

I'LL JUST PUT HIM TO BED. HE'LL BE FINE.

THAT'S ODD. MR. VOORHEES NEVER STRUCK ME AS THE TYPE WHO'D OVERINDULGE

AN' WHAT'S HE WEARIN' ON HIS FEET?

SNAKE-SKIN BOOTS?

SHORTLY, AFTER DR. ZABO HAS JIMMIED THE LOCK OF THE MULI-LEVELED PENTHOUSE...

MY! YOU HAVE DONE WELL FOR YOURSELF SINCE I LAST SAW YOU!

WELL, I GUESS IT TAKES ALL KINDS!

THOUGH I DARE SAY THAT YOU'D HAVE DONE FAR BETTER WITH THE HELP OF MY ALTER EGO.

14

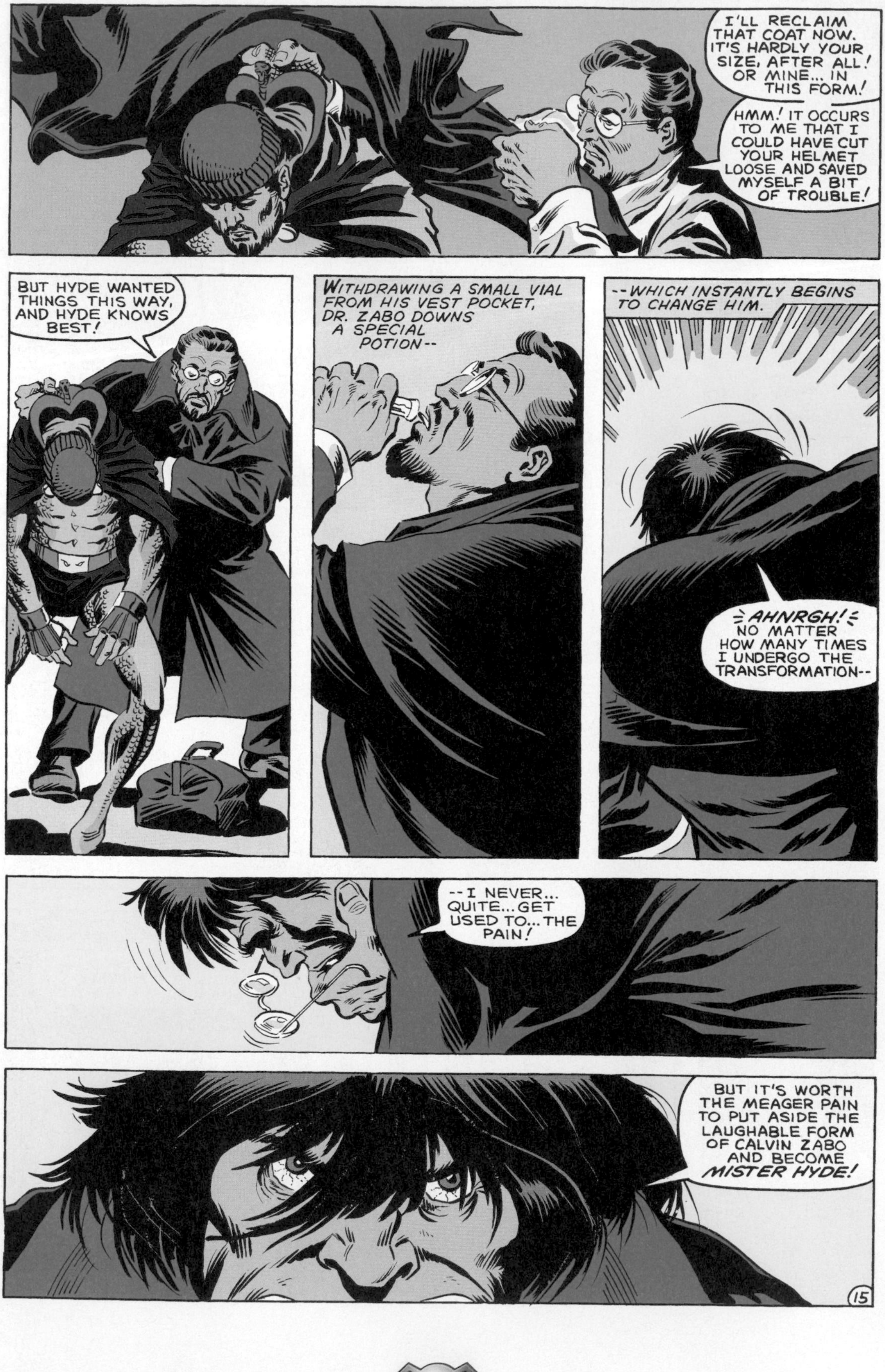
I'LL RECLAIM THAT COAT NOW. IT'S HARDLY YOUR SIZE, AFTER ALL! OR MINE... IN THIS FORM!
HMM! IT OCCURS TO ME THAT I COULD HAVE CUT YOUR HELMET LOOSE AND SAVED MYSELF A BIT OF TROUBLE!
BUT HYDE WANTED THINGS THIS WAY, AND HYDE KNOWS BEST!
WITHDRAWING A SMALL VIAL FROM HIS VEST POCKET, DR. ZABO DOWNS A SPECIAL POTION--
--WHICH INSTANTLY BEGINS TO CHANGE HIM.
AHNRGH! NO MATTER HOW MANY TIMES I UNDERGO THE TRANSFORMATION--
--I NEVER... QUITE... GET USED TO... THE PAIN!
BUT IT'S WORTH THE MEAGER PAIN TO PUT ASIDE THE LAUGHABLE FORM OF CALVIN ZABO AND BECOME MISTER HYDE!
15

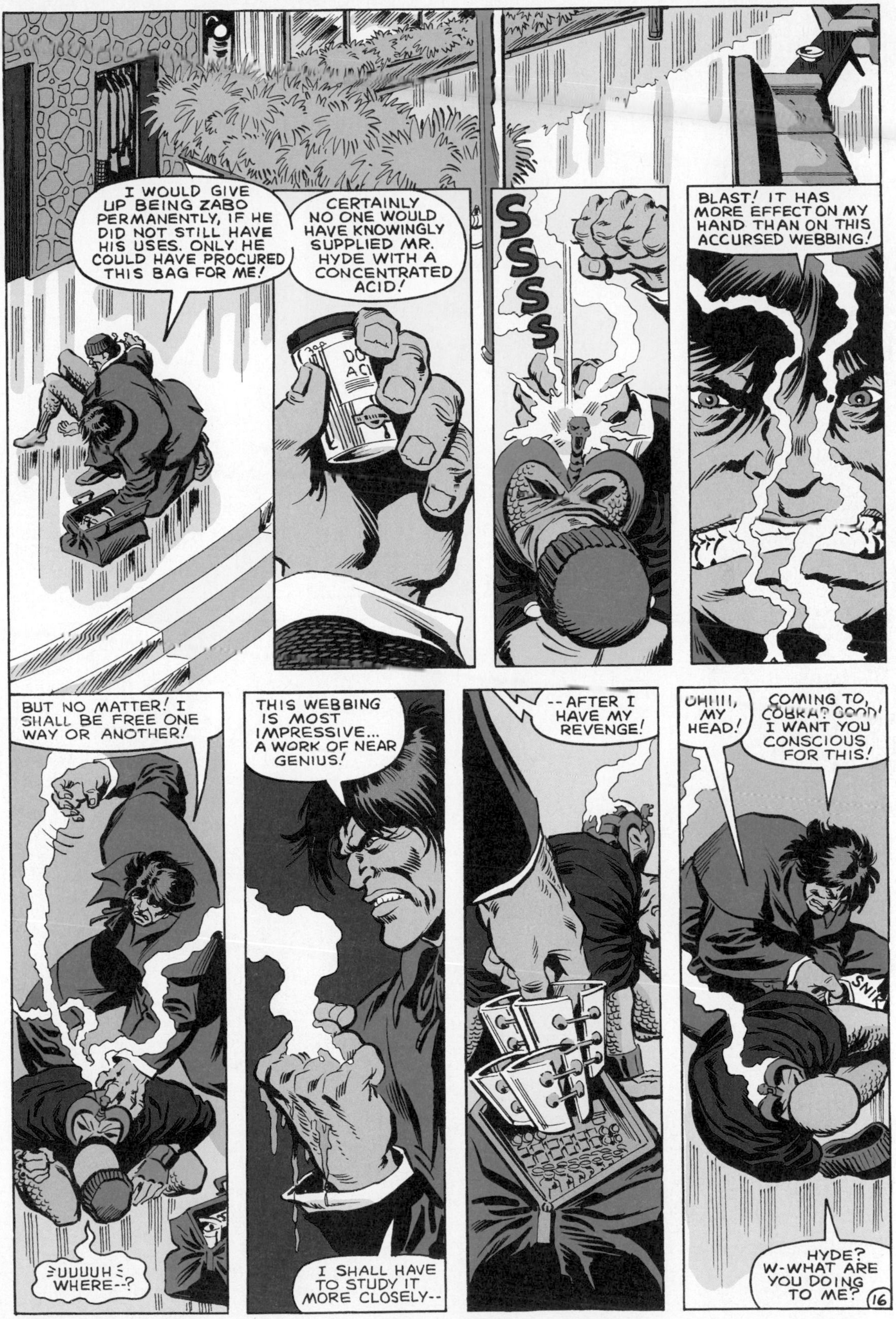
I WOULD GIVE UP BEING ZABO PERMANENTLY, IF HE DID NOT STILL HAVE HIS USES. ONLY HE COULD HAVE PROCURED THIS BAG FOR ME!
CERTAINLY NO ONE WOULD HAVE KNOWINGLY SUPPLIED MR. HYDE WITH A CONCENTRATED ACID!
SSSS
BLAST! IT HAS MORE EFFECT ON MY HAND THAN ON THIS ACCURSED WEBBING!
BUT NO MATTER! I SHALL BE FREE ONE WAY OR ANOTHER!
UUUUH WHERE--?
THIS WEBBING IS MOST IMPRESSIVE... A WORK OF NEAR GENIUS!
I SHALL HAVE TO STUDY IT MORE CLOSELY--
--AFTER I HAVE MY REVENGE!
OHHH, MY HEAD!
COMING TO, COBRA? GOOD! I WANT YOU CONSCIOUS FOR THIS!
HYDE? W-WHAT ARE YOU DOING TO ME?
16

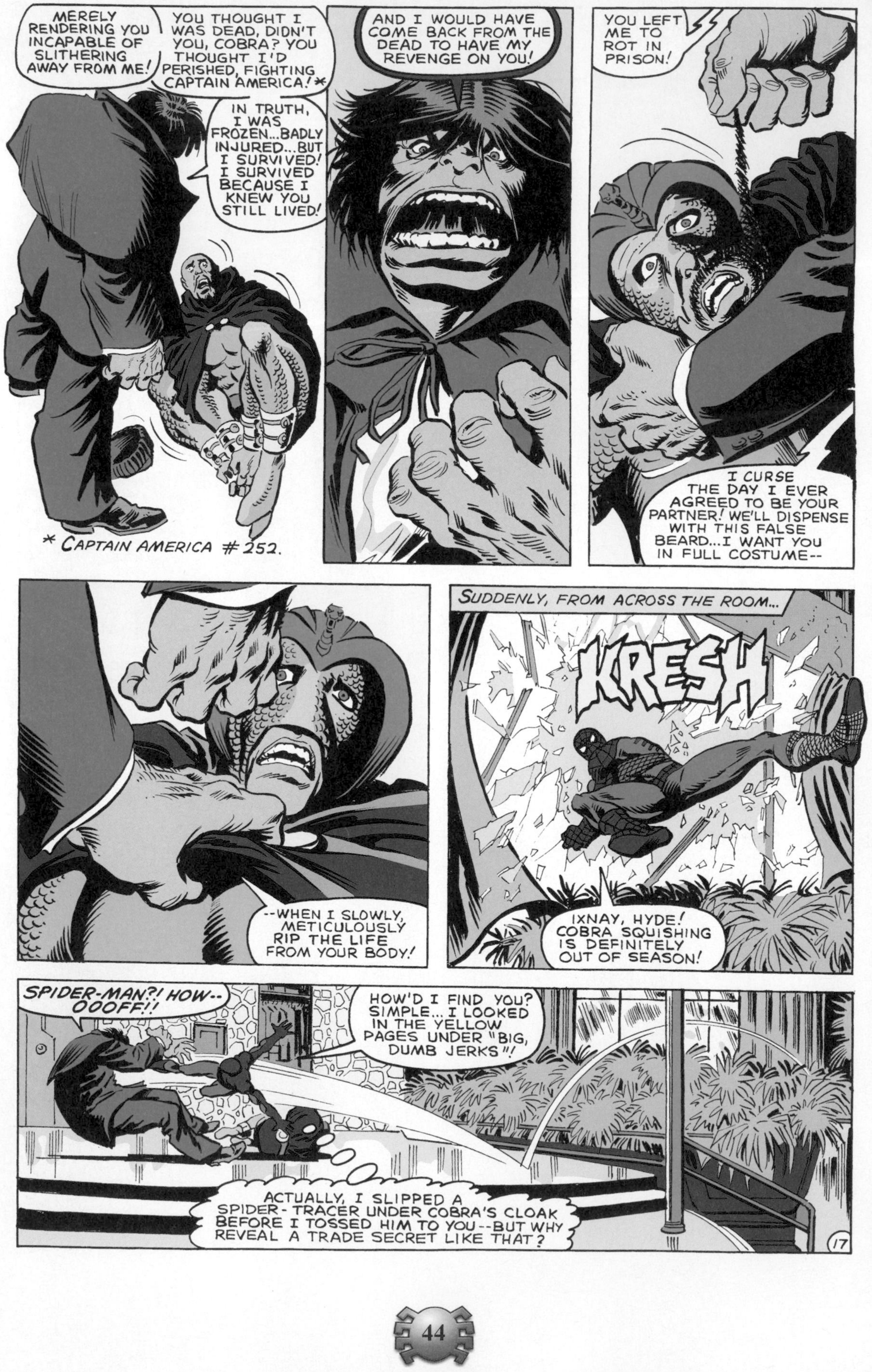
MERELY RENDERING YOU INCAPABLE OF SLITHERING AWAY FROM ME!
YOU THOUGHT I WAS DEAD, DIDN'T YOU, COBRA? YOU THOUGHT I'D PERISHED, FIGHTING CAPTAIN AMERICA! *
IN TRUTH, I WAS FROZEN...BADLY INJURED...BUT I SURVIVED! I SURVIVED BECAUSE I KNEW YOU STILL LIVED!
* CAPTAIN AMERICA #252.
AND I WOULD HAVE COME BACK FROM THE DEAD TO HAVE MY REVENGE ON YOU!
YOU LEFT ME TO ROT IN PRISON!
I CURSE THE DAY I EVER AGREED TO BE YOUR PARTNER! WE'LL DISPENSE WITH THIS FALSE BEARD...I WANT YOU IN FULL COSTUME--
--WHEN I SLOWLY, METICULOUSLY RIP THE LIFE FROM YOUR BODY!
SUDDENLY, FROM ACROSS THE ROOM...
KRESH
IXNAY, HYDE! COBRA SQUISHING IS DEFINITELY OUT OF SEASON!
SPIDER-MAN?! HOW-- OOOFF!!
HOW'D I FIND YOU? SIMPLE... I LOOKED IN THE YELLOW PAGES UNDER "BIG, DUMB JERKS"!
ACTUALLY, I SLIPPED A SPIDER-TRACER UNDER COBRA'S CLOAK BEFORE I TOSSED HIM TO YOU--BUT WHY REVEAL A TRADE SECRET LIKE THAT?
17

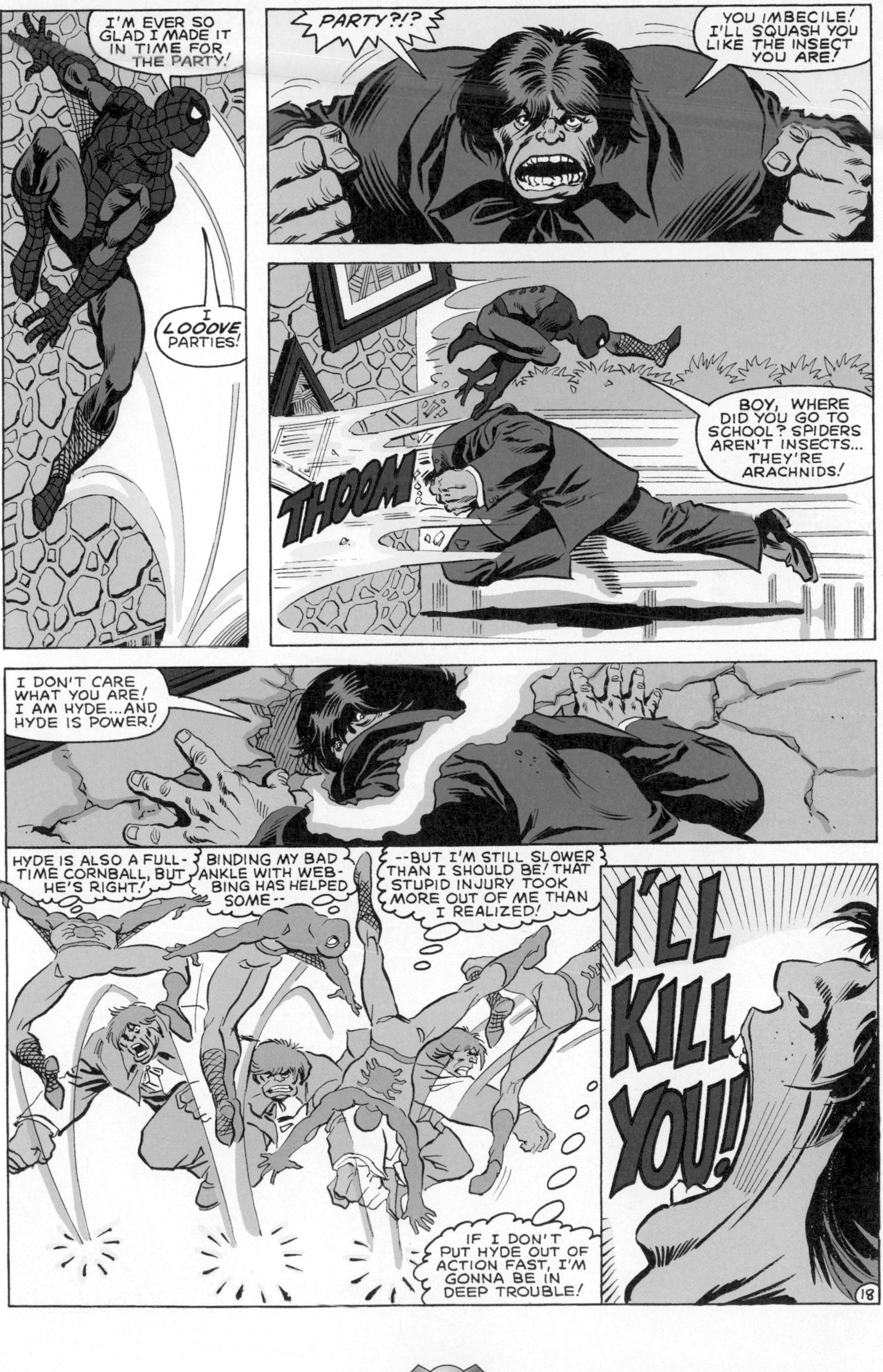
I'M EVER SO GLAD I MADE IT IN TIME FOR THE PARTY!
I LOOOVE PARTIES!
PARTY?!?
YOU IMBECILE! I'LL SQUASH YOU LIKE THE INSECT YOU ARE!
BOY, WHERE DID YOU GO TO SCHOOL? SPIDERS AREN'T INSECTS... THEY'RE ARACHNIDS!
THOOM
I DON'T CARE WHAT YOU ARE! I AM HYDE...AND HYDE IS POWER!
HYDE IS ALSO A FULL-TIME CORNBALL, BUT HE'S RIGHT!
BINDING MY BAD ANKLE WITH WEB-BING HAS HELPED SOME--
--BUT I'M STILL SLOWER THAN I SHOULD BE! THAT STUPID INJURY TOOK MORE OUT OF ME THAN I REALIZED!
IF I DON'T PUT HYDE OUT OF ACTION FAST, I'M GONNA BE IN DEEP TROUBLE!
I'LL KILL YOU!
18

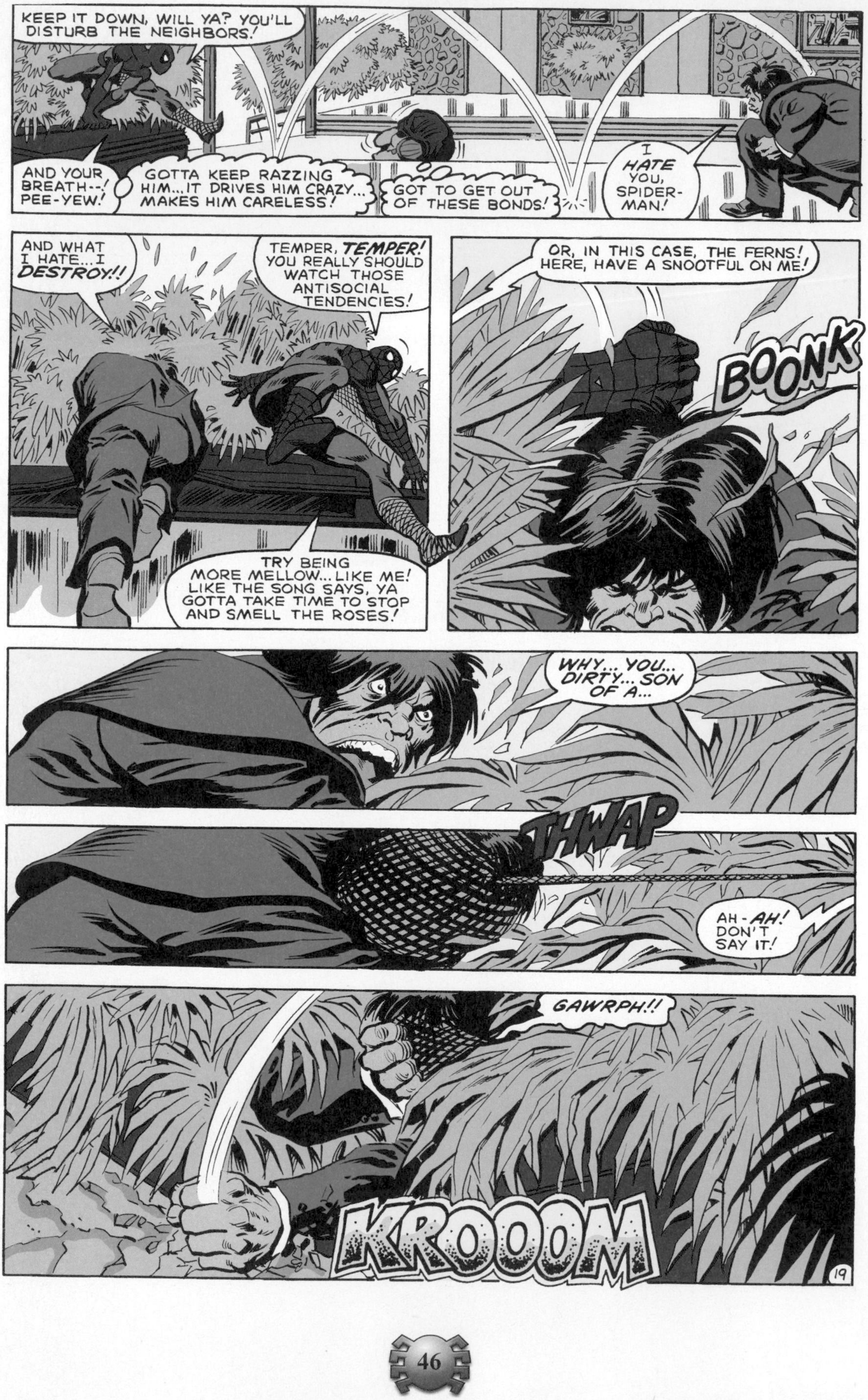
KEEP IT DOWN, WILL YA? YOU'LL DISTURB THE NEIGHBORS!
AND YOUR BREATH--! PEE-YEW!
GOTTA KEEP RAZZING HIM...IT DRIVES HIM CRAZY... MAKES HIM CARELESS!
GOT TO GET OUT OF THESE BONDS!
I HATE YOU, SPIDER-MAN!
AND WHAT I HATE...I DESTROY!!
TEMPER, TEMPER! YOU REALLY SHOULD WATCH THOSE ANTISOCIAL TENDENCIES!
TRY BEING MORE MELLOW...LIKE ME! LIKE THE SONG SAYS, YA GOTTA TAKE TIME TO STOP AND SMELL THE ROSES!
OR, IN THIS CASE, THE FERNS! HERE, HAVE A SNOOTFUL ON ME!
BOONK
WHY... YOU... DIRTY... SON OF A...
THWAP
AH-AH! DON'T SAY IT!
GAWRPH!!
KROOOM
19

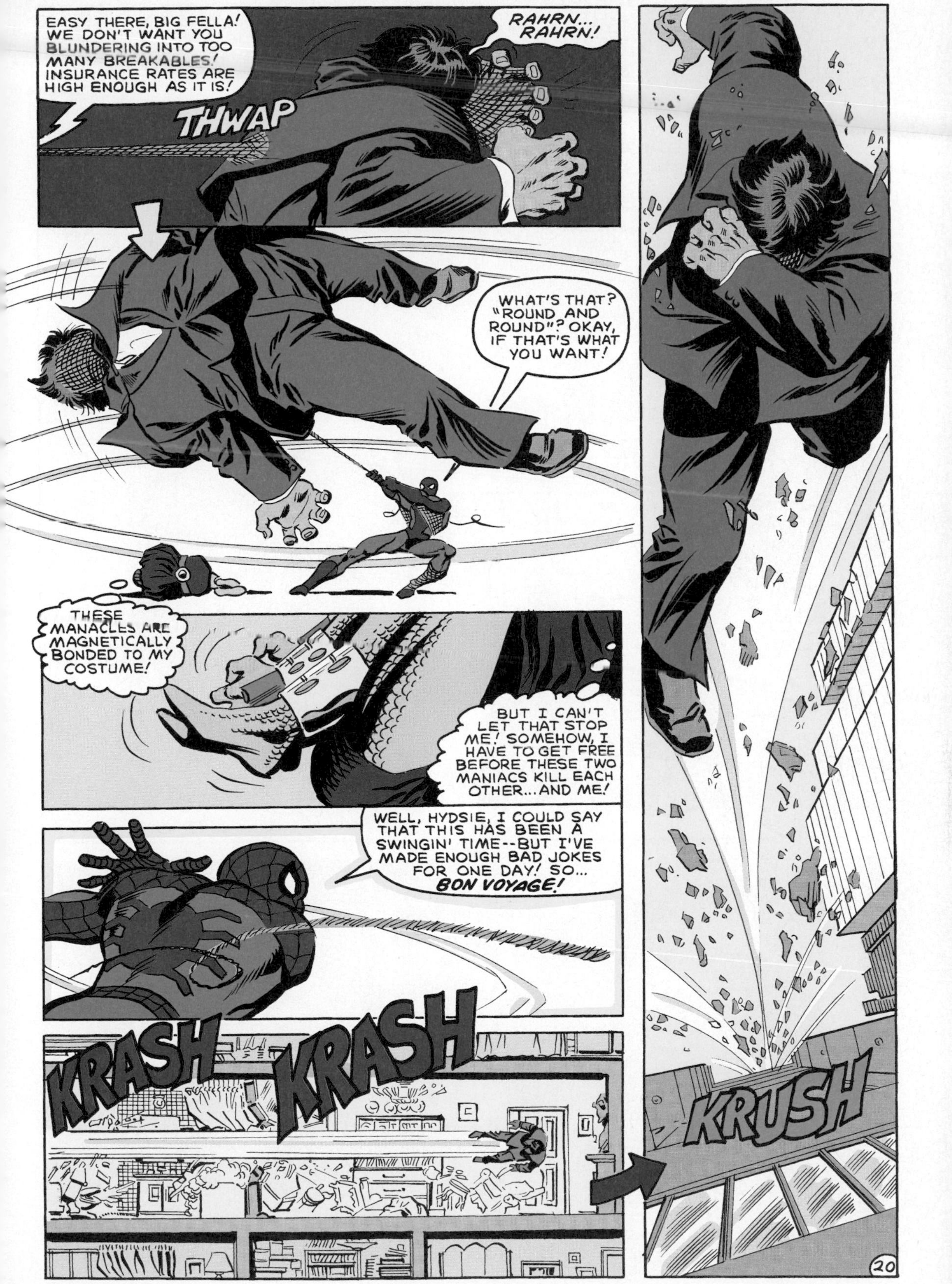

EASY THERE, BIG FELLA! WE DON'T WANT YOU BLUNDERING INTO TOO MANY BREAKABLES! INSURANCE RATES ARE HIGH ENOUGH AS IT IS!
RAHRN... RAHRN!
THWAP
WHAT'S THAT? "ROUND AND ROUND"? OKAY, IF THAT'S WHAT YOU WANT!
THESE MANACLES ARE MAGNETICALLY BONDED TO MY COSTUME!
BUT I CAN'T LET THAT STOP ME! SOMEHOW, I HAVE TO GET FREE BEFORE THESE TWO MANIACS KILL EACH OTHER... AND ME!
WELL, HYDSIE, I COULD SAY THAT THIS HAS BEEN A SWINGIN' TIME--BUT I'VE MADE ENOUGH BAD JOKES FOR ONE DAY! SO... BON VOYAGE!
KRASH
KRASH
KRUSH
20

PARK

PARK

PARKING

HOLEE--!

DON'T DUMP ON NEW YORK

KLA-BOOM

OH, *NO!* I-I EXPECTED AT LEAST ONE OF THOSE WALLS TO STOP HIM!

WHAT HAVE I DONE?!

FEARING THE WORST--

...*THE NIMBLE WEB-SLINGER SKITTERS DOWN TO STREET LEVEL WHERE...*

H-HE'S STILL ALIVE! WHAT A RELIEF!

OOPS! DID I SAY RELIEF?

YUUU!!

OKAY, HYDE, THIS IS IT! GIVE ME YOUR BEST SHOT AND... AND...

HEY, ALL OF A SUDDEN, I'M GETTING NARY A WARNING BUZZ FROM MY SPIDER-SENSE. THAT MUST MEAN HE'S--

--OUT COLD ON HIS FEET! WHEW! NIGHTY-NIGHT, LI'L ANGEL!

WHUMP

21

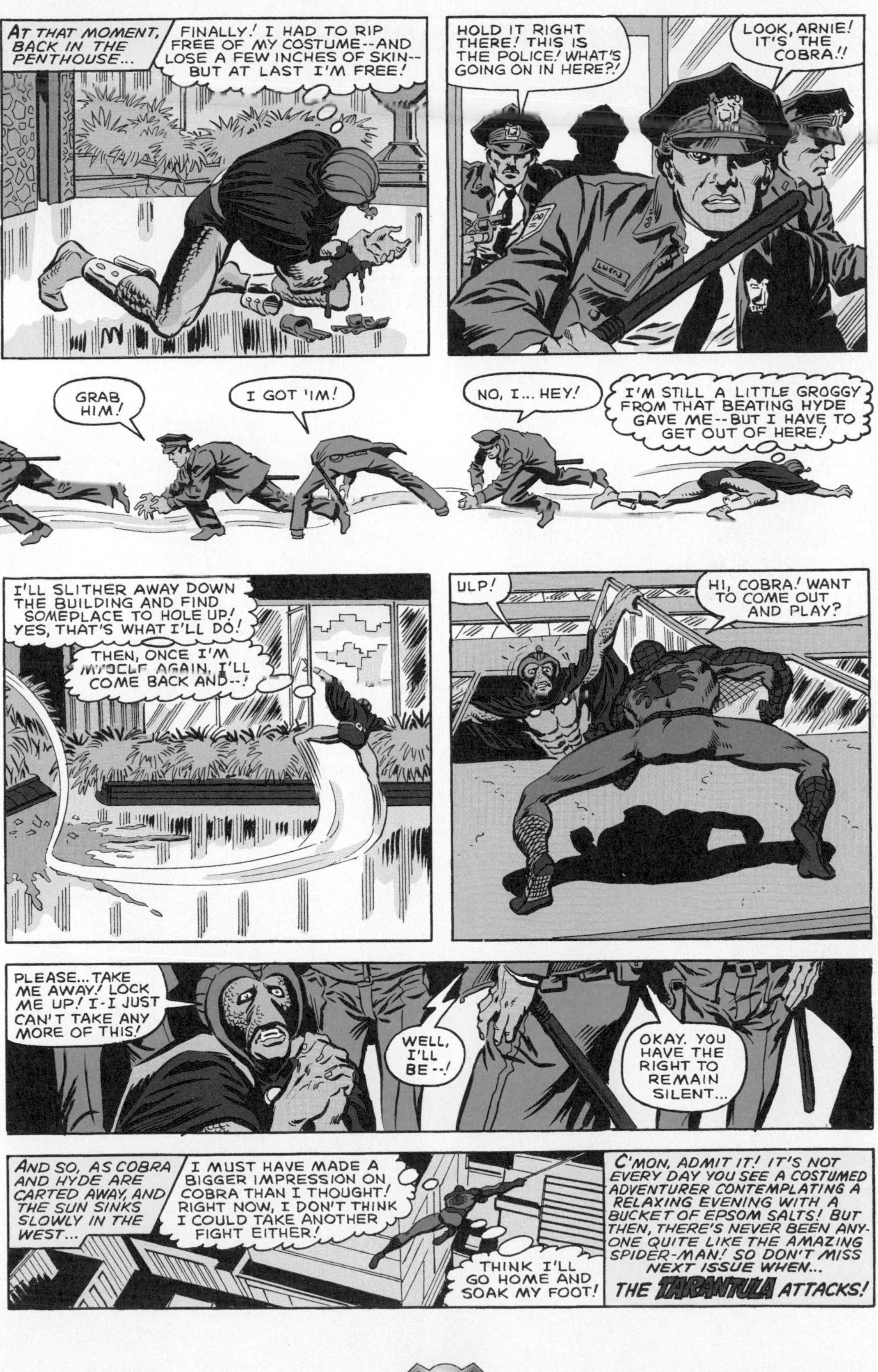
AT THAT MOMENT, BACK IN THE PENTHOUSE...
FINALLY! I HAD TO RIP FREE OF MY COSTUME--AND LOSE A FEW INCHES OF SKIN--BUT AT LAST I'M FREE!
HOLD IT RIGHT THERE! THIS IS THE POLICE! WHAT'S GOING ON IN HERE?!
LOOK, ARNIE! IT'S THE COBRA!!
GRAB HIM!
I GOT 'IM!
NO, I... HEY!
I'M STILL A LITTLE GROGGY FROM THAT BEATING HYDE GAVE ME--BUT I HAVE TO GET OUT OF HERE!
I'LL SLITHER AWAY DOWN THE BUILDING AND FIND SOMEPLACE TO HOLE UP! YES, THAT'S WHAT I'LL DO!
THEN, ONCE I'M MYSELF AGAIN, I'LL COME BACK AND--!
ULP!
HI, COBRA! WANT TO COME OUT AND PLAY?
PLEASE... TAKE ME AWAY! LOCK ME UP! I-I JUST CAN'T TAKE ANY MORE OF THIS!
WELL, I'LL BE--!
OKAY. YOU HAVE THE RIGHT TO REMAIN SILENT...
AND SO, AS COBRA AND HYDE ARE CARTED AWAY, AND THE SUN SINKS SLOWLY IN THE WEST...
I MUST HAVE MADE A BIGGER IMPRESSION ON COBRA THAN I THOUGHT! RIGHT NOW, I DON'T THINK I COULD TAKE ANOTHER FIGHT EITHER!
THINK I'LL GO HOME AND SOAK MY FOOT!
C'MON, ADMIT IT! IT'S NOT EVERY DAY YOU SEE A COSTUMED ADVENTURER CONTEMPLATING A RELAXING EVENING WITH A BUCKET OF EPSOM SALTS! BUT THEN, THERE'S NEVER BEEN ANYONE QUITE LIKE THE AMAZING SPIDER-MAN! SO DON'T MISS NEXT ISSUE WHEN...
THE TARANTULA ATTACKS!

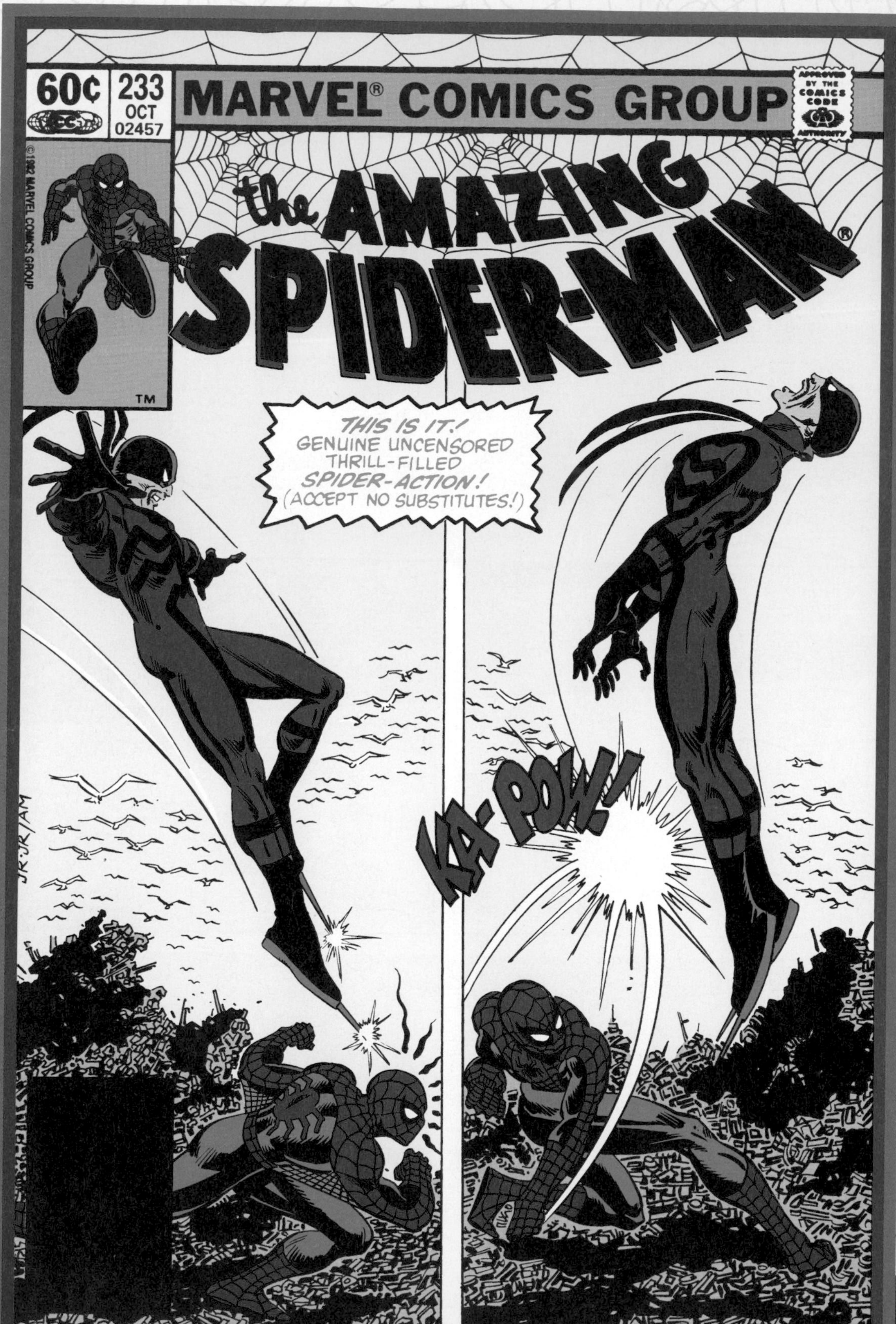

60¢
233
OCT
02457
MARVEL® COMICS GROUP
APPROVED BY THE COMICS CODE AUTHORITY
© 1982 MARVEL COMICS GROUP
the AMAZING SPIDER-MAN®
TM
THIS IS IT! GENUINE UNCENSORED THRILL-FILLED SPIDER-ACTION! (ACCEPT NO SUBSTITUTES!)
KA-POW!
JR.JR./AM

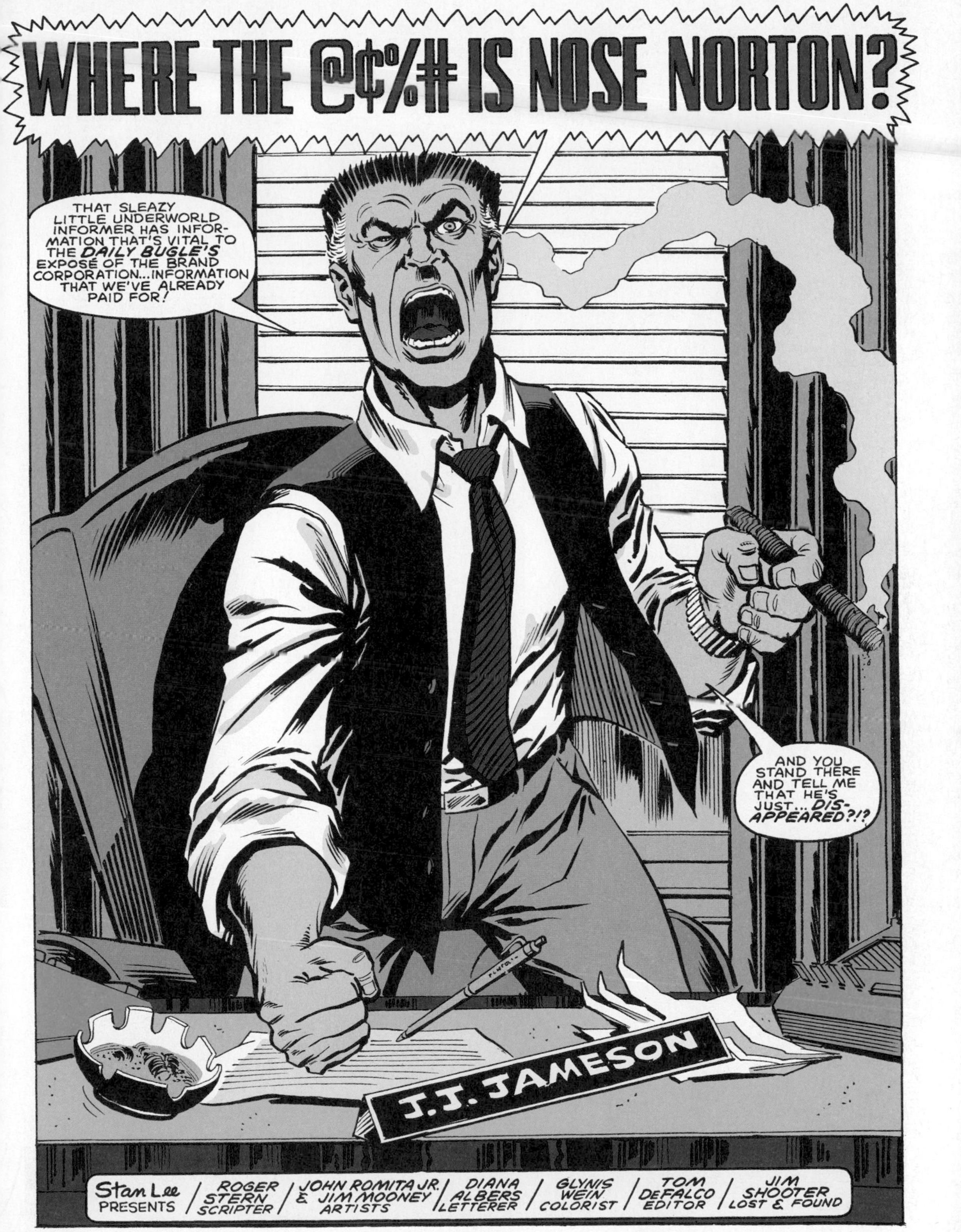
WHERE THE @¢%# IS NOSE NORTON?
THAT SLEAZY LITTLE UNDERWORLD INFORMER HAS INFORMATION THAT'S VITAL TO THE DAILY BUGLE'S EXPOSÉ OF THE BRAND CORPORATION...INFORMATION THAT WE'VE ALREADY PAID FOR!
AND YOU STAND THERE AND TELL ME THAT HE'S JUST... DISAPPEARED?!?
J.J. JAMESON
Stan Lee PRESENTS / ROGER STERN SCRIPTER / JOHN ROMITA JR. & JIM MOONEY ARTISTS / DIANA ALBERS LETTERER / GLYNIS WEIN COLORIST / TOM DeFALCO EDITOR / JIM SHOOTER LOST & FOUND

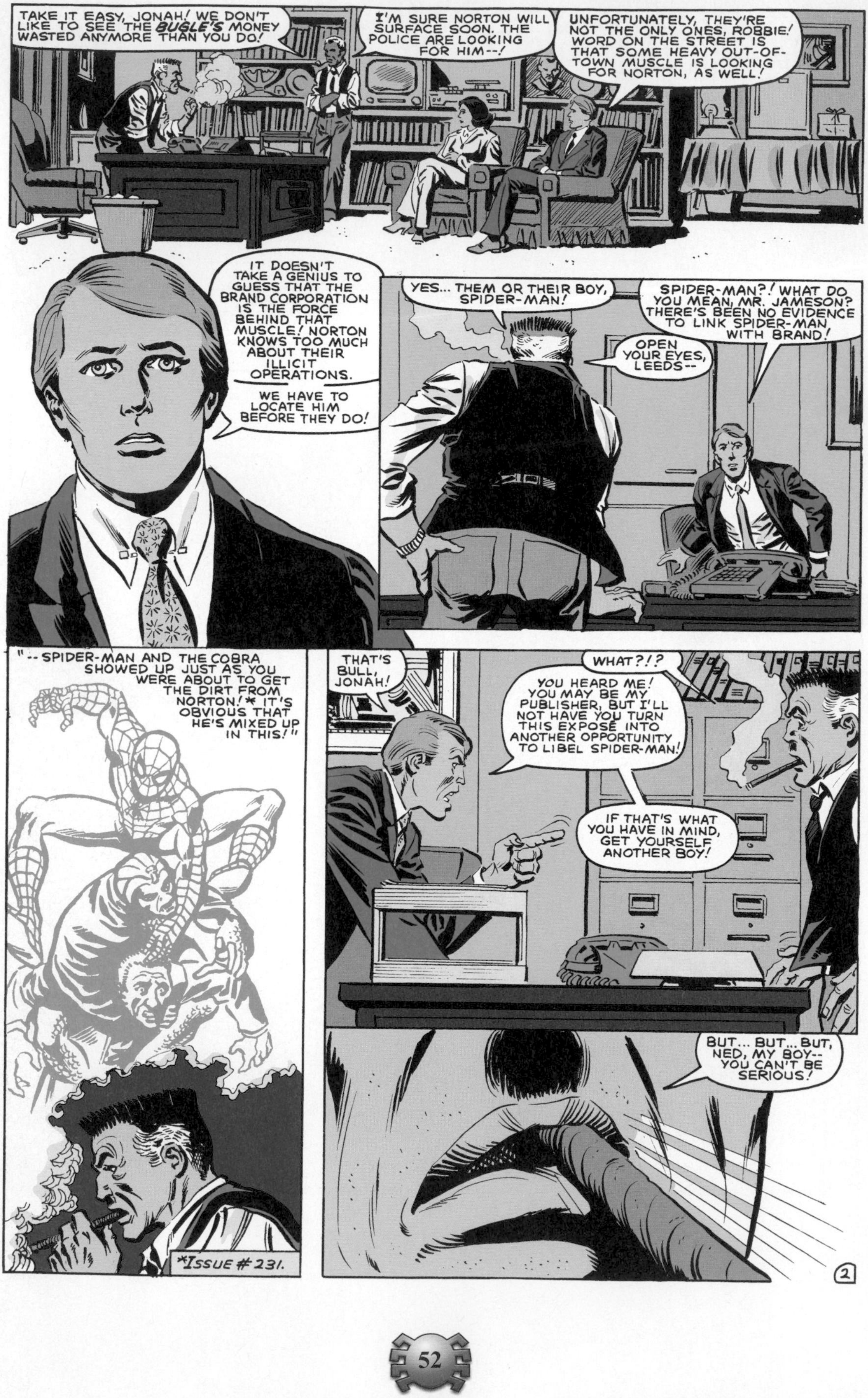
TAKE IT EASY, JONAH! WE DON'T LIKE TO SEE THE BUGLE'S MONEY WASTED ANYMORE THAN YOU DO!
I'M SURE NORTON WILL SURFACE SOON. THE POLICE ARE LOOKING FOR HIM--!
UNFORTUNATELY, THEY'RE NOT THE ONLY ONES, ROBBIE! WORD ON THE STREET IS THAT SOME HEAVY OUT-OF-TOWN MUSCLE IS LOOKING FOR NORTON, AS WELL!
IT DOESN'T TAKE A GENIUS TO GUESS THAT THE BRAND CORPORATION IS THE FORCE BEHIND THAT MUSCLE! NORTON KNOWS TOO MUCH ABOUT THEIR ILLICIT OPERATIONS.
WE HAVE TO LOCATE HIM BEFORE THEY DO!
YES... THEM OR THEIR BOY, SPIDER-MAN!
SPIDER-MAN?! WHAT DO YOU MEAN, MR. JAMESON? THERE'S BEEN NO EVIDENCE TO LINK SPIDER-MAN WITH BRAND!
OPEN YOUR EYES, LEEDS--
"--SPIDER-MAN AND THE COBRA SHOWED UP JUST AS YOU WERE ABOUT TO GET THE DIRT FROM NORTON!* IT'S OBVIOUS THAT HE'S MIXED UP IN THIS!"
*ISSUE #231.
THAT'S BULL, JONAH!
WHAT?!?
YOU HEARD ME! YOU MAY BE MY PUBLISHER, BUT I'LL NOT HAVE YOU TURN THIS EXPOSE INTO ANOTHER OPPORTUNITY TO LIBEL SPIDER-MAN!
IF THAT'S WHAT YOU HAVE IN MIND, GET YOURSELF ANOTHER BOY!
BUT... BUT... BUT, NED, MY BOY-- YOU CAN'T BE SERIOUS!
2

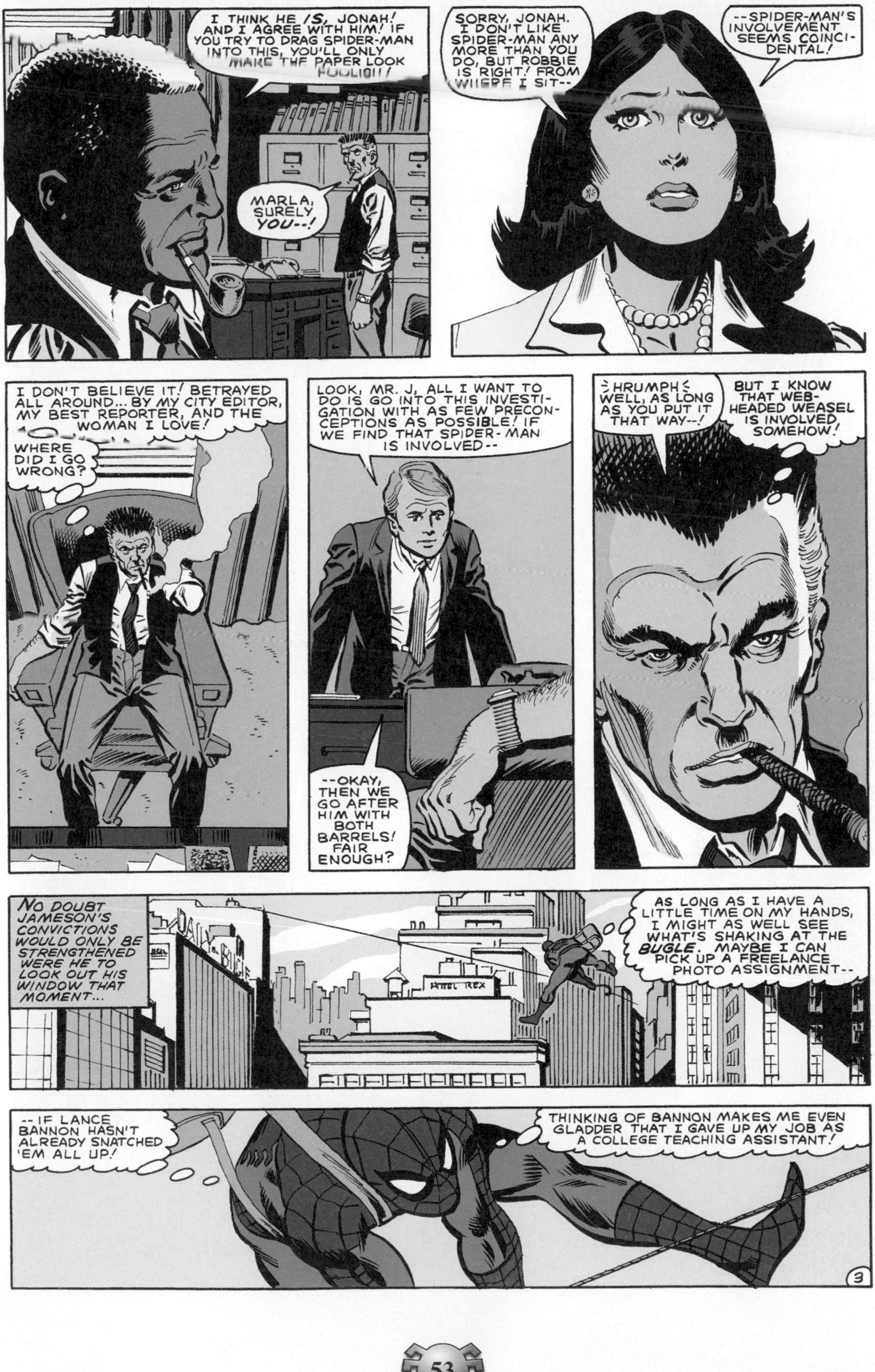

I THINK HE IS, JONAH! AND I AGREE WITH HIM! IF YOU TRY TO DRAG SPIDER-MAN INTO THIS, YOU'LL ONLY MAKE THE PAPER LOOK FOOLISH!
MARLA, SURELY YOU--!
SORRY, JONAH. I DON'T LIKE SPIDER-MAN ANY MORE THAN YOU DO, BUT ROBBIE IS RIGHT! FROM WHERE I SIT--
--SPIDER-MAN'S INVOLVEMENT SEEMS COINCI-DENTAL!
I DON'T BELIEVE IT! BETRAYED ALL AROUND... BY MY CITY EDITOR, MY BEST REPORTER, AND THE WOMAN I LOVE!
WHERE DID I GO WRONG?
LOOK, MR. J, ALL I WANT TO DO IS GO INTO THIS INVESTI-GATION WITH AS FEW PRECON-CEPTIONS AS POSSIBLE! IF WE FIND THAT SPIDER-MAN IS INVOLVED--
--OKAY, THEN WE GO AFTER HIM WITH BOTH BARRELS! FAIR ENOUGH?
HRUMPH WELL, AS LONG AS YOU PUT IT THAT WAY--!
BUT I KNOW THAT WEB-HEADED WEASEL IS INVOLVED SOMEHOW!
NO DOUBT JAMESON'S CONVICTIONS WOULD ONLY BE STRENGTHENED WERE HE TO LOOK OUT HIS WINDOW THAT MOMENT...
DAILY BUGLE
HOTEL REX
AS LONG AS I HAVE A LITTLE TIME ON MY HANDS, I MIGHT AS WELL SEE WHAT'S SHAKING AT THE BUGLE. MAYBE I CAN PICK UP A FREELANCE PHOTO ASSIGNMENT--
--IF LANCE BANNON HASN'T ALREADY SNATCHED 'EM ALL UP!
THINKING OF BANNON MAKES ME EVEN GLADDER THAT I GAVE UP MY JOB AS A COLLEGE TEACHING ASSISTANT!
3

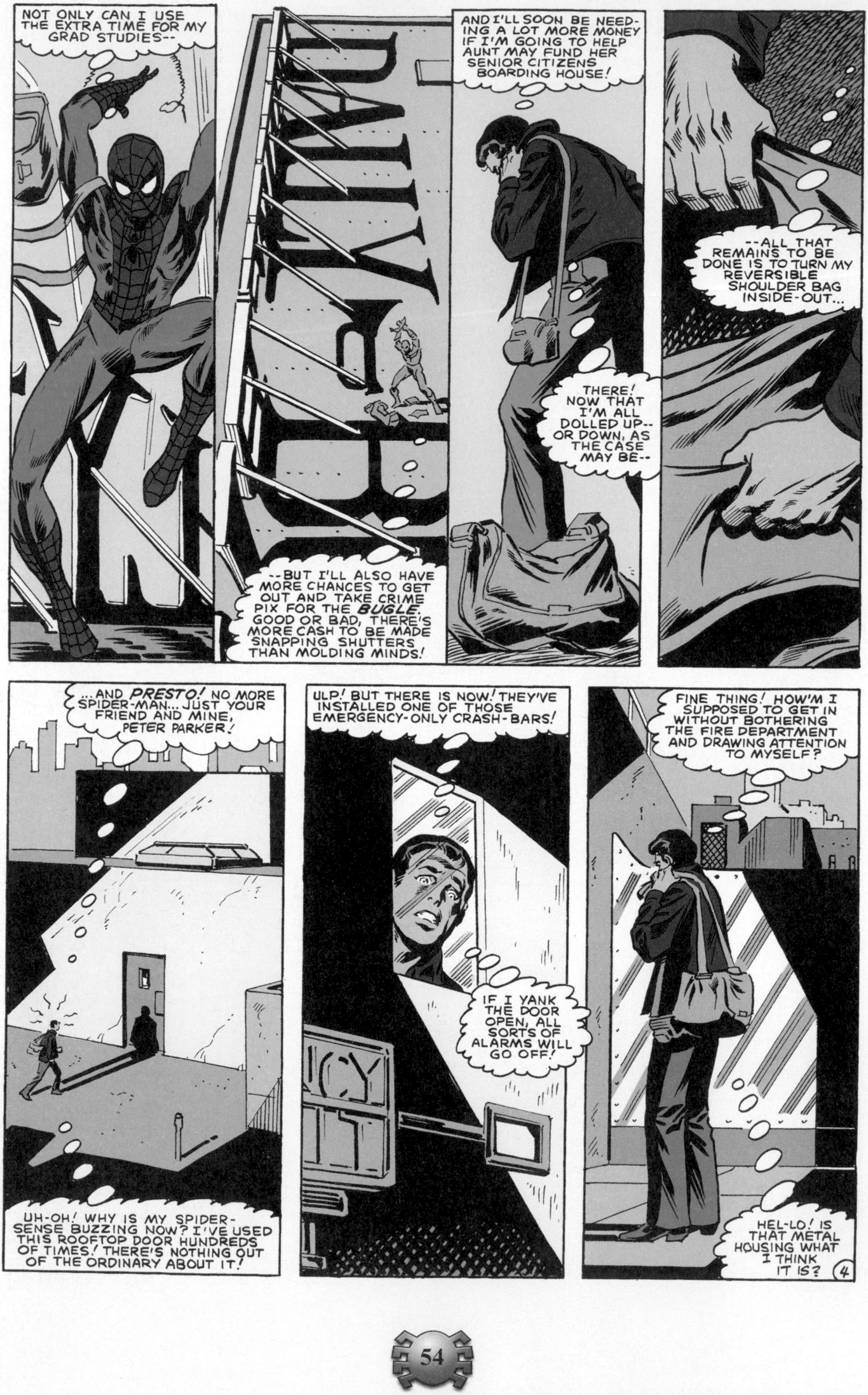
NOT ONLY CAN I USE THE EXTRA TIME FOR MY GRAD STUDIES--
--BUT I'LL ALSO HAVE MORE CHANCES TO GET OUT AND TAKE CRIME PIX FOR THE BUGLE. GOOD OR BAD, THERE'S MORE CASH TO BE MADE SNAPPING SHUTTERS THAN MOLDING MINDS!
AND I'LL SOON BE NEEDING A LOT MORE MONEY IF I'M GOING TO HELP AUNT MAY FUND HER SENIOR CITIZENS BOARDING HOUSE!
THERE! NOW THAT I'M ALL DOLLED UP-- OR DOWN, AS THE CASE MAY BE--
--ALL THAT REMAINS TO BE DONE IS TO TURN MY REVERSIBLE SHOULDER BAG INSIDE-OUT...
...AND PRESTO! NO MORE SPIDER-MAN... JUST YOUR FRIEND AND MINE, PETER PARKER!
UH-OH! WHY IS MY SPIDER-SENSE BUZZING NOW? I'VE USED THIS ROOFTOP DOOR HUNDREDS OF TIMES! THERE'S NOTHING OUT OF THE ORDINARY ABOUT IT!
ULP! BUT THERE IS NOW! THEY'VE INSTALLED ONE OF THOSE EMERGENCY-ONLY CRASH-BARS!
IF I YANK THE DOOR OPEN, ALL SORTS OF ALARMS WILL GO OFF!
FINE THING! HOW'M I SUPPOSED TO GET IN WITHOUT BOTHERING THE FIRE DEPARTMENT AND DRAWING ATTENTION TO MYSELF?
HEL-LO! IS THAT METAL HOUSING WHAT I THINK IT IS?
4

ONLY ONE WAY TO FIND OUT!

CHEE, WHAT CHINTZY CONSTRUCTION! THE METAL CAN'T BE MORE THAN AN INCH THICK!

GRINK

JACKPOT! I THOUGHT THE ELEVATOR SHAFT MIGHT BE ABOUT HERE!

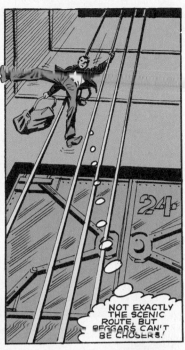

24

NOT EXACTLY THE SCENIC ROUTE, BUT BEGGARS CAN'T BE CHOSERS!

MOMENTS LATER, ON THE 17th FLOOR...

THIS IS THE RIGHT LEVEL, BUT FROM THE WAY MY SPIDER-SENSE IS HUMMING NOW, THE HALL MUST BE CROWDED.

LUCKILY, NO ONE RANG FOR THIS CAR. I'LL JUST HANG AROUND UNTIL IT'S...

...ALL CLEAR? YEAH.

SPIDER-SENSE, WHERE WOULD I BE WITHOUT YOU? YOU'VE SAVED MY HIDE SO MANY TIMES, I'VE LOST COUNT!

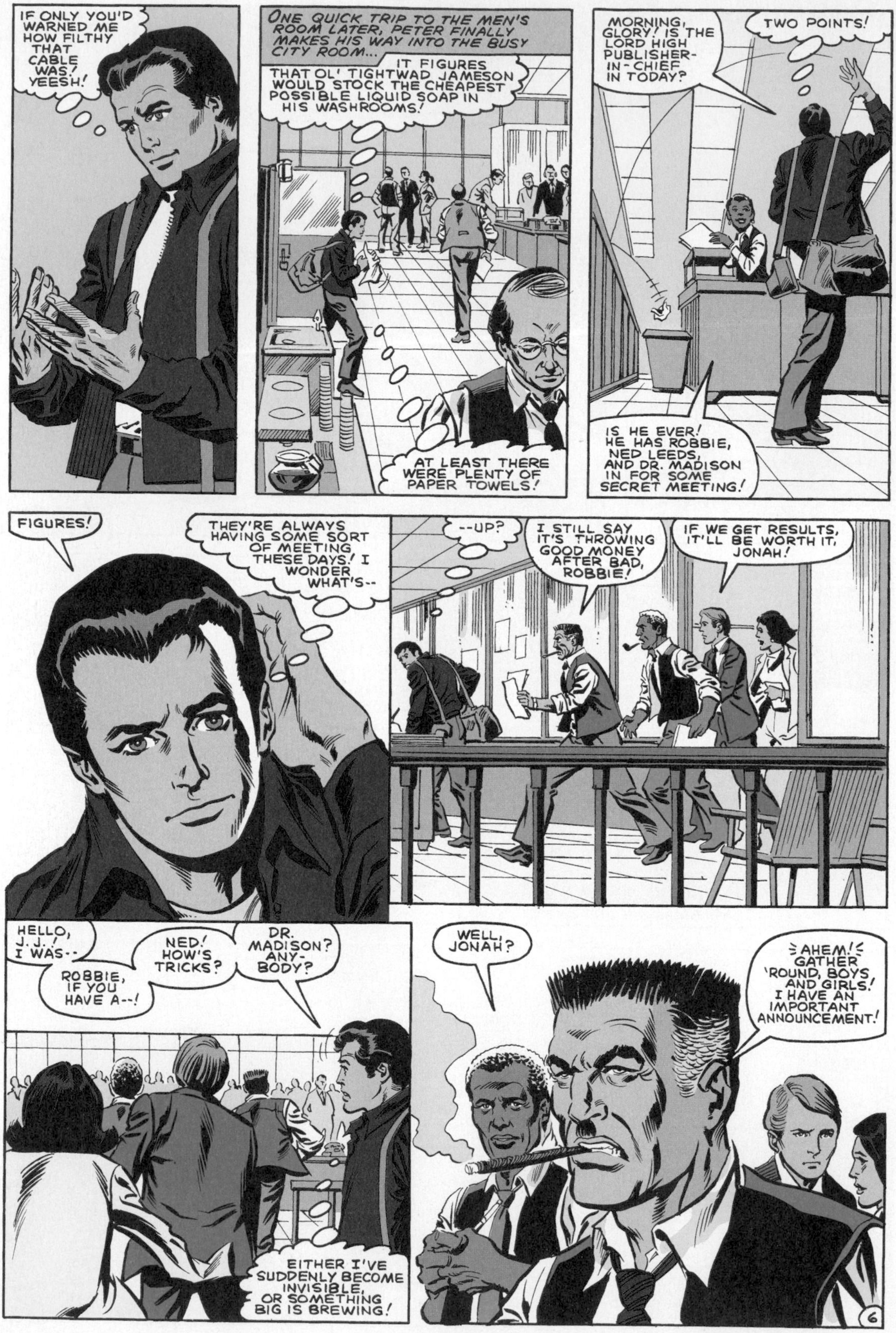
IF ONLY YOU'D WARNED ME HOW FILTHY THAT CABLE WAS! YEESH!
ONE QUICK TRIP TO THE MEN'S ROOM LATER, PETER FINALLY MAKES HIS WAY INTO THE BUSY CITY ROOM...
IT FIGURES THAT OL' TIGHTWAD JAMESON WOULD STOCK THE CHEAPEST POSSIBLE LIQUID SOAP IN HIS WASHROOMS!
AT LEAST THERE WERE PLENTY OF PAPER TOWELS!
MORNING, GLORY! IS THE LORD HIGH PUBLISHER-IN-CHIEF IN TODAY?
TWO POINTS!
IS HE EVER! HE HAS ROBBIE, NED LEEDS, AND DR. MADISON IN FOR SOME SECRET MEETING!
FIGURES!
THEY'RE ALWAYS HAVING SOME SORT OF MEETING THESE DAYS! I WONDER WHAT'S--
--UP?
I STILL SAY IT'S THROWING GOOD MONEY AFTER BAD, ROBBIE!
IF WE GET RESULTS, IT'LL BE WORTH IT, JONAH!
HELLO, J.J.! I WAS--
ROBBIE, IF YOU HAVE A--!
NED! HOW'S TRICKS?
DR. MADISON? ANY-BODY?
EITHER I'VE SUDDENLY BECOME INVISIBLE, OR SOMETHING BIG IS BREWING!
WELL, JONAH?
AHEM! GATHER 'ROUND, BOYS AND GIRLS! I HAVE AN IMPORTANT ANNOUNCEMENT!
6

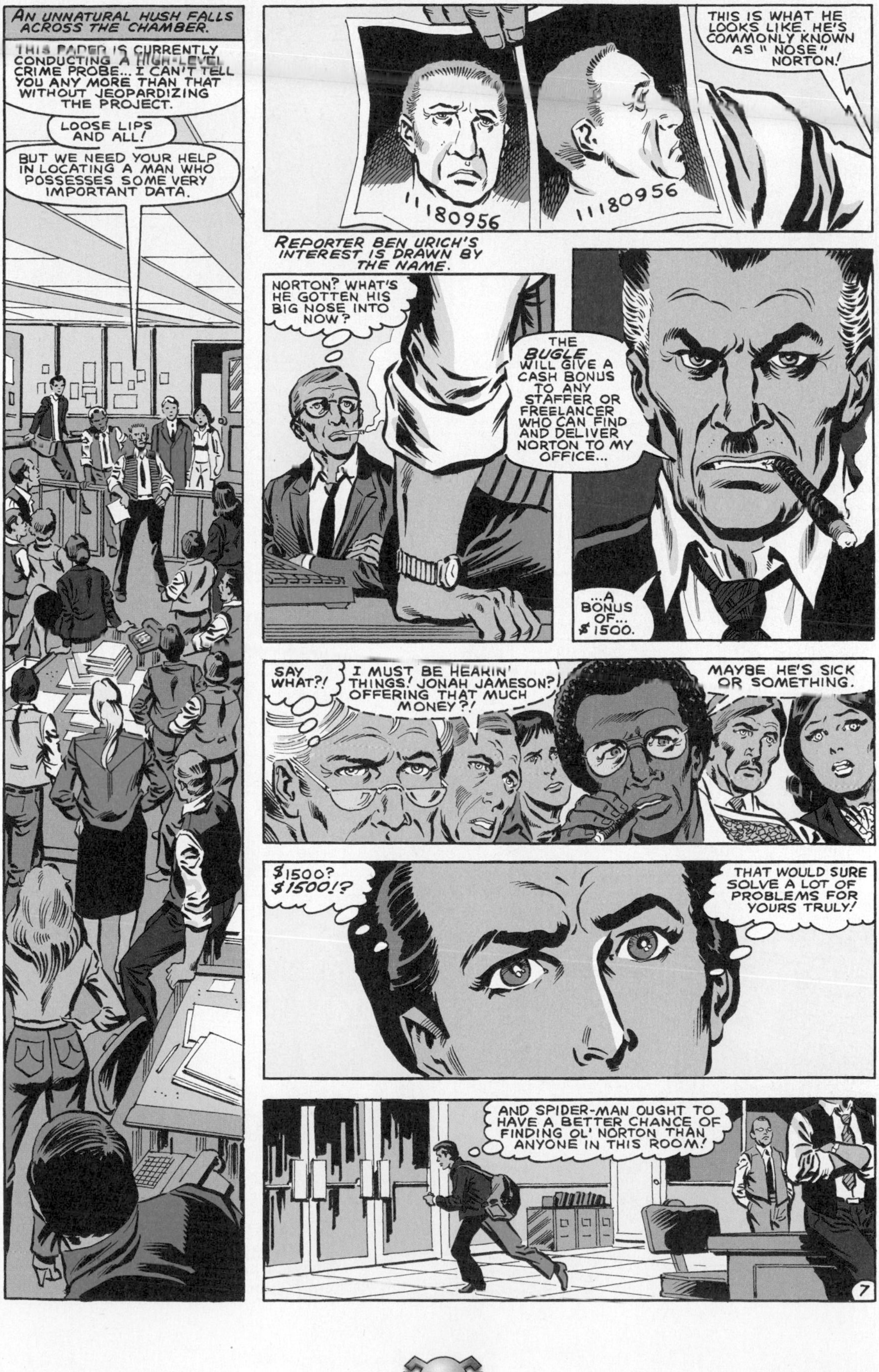
AN UNNATURAL HUSH FALLS ACROSS THE CHAMBER.
THIS PAPER IS CURRENTLY CONDUCTING A HIGH-LEVEL CRIME PROBE... I CAN'T TELL YOU ANY MORE THAN THAT WITHOUT JEOPARDIZING THE PROJECT.
LOOSE LIPS AND ALL!
BUT WE NEED YOUR HELP IN LOCATING A MAN WHO POSSESSES SOME VERY IMPORTANT DATA.
11180956
11180956
THIS IS WHAT HE LOOKS LIKE. HE'S COMMONLY KNOWN AS "NOSE" NORTON!
REPORTER BEN URICH'S INTEREST IS DRAWN BY THE NAME.
NORTON? WHAT'S HE GOTTEN HIS BIG NOSE INTO NOW?
THE BUGLE WILL GIVE A CASH BONUS TO ANY STAFFER OR FREELANCER WHO CAN FIND AND DELIVER NORTON TO MY OFFICE...
...A BONUS OF... $1500.
SAY WHAT?!
I MUST BE HEARIN' THINGS! JONAH JAMESON? OFFERING THAT MUCH MONEY?!
MAYBE HE'S SICK OR SOMETHING.
$1500? $1500!?
THAT WOULD SURE SOLVE A LOT OF PROBLEMS FOR YOURS TRULY!
AND SPIDER-MAN OUGHT TO HAVE A BETTER CHANCE OF FINDING OL' NORTON THAN ANYONE IN THIS ROOM!
7

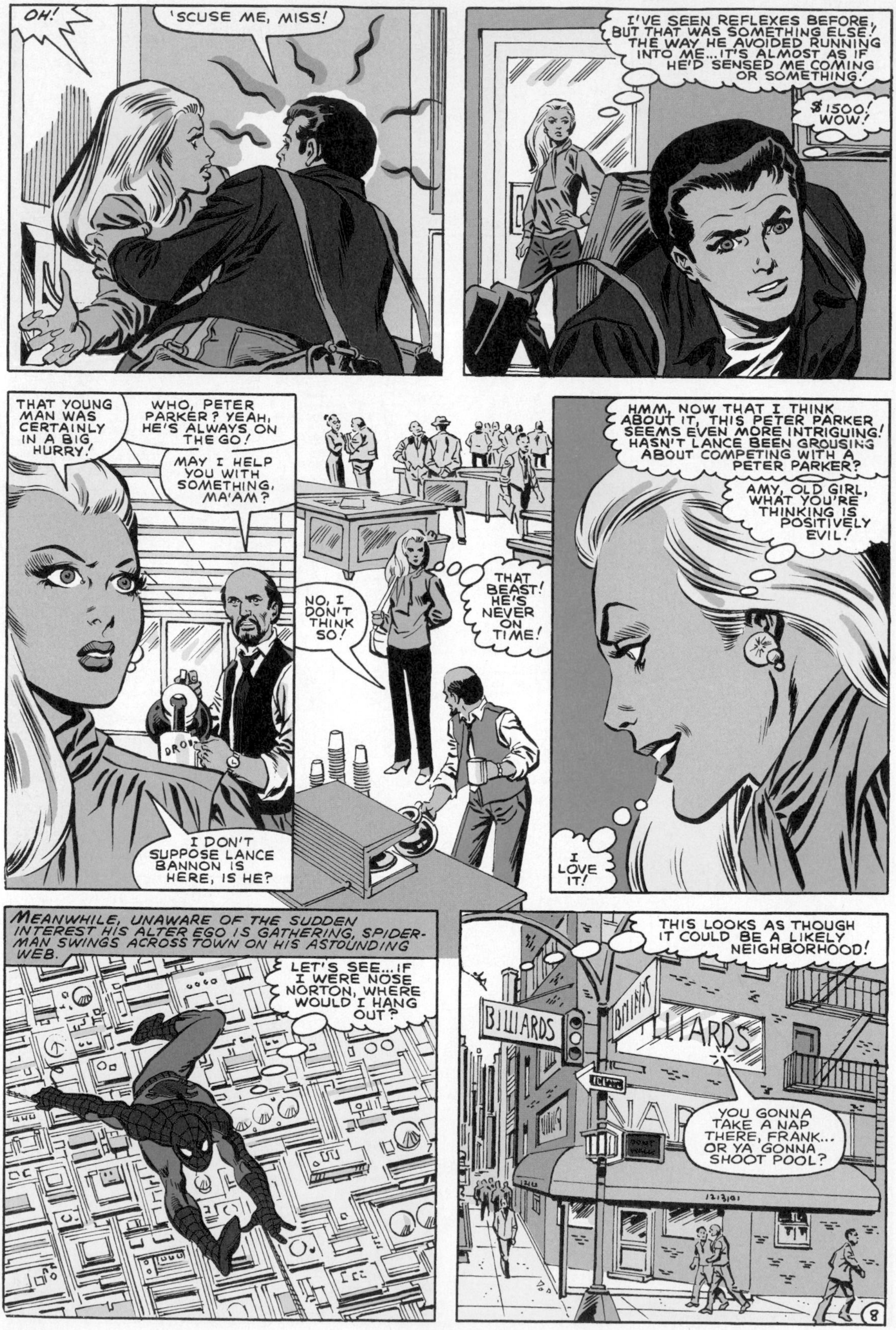
OH!
'SCUSE ME, MISS!
I'VE SEEN REFLEXES BEFORE, BUT THAT WAS SOMETHING ELSE! THE WAY HE AVOIDED RUNNING INTO ME...IT'S ALMOST AS IF HE'D SENSED ME COMING OR SOMETHING!
$1500! WOW!
THAT YOUNG MAN WAS CERTAINLY IN A BIG HURRY!
WHO, PETER PARKER? YEAH, HE'S ALWAYS ON THE GO!
MAY I HELP YOU WITH SOMETHING, MA'AM?
I DON'T SUPPOSE LANCE BANNON IS HERE, IS HE?
NO, I DON'T THINK SO!
THAT BEAST! HE'S NEVER ON TIME!
HMM, NOW THAT I THINK ABOUT IT, THIS PETER PARKER SEEMS EVEN MORE INTRIGUING! HASN'T LANCE BEEN GROUSING ABOUT COMPETING WITH A PETER PARKER?
AMY, OLD GIRL, WHAT YOU'RE THINKING IS POSITIVELY EVIL!
I LOVE IT!
MEANWHILE, UNAWARE OF THE SUDDEN INTEREST HIS ALTER EGO IS GATHERING, SPIDER-MAN SWINGS ACROSS TOWN ON HIS ASTOUNDING WEB.
LET'S SEE...IF I WERE NOSE NORTON, WHERE WOULD I HANG OUT?
THIS LOOKS AS THOUGH IT COULD BE A LIKELY NEIGHBORHOOD!
BILLIARDS
YOU GONNA TAKE A NAP THERE, FRANK... OR YA GONNA SHOOT POOL?
8

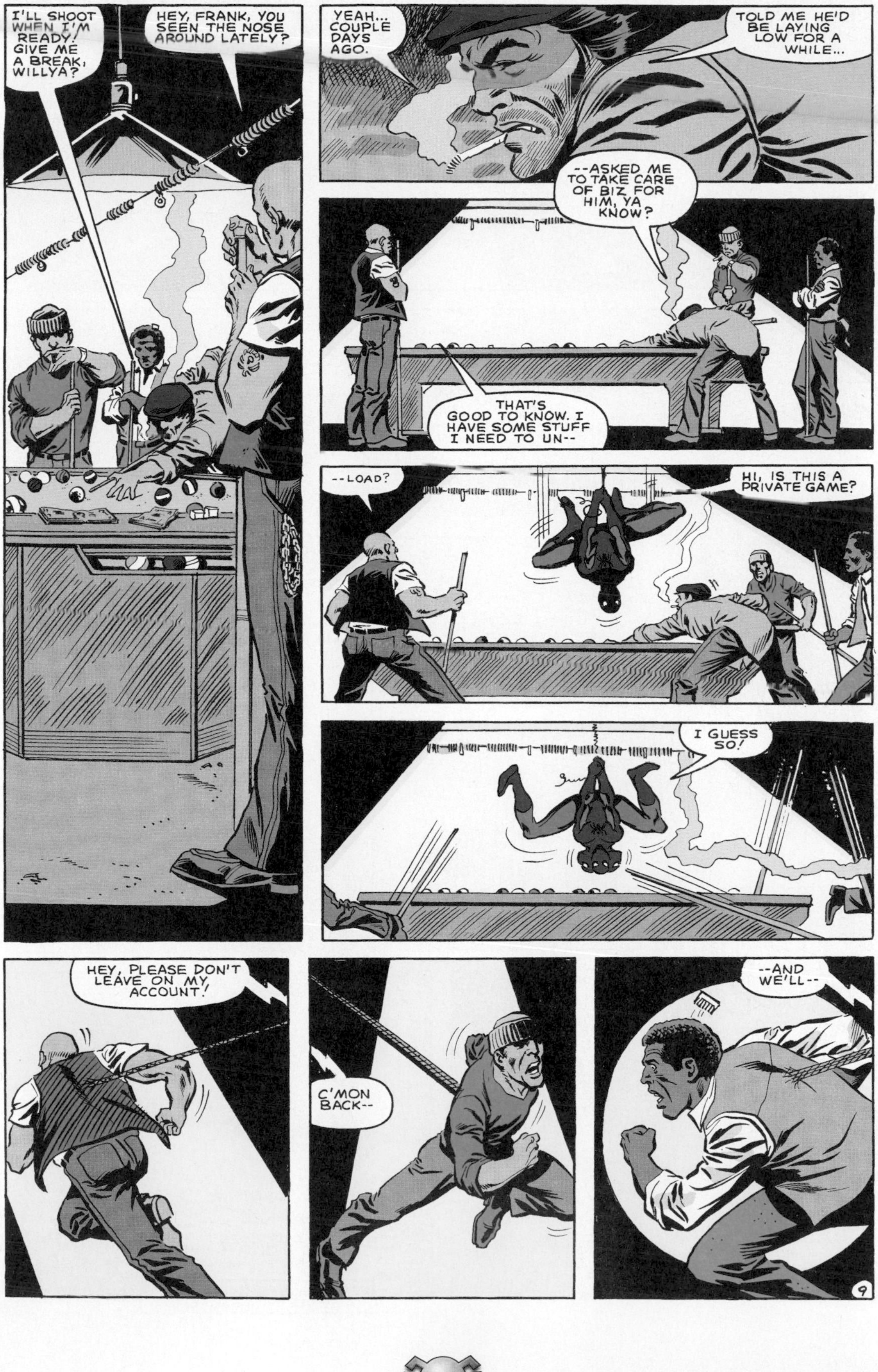
I'LL SHOOT WHEN I'M READY! GIVE ME A BREAK, WILLYA?
HEY, FRANK, YOU SEEN THE NOSE AROUND LATELY?
YEAH... COUPLE DAYS AGO.
TOLD ME HE'D BE LAYING LOW FOR A WHILE...
--ASKED ME TO TAKE CARE OF BIZ FOR HIM, YA KNOW?
THAT'S GOOD TO KNOW. I HAVE SOME STUFF I NEED TO UN--
--LOAD?
HI, IS THIS A PRIVATE GAME?
I GUESS SO!
HEY, PLEASE DON'T LEAVE ON MY ACCOUNT!
C'MON BACK--
--AND WE'LL--
9

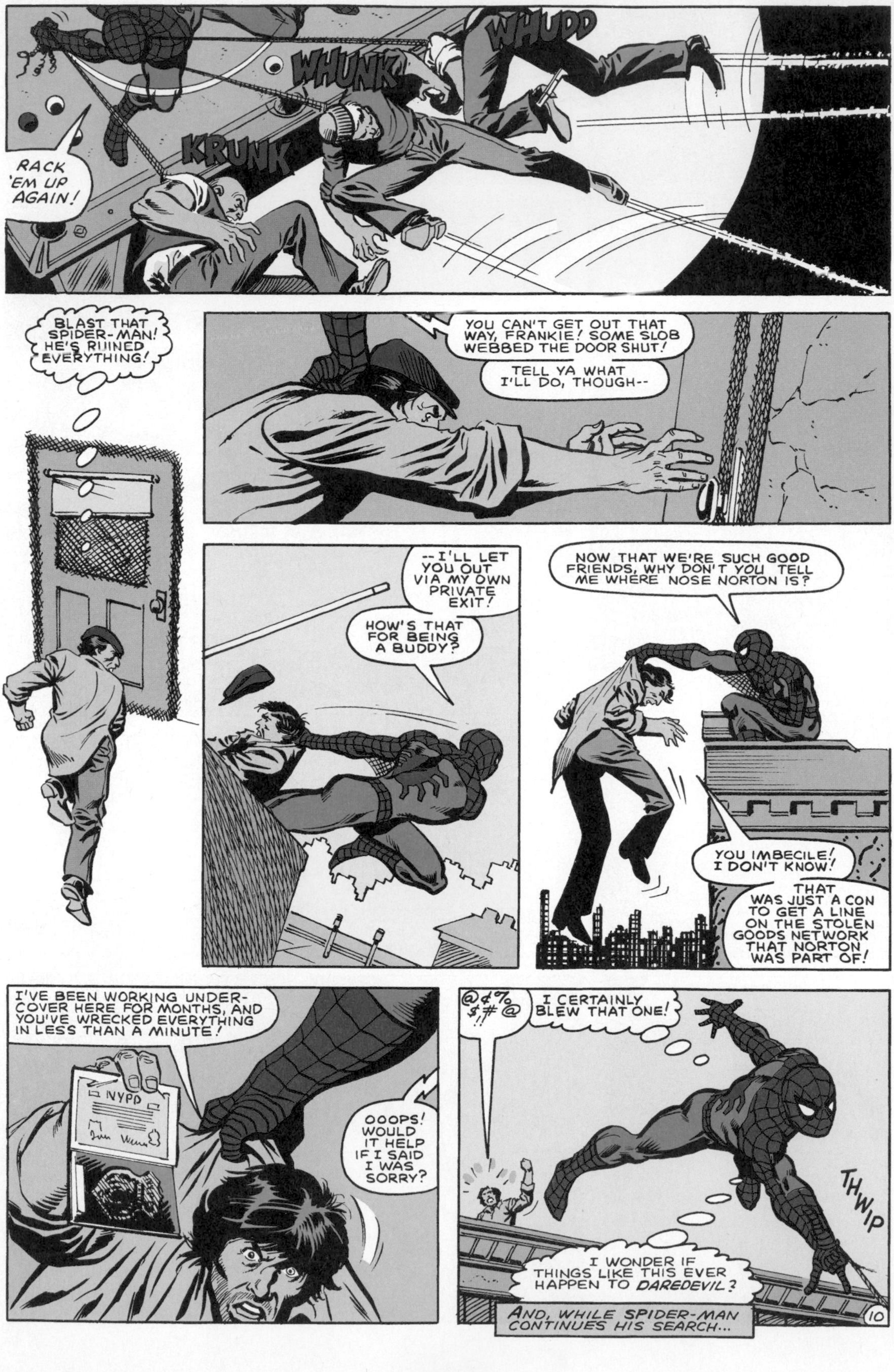
WHUDD
WHUNK
KRUNK
RACK 'EM UP AGAIN!
BLAST THAT SPIDER-MAN! HE'S RUINED EVERYTHING!
YOU CAN'T GET OUT THAT WAY, FRANKIE! SOME SLOB WEBBED THE DOOR SHUT!
TELL YA WHAT I'LL DO, THOUGH--
--I'LL LET YOU OUT VIA MY OWN PRIVATE EXIT!
HOW'S THAT FOR BEING A BUDDY?
NOW THAT WE'RE SUCH GOOD FRIENDS, WHY DON'T YOU TELL ME WHERE NOSE NORTON IS?
YOU IMBECILE! I DON'T KNOW!
THAT WAS JUST A CON TO GET A LINE ON THE STOLEN GOODS NETWORK THAT NORTON WAS PART OF!
I'VE BEEN WORKING UNDER-COVER HERE FOR MONTHS, AND YOU'VE WRECKED EVERYTHING IN LESS THAN A MINUTE!
NYPD
OOOPS! WOULD IT HELP IF I SAID I WAS SORRY?
@¢%$#@!!
I CERTAINLY BLEW THAT ONE!
THWIP
I WONDER IF THINGS LIKE THIS EVER HAPPEN TO DAREDEVIL?
AND, WHILE SPIDER-MAN CONTINUES HIS SEARCH...
10

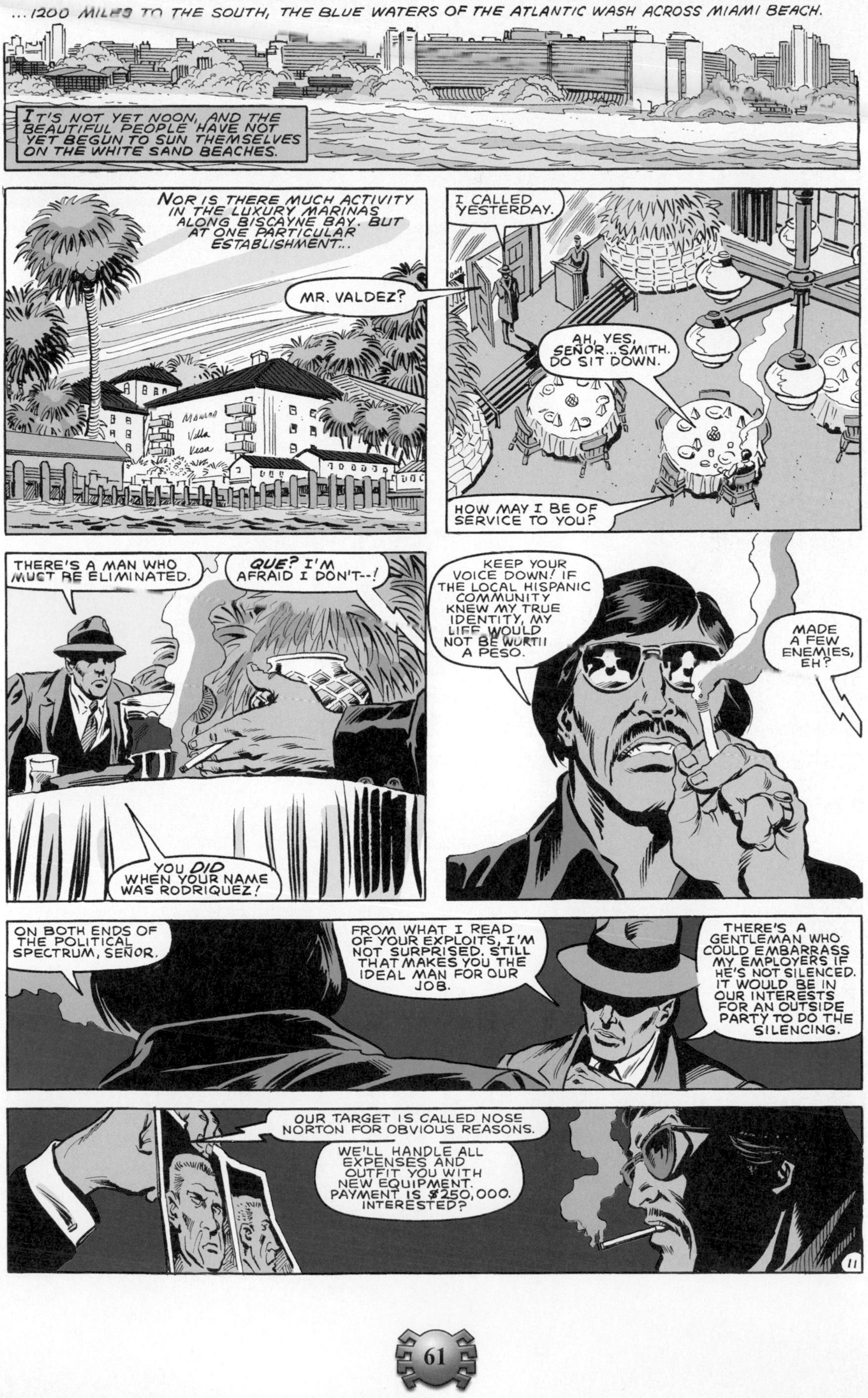
...1200 MILES TO THE SOUTH, THE BLUE WATERS OF THE ATLANTIC WASH ACROSS MIAMI BEACH.
IT'S NOT YET NOON, AND THE BEAUTIFUL PEOPLE HAVE NOT YET BEGUN TO SUN THEMSELVES ON THE WHITE SAND BEACHES.
NOR IS THERE MUCH ACTIVITY IN THE LUXURY MARINAS ALONG BISCAYNE BAY. BUT AT ONE PARTICULAR ESTABLISHMENT...
MR. VALDEZ?
I CALLED YESTERDAY.
AH, YES, SEÑOR... SMITH. DO SIT DOWN.
HOW MAY I BE OF SERVICE TO YOU?
THERE'S A MAN WHO MUST BE ELIMINATED.
QUE? I'M AFRAID I DON'T--!
YOU DID WHEN YOUR NAME WAS RODRIQUEZ!
KEEP YOUR VOICE DOWN! IF THE LOCAL HISPANIC COMMUNITY KNEW MY TRUE IDENTITY, MY LIFE WOULD NOT BE WORTH A PESO.
MADE A FEW ENEMIES, EH?
ON BOTH ENDS OF THE POLITICAL SPECTRUM, SEÑOR.
FROM WHAT I READ OF YOUR EXPLOITS, I'M NOT SURPRISED. STILL THAT MAKES YOU THE IDEAL MAN FOR OUR JOB.
THERE'S A GENTLEMAN WHO COULD EMBARRASS MY EMPLOYERS IF HE'S NOT SILENCED. IT WOULD BE IN OUR INTERESTS FOR AN OUTSIDE PARTY TO DO THE SILENCING.
OUR TARGET IS CALLED NOSE NORTON FOR OBVIOUS REASONS.
WE'LL HANDLE ALL EXPENSES AND OUTFIT YOU WITH NEW EQUIPMENT. PAYMENT IS $250,000. INTERESTED?
11

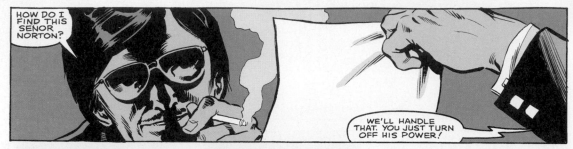

HOW DO I FIND THIS SENOR NORTON?

WE'LL HANDLE THAT. YOU JUST TURN OFF HIS POWER!

IN THE DAYS THAT FOLLOW, THE SEARCH FOR NOSE NORTON STRETCHES ACROSS THE ENTIRE EASTERN SEABOARD, INTO EVERY HOBO JUNGLE...

...EVERY WATERFRONT DIVE AND BACK ALLEY!

INTO EVERY GIN MILL IN A DOZEN STATES, THE QUEST GOES ON, BUT EVERYWHERE, THE ANSWER'S THE SAME.

NOPE! I AIN'T SEEN HIM.

WHERE IS NOSE NORTON? WHERE IS THIS LITTLE MAN WHO KNOWS TOO MUCH?

HERE! IN THE NEW YORK CITY BOROUGH OF RICHMOND, BETTER KNOWN AS STATEN ISLAND!

FOR OVER A WEEK, NORTON HAS HOLED UP IN A ONE ROOM APARTMENT OVER A DISREPUTABLE WATERFRONT BAR, JUST TWENTY MINUTES AWAY, BY FERRY, FROM MANHATTAN.

MURRAYS
MURRAYS

TODAY, HE HAS MADE A SERIOUS MISTAKE.

MAYBE I SHOULDN'T HAVE COME DOWNSTAIRS FOR A BREW, BUT I WAS GOING SQUIRRELLY, COOPED UP IN THERE!

AW, WHAT AM I WORRIED ABOUT?

12

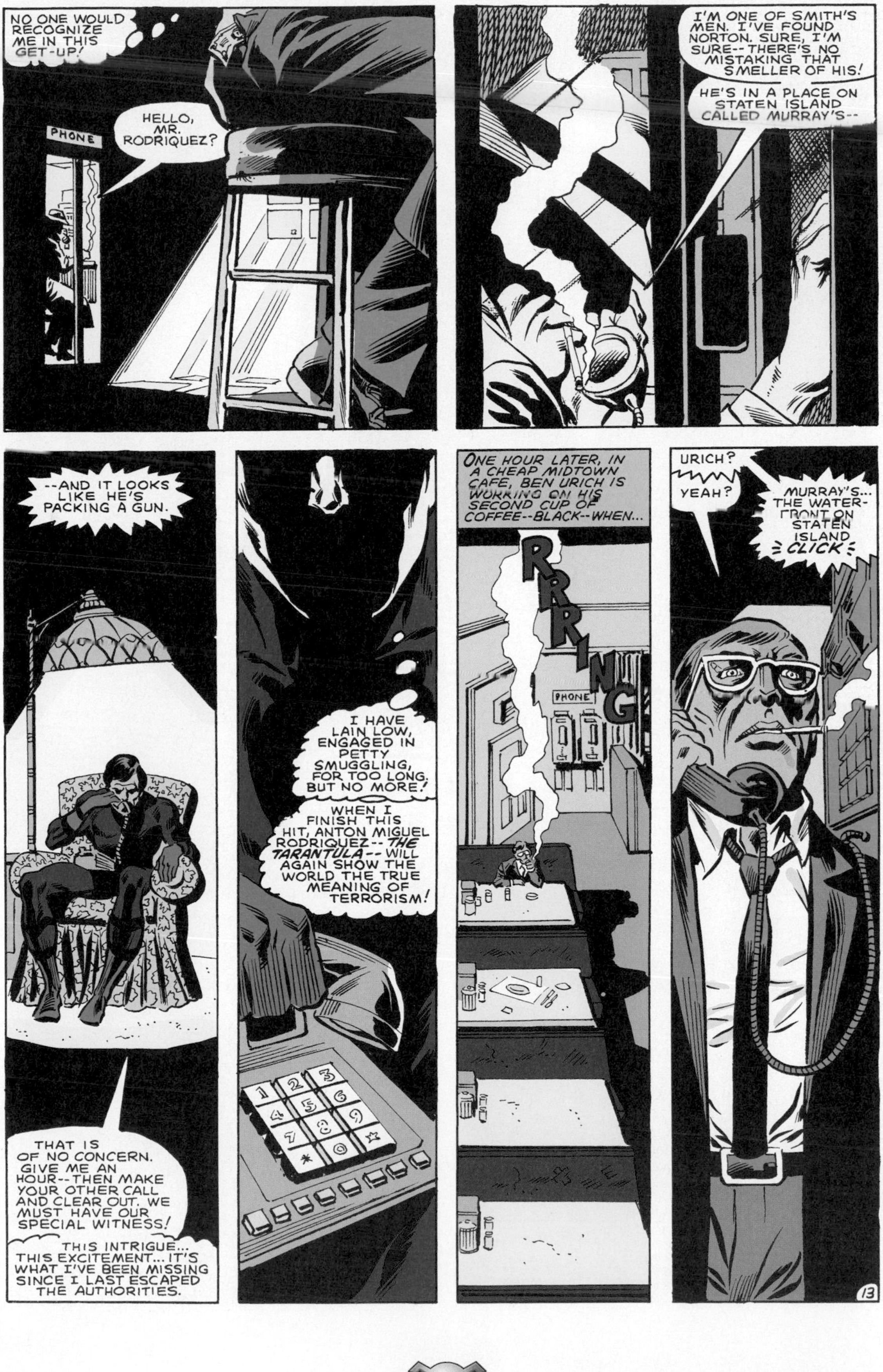
NO ONE WOULD RECOGNIZE ME IN THIS GET-UP!
PHONE
HELLO, MR. RODRIQUEZ?
I'M ONE OF SMITH'S MEN. I'VE FOUND NORTON. SURE, I'M SURE-- THERE'S NO MISTAKING THAT SMELLER OF HIS!
HE'S IN A PLACE ON STATEN ISLAND CALLED MURRAY'S--
--AND IT LOOKS LIKE HE'S PACKING A GUN.
THAT IS OF NO CONCERN. GIVE ME AN HOUR--THEN MAKE YOUR OTHER CALL AND CLEAR OUT. WE MUST HAVE OUR SPECIAL WITNESS!
THIS INTRIGUE... THIS EXCITEMENT... IT'S WHAT I'VE BEEN MISSING SINCE I LAST ESCAPED THE AUTHORITIES.
I HAVE LAIN LOW, ENGAGED IN PETTY SMUGGLING, FOR TOO LONG. BUT NO MORE!
WHEN I FINISH THIS HIT, ANTON MIGUEL RODRIQUEZ-- THE TARANTULA-- WILL AGAIN SHOW THE WORLD THE TRUE MEANING OF TERRORISM!
ONE HOUR LATER, IN A CHEAP MIDTOWN CAFE, BEN URICH IS WORKING ON HIS SECOND CUP OF COFFEE--BLACK--WHEN...
RRRING
PHONE
URICH?
YEAH?
MURRAY'S... THE WATER-FRONT ON STATEN ISLAND
CLICK
13

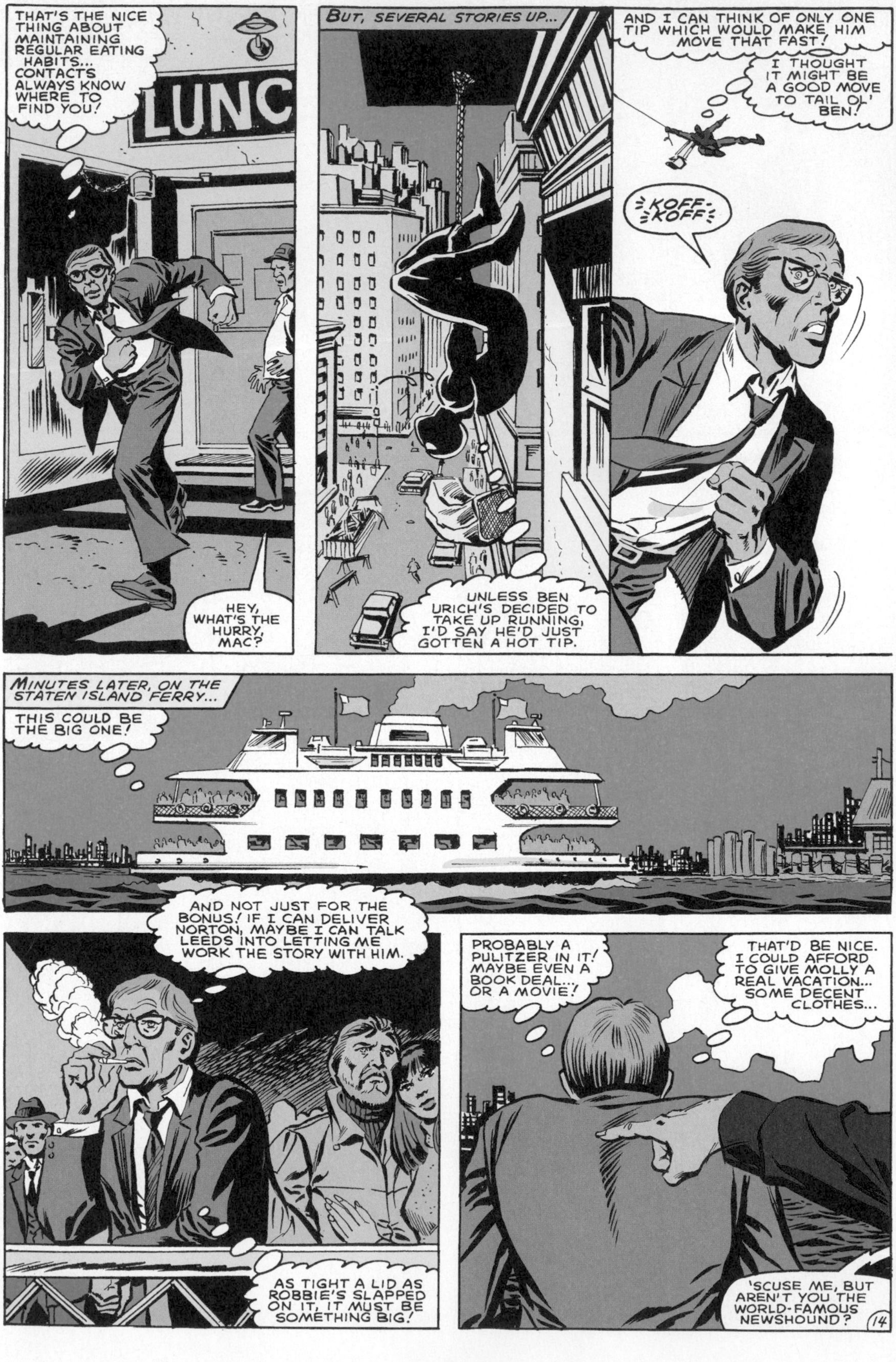
THAT'S THE NICE THING ABOUT MAINTAINING REGULAR EATING HABITS... CONTACTS ALWAYS KNOW WHERE TO FIND YOU!
LUNC
HEY, WHAT'S THE HURRY, MAC?
BUT, SEVERAL STORIES UP...
UNLESS BEN URICH'S DECIDED TO TAKE UP RUNNING, I'D SAY HE'D JUST GOTTEN A HOT TIP.
AND I CAN THINK OF ONLY ONE TIP WHICH WOULD MAKE HIM MOVE THAT FAST!
I THOUGHT IT MIGHT BE A GOOD MOVE TO TAIL OL' BEN!
KOFF-KOFF
MINUTES LATER, ON THE STATEN ISLAND FERRY...
THIS COULD BE THE BIG ONE!
AND NOT JUST FOR THE BONUS! IF I CAN DELIVER NORTON, MAYBE I CAN TALK LEEDS INTO LETTING ME WORK THE STORY WITH HIM.
AS TIGHT A LID AS ROBBIE'S SLAPPED ON IT, IT MUST BE SOMETHING BIG!
PROBABLY A PULITZER IN IT! MAYBE EVEN A BOOK DEAL... OR A MOVIE!
THAT'D BE NICE. I COULD AFFORD TO GIVE MOLLY A REAL VACATION... SOME DECENT CLOTHES...
'SCUSE ME, BUT AREN'T YOU THE WORLD-FAMOUS NEWSHOUND?
14

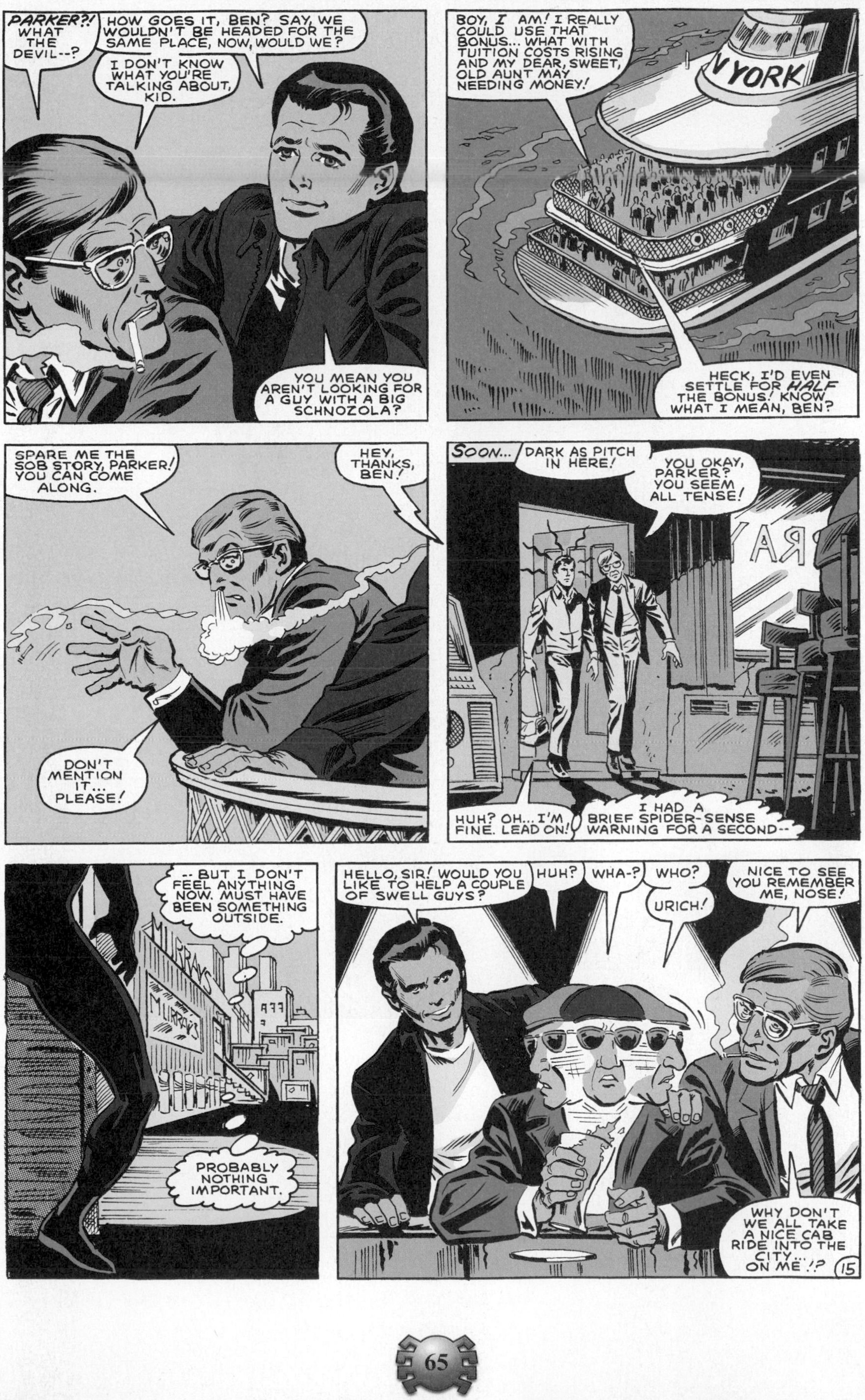
PARKER?! WHAT THE DEVIL--?
HOW GOES IT, BEN? SAY, WE WOULDN'T BE HEADED FOR THE SAME PLACE, NOW, WOULD WE?
I DON'T KNOW WHAT YOU'RE TALKING ABOUT, KID.
YOU MEAN YOU AREN'T LOOKING FOR A GUY WITH A BIG SCHNOZOLA?
BOY, I AM! I REALLY COULD USE THAT BONUS... WHAT WITH TUITION COSTS RISING AND MY DEAR, SWEET, OLD AUNT MAY NEEDING MONEY!
N YORK
HECK, I'D EVEN SETTLE FOR HALF THE BONUS! KNOW WHAT I MEAN, BEN?
SPARE ME THE SOB STORY, PARKER! YOU CAN COME ALONG.
HEY, THANKS, BEN!
DON'T MENTION IT... PLEASE!
SOON...
DARK AS PITCH IN HERE!
YOU OKAY, PARKER? YOU SEEM ALL TENSE!
HUH? OH... I'M FINE. LEAD ON!
I HAD A BRIEF SPIDER-SENSE WARNING FOR A SECOND--
-- BUT I DON'T FEEL ANYTHING NOW. MUST HAVE BEEN SOMETHING OUTSIDE.
MURRAY'S
MURRAY'S
PROBABLY NOTHING IMPORTANT.
HELLO, SIR! WOULD YOU LIKE TO HELP A COUPLE OF SWELL GUYS?
HUH?
WHA-?
WHO?
URICH!
NICE TO SEE YOU REMEMBER ME, NOSE!
WHY DON'T WE ALL TAKE A NICE CAB RIDE INTO THE CITY... ON ME!?
15

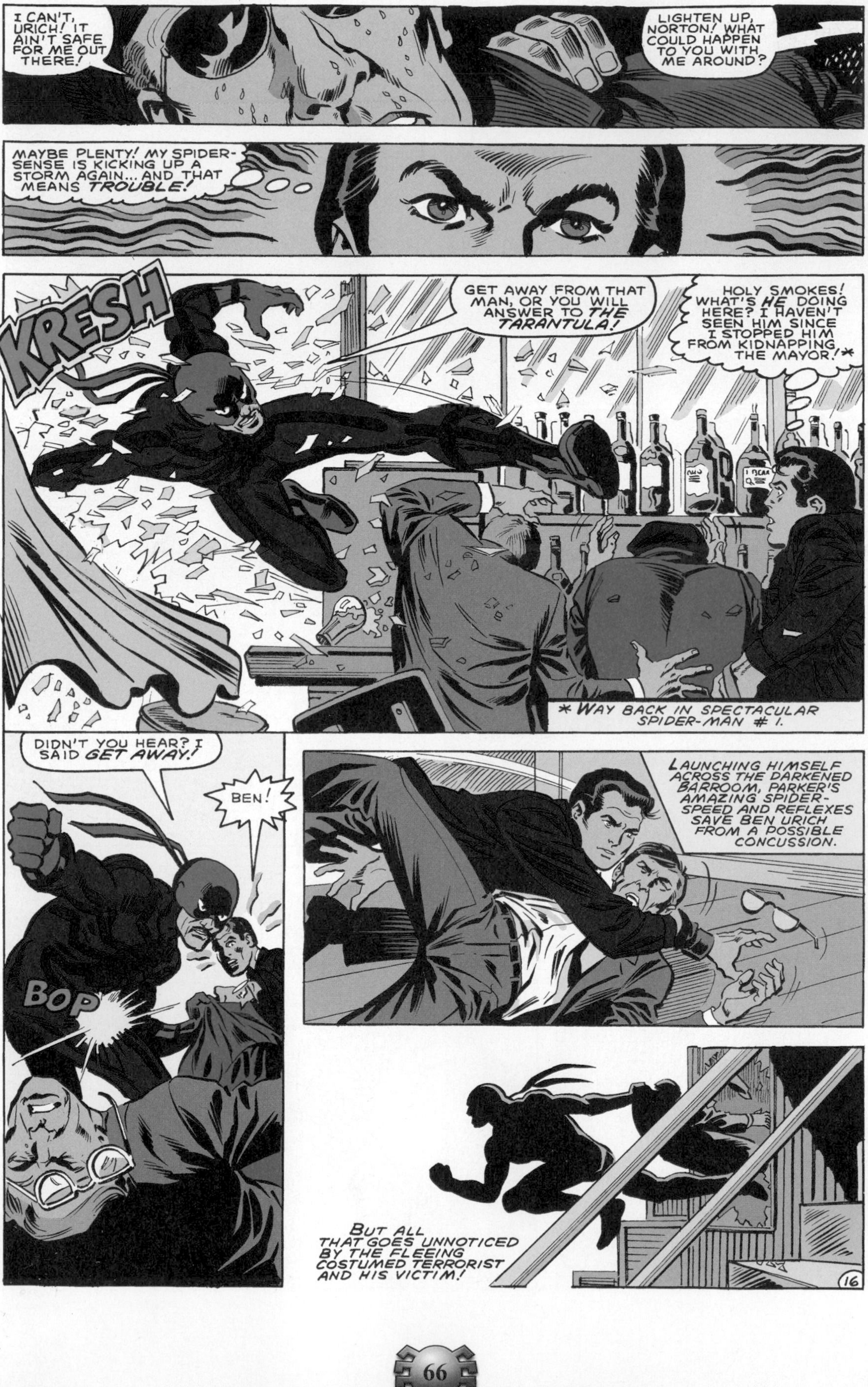

I CAN'T, URICH! IT AIN'T SAFE FOR ME OUT THERE!
LIGHTEN UP, NORTON! WHAT COULD HAPPEN TO YOU WITH ME AROUND?
MAYBE PLENTY! MY SPIDER-SENSE IS KICKING UP A STORM AGAIN... AND THAT MEANS TROUBLE!
KRESH
GET AWAY FROM THAT MAN, OR YOU WILL ANSWER TO THE TARANTULA!
HOLY SMOKES! WHAT'S HE DOING HERE? I HAVEN'T SEEN HIM SINCE I STOPPED HIM FROM KIDNAPPING THE MAYOR!*
* WAY BACK IN SPECTACULAR SPIDER-MAN # 1.
DIDN'T YOU HEAR? I SAID GET AWAY!
BEN!
BOP
LAUNCHING HIMSELF ACROSS THE DARKENED BARROOM, PARKER'S AMAZING SPIDER-SPEED AND REFLEXES SAVE BEN URICH FROM A POSSIBLE CONCUSSION.
BUT ALL THAT GOES UNNOTICED BY THE FLEEING COSTUMED TERRORIST AND HIS VICTIM!
16

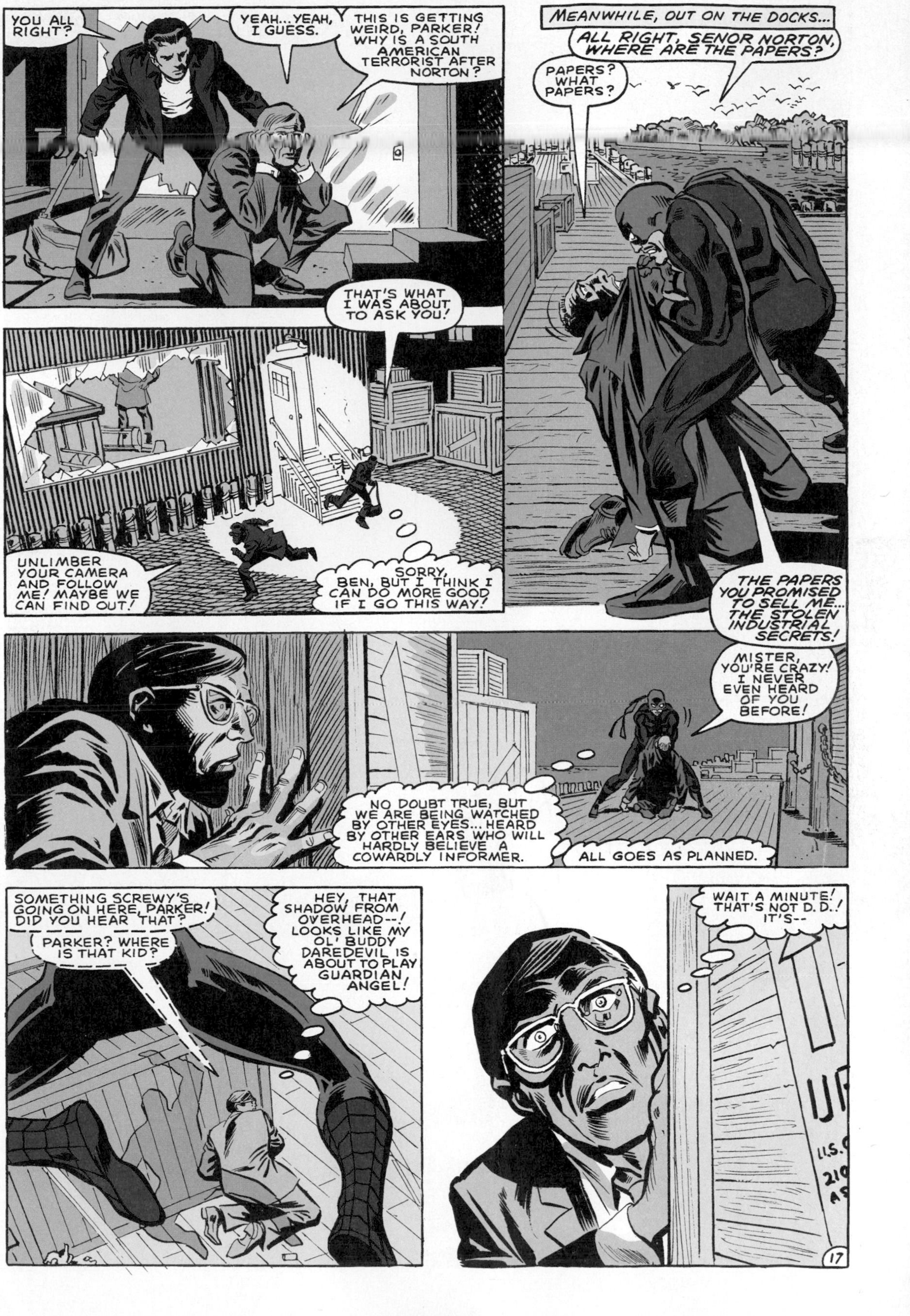
YOU ALL RIGHT?
YEAH...YEAH, I GUESS.
THIS IS GETTING WEIRD, PARKER! WHY IS A SOUTH AMERICAN TERRORIST AFTER NORTON?
THAT'S WHAT I WAS ABOUT TO ASK YOU!
UNLIMBER YOUR CAMERA AND FOLLOW ME! MAYBE WE CAN FIND OUT!
SORRY, BEN, BUT I THINK I CAN DO MORE GOOD IF I GO THIS WAY!
MEANWHILE, OUT ON THE DOCKS...
ALL RIGHT, SENOR NORTON, WHERE ARE THE PAPERS?
PAPERS? WHAT PAPERS?
THE PAPERS YOU PROMISED TO SELL ME... THE STOLEN INDUSTRIAL SECRETS!
MISTER, YOU'RE CRAZY! I NEVER EVEN HEARD OF YOU BEFORE!
NO DOUBT TRUE, BUT WE ARE BEING WATCHED BY OTHER EYES... HEARD BY OTHER EARS WHO WILL HARDLY BELIEVE A COWARDLY INFORMER.
ALL GOES AS PLANNED.
SOMETHING SCREWY'S GOING ON HERE, PARKER! DID YOU HEAR THAT?
PARKER? WHERE IS THAT KID?
HEY, THAT SHADOW FROM OVERHEAD--! LOOKS LIKE MY OL' BUDDY DAREDEVIL IS ABOUT TO PLAY GUARDIAN ANGEL!
WAIT A MINUTE! THAT'S NOT D.D.! IT'S--
17

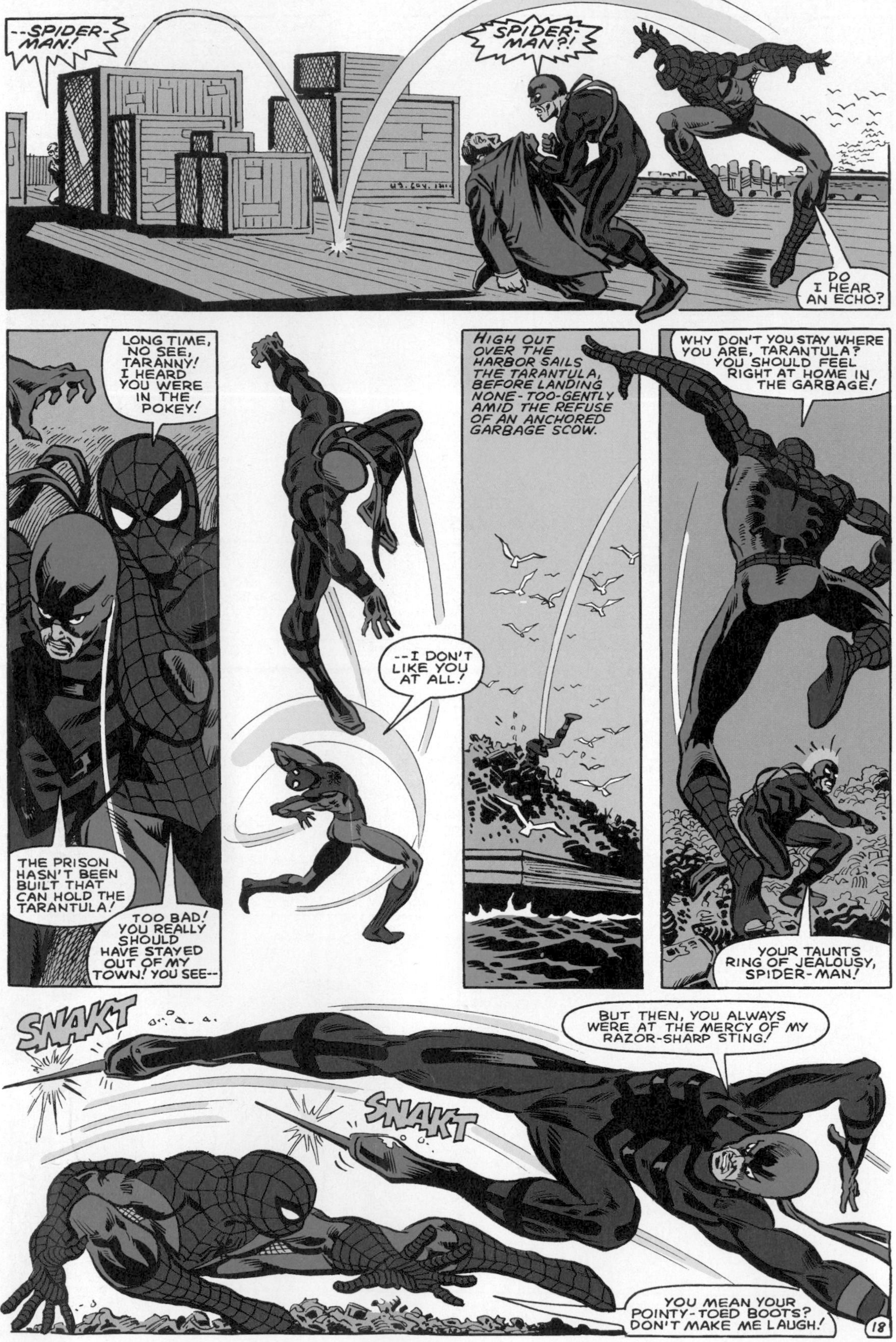
--SPIDER-MAN!
SPIDER-MAN?!
DO I HEAR AN ECHO?
LONG TIME, NO SEE, TARANNY! I HEARD YOU WERE IN THE POKEY!
THE PRISON HASN'T BEEN BUILT THAT CAN HOLD THE TARANTULA!
TOO BAD! YOU REALLY SHOULD HAVE STAYED OUT OF MY TOWN! YOU SEE--
--I DON'T LIKE YOU AT ALL!
HIGH OUT OVER THE HARBOR SAILS THE TARANTULA, BEFORE LANDING NONE-TOO-GENTLY AMID THE REFUSE OF AN ANCHORED GARBAGE SCOW.
WHY DON'T YOU STAY WHERE YOU ARE, TARANTULA? YOU SHOULD FEEL RIGHT AT HOME IN THE GARBAGE!
YOUR TAUNTS RING OF JEALOUSY, SPIDER-MAN!
SNAKT
BUT THEN, YOU ALWAYS WERE AT THE MERCY OF MY RAZOR-SHARP STING!
SNAKT
YOU MEAN YOUR POINTY-TOED BOOTS? DON'T MAKE ME LAUGH!
18

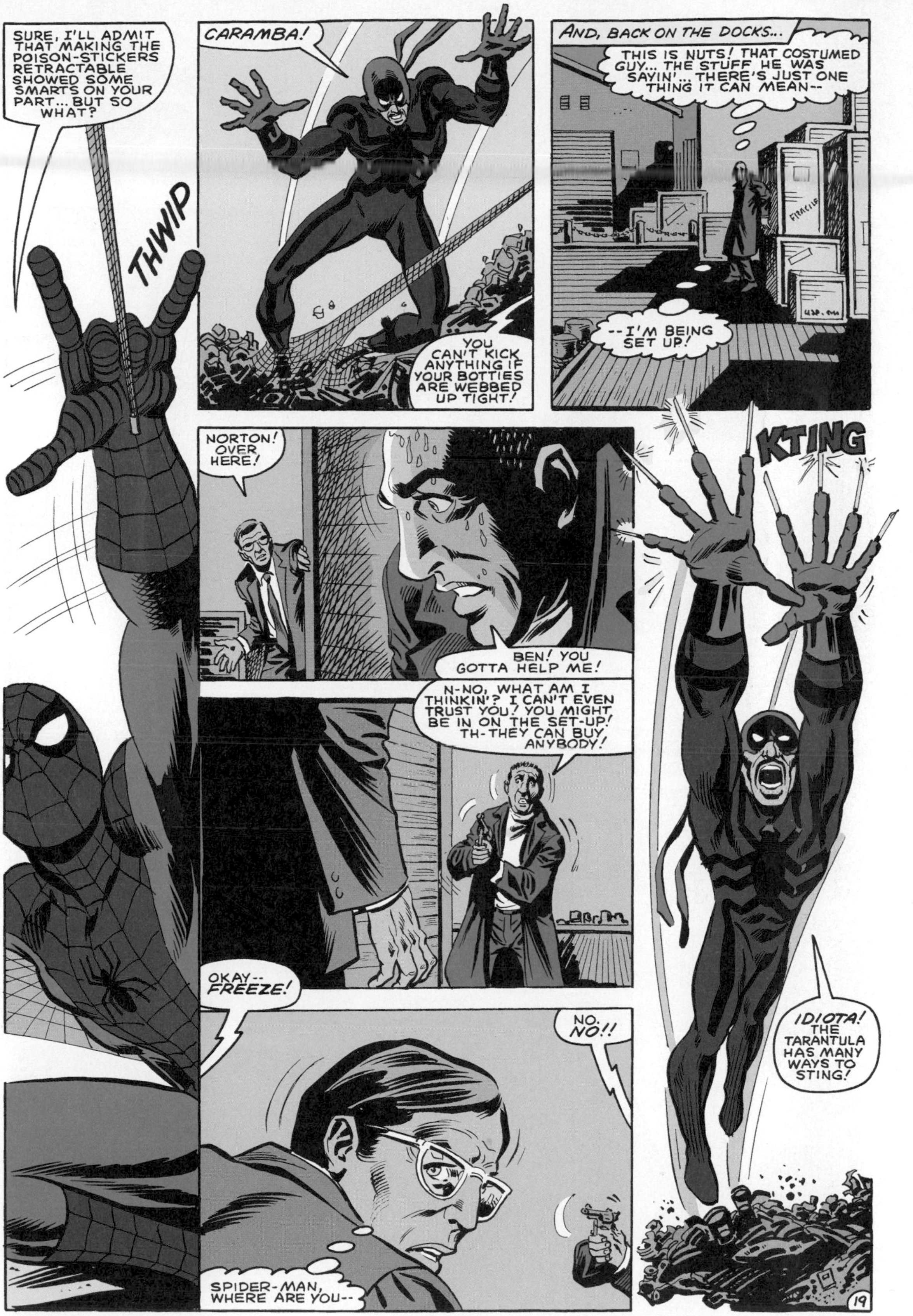
SURE, I'LL ADMIT THAT MAKING THE POISON-STICKERS RETRACTABLE SHOWED SOME SMARTS ON YOUR PART... BUT SO WHAT?
THWIP
CARAMBA!
YOU CAN'T KICK ANYTHING IF YOUR BOTTIES ARE WEBBED UP TIGHT!
AND, BACK ON THE DOCKS...
THIS IS NUTS! THAT COSTUMED GUY... THE STUFF HE WAS SAYIN'... THERE'S JUST ONE THING IT CAN MEAN--
--I'M BEING SET UP!
NORTON! OVER HERE!
BEN! YOU GOTTA HELP ME!
N-NO, WHAT AM I THINKIN'? I CAN'T EVEN TRUST YOU! YOU MIGHT BE IN ON THE SET-UP! TH-THEY CAN BUY ANYBODY!
OKAY-- FREEZE!
NO. NO!!
SPIDER-MAN, WHERE ARE YOU--
KTING
IDIOTA! THE TARANTULA HAS MANY WAYS TO STING!
19

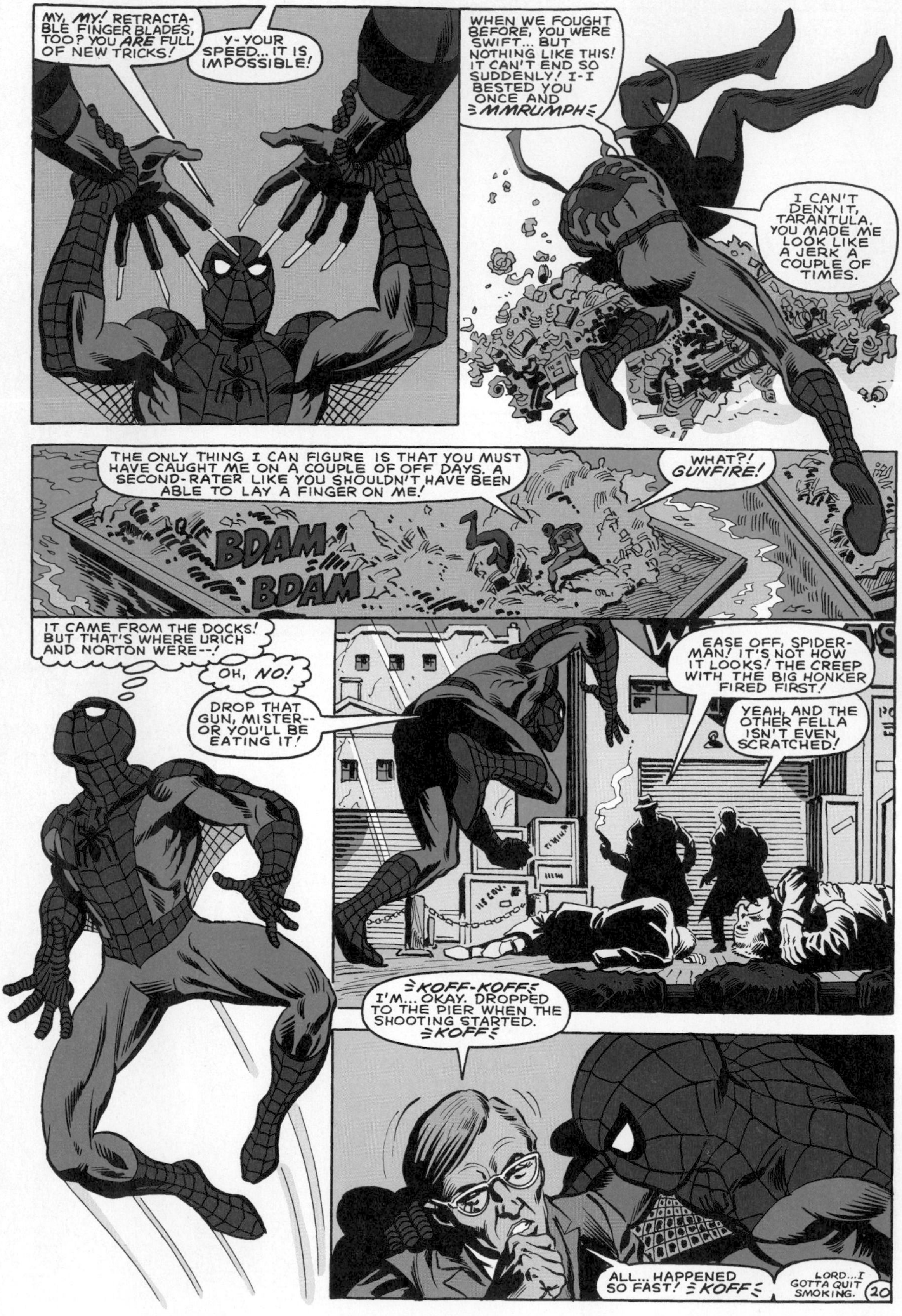
MY, MY! RETRACTABLE FINGER BLADES, TOO? YOU ARE FULL OF NEW TRICKS!
Y-YOUR SPEED... IT IS IMPOSSIBLE!
WHEN WE FOUGHT BEFORE, YOU WERE SWIFT... BUT NOTHING LIKE THIS! IT CAN'T END SO SUDDENLY! I-I BESTED YOU ONCE AND MMRUMPH
I CAN'T DENY IT, TARANTULA. YOU MADE ME LOOK LIKE A JERK A COUPLE OF TIMES.
THE ONLY THING I CAN FIGURE IS THAT YOU MUST HAVE CAUGHT ME ON A COUPLE OF OFF DAYS. A SECOND-RATER LIKE YOU SHOULDN'T HAVE BEEN ABLE TO LAY A FINGER ON ME!
WHAT?! GUNFIRE!
BDAM
BDAM
IT CAME FROM THE DOCKS! BUT THAT'S WHERE URICH AND NORTON WERE--!
OH, NO!
DROP THAT GUN, MISTER-- OR YOU'LL BE EATING IT!
EASE OFF, SPIDER-MAN! IT'S NOT HOW IT LOOKS! THE CREEP WITH THE BIG HONKER FIRED FIRST!
YEAH, AND THE OTHER FELLA ISN'T EVEN SCRATCHED!
KOFF-KOFF I'M... OKAY. DROPPED TO THE PIER WHEN THE SHOOTING STARTED. KOFF
ALL... HAPPENED SO FAST! KOFF
LORD... I GOTTA QUIT SMOKING.
20

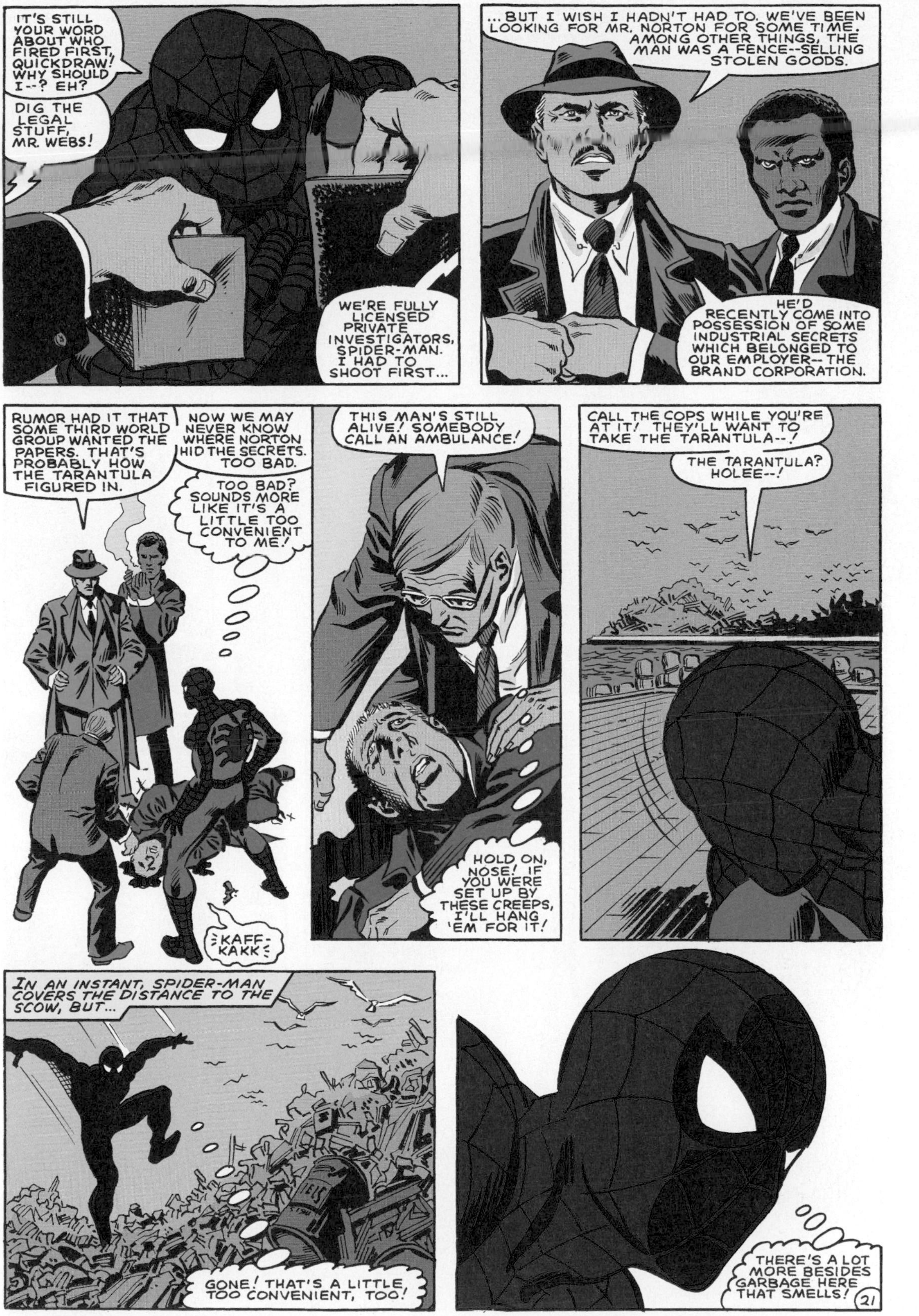

IT'S STILL YOUR WORD ABOUT WHO FIRED FIRST, QUICKDRAW! WHY SHOULD I--? EH?
DIG THE LEGAL STUFF, MR. WEBS!
WE'RE FULLY LICENSED PRIVATE INVESTIGATORS, SPIDER-MAN. I HAD TO SHOOT FIRST...
...BUT I WISH I HADN'T HAD TO. WE'VE BEEN LOOKING FOR MR. NORTON FOR SOME TIME. AMONG OTHER THINGS, THE MAN WAS A FENCE--SELLING STOLEN GOODS.
HE'D RECENTLY COME INTO POSSESSION OF SOME INDUSTRIAL SECRETS WHICH BELONGED TO OUR EMPLOYER-- THE BRAND CORPORATION.
RUMOR HAD IT THAT SOME THIRD WORLD GROUP WANTED THE PAPERS. THAT'S PROBABLY HOW THE TARANTULA FIGURED IN.
NOW WE MAY NEVER KNOW WHERE NORTON HID THE SECRETS. TOO BAD.
TOO BAD? SOUNDS MORE LIKE IT'S A LITTLE TOO CONVENIENT TO ME!
KAFF-KAKK
THIS MAN'S STILL ALIVE! SOMEBODY CALL AN AMBULANCE!
HOLD ON, NOSE! IF YOU WERE SET UP BY THESE CREEPS, I'LL HANG 'EM FOR IT!
CALL THE COPS WHILE YOU'RE AT IT! THEY'LL WANT TO TAKE THE TARANTULA--!
THE TARANTULA? HOLEE--!
IN AN INSTANT, SPIDER-MAN COVERS THE DISTANCE TO THE SCOW, BUT...
GONE! THAT'S A LITTLE, TOO CONVENIENT, TOO!
THERE'S A LOT MORE BESIDES GARBAGE HERE THAT SMELLS!
21

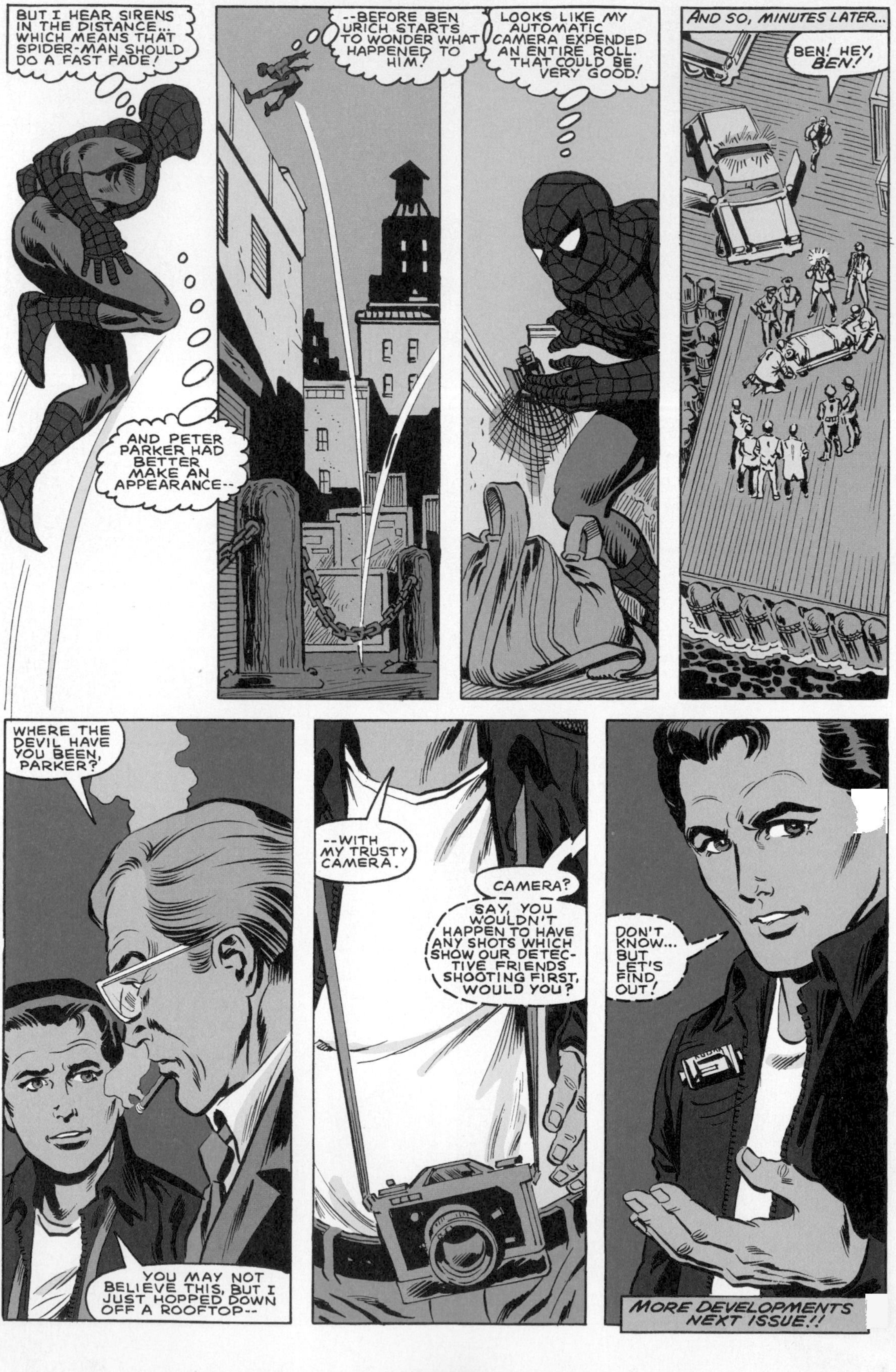

BUT I HEAR SIRENS IN THE DISTANCE... WHICH MEANS THAT SPIDER-MAN SHOULD DO A FAST FADE!
AND PETER PARKER HAD BETTER MAKE AN APPEARANCE--
--BEFORE BEN URICH STARTS TO WONDER WHAT HAPPENED TO HIM!
LOOKS LIKE MY AUTOMATIC CAMERA EXPENDED AN ENTIRE ROLL. THAT COULD BE VERY GOOD!
AND SO, MINUTES LATER...
BEN! HEY, BEN!
WHERE THE DEVIL HAVE YOU BEEN, PARKER?
YOU MAY NOT BELIEVE THIS, BUT I JUST HOPPED DOWN OFF A ROOFTOP--
--WITH MY TRUSTY CAMERA.
CAMERA?
SAY, YOU WOULDN'T HAPPEN TO HAVE ANY SHOTS WHICH SHOW OUR DETECTIVE FRIENDS SHOOTING FIRST, WOULD YOU?
DON'T KNOW... BUT LET'S FIND OUT!
MORE DEVELOPMENTS NEXT ISSUE!!

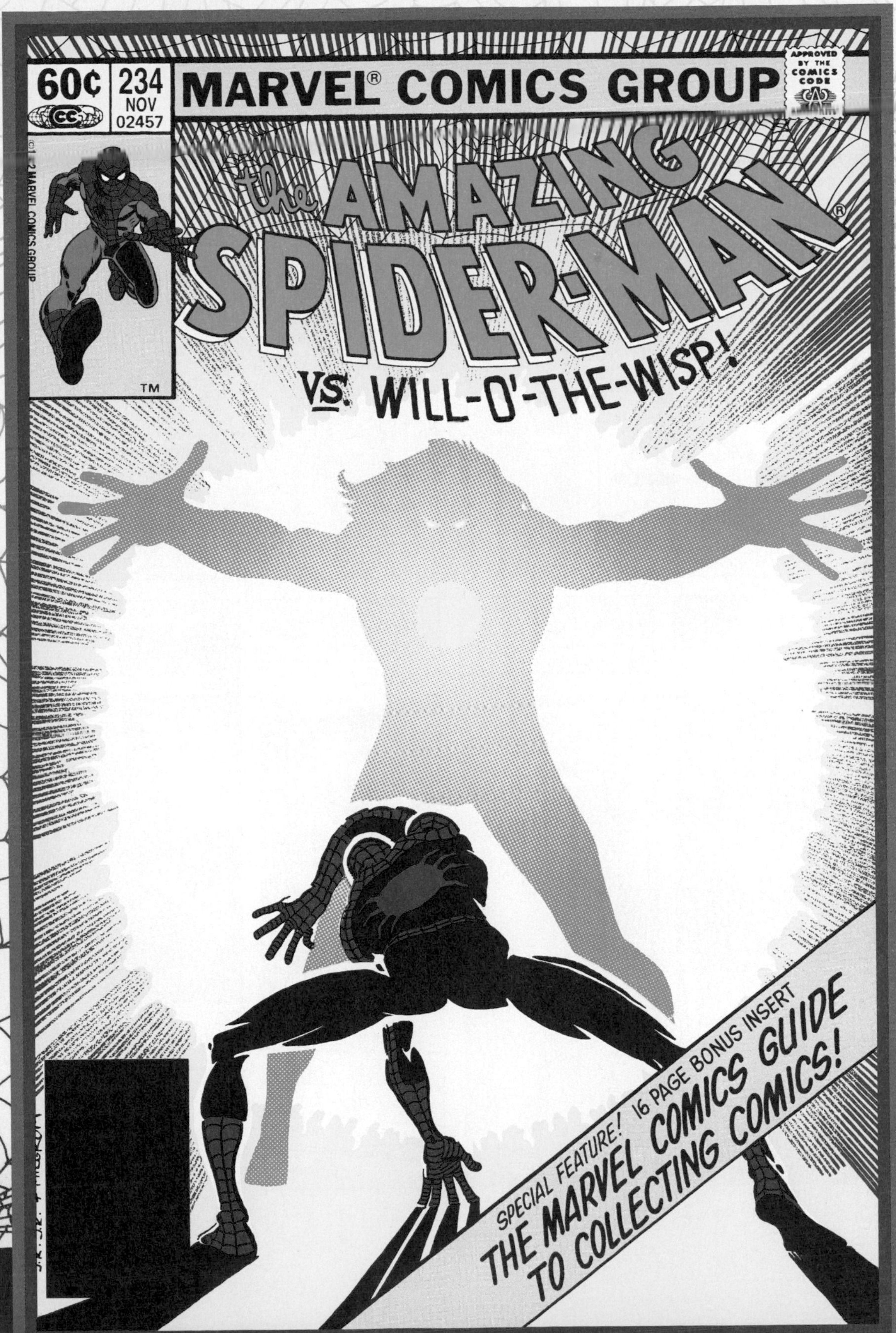
60¢
234
NOV
02457
MARVEL® COMICS GROUP
APPROVED BY THE COMICS CODE
the AMAZING SPIDER-MAN®
VS. WILL-O'-THE-WISP!
SPECIAL FEATURE! 16 PAGE BONUS INSERT
THE MARVEL COMICS GUIDE TO COLLECTING COMICS!
TM

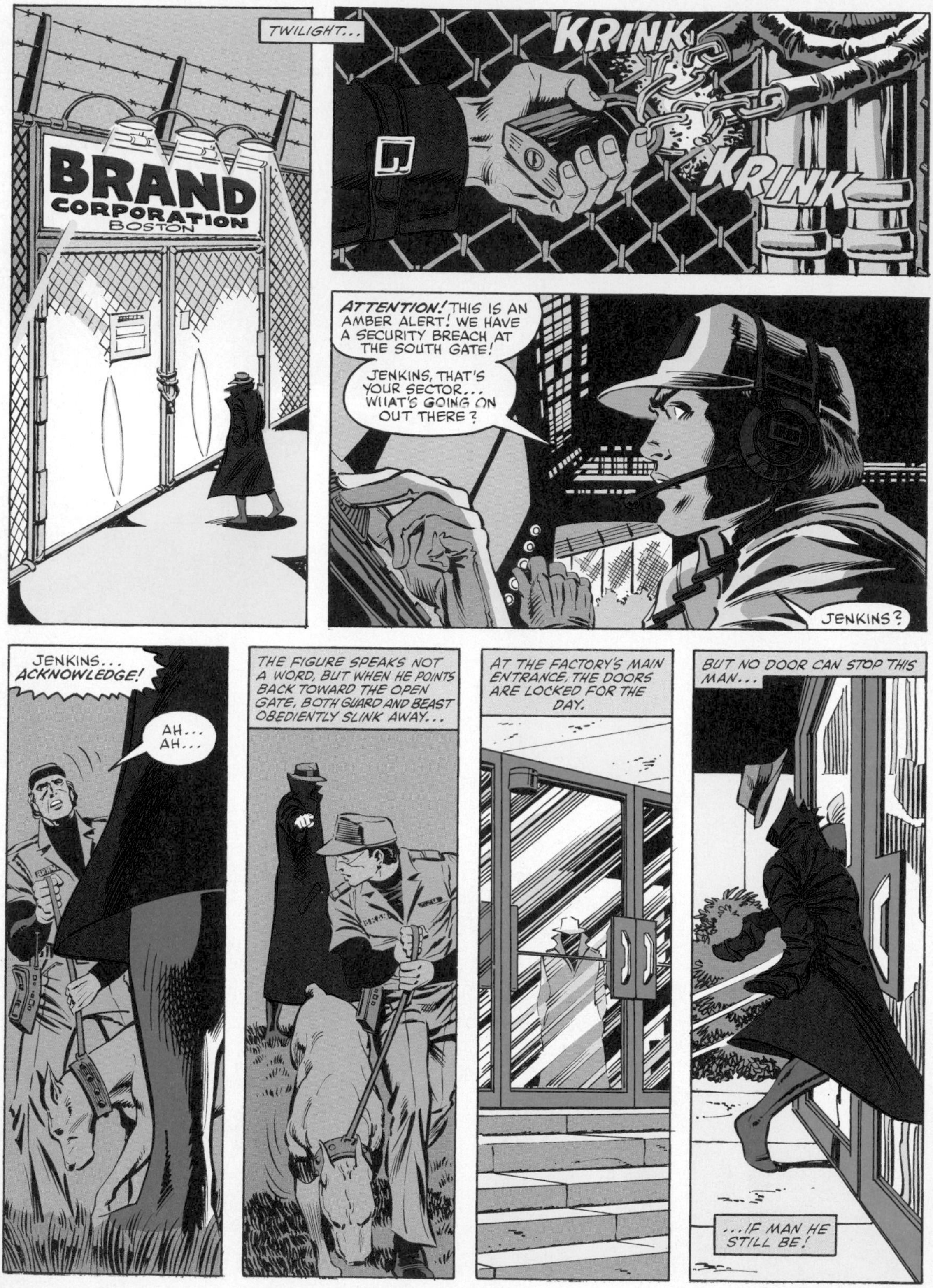

TWILIGHT...
BRAND CORPORATION BOSTON
KRINK
KRINK
ATTENTION! THIS IS AN AMBER ALERT! WE HAVE A SECURITY BREACH AT THE SOUTH GATE!
JENKINS, THAT'S YOUR SECTOR... WHAT'S GOING ON OUT THERE?
JENKINS?
JENKINS... ACKNOWLEDGE!
AH... AH...
THE FIGURE SPEAKS NOT A WORD, BUT WHEN HE POINTS BACK TOWARD THE OPEN GATE, BOTH GUARD AND BEAST OBEDIENTLY SLINK AWAY...
AT THE FACTORY'S MAIN ENTRANCE, THE DOORS ARE LOCKED FOR THE DAY.
BUT NO DOOR CAN STOP THIS MAN...
...IF MAN HE STILL BE!

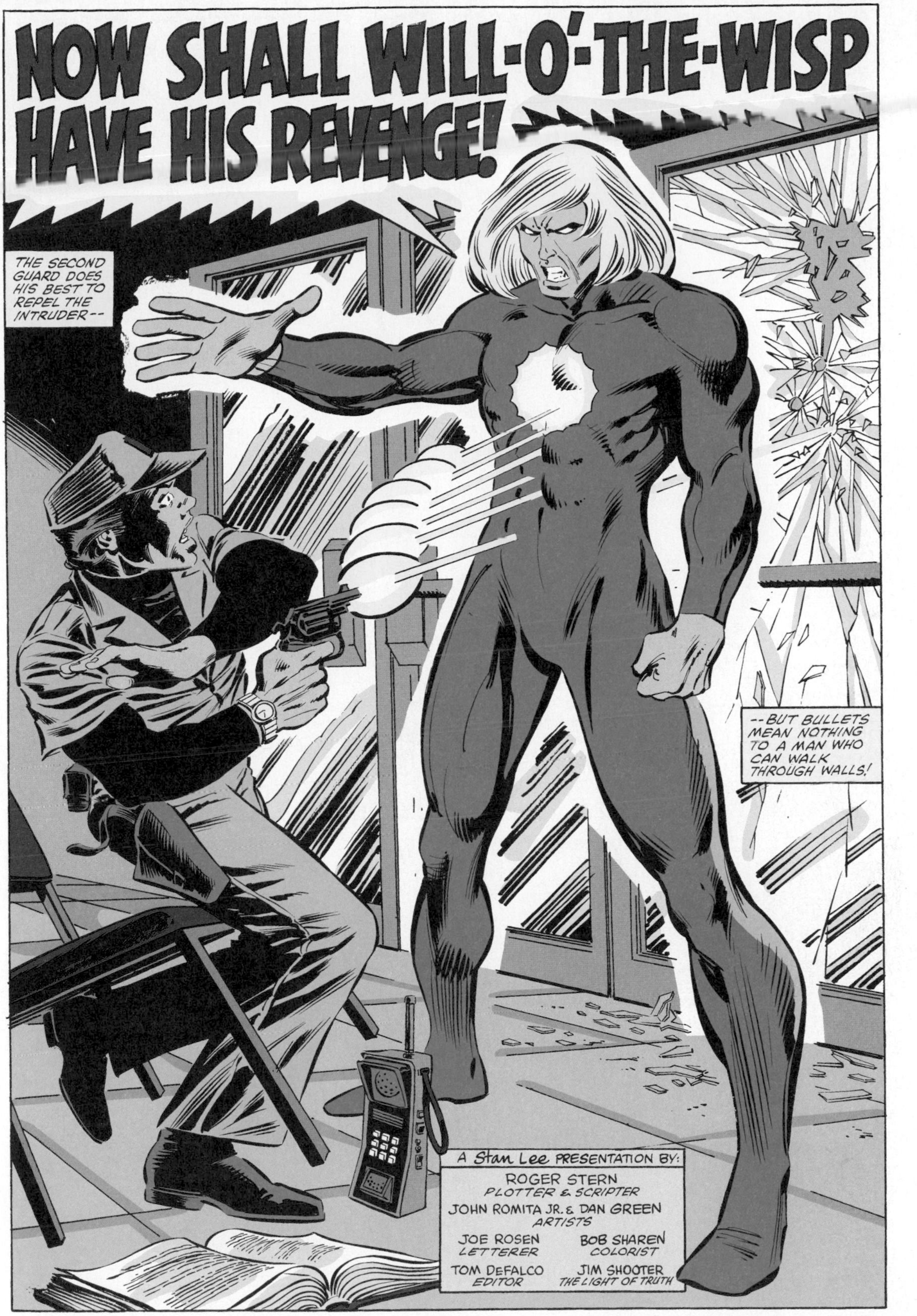
NOW SHALL WILL-O'-THE-WISP HAVE HIS REVENGE!
THE SECOND GUARD DOES HIS BEST TO REPEL THE INTRUDER--
--BUT BULLETS MEAN NOTHING TO A MAN WHO CAN WALK THROUGH WALLS!
A Stan Lee PRESENTATION BY:
ROGER STERN PLOTTER & SCRIPTER
JOHN ROMITA JR. & DAN GREEN ARTISTS
JOE ROSEN LETTERER
BOB SHAREN COLORIST
TOM DEFALCO EDITOR
JIM SHOOTER THE LIGHT OF TRUTH

STUMBLING TO THE FLOOR, THE TERRIFIED SENTRY BLINKS IN DISBELIEF AS THE GLOWING MAN BECOMES A PULSING BALL OF LIGHT!

MY GRIEVANCES ARE NOT WITH YOU, UNDERLING... NOR WITH YOUR FELLOWS!

I WILL ALLOW YOU ALL TO LIVE, IF YOU FLEE NOW!

GET EVERYONE OUT... BEFORE I LEVEL THIS PLACE!

EVACU-ALARM

HE WASN'T KIDDING!

...I THINK HE CAN DO IT!

AROO-AROO-AROO-AROO

IN LESS THAN A MINUTE, THE SMALL CREW OF GUARDS IS OUT OF THE COMPLEX.

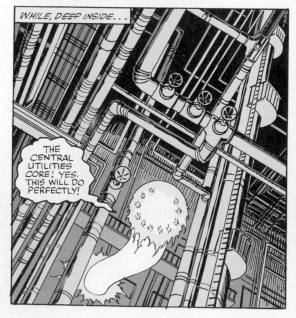

WHILE, DEEP INSIDE...

THE CENTRAL UTILITIES CORE! YES, THIS WILL DO PERFECTLY!

HIGH VOLTAGE

FOR YEARS, I WARNED THEM AGAINST RUNNING NATURAL GAS LINES IN SUCH CLOSE PROXIMITY TO THE HIGH VOLTAGE TERMINALS!

BUT THEY WOULDN'T LISTEN...

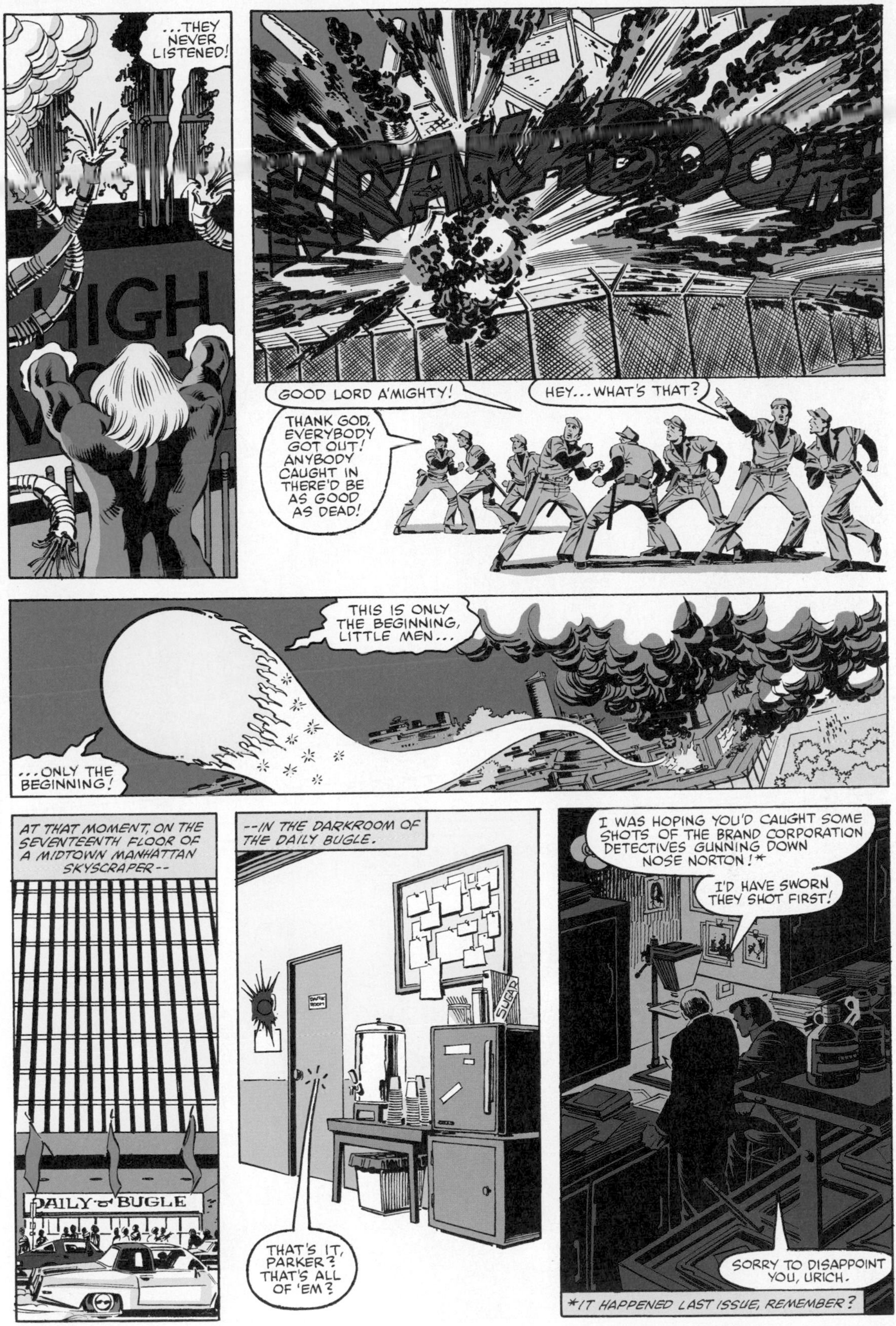
...THEY NEVER LISTENED!
HIGH
KRAKADOOM
GOOD LORD A'MIGHTY!
HEY... WHAT'S THAT?
THANK GOD, EVERYBODY GOT OUT! ANYBODY CAUGHT IN THERE'D BE AS GOOD AS DEAD!
THIS IS ONLY THE BEGINNING, LITTLE MEN...
...ONLY THE BEGINNING!
AT THAT MOMENT, ON THE SEVENTEENTH FLOOR OF A MIDTOWN MANHATTAN SKYSCRAPER--
DAILY BUGLE
--IN THE DARKROOM OF THE DAILY BUGLE.
SUGAR
THAT'S IT, PARKER? THAT'S ALL OF 'EM?
I WAS HOPING YOU'D CAUGHT SOME SHOTS OF THE BRAND CORPORATION DETECTIVES GUNNING DOWN NOSE NORTON!*
I'D HAVE SWORN THEY SHOT FIRST!
SORRY TO DISAPPOINT YOU, URICH.
*IT HAPPENED LAST ISSUE, REMEMBER?

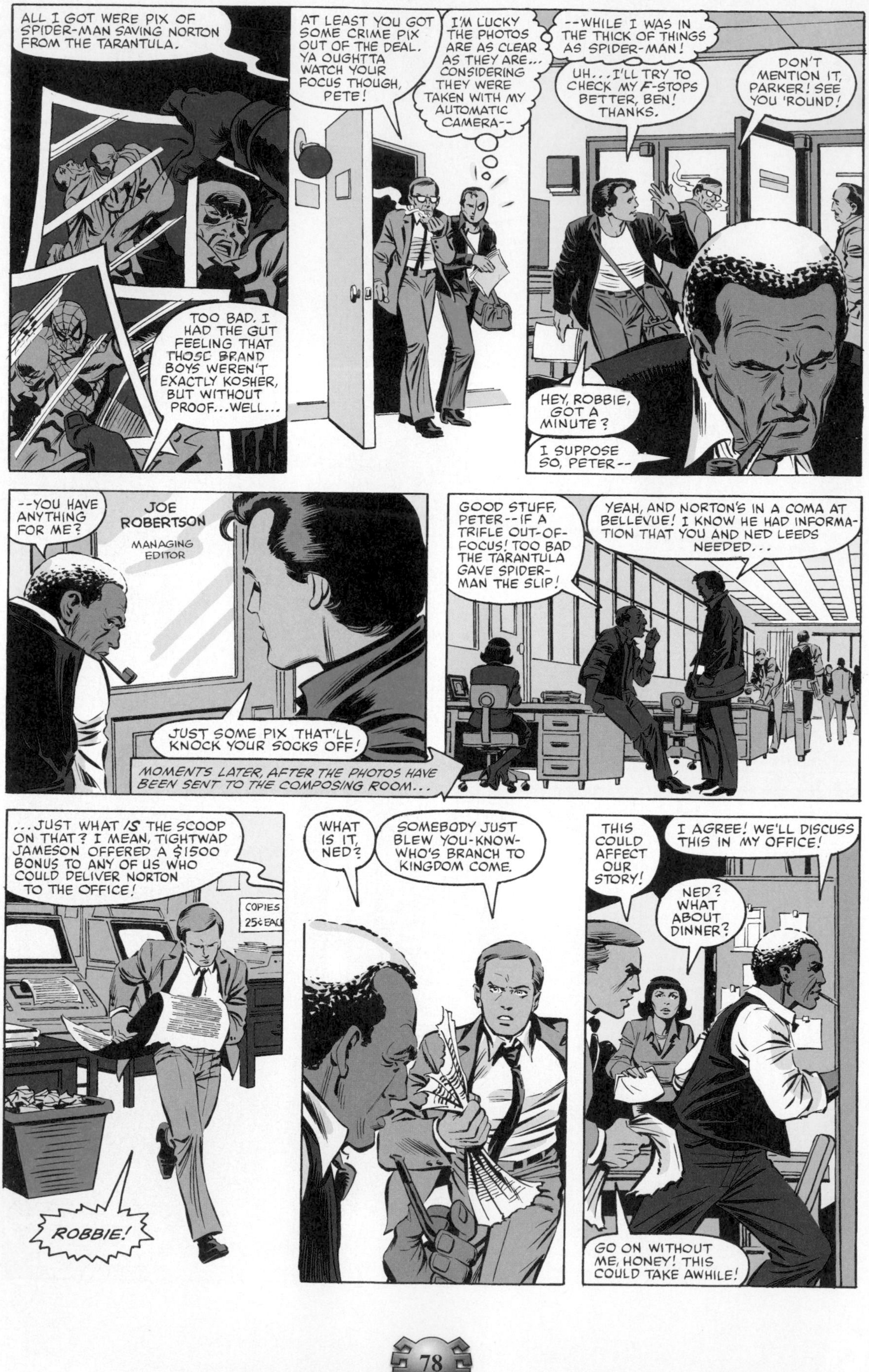
ALL I GOT WERE PIX OF SPIDER-MAN SAVING NORTON FROM THE TARANTULA.
TOO BAD. I HAD THE GUT FEELING THAT THOSE BRAND BOYS WEREN'T EXACTLY KOSHER, BUT WITHOUT PROOF... WELL...
AT LEAST YOU GOT SOME CRIME PIX OUT OF THE DEAL. YA OUGHTTA WATCH YOUR FOCUS THOUGH, PETE!
I'M LUCKY THE PHOTOS ARE AS CLEAR AS THEY ARE... CONSIDERING THEY WERE TAKEN WITH MY AUTOMATIC CAMERA--
--WHILE I WAS IN THE THICK OF THINGS AS SPIDER-MAN!
UH... I'LL TRY TO CHECK MY F-STOPS BETTER, BEN! THANKS.
DON'T MENTION IT, PARKER! SEE YOU 'ROUND!
HEY, ROBBIE, GOT A MINUTE?
I SUPPOSE SO, PETER--
--YOU HAVE ANYTHING FOR ME?
JOE ROBERTSON
MANAGING EDITOR
JUST SOME PIX THAT'LL KNOCK YOUR SOCKS OFF!
MOMENTS LATER, AFTER THE PHOTOS HAVE BEEN SENT TO THE COMPOSING ROOM...
GOOD STUFF, PETER--IF A TRIFLE OUT-OF-FOCUS! TOO BAD THE TARANTULA GAVE SPIDER-MAN THE SLIP!
YEAH, AND NORTON'S IN A COMA AT BELLEVUE! I KNOW HE HAD INFORMATION THAT YOU AND NED LEEDS NEEDED...
...JUST WHAT IS THE SCOOP ON THAT? I MEAN, TIGHTWAD JAMESON OFFERED A $1500 BONUS TO ANY OF US WHO COULD DELIVER NORTON TO THE OFFICE!
COPIES 25¢ EACH
ROBBIE!
WHAT IS IT, NED?
SOMEBODY JUST BLEW YOU-KNOW-WHO'S BRANCH TO KINGDOM COME.
THIS COULD AFFECT OUR STORY!
I AGREE! WE'LL DISCUSS THIS IN MY OFFICE!
NED? WHAT ABOUT DINNER?
GO ON WITHOUT ME, HONEY! THIS COULD TAKE AWHILE!

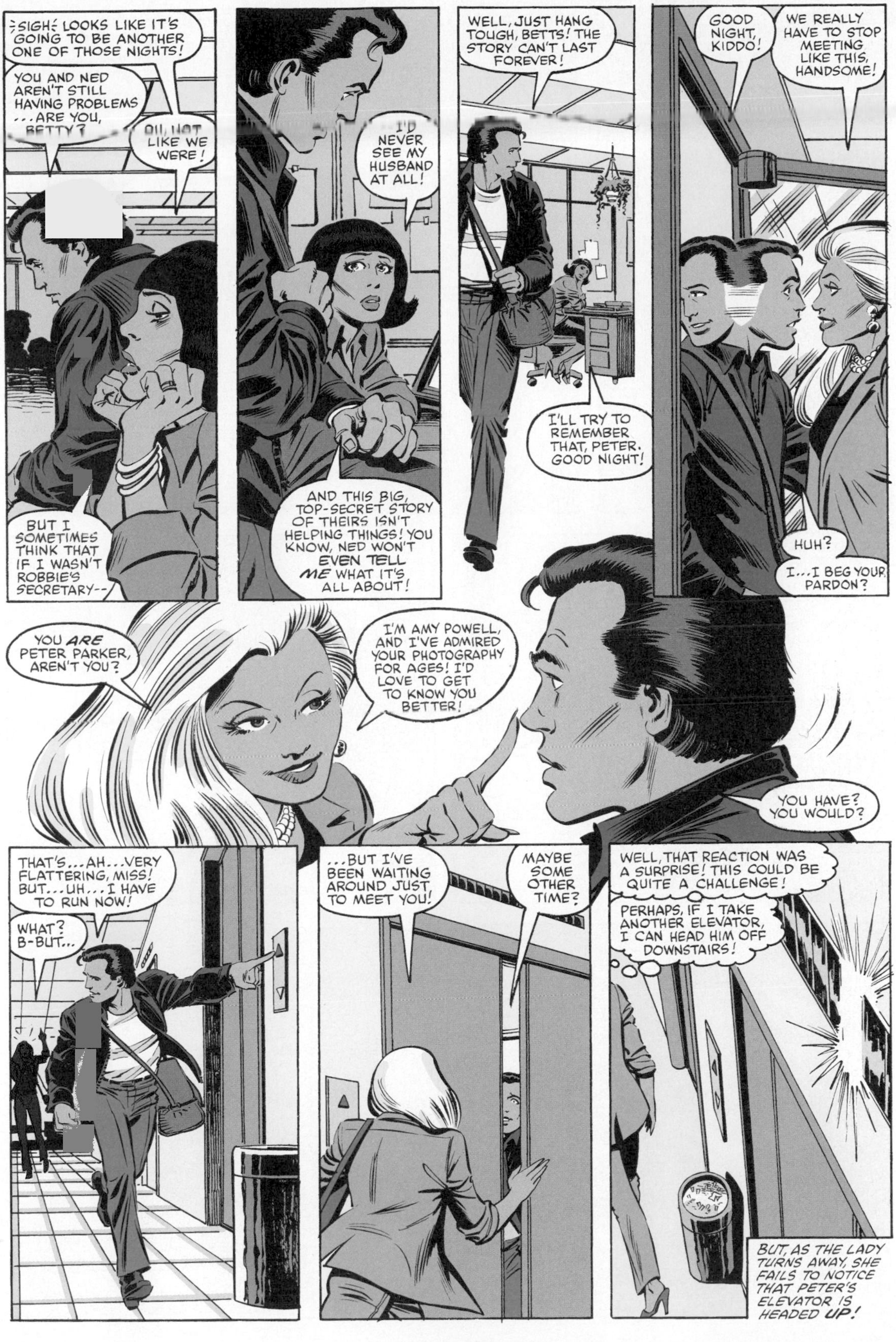

:SIGH: LOOKS LIKE IT'S GOING TO BE ANOTHER ONE OF THOSE NIGHTS!
YOU AND NED AREN'T STILL HAVING PROBLEMS ...ARE YOU, BETTY?
OH, NOT LIKE WE WERE!
BUT I SOMETIMES THINK THAT IF I WASN'T ROBBIE'S SECRETARY--
--I'D NEVER SEE MY HUSBAND AT ALL!
AND THIS BIG, TOP-SECRET STORY OF THEIRS ISN'T HELPING THINGS! YOU KNOW, NED WON'T EVEN TELL ME WHAT IT'S ALL ABOUT!
WELL, JUST HANG TOUGH, BETTS! THE STORY CAN'T LAST FOREVER!
I'LL TRY TO REMEMBER THAT, PETER. GOOD NIGHT!
GOOD NIGHT, KIDDO!
WE REALLY HAVE TO STOP MEETING LIKE THIS, HANDSOME!
HUH?
I...I BEG YOUR PARDON?
YOU ARE PETER PARKER, AREN'T YOU?
I'M AMY POWELL, AND I'VE ADMIRED YOUR PHOTOGRAPHY FOR AGES! I'D LOVE TO GET TO KNOW YOU BETTER!
YOU HAVE? YOU WOULD?
THAT'S...AH...VERY FLATTERING, MISS! BUT...UH...I HAVE TO RUN NOW!
WHAT? B-BUT...
...BUT I'VE BEEN WAITING AROUND JUST TO MEET YOU!
MAYBE SOME OTHER TIME?
WELL, THAT REACTION WAS A SURPRISE! THIS COULD BE QUITE A CHALLENGE!
PERHAPS, IF I TAKE ANOTHER ELEVATOR, I CAN HEAD HIM OFF DOWNSTAIRS!
BUT, AS THE LADY TURNS AWAY, SHE FAILS TO NOTICE THAT PETER'S ELEVATOR IS HEADED UP!

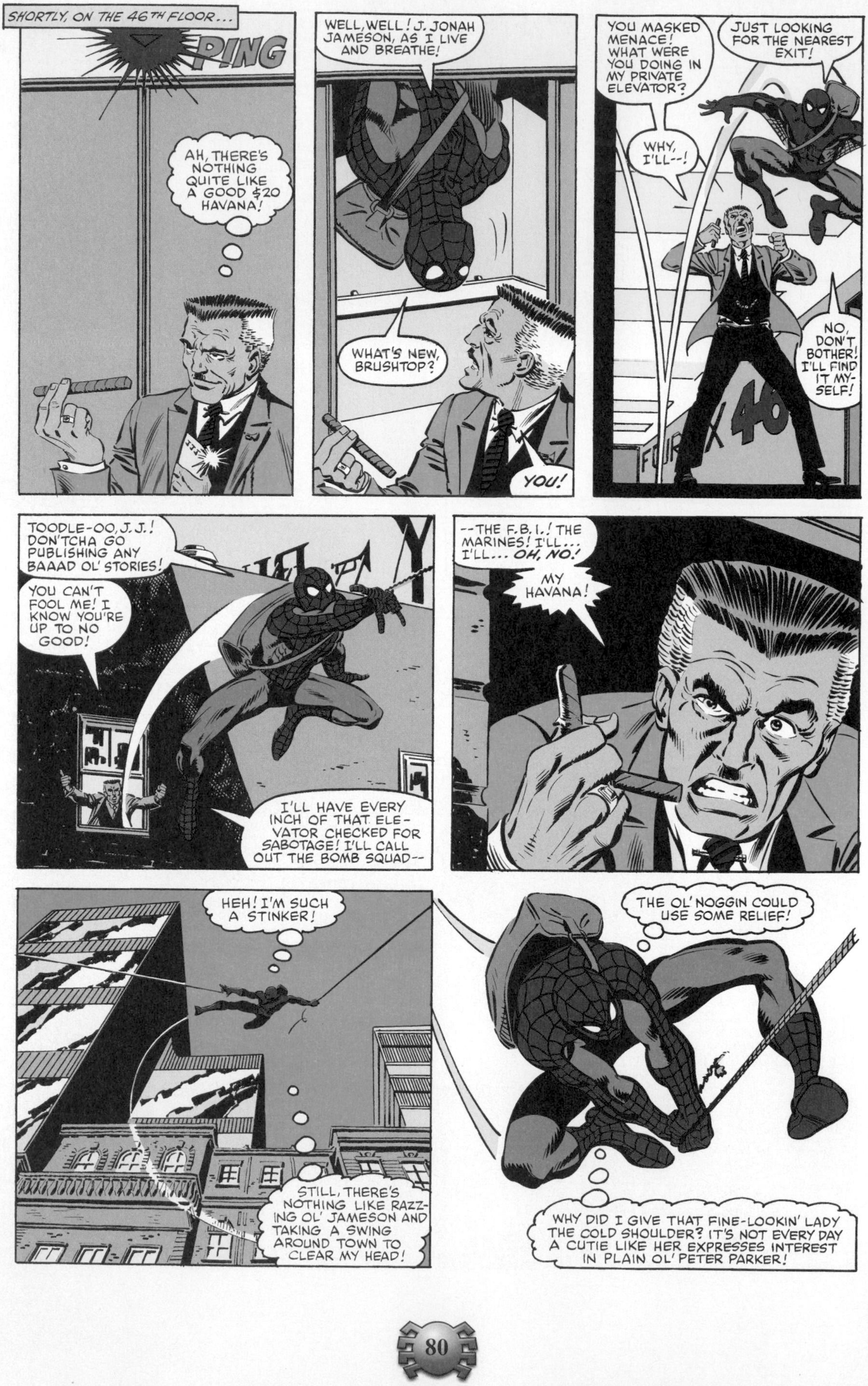
SHORTLY, ON THE 46TH FLOOR...
PING
AH, THERE'S NOTHING QUITE LIKE A GOOD $20 HAVANA!
WELL, WELL! J. JONAH JAMESON, AS I LIVE AND BREATHE!
WHAT'S NEW, BRUSHTOP?
YOU!
YOU MASKED MENACE! WHAT WERE YOU DOING IN MY PRIVATE ELEVATOR?
JUST LOOKING FOR THE NEAREST EXIT!
WHY, I'LL--!
NO, DON'T BOTHER! I'LL FIND IT MY-SELF!
TOODLE-OO, J.J.! DON'TCHA GO PUBLISHING ANY BAAAD OL' STORIES!
YOU CAN'T FOOL ME! I KNOW YOU'RE UP TO NO GOOD!
I'LL HAVE EVERY INCH OF THAT ELE-VATOR CHECKED FOR SABOTAGE! I'LL CALL OUT THE BOMB SQUAD--
--THE F.B.I.! THE MARINES! I'LL... I'LL... OH, NO!
MY HAVANA!
HEH! I'M SUCH A STINKER!
STILL, THERE'S NOTHING LIKE RAZZ-ING OL' JAMESON AND TAKING A SWING AROUND TOWN TO CLEAR MY HEAD!
THE OL' NOGGIN COULD USE SOME RELIEF!
WHY DID I GIVE THAT FINE-LOOKIN' LADY THE COLD SHOULDER? IT'S NOT EVERY DAY A CUTIE LIKE HER EXPRESSES INTEREST IN PLAIN OL' PETER PARKER!

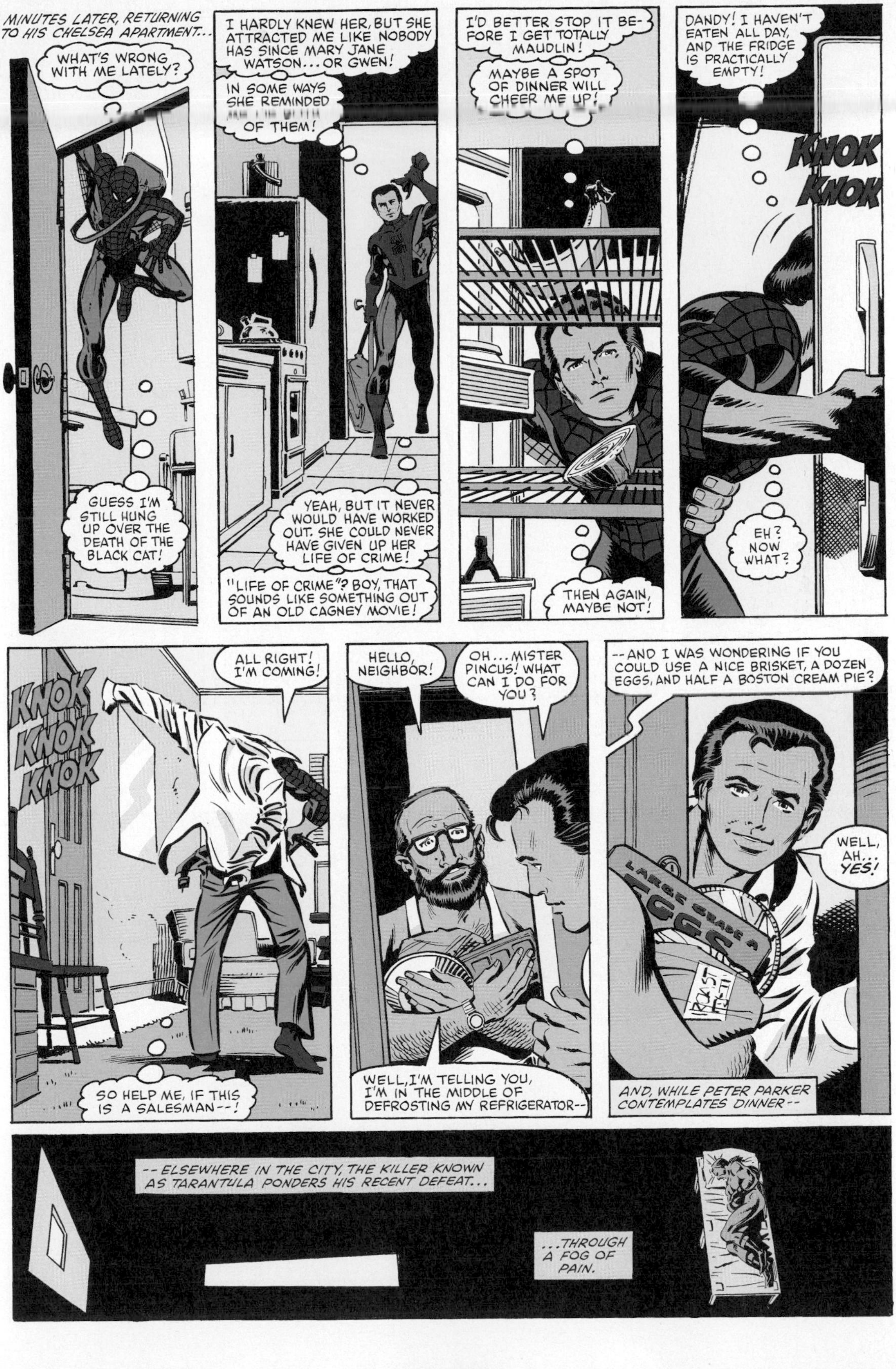
MINUTES LATER, RETURNING TO HIS CHELSEA APARTMENT...
WHAT'S WRONG WITH ME LATELY?
GUESS I'M STILL HUNG UP OVER THE DEATH OF THE BLACK CAT!
I HARDLY KNEW HER, BUT SHE ATTRACTED ME LIKE NOBODY HAS SINCE MARY JANE WATSON... OR GWEN!
IN SOME WAYS SHE REMINDED
OF THEM!
YEAH, BUT IT NEVER WOULD HAVE WORKED OUT. SHE COULD NEVER HAVE GIVEN UP HER LIFE OF CRIME!
"LIFE OF CRIME"? BOY, THAT SOUNDS LIKE SOMETHING OUT OF AN OLD CAGNEY MOVIE!
I'D BETTER STOP IT BEFORE I GET TOTALLY MAUDLIN!
MAYBE A SPOT OF DINNER WILL CHEER ME UP!
THEN AGAIN, MAYBE NOT!
DANDY! I HAVEN'T EATEN ALL DAY, AND THE FRIDGE IS PRACTICALLY EMPTY!
KNOK KNOK
EH? NOW WHAT?
KNOK KNOK KNOK
ALL RIGHT! I'M COMING!
SO HELP ME, IF THIS IS A SALESMAN--!
HELLO, NEIGHBOR!
OH... MISTER PINCUS! WHAT CAN I DO FOR YOU?
WELL, I'M TELLING YOU, I'M IN THE MIDDLE OF DEFROSTING MY REFRIGERATOR--
--AND I WAS WONDERING IF YOU COULD USE A NICE BRISKET, A DOZEN EGGS, AND HALF A BOSTON CREAM PIE?
WELL, AH... YES!
LARGE GRADE A EGGS
AND, WHILE PETER PARKER CONTEMPLATES DINNER--
--ELSEWHERE IN THE CITY, THE KILLER KNOWN AS TARANTULA PONDERS HIS RECENT DEFEAT...
...THROUGH A FOG OF PAIN.

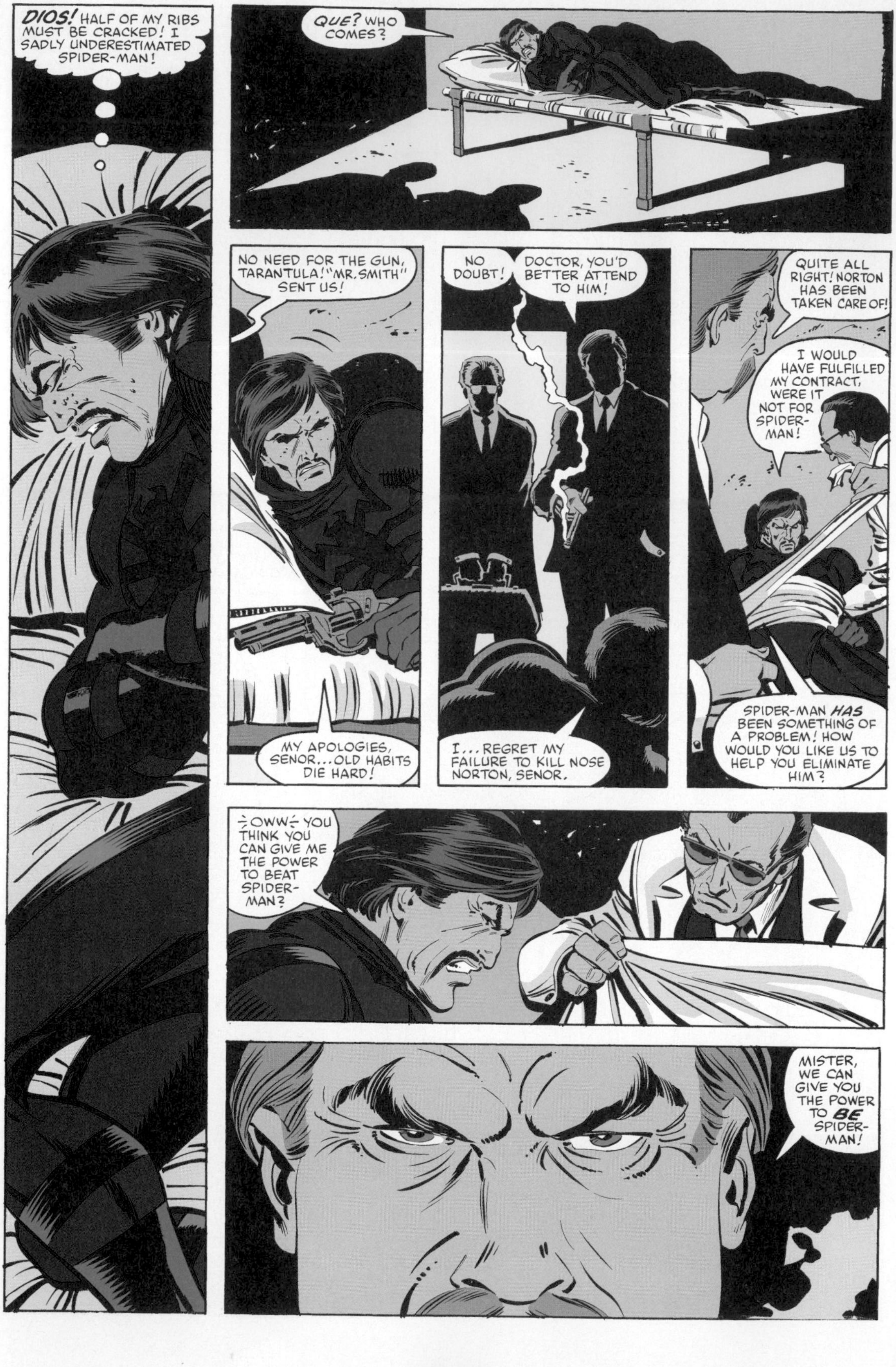
DIOS! HALF OF MY RIBS MUST BE CRACKED! I SADLY UNDERESTIMATED SPIDER-MAN!
QUE? WHO COMES?
NO NEED FOR THE GUN, TARANTULA! "MR. SMITH" SENT US!
MY APOLOGIES, SENOR... OLD HABITS DIE HARD!
NO DOUBT!
DOCTOR, YOU'D BETTER ATTEND TO HIM!
I... REGRET MY FAILURE TO KILL NOSE NORTON, SENOR.
QUITE ALL RIGHT! NORTON HAS BEEN TAKEN CARE OF!
I WOULD HAVE FULFILLED MY CONTRACT, WERE IT NOT FOR SPIDER-MAN!
SPIDER-MAN HAS BEEN SOMETHING OF A PROBLEM! HOW WOULD YOU LIKE US TO HELP YOU ELIMINATE HIM?
-OWW- YOU THINK YOU CAN GIVE ME THE POWER TO BEAT SPIDER-MAN?
MISTER, WE CAN GIVE YOU THE POWER TO BE SPIDER-MAN!

MORNING BRINGS AN UNCOMMONLY CLEAR AND PLEASANT DAY TO MANHATTAN...

...BUT EVEN THE NICEST WEATHER CAN'T BRIGHTEN THE MOOD OF SOME NEW YORKERS!

@××☆%#@!! YANKEES!

WHEN'LL THEY EVER LEARN?!

THWAP

AH, THE MORNING PAPER--RIGHT ON TIME!

I CAN'T WAIT TO FIND OUT WHAT "DOONESBURY" AND "JOHN DARLING" ARE UP TO TODAY!

BUT FIRST, LET'S SEE HOW MY PHOTOS PRINTED...

WHAT THE HEY--? THE TARANTULA STORY'S BEEN CROWDED OFF PAGE ONE!

DAI NEW YOR

BLAST I BOSTON

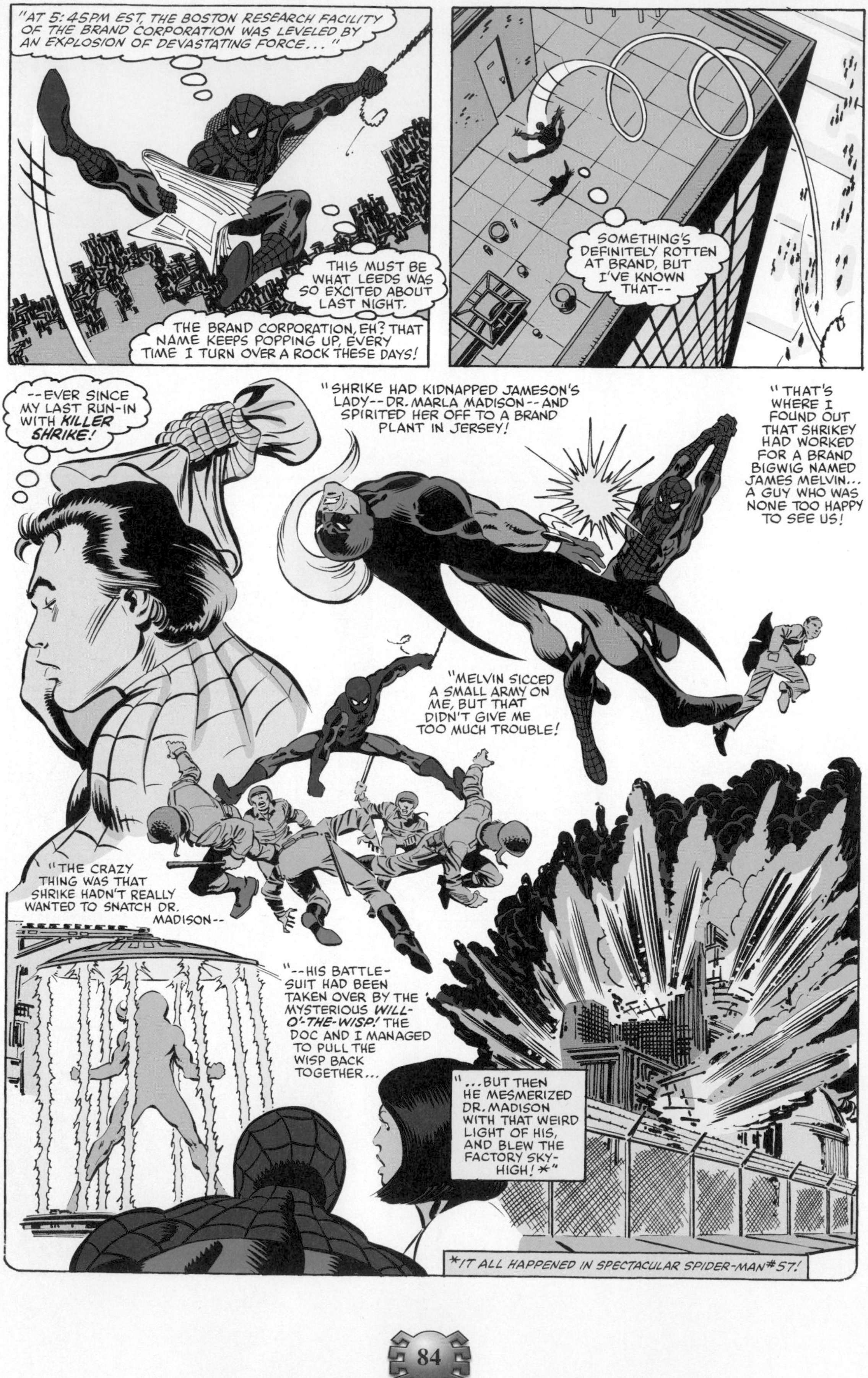
"AT 5:45PM EST, THE BOSTON RESEARCH FACILITY OF THE BRAND CORPORATION WAS LEVELED BY AN EXPLOSION OF DEVASTATING FORCE..."
THIS MUST BE WHAT LEEDS WAS SO EXCITED ABOUT LAST NIGHT.
THE BRAND CORPORATION, EH? THAT NAME KEEPS POPPING UP, EVERY TIME I TURN OVER A ROCK THESE DAYS!
SOMETHING'S DEFINITELY ROTTEN AT BRAND, BUT I'VE KNOWN THAT--
--EVER SINCE MY LAST RUN-IN WITH KILLER SHRIKE!
"SHRIKE HAD KIDNAPPED JAMESON'S LADY--DR. MARLA MADISON--AND SPIRITED HER OFF TO A BRAND PLANT IN JERSEY!
"THAT'S WHERE I FOUND OUT THAT SHRIKEY HAD WORKED FOR A BRAND BIGWIG NAMED JAMES MELVIN... A GUY WHO WAS NONE TOO HAPPY TO SEE US!
"MELVIN SICCED A SMALL ARMY ON ME, BUT THAT DIDN'T GIVE ME TOO MUCH TROUBLE!
"THE CRAZY THING WAS THAT SHRIKE HADN'T REALLY WANTED TO SNATCH DR. MADISON--
"--HIS BATTLE-SUIT HAD BEEN TAKEN OVER BY THE MYSTERIOUS WILL-O'-THE-WISP! THE DOC AND I MANAGED TO PULL THE WISP BACK TOGETHER...
"...BUT THEN HE MESMERIZED DR. MADISON WITH THAT WEIRD LIGHT OF HIS, AND BLEW THE FACTORY SKY-HIGH!*"
*IT ALL HAPPENED IN SPECTACULAR SPIDER-MAN #57!

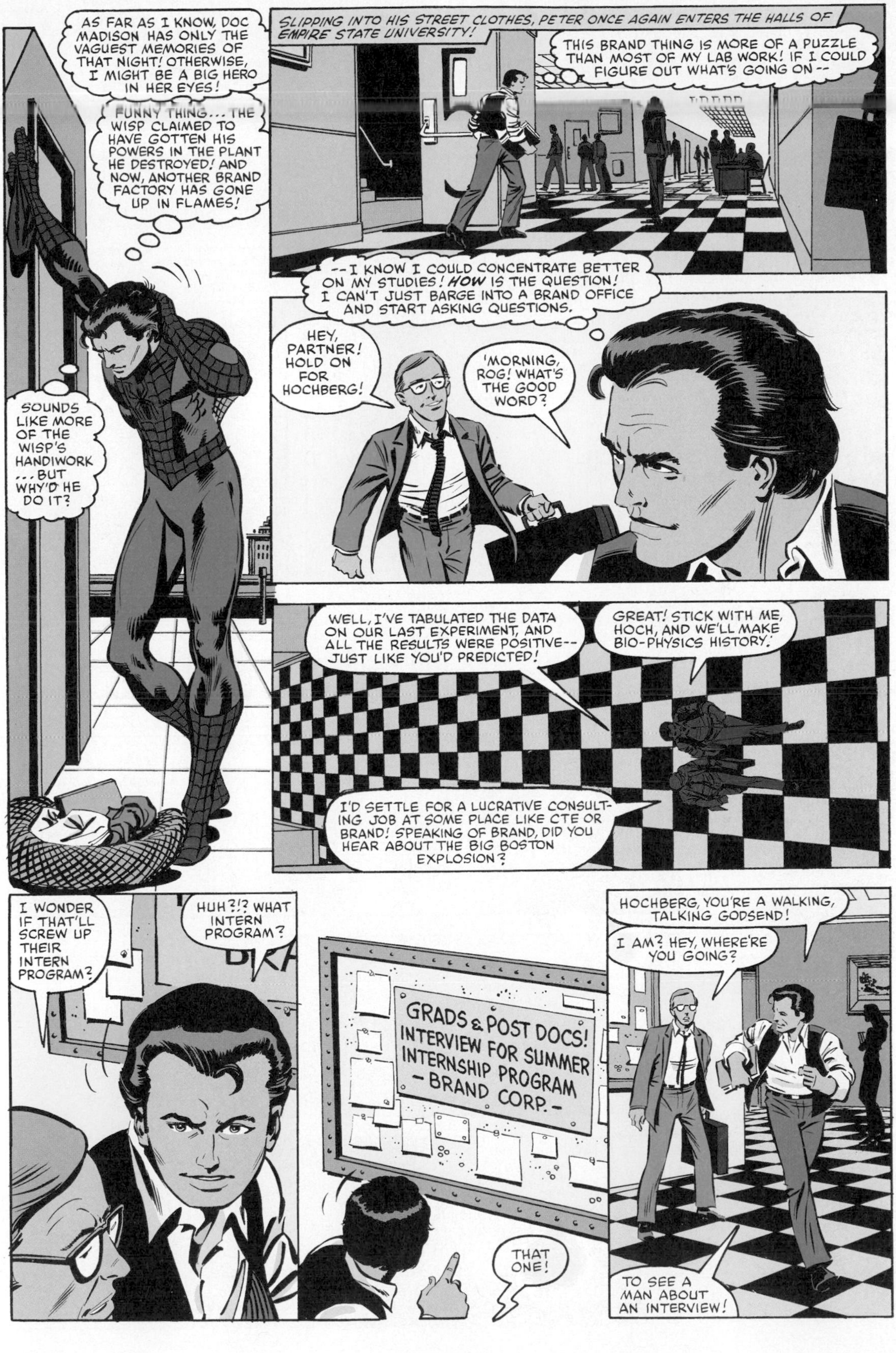
AS FAR AS I KNOW, DOC MADISON HAS ONLY THE VAGUEST MEMORIES OF THAT NIGHT! OTHERWISE, I MIGHT BE A BIG HERO IN HER EYES!
FUNNY THING... THE WISP CLAIMED TO HAVE GOTTEN HIS POWERS IN THE PLANT HE DESTROYED! AND NOW, ANOTHER BRAND FACTORY HAS GONE UP IN FLAMES!
SOUNDS LIKE MORE OF THE WISP'S HANDIWORK ... BUT WHY'D HE DO IT?
SLIPPING INTO HIS STREET CLOTHES, PETER ONCE AGAIN ENTERS THE HALLS OF EMPIRE STATE UNIVERSITY!
THIS BRAND THING IS MORE OF A PUZZLE THAN MOST OF MY LAB WORK! IF I COULD FIGURE OUT WHAT'S GOING ON --
-- I KNOW I COULD CONCENTRATE BETTER ON MY STUDIES! HOW IS THE QUESTION! I CAN'T JUST BARGE INTO A BRAND OFFICE AND START ASKING QUESTIONS.
HEY, PARTNER! HOLD ON FOR HOCHBERG!
'MORNING, ROG! WHAT'S THE GOOD WORD?
WELL, I'VE TABULATED THE DATA ON OUR LAST EXPERIMENT, AND ALL THE RESULTS WERE POSITIVE-- JUST LIKE YOU'D PREDICTED!
GREAT! STICK WITH ME, HOCH, AND WE'LL MAKE BIO-PHYSICS HISTORY!
I'D SETTLE FOR A LUCRATIVE CONSULTING JOB AT SOME PLACE LIKE CTE OR BRAND! SPEAKING OF BRAND, DID YOU HEAR ABOUT THE BIG BOSTON EXPLOSION?
I WONDER IF THAT'LL SCREW UP THEIR INTERN PROGRAM?
HUH?!? WHAT INTERN PROGRAM?
GRADS & POST DOCS! INTERVIEW FOR SUMMER INTERNSHIP PROGRAM - BRAND CORP. -
THAT ONE!
HOCHBERG, YOU'RE A WALKING, TALKING GODSEND!
I AM? HEY, WHERE'RE YOU GOING?
TO SEE A MAN ABOUT AN INTERVIEW!

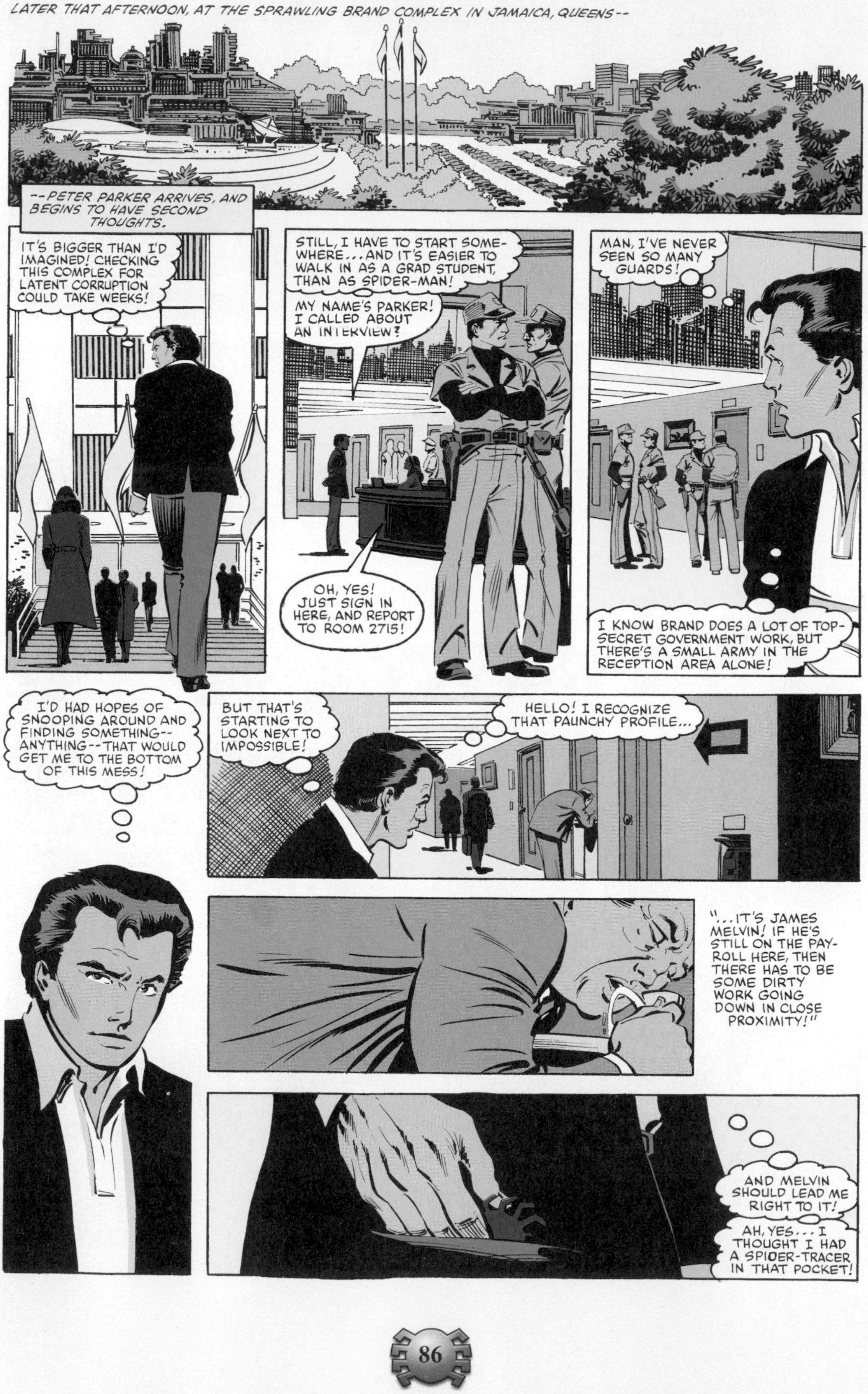

LATER THAT AFTERNOON, AT THE SPRAWLING BRAND COMPLEX IN JAMAICA, QUEENS--
--PETER PARKER ARRIVES, AND BEGINS TO HAVE SECOND THOUGHTS.
IT'S BIGGER THAN I'D IMAGINED! CHECKING THIS COMPLEX FOR LATENT CORRUPTION COULD TAKE WEEKS!
STILL, I HAVE TO START SOME-WHERE... AND IT'S EASIER TO WALK IN AS A GRAD STUDENT, THAN AS SPIDER-MAN!
MY NAME'S PARKER! I CALLED ABOUT AN INTERVIEW?
OH, YES! JUST SIGN IN HERE, AND REPORT TO ROOM 2715!
MAN, I'VE NEVER SEEN SO MANY GUARDS!
I KNOW BRAND DOES A LOT OF TOP-SECRET GOVERNMENT WORK, BUT THERE'S A SMALL ARMY IN THE RECEPTION AREA ALONE!
I'D HAD HOPES OF SNOOPING AROUND AND FINDING SOMETHING--ANYTHING--THAT WOULD GET ME TO THE BOTTOM OF THIS MESS!
BUT THAT'S STARTING TO LOOK NEXT TO IMPOSSIBLE!
HELLO! I RECOGNIZE THAT PAUNCHY PROFILE...
"...IT'S JAMES MELVIN! IF HE'S STILL ON THE PAY-ROLL HERE, THEN THERE HAS TO BE SOME DIRTY WORK GOING DOWN IN CLOSE PROXIMITY!"
AND MELVIN SHOULD LEAD ME RIGHT TO IT!
AH, YES... I THOUGHT I HAD A SPIDER-TRACER IN THAT POCKET!

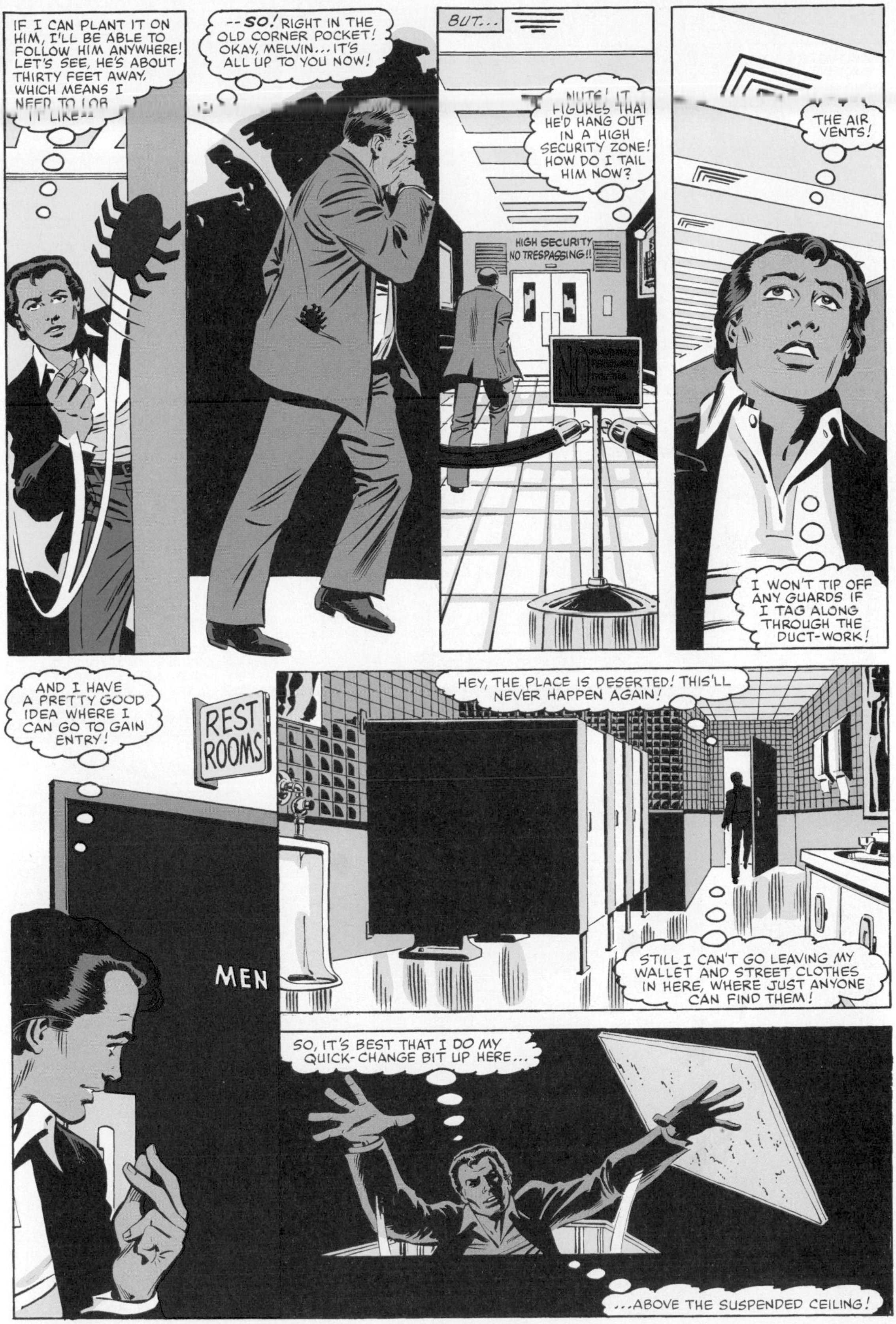
IF I CAN PLANT IT ON HIM, I'LL BE ABLE TO FOLLOW HIM ANYWHERE! LET'S SEE, HE'S ABOUT THIRTY FEET AWAY, WHICH MEANS I NEED TO LOB IT LIKE--
--SO! RIGHT IN THE OLD CORNER POCKET! OKAY, MELVIN... IT'S ALL UP TO YOU NOW!
BUT...
NUTS! IT FIGURES THAT HE'D HANG OUT IN A HIGH SECURITY ZONE! HOW DO I TAIL HIM NOW?
HIGH SECURITY NO TRESPASSING!!
THE AIR VENTS!
I WON'T TIP OFF ANY GUARDS IF I TAG ALONG THROUGH THE DUCT-WORK!
AND I HAVE A PRETTY GOOD IDEA WHERE I CAN GO TO GAIN ENTRY!
REST ROOMS
MEN
HEY, THE PLACE IS DESERTED! THIS'LL NEVER HAPPEN AGAIN!
STILL I CAN'T GO LEAVING MY WALLET AND STREET CLOTHES IN HERE, WHERE JUST ANYONE CAN FIND THEM!
SO, IT'S BEST THAT I DO MY QUICK-CHANGE BIT UP HERE...
...ABOVE THE SUSPENDED CEILING!

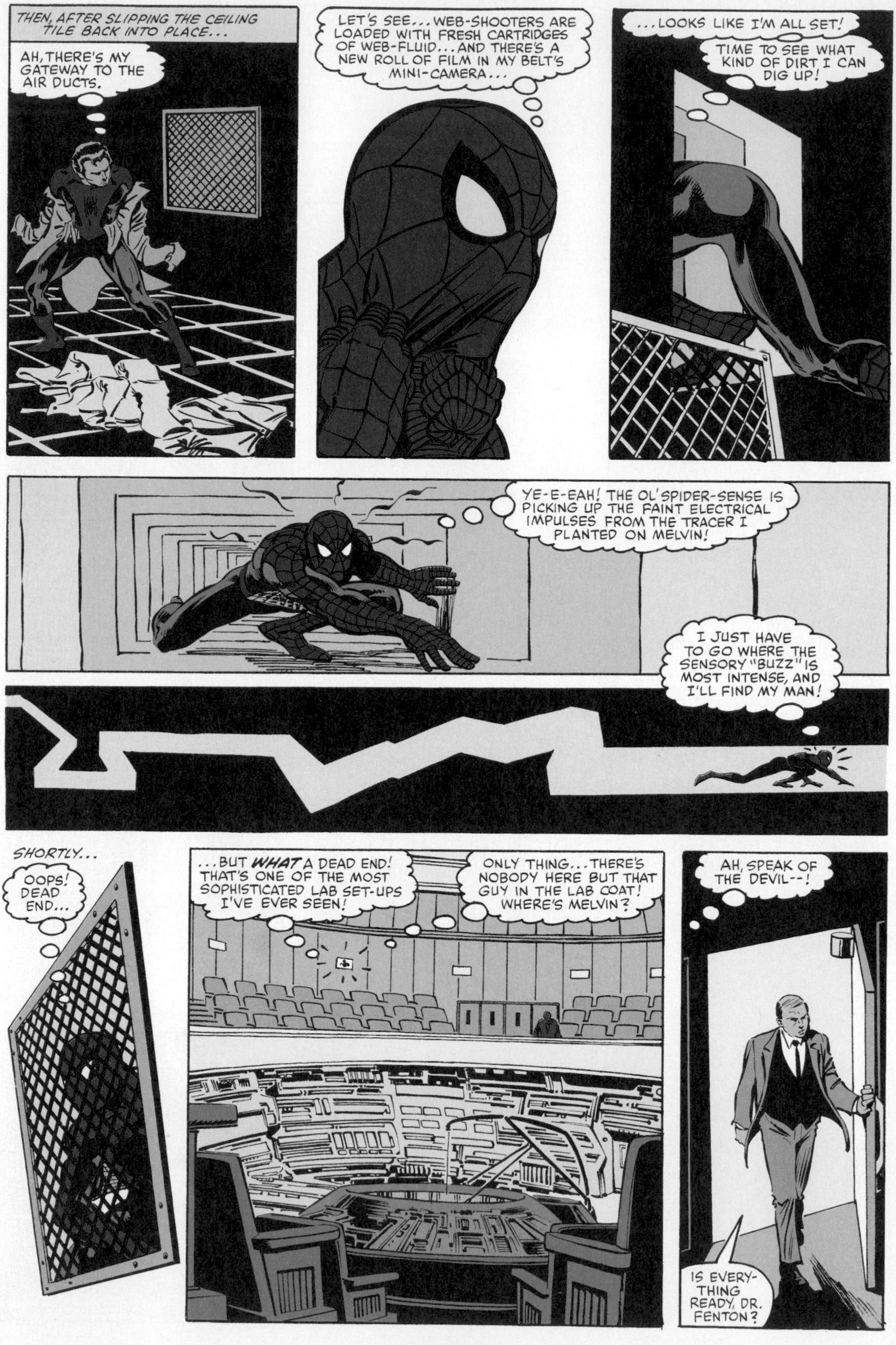
THEN, AFTER SLIPPING THE CEILING TILE BACK INTO PLACE...
AH, THERE'S MY GATEWAY TO THE AIR DUCTS.
LET'S SEE... WEB-SHOOTERS ARE LOADED WITH FRESH CARTRIDGES OF WEB-FLUID... AND THERE'S A NEW ROLL OF FILM IN MY BELT'S MINI-CAMERA...
...LOOKS LIKE I'M ALL SET!
TIME TO SEE WHAT KIND OF DIRT I CAN DIG UP!
YE-E-EAH! THE OL' SPIDER-SENSE IS PICKING UP THE FAINT ELECTRICAL IMPULSES FROM THE TRACER I PLANTED ON MELVIN!
I JUST HAVE TO GO WHERE THE SENSORY "BUZZ" IS MOST INTENSE, AND I'LL FIND MY MAN!
SHORTLY...
OOPS! DEAD END...
...BUT WHAT A DEAD END! THAT'S ONE OF THE MOST SOPHISTICATED LAB SET-UPS I'VE EVER SEEN!
ONLY THING... THERE'S NOBODY HERE BUT THAT GUY IN THE LAB COAT! WHERE'S MELVIN?
AH, SPEAK OF THE DEVIL--!
IS EVERY-THING READY, DR. FENTON?

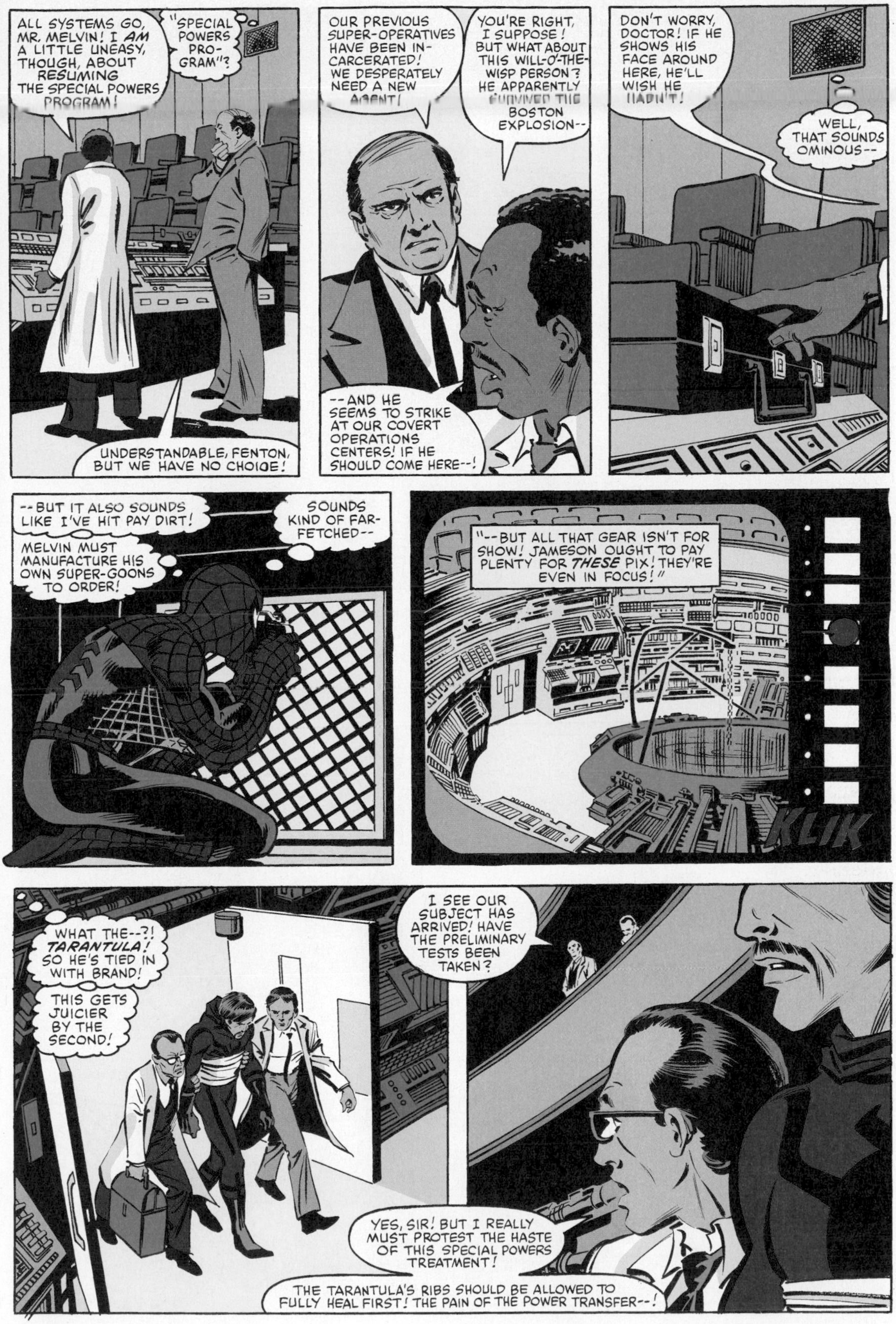
ALL SYSTEMS GO, MR. MELVIN! I AM A LITTLE UNEASY, THOUGH, ABOUT RESUMING THE SPECIAL POWERS PROGRAM!
"SPECIAL POWERS PROGRAM"?
UNDERSTANDABLE, FENTON, BUT WE HAVE NO CHOICE!
OUR PREVIOUS SUPER-OPERATIVES HAVE BEEN INCARCERATED! WE DESPERATELY NEED A NEW AGENT!
YOU'RE RIGHT, I SUPPOSE! BUT WHAT ABOUT THIS WILL-O'-THE-WISP PERSON? HE APPARENTLY SURVIVED THE BOSTON EXPLOSION--
--AND HE SEEMS TO STRIKE AT OUR COVERT OPERATIONS CENTERS! IF HE SHOULD COME HERE--!
DON'T WORRY, DOCTOR! IF HE SHOWS HIS FACE AROUND HERE, HE'LL WISH HE HADN'T!
WELL, THAT SOUNDS OMINOUS--
--BUT IT ALSO SOUNDS LIKE I'VE HIT PAY DIRT!
SOUNDS KIND OF FAR-FETCHED--
MELVIN MUST MANUFACTURE HIS OWN SUPER-GOONS TO ORDER!
"--BUT ALL THAT GEAR ISN'T FOR SHOW! JAMESON OUGHT TO PAY PLENTY FOR THESE PIX! THEY'RE EVEN IN FOCUS!"
KLIK
WHAT THE--?! TARANTULA! SO HE'S TIED IN WITH BRAND!
THIS GETS JUICIER BY THE SECOND!
I SEE OUR SUBJECT HAS ARRIVED! HAVE THE PRELIMINARY TESTS BEEN TAKEN?
YES, SIR! BUT I REALLY MUST PROTEST THE HASTE OF THIS SPECIAL POWERS TREATMENT!
THE TARANTULA'S RIBS SHOULD BE ALLOWED TO FULLY HEAL FIRST! THE PAIN OF THE POWER TRANSFER--!

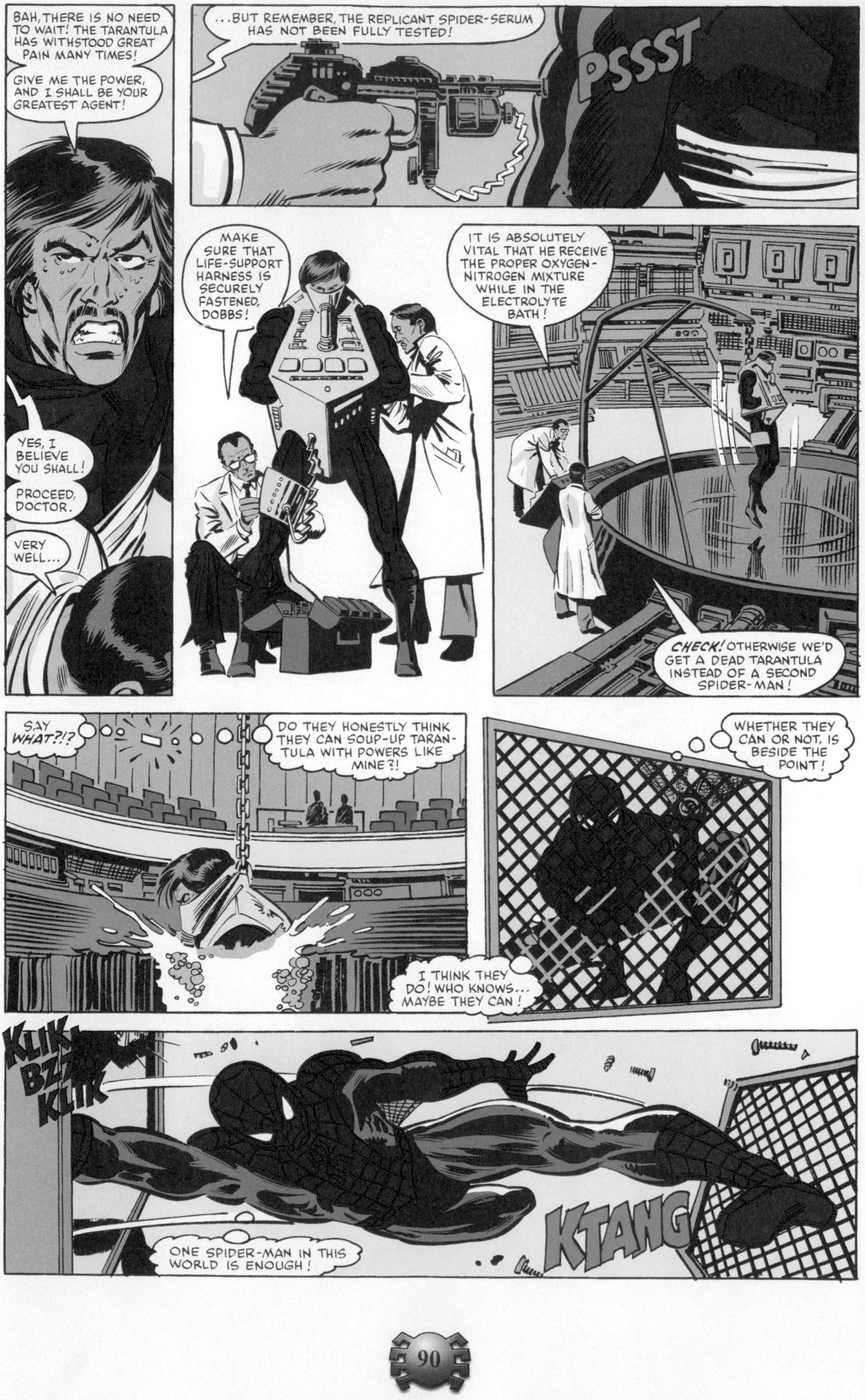
BAH, THERE IS NO NEED TO WAIT! THE TARANTULA HAS WITHSTOOD GREAT PAIN MANY TIMES!
GIVE ME THE POWER, AND I SHALL BE YOUR GREATEST AGENT!
YES, I BELIEVE YOU SHALL!
PROCEED, DOCTOR.
VERY WELL...
...BUT REMEMBER, THE REPLICANT SPIDER-SERUM HAS NOT BEEN FULLY TESTED!
PSSST
MAKE SURE THAT LIFE-SUPPORT HARNESS IS SECURELY FASTENED, DOBBS!
IT IS ABSOLUTELY VITAL THAT HE RECEIVE THE PROPER OXYGEN-NITROGEN MIXTURE WHILE IN THE ELECTROLYTE BATH!
CHECK! OTHERWISE WE'D GET A DEAD TARANTULA INSTEAD OF A SECOND SPIDER-MAN!
SAY WHAT?!?
DO THEY HONESTLY THINK THEY CAN SOUP-UP TARANTULA WITH POWERS LIKE MINE?!
I THINK THEY DO! WHO KNOWS... MAYBE THEY CAN!
WHETHER THEY CAN OR NOT, IS BESIDE THE POINT!
KLIK BZZT KLIK
ONE SPIDER-MAN IN THIS WORLD IS ENOUGH!
KTANG

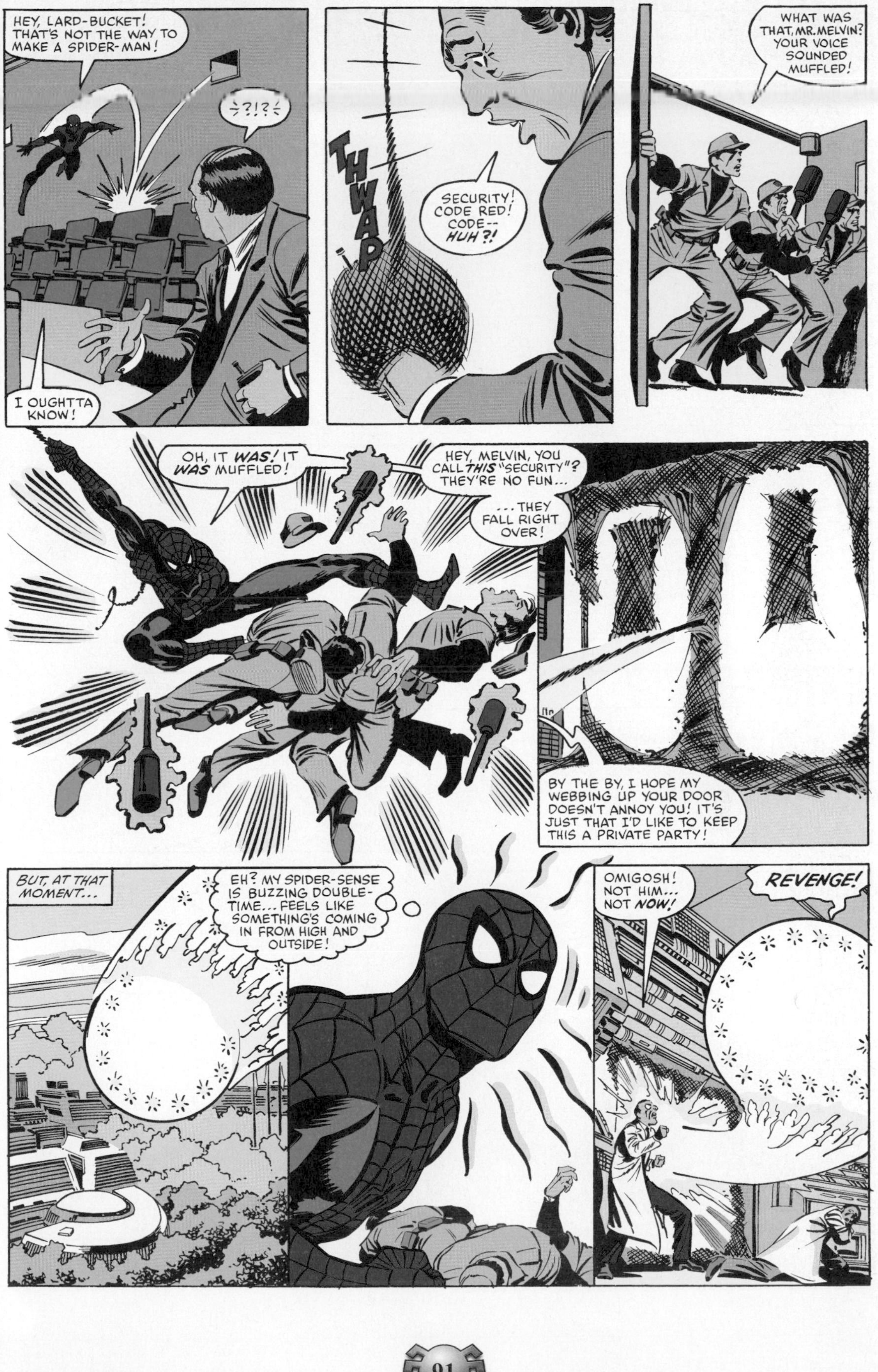
HEY, LARD-BUCKET! THAT'S NOT THE WAY TO MAKE A SPIDER-MAN!
?!?
I OUGHTTA KNOW!
THWAP
SECURITY! CODE RED! CODE-- HUH?!
WHAT WAS THAT, MR. MELVIN? YOUR VOICE SOUNDED MUFFLED!
OH, IT WAS! IT WAS MUFFLED!
HEY, MELVIN, YOU CALL THIS "SECURITY"? THEY'RE NO FUN...
...THEY FALL RIGHT OVER!
BY THE BY, I HOPE MY WEBBING UP YOUR DOOR DOESN'T ANNOY YOU! IT'S JUST THAT I'D LIKE TO KEEP THIS A PRIVATE PARTY!
BUT, AT THAT MOMENT...
EH? MY SPIDER-SENSE IS BUZZING DOUBLE-TIME... FEELS LIKE SOMETHING'S COMING IN FROM HIGH AND OUTSIDE!
OMIGOSH! NOT HIM... NOT NOW!
REVENGE!

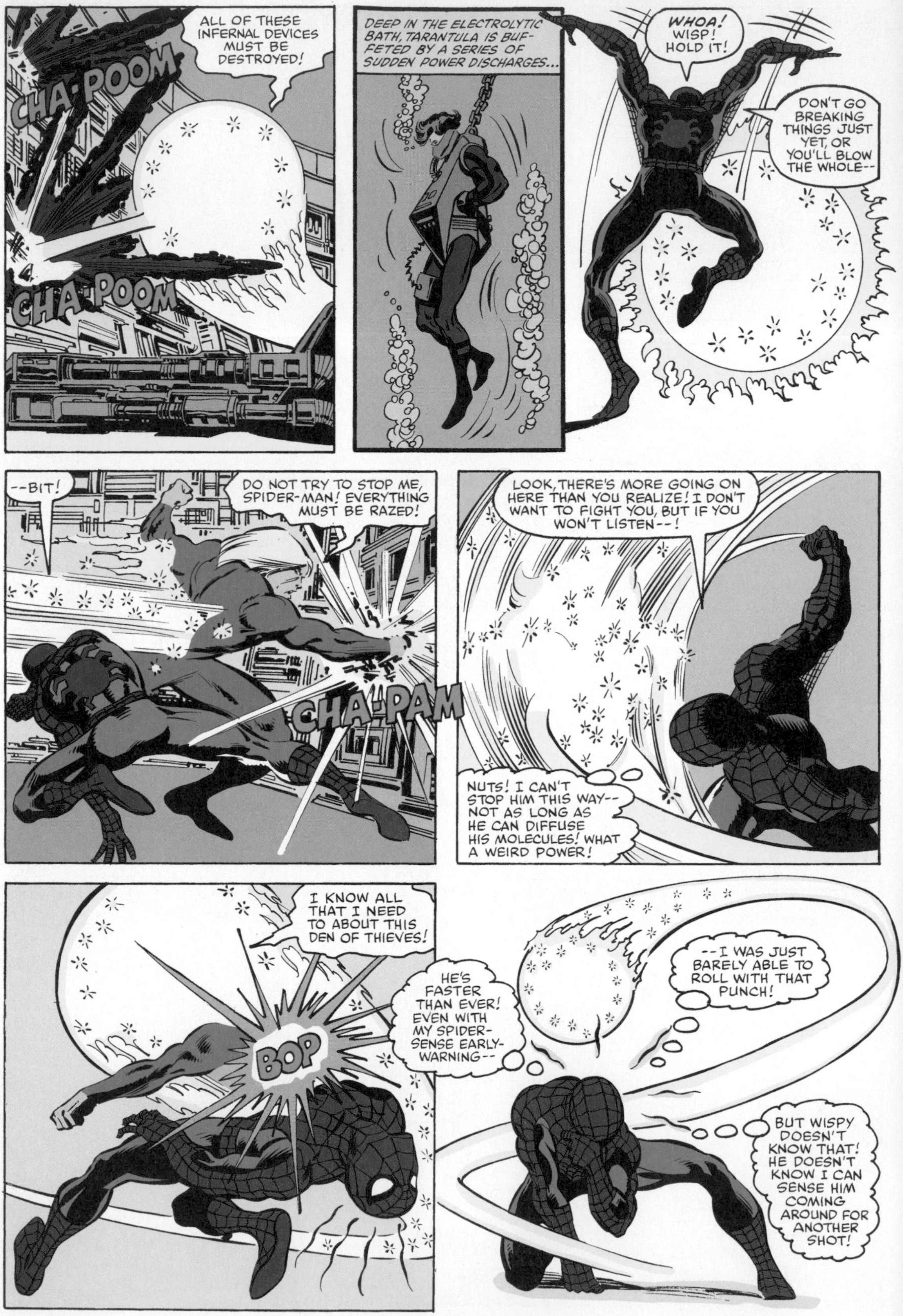
ALL OF THESE INFERNAL DEVICES MUST BE DESTROYED!
CHA-POOM
CHA-POOM
DEEP IN THE ELECTROLYTIC BATH, TARANTULA IS BUFFETED BY A SERIES OF SUDDEN POWER DISCHARGES...
WHOA! WISP! HOLD IT!
DON'T GO BREAKING THINGS JUST YET, OR YOU'LL BLOW THE WHOLE--
--BIT!
DO NOT TRY TO STOP ME, SPIDER-MAN! EVERYTHING MUST BE RAZED!
CHA-PAM
LOOK, THERE'S MORE GOING ON HERE THAN YOU REALIZE! I DON'T WANT TO FIGHT YOU, BUT IF YOU WON'T LISTEN--!
NUTS! I CAN'T STOP HIM THIS WAY--NOT AS LONG AS HE CAN DIFFUSE HIS MOLECULES! WHAT A WEIRD POWER!
I KNOW ALL THAT I NEED TO ABOUT THIS DEN OF THIEVES!
BOP
HE'S FASTER THAN EVER! EVEN WITH MY SPIDER-SENSE EARLY-WARNING--
--I WAS JUST BARELY ABLE TO ROLL WITH THAT PUNCH!
BUT WISPY DOESN'T KNOW THAT! HE DOESN'T KNOW I CAN SENSE HIM COMING AROUND FOR ANOTHER SHOT!

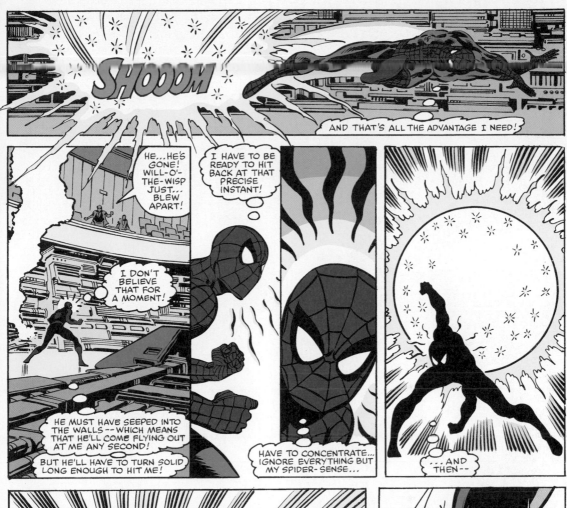

SHOOOM

AND THAT'S ALL THE ADVANTAGE I NEED!

HE...HE'S GONE! WILL-O'-THE-WISP... JUST... BLEW APART!

I DON'T BELIEVE THAT FOR A MOMENT!

I HAVE TO BE READY TO HIT BACK AT THAT PRECISE INSTANT!

HE MUST HAVE SEEPED INTO THE WALLS -- WHICH MEANS THAT HE'LL COME FLYING OUT AT ME ANY SECOND!

BUT HE'LL HAVE TO TURN SOLID LONG ENOUGH TO HIT ME!

HAVE TO CONCENTRATE... IGNORE EVERYTHING BUT MY SPIDER-SENSE...

...AND THEN--

KROOM

--LET 'IM HAVE IT!

YOU OKAY, WISP?

I PULLED MY PUNCH AS MUCH AS I DARED!

UNNGH: WHA--?

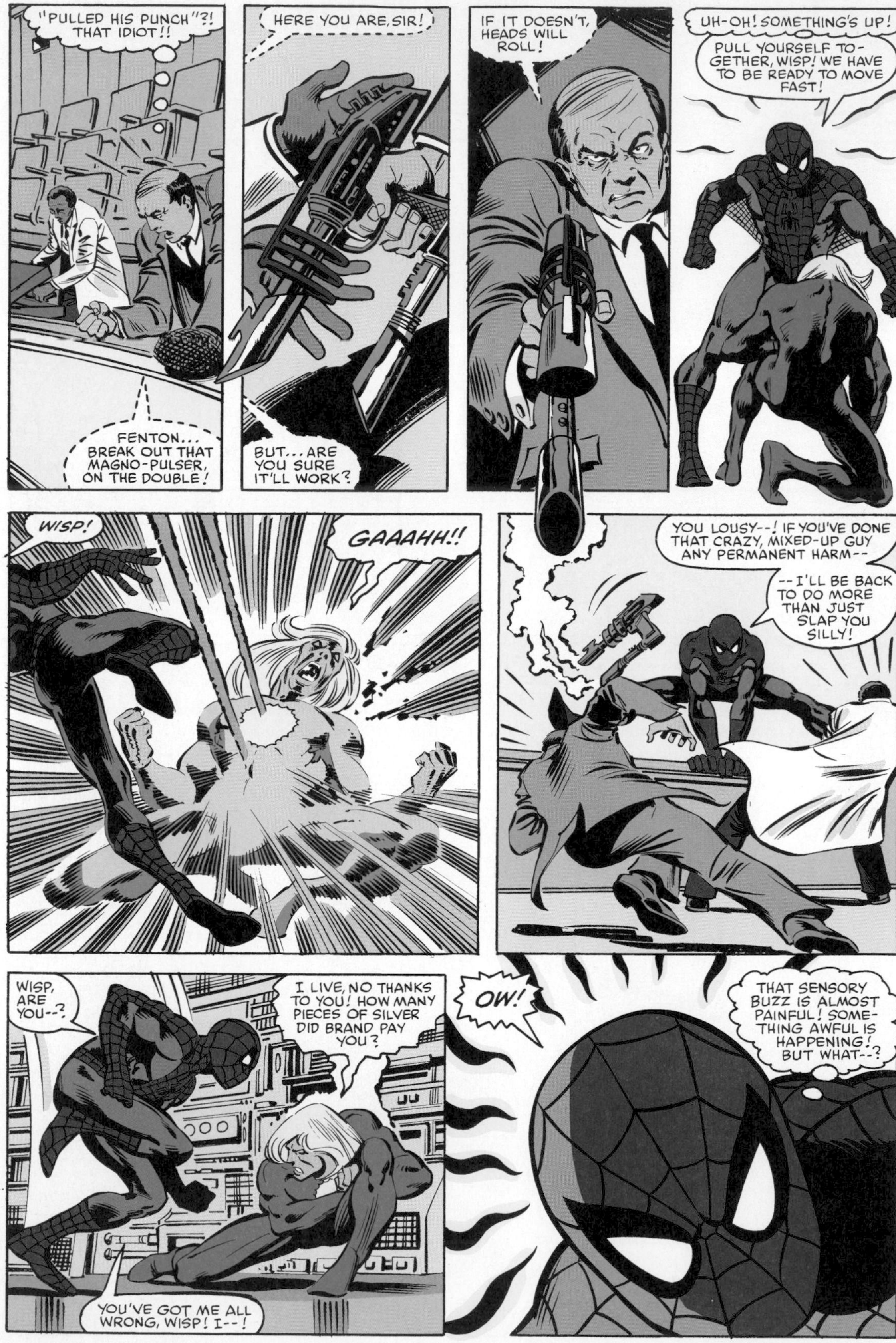
"PULLED HIS PUNCH"?! THAT IDIOT!!
FENTON... BREAK OUT THAT MAGNO-PULSER, ON THE DOUBLE!
HERE YOU ARE, SIR!
BUT... ARE YOU SURE IT'LL WORK?
IF IT DOESN'T, HEADS WILL ROLL!
UH-OH! SOMETHING'S UP!
PULL YOURSELF TOGETHER, WISP! WE HAVE TO BE READY TO MOVE FAST!
WISP!
GAAAHH!!
YOU LOUSY--! IF YOU'VE DONE THAT CRAZY, MIXED-UP GUY ANY PERMANENT HARM--
--I'LL BE BACK TO DO MORE THAN JUST SLAP YOU SILLY!
WISP, ARE YOU--?
I LIVE, NO THANKS TO YOU! HOW MANY PIECES OF SILVER DID BRAND PAY YOU?
YOU'VE GOT ME ALL WRONG, WISP! I--!
OW!
THAT SENSORY BUZZ IS ALMOST PAINFUL! SOMETHING AWFUL IS HAPPENING! BUT WHAT--?

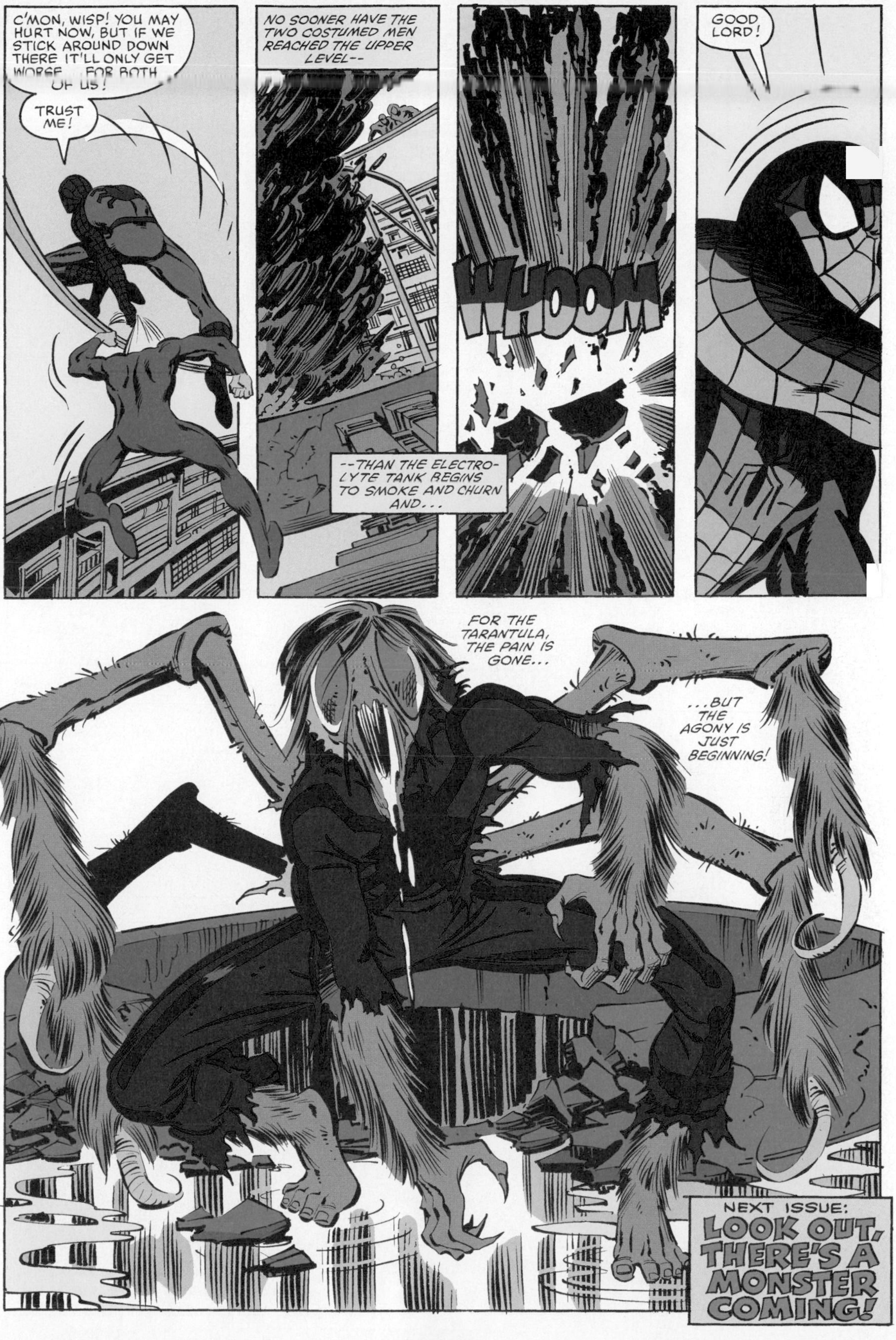

C'MON, WISP! YOU MAY HURT NOW, BUT IF WE STICK AROUND DOWN THERE IT'LL ONLY GET WORSE... FOR BOTH OF US!
TRUST ME!
NO SOONER HAVE THE TWO COSTUMED MEN REACHED THE UPPER LEVEL--
--THAN THE ELECTROLYTE TANK BEGINS TO SMOKE AND CHURN AND...
WHOOM
GOOD LORD!
FOR THE TARANTULA, THE PAIN IS GONE...
...BUT THE AGONY IS JUST BEGINNING!
NEXT ISSUE:
LOOK OUT, THERE'S A MONSTER COMING!

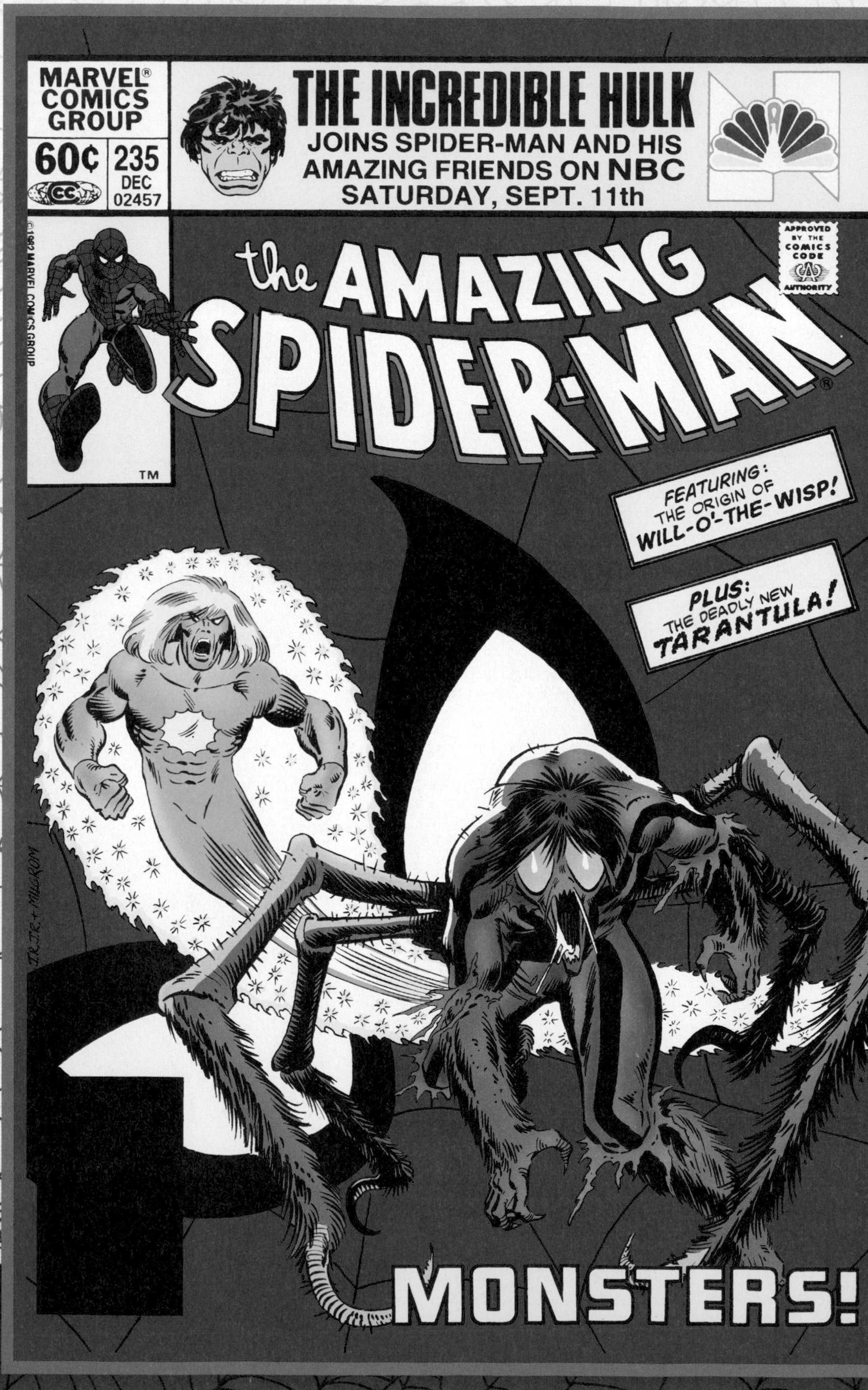
MARVEL® COMICS GROUP
60¢ 235 DEC 02457
THE INCREDIBLE HULK
JOINS SPIDER-MAN AND HIS AMAZING FRIENDS ON NBC SATURDAY, SEPT. 11th
APPROVED BY THE COMICS CODE AUTHORITY
the AMAZING SPIDER-MAN®
TM
FEATURING: THE ORIGIN OF WILL-O'-THE-WISP!
PLUS: THE DEADLY NEW TARANTULA!
MONSTERS!

LOOK OUT THERE'S A MONSTER COMING!

AMAZING SPIDER-MAN!

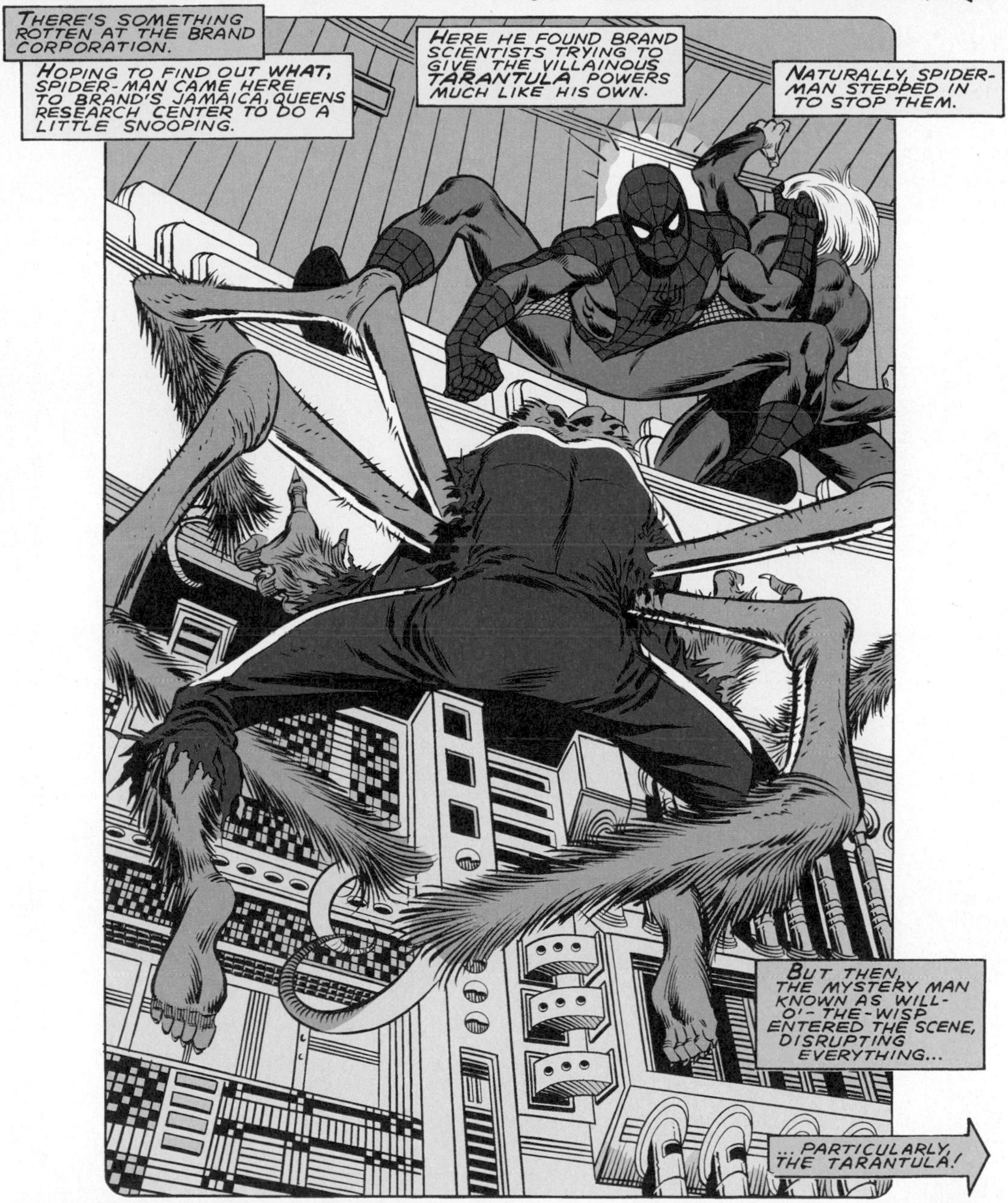

THERE'S SOMETHING ROTTEN AT THE BRAND CORPORATION.
HOPING TO FIND OUT WHAT, SPIDER-MAN CAME HERE TO BRAND'S JAMAICA, QUEENS RESEARCH CENTER TO DO A LITTLE SNOOPING.
HERE HE FOUND BRAND SCIENTISTS TRYING TO GIVE THE VILLAINOUS TARANTULA POWERS MUCH LIKE HIS OWN.
NATURALLY, SPIDER-MAN STEPPED IN TO STOP THEM.
BUT THEN, THE MYSTERY MAN KNOWN AS WILL-O'-THE-WISP ENTERED THE SCENE, DISRUPTING EVERYTHING...
...PARTICULARLY, THE TARANTULA!

ROGER STERN WRITER / JOHN ROMITA JR. & FRANK GIACOIA ARTISTS / DIANA ALBERS LETTERER / GLYNIS WEIN COLORIST / TOM DeFALCO EDITOR / JIM SHOOTER BOSS-MAN / STAN LEE PRESENTER EMERITUS

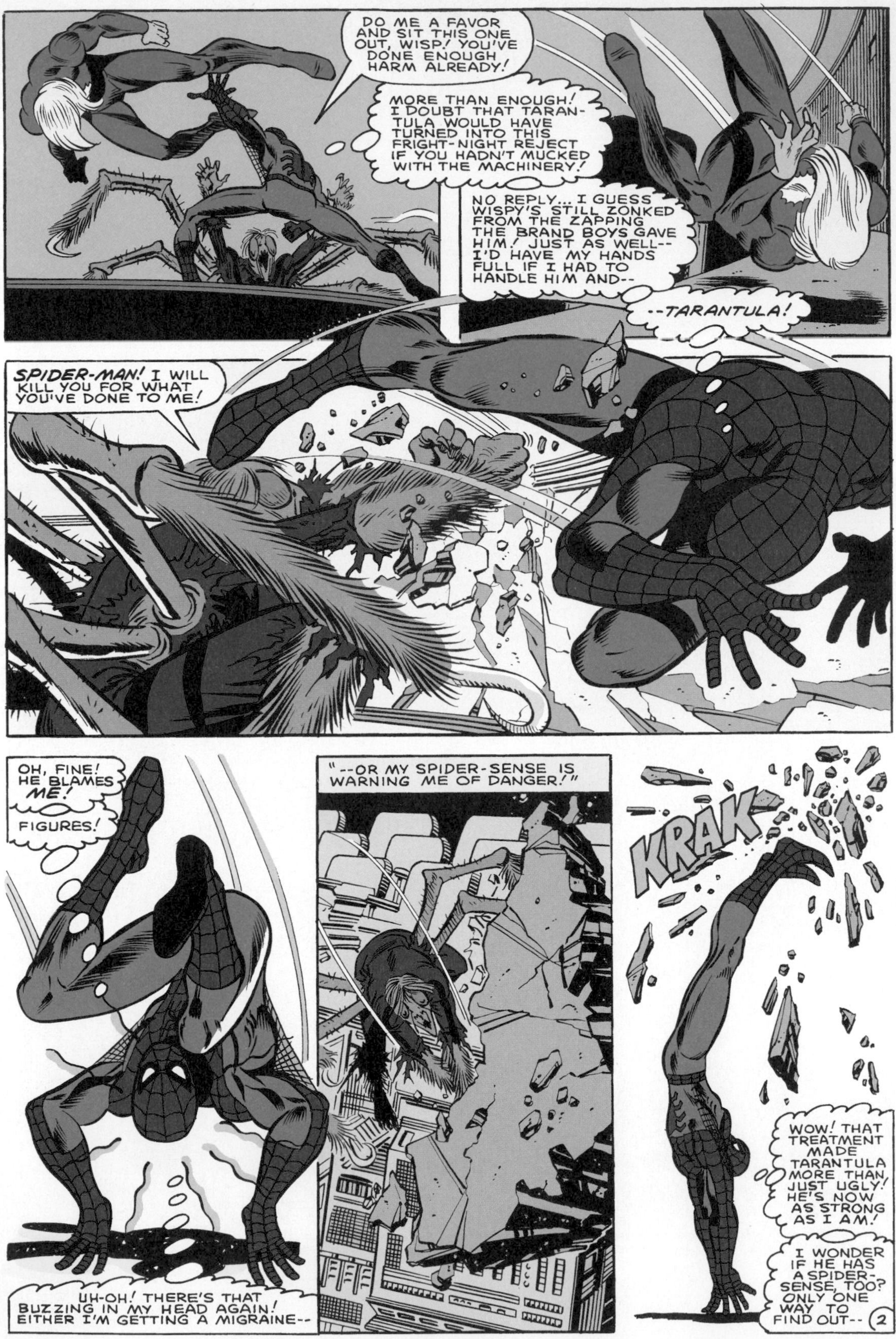
DO ME A FAVOR AND SIT THIS ONE OUT, WISP! YOU'VE DONE ENOUGH HARM ALREADY!
MORE THAN ENOUGH! I DOUBT THAT TARANTULA WOULD HAVE TURNED INTO THIS FRIGHT-NIGHT REJECT IF YOU HADN'T MUCKED WITH THE MACHINERY!
NO REPLY... I GUESS WISPY'S STILL ZONKED FROM THE ZAPPING THE BRAND BOYS GAVE HIM! JUST AS WELL-- I'D HAVE MY HANDS FULL IF I HAD TO HANDLE HIM AND--
--TARANTULA!
SPIDER-MAN! I WILL KILL YOU FOR WHAT YOU'VE DONE TO ME!
OH, FINE! HE BLAMES ME!
FIGURES!
UH-OH! THERE'S THAT BUZZING IN MY HEAD AGAIN! EITHER I'M GETTING A MIGRAINE--
"--OR MY SPIDER-SENSE IS WARNING ME OF DANGER!"
KRAK
WOW! THAT TREATMENT MADE TARANTULA MORE THAN JUST UGLY! HE'S NOW AS STRONG AS I AM!
I WONDER IF HE HAS A SPIDER-SENSE, TOO? ONLY ONE WAY TO FIND OUT--
2

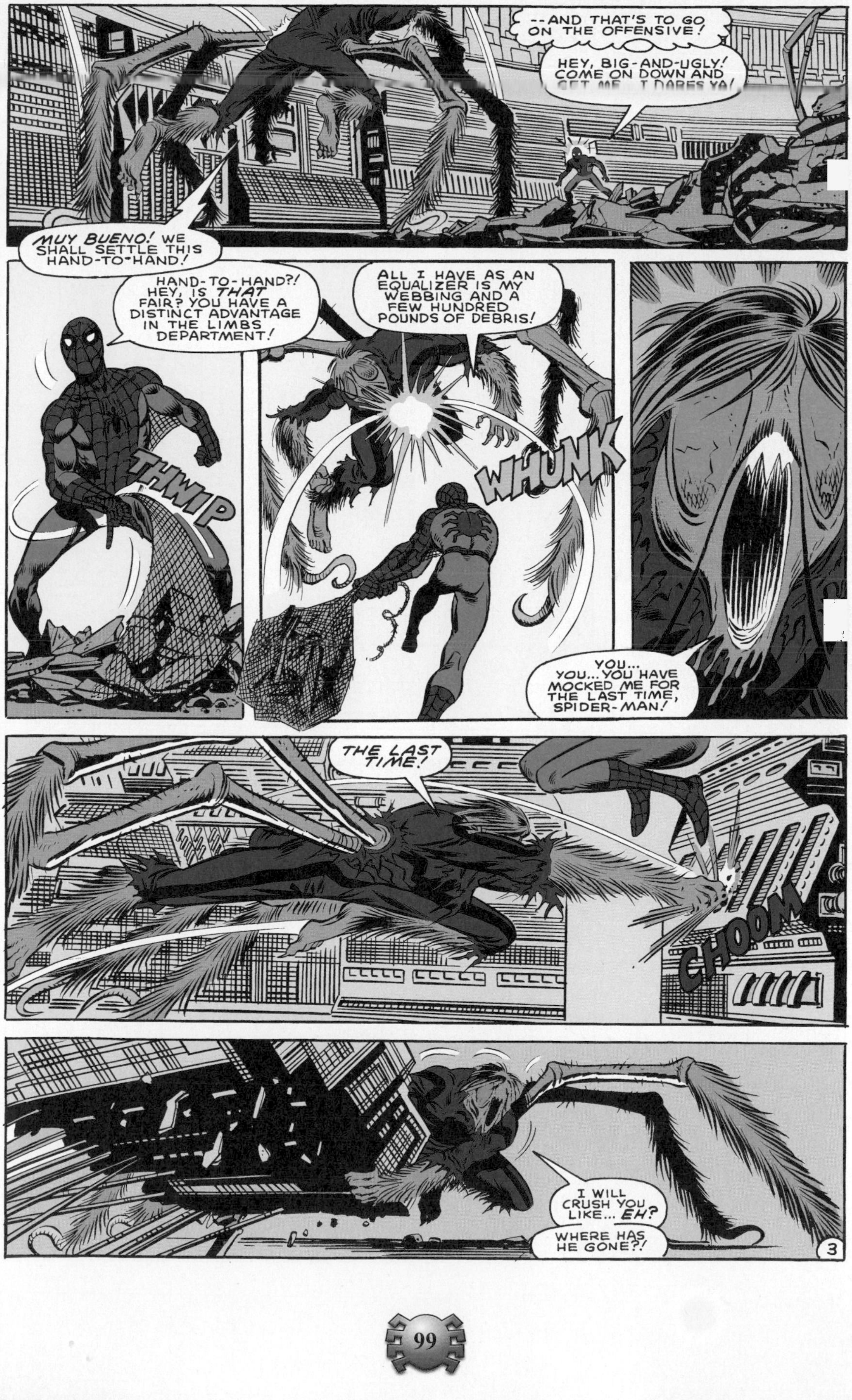
--AND THAT'S TO GO ON THE OFFENSIVE!
HEY, BIG-AND-UGLY! COME ON DOWN AND GET ME... I DARES YA!
MUY BUENO! WE SHALL SETTLE THIS HAND-TO-HAND!
HAND-TO-HAND?! HEY, IS THAT FAIR? YOU HAVE A DISTINCT ADVANTAGE IN THE LIMBS DEPARTMENT!
THWIP
ALL I HAVE AS AN EQUALIZER IS MY WEBBING AND A FEW HUNDRED POUNDS OF DEBRIS!
WHUNK
YOU... YOU... YOU HAVE MOCKED ME FOR THE LAST TIME, SPIDER-MAN!
THE LAST TIME!
CHOOM
I WILL CRUSH YOU LIKE... EH?
WHERE HAS HE GONE?!
3

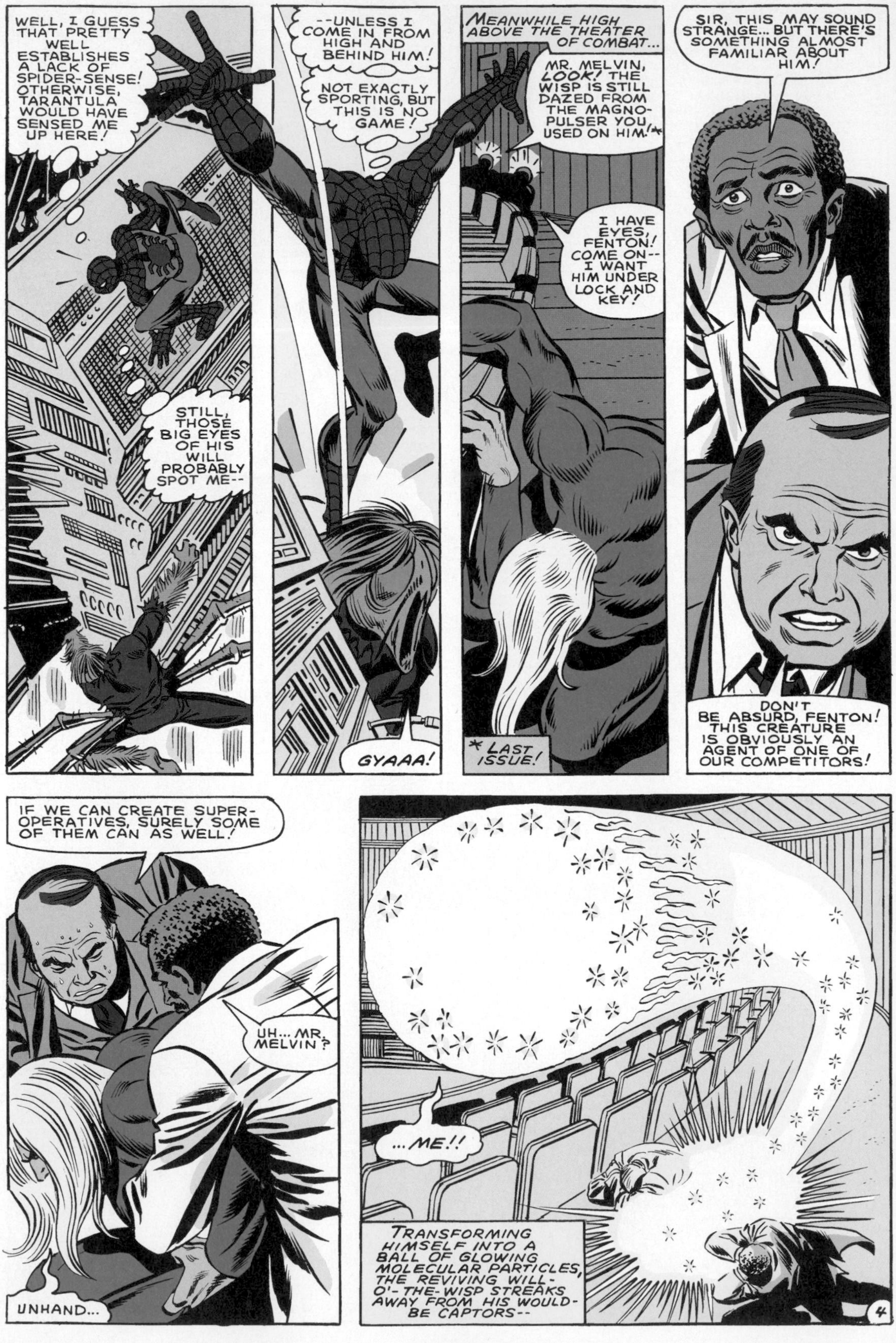

WELL, I GUESS THAT PRETTY WELL ESTABLISHES A LACK OF SPIDER-SENSE! OTHERWISE, TARANTULA WOULD HAVE SENSED ME UP HERE!
STILL, THOSE BIG EYES OF HIS WILL PROBABLY SPOT ME--
--UNLESS I COME IN FROM HIGH AND BEHIND HIM!
NOT EXACTLY SPORTING, BUT THIS IS NO GAME!
GYAAA!
MEANWHILE HIGH ABOVE THE THEATER OF COMBAT...
MR. MELVIN, LOOK! THE WISP IS STILL DAZED FROM THE MAGNO-PULSER YOU USED ON HIM!*
I HAVE EYES, FENTON! COME ON-- I WANT HIM UNDER LOCK AND KEY!
*LAST ISSUE!
SIR, THIS MAY SOUND STRANGE... BUT THERE'S SOMETHING ALMOST FAMILIAR ABOUT HIM!
DON'T BE ABSURD, FENTON! THIS CREATURE IS OBVIOUSLY AN AGENT OF ONE OF OUR COMPETITORS!
IF WE CAN CREATE SUPER-OPERATIVES, SURELY SOME OF THEM CAN AS WELL!
UH... MR. MELVIN?
UNHAND...
...ME!!
TRANSFORMING HIMSELF INTO A BALL OF GLOWING MOLECULAR PARTICLES, THE REVIVING WILL-O'-THE-WISP STREAKS AWAY FROM HIS WOULD-BE CAPTORS--
4

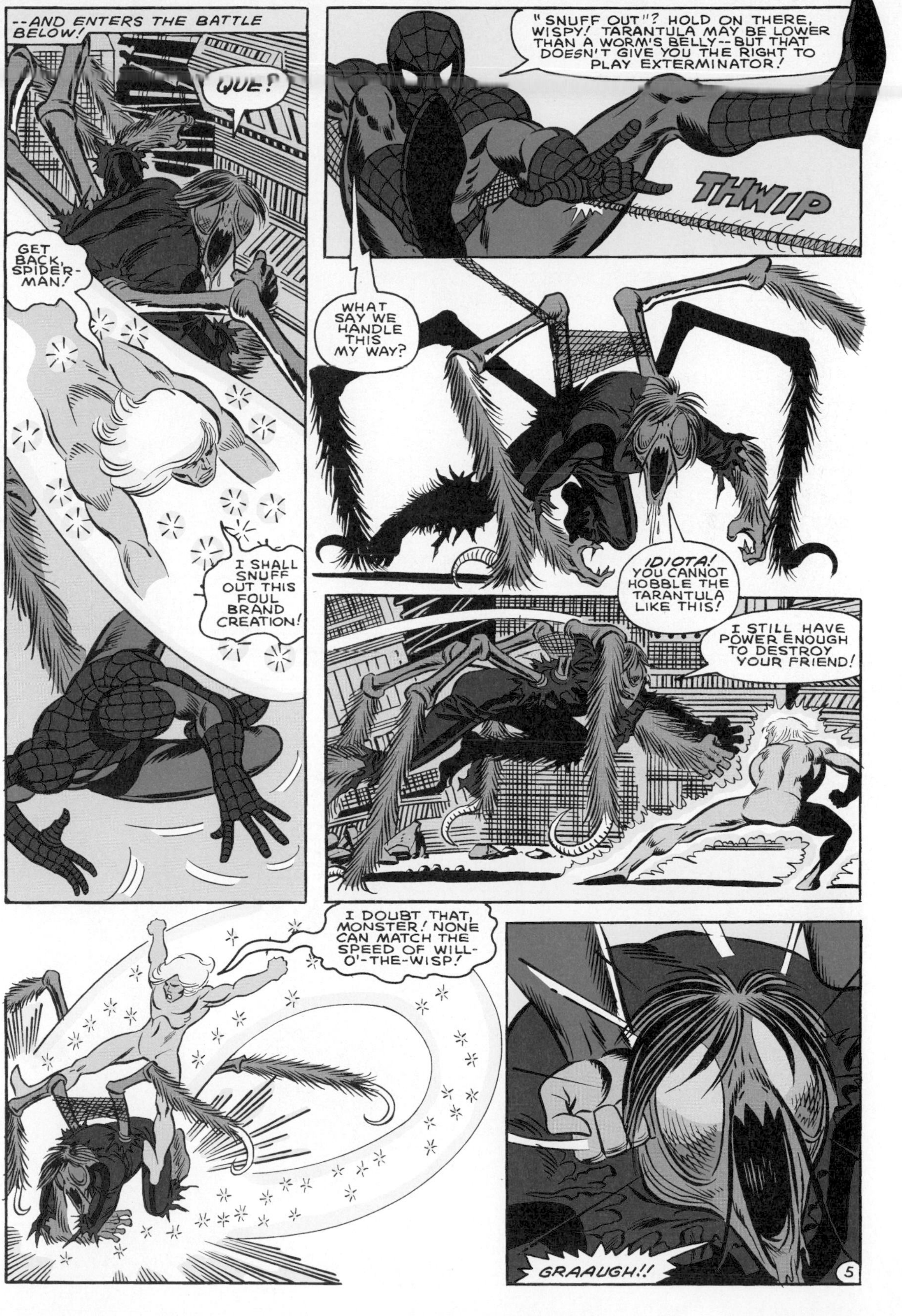
--AND ENTERS THE BATTLE BELOW!
QUE!
GET BACK, SPIDER-MAN!
I SHALL SNUFF OUT THIS FOUL BRAND CREATION!
"SNUFF OUT"? HOLD ON THERE, WISPY! TARANTULA MAY BE LOWER THAN A WORM'S BELLY--BUT THAT DOESN'T GIVE YOU THE RIGHT TO PLAY EXTERMINATOR!
THWIP
WHAT SAY WE HANDLE THIS MY WAY?
¡IDIOTA! YOU CANNOT HOBBLE THE TARANTULA LIKE THIS!
I STILL HAVE POWER ENOUGH TO DESTROY YOUR FRIEND!
I DOUBT THAT, MONSTER! NONE CAN MATCH THE SPEED OF WILL-O'-THE-WISP!
GRAAUGH!!
5

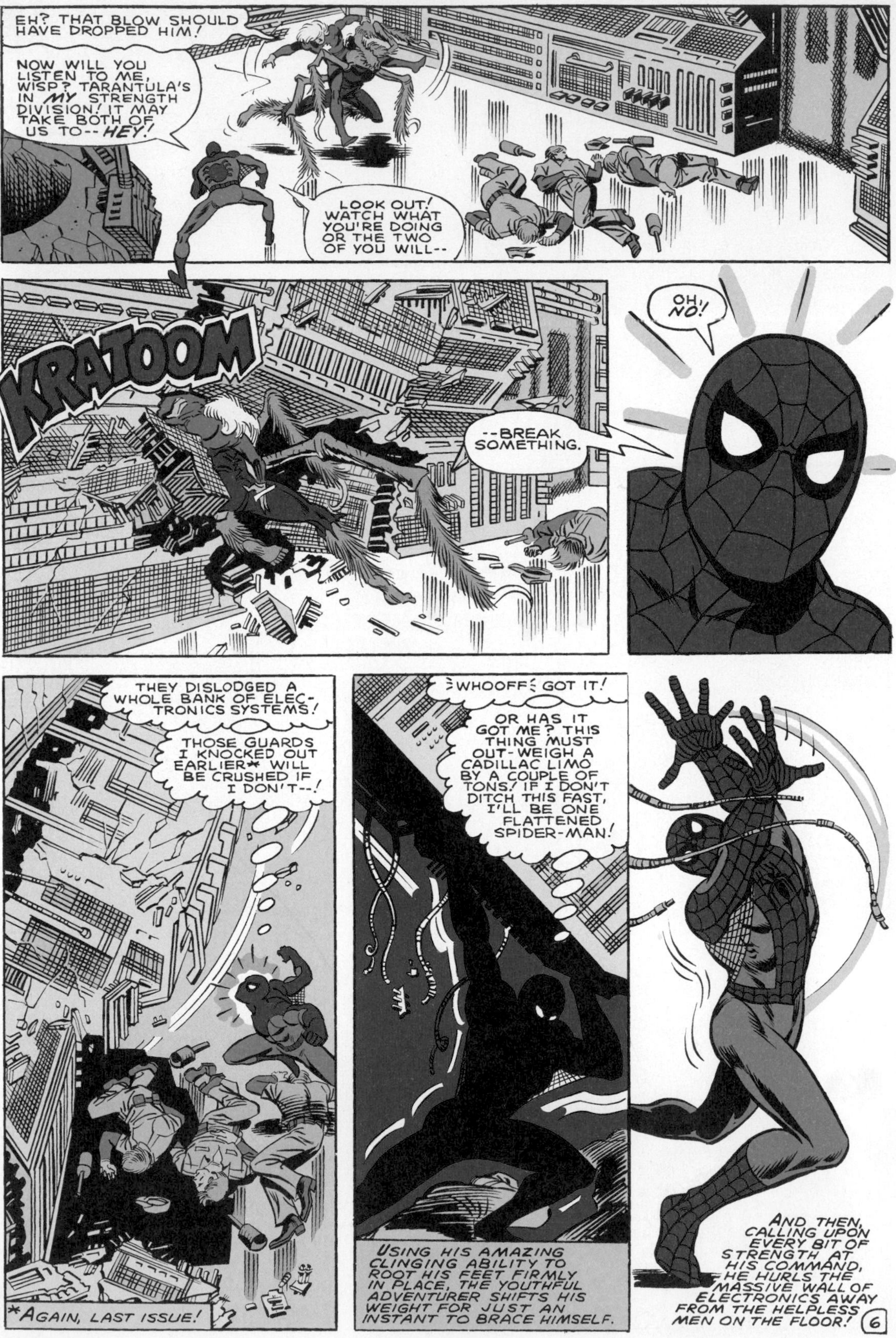
EH? THAT BLOW SHOULD HAVE DROPPED HIM!
NOW WILL YOU LISTEN TO ME, WISP? TARANTULA'S IN MY STRENGTH DIVISION! IT MAY TAKE BOTH OF US TO--HEY!
LOOK OUT! WATCH WHAT YOU'RE DOING OR THE TWO OF YOU WILL--
KRATOOM
--BREAK SOMETHING.
OH, NO!
THEY DISLODGED A WHOLE BANK OF ELEC-TRONICS SYSTEMS!
THOSE GUARDS I KNOCKED OUT EARLIER* WILL BE CRUSHED IF I DON'T--!
*AGAIN, LAST ISSUE!
WHOOFF! GOT IT!
OR HAS IT GOT ME? THIS THING MUST OUT-WEIGH A CADILLAC LIMO BY A COUPLE OF TONS! IF I DON'T DITCH THIS FAST, I'LL BE ONE FLATTENED SPIDER-MAN!
USING HIS AMAZING CLINGING ABILITY TO ROOT HIS FEET FIRMLY IN PLACE, THE YOUTHFUL ADVENTURER SHIFTS HIS WEIGHT FOR JUST AN INSTANT TO BRACE HIMSELF.
AND THEN, CALLING UPON EVERY BIT OF STRENGTH AT HIS COMMAND, HE HURLS THE MASSIVE WALL OF ELECTRONICS AWAY FROM THE HELPLESS MEN ON THE FLOOR!
6

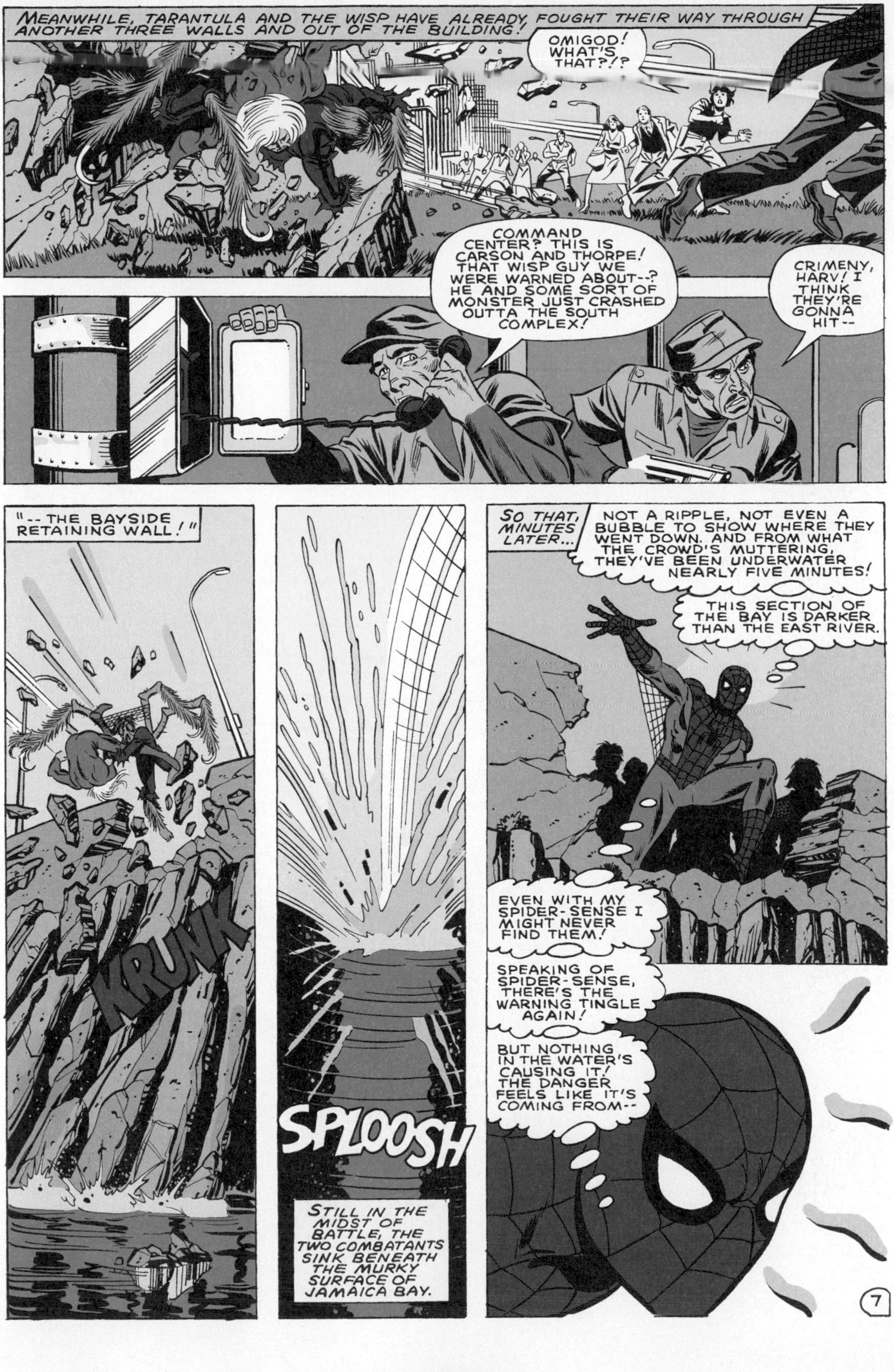
MEANWHILE, TARANTULA AND THE WISP HAVE ALREADY FOUGHT THEIR WAY THROUGH ANOTHER THREE WALLS AND OUT OF THE BUILDING!
OMIGOD! WHAT'S THAT?!?
COMMAND CENTER? THIS IS CARSON AND THORPE! THAT WISP GUY WE WERE WARNED ABOUT--? HE AND SOME SORT OF MONSTER JUST CRASHED OUTTA THE SOUTH COMPLEX!
CRIMENY, HARV! I THINK THEY'RE GONNA HIT--
"--THE BAYSIDE RETAINING WALL!"
KRUNK
SPLOOSH
STILL IN THE MIDST OF BATTLE, THE TWO COMBATANTS SINK BENEATH THE MURKY SURFACE OF JAMAICA BAY.
SO THAT, MINUTES LATER...
NOT A RIPPLE, NOT EVEN A BUBBLE TO SHOW WHERE THEY WENT DOWN. AND FROM WHAT THE CROWD'S MUTTERING, THEY'VE BEEN UNDERWATER NEARLY FIVE MINUTES!
THIS SECTION OF THE BAY IS DARKER THAN THE EAST RIVER.
EVEN WITH MY SPIDER-SENSE I MIGHT NEVER FIND THEM!
SPEAKING OF SPIDER-SENSE, THERE'S THE WARNING TINGLE AGAIN!
BUT NOTHING IN THE WATER'S CAUSING IT! THE DANGER FEELS LIKE IT'S COMING FROM--
7

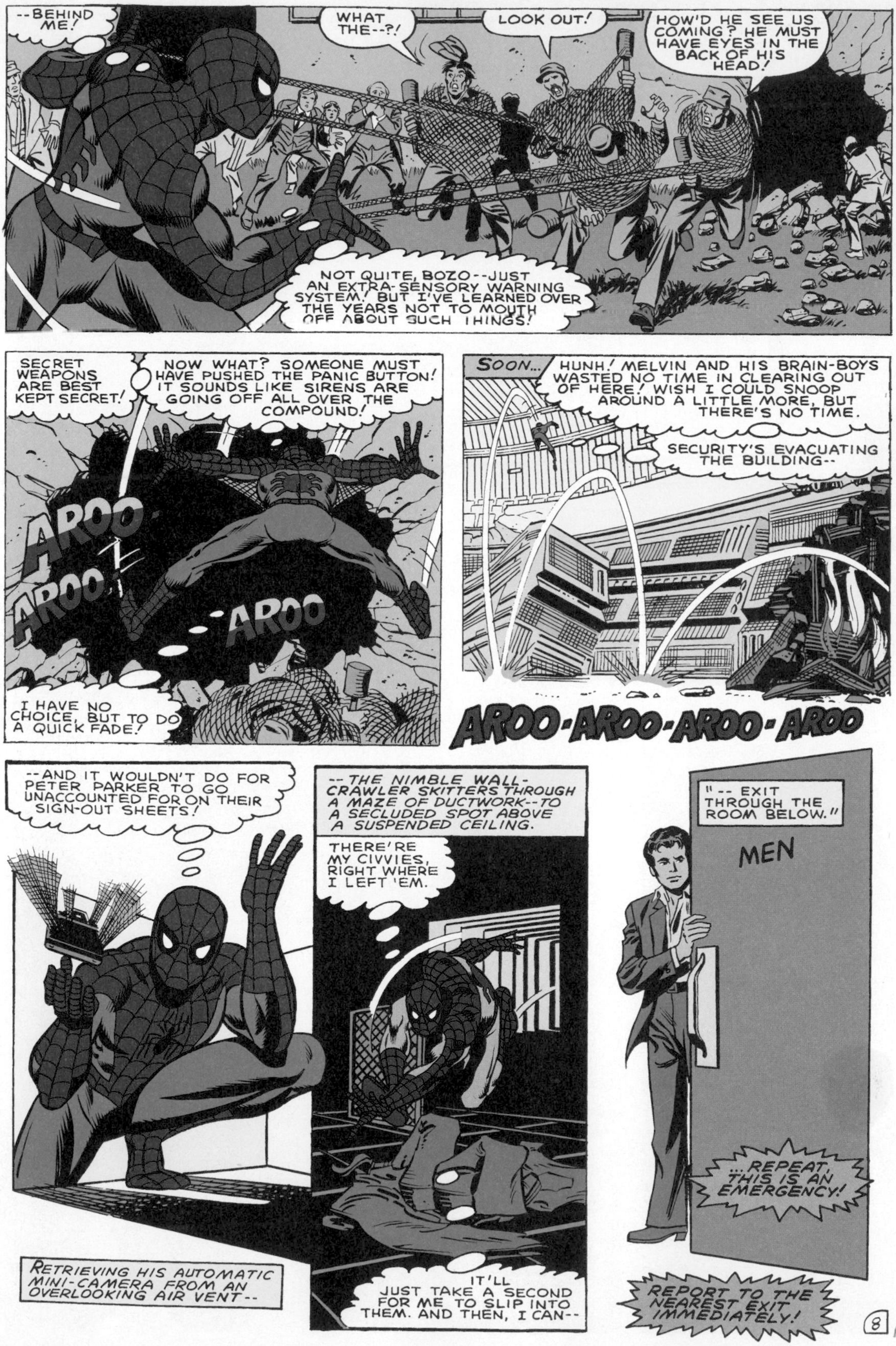
--BEHIND ME!
WHAT THE--?!
LOOK OUT!
HOW'D HE SEE US COMING? HE MUST HAVE EYES IN THE BACK OF HIS HEAD!
NOT QUITE, BOZO--JUST AN EXTRA-SENSORY WARNING SYSTEM! BUT I'VE LEARNED OVER THE YEARS NOT TO MOUTH OFF ABOUT SUCH THINGS!
SECRET WEAPONS ARE BEST KEPT SECRET!
NOW WHAT? SOMEONE MUST HAVE PUSHED THE PANIC BUTTON! IT SOUNDS LIKE SIRENS ARE GOING OFF ALL OVER THE COMPOUND!
AROO-
AROO-
AROO
I HAVE NO CHOICE, BUT TO DO A QUICK FADE!
SOON...
HUNH! MELVIN AND HIS BRAIN-BOYS WASTED NO TIME IN CLEARING OUT OF HERE! WISH I COULD SNOOP AROUND A LITTLE MORE, BUT THERE'S NO TIME.
SECURITY'S EVACUATING THE BUILDING--
AROO-AROO-AROO-AROO
--AND IT WOULDN'T DO FOR PETER PARKER TO GO UNACCOUNTED FOR ON THEIR SIGN-OUT SHEETS!
RETRIEVING HIS AUTOMATIC MINI-CAMERA FROM AN OVERLOOKING AIR VENT--
--THE NIMBLE WALL-CRAWLER SKITTERS THROUGH A MAZE OF DUCTWORK--TO A SECLUDED SPOT ABOVE A SUSPENDED CEILING.
THERE'RE MY CIVVIES, RIGHT WHERE I LEFT 'EM.
IT'LL JUST TAKE A SECOND FOR ME TO SLIP INTO THEM. AND THEN, I CAN--
"--EXIT THROUGH THE ROOM BELOW."
MEN
...REPEAT, THIS IS AN EMERGENCY!
REPORT TO THE NEAREST EXIT IMMEDIATELY!
8

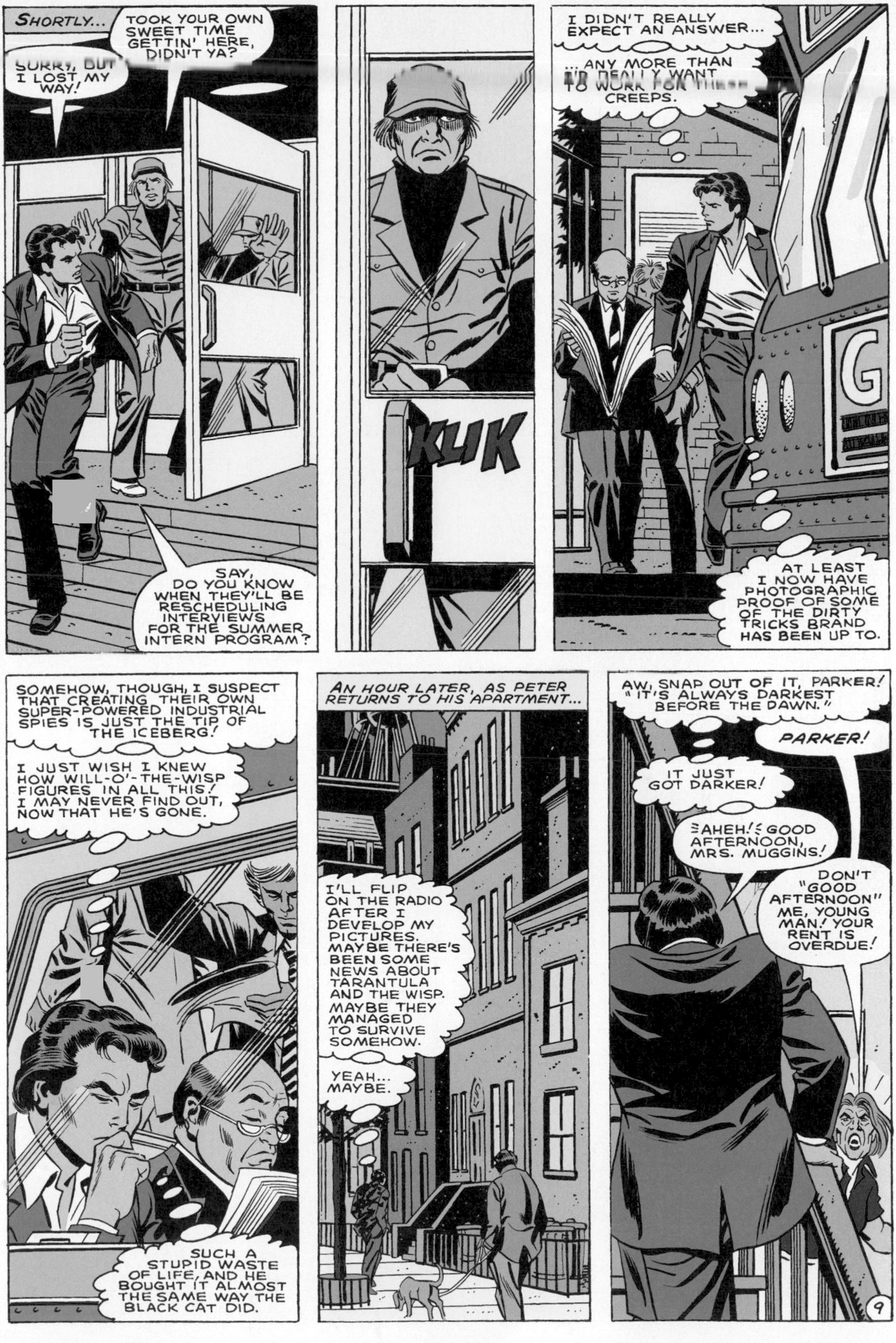
SHORTLY...
TOOK YOUR OWN SWEET TIME GETTIN' HERE, DIDN'T YA?
SORRY, BUT I LOST MY WAY!
SAY, DO YOU KNOW WHEN THEY'LL BE RESCHEDULING INTERVIEWS FOR THE SUMMER INTERN PROGRAM?
KLIK
I DIDN'T REALLY EXPECT AN ANSWER...
...ANY MORE THAN I'D REALLY WANT TO WORK FOR THESE CREEPS.
AT LEAST I NOW HAVE PHOTOGRAPHIC PROOF OF SOME OF THE DIRTY TRICKS BRAND HAS BEEN UP TO.
SOMEHOW, THOUGH, I SUSPECT THAT CREATING THEIR OWN SUPER-POWERED INDUSTRIAL SPIES IS JUST THE TIP OF THE ICEBERG!
I JUST WISH I KNEW HOW WILL-O'-THE-WISP FIGURES IN ALL THIS! I MAY NEVER FIND OUT, NOW THAT HE'S GONE.
SUCH A STUPID WASTE OF LIFE, AND HE BOUGHT IT ALMOST THE SAME WAY THE BLACK CAT DID.
AN HOUR LATER, AS PETER RETURNS TO HIS APARTMENT...
I'LL FLIP ON THE RADIO AFTER I DEVELOP MY PICTURES. MAYBE THERE'S BEEN SOME NEWS ABOUT TARANTULA AND THE WISP. MAYBE THEY MANAGED TO SURVIVE SOMEHOW.
YEAH... MAYBE.
AW, SNAP OUT OF IT, PARKER! "IT'S ALWAYS DARKEST BEFORE THE DAWN."
PARKER!
IT JUST GOT DARKER!
AHEH! GOOD AFTERNOON, MRS. MUGGINS!
DON'T "GOOD AFTERNOON" ME, YOUNG MAN! YOUR RENT IS OVERDUE!
9

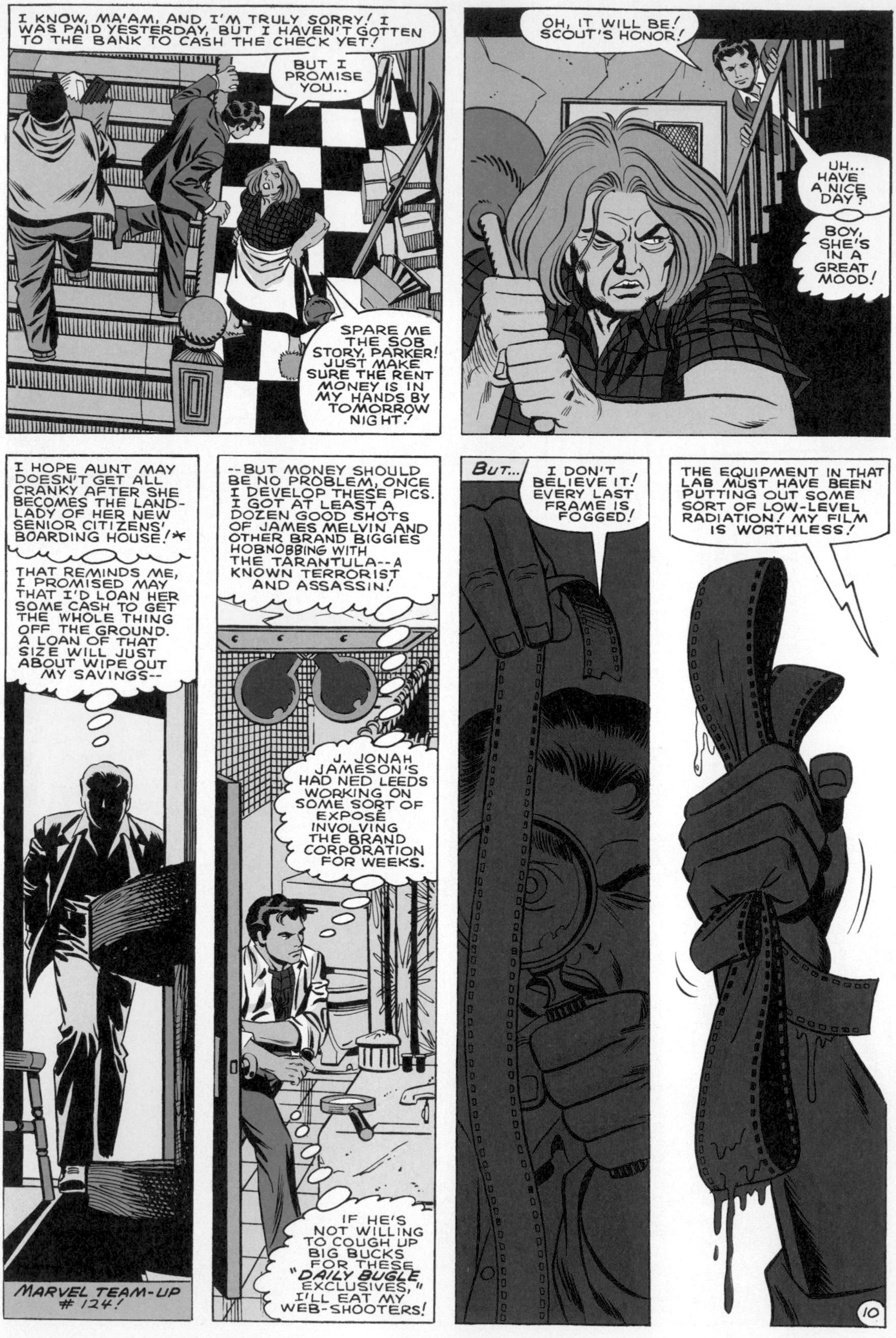
I KNOW, MA'AM, AND I'M TRULY SORRY! I WAS PAID YESTERDAY, BUT I HAVEN'T GOTTEN TO THE BANK TO CASH THE CHECK YET!
BUT I PROMISE YOU...
SPARE ME THE SOB STORY, PARKER! JUST MAKE SURE THE RENT MONEY IS IN MY HANDS BY TOMORROW NIGHT!
OH, IT WILL BE! SCOUT'S HONOR!
UH... HAVE A NICE DAY?
BOY, SHE'S IN A GREAT MOOD!
I HOPE AUNT MAY DOESN'T GET ALL CRANKY AFTER SHE BECOMES THE LANDLADY OF HER NEW SENIOR CITIZENS' BOARDING HOUSE!*
THAT REMINDS ME, I PROMISED MAY THAT I'D LOAN HER SOME CASH TO GET THE WHOLE THING OFF THE GROUND. A LOAN OF THAT SIZE WILL JUST ABOUT WIPE OUT MY SAVINGS--
*MARVEL TEAM-UP # 124!
--BUT MONEY SHOULD BE NO PROBLEM, ONCE I DEVELOP THESE PICS. I GOT AT LEAST A DOZEN GOOD SHOTS OF JAMES MELVIN AND OTHER BRAND BIGGIES HOBNOBBING WITH THE TARANTULA--A KNOWN TERRORIST AND ASSASSIN!
J. JONAH JAMESON'S HAD NED LEEDS WORKING ON SOME SORT OF EXPOSÉ INVOLVING THE BRAND CORPORATION FOR WEEKS.
IF HE'S NOT WILLING TO COUGH UP BIG BUCKS FOR THESE "DAILY BUGLE EXCLUSIVES," I'LL EAT MY WEB-SHOOTERS!
BUT...
I DON'T BELIEVE IT! EVERY LAST FRAME IS FOGGED!
THE EQUIPMENT IN THAT LAB MUST HAVE BEEN PUTTING OUT SOME SORT OF LOW-LEVEL RADIATION! MY FILM IS WORTHLESS!
10

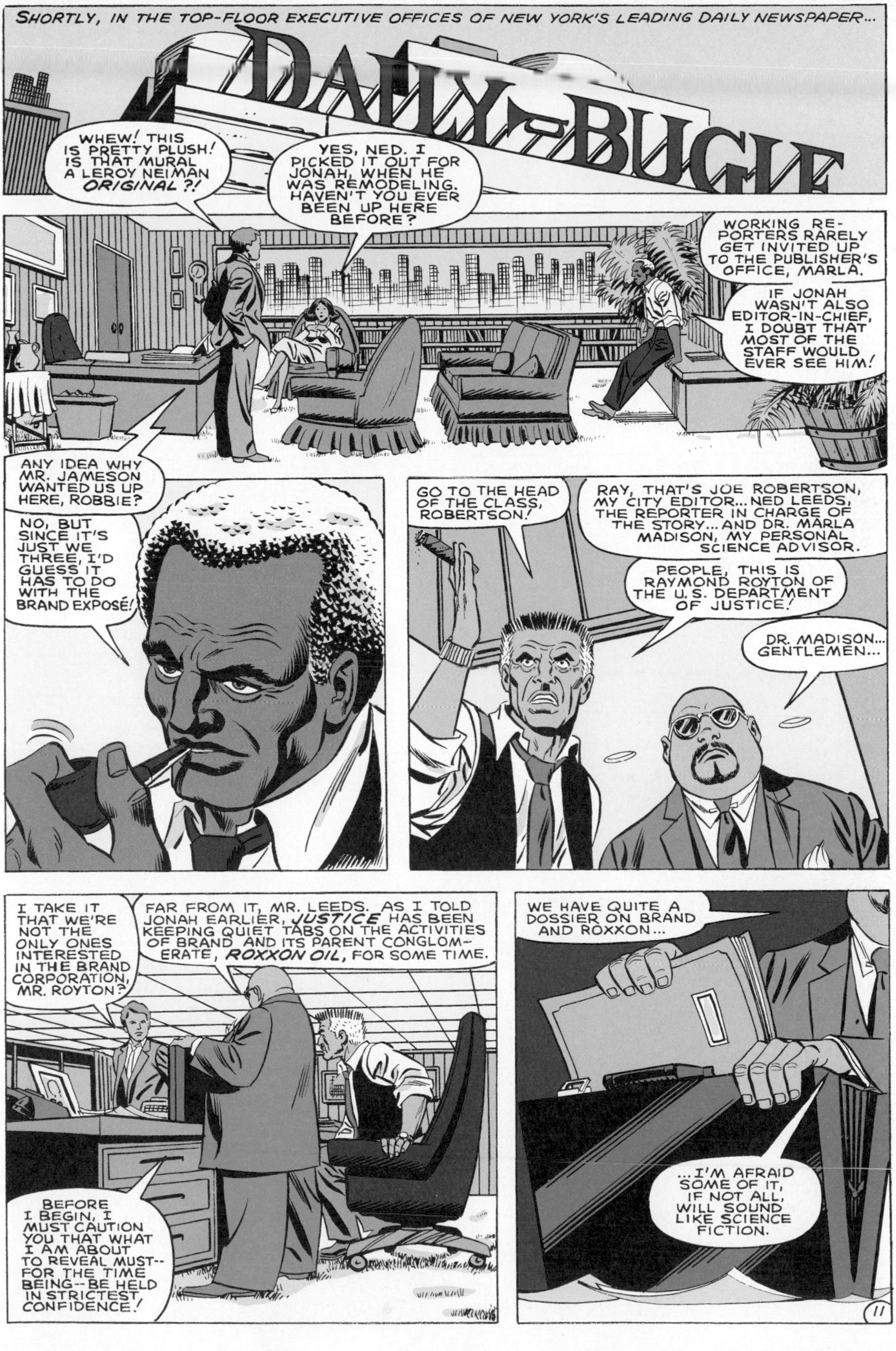
SHORTLY, IN THE TOP-FLOOR EXECUTIVE OFFICES OF NEW YORK'S LEADING DAILY NEWSPAPER...
DAILY BUGLE
WHEW! THIS IS PRETTY PLUSH! IS THAT MURAL A LEROY NEIMAN ORIGINAL?!
YES, NED. I PICKED IT OUT FOR JONAH, WHEN HE WAS REMODELING. HAVEN'T YOU EVER BEEN UP HERE BEFORE?
WORKING REPORTERS RARELY GET INVITED UP TO THE PUBLISHER'S OFFICE, MARLA.
IF JONAH WASN'T ALSO EDITOR-IN-CHIEF, I DOUBT THAT MOST OF THE STAFF WOULD EVER SEE HIM!
ANY IDEA WHY MR. JAMESON WANTED US UP HERE, ROBBIE?
NO, BUT SINCE IT'S JUST WE THREE, I'D GUESS IT HAS TO DO WITH THE BRAND EXPOSÉ!
GO TO THE HEAD OF THE CLASS, ROBERTSON!
RAY, THAT'S JOE ROBERTSON, MY CITY EDITOR... NED LEEDS, THE REPORTER IN CHARGE OF THE STORY... AND DR. MARLA MADISON, MY PERSONAL SCIENCE ADVISOR.
PEOPLE, THIS IS RAYMOND ROYTON OF THE U.S. DEPARTMENT OF JUSTICE!
DR. MADISON... GENTLEMEN...
I TAKE IT THAT WE'RE NOT THE ONLY ONES INTERESTED IN THE BRAND CORPORATION, MR. ROYTON?
FAR FROM IT, MR. LEEDS. AS I TOLD JONAH EARLIER, JUSTICE HAS BEEN KEEPING QUIET TABS ON THE ACTIVITIES OF BRAND AND ITS PARENT CONGLOMERATE, ROXXON OIL, FOR SOME TIME.
BEFORE I BEGIN, I MUST CAUTION YOU THAT WHAT I AM ABOUT TO REVEAL MUST--FOR THE TIME BEING--BE HELD IN STRICTEST CONFIDENCE!
WE HAVE QUITE A DOSSIER ON BRAND AND ROXXON...
...I'M AFRAID SOME OF IT, IF NOT ALL, WILL SOUND LIKE SCIENCE FICTION.
11

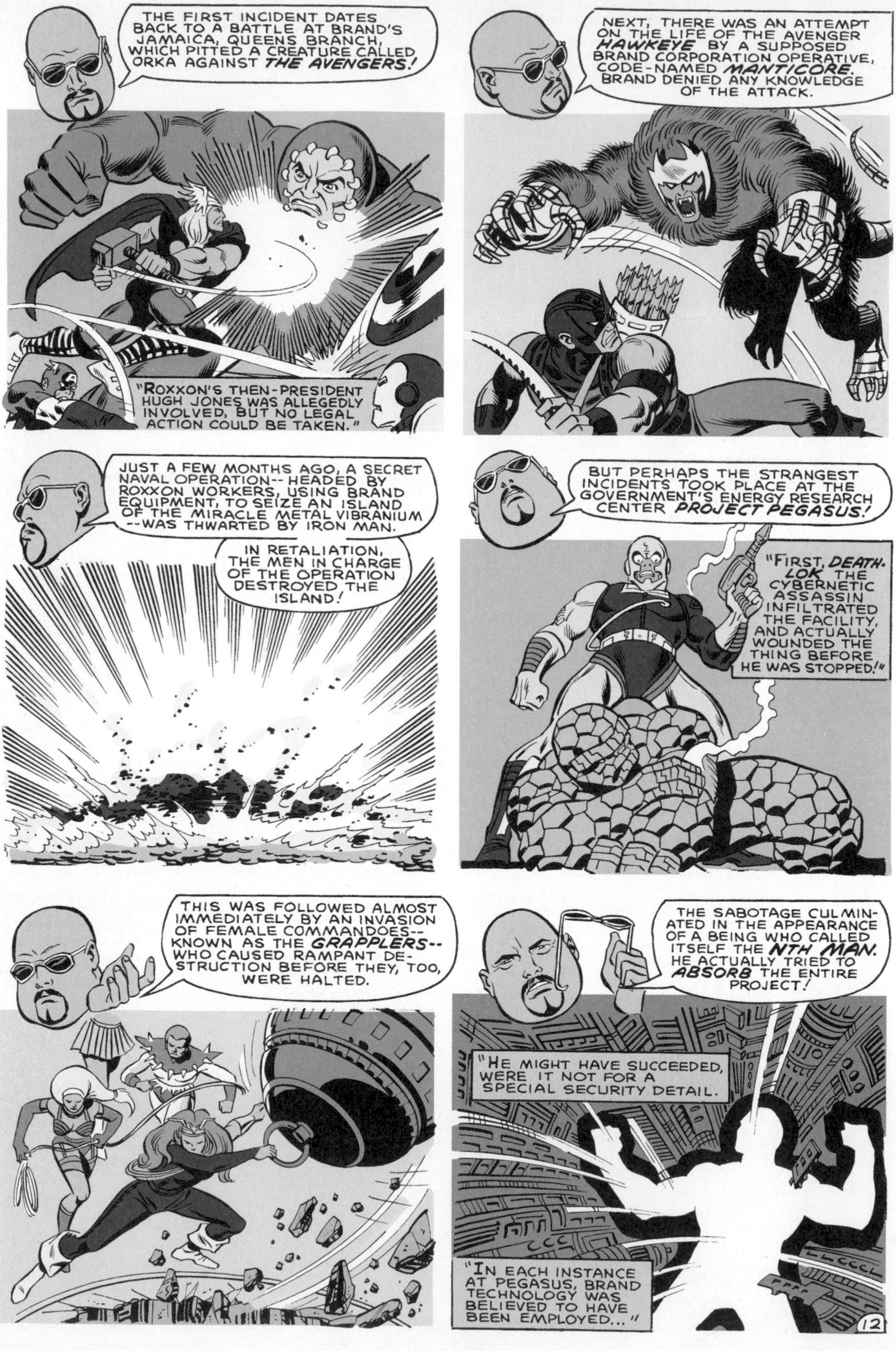
THE FIRST INCIDENT DATES BACK TO A BATTLE AT BRAND'S JAMAICA, QUEENS BRANCH, WHICH PITTED A CREATURE CALLED ORKA AGAINST THE AVENGERS!
"ROXXON'S THEN-PRESIDENT HUGH JONES WAS ALLEGEDLY INVOLVED, BUT NO LEGAL ACTION COULD BE TAKEN."
NEXT, THERE WAS AN ATTEMPT ON THE LIFE OF THE AVENGER HAWKEYE BY A SUPPOSED BRAND CORPORATION OPERATIVE, CODE-NAMED MANTICORE. BRAND DENIED ANY KNOWLEDGE OF THE ATTACK.
JUST A FEW MONTHS AGO, A SECRET NAVAL OPERATION-- HEADED BY ROXXON WORKERS, USING BRAND EQUIPMENT, TO SEIZE AN ISLAND OF THE MIRACLE METAL VIBRANIUM --WAS THWARTED BY IRON MAN.
IN RETALIATION, THE MEN IN CHARGE OF THE OPERATION DESTROYED THE ISLAND!
BUT PERHAPS THE STRANGEST INCIDENTS TOOK PLACE AT THE GOVERNMENT'S ENERGY RESEARCH CENTER PROJECT PEGASUS!
"FIRST, DEATHLOK THE CYBERNETIC ASSASSIN INFILTRATED THE FACILITY, AND ACTUALLY WOUNDED THE THING BEFORE HE WAS STOPPED!"
THIS WAS FOLLOWED ALMOST IMMEDIATELY BY AN INVASION OF FEMALE COMMANDOES-- KNOWN AS THE GRAPPLERS-- WHO CAUSED RAMPANT DESTRUCTION BEFORE THEY, TOO, WERE HALTED.
THE SABOTAGE CULMINATED IN THE APPEARANCE OF A BEING WHO CALLED ITSELF THE NTH MAN. HE ACTUALLY TRIED TO ABSORB THE ENTIRE PROJECT!
"HE MIGHT HAVE SUCCEEDED, WERE IT NOT FOR A SPECIAL SECURITY DETAIL.
"IN EACH INSTANCE AT PEGASUS, BRAND TECHNOLOGY WAS BELIEVED TO HAVE BEEN EMPLOYED..."
12

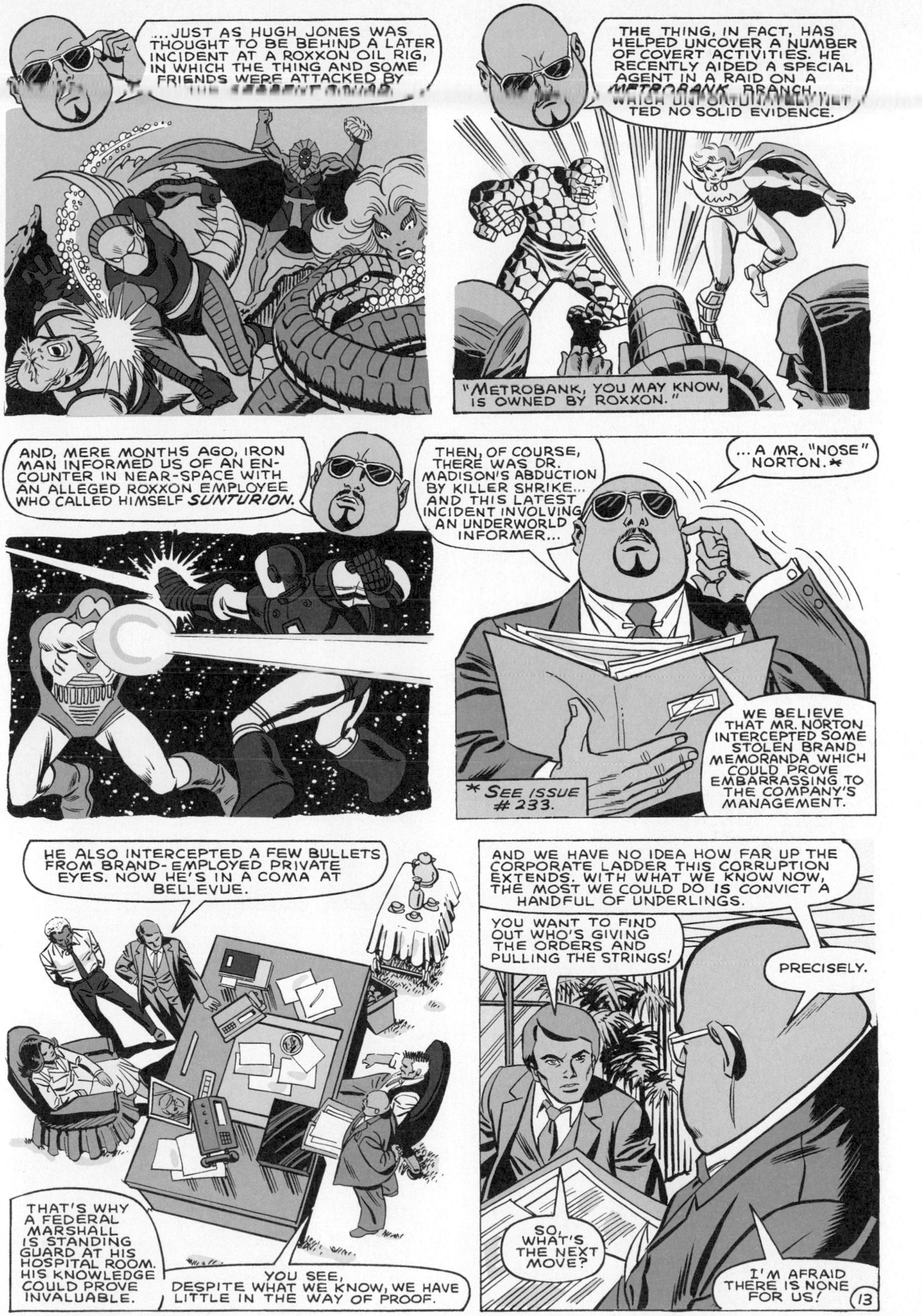
...JUST AS HUGH JONES WAS THOUGHT TO BE BEHIND A LATER INCIDENT AT A ROXXON OIL RIG, IN WHICH THE THING AND SOME FRIENDS WERE ATTACKED BY
THE THING, IN FACT, HAS HELPED UNCOVER A NUMBER OF COVERT ACTIVITIES. HE RECENTLY AIDED A SPECIAL AGENT IN A RAID ON A METROBANK BRANCH...
TED NO SOLID EVIDENCE.
"METROBANK, YOU MAY KNOW, IS OWNED BY ROXXON."
AND, MERE MONTHS AGO, IRON MAN INFORMED US OF AN ENCOUNTER IN NEAR-SPACE WITH AN ALLEGED ROXXON EMPLOYEE WHO CALLED HIMSELF SUNTURION.
THEN, OF COURSE, THERE WAS DR. MADISON'S ABDUCTION BY KILLER SHRIKE... AND THIS LATEST INCIDENT INVOLVING AN UNDERWORLD INFORMER...
...A MR. "NOSE" NORTON.*
WE BELIEVE THAT MR. NORTON INTERCEPTED SOME STOLEN BRAND MEMORANDA WHICH COULD PROVE EMBARRASSING TO THE COMPANY'S MANAGEMENT.
*SEE ISSUE #233.
HE ALSO INTERCEPTED A FEW BULLETS FROM BRAND-EMPLOYED PRIVATE EYES. NOW HE'S IN A COMA AT BELLEVUE.
THAT'S WHY A FEDERAL MARSHALL IS STANDING GUARD AT HIS HOSPITAL ROOM. HIS KNOWLEDGE COULD PROVE INVALUABLE.
YOU SEE, DESPITE WHAT WE KNOW, WE HAVE LITTLE IN THE WAY OF PROOF.
AND WE HAVE NO IDEA HOW FAR UP THE CORPORATE LADDER THIS CORRUPTION EXTENDS. WITH WHAT WE KNOW NOW, THE MOST WE COULD DO IS CONVICT A HANDFUL OF UNDERLINGS.
YOU WANT TO FIND OUT WHO'S GIVING THE ORDERS AND PULLING THE STRINGS!
PRECISELY.
SO, WHAT'S THE NEXT MOVE?
I'M AFRAID THERE IS NONE FOR US!
13

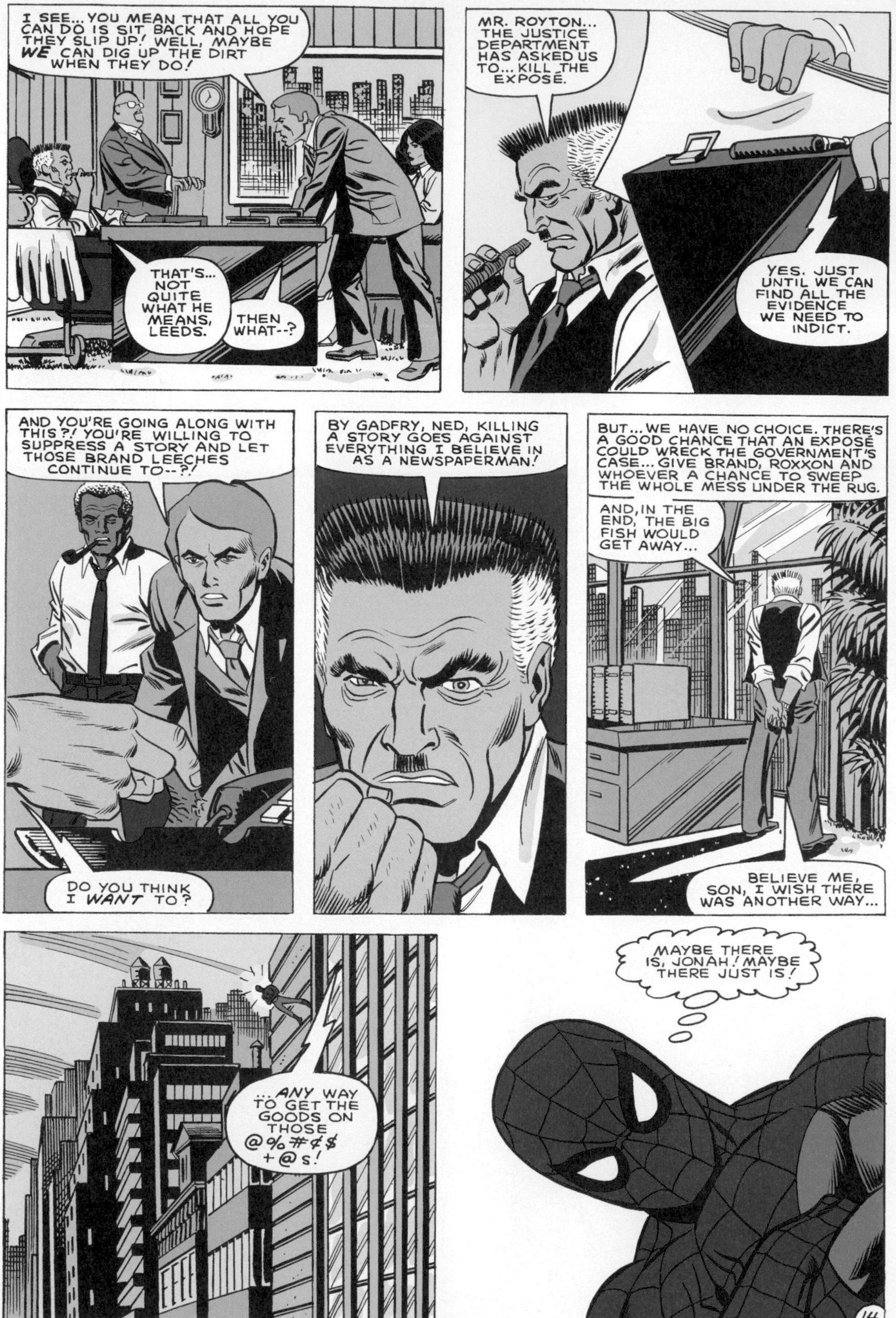
I SEE...YOU MEAN THAT ALL YOU CAN DO IS SIT BACK AND HOPE THEY SLIP UP! WELL, MAYBE WE CAN DIG UP THE DIRT WHEN THEY DO!
THAT'S... NOT QUITE WHAT HE MEANS, LEEDS.
THEN WHAT--?
MR. ROYTON... THE JUSTICE DEPARTMENT HAS ASKED US TO... KILL THE EXPOSÉ.
YES. JUST UNTIL WE CAN FIND ALL THE EVIDENCE WE NEED TO INDICT.
AND YOU'RE GOING ALONG WITH THIS?! YOU'RE WILLING TO SUPPRESS A STORY AND LET THOSE BRAND LEECHES CONTINUE TO--?!
DO YOU THINK I WANT TO?
BY GADFRY, NED, KILLING A STORY GOES AGAINST EVERYTHING I BELIEVE IN AS A NEWSPAPERMAN!
BUT...WE HAVE NO CHOICE. THERE'S A GOOD CHANCE THAT AN EXPOSÉ COULD WRECK THE GOVERNMENT'S CASE...GIVE BRAND, ROXXON AND WHOEVER A CHANCE TO SWEEP THE WHOLE MESS UNDER THE RUG.
AND, IN THE END, THE BIG FISH WOULD GET AWAY...
BELIEVE ME, SON, I WISH THERE WAS ANOTHER WAY...
...ANY WAY TO GET THE GOODS ON THOSE @%#¢$ +@s!
MAYBE THERE IS, JONAH! MAYBE THERE JUST IS!
14

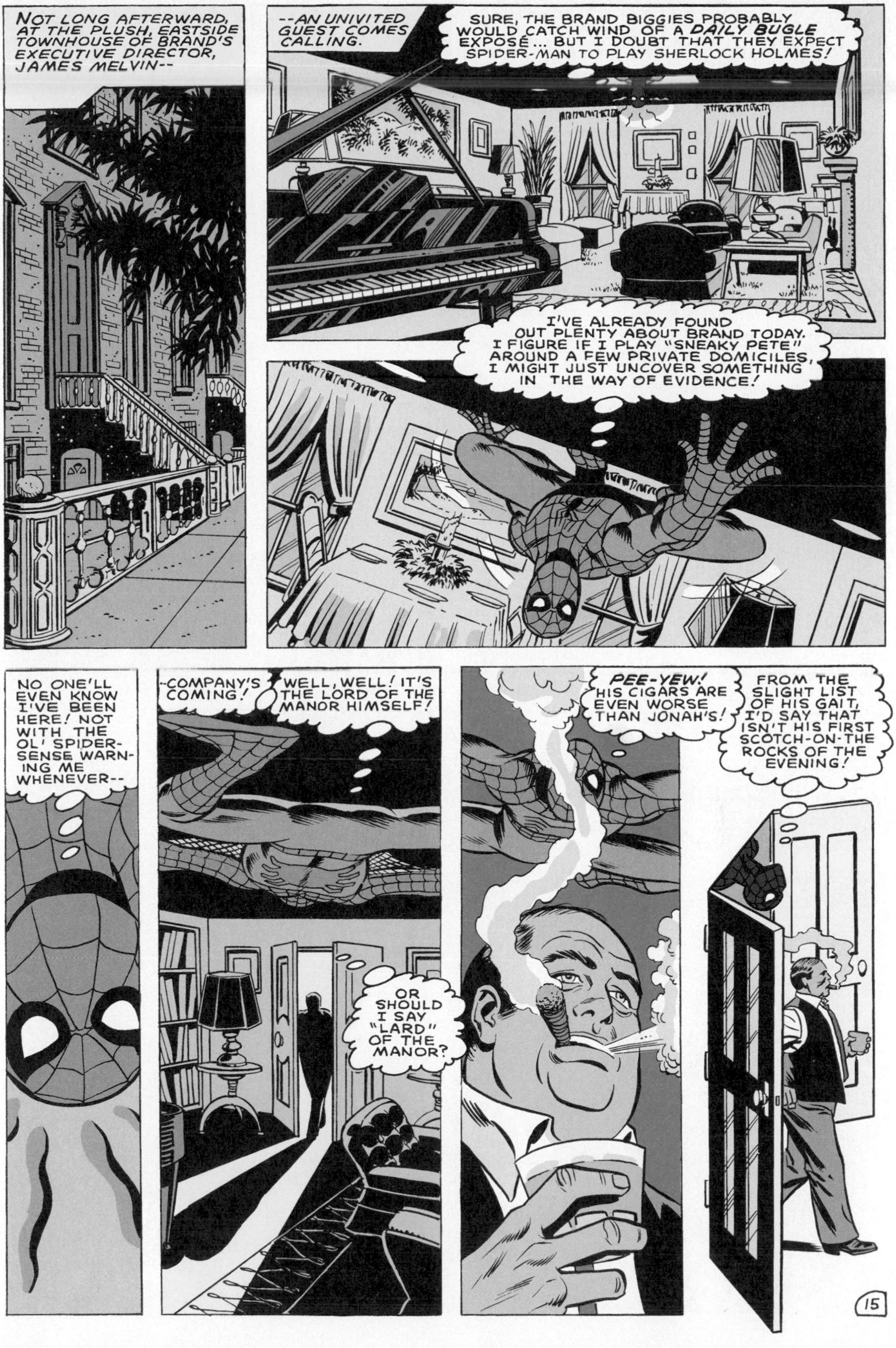
NOT LONG AFTERWARD, AT THE PLUSH, EASTSIDE TOWNHOUSE OF BRAND'S EXECUTIVE DIRECTOR, JAMES MELVIN--
--AN UNIVITED GUEST COMES CALLING.
SURE, THE BRAND BIGGIES PROBABLY WOULD CATCH WIND OF A DAILY BUGLE EXPOSÉ ... BUT I DOUBT THAT THEY EXPECT SPIDER-MAN TO PLAY SHERLOCK HOLMES!
I'VE ALREADY FOUND OUT PLENTY ABOUT BRAND TODAY. I FIGURE IF I PLAY "SNEAKY PETE" AROUND A FEW PRIVATE DOMICILES, I MIGHT JUST UNCOVER SOMETHING IN THE WAY OF EVIDENCE!
NO ONE'LL EVEN KNOW I'VE BEEN HERE! NOT WITH THE OL' SPIDER-SENSE WARNING ME WHENEVER--
--COMPANY'S COMING!
WELL, WELL! IT'S THE LORD OF THE MANOR HIMSELF!
OR SHOULD I SAY "LARD" OF THE MANOR?
PEE-YEW! HIS CIGARS ARE EVEN WORSE THAN JONAH'S!
FROM THE SLIGHT LIST OF HIS GAIT, I'D SAY THAT ISN'T HIS FIRST SCOTCH-ON-THE ROCKS OF THE EVENING!
15

LOOKS LIKE TODAY'S LITTLE FRACAS AT THE PLANT HAS MELLY-BELLY BUGGED!

HE *WOULD* HAVE TO PLOP DOWN IN HIS STUDY! IF THERE'S ANYTHING TO BE FOUND, IT WOULD BE IN THERE!

MEEP MEEP

PRIORITY CALL...

...PRIORITY CALL... PRIORITY

KLIK

ALL RIGHT, ALREADY!

VIDEOPHONE DEPLOYED

INCOMING CALL... FROM... JOHN T. GAMELIN... PRESIDENT... ROXXON OIL. SECURITY SCRAMBLER ON!

MELVIN, I JUST GOT OFF THE LINE WITH THE CHAIRMAN OF THE BOARD! WHAT IN BLAZES IS GOING ON? YOUR QUEENS PLANT EVAC-UATION IS ALL OVER THE EVENING NEWS!!

I CAN EXPLAIN EVERYTHING, J.T.

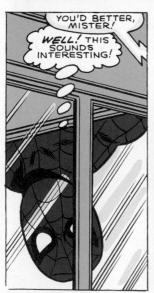

YOU'D BETTER, MISTER!

WELL! THIS SOUNDS INTERESTING!

IT WAS WILL-O'-THE-WISP AGAIN, SIR! HE WRECKED A NEW SUPER-OPERATIVE EXPERIMENT!

BUT HE WON'T BE BOTHERING US ANYMORE! HE WAS WEAKENED BY A MAGNO-PULSE GUN --

--AND DROWNED... IN JAMAICA... BAY.

YOU'RE CERTAIN OF THAT, MELVIN? MELVIN?

16

BUT THE BRAND EXECUTIVE DOES NOT REPLY, SO DRAWN IS HIS ATTENTION TO THE BALL OF LIGHT WHICH SEEMS TO OOZE THROUGH THE VERY SUBSTANCE OF THE FAR WALL...

...THE BALL OF LIGHT WHICH QUICKLY ASSUMES THE FORM OF MAN!

GOOD EVENING, MR. MELVIN.

WE HAVE SOME UNFINISHED BUSINESS TO ATTEND TO!

NO! IT'S NOT POSSIBLE! YOU DROWNED!

GET BACK!

I CANNOT DROWN, MELVIN. I DO NOT BREATHE...

...I AM NO LONGER QUITE SO HUMAN!

AS FOR GETTING BACK... I THINK NOT!

PUT THE GUN DOWN, MELVIN.

BE SEATED.

PUT... GUN... DOWN. BE... SEATED.

17

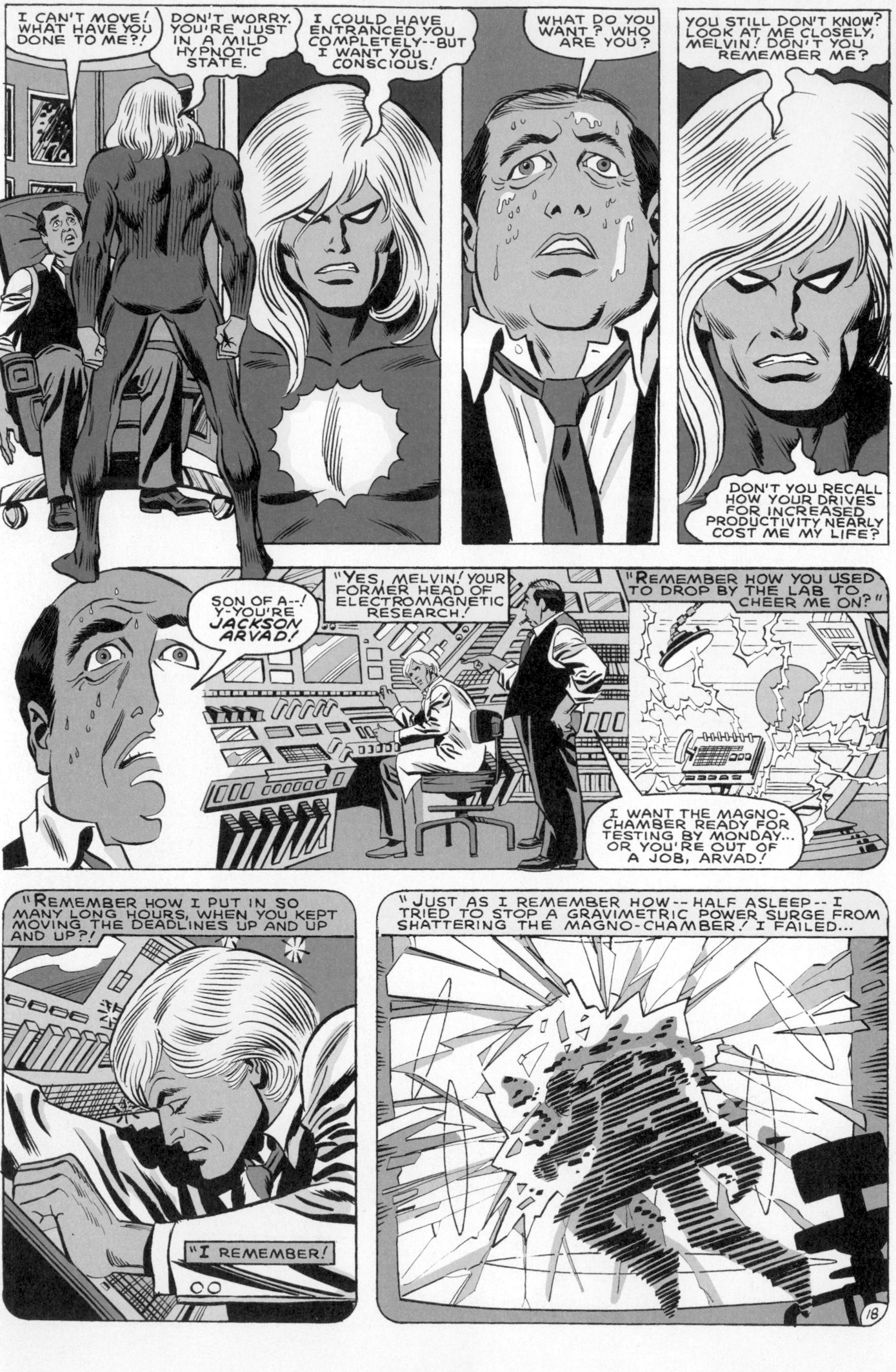
I CAN'T MOVE! WHAT HAVE YOU DONE TO ME?!
DON'T WORRY. YOU'RE JUST IN A MILD HYPNOTIC STATE.
I COULD HAVE ENTRANCED YOU COMPLETELY--BUT I WANT YOU CONSCIOUS!
WHAT DO YOU WANT? WHO ARE YOU?
YOU STILL DON'T KNOW? LOOK AT ME CLOSELY, MELVIN! DON'T YOU REMEMBER ME?
DON'T YOU RECALL HOW YOUR DRIVES FOR INCREASED PRODUCTIVITY NEARLY COST ME MY LIFE?
SON OF A--! Y-YOU'RE JACKSON ARVAD!
"YES, MELVIN! YOUR FORMER HEAD OF ELECTROMAGNETIC RESEARCH!
"REMEMBER HOW YOU USED TO DROP BY THE LAB TO CHEER ME ON?"
I WANT THE MAGNO-CHAMBER READY FOR TESTING BY MONDAY... OR YOU'RE OUT OF A JOB, ARVAD!
"REMEMBER HOW I PUT IN SO MANY LONG HOURS, WHEN YOU KEPT MOVING THE DEADLINES UP AND UP AND UP?!
"I REMEMBER!
"JUST AS I REMEMBER HOW--HALF ASLEEP--I TRIED TO STOP A GRAVIMETRIC POWER SURGE FROM SHATTERING THE MAGNO-CHAMBER! I FAILED...
18

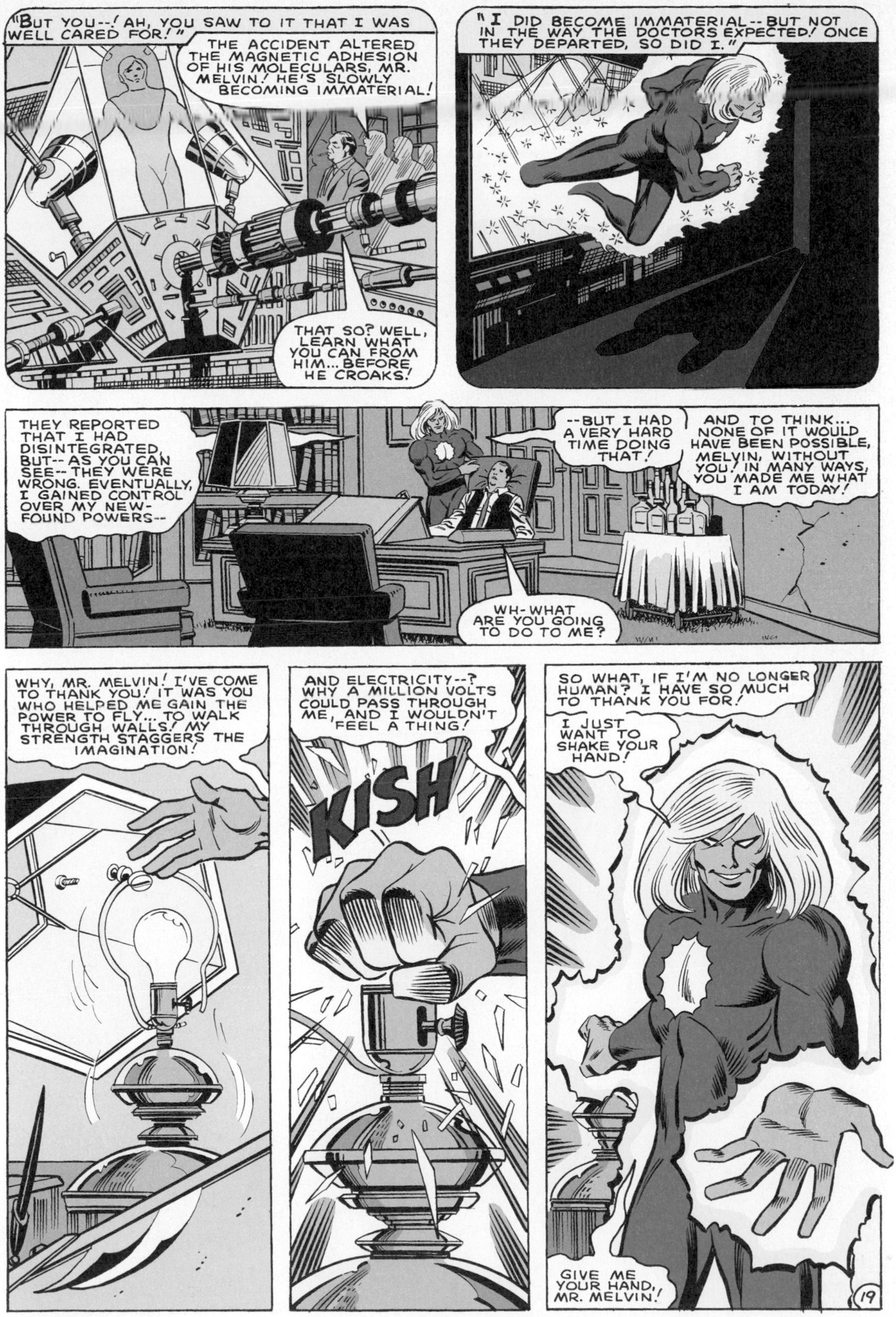
"BUT YOU--! AH, YOU SAW TO IT THAT I WAS WELL CARED FOR!"
THE ACCIDENT ALTERED THE MAGNETIC ADHESION OF HIS MOLECULARS, MR. MELVIN! HE'S SLOWLY BECOMING IMMATERIAL!
THAT SO? WELL, LEARN WHAT YOU CAN FROM HIM... BEFORE HE CROAKS!
"I DID BECOME IMMATERIAL--BUT NOT IN THE WAY THE DOCTORS EXPECTED! ONCE THEY DEPARTED, SO DID I."
THEY REPORTED THAT I HAD DISINTEGRATED, BUT--AS YOU CAN SEE--THEY WERE WRONG. EVENTUALLY, I GAINED CONTROL OVER MY NEW-FOUND POWERS--
--BUT I HAD A VERY HARD TIME DOING THAT!
AND TO THINK... NONE OF IT WOULD HAVE BEEN POSSIBLE, MELVIN, WITHOUT YOU! IN MANY WAYS, YOU MADE ME WHAT I AM TODAY!
WH-WHAT ARE YOU GOING TO DO TO ME?
WHY, MR. MELVIN! I'VE COME TO THANK YOU! IT WAS YOU WHO HELPED ME GAIN THE POWER TO FLY... TO WALK THROUGH WALLS! MY STRENGTH STAGGERS THE IMAGINATION!
AND ELECTRICITY--? WHY A MILLION VOLTS COULD PASS THROUGH ME, AND I WOULDN'T FEEL A THING!
KISH
SO WHAT, IF I'M NO LONGER HUMAN? I HAVE SO MUCH TO THANK YOU FOR!
I JUST WANT TO SHAKE YOUR HAND!
GIVE ME YOUR HAND, MR. MELVIN!
19

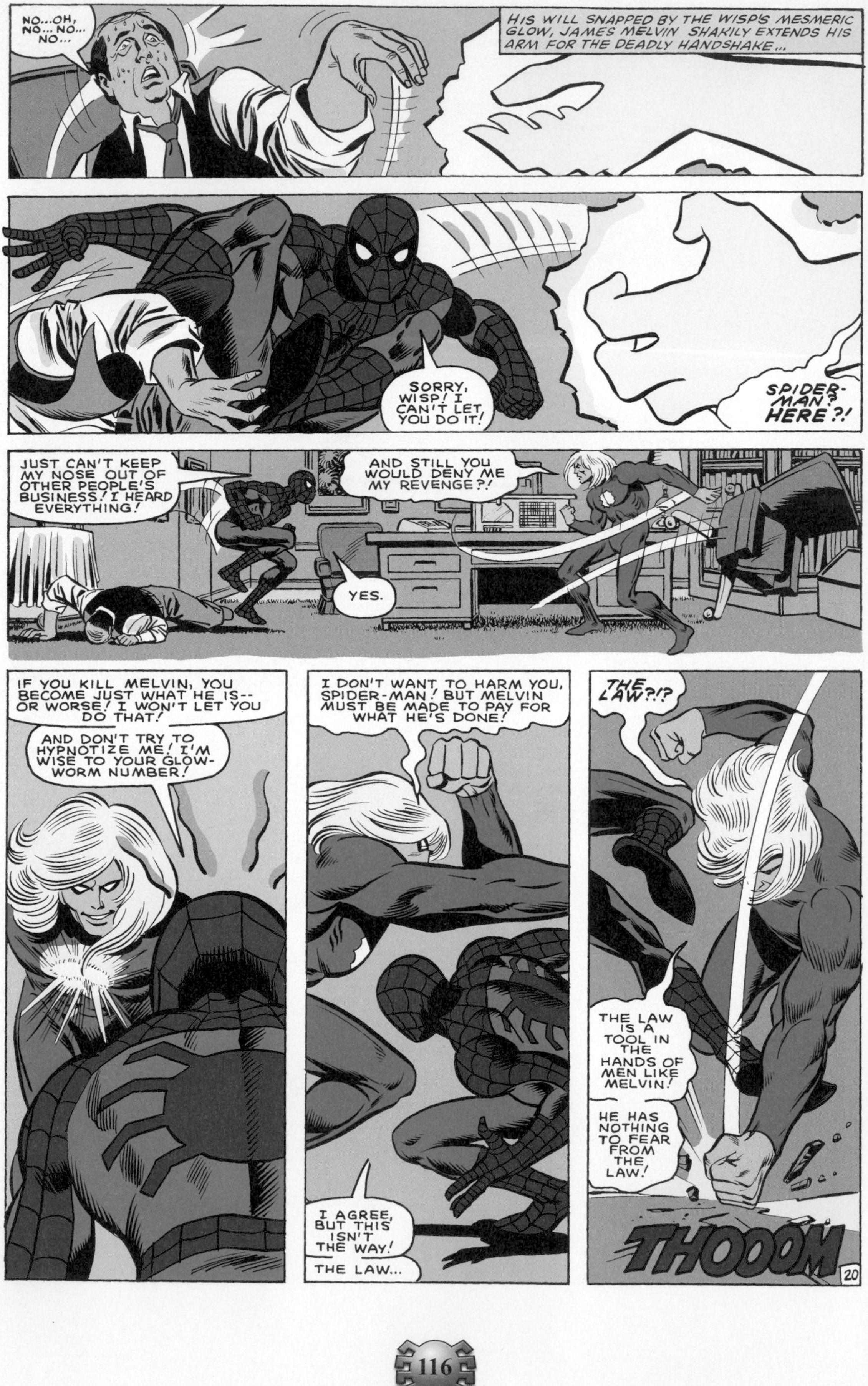
NO...OH, NO...NO... NO...
HIS WILL SNAPPED BY THE WISP'S MESMERIC GLOW, JAMES MELVIN SHAKILY EXTENDS HIS ARM FOR THE DEADLY HANDSHAKE...
SORRY, WISP! I CAN'T LET YOU DO IT!
SPIDER-MAN? HERE?!
JUST CAN'T KEEP MY NOSE OUT OF OTHER PEOPLE'S BUSINESS! I HEARD EVERYTHING!
AND STILL YOU WOULD DENY ME MY REVENGE?!
YES.
IF YOU KILL MELVIN, YOU BECOME JUST WHAT HE IS-- OR WORSE! I WON'T LET YOU DO THAT!
AND DON'T TRY TO HYPNOTIZE ME! I'M WISE TO YOUR GLOW-WORM NUMBER!
I DON'T WANT TO HARM YOU, SPIDER-MAN! BUT MELVIN MUST BE MADE TO PAY FOR WHAT HE'S DONE!
I AGREE, BUT THIS ISN'T THE WAY!
THE LAW...
THE LAW?!?
THE LAW IS A TOOL IN THE HANDS OF MEN LIKE MELVIN!
HE HAS NOTHING TO FEAR FROM THE LAW!
THOOOM
20

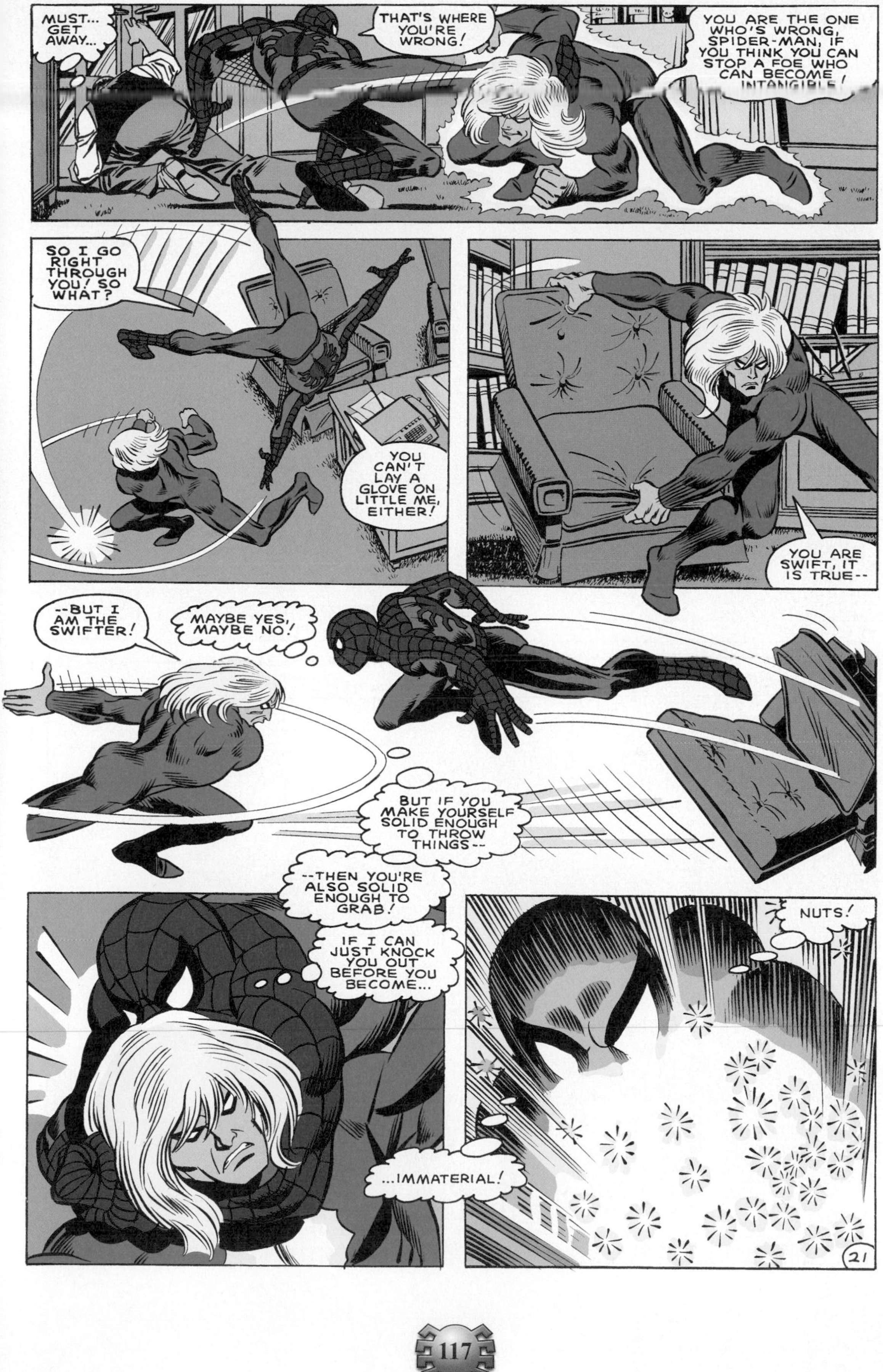
MUST... GET AWAY...
THAT'S WHERE YOU'RE WRONG!
YOU ARE THE ONE WHO'S WRONG, SPIDER-MAN, IF YOU THINK YOU CAN STOP A FOE WHO CAN BECOME INTANGIBLE!
SO I GO RIGHT THROUGH YOU! SO WHAT?
YOU CAN'T LAY A GLOVE ON LITTLE ME, EITHER!
YOU ARE SWIFT, IT IS TRUE--
--BUT I AM THE SWIFTER!
MAYBE YES, MAYBE NO!
BUT IF YOU MAKE YOURSELF SOLID ENOUGH TO THROW THINGS--
--THEN YOU'RE ALSO SOLID ENOUGH TO GRAB!
IF I CAN JUST KNOCK YOU OUT BEFORE YOU BECOME...
...IMMATERIAL!
NUTS!
21

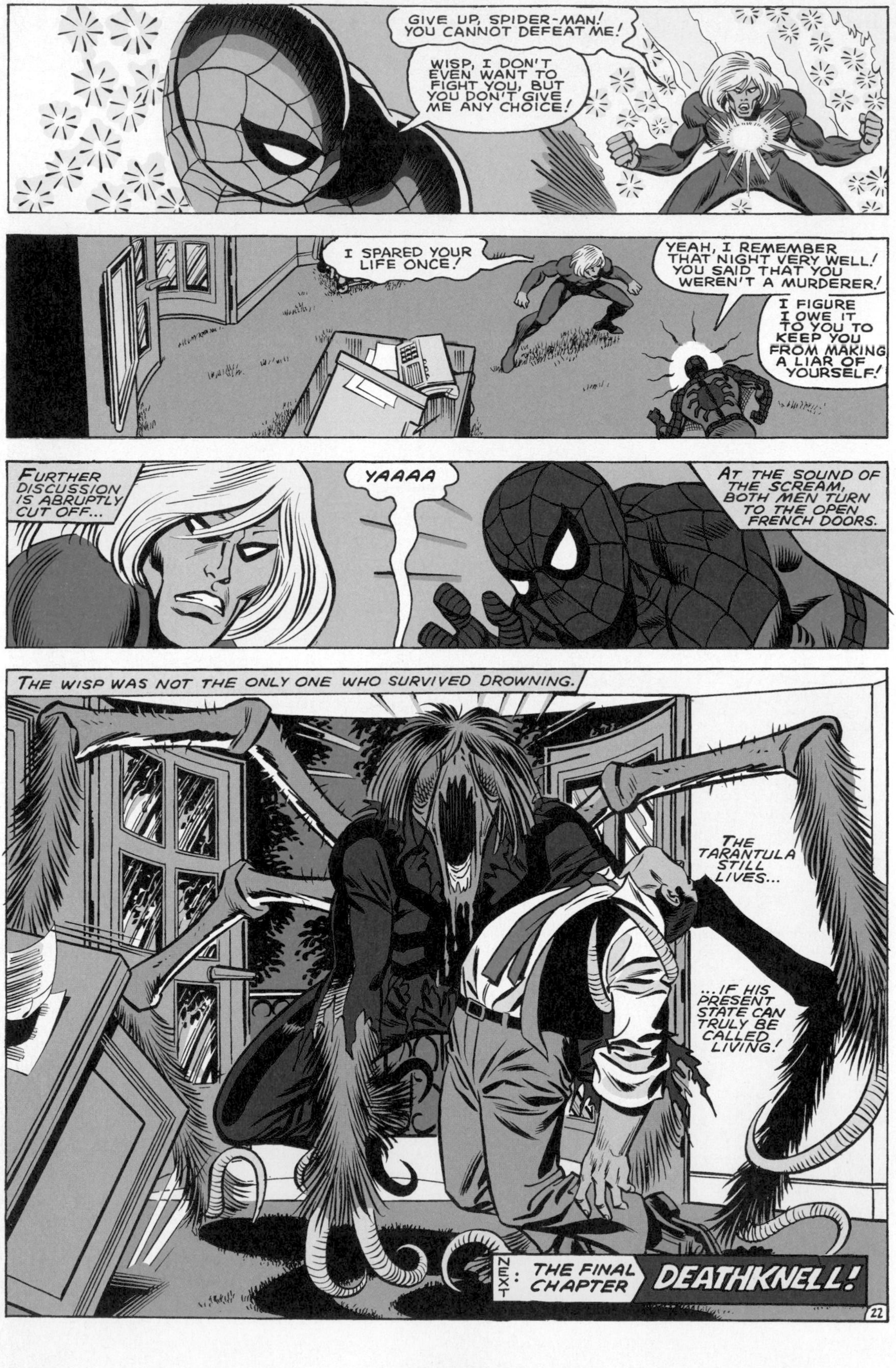
GIVE UP, SPIDER-MAN! YOU CANNOT DEFEAT ME!
WISP, I DON'T EVEN WANT TO FIGHT YOU, BUT YOU DON'T GIVE ME ANY CHOICE!
I SPARED YOUR LIFE ONCE!
YEAH, I REMEMBER THAT NIGHT VERY WELL! YOU SAID THAT YOU WEREN'T A MURDERER!
I FIGURE I OWE IT TO YOU TO KEEP YOU FROM MAKING A LIAR OF YOURSELF!
FURTHER DISCUSSION IS ABRUPTLY CUT OFF...
YAAAA
AT THE SOUND OF THE SCREAM, BOTH MEN TURN TO THE OPEN FRENCH DOORS.
THE WISP WAS NOT THE ONLY ONE WHO SURVIVED DROWNING.
THE TARANTULA STILL LIVES...
...IF HIS PRESENT STATE CAN TRULY BE CALLED LIVING!
NEXT: THE FINAL CHAPTER DEATHKNELL!
22

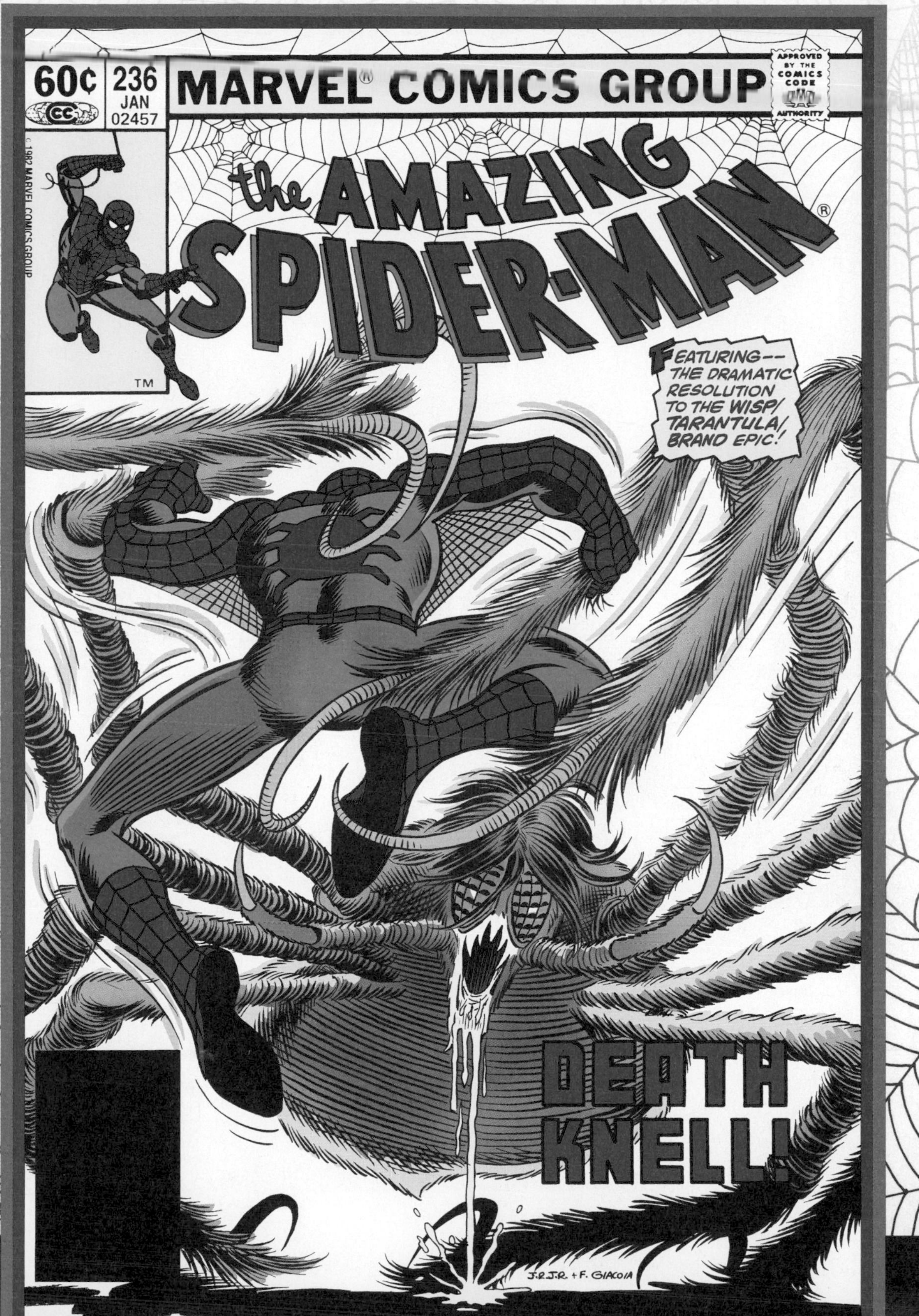
60¢
236
JAN
02457
MARVEL COMICS GROUP
APPROVED BY THE COMICS CODE AUTHORITY
© 1982 MARVEL COMICS GROUP
the AMAZING SPIDER-MAN
TM
FEATURING-- THE DRAMATIC RESOLUTION TO THE WISP/ TARANTULA/ BRAND EPIC!
DEATH KNELL!
J.R.JR. + F. GIACOIA

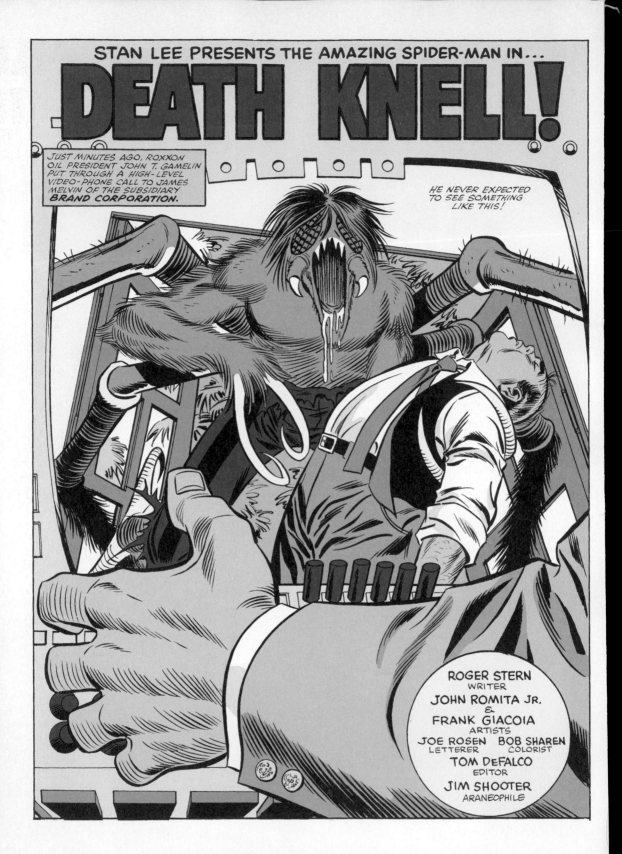

STAN LEE PRESENTS THE AMAZING SPIDER-MAN IN...

DEATH KNELL!

JUST MINUTES AGO, ROXXON OIL PRESIDENT JOHN T. GAMELIN PUT THROUGH A HIGH-LEVEL VIDEO-PHONE CALL TO JAMES MELVIN OF THE SUBSIDIARY **BRAND CORPORATION.**

HE NEVER EXPECTED TO SEE SOMETHING LIKE THIS!

ROGER STERN
WRITER

JOHN ROMITA JR.
&
FRANK GIACOIA
ARTISTS

JOE ROSEN   BOB SHAREN
LETTERER   COLORIST

TOM DEFALCO
EDITOR

JIM SHOOTER
ARANEOPHILE

120

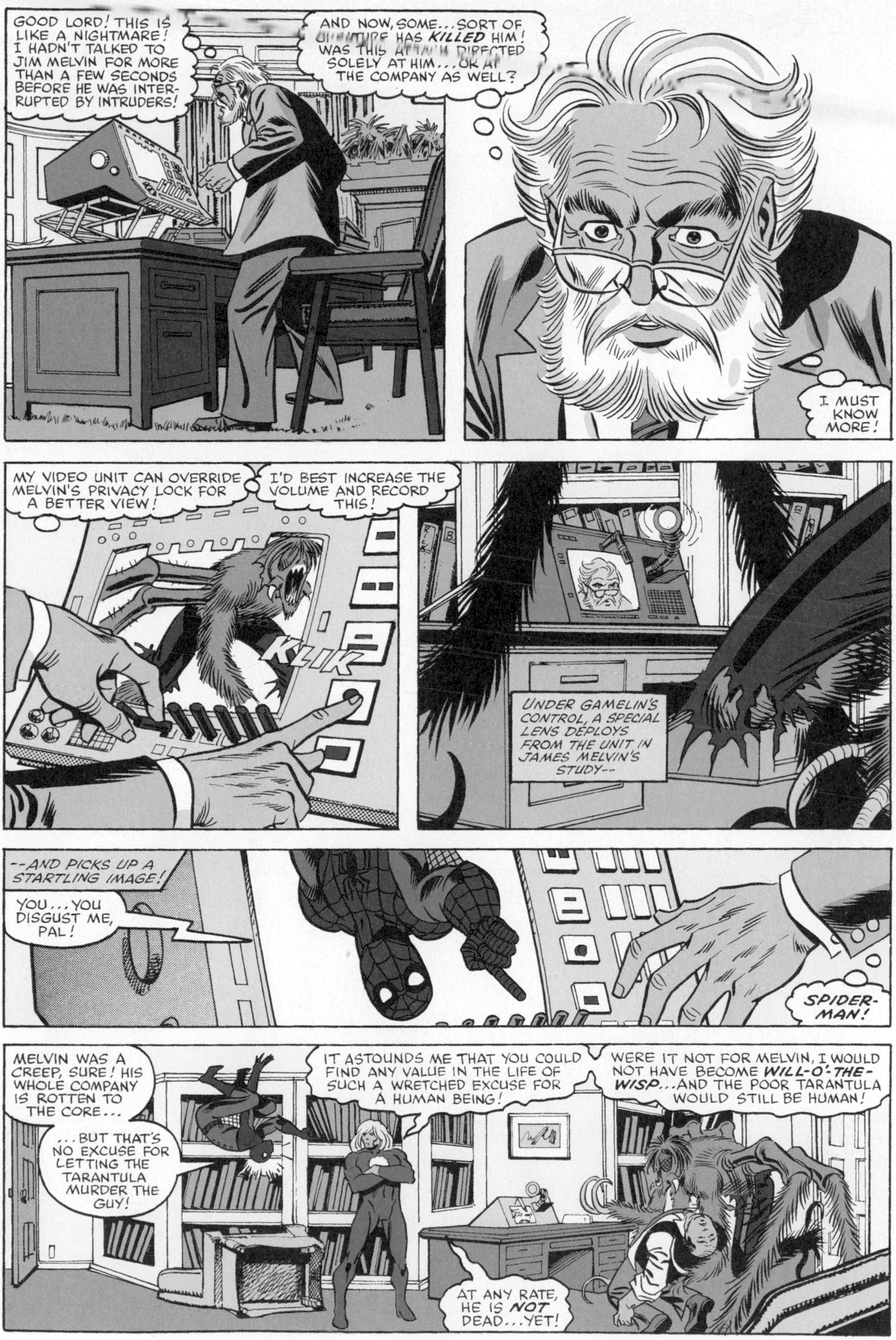
GOOD LORD! THIS IS LIKE A NIGHTMARE! I HADN'T TALKED TO JIM MELVIN FOR MORE THAN A FEW SECONDS BEFORE HE WAS INTERRUPTED BY INTRUDERS!
AND NOW, SOME...SORT OF CREATURE HAS KILLED HIM! WAS THIS ATTACK DIRECTED SOLELY AT HIM...OR AT THE COMPANY AS WELL?
I MUST KNOW MORE!
MY VIDEO UNIT CAN OVERRIDE MELVIN'S PRIVACY LOCK FOR A BETTER VIEW!
I'D BEST INCREASE THE VOLUME AND RECORD THIS!
KLIK
UNDER GAMELIN'S CONTROL, A SPECIAL LENS DEPLOYS FROM THE UNIT IN JAMES MELVIN'S STUDY--
--AND PICKS UP A STARTLING IMAGE!
YOU...YOU DISGUST ME, PAL!
SPIDER-MAN!
MELVIN WAS A CREEP, SURE! HIS WHOLE COMPANY IS ROTTEN TO THE CORE...
...BUT THAT'S NO EXCUSE FOR LETTING THE TARANTULA MURDER THE GUY!
IT ASTOUNDS ME THAT YOU COULD FIND ANY VALUE IN THE LIFE OF SUCH A WRETCHED EXCUSE FOR A HUMAN BEING!
WERE IT NOT FOR MELVIN, I WOULD NOT HAVE BECOME WILL-O'-THE-WISP...AND THE POOR TARANTULA WOULD STILL BE HUMAN!
AT ANY RATE, HE IS NOT DEAD...YET!

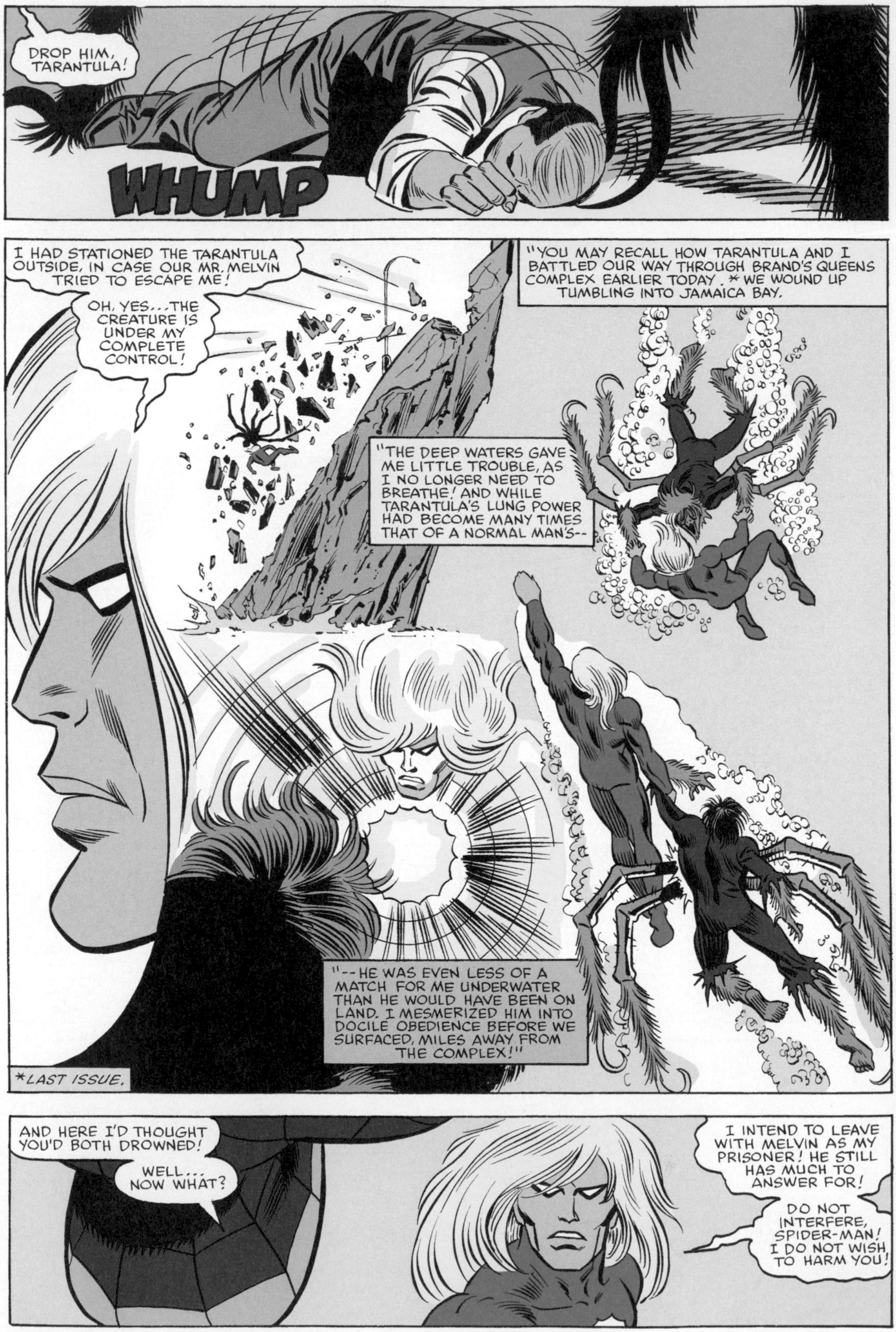
DROP HIM, TARANTULA!
WHUMP
I HAD STATIONED THE TARANTULA OUTSIDE, IN CASE OUR MR. MELVIN TRIED TO ESCAPE ME!
OH, YES... THE CREATURE IS UNDER MY COMPLETE CONTROL!
"YOU MAY RECALL HOW TARANTULA AND I BATTLED OUR WAY THROUGH BRAND'S QUEENS COMPLEX EARLIER TODAY.* WE WOUND UP TUMBLING INTO JAMAICA BAY.
"THE DEEP WATERS GAVE ME LITTLE TROUBLE, AS I NO LONGER NEED TO BREATHE! AND WHILE TARANTULA'S LUNG POWER HAD BECOME MANY TIMES THAT OF A NORMAL MAN'S--
"--HE WAS EVEN LESS OF A MATCH FOR ME UNDERWATER THAN HE WOULD HAVE BEEN ON LAND. I MESMERIZED HIM INTO DOCILE OBEDIENCE BEFORE WE SURFACED, MILES AWAY FROM THE COMPLEX!"
*LAST ISSUE.
AND HERE I'D THOUGHT YOU'D BOTH DROWNED!
WELL... NOW WHAT?
I INTEND TO LEAVE WITH MELVIN AS MY PRISONER! HE STILL HAS MUCH TO ANSWER FOR!
DO NOT INTERFERE, SPIDER-MAN! I DO NOT WISH TO HARM YOU!

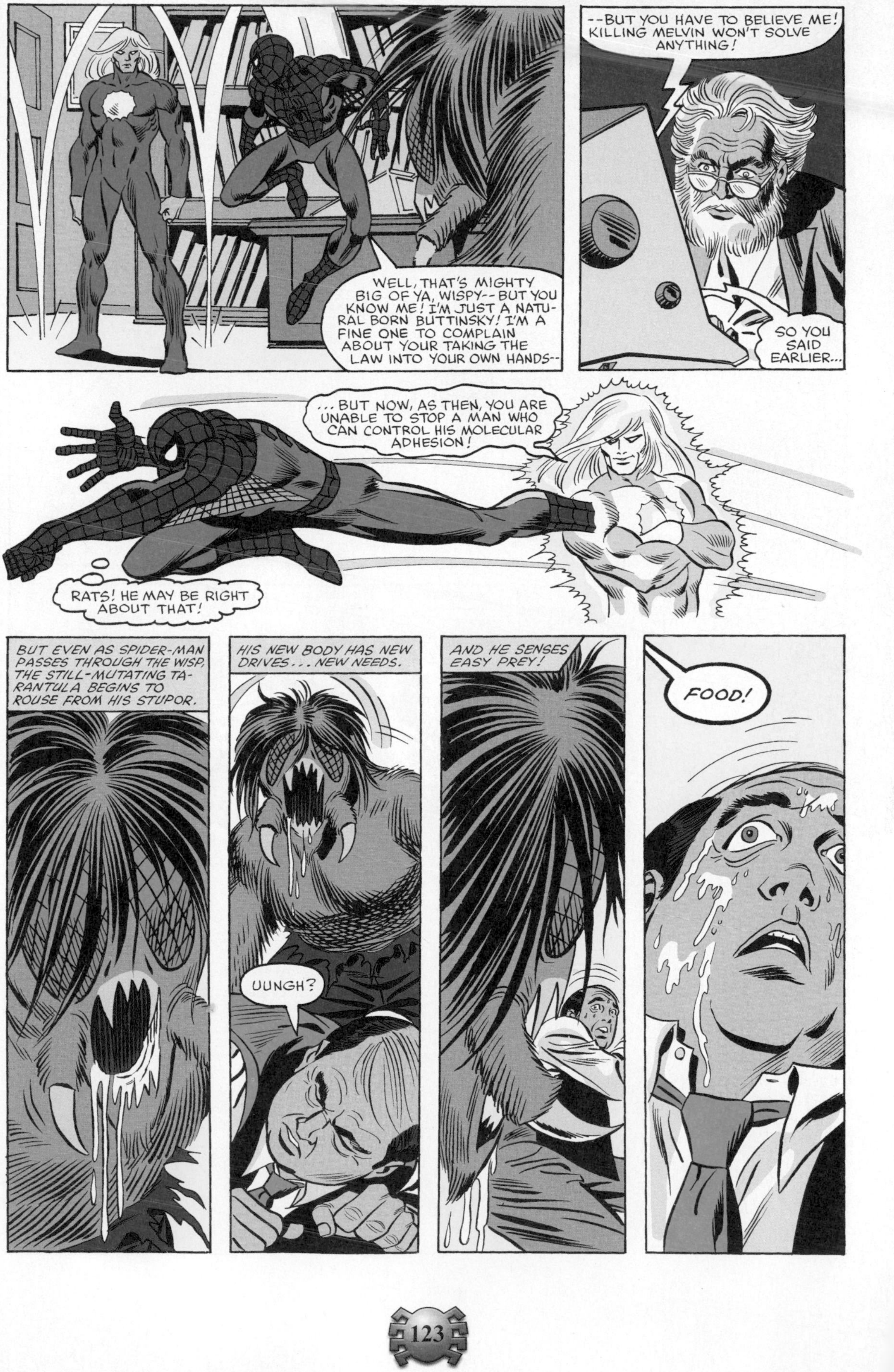

WELL, THAT'S MIGHTY BIG OF YA, WISPY-- BUT YOU KNOW ME! I'M JUST A NATURAL BORN BUTTINSKY! I'M A FINE ONE TO COMPLAIN ABOUT YOUR TAKING THE LAW INTO YOUR OWN HANDS--
--BUT YOU HAVE TO BELIEVE ME! KILLING MELVIN WON'T SOLVE ANYTHING!
SO YOU SAID EARLIER...
...BUT NOW, AS THEN, YOU ARE UNABLE TO STOP A MAN WHO CAN CONTROL HIS MOLECULAR ADHESION!
RATS! HE MAY BE RIGHT ABOUT THAT!
BUT EVEN AS SPIDER-MAN PASSES THROUGH THE WISP, THE STILL-MUTATING TARANTULA BEGINS TO ROUSE FROM HIS STUPOR.
HIS NEW BODY HAS NEW DRIVES... NEW NEEDS.
UUNGH?
AND HE SENSES EASY PREY!
FOOD!

NO! MELVIN IS MINE! YOU'RE NOT TO TOUCH HIM UNTIL I'VE HAD MY REVENGE!

YOU... WILL NOT LET ME FEED ON HIM?!?

THEN... I... WILL FEED ON **YOU**!!

WHEW! TARANTULA'S REALLY GONE BUG-HOUSE! I HAVE TO HOPE THE WISP CAN HANDLE HIM...

...I CAN'T PASS UP THIS DIVERSION!

HEY! LEGGO--!

PUT A SOCK IN IT, MELVIN, OR I MIGHT JUST BE TEMPTED TO THINK TWICE ABOUT SAVING YOUR BEHIND!

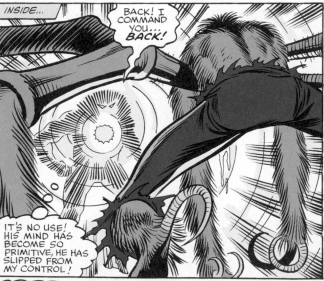

INSIDE...

BACK! I COMMAND YOU... **BACK**!

IT'S NO USE! HIS MIND HAS BECOME SO PRIMITIVE, HE HAS SLIPPED FROM MY CONTROL!

FORCE IS MY ONLY OPTION!

WHUD

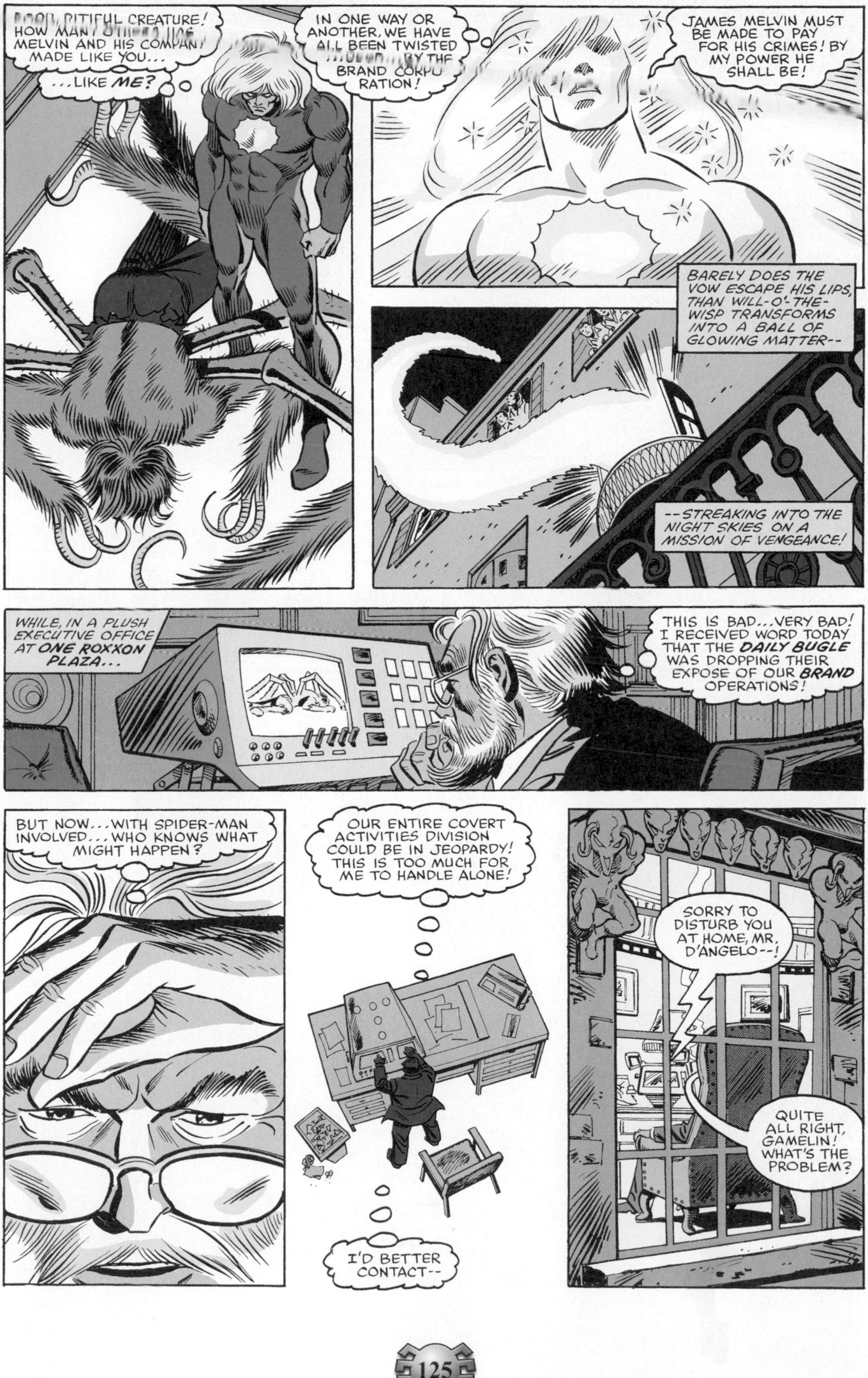
PITIFUL CREATURE! HOW MAN... MELVIN AND HIS COMPAN... MADE LIKE YOU...
...LIKE ME?
IN ONE WAY OR ANOTHER, WE HAVE ALL BEEN TWISTED ... BY THE BRAND CORPORATION!
JAMES MELVIN MUST BE MADE TO PAY FOR HIS CRIMES! BY MY POWER HE SHALL BE!
BARELY DOES THE VOW ESCAPE HIS LIPS, THAN WILL-O'-THE-WISP TRANSFORMS INTO A BALL OF GLOWING MATTER--
--STREAKING INTO THE NIGHT SKIES ON A MISSION OF VENGEANCE!
WHILE, IN A PLUSH EXECUTIVE OFFICE AT ONE ROXXON PLAZA...
THIS IS BAD...VERY BAD! I RECEIVED WORD TODAY THAT THE DAILY BUGLE WAS DROPPING THEIR EXPOSE OF OUR BRAND OPERATIONS!
BUT NOW...WITH SPIDER-MAN INVOLVED...WHO KNOWS WHAT MIGHT HAPPEN?
OUR ENTIRE COVERT ACTIVITIES DIVISION COULD BE IN JEOPARDY! THIS IS TOO MUCH FOR ME TO HANDLE ALONE!
I'D BETTER CONTACT--
SORRY TO DISTURB YOU AT HOME, MR. D'ANGELO--!
QUITE ALL RIGHT, GAMELIN! WHAT'S THE PROBLEM?

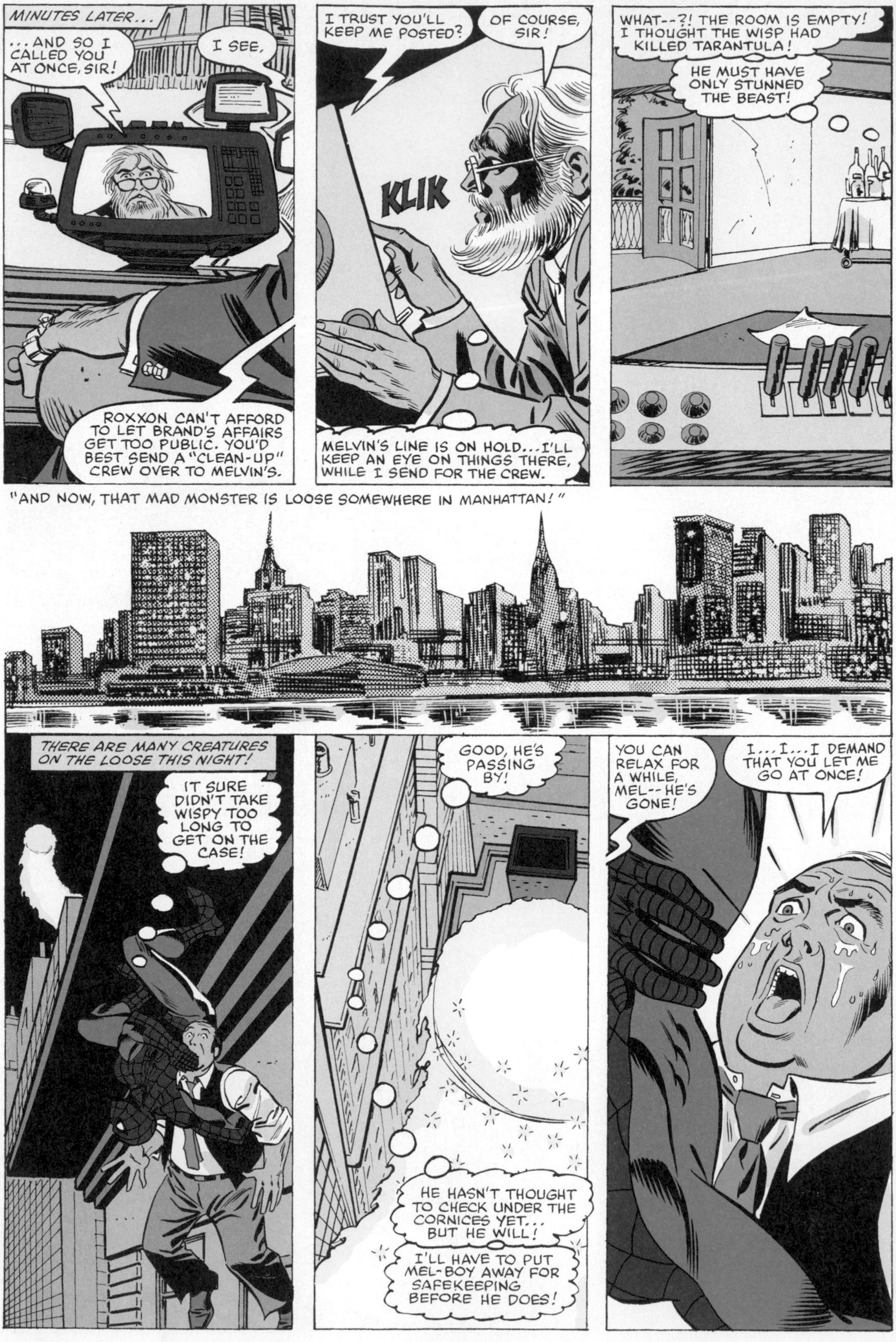
MINUTES LATER...
...AND SO I CALLED YOU AT ONCE, SIR!
I SEE,
ROXXON CAN'T AFFORD TO LET BRAND'S AFFAIRS GET TOO PUBLIC. YOU'D BEST SEND A "CLEAN-UP" CREW OVER TO MELVIN'S.
I TRUST YOU'LL KEEP ME POSTED?
OF COURSE, SIR!
KLIK
MELVIN'S LINE IS ON HOLD... I'LL KEEP AN EYE ON THINGS THERE, WHILE I SEND FOR THE CREW.
WHAT--?! THE ROOM IS EMPTY! I THOUGHT THE WISP HAD KILLED TARANTULA!
HE MUST HAVE ONLY STUNNED THE BEAST!
"AND NOW, THAT MAD MONSTER IS LOOSE SOMEWHERE IN MANHATTAN!"
THERE ARE MANY CREATURES ON THE LOOSE THIS NIGHT!
IT SURE DIDN'T TAKE WISPY TOO LONG TO GET ON THE CASE!
GOOD, HE'S PASSING BY!
HE HASN'T THOUGHT TO CHECK UNDER THE CORNICES YET... BUT HE WILL!
I'LL HAVE TO PUT MEL-BOY AWAY FOR SAFEKEEPING BEFORE HE DOES!
YOU CAN RELAX FOR A WHILE, MEL-- HE'S GONE!
I... I... I DEMAND THAT YOU LET ME GO AT ONCE!

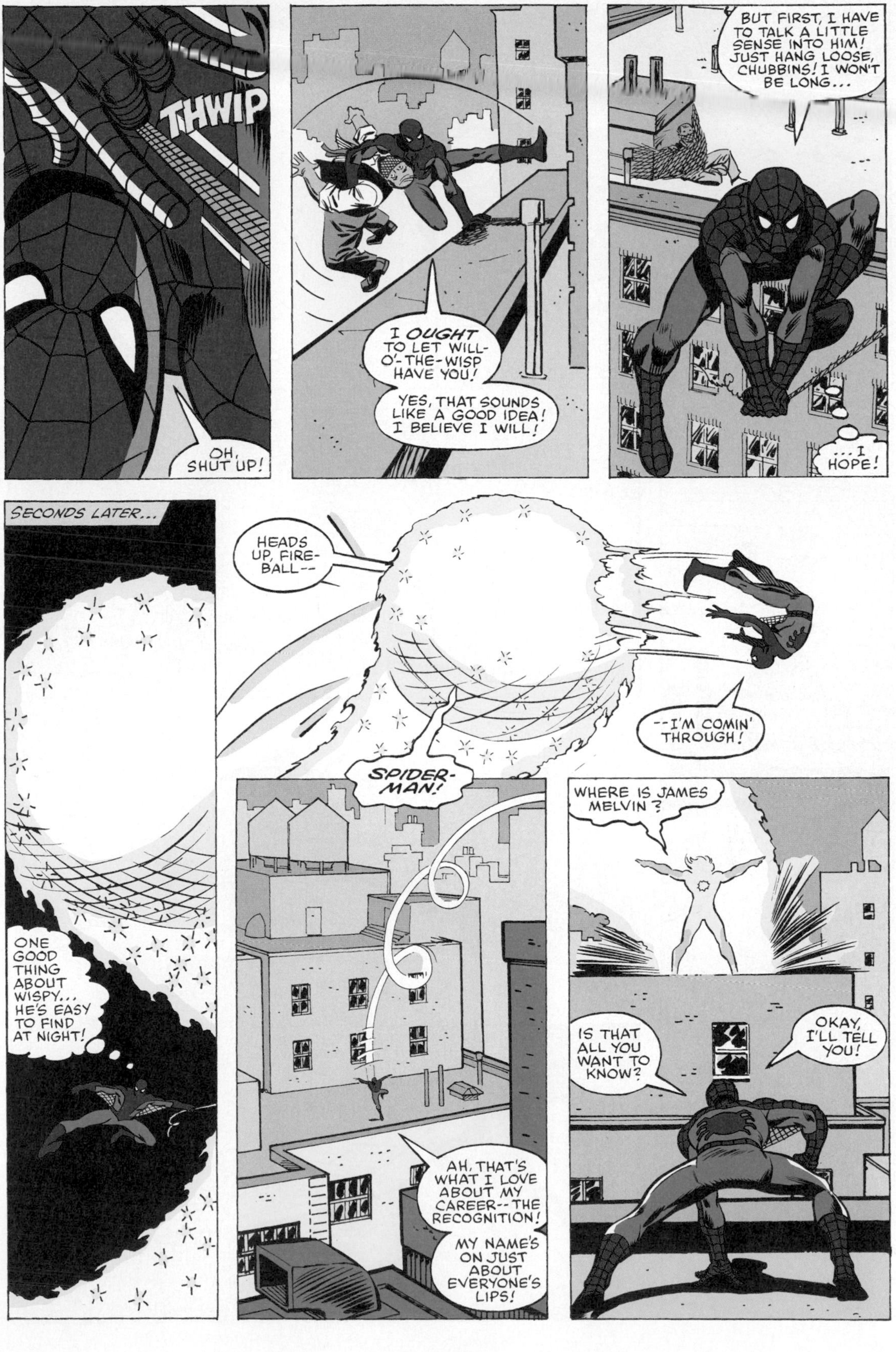
THWIP
OH, SHUT UP!
I OUGHT TO LET WILL-O'-THE-WISP HAVE YOU!
YES, THAT SOUNDS LIKE A GOOD IDEA! I BELIEVE I WILL!
BUT FIRST, I HAVE TO TALK A LITTLE SENSE INTO HIM! JUST HANG LOOSE, CHUBBINS! I WON'T BE LONG...
...I HOPE!
SECONDS LATER...
ONE GOOD THING ABOUT WISPY... HE'S EASY TO FIND AT NIGHT!
HEADS UP, FIRE-BALL--
--I'M COMIN' THROUGH!
SPIDER-MAN!
AH, THAT'S WHAT I LOVE ABOUT MY CAREER--THE RECOGNITION!
MY NAME'S ON JUST ABOUT EVERYONE'S LIPS!
WHERE IS JAMES MELVIN?
IS THAT ALL YOU WANT TO KNOW?
OKAY, I'LL TELL YOU!

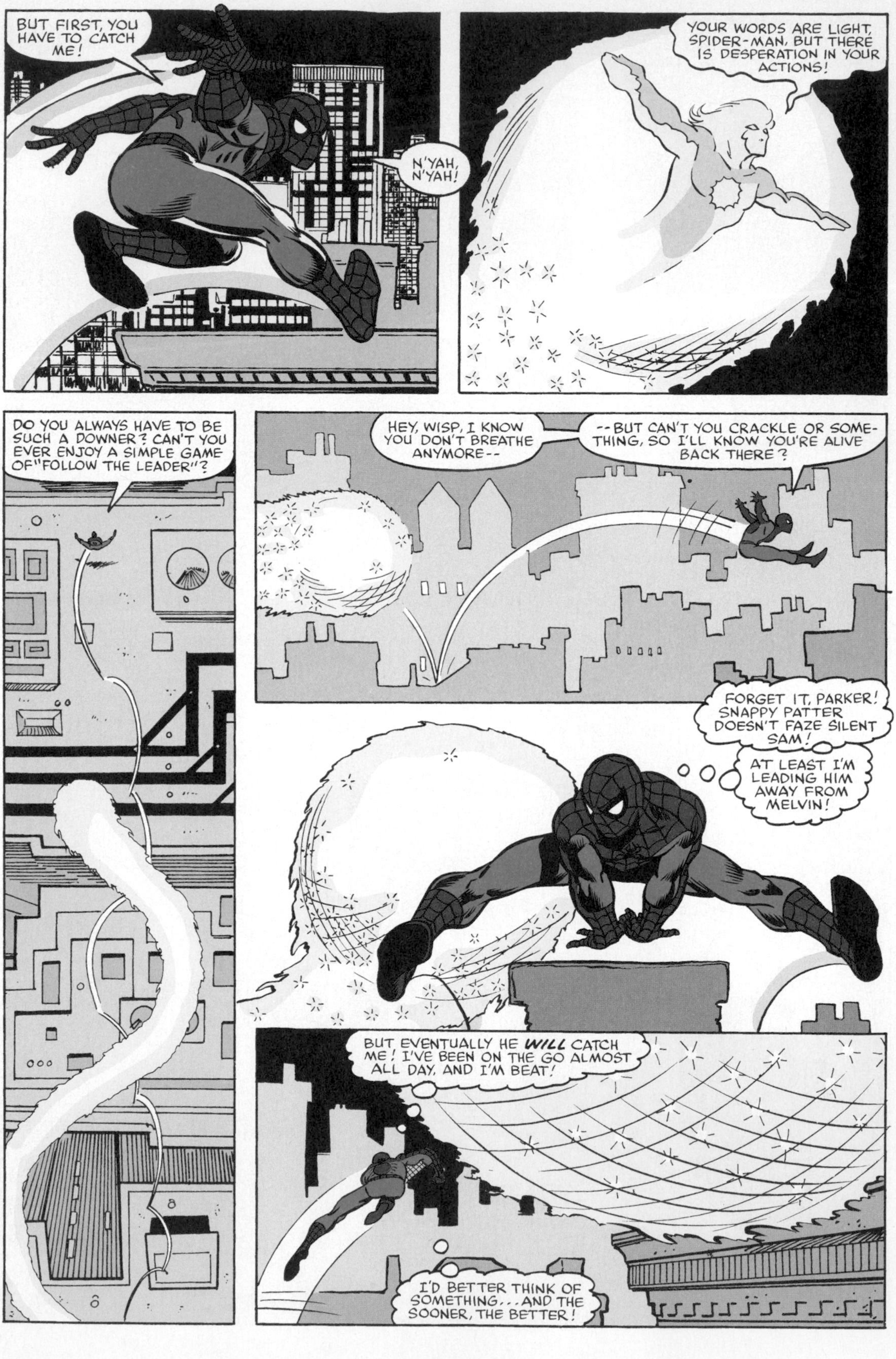

BUT FIRST, YOU HAVE TO CATCH ME!
N'YAH, N'YAH!
YOUR WORDS ARE LIGHT, SPIDER-MAN, BUT THERE IS DESPERATION IN YOUR ACTIONS!
DO YOU ALWAYS HAVE TO BE SUCH A DOWNER? CAN'T YOU EVER ENJOY A SIMPLE GAME OF "FOLLOW THE LEADER"?
HEY, WISP, I KNOW YOU DON'T BREATHE ANYMORE--
--BUT CAN'T YOU CRACKLE OR SOMETHING, SO I'LL KNOW YOU'RE ALIVE BACK THERE?
FORGET IT, PARKER! SNAPPY PATTER DOESN'T FAZE SILENT SAM!
AT LEAST I'M LEADING HIM AWAY FROM MELVIN!
BUT EVENTUALLY HE WILL CATCH ME! I'VE BEEN ON THE GO ALMOST ALL DAY, AND I'M BEAT!
I'D BETTER THINK OF SOMETHING... AND THE SOONER, THE BETTER!

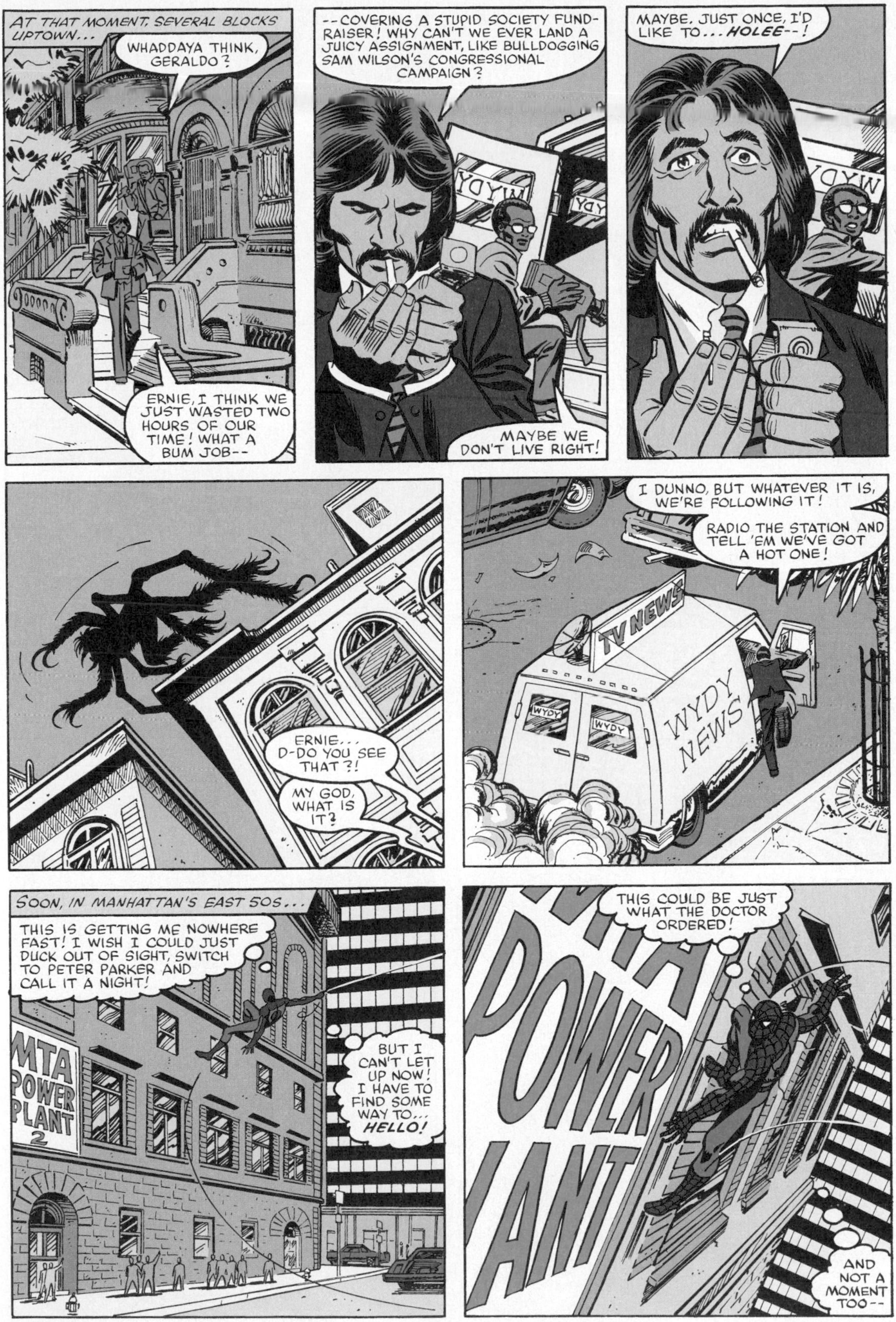
AT THAT MOMENT, SEVERAL BLOCKS UPTOWN...
WHADDAYA THINK, GERALDO?
ERNIE, I THINK WE JUST WASTED TWO HOURS OF OUR TIME! WHAT A BUM JOB--
--COVERING A STUPID SOCIETY FUND-RAISER! WHY CAN'T WE EVER LAND A JUICY ASSIGNMENT, LIKE BULLDOGGING SAM WILSON'S CONGRESSIONAL CAMPAIGN?
MAYBE WE DON'T LIVE RIGHT!
MAYBE, JUST ONCE, I'D LIKE TO... HOLEE--!
ERNIE... D-DO YOU SEE THAT?!
MY GOD, WHAT IS IT?
I DUNNO, BUT WHATEVER IT IS, WE'RE FOLLOWING IT!
RADIO THE STATION AND TELL 'EM WE'VE GOT A HOT ONE!
TV NEWS
WYDY
WYDY
WYDY NEWS
SOON, IN MANHATTAN'S EAST 50S...
THIS IS GETTING ME NOWHERE FAST! I WISH I COULD JUST DUCK OUT OF SIGHT, SWITCH TO PETER PARKER AND CALL IT A NIGHT!
MTA POWER PLANT 2
BUT I CAN'T LET UP NOW! I HAVE TO FIND SOME WAY TO... HELLO!
THIS COULD BE JUST WHAT THE DOCTOR ORDERED!
POWER LANT
AND NOT A MOMENT TOO--

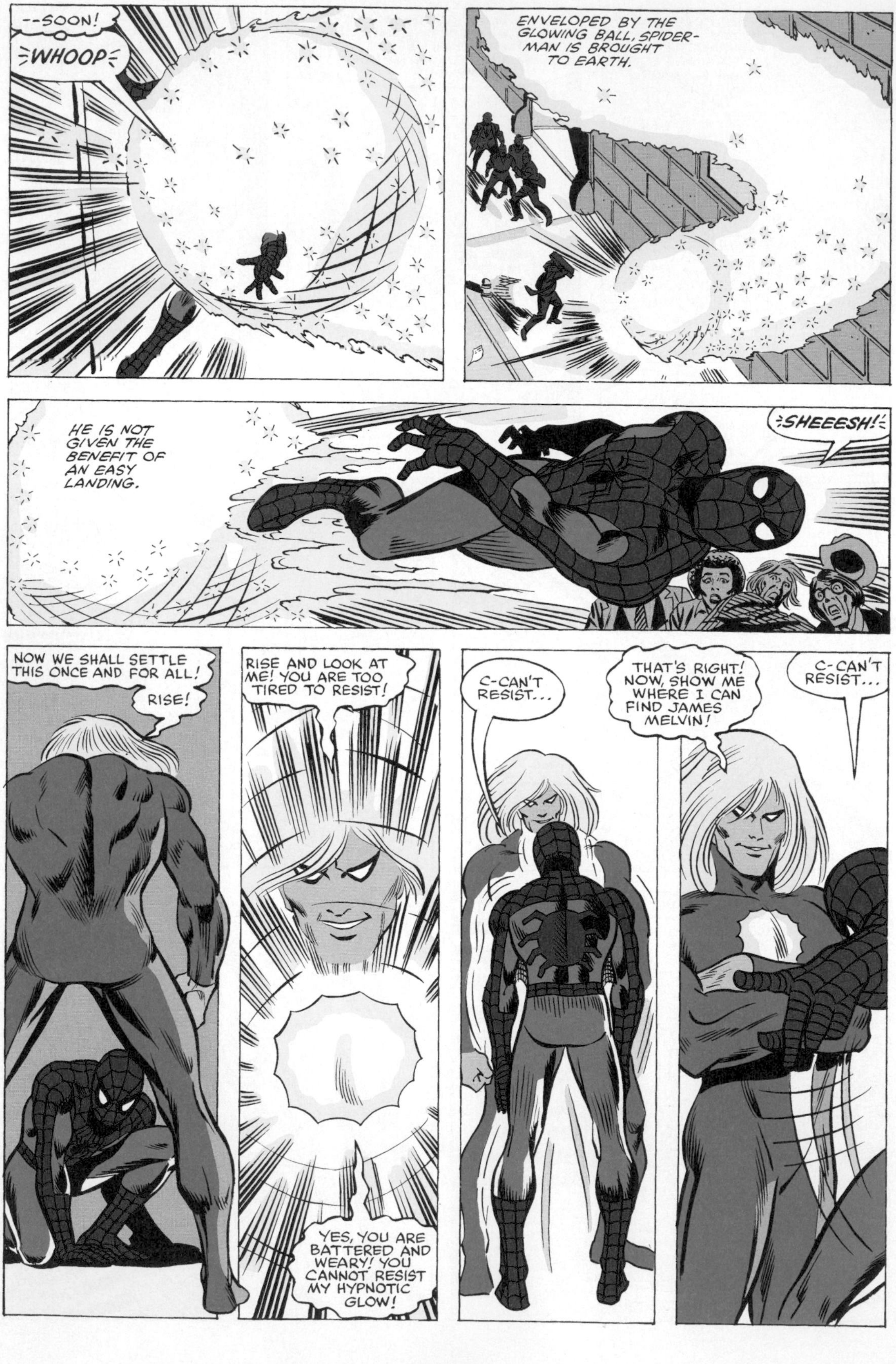
--SOON!
WHOOP
ENVELOPED BY THE GLOWING BALL, SPIDER-MAN IS BROUGHT TO EARTH.
HE IS NOT GIVEN THE BENEFIT OF AN EASY LANDING.
SHEEESH!
NOW WE SHALL SETTLE THIS ONCE AND FOR ALL!
RISE!
RISE AND LOOK AT ME! YOU ARE TOO TIRED TO RESIST!
YES, YOU ARE BATTERED AND WEARY! YOU CANNOT RESIST MY HYPNOTIC GLOW!
C-CAN'T RESIST...
THAT'S RIGHT! NOW, SHOW ME WHERE I CAN FIND JAMES MELVIN!
C-CAN'T RESIST...

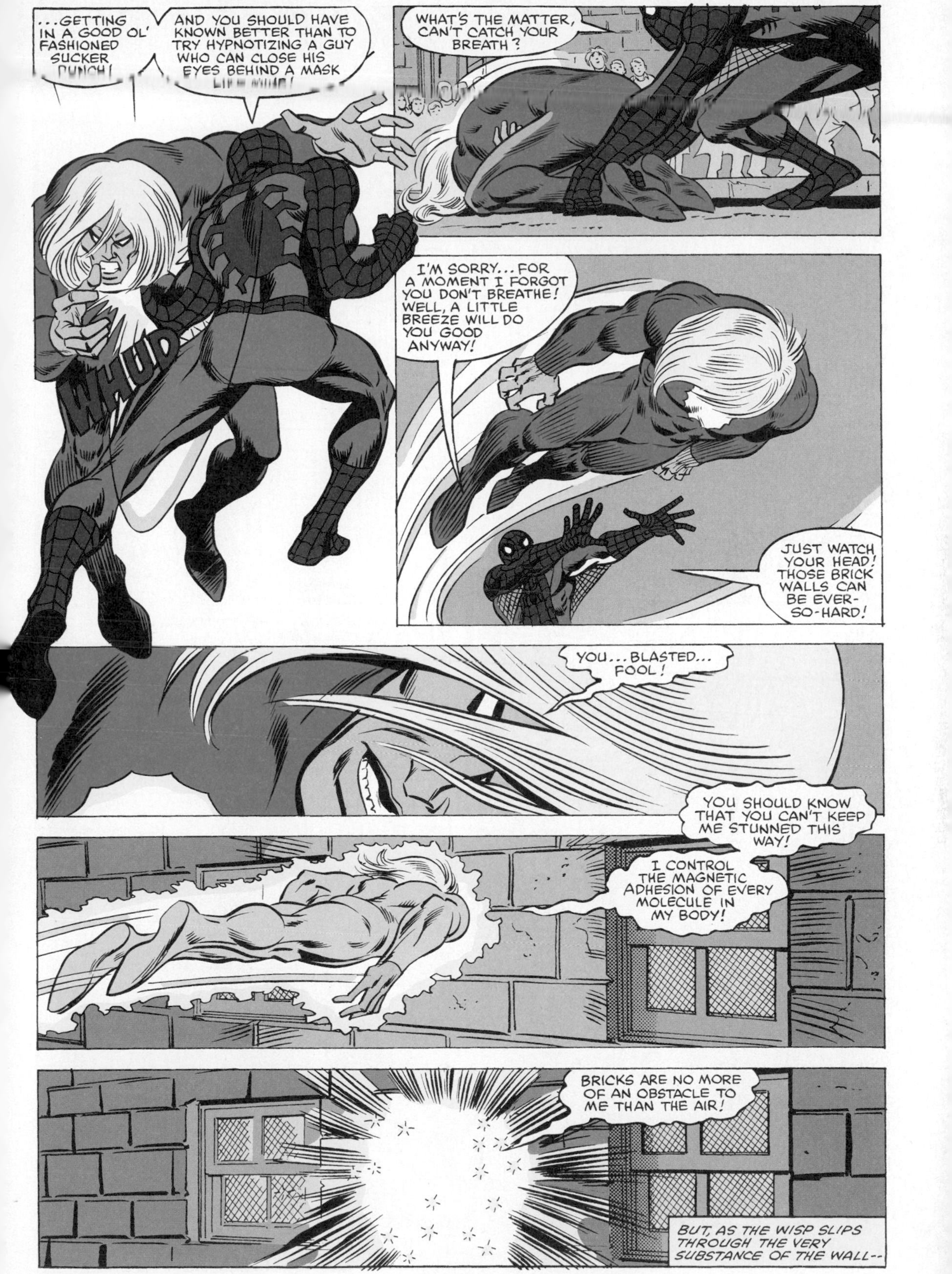

...GETTING IN A GOOD OL' FASHIONED SUCKER PUNCH!
AND YOU SHOULD HAVE KNOWN BETTER THAN TO TRY HYPNOTIZING A GUY WHO CAN CLOSE HIS EYES BEHIND A MASK
WHUD
WHAT'S THE MATTER, CAN'T CATCH YOUR BREATH?
I'M SORRY... FOR A MOMENT I FORGOT YOU DON'T BREATHE! WELL, A LITTLE BREEZE WILL DO YOU GOOD ANYWAY!
JUST WATCH YOUR HEAD! THOSE BRICK WALLS CAN BE EVER-SO-HARD!
YOU... BLASTED... FOOL!
YOU SHOULD KNOW THAT YOU CAN'T KEEP ME STUNNED THIS WAY!
I CONTROL THE MAGNETIC ADHESION OF EVERY MOLECULE IN MY BODY!
BRICKS ARE NO MORE OF AN OBSTACLE TO ME THAN THE AIR!
BUT, AS THE WISP SLIPS THROUGH THE VERY SUBSTANCE OF THE WALL--

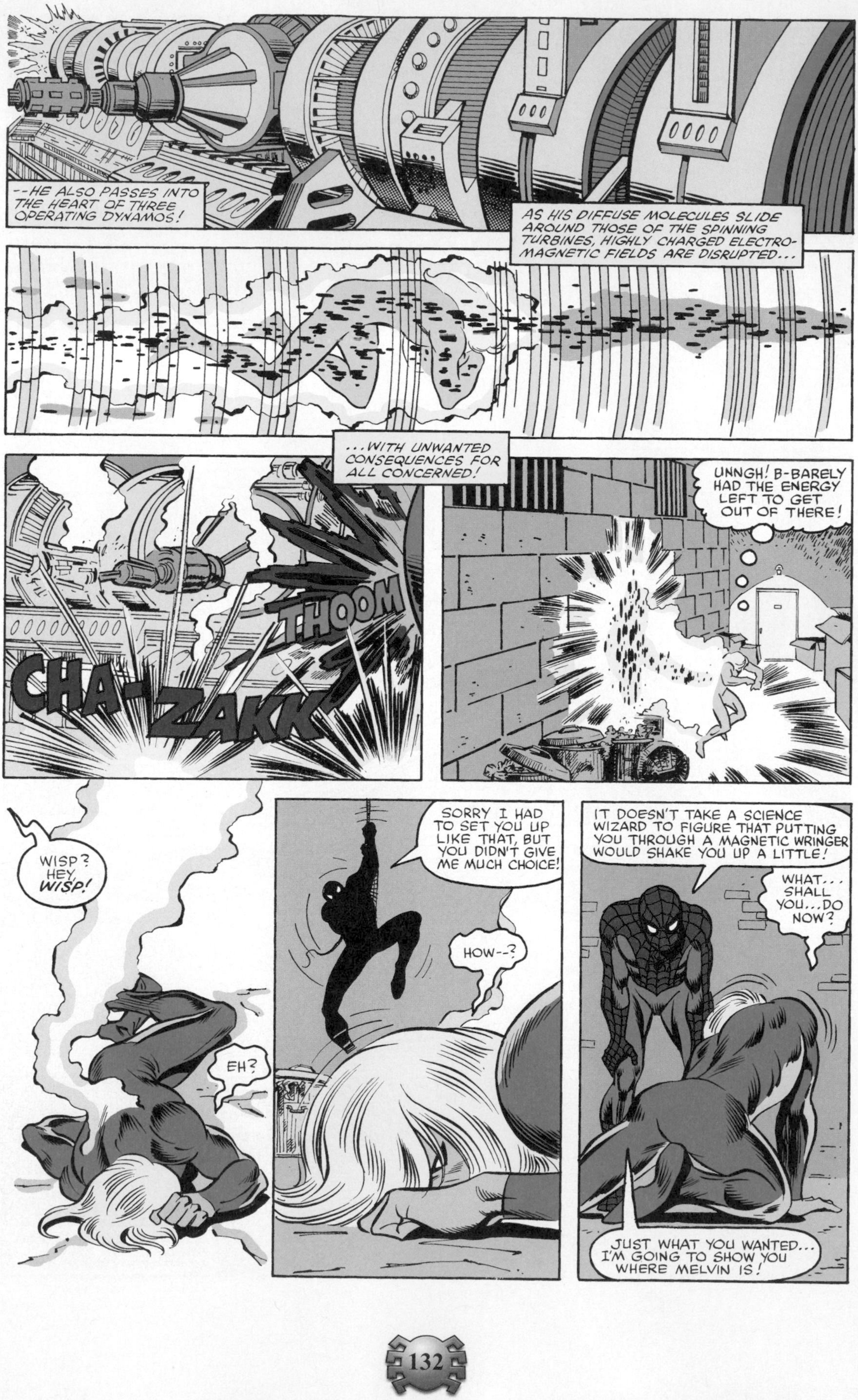
--HE ALSO PASSES INTO THE HEART OF THREE OPERATING DYNAMOS!
AS HIS DIFFUSE MOLECULES SLIDE AROUND THOSE OF THE SPINNING TURBINES, HIGHLY CHARGED ELECTRO-MAGNETIC FIELDS ARE DISRUPTED...
...WITH UNWANTED CONSEQUENCES FOR ALL CONCERNED!
THOOM
CHA-ZAKK
UNNGH! B-BARELY HAD THE ENERGY LEFT TO GET OUT OF THERE!
WISP? HEY, WISP!
EH?
SORRY I HAD TO SET YOU UP LIKE THAT, BUT YOU DIDN'T GIVE ME MUCH CHOICE!
HOW--?
IT DOESN'T TAKE A SCIENCE WIZARD TO FIGURE THAT PUTTING YOU THROUGH A MAGNETIC WRINGER WOULD SHAKE YOU UP A LITTLE!
WHAT... SHALL YOU...DO NOW?
JUST WHAT YOU WANTED... I'M GOING TO SHOW YOU WHERE MELVIN IS!

MERE MOMENTS LATER...

NOW THAT *YOU* DON'T HAVE ANY CHOICE, MAYBE YOU'LL WISE UP AND LISTEN TO ME, WISP!

THE JUSTICE DEPARTMENT IS TRYING TO BUILD A CASE AGAINST THE BRAND CORPORATION AND THE LOW LIFES WHO RUN IT!* WITH WHAT YOU COULD TELL THEM ABOUT MELVIN AND THE CREW--!

*SEE LAST ISSUE.

IT WOULD DO NO GOOD! MEN LIKE MELVIN TWIST THE LAWS AS THEY WISH!

THWIP

ONLY IF YOU LET THEM! WHY NOT GIVE THE FEDS A FIGHTING CHANCE?

IF YOU WERE TO WALTZ MELVIN INTO THE FEDERAL D.A.'S OFFICE, HE'D SPILL EVERYTHING!

YOU KNOW HE WOULD!

ON THE OTHER HAND, YOU COULD KILL MELVIN! BUT THEN YOU WOULD HAVE TO RUN FROM THE LAW FOR THE REST OF YOUR LIFE!

AND EVENTUALLY THEY WOULD HUNT YOU DOWN LIKE SOME SORT OF... MONSTER!

HOLY SMOKES!!

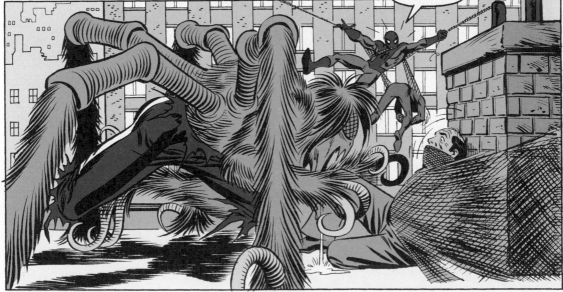

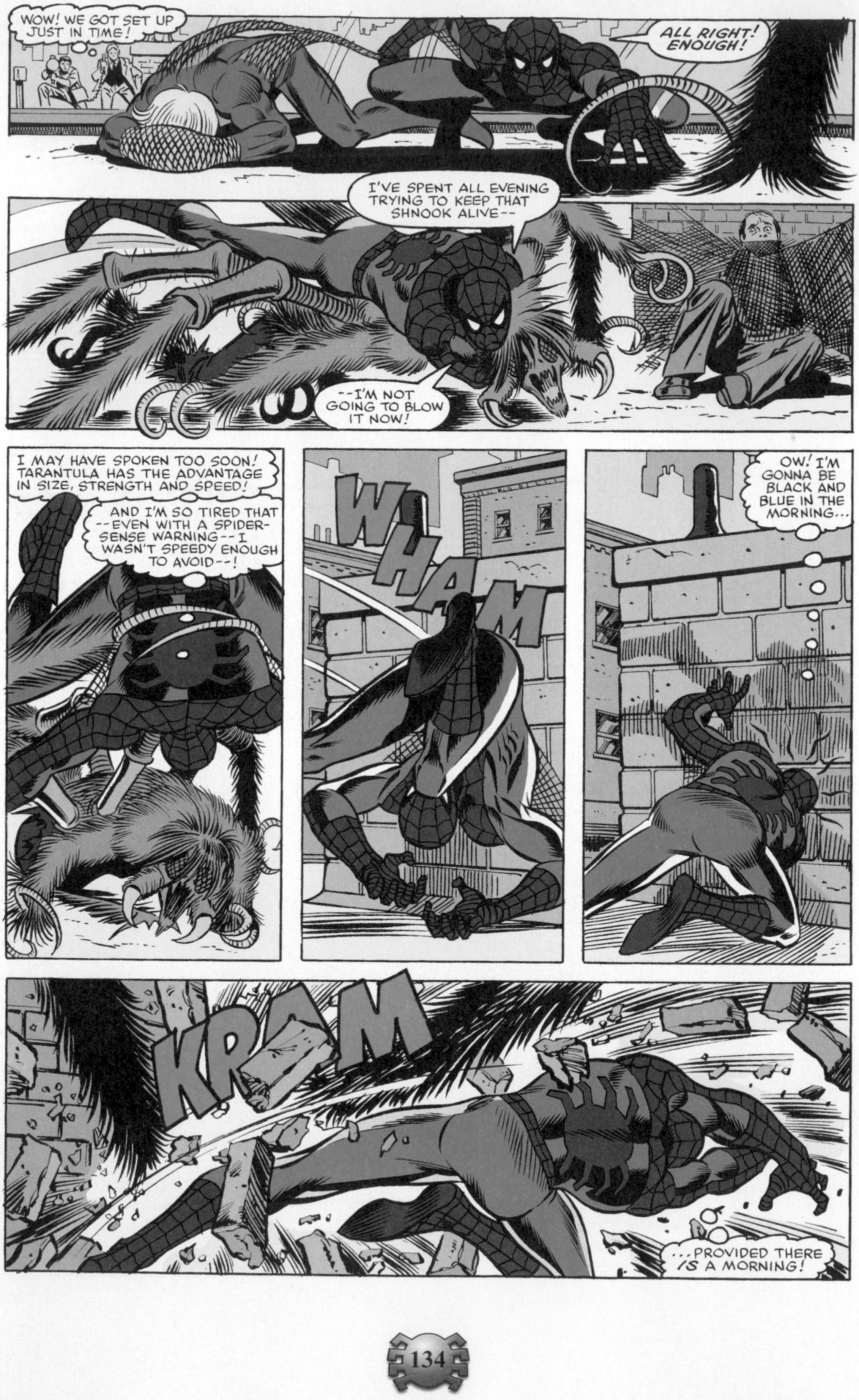
WOW! WE GOT SET UP JUST IN TIME!
ALL RIGHT! ENOUGH!
I'VE SPENT ALL EVENING TRYING TO KEEP THAT SHNOOK ALIVE--
--I'M NOT GOING TO BLOW IT NOW!
I MAY HAVE SPOKEN TOO SOON! TARANTULA HAS THE ADVANTAGE IN SIZE, STRENGTH AND SPEED!
AND I'M SO TIRED THAT --EVEN WITH A SPIDER-SENSE WARNING--I WASN'T SPEEDY ENOUGH TO AVOID--!
WHAM
OW! I'M GONNA BE BLACK AND BLUE IN THE MORNING...
KRAM
...PROVIDED THERE IS A MORNING!

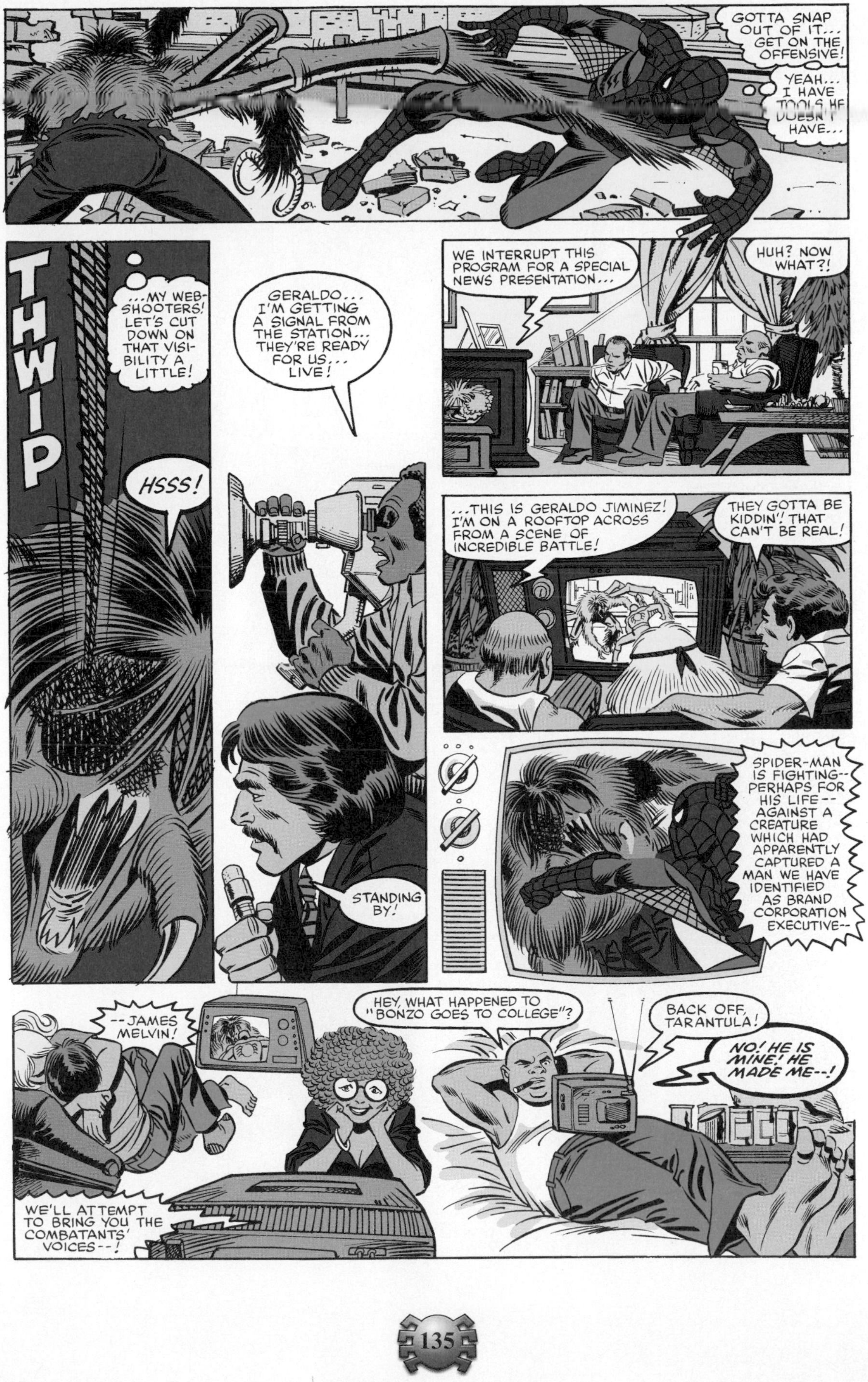
GOTTA SNAP OUT OF IT... GET ON THE OFFENSIVE!
YEAH... I HAVE TOOLS HE DOESN'T HAVE...
...MY WEB-SHOOTERS! LET'S CUT DOWN ON THAT VISIBILITY A LITTLE!
THWIP
GERALDO... I'M GETTING A SIGNAL FROM THE STATION... THEY'RE READY FOR US... LIVE!
WE INTERRUPT THIS PROGRAM FOR A SPECIAL NEWS PRESENTATION...
HUH? NOW WHAT?!
HSSS!
...THIS IS GERALDO JIMINEZ! I'M ON A ROOFTOP ACROSS FROM A SCENE OF INCREDIBLE BATTLE!
THEY GOTTA BE KIDDIN'! THAT CAN'T BE REAL!
SPIDER-MAN IS FIGHTING--PERHAPS FOR HIS LIFE--AGAINST A CREATURE WHICH HAD APPARENTLY CAPTURED A MAN WE HAVE IDENTIFIED AS BRAND CORPORATION EXECUTIVE--
STANDING BY!
--JAMES MELVIN!
HEY, WHAT HAPPENED TO "BONZO GOES TO COLLEGE"?
BACK OFF, TARANTULA!
NO! HE IS MINE! HE MADE ME--!
WE'LL ATTEMPT TO BRING YOU THE COMBATANTS' VOICES--!

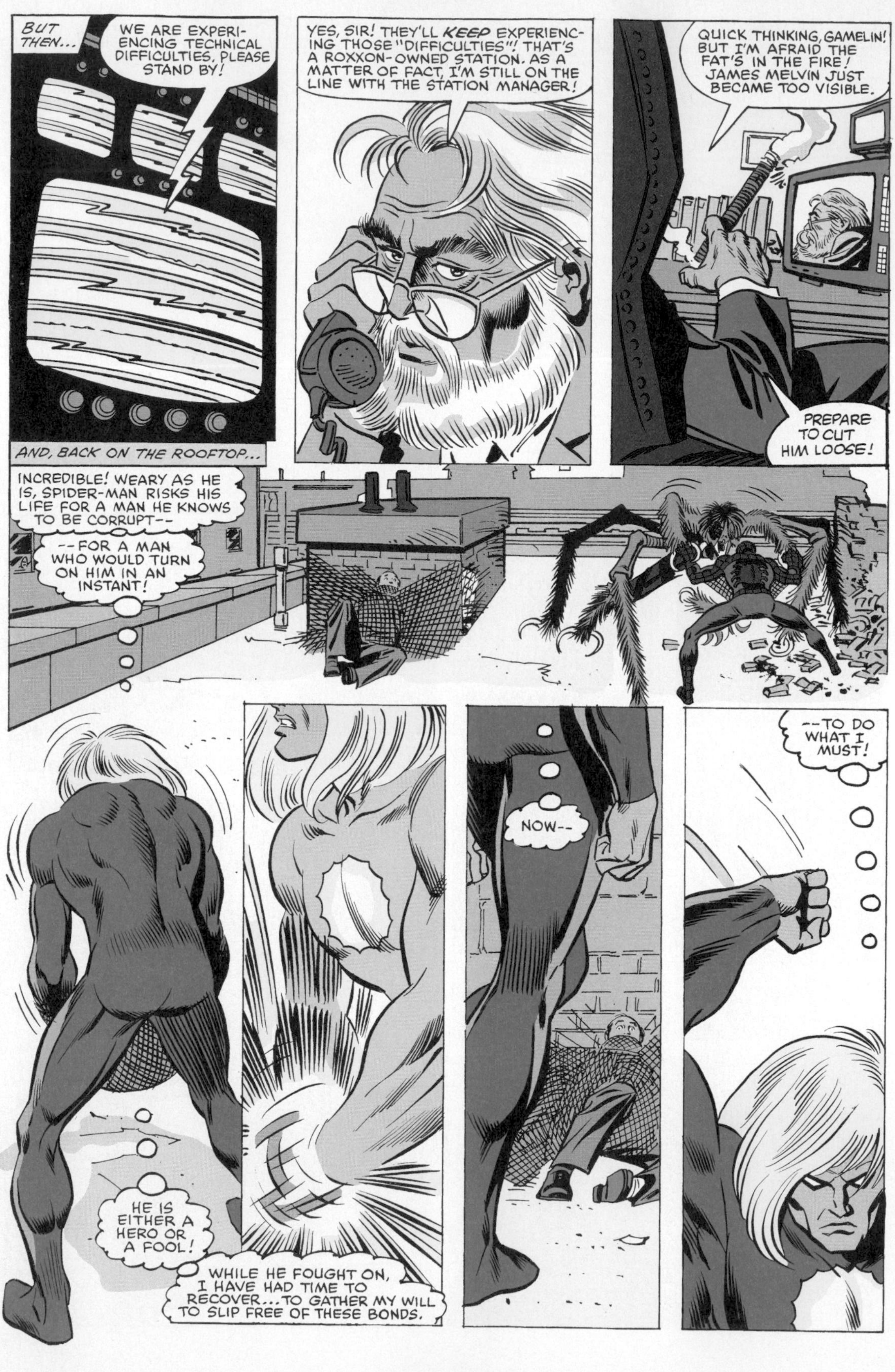
BUT THEN...
WE ARE EXPERIENCING TECHNICAL DIFFICULTIES, PLEASE STAND BY!
YES, SIR! THEY'LL KEEP EXPERIENCING THOSE "DIFFICULTIES"! THAT'S A ROXXON-OWNED STATION. AS A MATTER OF FACT, I'M STILL ON THE LINE WITH THE STATION MANAGER!
QUICK THINKING, GAMELIN! BUT I'M AFRAID THE FAT'S IN THE FIRE! JAMES MELVIN JUST BECAME TOO VISIBLE.
PREPARE TO CUT HIM LOOSE!
AND, BACK ON THE ROOFTOP...
INCREDIBLE! WEARY AS HE IS, SPIDER-MAN RISKS HIS LIFE FOR A MAN HE KNOWS TO BE CORRUPT--
--FOR A MAN WHO WOULD TURN ON HIM IN AN INSTANT!
HE IS EITHER A HERO OR A FOOL!
WHILE HE FOUGHT ON, I HAVE HAD TIME TO RECOVER...TO GATHER MY WILL TO SLIP FREE OF THESE BONDS.
NOW--
--TO DO WHAT I MUST!

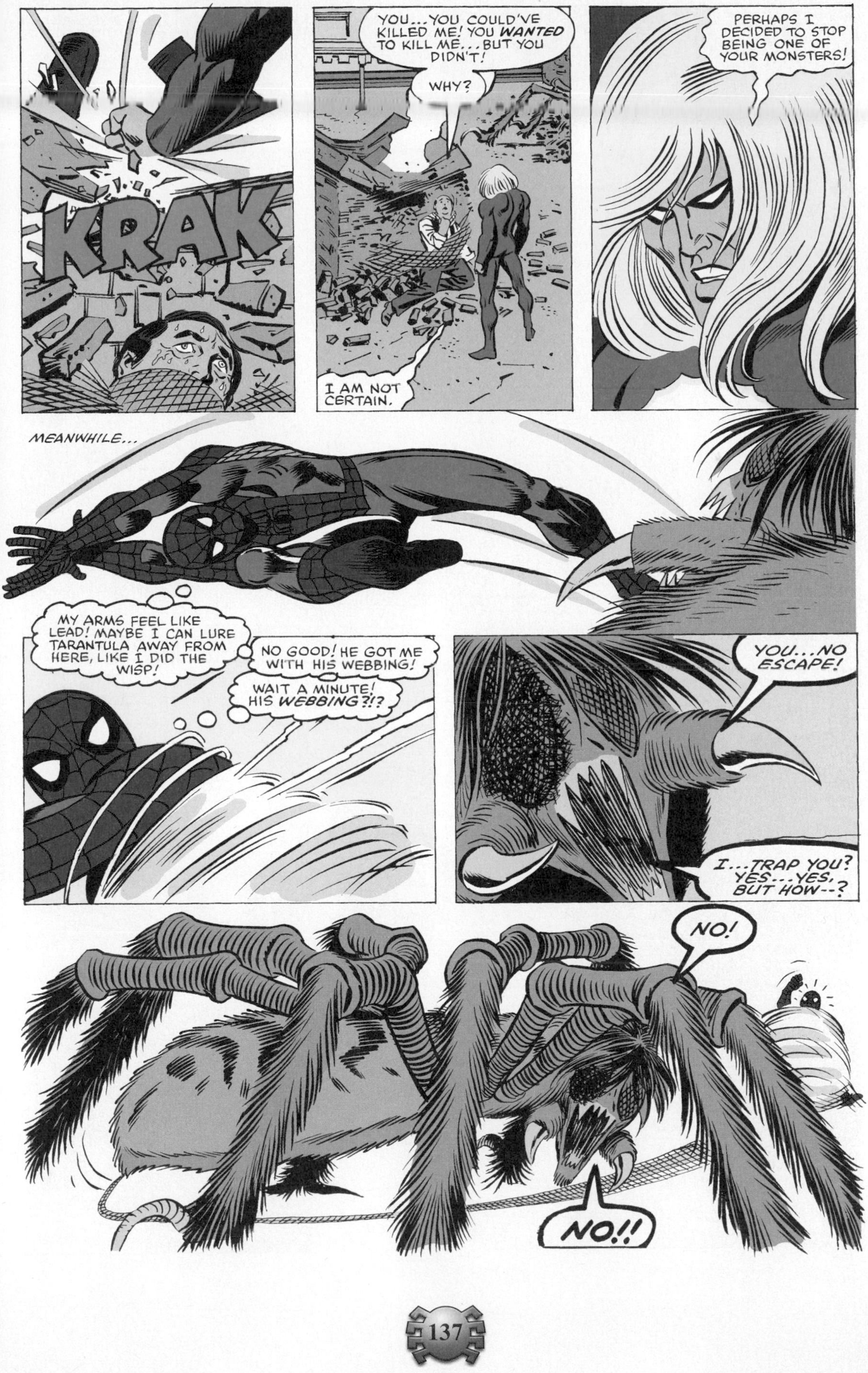
KRAK
YOU...YOU COULD'VE KILLED ME! YOU WANTED TO KILL ME...BUT YOU DIDN'T!
WHY?
I AM NOT CERTAIN.
PERHAPS I DECIDED TO STOP BEING ONE OF YOUR MONSTERS!
MEANWHILE...
MY ARMS FEEL LIKE LEAD! MAYBE I CAN LURE TARANTULA AWAY FROM HERE, LIKE I DID THE WISP!
NO GOOD! HE GOT ME WITH HIS WEBBING!
WAIT A MINUTE! HIS WEBBING?!?
YOU...NO ESCAPE!
I...TRAP YOU? YES...YES, BUT HOW--?
NO!
NO!!

WHAT...WHAT HAS BECOME ME?!?

MONSTER! YOU MADE ME... MONSTER! KILL!

NO, YOU'LL NOT KILL HIM! NO ONE SHALL!

AND BEFORE THE STARTLED EXECUTIVE CAN BLINK--

--HE'S CARRIED OFF TO SAFETY, BEHIND THE BARRICADES OF THE POLICE LINES BEING HASTILY ERECTED BELOW!

NO...NO! NOT END NOW...NOT LIKE THIS! KILL... KILL...

SOUNDS LIKE HIS MIND IS JUST ABOUT COMPLETELY GONE-- AND NO WONDER!

UNGH! GOTTA GET OUT OF THIS WEB OF HIS!

IT'S NOT AS STRONG AS MINE, BUT IT'S STICKY ENOUGH!

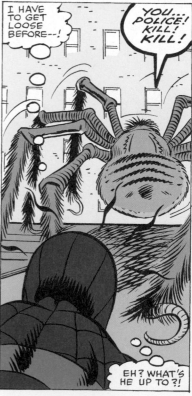

I HAVE TO GET LOOSE BEFORE--!

YOU...POLICE! KILL! KILL!

EH? WHAT'S HE UP TO?!

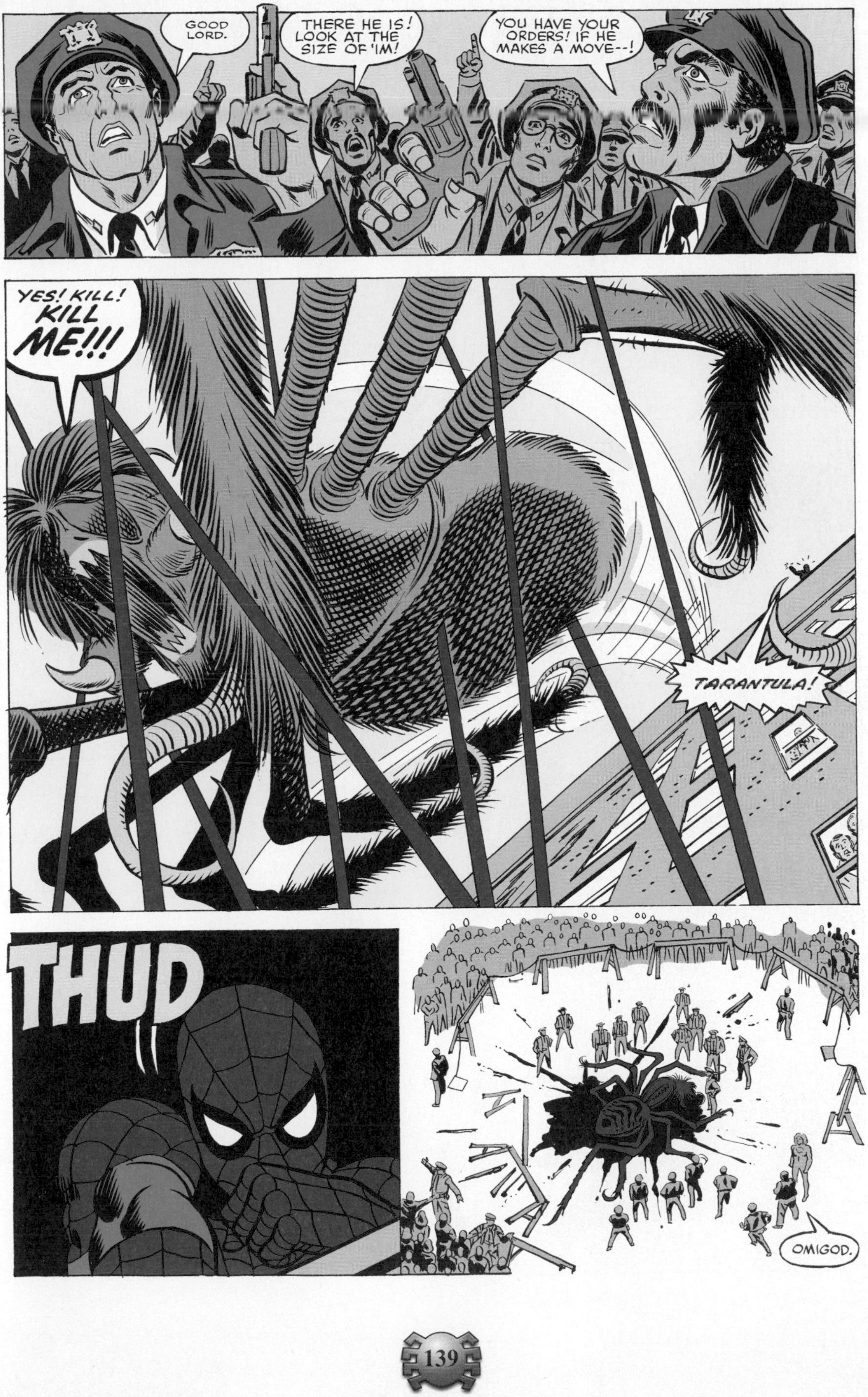
GOOD LORD.
THERE HE IS! LOOK AT THE SIZE OF 'IM!
YOU HAVE YOUR ORDERS! IF HE MAKES A MOVE--!
YES! KILL! KILL ME!!!
TARANTULA!
THUD
OMIGOD.

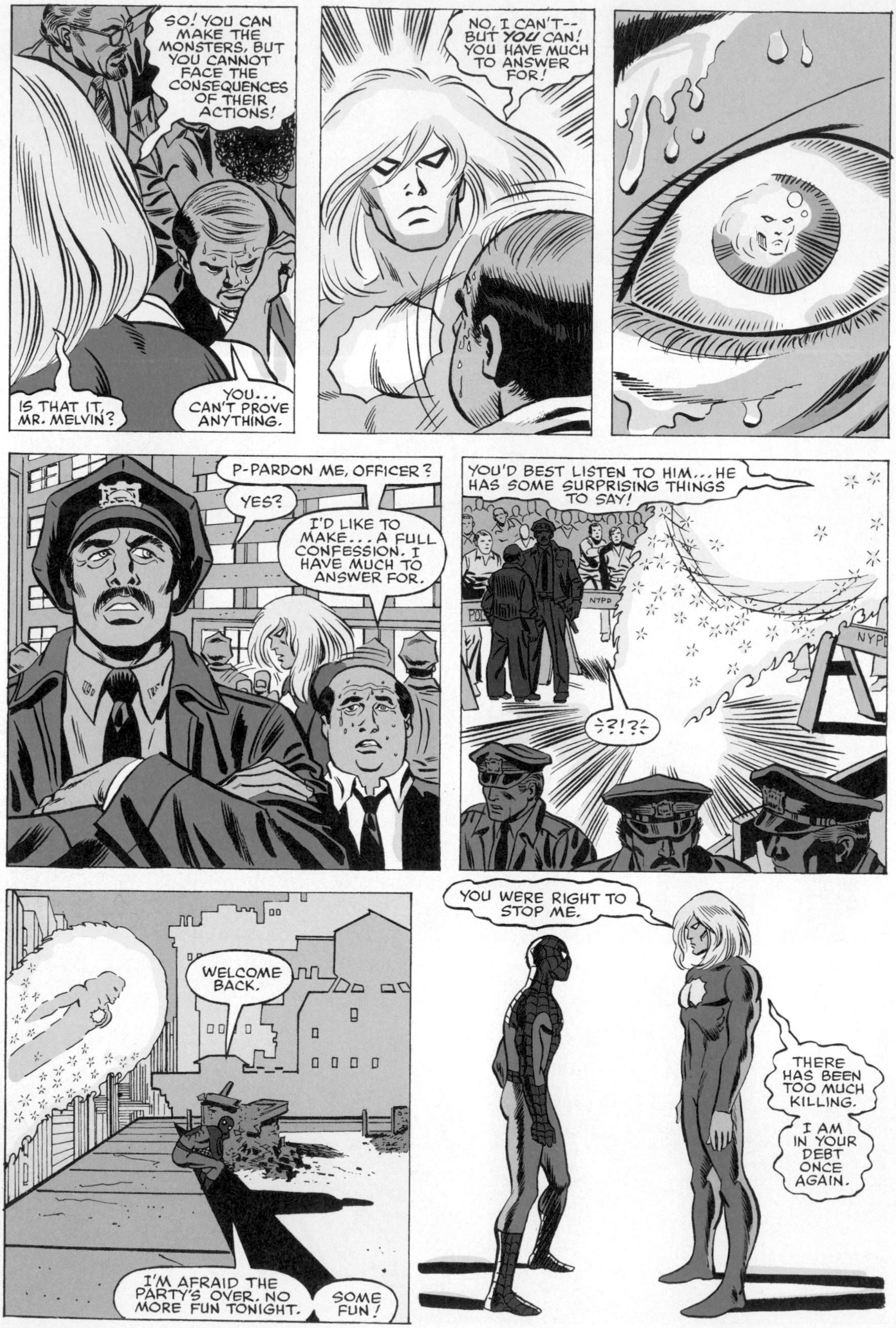
SO! YOU CAN MAKE THE MONSTERS, BUT YOU CANNOT FACE THE CONSEQUENCES OF THEIR ACTIONS!
IS THAT IT, MR. MELVIN?
YOU... CAN'T PROVE ANYTHING.
NO, I CAN'T-- BUT YOU CAN! YOU HAVE MUCH TO ANSWER FOR!
P-PARDON ME, OFFICER?
YES?
I'D LIKE TO MAKE... A FULL CONFESSION. I HAVE MUCH TO ANSWER FOR.
YOU'D BEST LISTEN TO HIM... HE HAS SOME SURPRISING THINGS TO SAY!
?!?
NYPD
WELCOME BACK.
I'M AFRAID THE PARTY'S OVER. NO MORE FUN TONIGHT.
SOME FUN!
YOU WERE RIGHT TO STOP ME.
THERE HAS BEEN TOO MUCH KILLING.
I AM IN YOUR DEBT ONCE AGAIN.

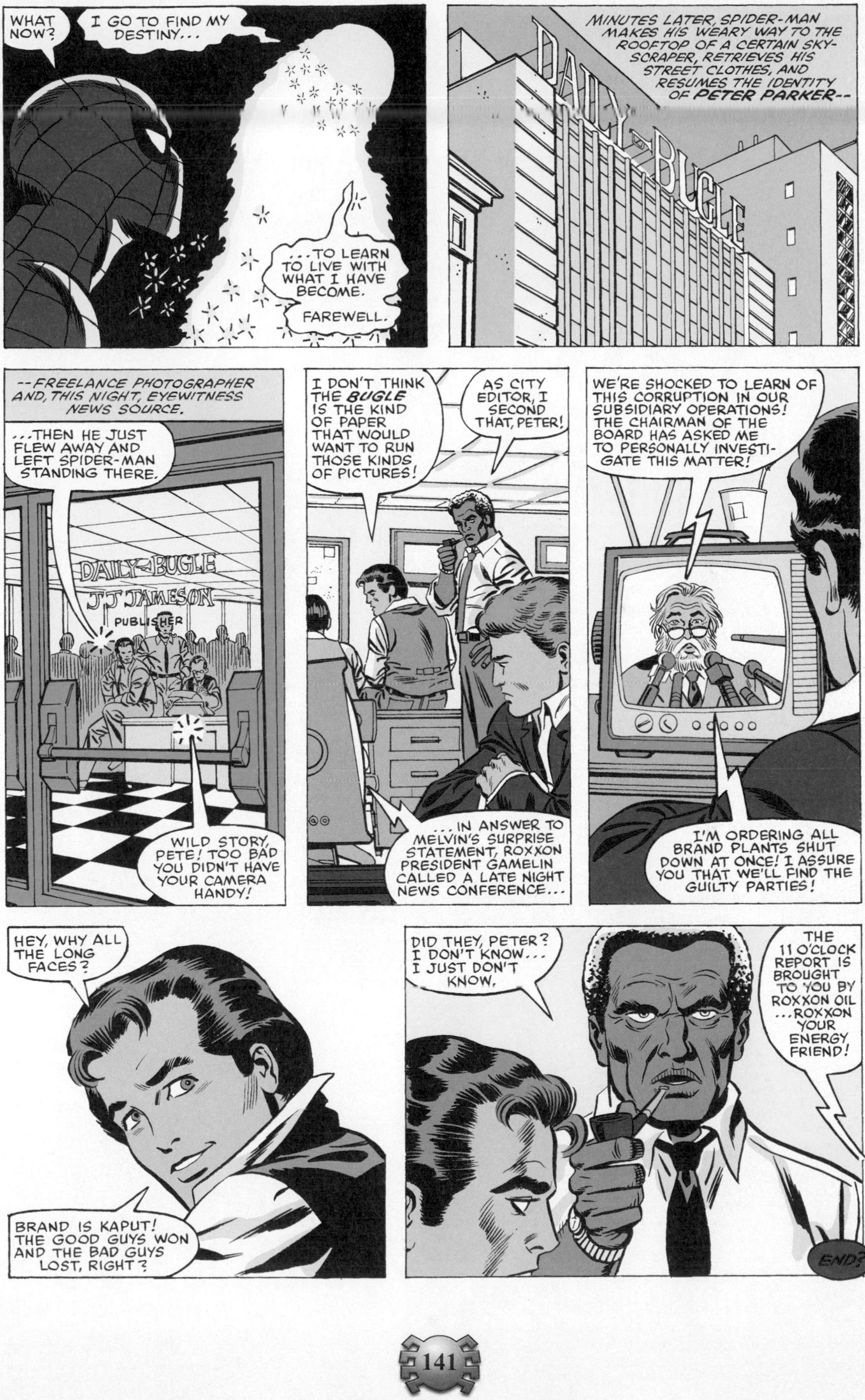
WHAT NOW?
I GO TO FIND MY DESTINY...
...TO LEARN TO LIVE WITH WHAT I HAVE BECOME.
FAREWELL.
MINUTES LATER, SPIDER-MAN MAKES HIS WEARY WAY TO THE ROOFTOP OF A CERTAIN SKY-SCRAPER, RETRIEVES HIS STREET CLOTHES, AND RESUMES THE IDENTITY OF PETER PARKER--
DAILY BUGLE
--FREELANCE PHOTOGRAPHER AND, THIS NIGHT, EYEWITNESS NEWS SOURCE.
...THEN HE JUST FLEW AWAY AND LEFT SPIDER-MAN STANDING THERE.
DAILY BUGLE
J J JAMESON
PUBLISHER
WILD STORY, PETE! TOO BAD YOU DIDN'T HAVE YOUR CAMERA HANDY!
I DON'T THINK THE BUGLE IS THE KIND OF PAPER THAT WOULD WANT TO RUN THOSE KINDS OF PICTURES!
AS CITY EDITOR, I SECOND THAT, PETER!
...IN ANSWER TO MELVIN'S SURPRISE STATEMENT, ROXXON PRESIDENT GAMELIN CALLED A LATE NIGHT NEWS CONFERENCE...
WE'RE SHOCKED TO LEARN OF THIS CORRUPTION IN OUR SUBSIDIARY OPERATIONS! THE CHAIRMAN OF THE BOARD HAS ASKED ME TO PERSONALLY INVESTIGATE THIS MATTER!
I'M ORDERING ALL BRAND PLANTS SHUT DOWN AT ONCE! I ASSURE YOU THAT WE'LL FIND THE GUILTY PARTIES!
HEY, WHY ALL THE LONG FACES?
BRAND IS KAPUT! THE GOOD GUYS WON AND THE BAD GUYS LOST, RIGHT?
DID THEY, PETER? I DON'T KNOW... I JUST DON'T KNOW.
THE 11 O'CLOCK REPORT IS BROUGHT TO YOU BY ROXXON OIL ...ROXXON YOUR ENERGY FRIEND!
END?

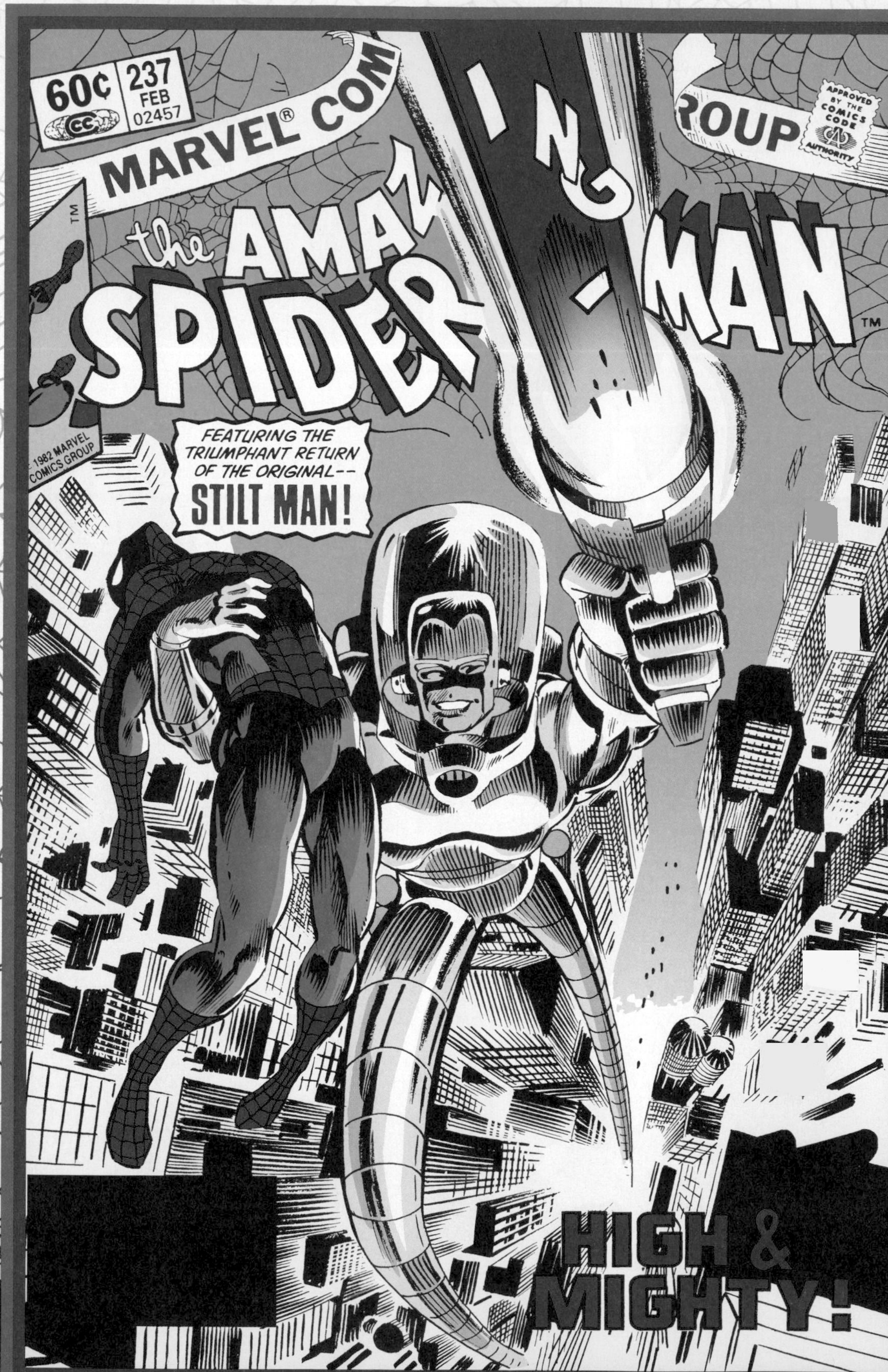
60¢
237
FEB
02457
MARVEL® COM
ROUP
APPROVED BY THE COMICS CODE AUTHORITY
the AMAZ
I NG
SPIDER-MAN™
© 1982 MARVEL COMICS GROUP
FEATURING THE TRIUMPHANT RETURN OF THE ORIGINAL--
STILT MAN!
HIGH & MIGHTY!

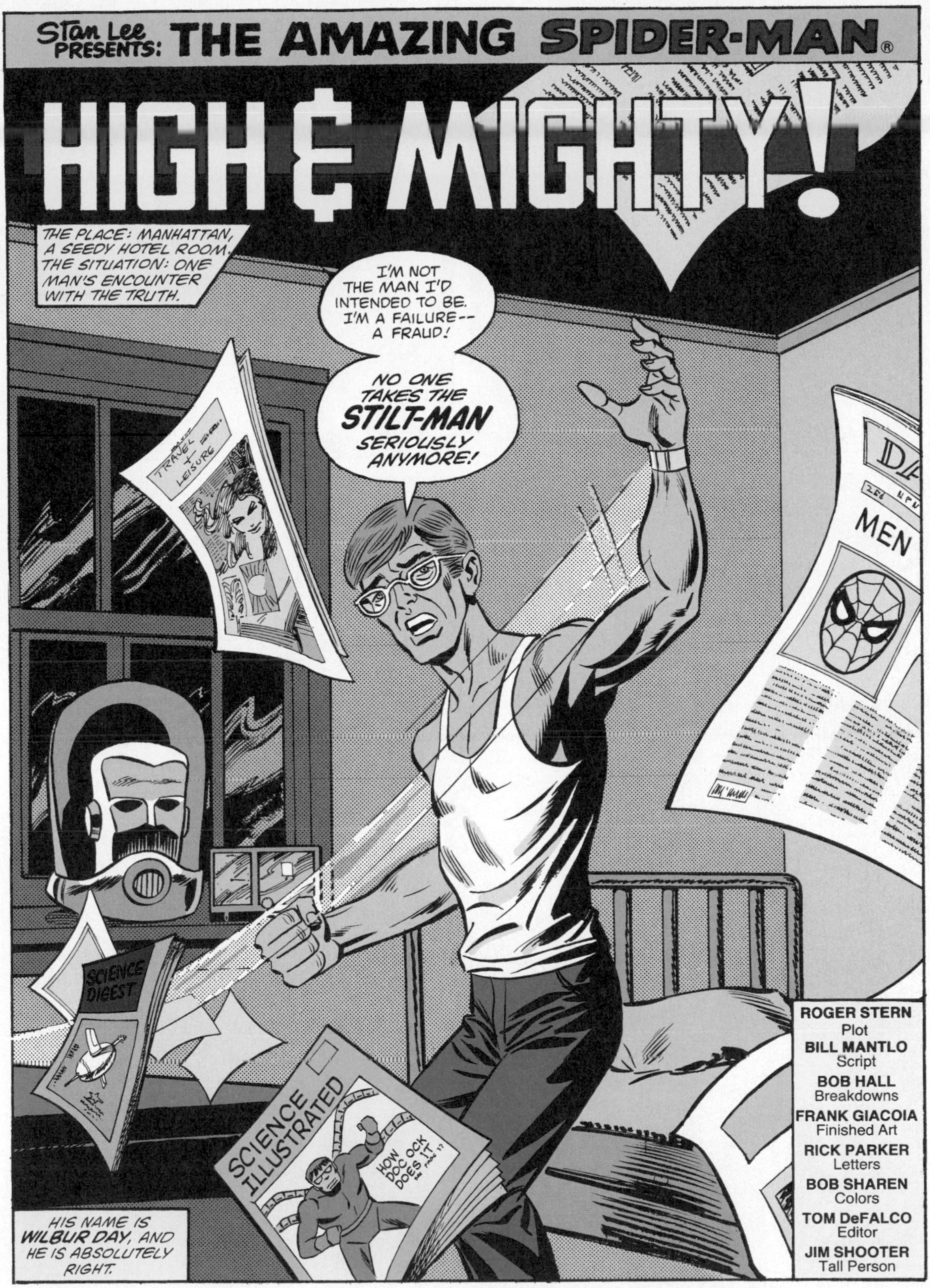
Stan Lee PRESENTS: THE AMAZING SPIDER-MAN®
HIGH & MIGHTY!
THE PLACE: MANHATTAN, A SEEDY HOTEL ROOM. THE SITUATION: ONE MAN'S ENCOUNTER WITH THE TRUTH.
I'M NOT THE MAN I'D INTENDED TO BE. I'M A FAILURE-- A FRAUD!
NO ONE TAKES THE STILT-MAN SERIOUSLY ANYMORE!
TRAVEL + LEISURE
MEN
SCIENCE DIGEST
SCIENCE ILLUSTRATED
HOW DOC OCK DOES IT
HIS NAME IS WILBUR DAY, AND HE IS ABSOLUTELY RIGHT.
ROGER STERN Plot
BILL MANTLO Script
BOB HALL Breakdowns
FRANK GIACOIA Finished Art
RICK PARKER Letters
BOB SHAREN Colors
TOM DeFALCO Editor
JIM SHOOTER Tall Person

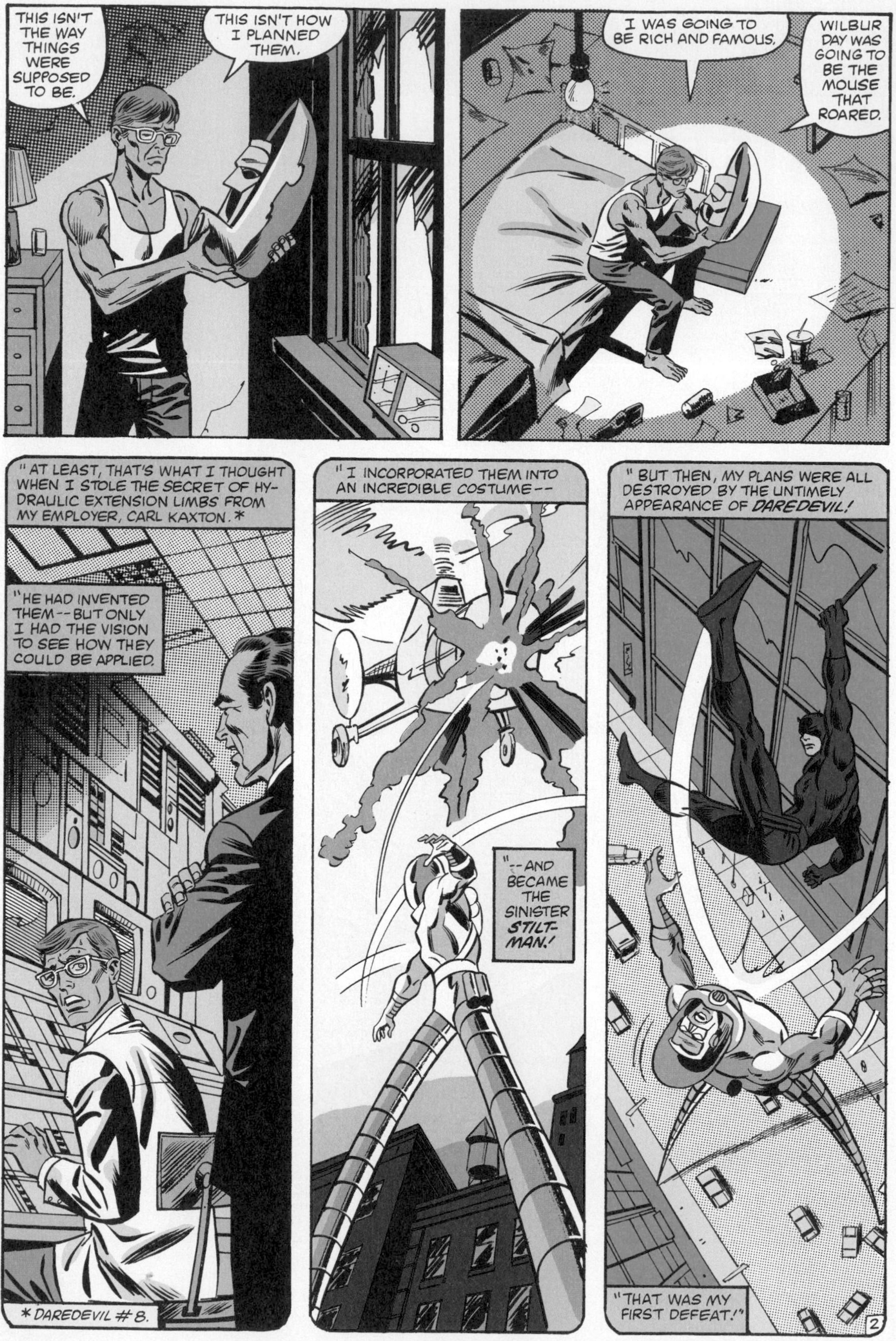
THIS ISN'T THE WAY THINGS WERE SUPPOSED TO BE.
THIS ISN'T HOW I PLANNED THEM.
I WAS GOING TO BE RICH AND FAMOUS.
WILBUR DAY WAS GOING TO BE THE MOUSE THAT ROARED.
"AT LEAST, THAT'S WHAT I THOUGHT WHEN I STOLE THE SECRET OF HYDRAULIC EXTENSION LIMBS FROM MY EMPLOYER, CARL KAXTON.*
"HE HAD INVENTED THEM--BUT ONLY I HAD THE VISION TO SEE HOW THEY COULD BE APPLIED.
*DAREDEVIL #8.
"I INCORPORATED THEM INTO AN INCREDIBLE COSTUME--
"--AND BECAME THE SINISTER STILT-MAN!
"BUT THEN, MY PLANS WERE ALL DESTROYED BY THE UNTIMELY APPEARANCE OF DAREDEVIL!
"THAT WAS MY FIRST DEFEAT!"
2

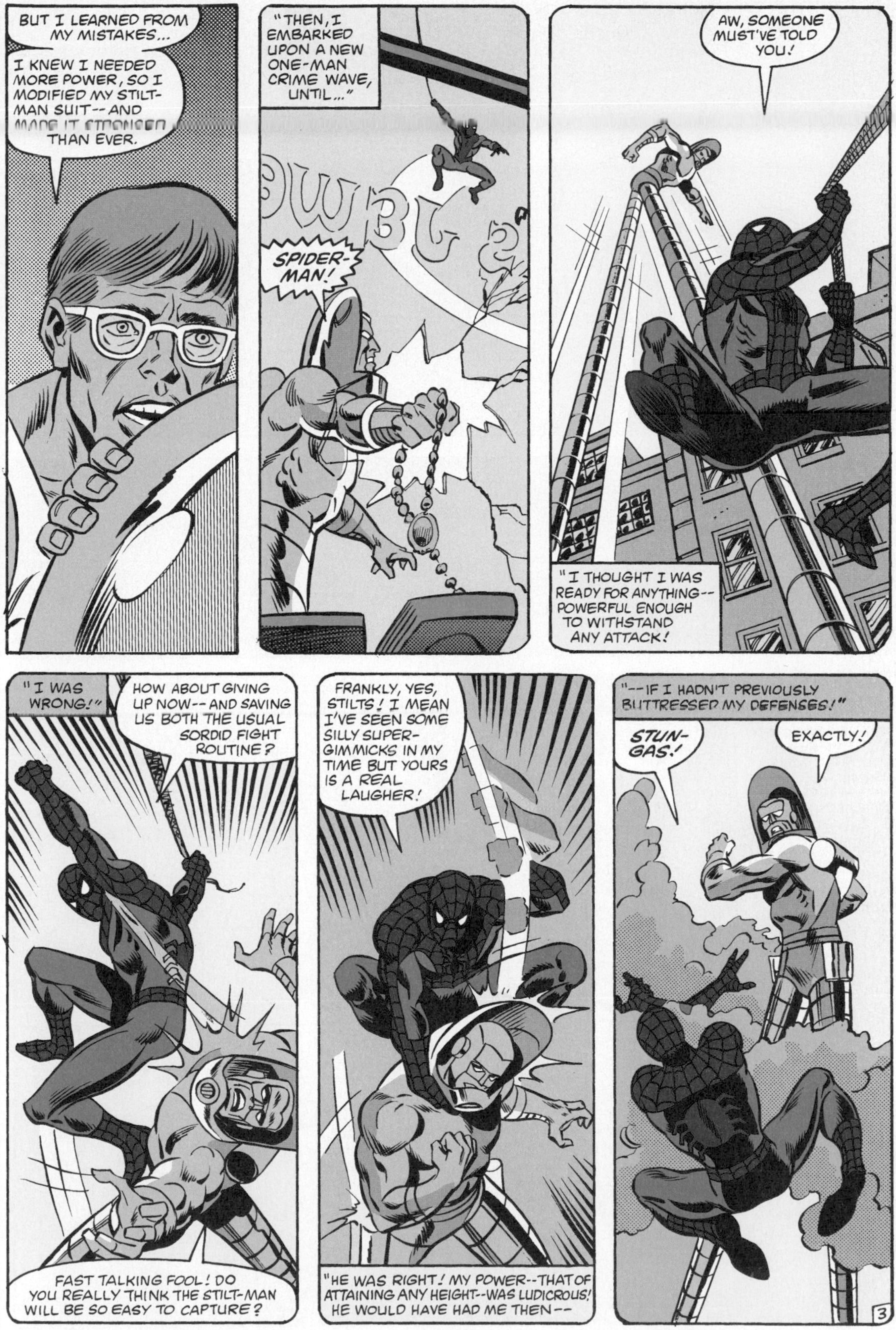
BUT I LEARNED FROM MY MISTAKES...
I KNEW I NEEDED MORE POWER, SO I MODIFIED MY STILT-MAN SUIT--AND MADE IT STRONGER THAN EVER.
"THEN, I EMBARKED UPON A NEW ONE-MAN CRIME WAVE, UNTIL..."
SPIDER-MAN!
AW, SOMEONE MUST'VE TOLD YOU!
"I THOUGHT I WAS READY FOR ANYTHING--POWERFUL ENOUGH TO WITHSTAND ANY ATTACK!
"I WAS WRONG!"
HOW ABOUT GIVING UP NOW--AND SAVING US BOTH THE USUAL SORDID FIGHT ROUTINE?
FAST TALKING FOOL! DO YOU REALLY THINK THE STILT-MAN WILL BE SO EASY TO CAPTURE?
FRANKLY, YES, STILTS! I MEAN I'VE SEEN SOME SILLY SUPER-GIMMICKS IN MY TIME BUT YOURS IS A REAL LAUGHER!
"HE WAS RIGHT! MY POWER--THAT OF ATTAINING ANY HEIGHT--WAS LUDICROUS! HE WOULD HAVE HAD ME THEN--
"--IF I HADN'T PREVIOUSLY BUTTRESSED MY DEFENSES!"
STUN-GAS!
EXACTLY!
3

NO ONE WILL EVER RECAPTURE ME NOW!

"BUT, MERE MOMENTS LATER, DAREDEVIL DID AGAIN.*"

*AS SHOWN IN DAREDEVIL #27.

AFTER THAT, MY LIFE BECAME ONE SUCCEEDING SERIES OF DEFEATS.

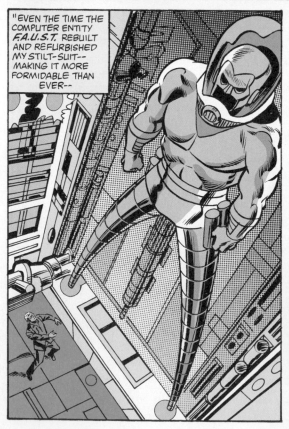

"EVEN THE TIME THE COMPUTER ENTITY F.A.U.S.T. REBUILT AND REFURBISHED MY STILT-SUIT-- MAKING IT MORE FORMIDABLE THAN EVER--

"--I STILL WENT DOWN IN DISGRACE BEFORE THE MIGHTY MALLET OF THE THUNDER GOD, THOR!*

*THOR #269.

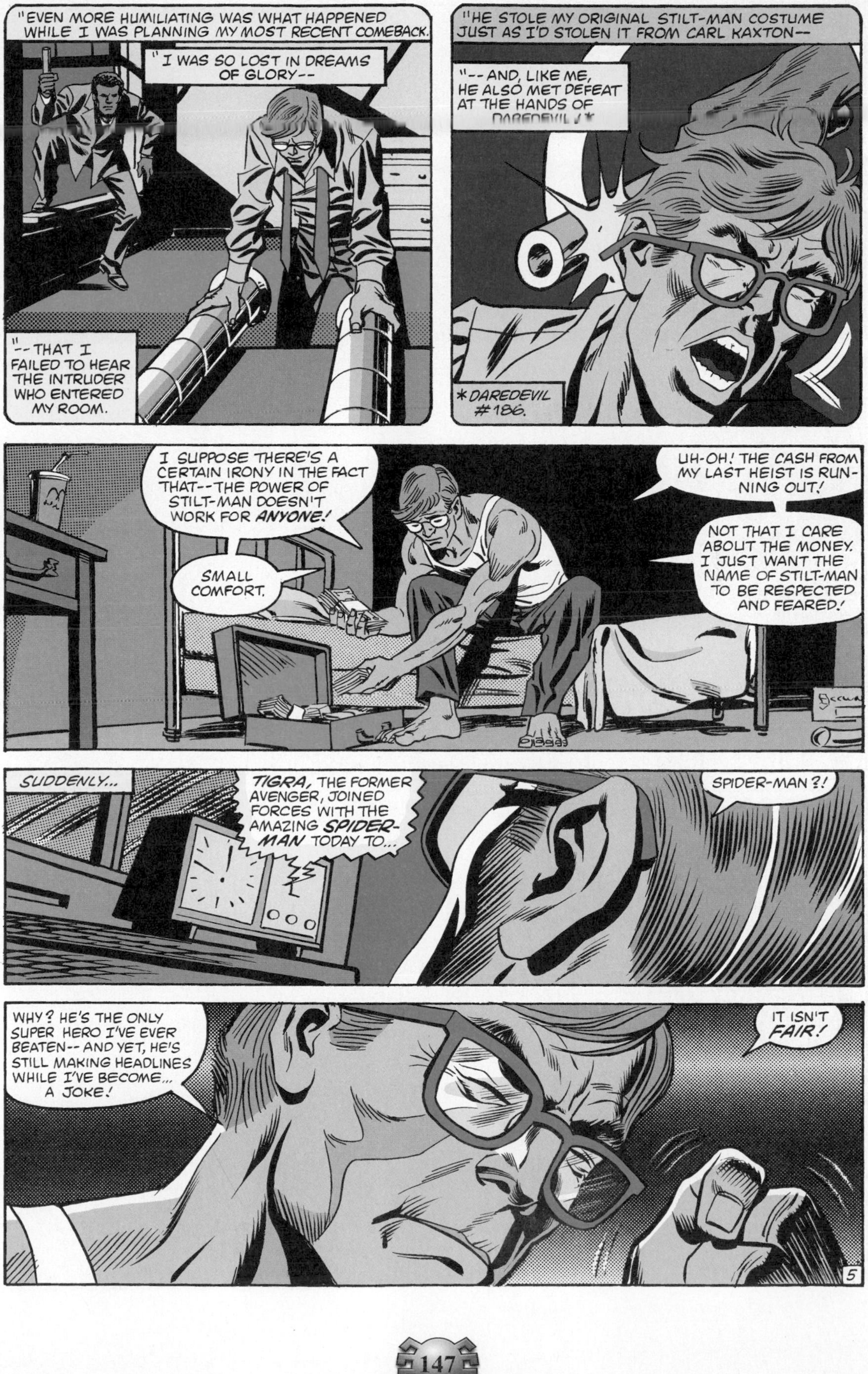
"EVEN MORE HUMILIATING WAS WHAT HAPPENED WHILE I WAS PLANNING MY MOST RECENT COMEBACK.
"I WAS SO LOST IN DREAMS OF GLORY--
"--THAT I FAILED TO HEAR THE INTRUDER WHO ENTERED MY ROOM.
"HE STOLE MY ORIGINAL STILT-MAN COSTUME JUST AS I'D STOLEN IT FROM CARL KAXTON--
"--AND, LIKE ME, HE ALSO MET DEFEAT AT THE HANDS OF DAREDEVIL!*
*DAREDEVIL #186.
I SUPPOSE THERE'S A CERTAIN IRONY IN THE FACT THAT--THE POWER OF STILT-MAN DOESN'T WORK FOR ANYONE!
SMALL COMFORT.
UH-OH! THE CASH FROM MY LAST HEIST IS RUNNING OUT!
NOT THAT I CARE ABOUT THE MONEY. I JUST WANT THE NAME OF STILT-MAN TO BE RESPECTED AND FEARED!
SUDDENLY...
TIGRA, THE FORMER AVENGER, JOINED FORCES WITH THE AMAZING SPIDER-MAN TODAY TO...
SPIDER-MAN?!
WHY? HE'S THE ONLY SUPER HERO I'VE EVER BEATEN-- AND YET, HE'S STILL MAKING HEADLINES WHILE I'VE BECOME... A JOKE!
IT ISN'T FAIR!
5

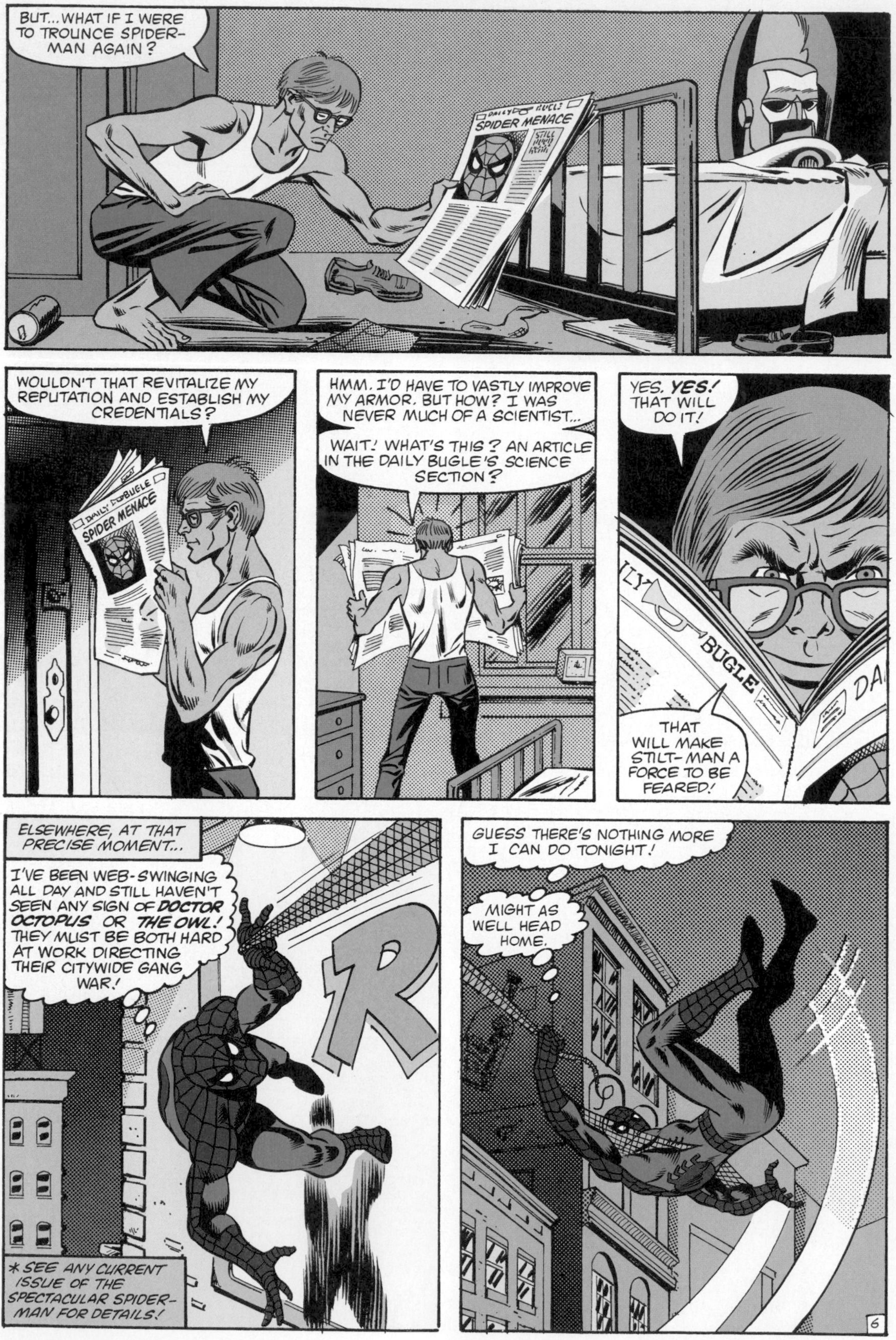

BUT... WHAT IF I WERE TO TROUNCE SPIDER-MAN AGAIN?
SPIDER MENACE
WOULDN'T THAT REVITALIZE MY REPUTATION AND ESTABLISH MY CREDENTIALS?
SPIDER MENACE
HMM. I'D HAVE TO VASTLY IMPROVE MY ARMOR. BUT HOW? I WAS NEVER MUCH OF A SCIENTIST...
WAIT! WHAT'S THIS? AN ARTICLE IN THE DAILY BUGLE'S SCIENCE SECTION?
YES. YES! THAT WILL DO IT!
BUGLE
THAT WILL MAKE STILT-MAN A FORCE TO BE FEARED!
ELSEWHERE, AT THAT PRECISE MOMENT...
I'VE BEEN WEB-SWINGING ALL DAY AND STILL HAVEN'T SEEN ANY SIGN OF DOCTOR OCTOPUS OR THE OWL! THEY MUST BE BOTH HARD AT WORK DIRECTING THEIR CITYWIDE GANG WAR!
* SEE ANY CURRENT ISSUE OF THE SPECTACULAR SPIDER-MAN FOR DETAILS!
GUESS THERE'S NOTHING MORE I CAN DO TONIGHT!
MIGHT AS WELL HEAD HOME.
6

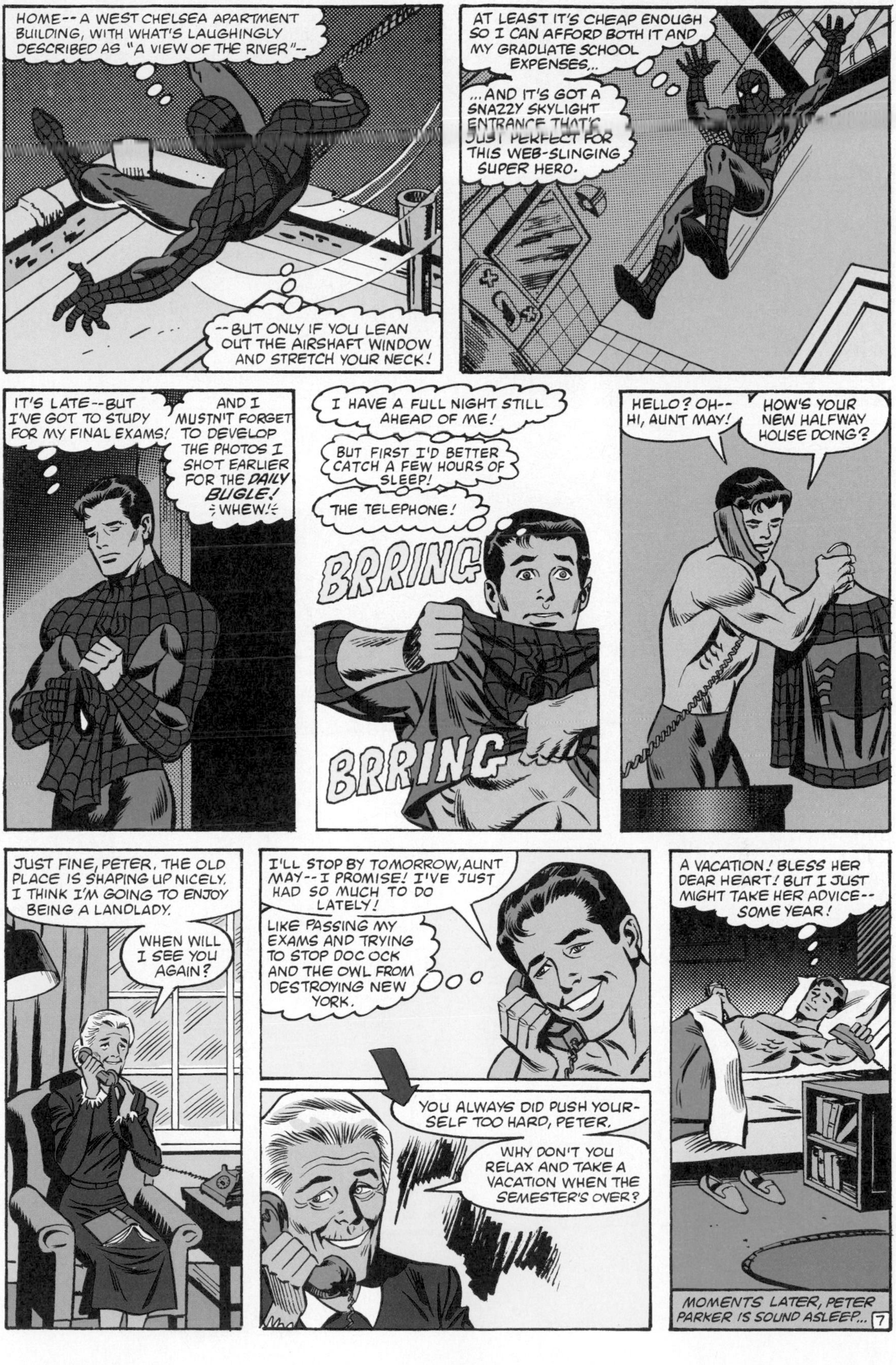
HOME-- A WEST CHELSEA APARTMENT BUILDING, WITH WHAT'S LAUGHINGLY DESCRIBED AS "A VIEW OF THE RIVER"--
--BUT ONLY IF YOU LEAN OUT THE AIRSHAFT WINDOW AND STRETCH YOUR NECK!
AT LEAST IT'S CHEAP ENOUGH SO I CAN AFFORD BOTH IT AND MY GRADUATE SCHOOL EXPENSES...
...AND IT'S GOT A SNAZZY SKYLIGHT ENTRANCE THAT'S JUST PERFECT FOR THIS WEB-SLINGING SUPER HERO.
IT'S LATE--BUT I'VE GOT TO STUDY FOR MY FINAL EXAMS!
AND I MUSTN'T FORGET TO DEVELOP THE PHOTOS I SHOT EARLIER FOR THE DAILY BUGLE! WHEW!
I HAVE A FULL NIGHT STILL AHEAD OF ME!
BUT FIRST I'D BETTER CATCH A FEW HOURS OF SLEEP!
THE TELEPHONE!
BRRING
BRRING
HELLO? OH-- HI, AUNT MAY!
HOW'S YOUR NEW HALFWAY HOUSE DOING?
JUST FINE, PETER. THE OLD PLACE IS SHAPING UP NICELY. I THINK I'M GOING TO ENJOY BEING A LANDLADY.
WHEN WILL I SEE YOU AGAIN?
I'LL STOP BY TOMORROW, AUNT MAY-- I PROMISE! I'VE JUST HAD SO MUCH TO DO LATELY!
LIKE PASSING MY EXAMS AND TRYING TO STOP DOC OCK AND THE OWL FROM DESTROYING NEW YORK.
YOU ALWAYS DID PUSH YOURSELF TOO HARD, PETER.
WHY DON'T YOU RELAX AND TAKE A VACATION WHEN THE SEMESTER'S OVER?
A VACATION! BLESS HER DEAR HEART! BUT I JUST MIGHT TAKE HER ADVICE-- SOME YEAR!
MOMENTS LATER, PETER PARKER IS SOUND ASLEEP...
7

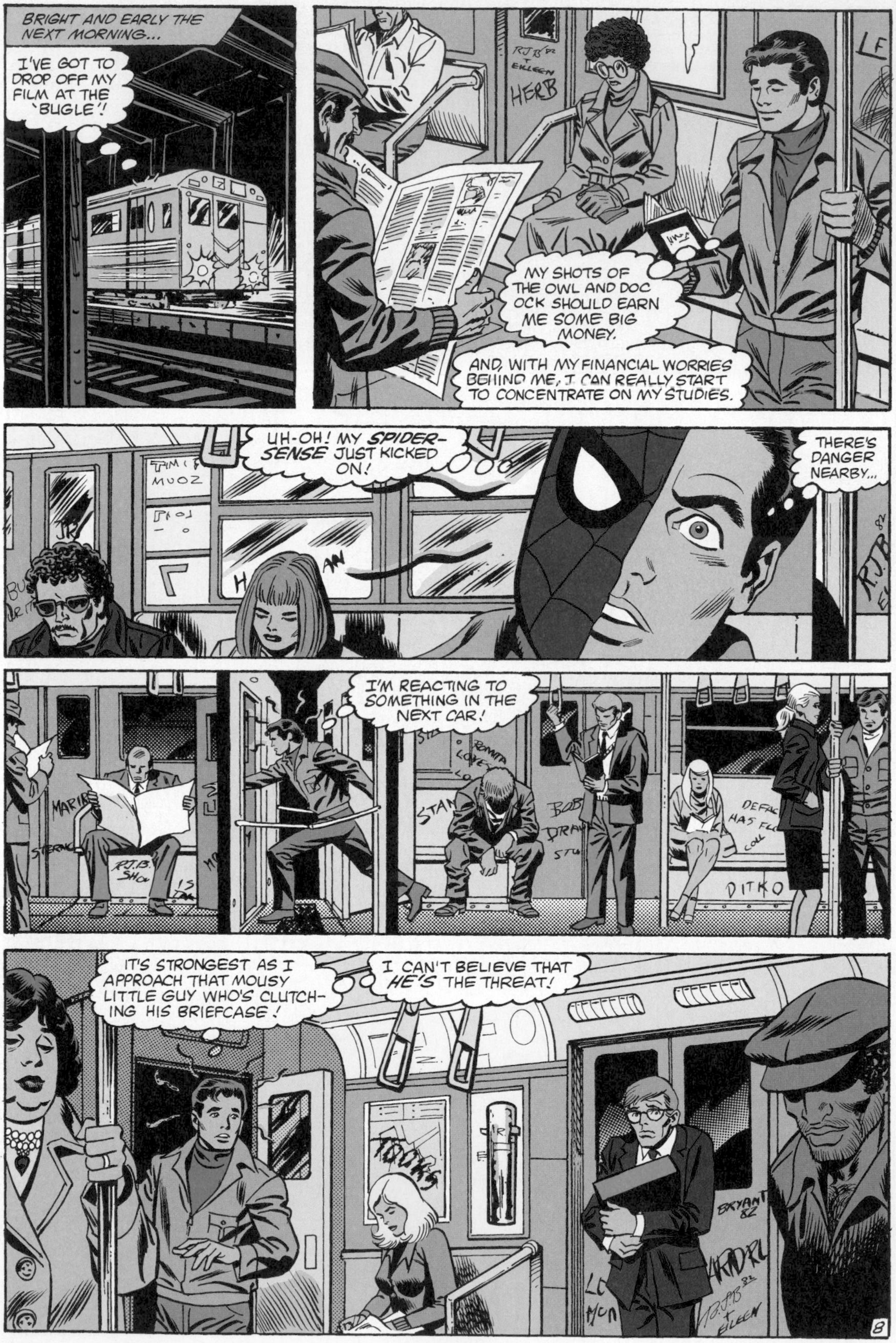
BRIGHT AND EARLY THE NEXT MORNING...
I'VE GOT TO DROP OFF MY FILM AT THE 'BUGLE'!
MY SHOTS OF THE OWL AND DOC OCK SHOULD EARN ME SOME BIG MONEY.
AND, WITH MY FINANCIAL WORRIES BEHIND ME, I CAN REALLY START TO CONCENTRATE ON MY STUDIES.
UH-OH! MY SPIDER-SENSE JUST KICKED ON!
THERE'S DANGER NEARBY...
I'M REACTING TO SOMETHING IN THE NEXT CAR!
IT'S STRONGEST AS I APPROACH THAT MOUSY LITTLE GUY WHO'S CLUTCHING HIS BRIEFCASE!
I CAN'T BELIEVE THAT HE'S THE THREAT!
DITKO
8

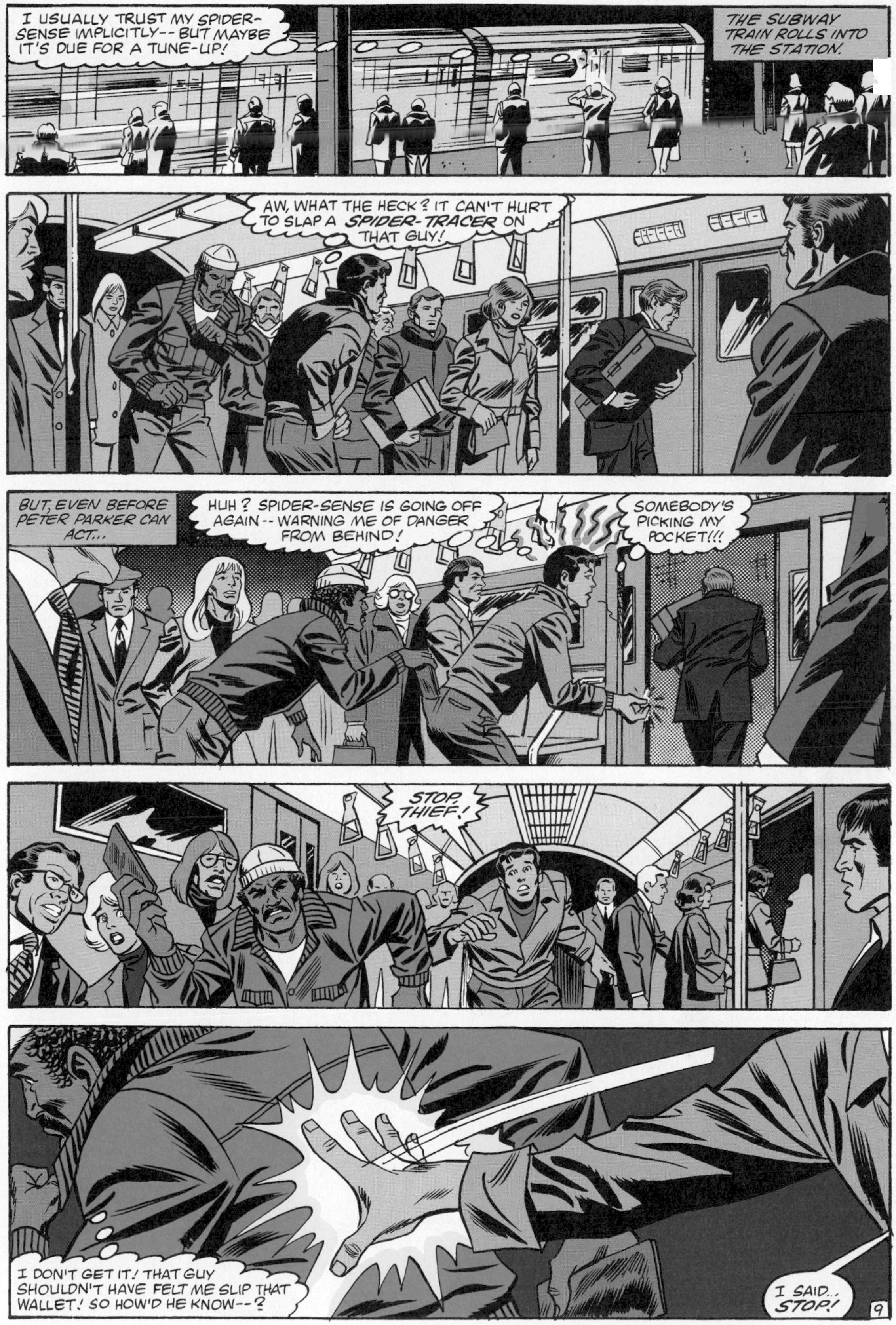

I USUALLY TRUST MY SPIDER-SENSE IMPLICITLY-- BUT MAYBE IT'S DUE FOR A TUNE-UP!
THE SUBWAY TRAIN ROLLS INTO THE STATION.
AW, WHAT THE HECK? IT CAN'T HURT TO SLAP A SPIDER-TRACER ON THAT GUY!
BUT, EVEN BEFORE PETER PARKER CAN ACT...
HUH? SPIDER-SENSE IS GOING OFF AGAIN-- WARNING ME OF DANGER FROM BEHIND!
SOMEBODY'S PICKING MY POCKET!!!
STOP, THIEF!
I DON'T GET IT! THAT GUY SHOULDN'T HAVE FELT ME SLIP THAT WALLET! SO HOW'D HE KNOW--?
I SAID... STOP!
9

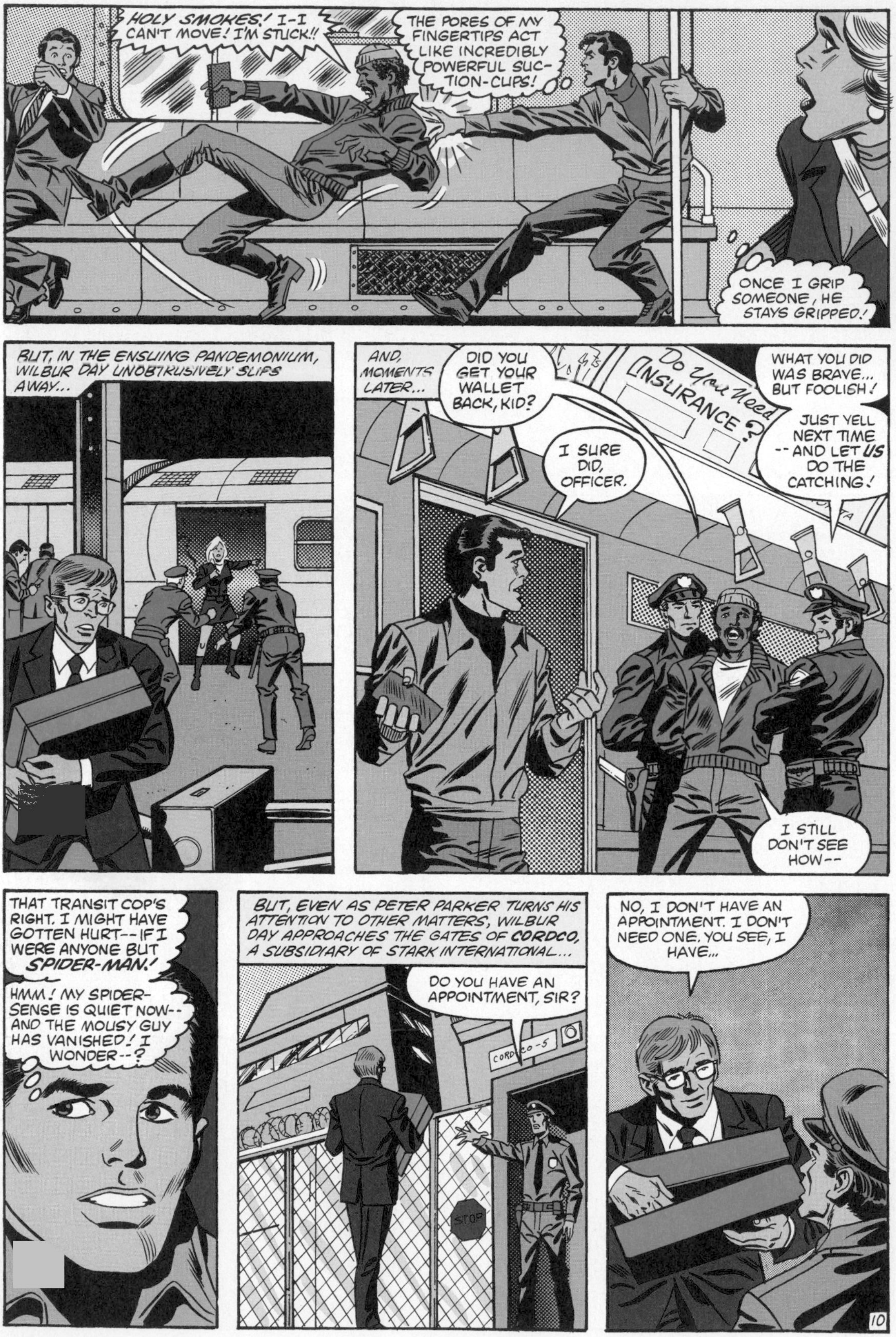
HOLY SMOKES! I-I CAN'T MOVE! I'M STUCK!!
THE PORES OF MY FINGERTIPS ACT LIKE INCREDIBLY POWERFUL SUC-TION-CUPS!
ONCE I GRIP SOMEONE, HE STAYS GRIPPED!
BUT, IN THE ENSUING PANDEMONIUM, WILBUR DAY UNOBTRUSIVELY SLIPS AWAY...
AND, MOMENTS LATER...
DID YOU GET YOUR WALLET BACK, KID?
Do You Need INSURANCE?
WHAT YOU DID WAS BRAVE... BUT FOOLISH!
JUST YELL NEXT TIME -- AND LET US DO THE CATCHING!
I SURE DID, OFFICER.
I STILL DON'T SEE HOW--
THAT TRANSIT COP'S RIGHT. I MIGHT HAVE GOTTEN HURT--IF I WERE ANYONE BUT SPIDER-MAN!
HMM! MY SPIDER-SENSE IS QUIET NOW--AND THE MOUSY GUY HAS VANISHED! I WONDER--?
BUT, EVEN AS PETER PARKER TURNS HIS ATTENTION TO OTHER MATTERS, WILBUR DAY APPROACHES THE GATES OF CORDCO, A SUBSIDIARY OF STARK INTERNATIONAL...
DO YOU HAVE AN APPOINTMENT, SIR?
STOP
NO, I DON'T HAVE AN APPOINTMENT. I DON'T NEED ONE. YOU SEE, I HAVE...
10

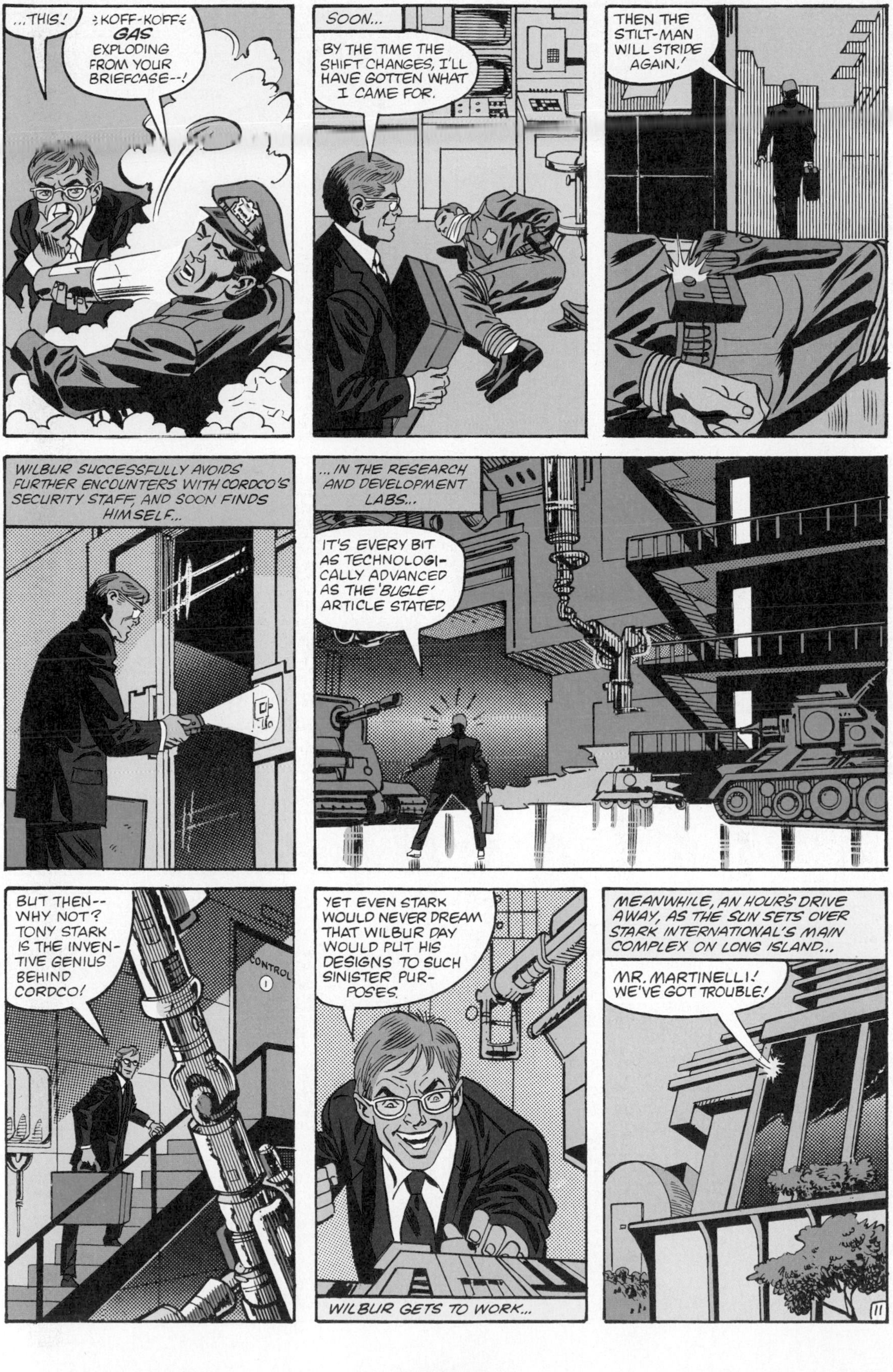
...THIS!
KOFF-KOFF
GAS
EXPLODING FROM YOUR BRIEFCASE--!
SOON...
BY THE TIME THE SHIFT CHANGES, I'LL HAVE GOTTEN WHAT I CAME FOR.
THEN THE STILT-MAN WILL STRIDE AGAIN!
WILBUR SUCCESSFULLY AVOIDS FURTHER ENCOUNTERS WITH CORDCO'S SECURITY STAFF, AND SOON FINDS HIMSELF...
...IN THE RESEARCH AND DEVELOPMENT LABS...
IT'S EVERY BIT AS TECHNOLOGICALLY ADVANCED AS THE 'BUGLE' ARTICLE STATED.
BUT THEN--WHY NOT? TONY STARK IS THE INVENTIVE GENIUS BEHIND CORDCO!
CONTROL
YET EVEN STARK WOULD NEVER DREAM THAT WILBUR DAY WOULD PUT HIS DESIGNS TO SUCH SINISTER PURPOSES.
WILBUR GETS TO WORK...
MEANWHILE, AN HOUR'S DRIVE AWAY, AS THE SUN SETS OVER STARK INTERNATIONAL'S MAIN COMPLEX ON LONG ISLAND...
MR. MARTINELLI! WE'VE GOT TROUBLE!
11

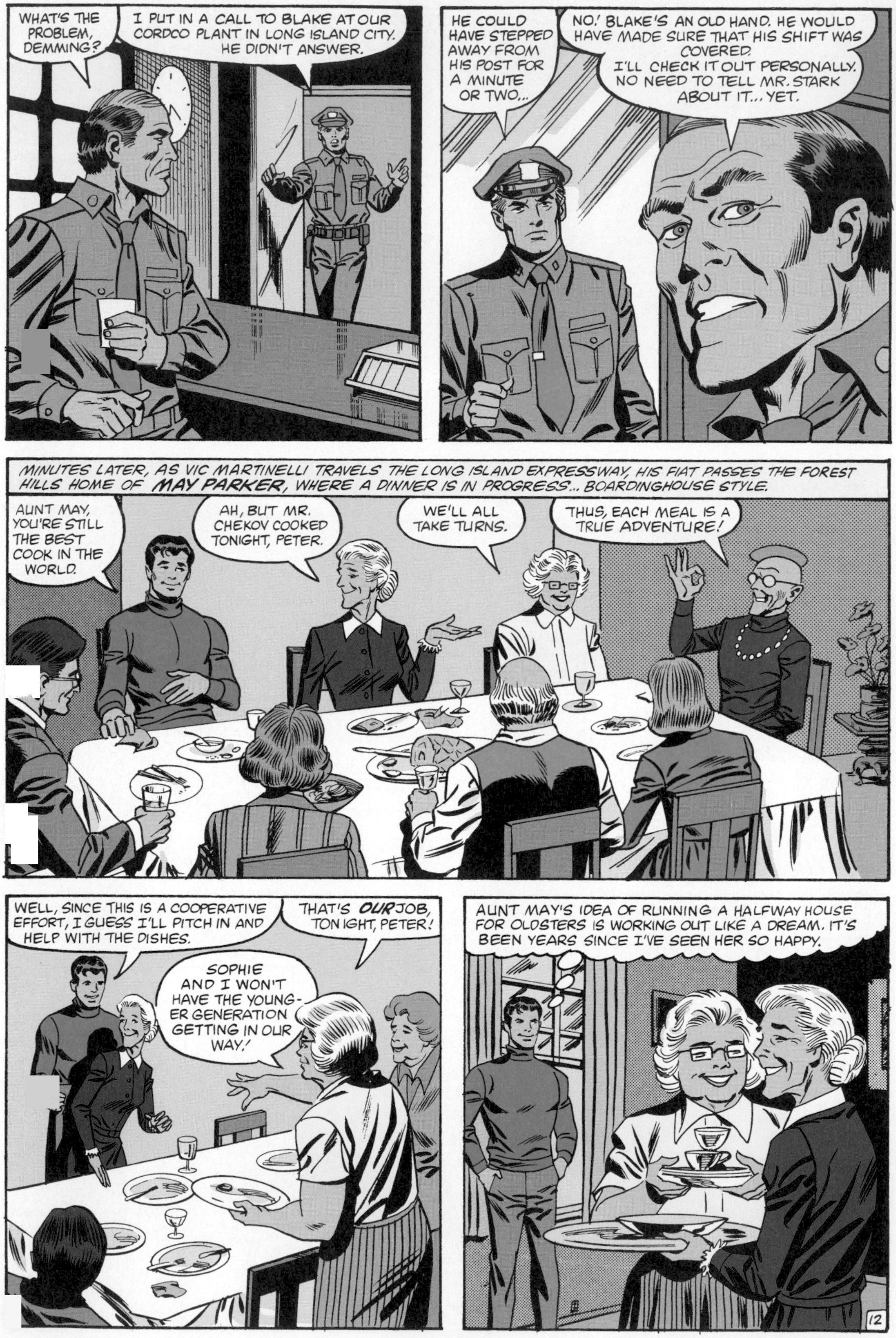

WHAT'S THE PROBLEM, DEMMING?
I PUT IN A CALL TO BLAKE AT OUR CORDCO PLANT IN LONG ISLAND CITY. HE DIDN'T ANSWER.
HE COULD HAVE STEPPED AWAY FROM HIS POST FOR A MINUTE OR TWO...
NO! BLAKE'S AN OLD HAND. HE WOULD HAVE MADE SURE THAT HIS SHIFT WAS COVERED. I'LL CHECK IT OUT PERSONALLY. NO NEED TO TELL MR. STARK ABOUT IT... YET.
MINUTES LATER, AS VIC MARTINELLI TRAVELS THE LONG ISLAND EXPRESSWAY, HIS FIAT PASSES THE FOREST HILLS HOME OF MAY PARKER, WHERE A DINNER IS IN PROGRESS... BOARDINGHOUSE STYLE.
AUNT MAY, YOU'RE STILL THE BEST COOK IN THE WORLD.
AH, BUT MR. CHEKOV COOKED TONIGHT, PETER.
WE'LL ALL TAKE TURNS.
THUS, EACH MEAL IS A TRUE ADVENTURE!
WELL, SINCE THIS IS A COOPERATIVE EFFORT, I GUESS I'LL PITCH IN AND HELP WITH THE DISHES.
THAT'S OUR JOB, TONIGHT, PETER!
SOPHIE AND I WON'T HAVE THE YOUNGER GENERATION GETTING IN OUR WAY!
AUNT MAY'S IDEA OF RUNNING A HALFWAY HOUSE FOR OLDSTERS IS WORKING OUT LIKE A DREAM. IT'S BEEN YEARS SINCE I'VE SEEN HER SO HAPPY.
12

BUT THAT ISN'T GOING TO HELP HER PAY THE MORTGAGE AND TAXES ON THIS PLACE.

WHY THE LONG FACE, PETE?

NO REAL REASON, NATHAN-- I JUST HAVE A FEW THINGS ON MY MIND AT THE MOMENT.

GET RID OF THEM-- BY GOING OUT AND TAKING CARE OF THEM!

TROUBLE WITH THE WORLD TODAY-- IS THAT PEOPLE SPEND TOO MUCH TIME THINKING-- AND NOT ENOUGH TIME DOING!

LOOK AT YOUR AUNT! SHE'S GOT SOMETHING TO DO....

AND SHE LOOKS BETTER THAN EVER!

YOU'RE RIGHT, NATHAN-- HAVING A GOAL DOES MAKE LIFE A LOT BRIGHTER.

AND MY GOAL IS TO HELP AUNT MAY ATTAIN HERS!

PETER LEFT IN SUCH HIGH SPIRITS, NATHAN. WHAT DID YOU SAY TO HIM?

JUST A LITTLE PEP TALK, MY DEAR! IF PETER TAKES IT TO HEART-- --HE'LL GO FAR!

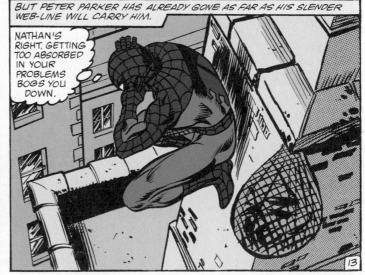

BUT PETER PARKER HAS ALREADY GONE AS FAR AS HIS SLENDER WEB-LINE WILL CARRY HIM.

NATHAN'S RIGHT. GETTING TOO ABSORBED IN YOUR PROBLEMS BOGS YOU DOWN.

155

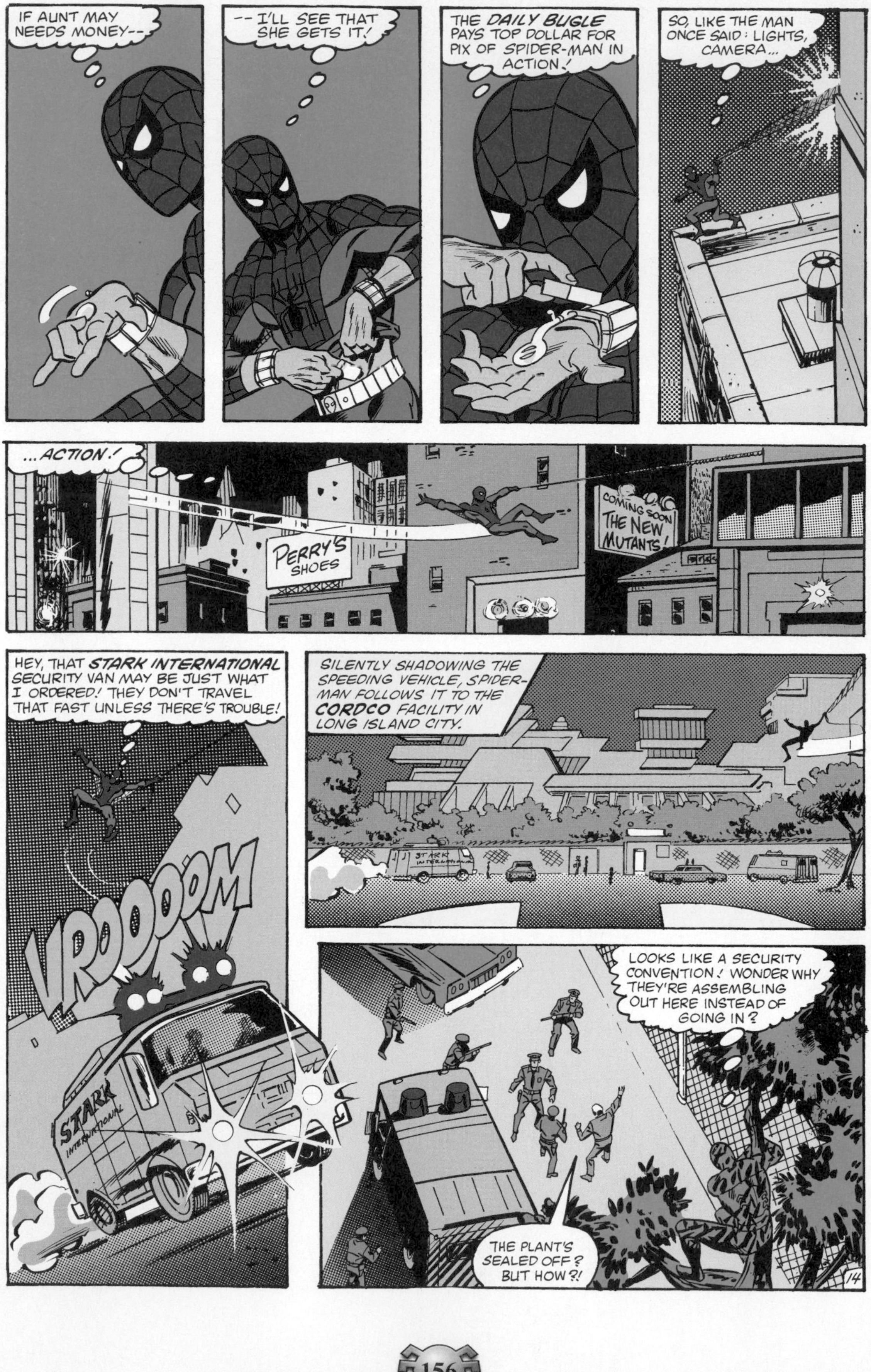
IF AUNT MAY NEEDS MONEY--
-- I'LL SEE THAT SHE GETS IT!
THE DAILY BUGLE PAYS TOP DOLLAR FOR PIX OF SPIDER-MAN IN ACTION!
SO, LIKE THE MAN ONCE SAID: LIGHTS, CAMERA...
...ACTION!
PERRY'S SHOES
COMING SOON THE NEW MUTANTS!
HEY, THAT STARK INTERNATIONAL SECURITY VAN MAY BE JUST WHAT I ORDERED! THEY DON'T TRAVEL THAT FAST UNLESS THERE'S TROUBLE!
VROOOOM
STARK INTERNATIONAL
SILENTLY SHADOWING THE SPEEDING VEHICLE, SPIDER-MAN FOLLOWS IT TO THE CORDCO FACILITY IN LONG ISLAND CITY.
LOOKS LIKE A SECURITY CONVENTION! WONDER WHY THEY'RE ASSEMBLING OUT HERE INSTEAD OF GOING IN?
THE PLANT'S SEALED OFF? BUT HOW?!
14

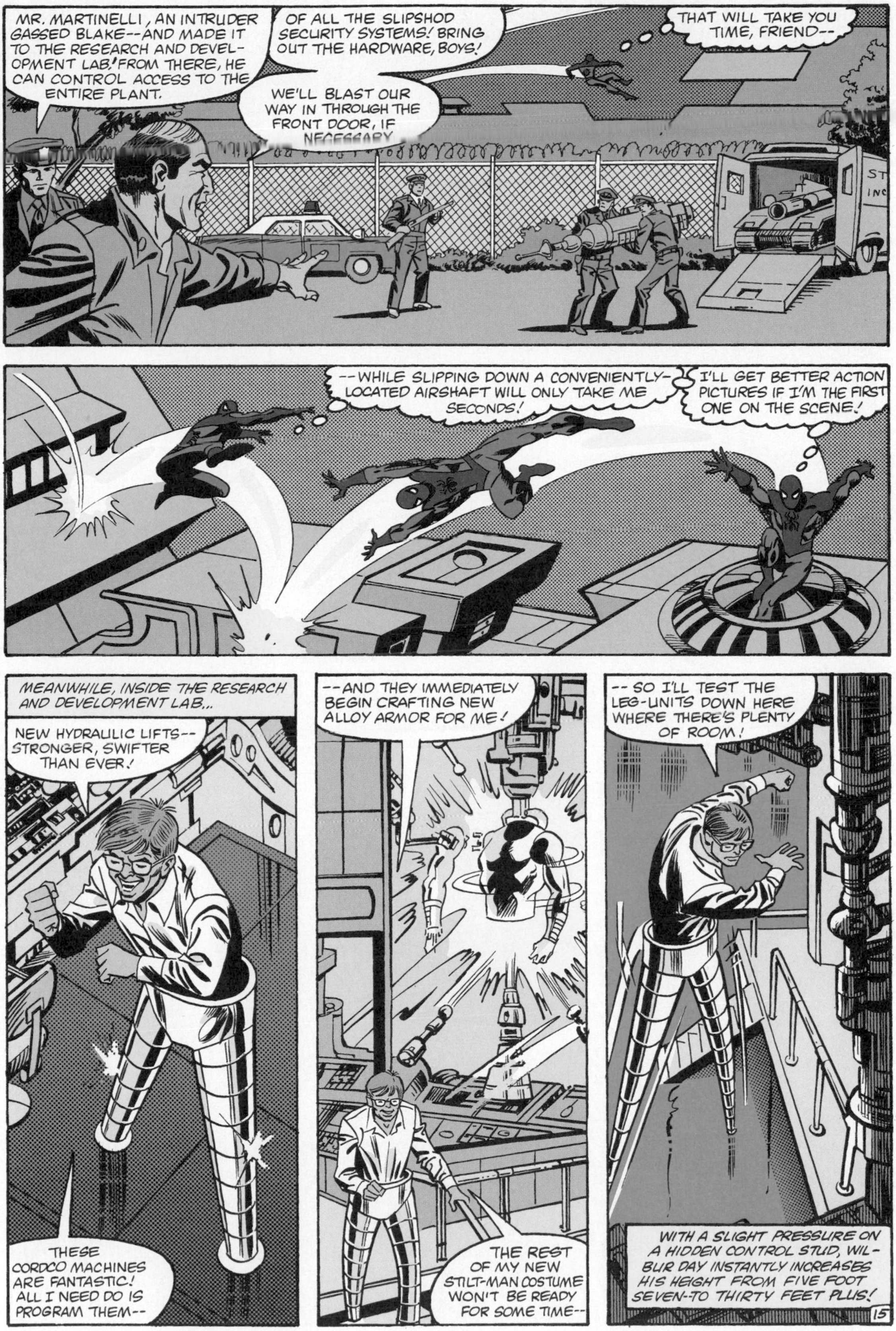

MR. MARTINELLI, AN INTRUDER GASSED BLAKE--AND MADE IT TO THE RESEARCH AND DEVELOPMENT LAB! FROM THERE, HE CAN CONTROL ACCESS TO THE ENTIRE PLANT.
OF ALL THE SLIPSHOD SECURITY SYSTEMS! BRING OUT THE HARDWARE, BOYS!
WE'LL BLAST OUR WAY IN THROUGH THE FRONT DOOR, IF NECESSARY.
THAT WILL TAKE YOU TIME, FRIEND--
--WHILE SLIPPING DOWN A CONVENIENTLY-LOCATED AIRSHAFT WILL ONLY TAKE ME SECONDS!
I'LL GET BETTER ACTION PICTURES IF I'M THE FIRST ONE ON THE SCENE!
MEANWHILE, INSIDE THE RESEARCH AND DEVELOPMENT LAB...
NEW HYDRAULIC LIFTS--STRONGER, SWIFTER THAN EVER!
THESE CORDCO MACHINES ARE FANTASTIC! ALL I NEED DO IS PROGRAM THEM--
--AND THEY IMMEDIATELY BEGIN CRAFTING NEW ALLOY ARMOR FOR ME!
THE REST OF MY NEW STILT-MAN COSTUME WON'T BE READY FOR SOME TIME--
-- SO I'LL TEST THE LEG-UNITS DOWN HERE WHERE THERE'S PLENTY OF ROOM!
WITH A SLIGHT PRESSURE ON A HIDDEN CONTROL STUD, WILBUR DAY INSTANTLY INCREASES HIS HEIGHT FROM FIVE FOOT SEVEN-TO THIRTY FEET PLUS!
15

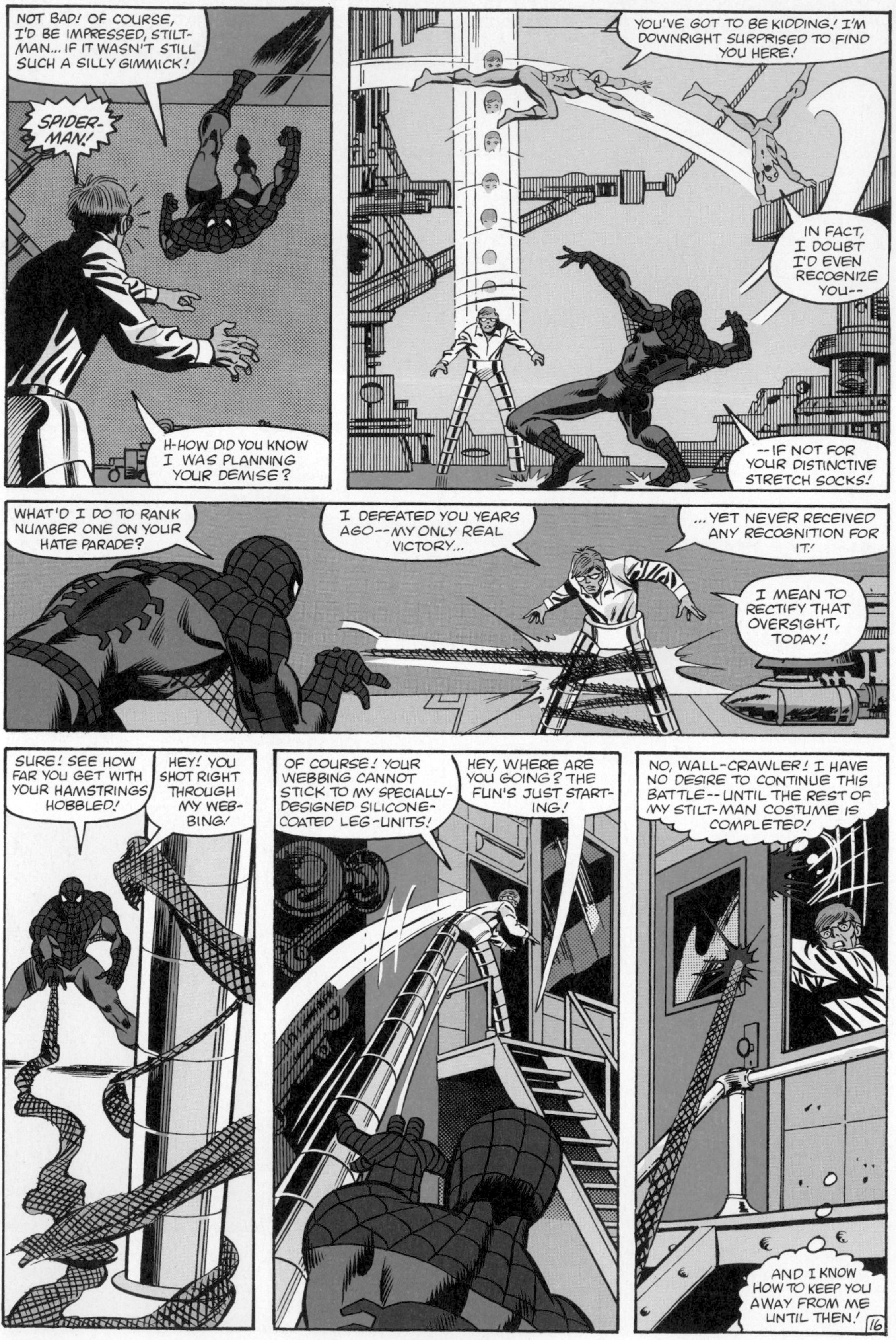
NOT BAD! OF COURSE, I'D BE IMPRESSED, STILT-MAN... IF IT WASN'T STILL SUCH A SILLY GIMMICK!
SPIDER-MAN!
H-HOW DID YOU KNOW I WAS PLANNING YOUR DEMISE?
YOU'VE GOT TO BE KIDDING! I'M DOWNRIGHT SURPRISED TO FIND YOU HERE!
IN FACT, I DOUBT I'D EVEN RECOGNIZE YOU--
--IF NOT FOR YOUR DISTINCTIVE STRETCH SOCKS!
WHAT'D I DO TO RANK NUMBER ONE ON YOUR HATE PARADE?
I DEFEATED YOU YEARS AGO--MY ONLY REAL VICTORY...
...YET NEVER RECEIVED ANY RECOGNITION FOR IT!
I MEAN TO RECTIFY THAT OVERSIGHT, TODAY!
SURE! SEE HOW FAR YOU GET WITH YOUR HAMSTRINGS HOBBLED!
HEY! YOU SHOT RIGHT THROUGH MY WEB-BING!
OF COURSE! YOUR WEBBING CANNOT STICK TO MY SPECIALLY-DESIGNED SILICONE-COATED LEG-UNITS!
HEY, WHERE ARE YOU GOING? THE FUN'S JUST START-ING!
NO, WALL-CRAWLER! I HAVE NO DESIRE TO CONTINUE THIS BATTLE--UNTIL THE REST OF MY STILT-MAN COSTUME IS COMPLETED!
AND I KNOW HOW TO KEEP YOU AWAY FROM ME UNTIL THEN!
16

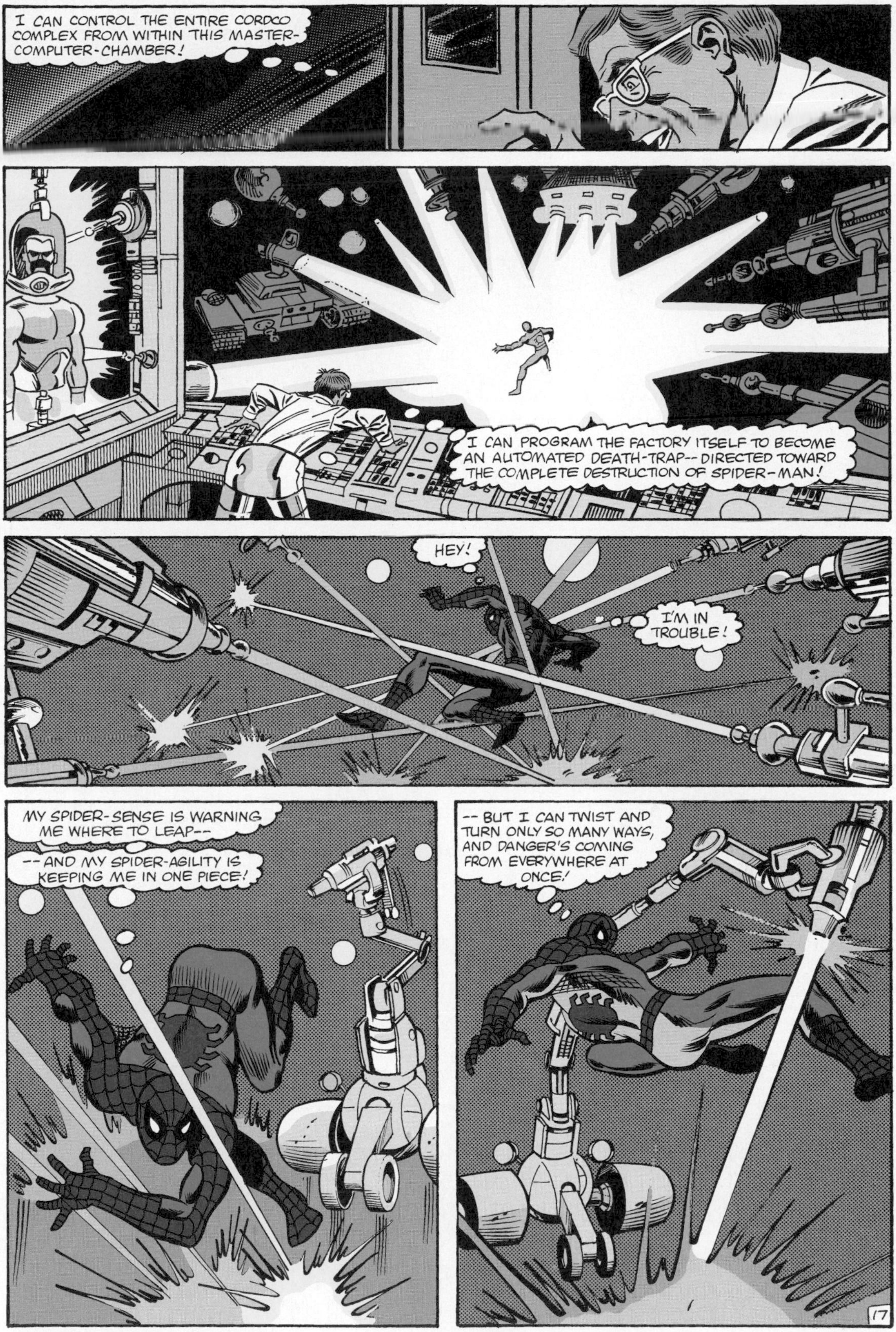
I CAN CONTROL THE ENTIRE CORDCO COMPLEX FROM WITHIN THIS MASTER-COMPUTER-CHAMBER!
I CAN PROGRAM THE FACTORY ITSELF TO BECOME AN AUTOMATED DEATH-TRAP-- DIRECTED TOWARD THE COMPLETE DESTRUCTION OF SPIDER-MAN!
HEY!
I'M IN TROUBLE!
MY SPIDER-SENSE IS WARNING ME WHERE TO LEAP--
-- AND MY SPIDER-AGILITY IS KEEPING ME IN ONE PIECE!
-- BUT I CAN TWIST AND TURN ONLY SO MANY WAYS, AND DANGER'S COMING FROM EVERYWHERE AT ONCE!
17

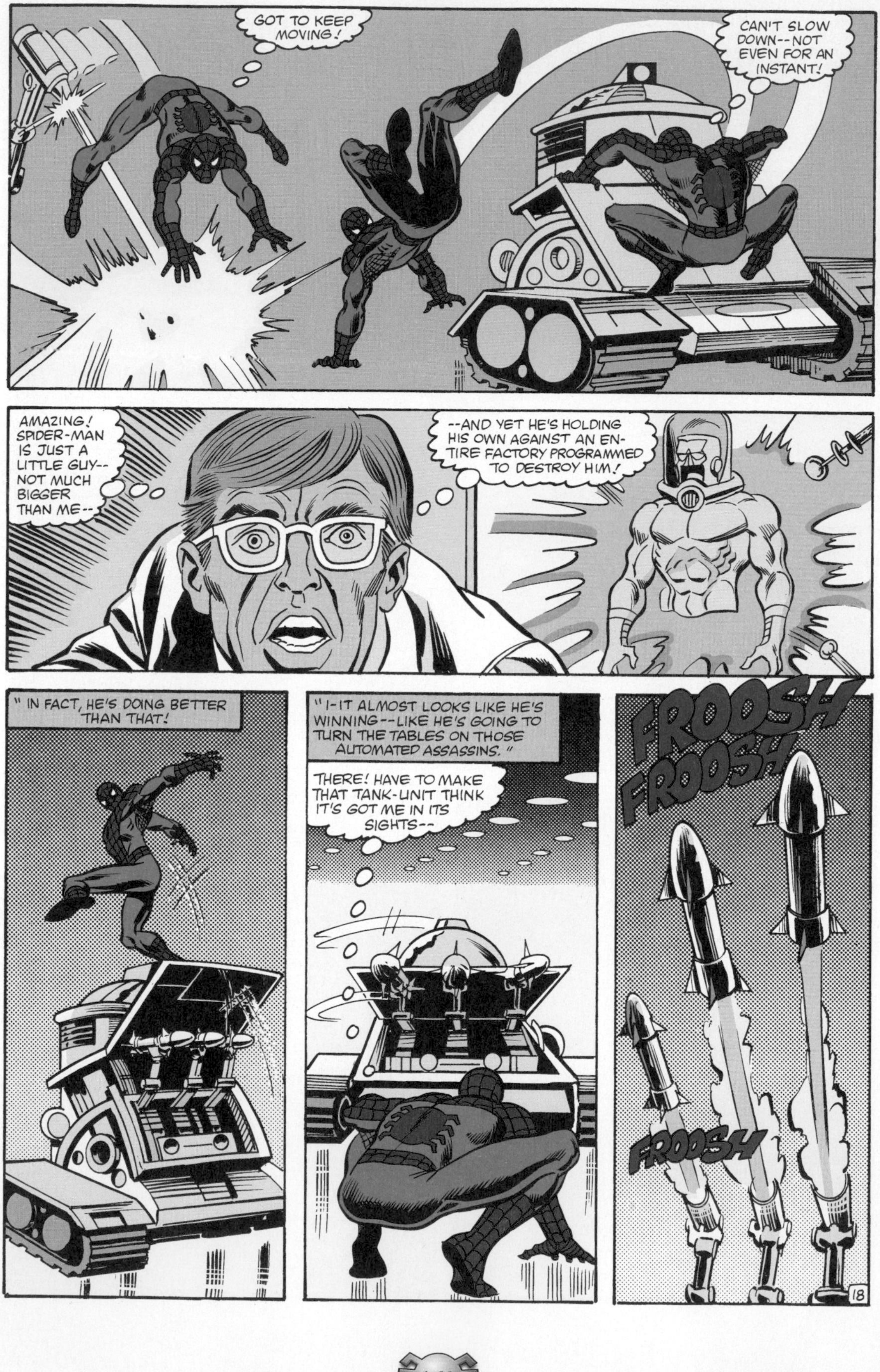
GOT TO KEEP MOVING!
CAN'T SLOW DOWN--NOT EVEN FOR AN INSTANT!
AMAZING! SPIDER-MAN IS JUST A LITTLE GUY--NOT MUCH BIGGER THAN ME--
--AND YET HE'S HOLDING HIS OWN AGAINST AN EN-TIRE FACTORY PROGRAMMED TO DESTROY HIM!
" IN FACT, HE'S DOING BETTER THAN THAT!
" I-IT ALMOST LOOKS LIKE HE'S WINNING--LIKE HE'S GOING TO TURN THE TABLES ON THOSE AUTOMATED ASSASSINS."
THERE! HAVE TO MAKE THAT TANK-UNIT THINK IT'S GOT ME IN ITS SIGHTS--
FROOSH
FROOSH
FROOSH
18

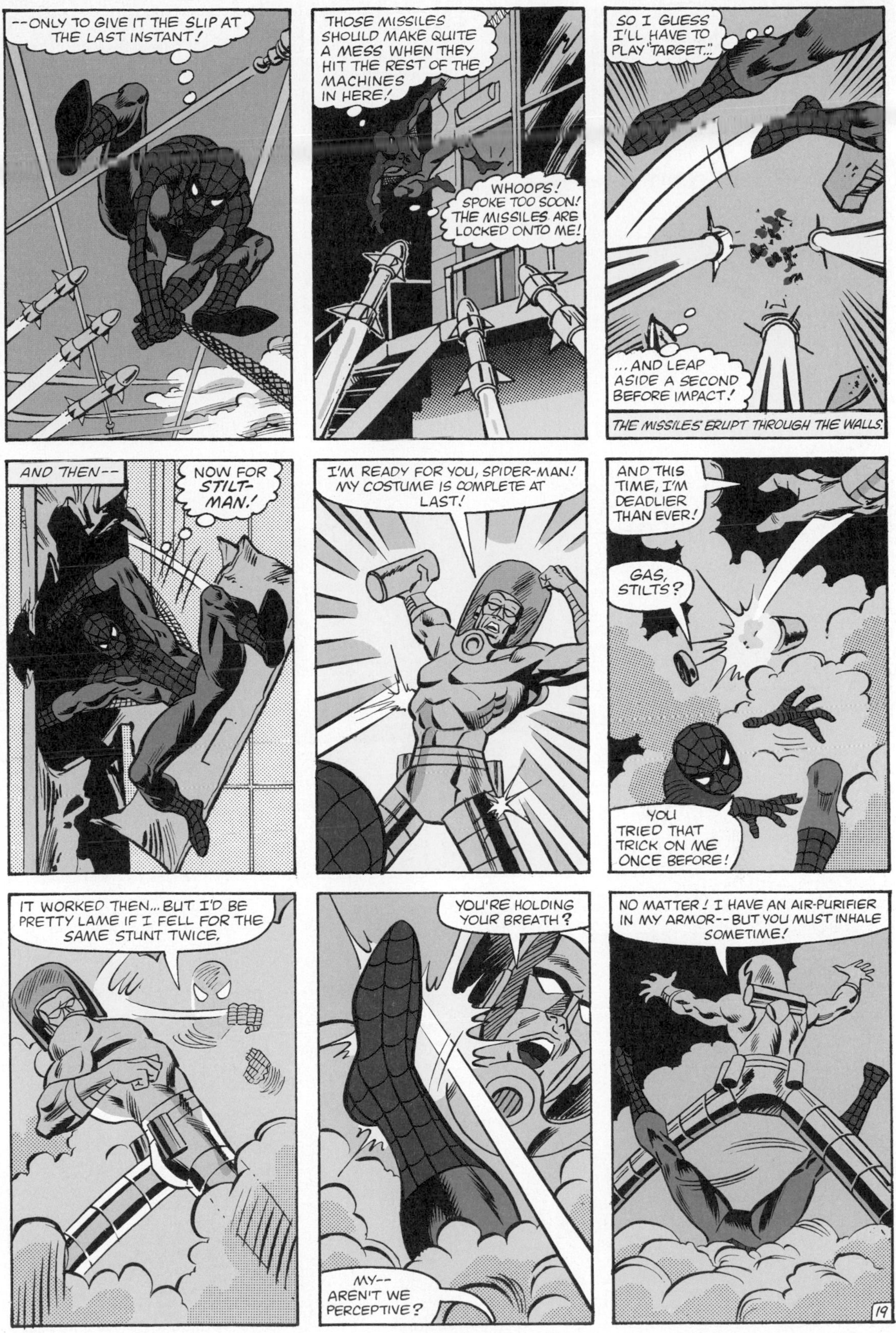
--ONLY TO GIVE IT THE SLIP AT THE LAST INSTANT!
THOSE MISSILES SHOULD MAKE QUITE A MESS WHEN THEY HIT THE REST OF THE MACHINES IN HERE!
WHOOPS! SPOKE TOO SOON! THE MISSILES ARE LOCKED ONTO ME!
SO I GUESS I'LL HAVE TO PLAY "TARGET..."
...AND LEAP ASIDE A SECOND BEFORE IMPACT!
THE MISSILES ERUPT THROUGH THE WALLS.
AND THEN--
NOW FOR STILT-MAN!
I'M READY FOR YOU, SPIDER-MAN! MY COSTUME IS COMPLETE AT LAST!
AND THIS TIME, I'M DEADLIER THAN EVER!
GAS, STILTS?
YOU TRIED THAT TRICK ON ME ONCE BEFORE!
IT WORKED THEN... BUT I'D BE PRETTY LAME IF I FELL FOR THE SAME STUNT TWICE.
YOU'RE HOLDING YOUR BREATH?
MY-- AREN'T WE PERCEPTIVE?
NO MATTER! I HAVE AN AIR-PURIFIER IN MY ARMOR--BUT YOU MUST INHALE SOMETIME!
19

I CAN HOLD MY BREATH A LONG TIME-- BUT NOT FOREVER!

YOU'RE RIGHT, STILTS!

BUT IT WON'T TAKE ME THAT LONG TO FIND THE EXHAUST FANS THAT VENTILATE THIS LAB!

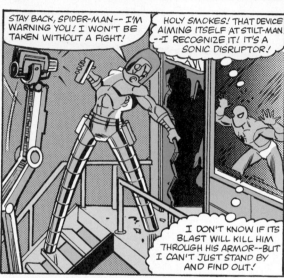

STAY BACK, SPIDER-MAN-- I'M WARNING YOU! I WON'T BE TAKEN WITHOUT A FIGHT!

HOLY SMOKES! THAT DEVICE AIMING ITSELF AT STILT-MAN --I RECOGNIZE IT! IT'S A SONIC DISRUPTOR!

I DON'T KNOW IF ITS BLAST WILL KILL HIM THROUGH HIS ARMOR--BUT I CAN'T JUST STAND BY AND FIND OUT!

STILT-MAN-- LOOK OUT!

WHAT? IS THIS SOME KIND OF TRICK--?

THE DISRUPTOR THAT WILBUR DAY HAD HIM-SELF SET IN MOTION, FIRES--

--CATCHING THE AMAZING SPIDER-MAN WITH ITS FULL FORCE.

SECONDS LATER, AS THE STILT-MAN DISMANTLES THE DISRUPTOR BEFORE IT CAN FIRE AGAIN.

SPIDER-MAN TOOK A BLAST AIMED AT ME! H-HE MAY HAVE SAVED MY LIFE!

BUT THERE WAS NO ONE HERE TO WITNESS...

20

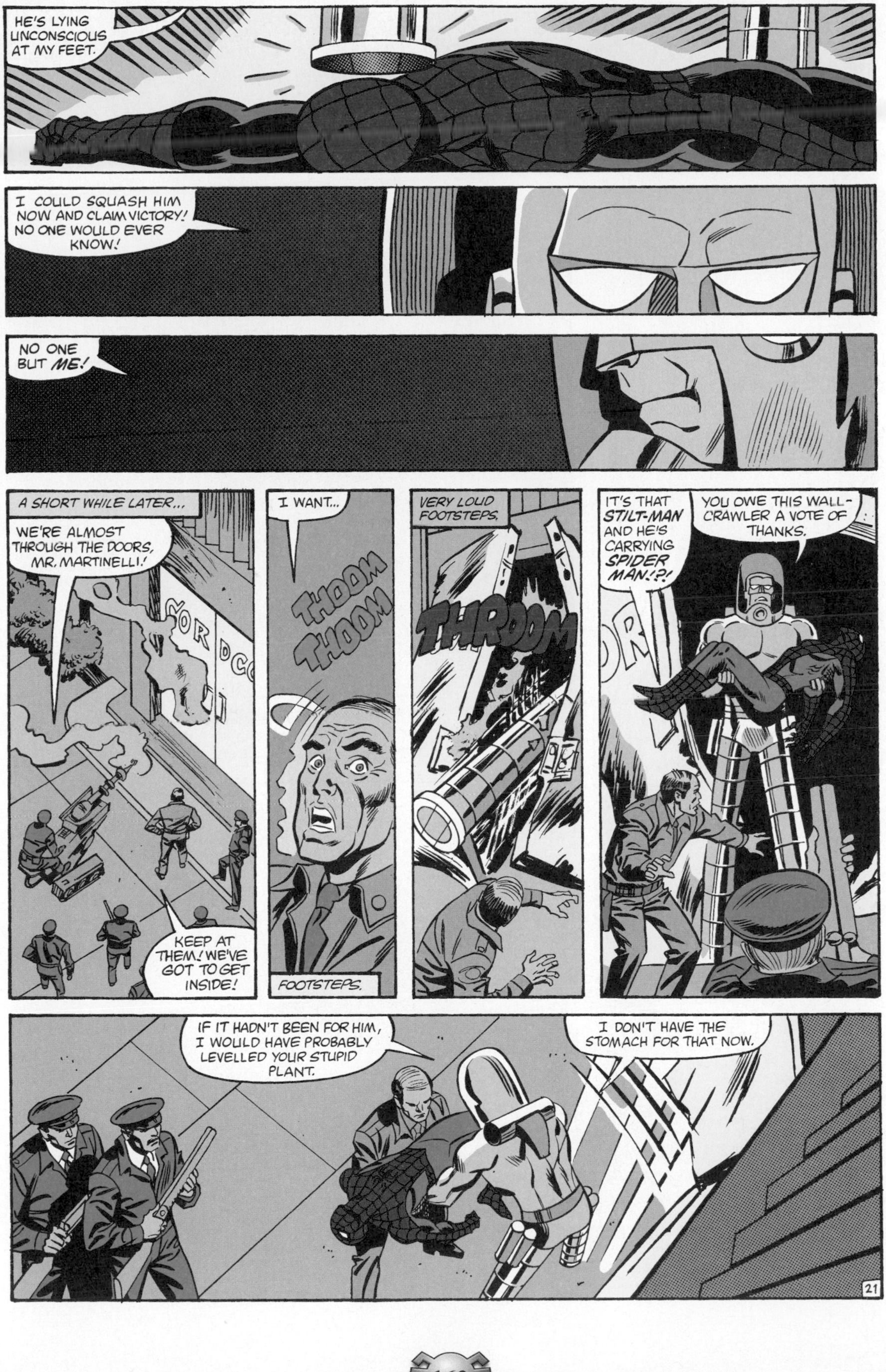
HE'S LYING UNCONSCIOUS AT MY FEET.
I COULD SQUASH HIM NOW AND CLAIM VICTORY! NO ONE WOULD EVER KNOW!
NO ONE BUT ME!
A SHORT WHILE LATER...
WE'RE ALMOST THROUGH THE DOORS, MR. MARTINELLI!
KEEP AT THEM! WE'VE GOT TO GET INSIDE!
I WANT...
THOOM THOOM
FOOTSTEPS.
VERY LOUD FOOTSTEPS.
THROOM
IT'S THAT STILT-MAN AND HE'S CARRYING SPIDER MAN!?!
YOU OWE THIS WALL-CRAWLER A VOTE OF THANKS.
IF IT HADN'T BEEN FOR HIM, I WOULD HAVE PROBABLY LEVELLED YOUR STUPID PLANT.
I DON'T HAVE THE STOMACH FOR THAT NOW.
21

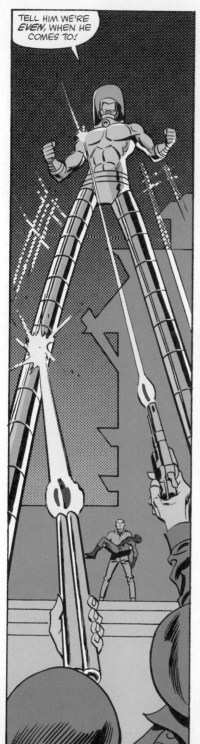

TELL HIM WE'RE *EVEN*, WHEN HE COMES TO!

IGNORING THE SECURITY STAFF -- AND THE BULLETS THAT SHRIEK OFF HIS ARMOR, THE STILT-MAN TURNS AND STRIDES AWAY...

...AS ONLY HE CAN.

LEAVING BEHIND A REVIVING SPIDER-MAN AND A MYSTIFIED VIC MARTINELLI...

DO YOU KNOW WHAT HE MEANT, WEB-SLINGER -- ABOUT YOU TWO BEING *EVEN*?

I SAVED STILT-MAN'S LIFE IN THERE, FRIEND... AND, IN RETURN, HE DIDN'T TAKE MINE.

FUNNY WAY OF EVENING THE ODDS, HUH?

YEAH... FUNNY.

END

NEXT ISSUE: AN *OLD* GIRLFRIEND (GUESS WHO) MAKES A BRIEF APPEARANCE -- AND A *NEW* VILLAIN ENTERS THE SCENE!

SHADOW OF EVILS PAST!

DON'T MISS IT!

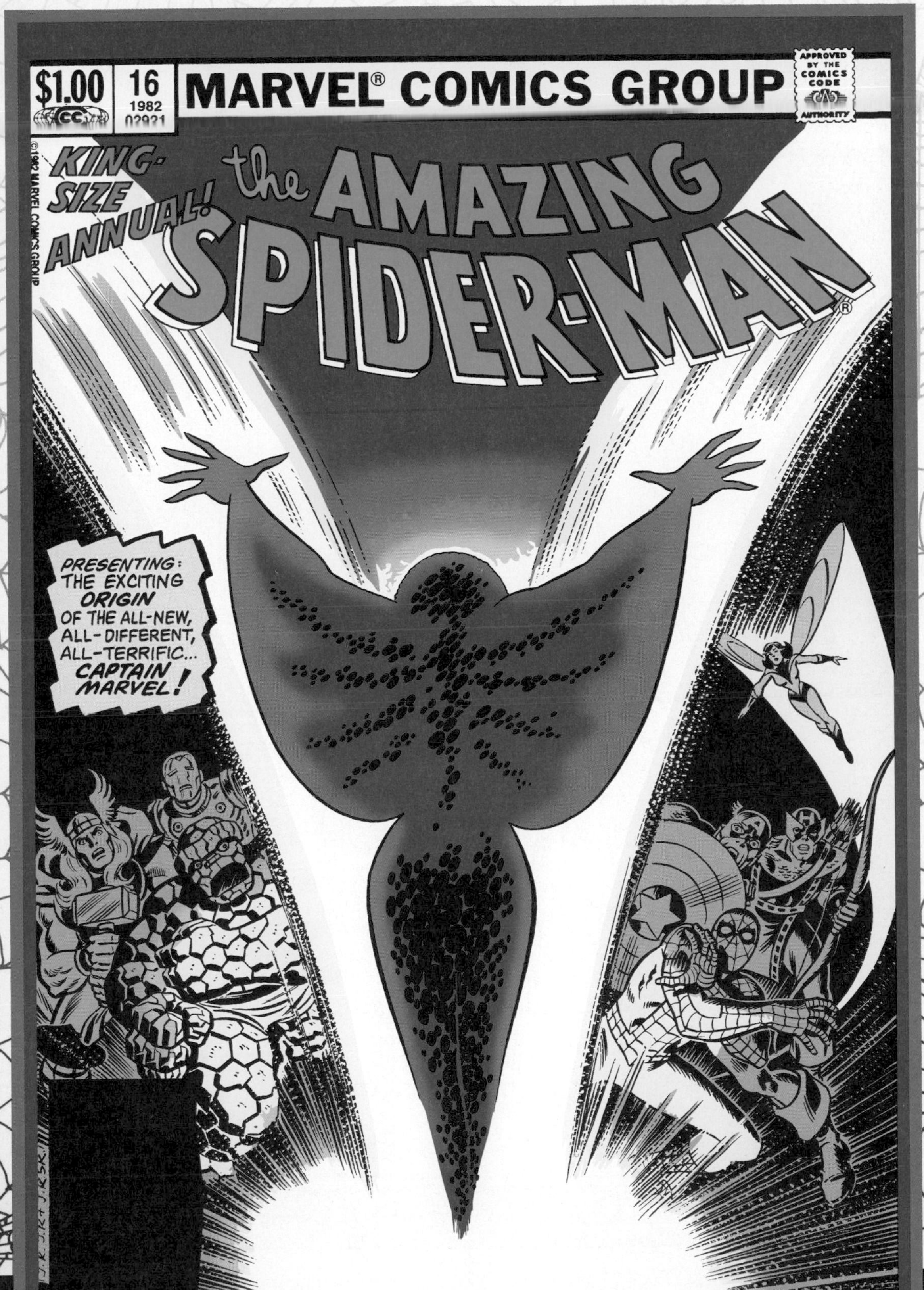
$1.00
16
1982
02921
MARVEL® COMICS GROUP
APPROVED BY THE COMICS CODE AUTHORITY
© 1982 MARVEL COMICS GROUP
KING-SIZE ANNUAL!
the AMAZING SPIDER-MAN®
PRESENTING: THE EXCITING ORIGIN OF THE ALL-NEW, ALL-DIFFERENT, ALL-TERRIFIC... CAPTAIN MARVEL!

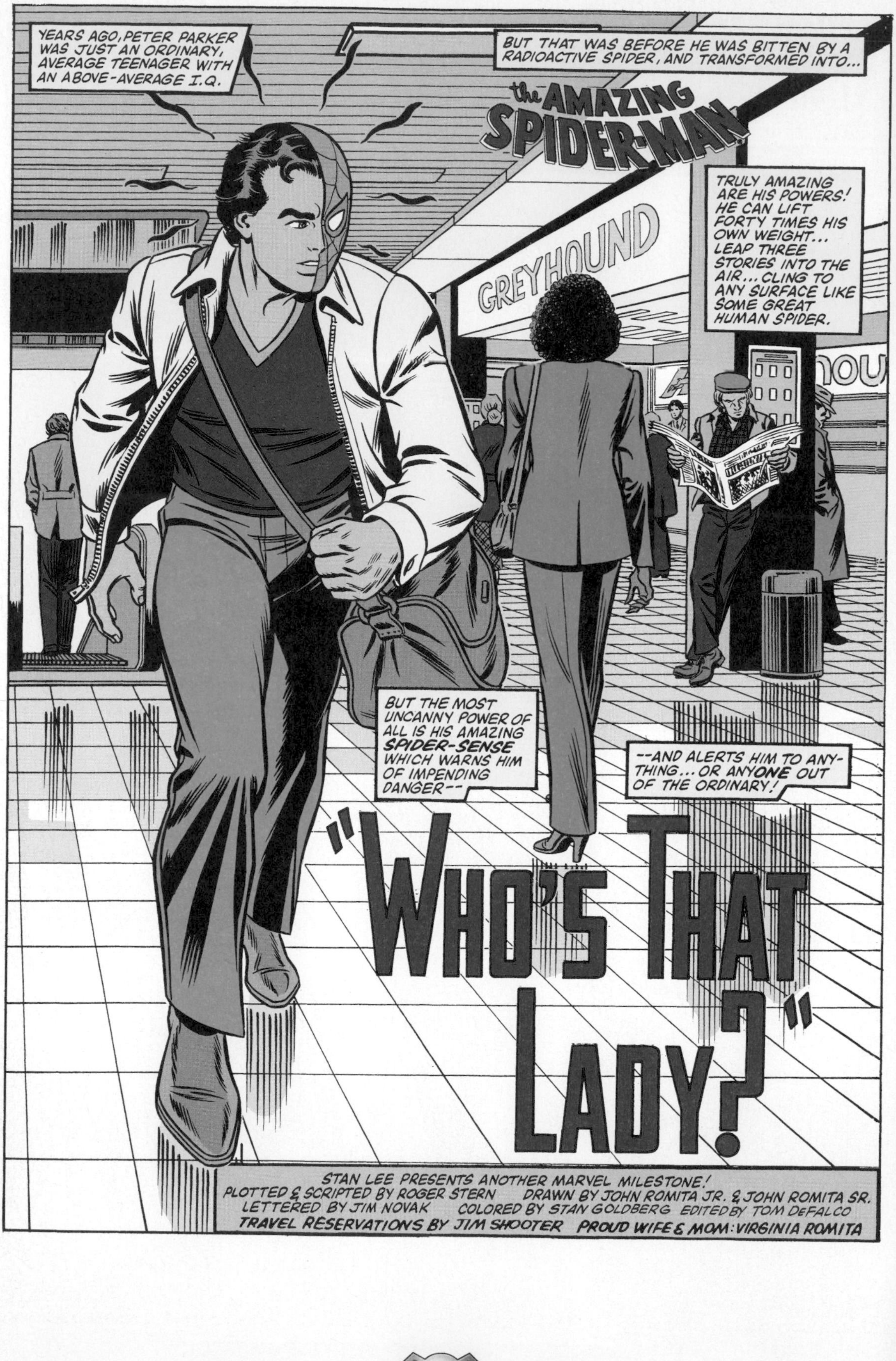
YEARS AGO, PETER PARKER WAS JUST AN ORDINARY, AVERAGE TEENAGER WITH AN ABOVE-AVERAGE I.Q.
BUT THAT WAS BEFORE HE WAS BITTEN BY A RADIOACTIVE SPIDER, AND TRANSFORMED INTO...
the AMAZING SPIDER-MAN
TRULY AMAZING ARE HIS POWERS! HE CAN LIFT FORTY TIMES HIS OWN WEIGHT... LEAP THREE STORIES INTO THE AIR... CLING TO ANY SURFACE LIKE SOME GREAT HUMAN SPIDER.
GREYHOUND
BUT THE MOST UNCANNY POWER OF ALL IS HIS AMAZING SPIDER-SENSE WHICH WARNS HIM OF IMPENDING DANGER--
--AND ALERTS HIM TO ANYTHING... OR ANYONE OUT OF THE ORDINARY!
"WHO'S THAT LADY?"
STAN LEE PRESENTS ANOTHER MARVEL MILESTONE!
PLOTTED & SCRIPTED BY ROGER STERN DRAWN BY JOHN ROMITA JR. & JOHN ROMITA SR.
LETTERED BY JIM NOVAK COLORED BY STAN GOLDBERG EDITED BY TOM DeFALCO
TRAVEL RESERVATIONS BY JIM SHOOTER PROUD WIFE & MOM: VIRGINIA ROMITA

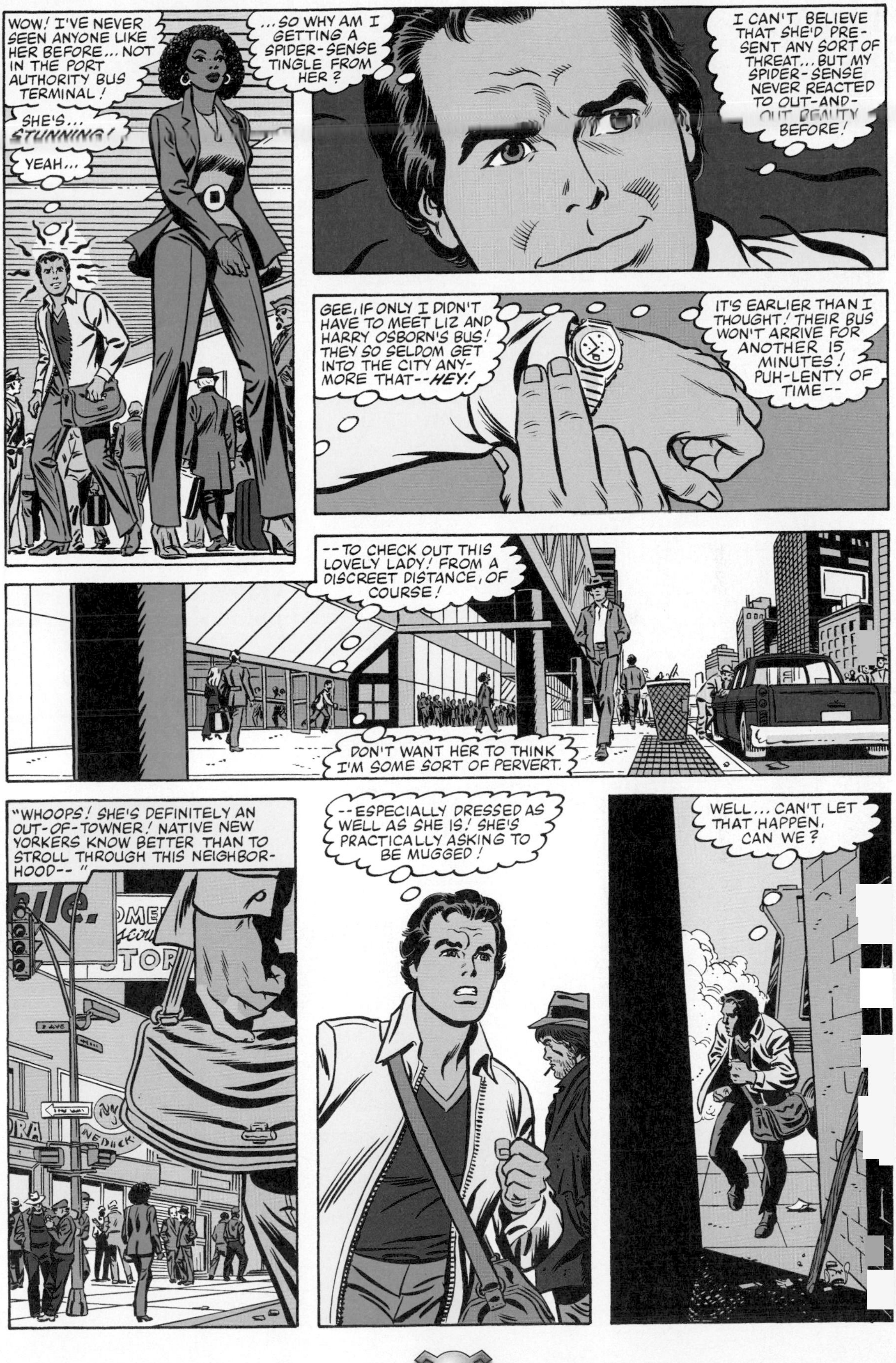
WOW! I'VE NEVER SEEN ANYONE LIKE HER BEFORE... NOT IN THE PORT AUTHORITY BUS TERMINAL!
SHE'S... STUNNING!
YEAH...
...SO WHY AM I GETTING A SPIDER-SENSE TINGLE FROM HER?
I CAN'T BELIEVE THAT SHE'D PRESENT ANY SORT OF THREAT... BUT MY SPIDER-SENSE NEVER REACTED TO OUT-AND-OUT BEAUTY BEFORE!
GEE, IF ONLY I DIDN'T HAVE TO MEET LIZ AND HARRY OSBORN'S BUS! THEY SO SELDOM GET INTO THE CITY ANYMORE THAT--HEY!
IT'S EARLIER THAN I THOUGHT! THEIR BUS WON'T ARRIVE FOR ANOTHER 15 MINUTES! PUH-LENTY OF TIME--
--TO CHECK OUT THIS LOVELY LADY! FROM A DISCREET DISTANCE, OF COURSE!
DON'T WANT HER TO THINK I'M SOME SORT OF PERVERT.
"WHOOPS! SHE'S DEFINITELY AN OUT-OF-TOWNER! NATIVE NEW YORKERS KNOW BETTER THAN TO STROLL THROUGH THIS NEIGHBORHOOD--"
--ESPECIALLY DRESSED AS WELL AS SHE IS! SHE'S PRACTICALLY ASKING TO BE MUGGED!
WELL... CAN'T LET THAT HAPPEN, CAN WE?

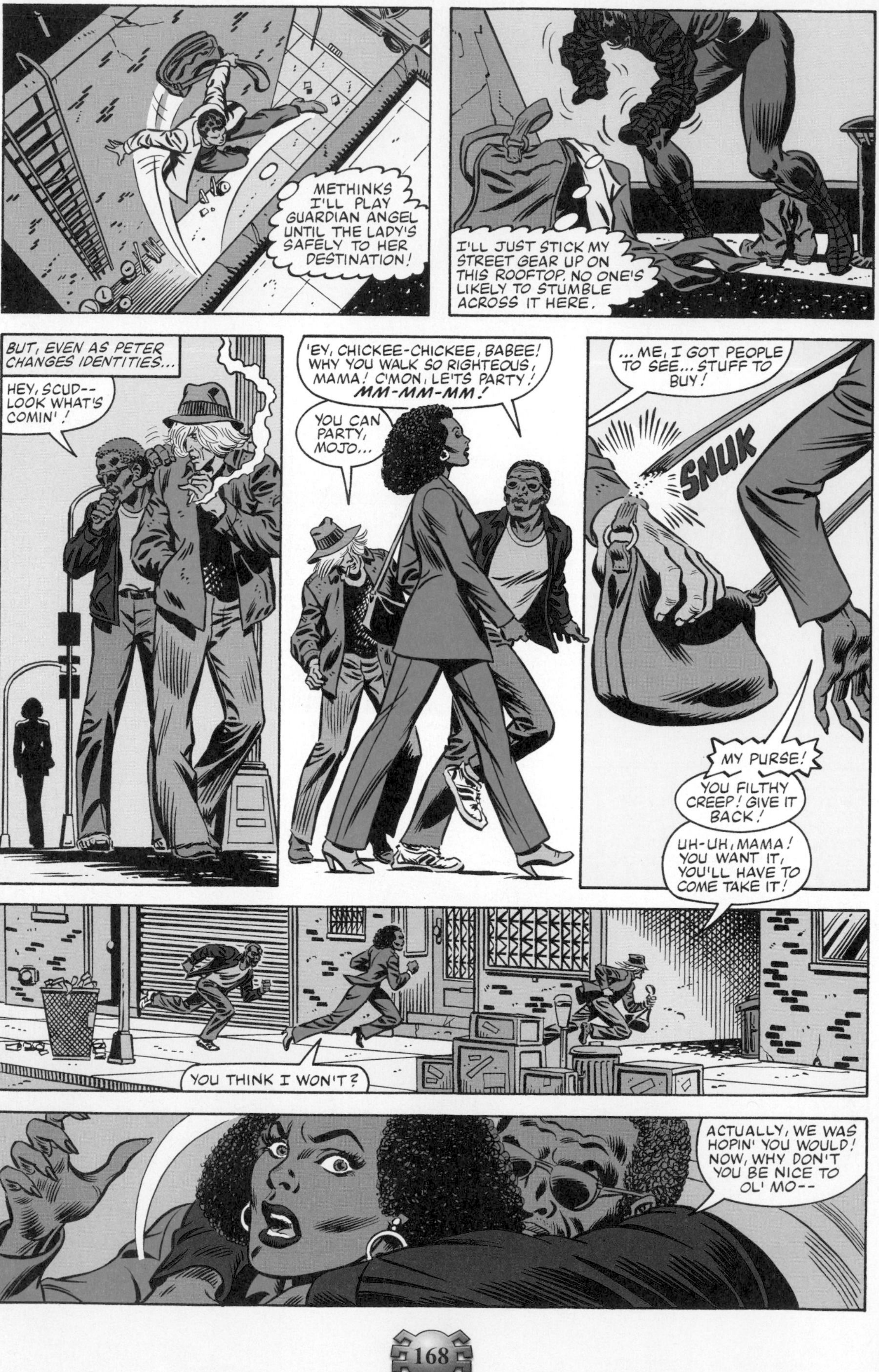
METHINKS I'LL PLAY GUARDIAN ANGEL UNTIL THE LADY'S SAFELY TO HER DESTINATION!
I'LL JUST STICK MY STREET GEAR UP ON THIS ROOFTOP. NO ONE'S LIKELY TO STUMBLE ACROSS IT HERE.
BUT, EVEN AS PETER CHANGES IDENTITIES...
HEY, SCUD-- LOOK WHAT'S COMIN'!
'EY, CHICKEE-CHICKEE, BABEE! WHY YOU WALK SO RIGHTEOUS, MAMA! C'MON, LET'S PARTY! MM-MM-MM!
YOU CAN PARTY, MOJO...
...ME, I GOT PEOPLE TO SEE... STUFF TO BUY!
SNUK
MY PURSE!
YOU FILTHY CREEP! GIVE IT BACK!
UH-UH, MAMA! YOU WANT IT, YOU'LL HAVE TO COME TAKE IT!
YOU THINK I WON'T?
ACTUALLY, WE WAS HOPIN' YOU WOULD! NOW, WHY DON'T YOU BE NICE TO OL' MO--

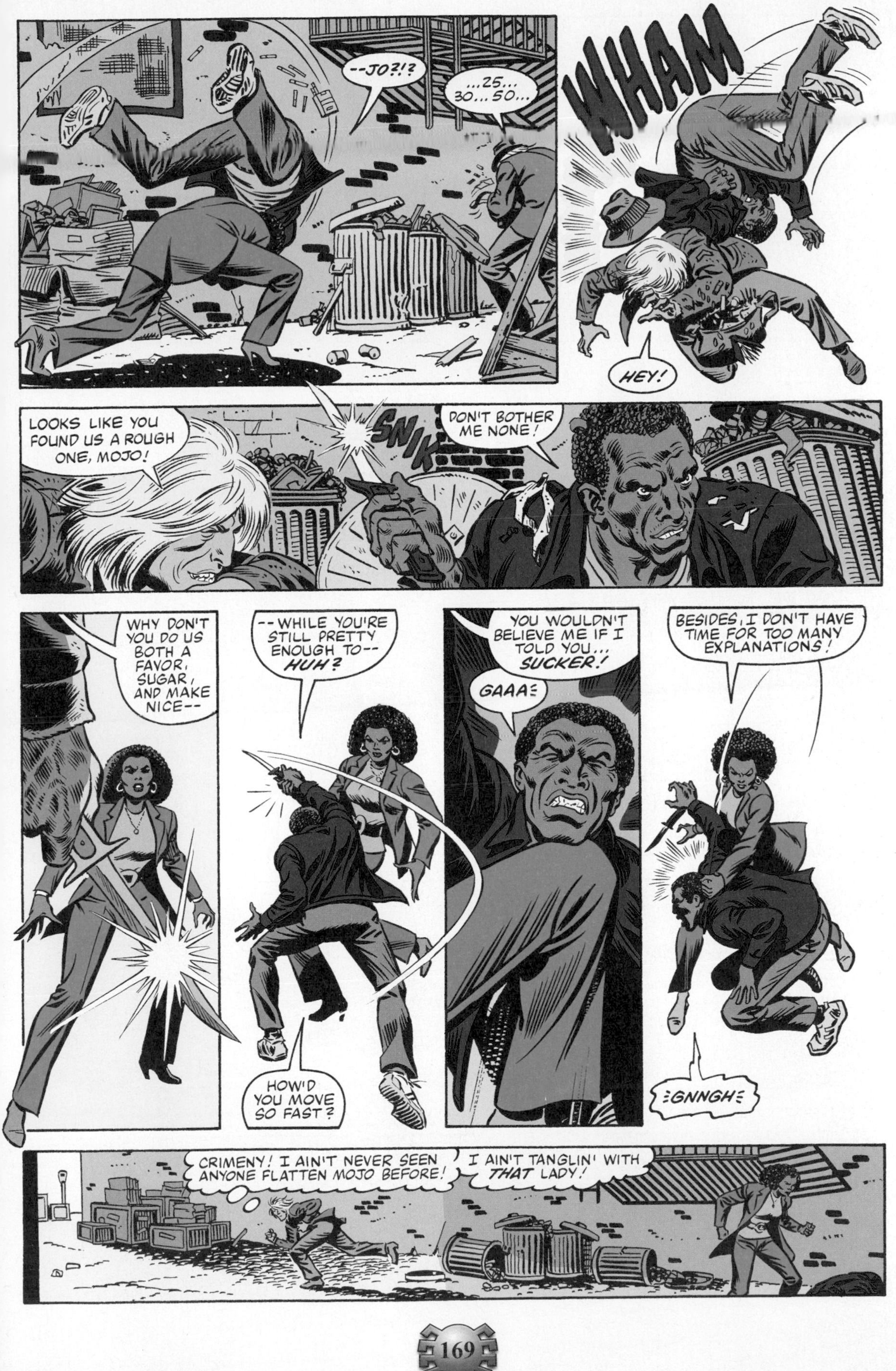
--JO?!?
...25... 30...50...
WHAM
HEY!
LOOKS LIKE YOU FOUND US A ROUGH ONE, MOJO!
SNIK
DON'T BOTHER ME NONE!
WHY DON'T YOU DO US BOTH A FAVOR, SUGAR, AND MAKE NICE--
--WHILE YOU'RE STILL PRETTY ENOUGH TO-- HUH?
HOW'D YOU MOVE SO FAST?
YOU WOULDN'T BELIEVE ME IF I TOLD YOU... SUCKER!
GAAA
BESIDES, I DON'T HAVE TIME FOR TOO MANY EXPLANATIONS!
GNNGH
CRIMENY! I AIN'T NEVER SEEN ANYONE FLATTEN MOJO BEFORE!
I AIN'T TANGLIN' WITH THAT LADY!

WHAT'S YOUR HURRY, DOG-BREATH?

UH-OH.

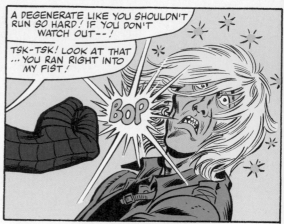

A DEGENERATE LIKE YOU SHOULDN'T RUN SO HARD! IF YOU DON'T WATCH OUT--!

TSK-TSK! LOOK AT THAT ...YOU RAN RIGHT INTO MY FIST!

BOP

SO MUCH FOR THOSE TWO. THE LADY LOOKS OKAY ...BUT MY SPIDER-SENSE IS BUZZING MORE THAN EVER!

WHY?! SHE'S A GOOD FIGHTER, BUT SHE'S SURELY NO DANGER TO ME!

MAYBE IF I COME RIGHT OUT AND CONFRONT HER--!

HEY, LADY, YOU HANDLE YOURSELF--

--PRETTY--

CART

IT HAPPENS IN A SPLIT-SECOND!

EVEN BEFORE SPIDER-MAN'S FEET CAN TOUCH THE GROUND...

...EVEN AS HIS SPECIAL SENSES TELL HIM THAT HE'S MADE A SERIOUS MISTAKE...

...A SUDDEN BURST OF PURE FORCE SENDS HIM FLYING!

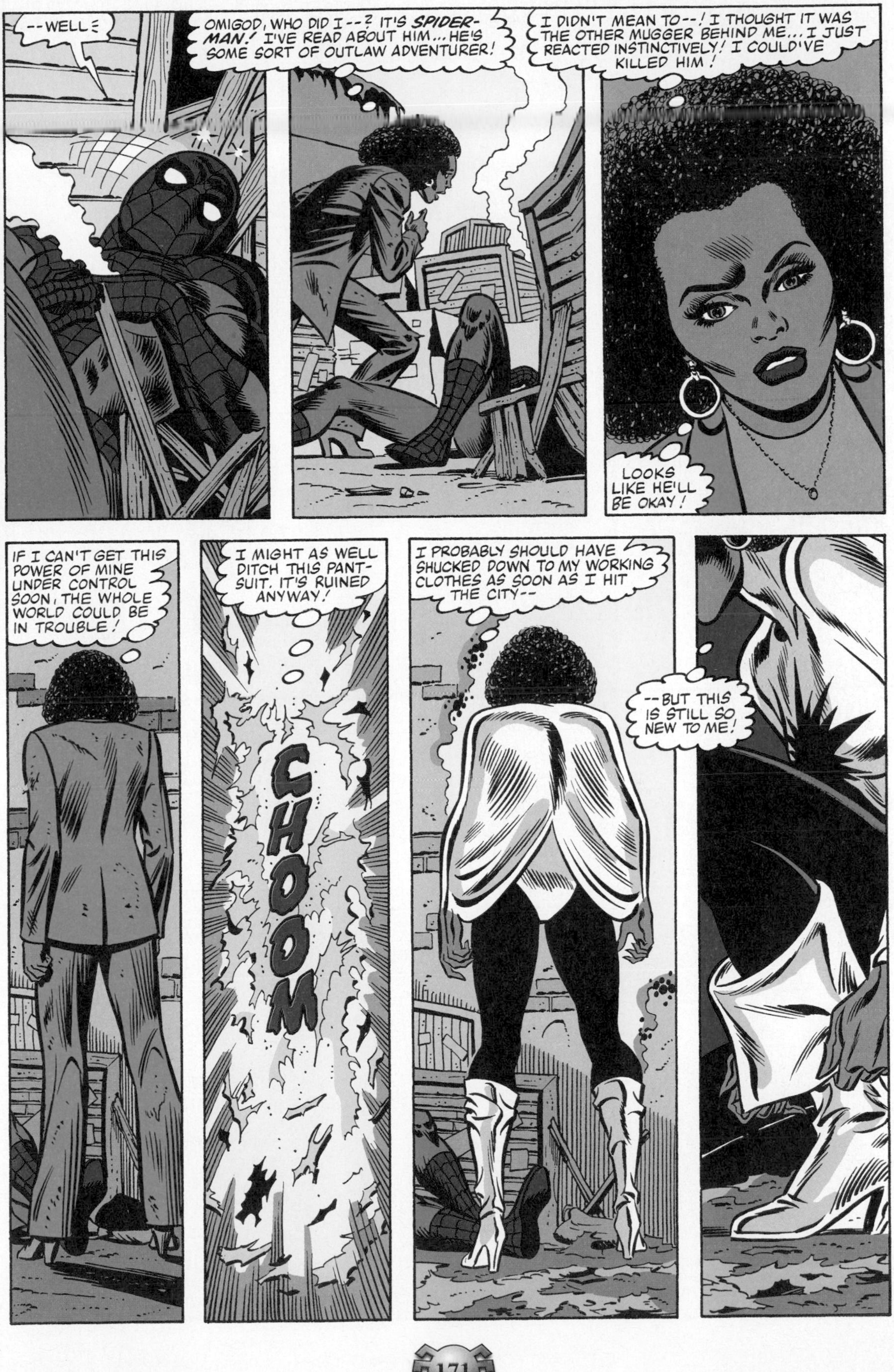

--WELL--?
OMIGOD, WHO DID I--? IT'S SPIDER-MAN! I'VE READ ABOUT HIM... HE'S SOME SORT OF OUTLAW ADVENTURER!
I DIDN'T MEAN TO--! I THOUGHT IT WAS THE OTHER MUGGER BEHIND ME... I JUST REACTED INSTINCTIVELY! I COULD'VE KILLED HIM!
LOOKS LIKE HE'LL BE OKAY!
IF I CAN'T GET THIS POWER OF MINE UNDER CONTROL SOON, THE WHOLE WORLD COULD BE IN TROUBLE!
I MIGHT AS WELL DITCH THIS PANT-SUIT. IT'S RUINED ANYWAY!
CHOOM
I PROBABLY SHOULD HAVE SHUCKED DOWN TO MY WORKING CLOTHES AS SOON AS I HIT THE CITY--
--BUT THIS IS STILL SO NEW TO ME!

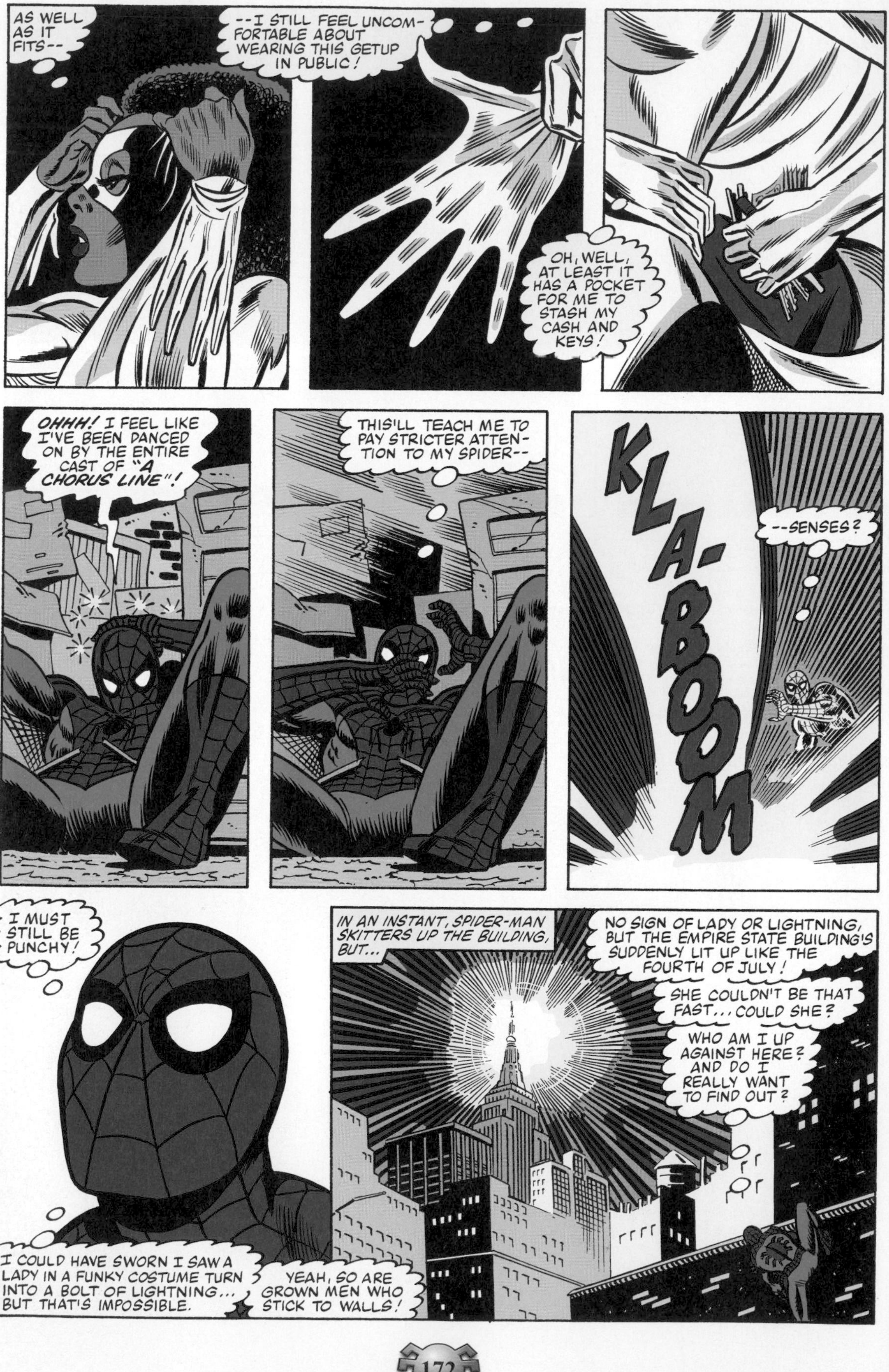
AS WELL AS IT FITS--
--I STILL FEEL UNCOMFORTABLE ABOUT WEARING THIS GETUP IN PUBLIC!
OH, WELL, AT LEAST IT HAS A POCKET FOR ME TO STASH MY CASH AND KEYS!
OHHH! I FEEL LIKE I'VE BEEN DANCED ON BY THE ENTIRE CAST OF "A CHORUS LINE"!
THIS'LL TEACH ME TO PAY STRICTER ATTENTION TO MY SPIDER--
KLA-BOOM
--SENSES?
I MUST STILL BE PUNCHY!
I COULD HAVE SWORN I SAW A LADY IN A FUNKY COSTUME TURN INTO A BOLT OF LIGHTNING... BUT THAT'S IMPOSSIBLE.
YEAH, SO ARE GROWN MEN WHO STICK TO WALLS!
IN AN INSTANT, SPIDER-MAN SKITTERS UP THE BUILDING, BUT...
NO SIGN OF LADY OR LIGHTNING, BUT THE EMPIRE STATE BUILDING'S SUDDENLY LIT UP LIKE THE FOURTH OF JULY!
SHE COULDN'T BE THAT FAST... COULD SHE?
WHO AM I UP AGAINST HERE? AND DO I REALLY WANT TO FIND OUT?

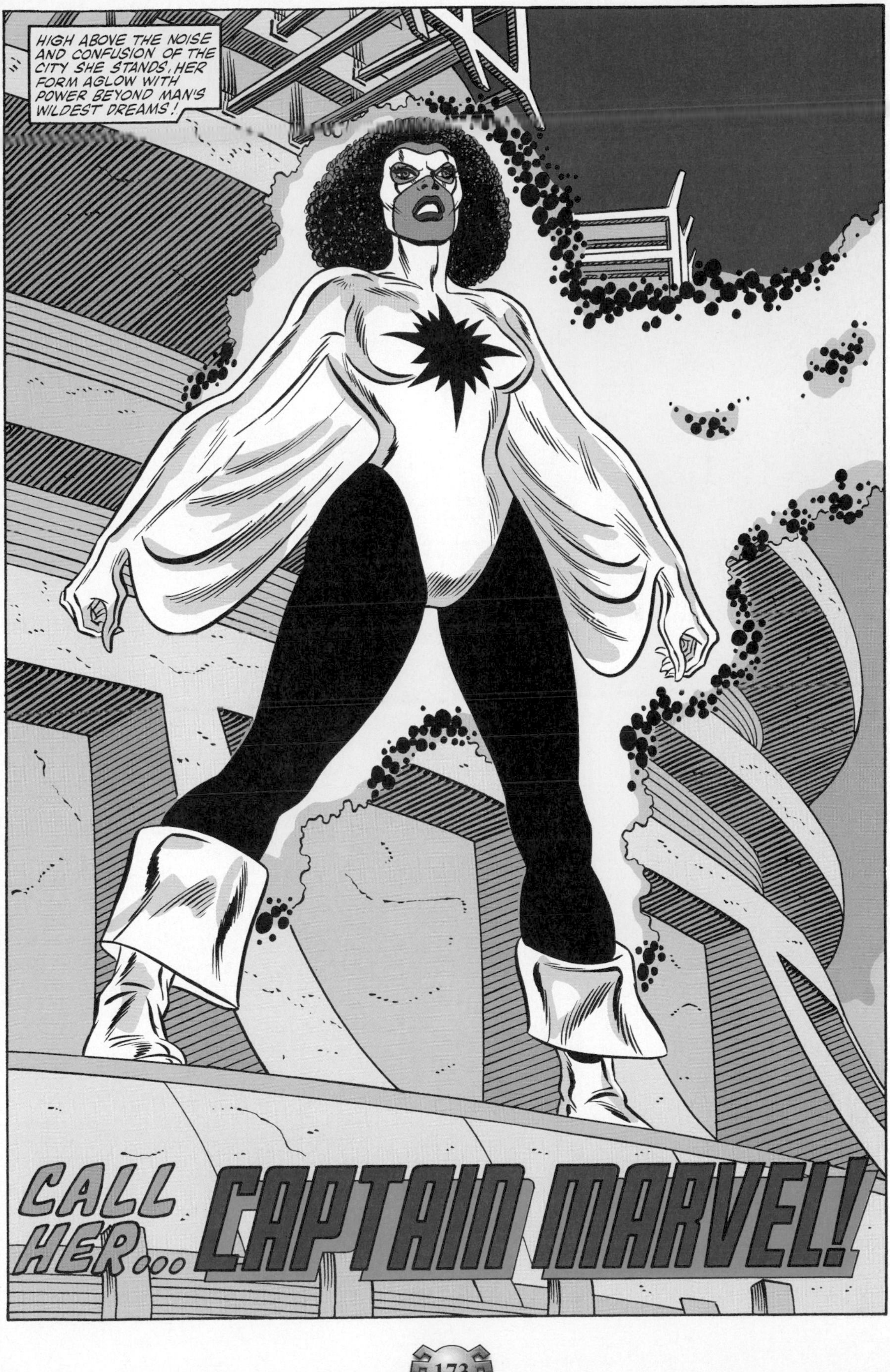
HIGH ABOVE THE NOISE AND CONFUSION OF THE CITY SHE STANDS, HER FORM AGLOW WITH POWER BEYOND MAN'S WILDEST DREAMS!
CALL HER... CAPTAIN MARVEL!

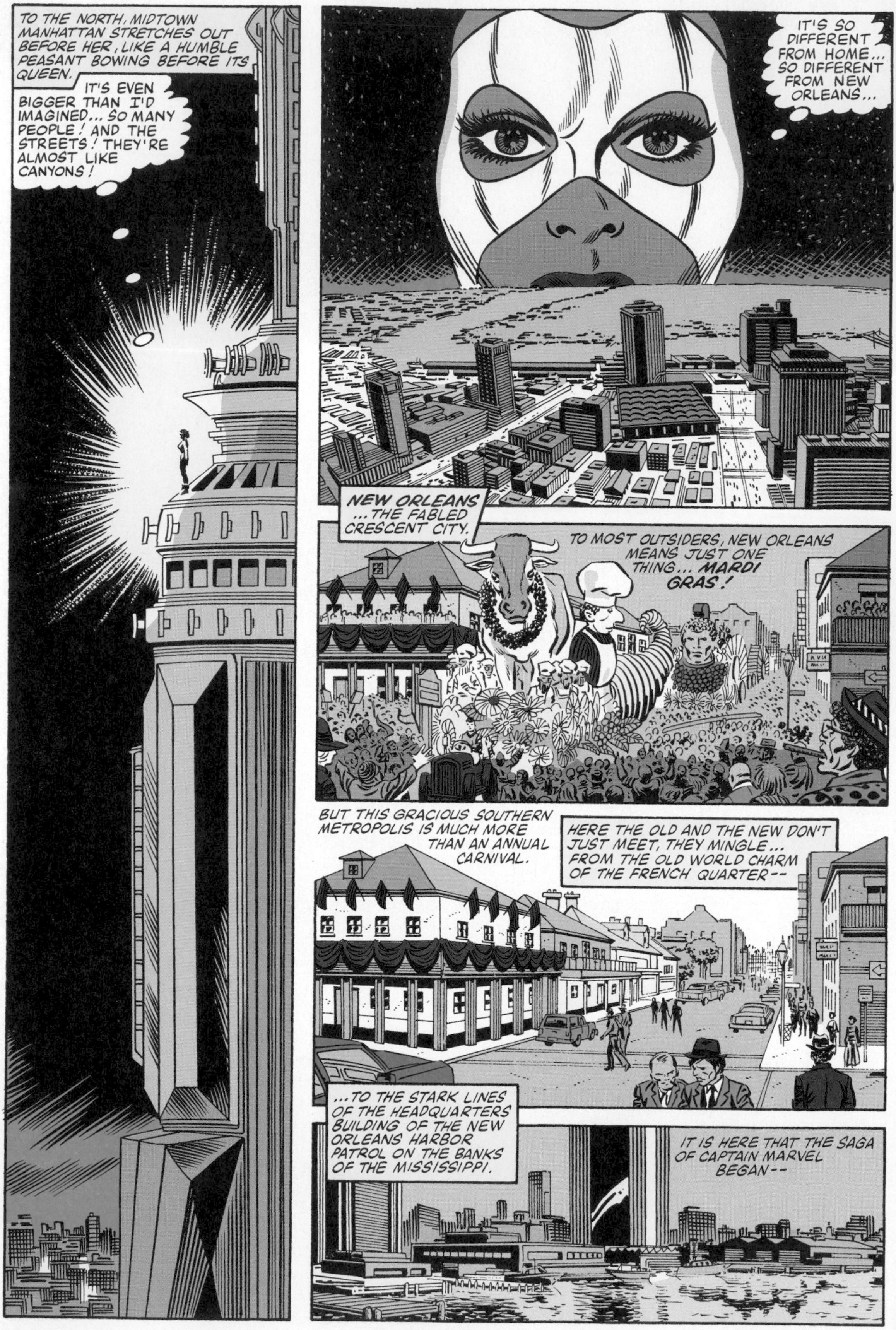
TO THE NORTH, MIDTOWN MANHATTAN STRETCHES OUT BEFORE HER, LIKE A HUMBLE PEASANT BOWING BEFORE ITS QUEEN.
IT'S EVEN BIGGER THAN I'D IMAGINED... SO MANY PEOPLE! AND THE STREETS! THEY'RE ALMOST LIKE CANYONS!
IT'S SO DIFFERENT FROM HOME... SO DIFFERENT FROM NEW ORLEANS...
NEW ORLEANS ...THE FABLED CRESCENT CITY.
TO MOST OUTSIDERS, NEW ORLEANS MEANS JUST ONE THING... MARDI GRAS!
BUT THIS GRACIOUS SOUTHERN METROPOLIS IS MUCH MORE THAN AN ANNUAL CARNIVAL.
HERE THE OLD AND THE NEW DON'T JUST MEET, THEY MINGLE... FROM THE OLD WORLD CHARM OF THE FRENCH QUARTER--
...TO THE STARK LINES OF THE HEADQUARTERS BUILDING OF THE NEW ORLEANS HARBOR PATROL ON THE BANKS OF THE MISSISSIPPI.
IT IS HERE THAT THE SAGA OF CAPTAIN MARVEL BEGAN--

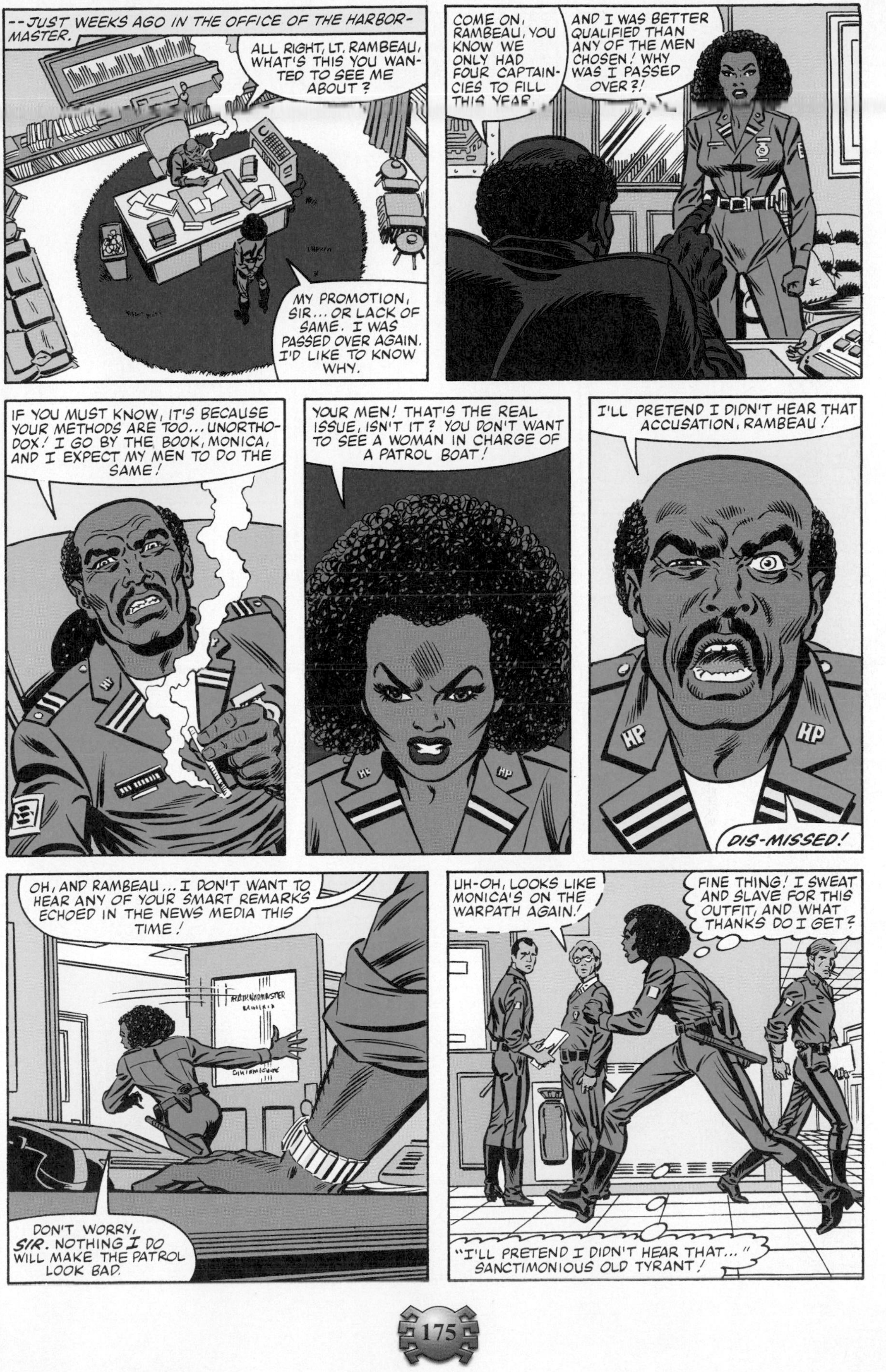
--JUST WEEKS AGO IN THE OFFICE OF THE HARBOR-MASTER.
ALL RIGHT, LT. RAMBEAU, WHAT'S THIS YOU WANTED TO SEE ME ABOUT?
MY PROMOTION, SIR... OR LACK OF SAME. I WAS PASSED OVER AGAIN. I'D LIKE TO KNOW WHY.
COME ON, RAMBEAU, YOU KNOW WE ONLY HAD FOUR CAPTAINCIES TO FILL THIS YEAR.
AND I WAS BETTER QUALIFIED THAN ANY OF THE MEN CHOSEN! WHY WAS I PASSED OVER?!
IF YOU MUST KNOW, IT'S BECAUSE YOUR METHODS ARE TOO... UNORTHODOX! I GO BY THE BOOK, MONICA, AND I EXPECT MY MEN TO DO THE SAME!
YOUR MEN! THAT'S THE REAL ISSUE, ISN'T IT? YOU DON'T WANT TO SEE A WOMAN IN CHARGE OF A PATROL BOAT!
I'LL PRETEND I DIDN'T HEAR THAT ACCUSATION, RAMBEAU!
DIS-MISSED!
OH, AND RAMBEAU... I DON'T WANT TO HEAR ANY OF YOUR SMART REMARKS ECHOED IN THE NEWS MEDIA THIS TIME!
DON'T WORRY, SIR. NOTHING I DO WILL MAKE THE PATROL LOOK BAD.
UH-OH, LOOKS LIKE MONICA'S ON THE WARPATH AGAIN!
FINE THING! I SWEAT AND SLAVE FOR THIS OUTFIT, AND WHAT THANKS DO I GET?
"I'LL PRETEND I DIDN'T HEAR THAT..." SANCTIMONIOUS OLD TYRANT!

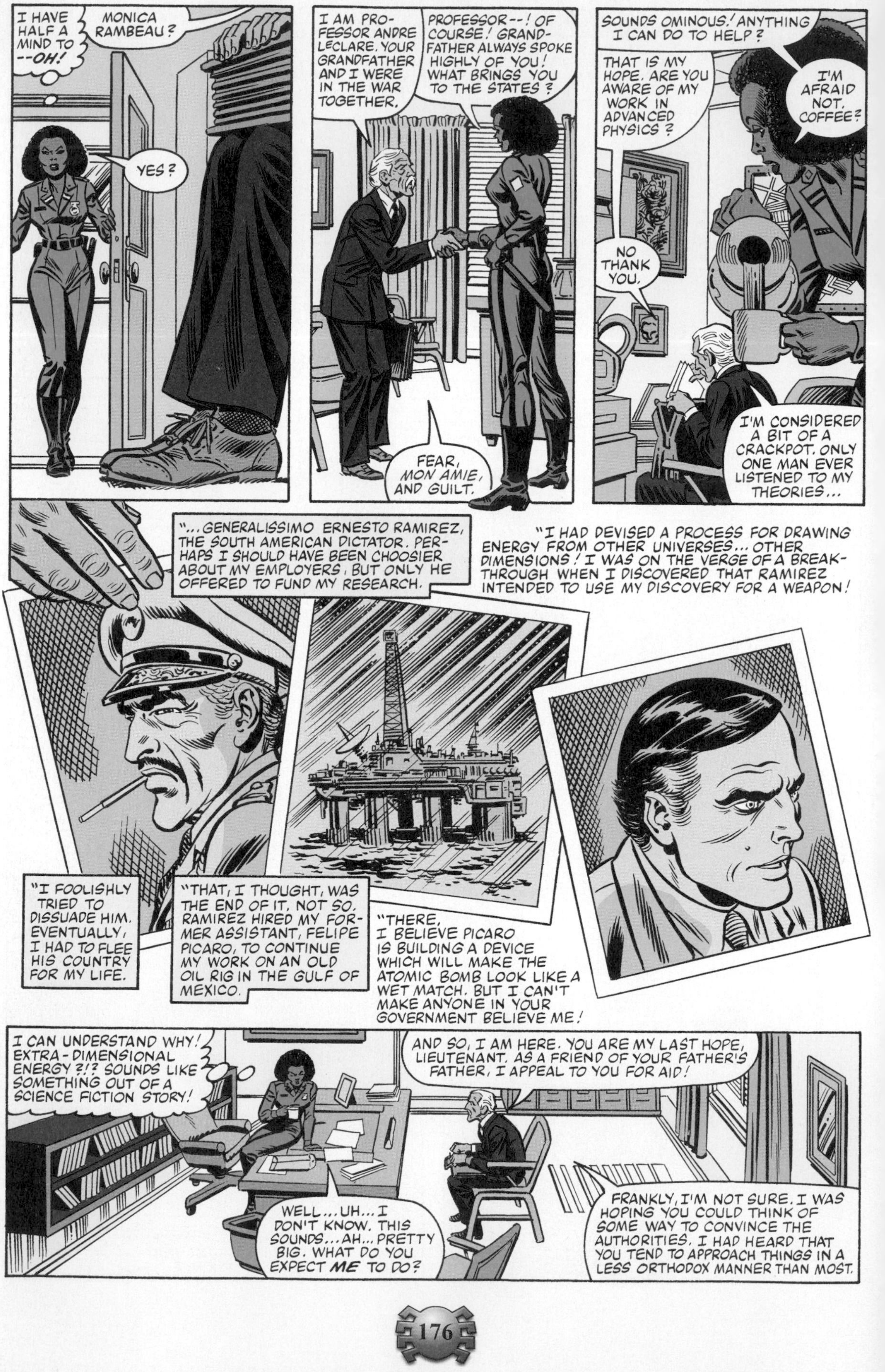
I HAVE HALF A MIND TO --OH!
MONICA RAMBEAU?
YES?
I AM PROFESSOR ANDRE LeCLARE. YOUR GRANDFATHER AND I WERE IN THE WAR TOGETHER.
PROFESSOR--! OF COURSE! GRANDFATHER ALWAYS SPOKE HIGHLY OF YOU! WHAT BRINGS YOU TO THE STATES?
FEAR, MON AMIE, AND GUILT.
SOUNDS OMINOUS! ANYTHING I CAN DO TO HELP?
THAT IS MY HOPE. ARE YOU AWARE OF MY WORK IN ADVANCED PHYSICS?
I'M AFRAID NOT. COFFEE?
NO THANK YOU.
I'M CONSIDERED A BIT OF A CRACKPOT. ONLY ONE MAN EVER LISTENED TO MY THEORIES...
"...GENERALISSIMO ERNESTO RAMIREZ, THE SOUTH AMERICAN DICTATOR. PERHAPS I SHOULD HAVE BEEN CHOOSIER ABOUT MY EMPLOYERS, BUT ONLY HE OFFERED TO FUND MY RESEARCH.
"I HAD DEVISED A PROCESS FOR DRAWING ENERGY FROM OTHER UNIVERSES... OTHER DIMENSIONS! I WAS ON THE VERGE OF A BREAKTHROUGH WHEN I DISCOVERED THAT RAMIREZ INTENDED TO USE MY DISCOVERY FOR A WEAPON!
"I FOOLISHLY TRIED TO DISSUADE HIM. EVENTUALLY, I HAD TO FLEE HIS COUNTRY FOR MY LIFE.
"THAT, I THOUGHT, WAS THE END OF IT. NOT SO. RAMIREZ HIRED MY FORMER ASSISTANT, FELIPE PICARO, TO CONTINUE MY WORK ON AN OLD OIL RIG IN THE GULF OF MEXICO.
"THERE, I BELIEVE PICARO IS BUILDING A DEVICE WHICH WILL MAKE THE ATOMIC BOMB LOOK LIKE A WET MATCH. BUT I CAN'T MAKE ANYONE IN YOUR GOVERNMENT BELIEVE ME!
I CAN UNDERSTAND WHY! EXTRA-DIMENSIONAL ENERGY ?!? SOUNDS LIKE SOMETHING OUT OF A SCIENCE FICTION STORY!
AND SO, I AM HERE. YOU ARE MY LAST HOPE, LIEUTENANT. AS A FRIEND OF YOUR FATHER'S FATHER, I APPEAL TO YOU FOR AID!
WELL...UH...I DON'T KNOW. THIS SOUNDS...AH...PRETTY BIG. WHAT DO YOU EXPECT ME TO DO?
FRANKLY, I'M NOT SURE. I WAS HOPING YOU COULD THINK OF SOME WAY TO CONVINCE THE AUTHORITIES. I HAD HEARD THAT YOU TEND TO APPROACH THINGS IN A LESS ORTHODOX MANNER THAN MOST.

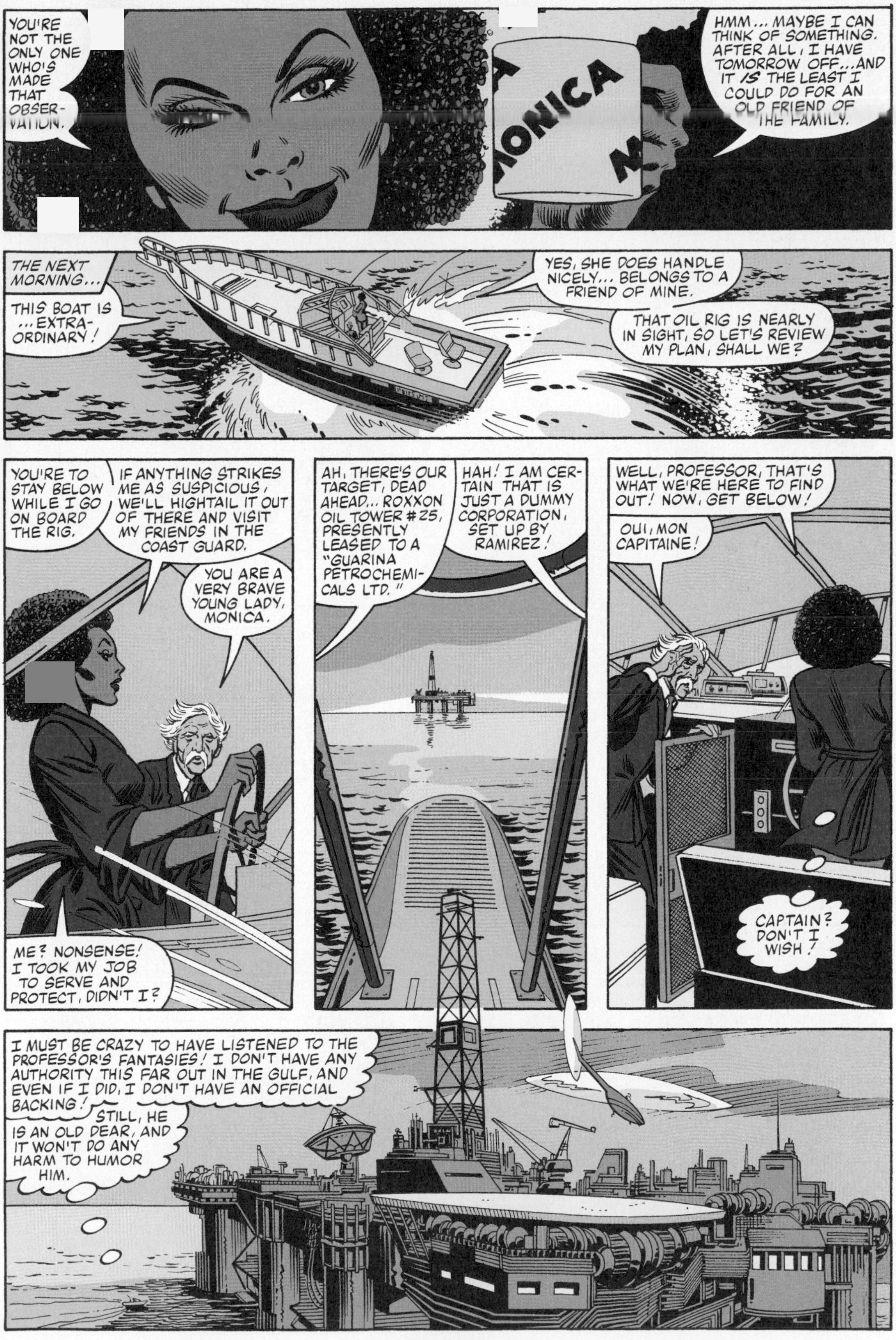

YOU'RE NOT THE ONLY ONE WHO'S MADE THAT OBSER-VATION.
MONICA
HMM... MAYBE I CAN THINK OF SOMETHING. AFTER ALL, I HAVE TOMORROW OFF... AND IT IS THE LEAST I COULD DO FOR AN OLD FRIEND OF THE FAMILY.
THE NEXT MORNING...
THIS BOAT IS ...EXTRA-ORDINARY!
YES, SHE DOES HANDLE NICELY... BELONGS TO A FRIEND OF MINE.
THAT OIL RIG IS NEARLY IN SIGHT, SO LET'S REVIEW MY PLAN, SHALL WE?
YOU'RE TO STAY BELOW WHILE I GO ON BOARD THE RIG.
IF ANYTHING STRIKES ME AS SUSPICIOUS, WE'LL HIGHTAIL IT OUT OF THERE AND VISIT MY FRIENDS IN THE COAST GUARD.
YOU ARE A VERY BRAVE YOUNG LADY, MONICA.
ME? NONSENSE! I TOOK MY JOB TO SERVE AND PROTECT, DIDN'T I?
AH, THERE'S OUR TARGET, DEAD AHEAD... ROXXON OIL TOWER #25, PRESENTLY LEASED TO A "GUARINA PETROCHEMI-CALS LTD."
HAH! I AM CER-TAIN THAT IS JUST A DUMMY CORPORATION, SET UP BY RAMIREZ!
WELL, PROFESSOR, THAT'S WHAT WE'RE HERE TO FIND OUT! NOW, GET BELOW!
OUI, MON CAPITAINE!
CAPTAIN? DON'T I WISH!
I MUST BE CRAZY TO HAVE LISTENED TO THE PROFESSOR'S FANTASIES! I DON'T HAVE ANY AUTHORITY THIS FAR OUT IN THE GULF, AND EVEN IF I DID, I DON'T HAVE AN OFFICIAL BACKING!
STILL, HE IS AN OLD DEAR, AND IT WON'T DO ANY HARM TO HUMOR HIM.

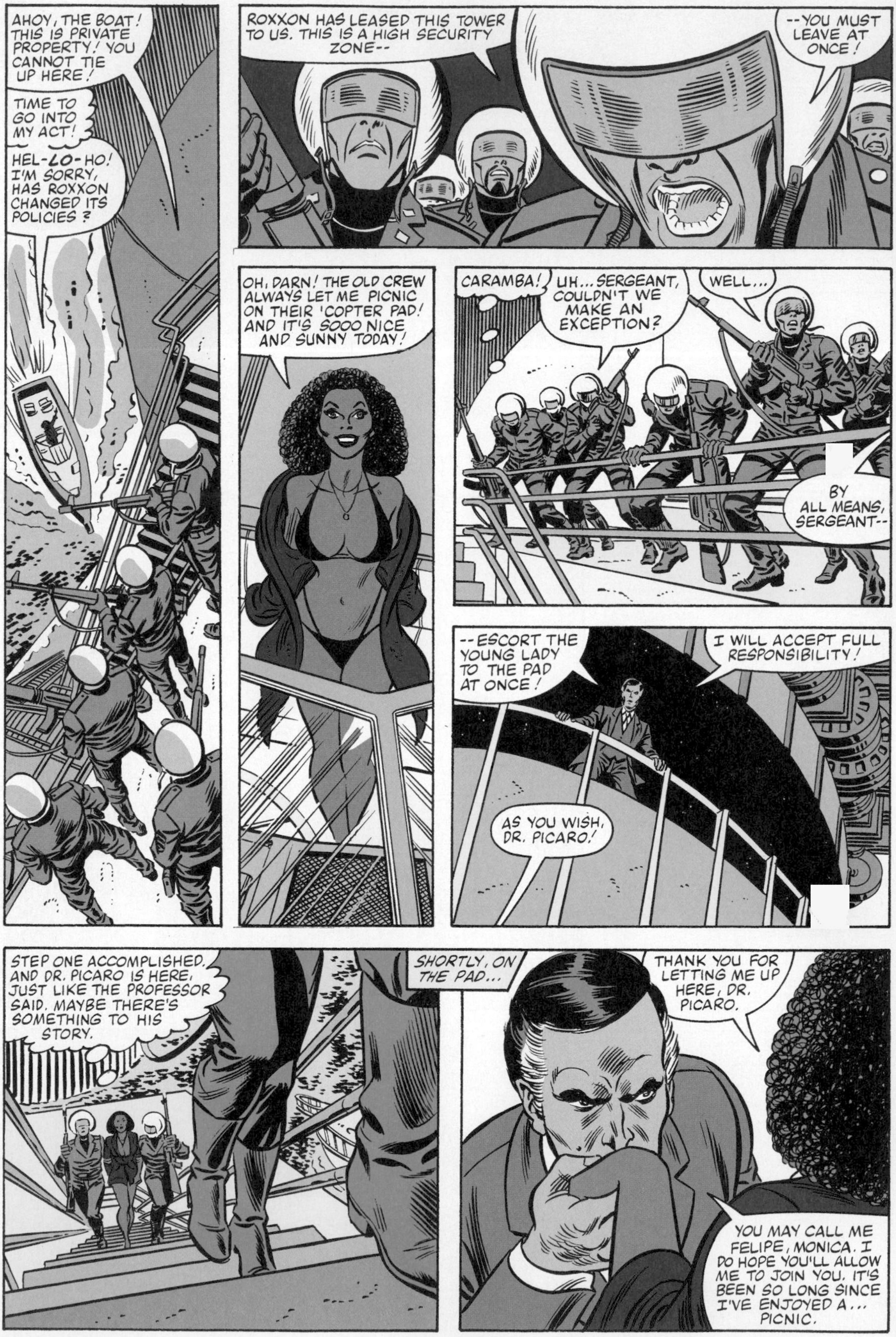
AHOY, THE BOAT! THIS IS PRIVATE PROPERTY! YOU CANNOT TIE UP HERE!
TIME TO GO INTO MY ACT!
HEL-LO-HO! I'M SORRY, HAS ROXXON CHANGED ITS POLICIES?
ROXXON HAS LEASED THIS TOWER TO US. THIS IS A HIGH SECURITY ZONE--
--YOU MUST LEAVE AT ONCE!
OH, DARN! THE OLD CREW ALWAYS LET ME PICNIC ON THEIR 'COPTER PAD! AND IT'S SOOO NICE AND SUNNY TODAY!
CARAMBA!
UH... SERGEANT, COULDN'T WE MAKE AN EXCEPTION?
WELL...
BY ALL MEANS, SERGEANT--
--ESCORT THE YOUNG LADY TO THE PAD AT ONCE!
I WILL ACCEPT FULL RESPONSIBILITY!
AS YOU WISH, DR. PICARO!
STEP ONE ACCOMPLISHED. AND DR. PICARO IS HERE, JUST LIKE THE PROFESSOR SAID. MAYBE THERE'S SOMETHING TO HIS STORY.
SHORTLY, ON THE PAD...
THANK YOU FOR LETTING ME UP HERE, DR. PICARO.
YOU MAY CALL ME FELIPE, MONICA. I DO HOPE YOU'LL ALLOW ME TO JOIN YOU. IT'S BEEN SO LONG SINCE I'VE ENJOYED A... PICNIC.

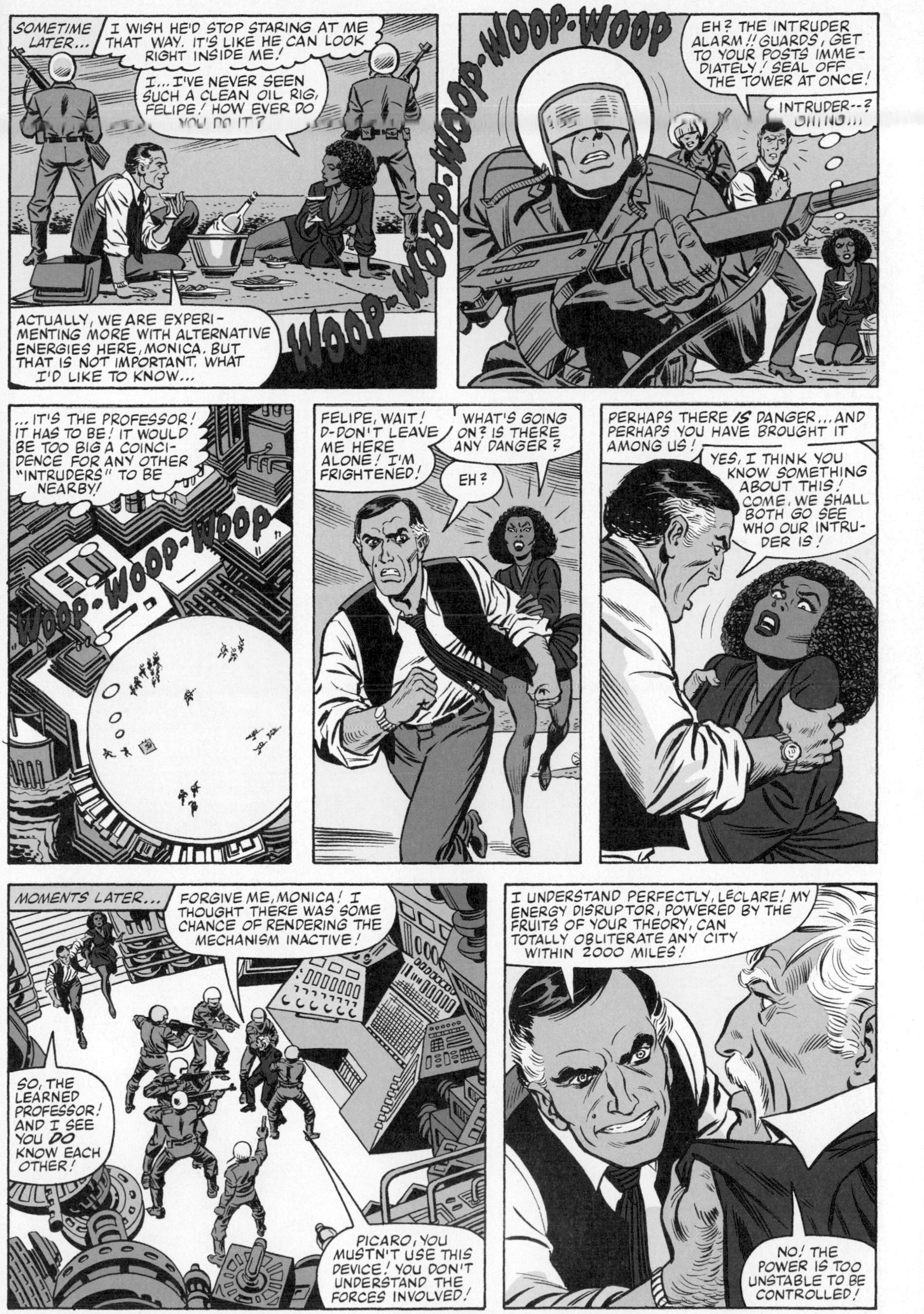

SOMETIME LATER...
I WISH HE'D STOP STARING AT ME THAT WAY. IT'S LIKE HE CAN LOOK RIGHT INSIDE ME!
I... I'VE NEVER SEEN SUCH A CLEAN OIL RIG, FELIPE! HOW EVER DO YOU DO IT?
ACTUALLY, WE ARE EXPERIMENTING MORE WITH ALTERNATIVE ENERGIES HERE, MONICA. BUT THAT IS NOT IMPORTANT. WHAT I'D LIKE TO KNOW...
WOOP-WOOP-WOOP-WOOP-WOOP
EH? THE INTRUDER ALARM!! GUARDS, GET TO YOUR POSTS IMMEDIATELY! SEAL OFF THE TOWER AT ONCE!
INTRUDER--? OH NO...!
...IT'S THE PROFESSOR! IT HAS TO BE! IT WOULD BE TOO BIG A COINCIDENCE FOR ANY OTHER "INTRUDERS" TO BE NEARBY!
WOOP-WOOP-WOOP-WOOP
FELIPE, WAIT! D-DON'T LEAVE ME HERE ALONE! I'M FRIGHTENED!
WHAT'S GOING ON? IS THERE ANY DANGER?
EH?
PERHAPS THERE IS DANGER... AND PERHAPS YOU HAVE BROUGHT IT AMONG US!
YES, I THINK YOU KNOW SOMETHING ABOUT THIS! COME. WE SHALL BOTH GO SEE WHO OUR INTRUDER IS!
MOMENTS LATER...
FORGIVE ME, MONICA! I THOUGHT THERE WAS SOME CHANCE OF RENDERING THE MECHANISM INACTIVE!
SO, THE LEARNED PROFESSOR! AND I SEE YOU DO KNOW EACH OTHER!
PICARO, YOU MUSTN'T USE THIS DEVICE! YOU DON'T UNDERSTAND THE FORCES INVOLVED!
I UNDERSTAND PERFECTLY, LECLARE! MY ENERGY DISRUPTOR, POWERED BY THE FRUITS OF YOUR THEORY, CAN TOTALLY OBLITERATE ANY CITY WITHIN 2000 MILES!
NO! THE POWER IS TOO UNSTABLE TO BE CONTROLLED!

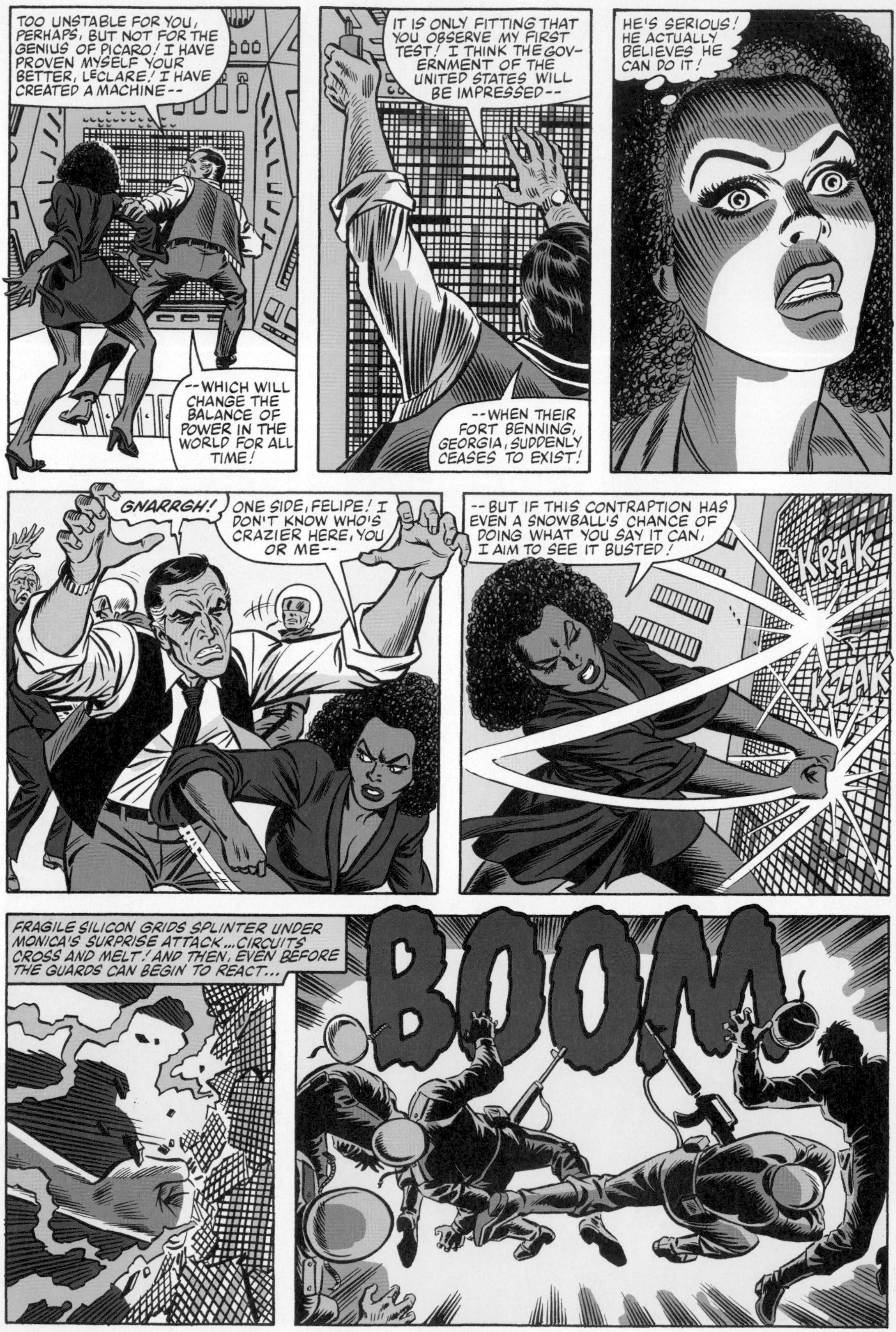

TOO UNSTABLE FOR YOU, PERHAPS, BUT NOT FOR THE GENIUS OF PICARO! I HAVE PROVEN MYSELF YOUR BETTER, LECLARE! I HAVE CREATED A MACHINE--
--WHICH WILL CHANGE THE BALANCE OF POWER IN THE WORLD FOR ALL TIME!
IT IS ONLY FITTING THAT YOU OBSERVE MY FIRST TEST! I THINK THE GOVERNMENT OF THE UNITED STATES WILL BE IMPRESSED--
--WHEN THEIR FORT BENNING, GEORGIA, SUDDENLY CEASES TO EXIST!
HE'S SERIOUS! HE ACTUALLY BELIEVES HE CAN DO IT!
GNARRGH!
ONE SIDE, FELIPE! I DON'T KNOW WHO'S CRAZIER HERE, YOU OR ME--
--BUT IF THIS CONTRAPTION HAS EVEN A SNOWBALL'S CHANCE OF DOING WHAT YOU SAY IT CAN, I AIM TO SEE IT BUSTED!
KRAK
KZAK
FRAGILE SILICON GRIDS SPLINTER UNDER MONICA'S SURPRISE ATTACK...CIRCUITS CROSS AND MELT! AND THEN, EVEN BEFORE THE GUARDS CAN BEGIN TO REACT...
BOOM

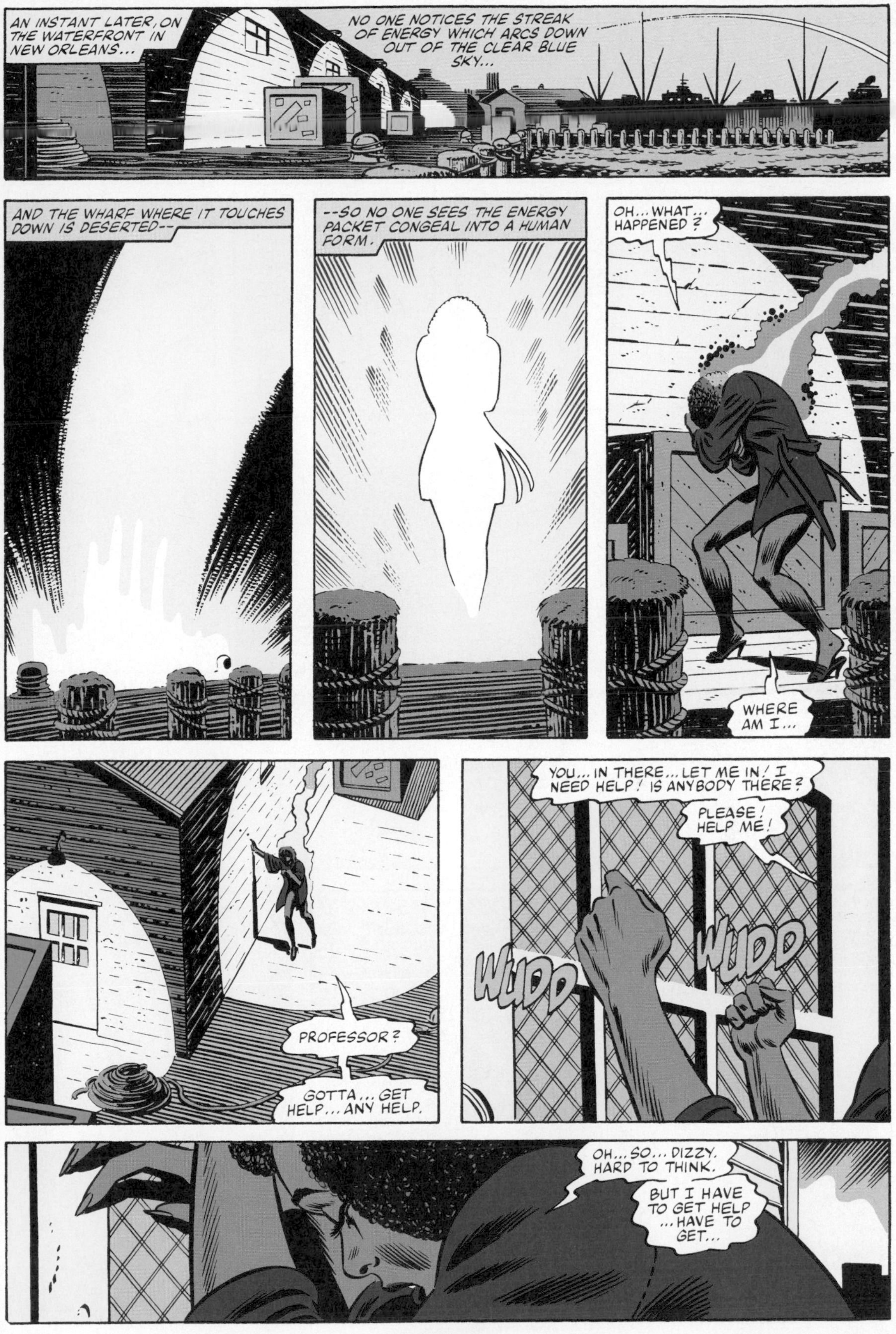
AN INSTANT LATER, ON THE WATERFRONT IN NEW ORLEANS...
NO ONE NOTICES THE STREAK OF ENERGY WHICH ARCS DOWN OUT OF THE CLEAR BLUE SKY...
AND THE WHARF WHERE IT TOUCHES DOWN IS DESERTED--
--SO NO ONE SEES THE ENERGY PACKET CONGEAL INTO A HUMAN FORM.
OH... WHAT... HAPPENED?
WHERE AM I...
PROFESSOR?
GOTTA... GET HELP... ANY HELP.
YOU... IN THERE... LET ME IN! I NEED HELP! IS ANYBODY THERE?
PLEASE! HELP ME!
WUDD
WUDD
OH... SO... DIZZY. HARD TO THINK.
BUT I HAVE TO GET HELP ...HAVE TO GET...

...INSIDE!

FOR AN INSTANT, MONICA EXPERIENCES AN EERIE, SHIMMERING SENSATION... SHE FEELS LIGHT, AIRY. THE DOOR NO LONGER FEELS SO HARD BENEATH HER HAND. AND WHEN SHE STRAIGHTENS UP...

WHAT?!?

I'M INSIDE! BUT HOW... WHERE -- ?

OH, I'LL WORRY ABOUT THAT LATER! FIRST, I HAVE TO GET HELP AND... HEY, A RADIO!

GREAT, IT BROADCASTS ON NAVAL FREQUENCIES!

MAYDAY! MAYDAY! ALL STATIONS PLEASE COPY!

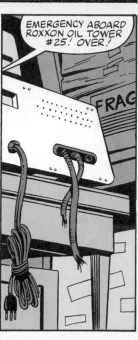

EMERGENCY ABOARD ROXXON OIL TOWER #25! OVER!

MAYDAY! MAYDAY! PLEASE! CAN'T ANYONE HEAR ME?

AT THAT MOMENT, OUT IN THE GULF OF MEXICO...

MAYDAY! MAYDAY!

YEEOOW!

EMERGENCY ABOARD ROXXON OIL TOWER #25!

OKAY! OKAY! ACKNOWLEDGED!

LORDY, WHAT KIND OF POWER IS SHE USING?

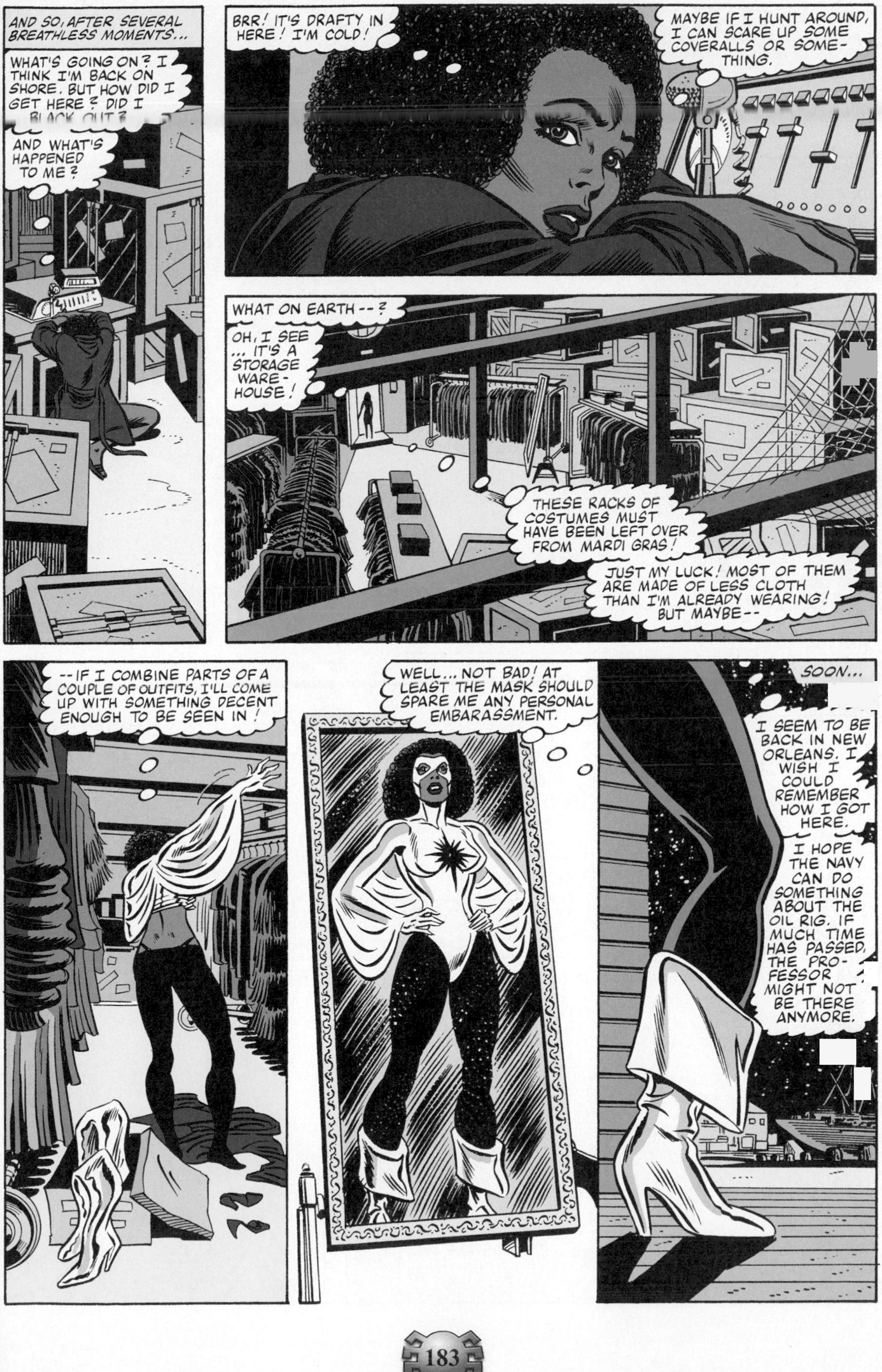
AND SO, AFTER SEVERAL BREATHLESS MOMENTS...
WHAT'S GOING ON? I THINK I'M BACK ON SHORE. BUT HOW DID I GET HERE? DID I BLACK OUT?
AND WHAT'S HAPPENED TO ME?
BRR! IT'S DRAFTY IN HERE! I'M COLD!
MAYBE IF I HUNT AROUND, I CAN SCARE UP SOME COVERALLS OR SOMETHING.
WHAT ON EARTH --?
OH, I SEE ... IT'S A STORAGE WAREHOUSE!
THESE RACKS OF COSTUMES MUST HAVE BEEN LEFT OVER FROM MARDI GRAS!
JUST MY LUCK! MOST OF THEM ARE MADE OF LESS CLOTH THAN I'M ALREADY WEARING! BUT MAYBE--
--IF I COMBINE PARTS OF A COUPLE OF OUTFITS, I'LL COME UP WITH SOMETHING DECENT ENOUGH TO BE SEEN IN!
WELL... NOT BAD! AT LEAST THE MASK SHOULD SPARE ME ANY PERSONAL EMBARASSMENT.
SOON...
I SEEM TO BE BACK IN NEW ORLEANS. I WISH I COULD REMEMBER HOW I GOT HERE.
I HOPE THE NAVY CAN DO SOMETHING ABOUT THE OIL RIG. IF MUCH TIME HAS PASSED, THE PROFESSOR MIGHT NOT BE THERE ANYMORE.

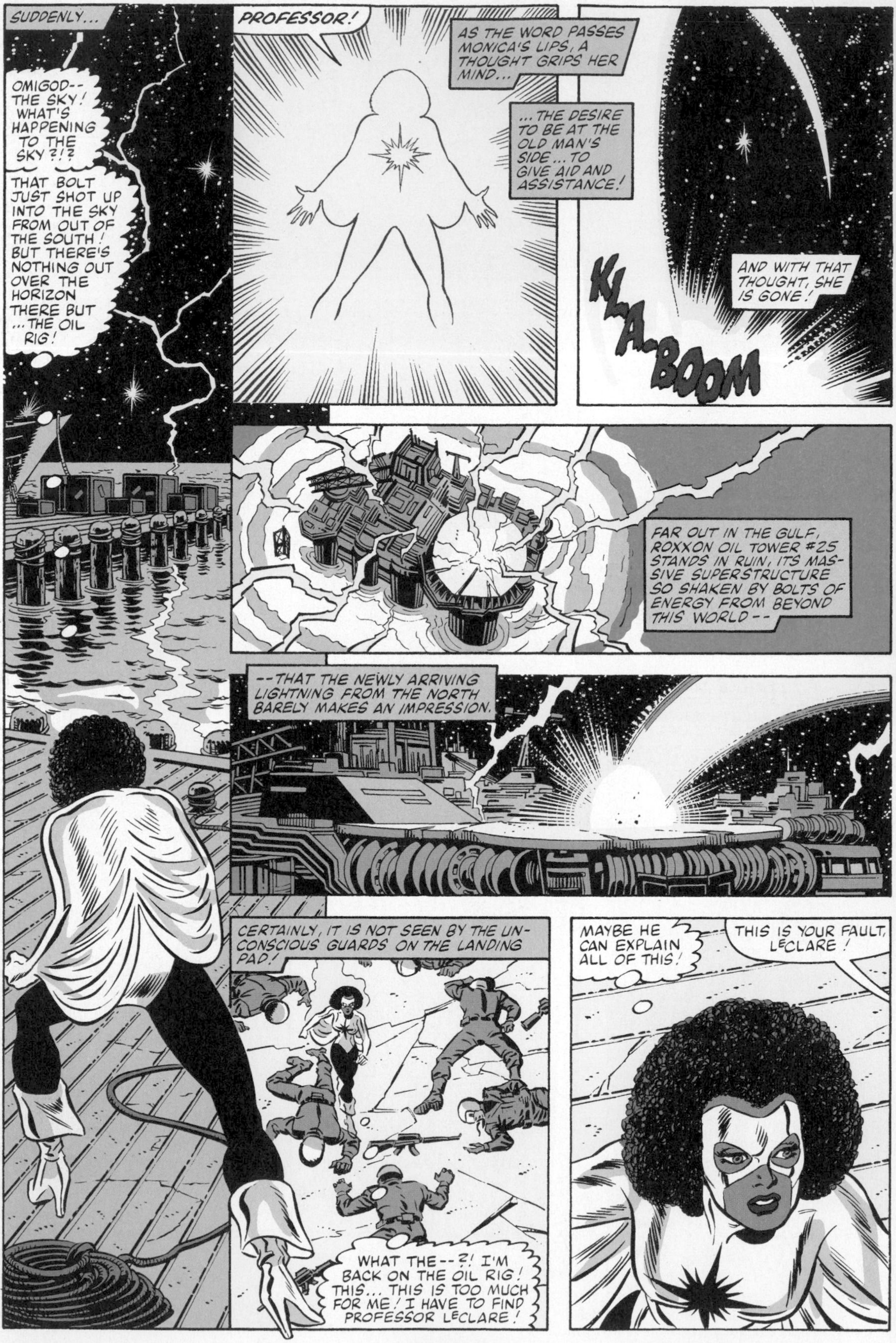

SUDDENLY...
OMIGOD-- THE SKY! WHAT'S HAPPENING TO THE SKY?!?
THAT BOLT JUST SHOT UP INTO THE SKY FROM OUT OF THE SOUTH! BUT THERE'S NOTHING OUT OVER THE HORIZON THERE BUT ...THE OIL RIG!
PROFESSOR!
AS THE WORD PASSES MONICA'S LIPS, A THOUGHT GRIPS HER MIND...
...THE DESIRE TO BE AT THE OLD MAN'S SIDE... TO GIVE AID AND ASSISTANCE!
KLA-BOOM
AND WITH THAT THOUGHT, SHE IS GONE!
FAR OUT IN THE GULF, ROXXON OIL TOWER #25 STANDS IN RUIN, ITS MASSIVE SUPERSTRUCTURE SO SHAKEN BY BOLTS OF ENERGY FROM BEYOND THIS WORLD--
--THAT THE NEWLY ARRIVING LIGHTNING FROM THE NORTH BARELY MAKES AN IMPRESSION.
CERTAINLY, IT IS NOT SEEN BY THE UNCONSCIOUS GUARDS ON THE LANDING PAD!
WHAT THE--?! I'M BACK ON THE OIL RIG! THIS... THIS IS TOO MUCH FOR ME! I HAVE TO FIND PROFESSOR LECLARE!
MAYBE HE CAN EXPLAIN ALL OF THIS!
THIS IS YOUR FAULT, LECLARE!

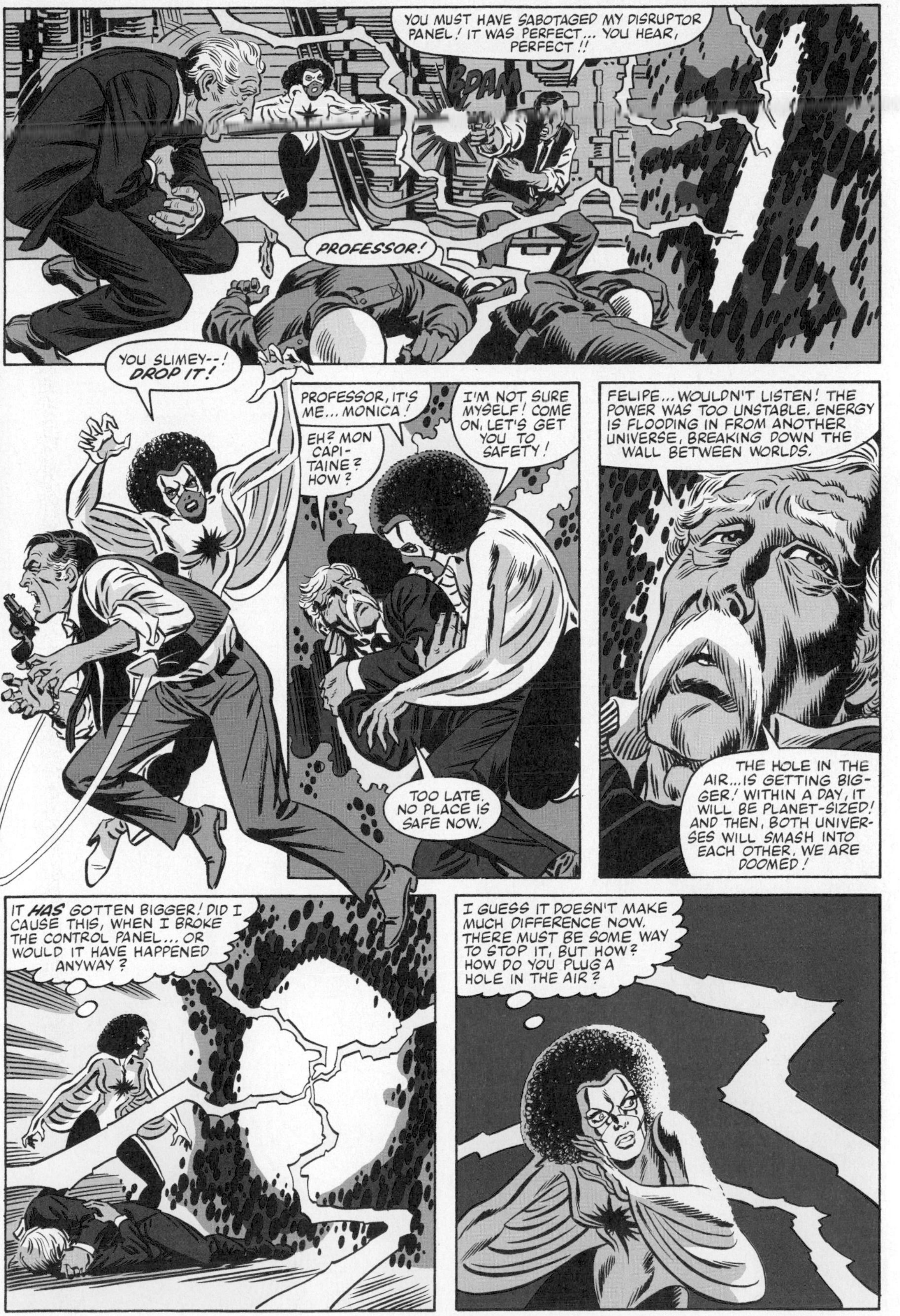

YOU MUST HAVE SABOTAGED MY DISRUPTOR PANEL! IT WAS PERFECT... YOU HEAR, PERFECT!!
BDAM
PROFESSOR!
YOU SLIMEY--! DROP IT!
PROFESSOR, IT'S ME... MONICA!
EH? MON CAPITAINE? HOW?
I'M NOT SURE MYSELF! COME ON, LET'S GET YOU TO SAFETY!
TOO LATE. NO PLACE IS SAFE NOW.
FELIPE... WOULDN'T LISTEN! THE POWER WAS TOO UNSTABLE. ENERGY IS FLOODING IN FROM ANOTHER UNIVERSE, BREAKING DOWN THE WALL BETWEEN WORLDS.
THE HOLE IN THE AIR... IS GETTING BIGGER! WITHIN A DAY, IT WILL BE PLANET-SIZED! AND THEN, BOTH UNIVERSES WILL SMASH INTO EACH OTHER. WE ARE DOOMED!
IT HAS GOTTEN BIGGER! DID I CAUSE THIS, WHEN I BROKE THE CONTROL PANEL... OR WOULD IT HAVE HAPPENED ANYWAY?
I GUESS IT DOESN'T MAKE MUCH DIFFERENCE NOW. THERE MUST BE SOME WAY TO STOP IT, BUT HOW? HOW DO YOU PLUG A HOLE IN THE AIR?

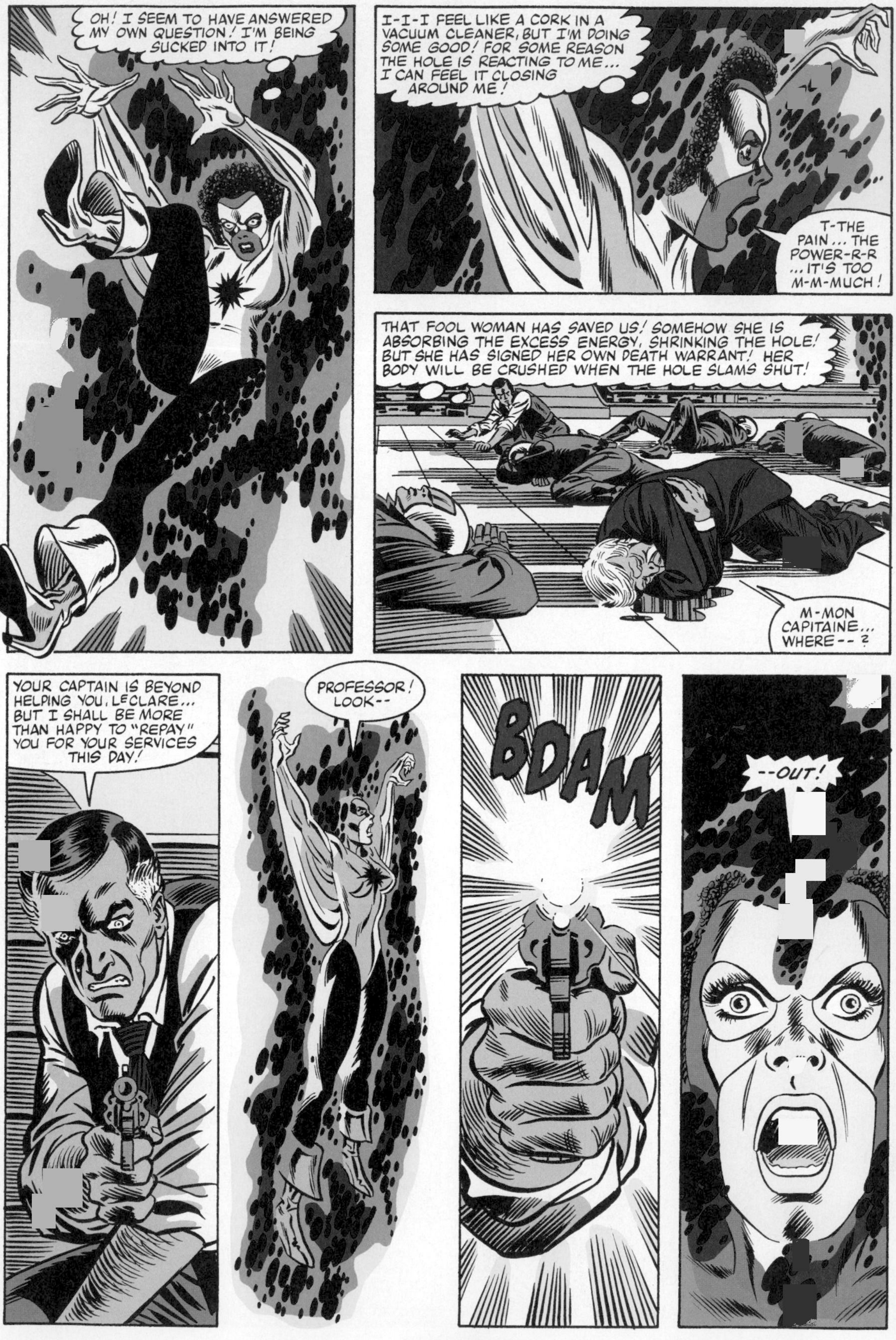

OH! I SEEM TO HAVE ANSWERED MY OWN QUESTION! I'M BEING SUCKED INTO IT!
I-I-I FEEL LIKE A CORK IN A VACUUM CLEANER, BUT I'M DOING SOME GOOD! FOR SOME REASON THE HOLE IS REACTING TO ME... I CAN FEEL IT CLOSING AROUND ME!
T-THE PAIN... THE POWER-R-R ...IT'S TOO M-M-MUCH!
THAT FOOL WOMAN HAS SAVED US! SOMEHOW SHE IS ABSORBING THE EXCESS ENERGY, SHRINKING THE HOLE! BUT SHE HAS SIGNED HER OWN DEATH WARRANT! HER BODY WILL BE CRUSHED WHEN THE HOLE SLAMS SHUT!
M-MON CAPITAINE... WHERE--?
YOUR CAPTAIN IS BEYOND HELPING YOU, LECLARE... BUT I SHALL BE MORE THAN HAPPY TO "REPAY" YOU FOR YOUR SERVICES THIS DAY!
PROFESSOR! LOOK--
BDAM
--OUT!

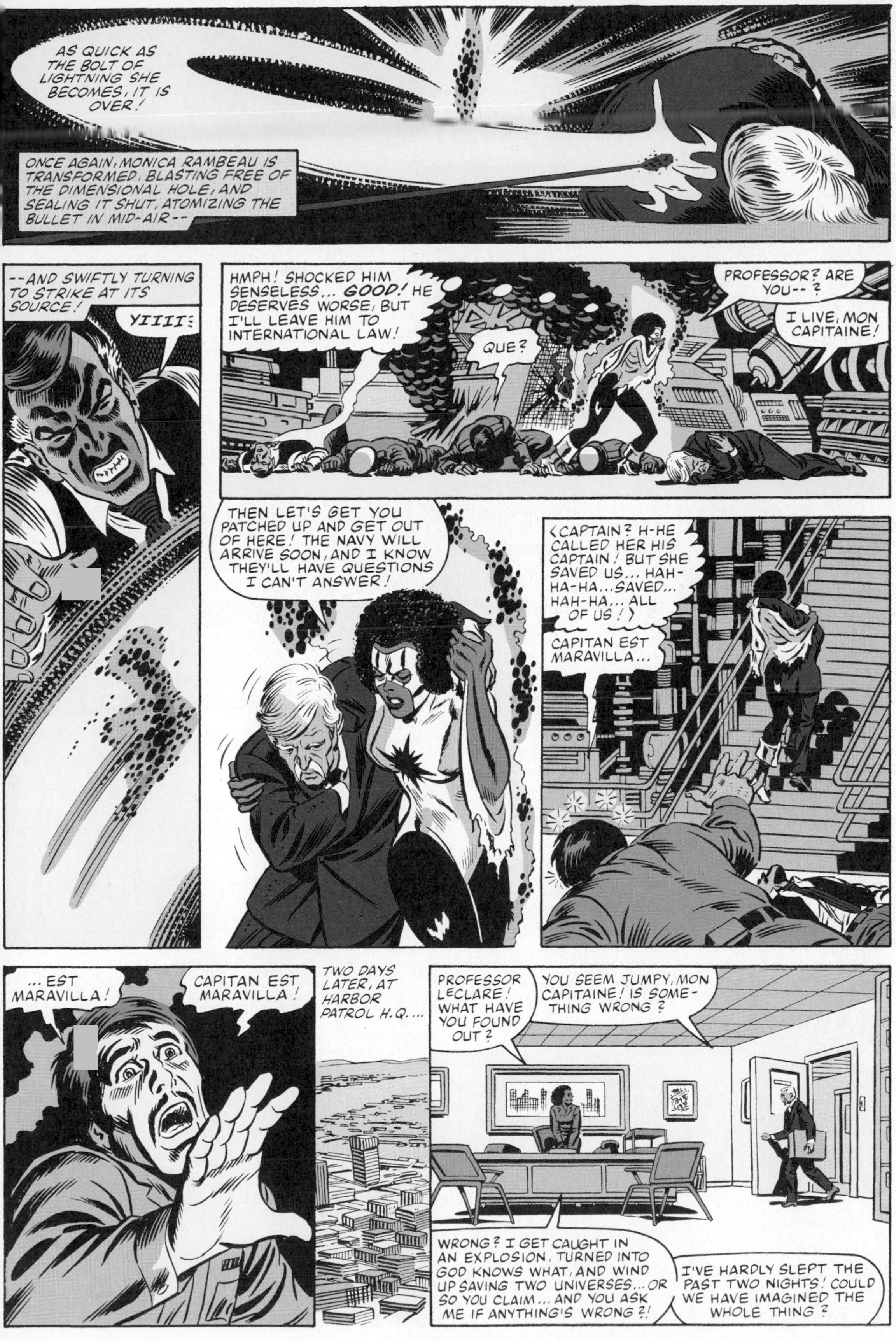
AS QUICK AS THE BOLT OF LIGHTNING SHE BECOMES, IT IS OVER!
ONCE AGAIN, MONICA RAMBEAU IS TRANSFORMED, BLASTING FREE OF THE DIMENSIONAL HOLE, AND SEALING IT SHUT, ATOMIZING THE BULLET IN MID-AIR--
--AND SWIFTLY TURNING TO STRIKE AT ITS SOURCE!
YIIIII!
HMPH! SHOCKED HIM SENSELESS... GOOD! HE DESERVES WORSE, BUT I'LL LEAVE HIM TO INTERNATIONAL LAW!
QUE?
PROFESSOR? ARE YOU--?
I LIVE, MON CAPITAINE!
THEN LET'S GET YOU PATCHED UP AND GET OUT OF HERE! THE NAVY WILL ARRIVE SOON, AND I KNOW THEY'LL HAVE QUESTIONS I CAN'T ANSWER!
‹CAPTAIN? H-HE CALLED HER HIS CAPTAIN! BUT SHE SAVED US... HAH-HA-HA... SAVED... HAH-HA... ALL OF US!›
CAPITAN EST MARAVILLA...
...EST MARAVILLA!
CAPITAN EST MARAVILLA!
TWO DAYS LATER, AT HARBOR PATROL H.Q....
PROFESSOR LECLARE! WHAT HAVE YOU FOUND OUT?
YOU SEEM JUMPY, MON CAPITAINE! IS SOMETHING WRONG?
WRONG? I GET CAUGHT IN AN EXPLOSION, TURNED INTO GOD KNOWS WHAT, AND WIND UP SAVING TWO UNIVERSES... OR SO YOU CLAIM... AND YOU ASK ME IF ANYTHING'S WRONG?!
I'VE HARDLY SLEPT THE PAST TWO NIGHTS! COULD WE HAVE IMAGINED THE WHOLE THING?

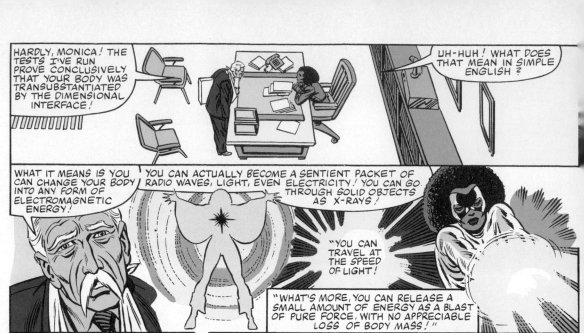

HARDLY, MONICA! THE TESTS I'VE RUN PROVE CONCLUSIVELY THAT YOUR BODY WAS TRANSUBSTANTIATED BY THE DIMENSIONAL INTERFACE!

UH-HUH! WHAT DOES THAT MEAN IN SIMPLE ENGLISH?

WHAT IT MEANS IS YOU CAN CHANGE YOUR BODY INTO ANY FORM OF ELECTROMAGNETIC ENERGY!

YOU CAN ACTUALLY BECOME A SENTIENT PACKET OF RADIO WAVES, LIGHT, EVEN ELECTRICITY! YOU CAN GO THROUGH SOLID OBJECTS AS X-RAYS!

"YOU CAN TRAVEL AT THE SPEED OF LIGHT!"

"WHAT'S MORE, YOU CAN RELEASE A SMALL AMOUNT OF ENERGY AS A BLAST OF PURE FORCE, WITH NO APPRECIABLE LOSS OF BODY MASS!"

BUT I FORGET MYSELF! HERE... FOR YOU!

WHAT IS IT?

I HAD A COPY OF YOUR COSTUME FABRICATED FROM CLOTH COMPOSED OF UNSTABLE MOLECULES.

I THINK YOU'LL FIND IT FAR MORE DURABLE THAN THE ORIGINAL.

GREAT.

PROFESSOR, I'M NOT SO SURE I NEED A COSTUME. I'M NOT CERTAIN I WANT TO EVER USE THOSE POWERS AGAIN!

WE ALL HAVE A DESTINY TO FULFILL, MON CAPITAINE.

WILL YOU STOP CALLING ME THAT? YOU KNOW DARN WELL THAT I'M ONLY A LIEUTENANT!

OH? NOT IN THE EYES OF SOME!

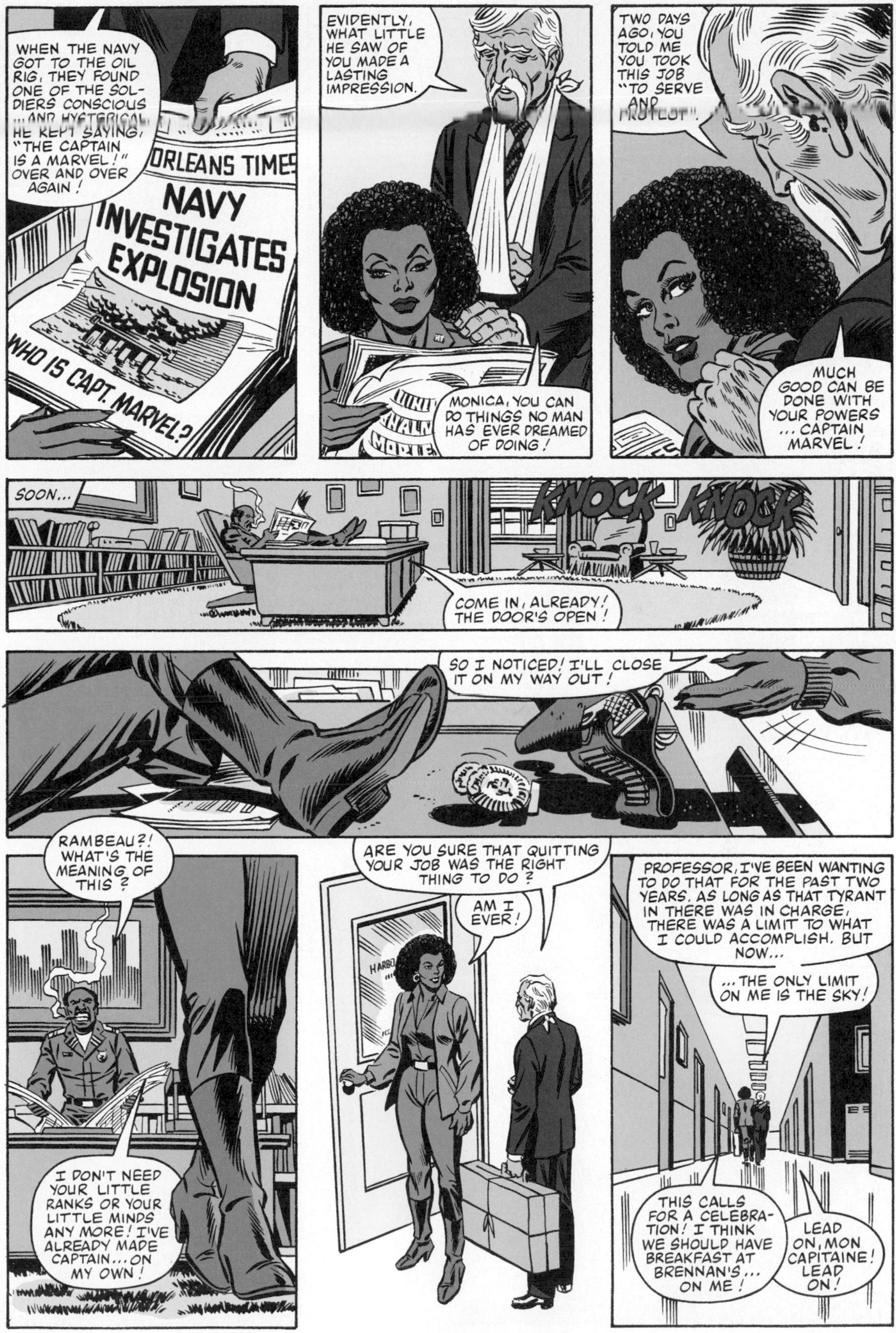
WHEN THE NAVY GOT TO THE OIL RIG, THEY FOUND ONE OF THE SOLDIERS CONSCIOUS ...AND HYSTERICAL. HE KEPT SAYING, "THE CAPTAIN IS A MARVEL!" OVER AND OVER AGAIN!
ORLEANS TIMES
NAVY INVESTIGATES EXPLOSION
WHO IS CAPT. MARVEL?
EVIDENTLY, WHAT LITTLE HE SAW OF YOU MADE A LASTING IMPRESSION.
MONICA, YOU CAN DO THINGS NO MAN HAS EVER DREAMED OF DOING!
TWO DAYS AGO, YOU TOLD ME YOU TOOK THIS JOB "TO SERVE AND PROTECT".
MUCH GOOD CAN BE DONE WITH YOUR POWERS ...CAPTAIN MARVEL!
SOON...
KNOCK KNOCK
COME IN, ALREADY! THE DOOR'S OPEN!
SO I NOTICED! I'LL CLOSE IT ON MY WAY OUT!
RAMBEAU?! WHAT'S THE MEANING OF THIS?
I DON'T NEED YOUR LITTLE RANKS OR YOUR LITTLE MINDS ANY MORE! I'VE ALREADY MADE CAPTAIN... ON MY OWN!
ARE YOU SURE THAT QUITTING YOUR JOB WAS THE RIGHT THING TO DO?
AM I EVER!
PROFESSOR, I'VE BEEN WANTING TO DO THAT FOR THE PAST TWO YEARS. AS LONG AS THAT TYRANT IN THERE WAS IN CHARGE, THERE WAS A LIMIT TO WHAT I COULD ACCOMPLISH. BUT NOW...
...THE ONLY LIMIT ON ME IS THE SKY!
THIS CALLS FOR A CELEBRATION! I THINK WE SHOULD HAVE BREAKFAST AT BRENNAN'S... ON ME!
LEAD ON, MON CAPITAINE! LEAD ON!

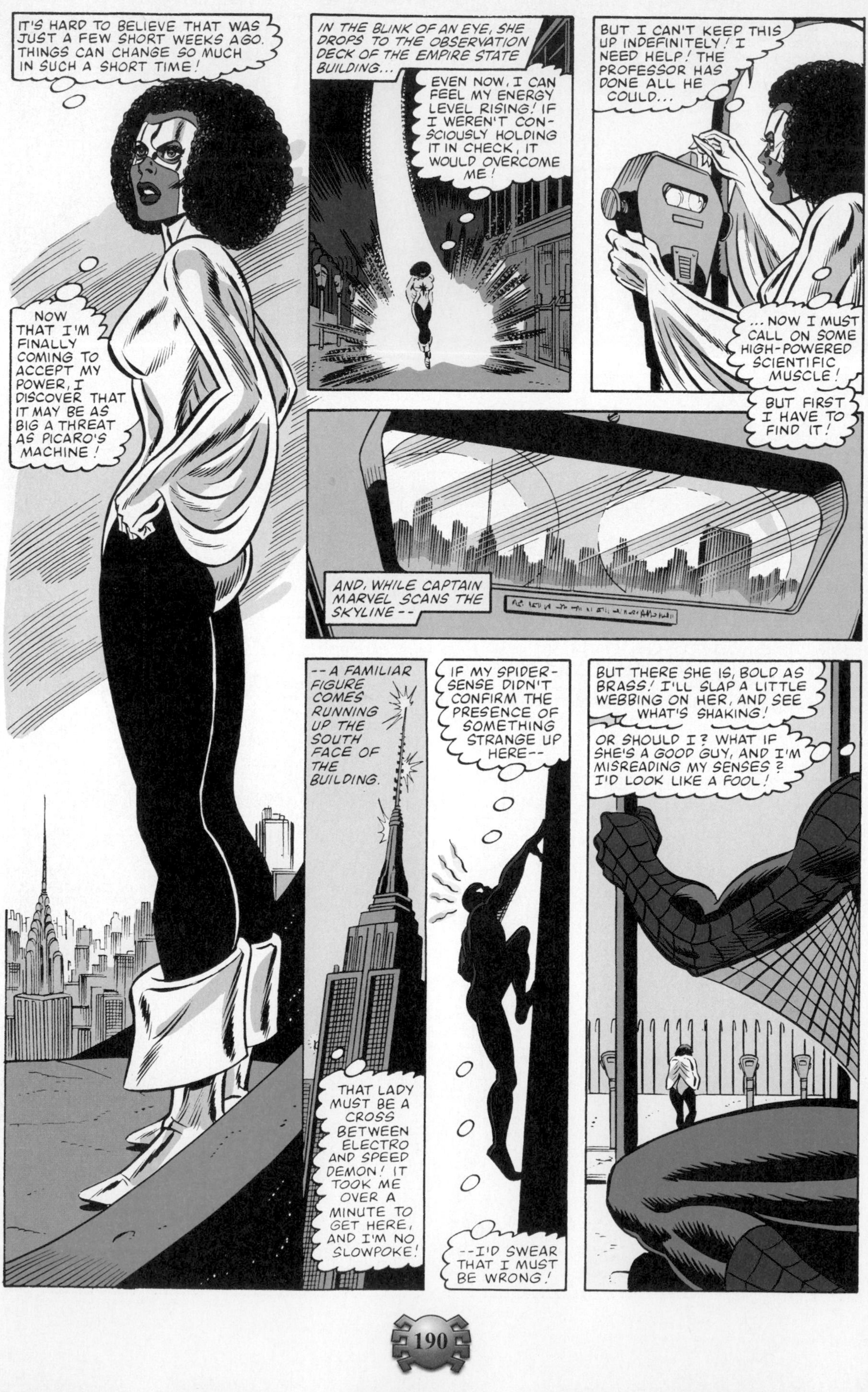
IT'S HARD TO BELIEVE THAT WAS JUST A FEW SHORT WEEKS AGO. THINGS CAN CHANGE SO MUCH IN SUCH A SHORT TIME!
NOW THAT I'M FINALLY COMING TO ACCEPT MY POWER, I DISCOVER THAT IT MAY BE AS BIG A THREAT AS PICARO'S MACHINE!
IN THE BLINK OF AN EYE, SHE DROPS TO THE OBSERVATION DECK OF THE EMPIRE STATE BUILDING...
EVEN NOW, I CAN FEEL MY ENERGY LEVEL RISING! IF I WEREN'T CONSCIOUSLY HOLDING IT IN CHECK, IT WOULD OVERCOME ME!
BUT I CAN'T KEEP THIS UP INDEFINITELY! I NEED HELP! THE PROFESSOR HAS DONE ALL HE COULD...
...NOW I MUST CALL ON SOME HIGH-POWERED SCIENTIFIC MUSCLE!
BUT FIRST I HAVE TO FIND IT!
AND, WHILE CAPTAIN MARVEL SCANS THE SKYLINE--
--A FAMILIAR FIGURE COMES RUNNING UP THE SOUTH FACE OF THE BUILDING.
THAT LADY MUST BE A CROSS BETWEEN ELECTRO AND SPEED DEMON! IT TOOK ME OVER A MINUTE TO GET HERE, AND I'M NO SLOWPOKE!
IF MY SPIDER-SENSE DIDN'T CONFIRM THE PRESENCE OF SOMETHING STRANGE UP HERE--
--I'D SWEAR THAT I MUST BE WRONG!
BUT THERE SHE IS, BOLD AS BRASS! I'LL SLAP A LITTLE WEBBING ON HER, AND SEE WHAT'S SHAKING!
OR SHOULD I? WHAT IF SHE'S A GOOD GUY, AND I'M MISREADING MY SENSES? I'D LOOK LIKE A FOOL!

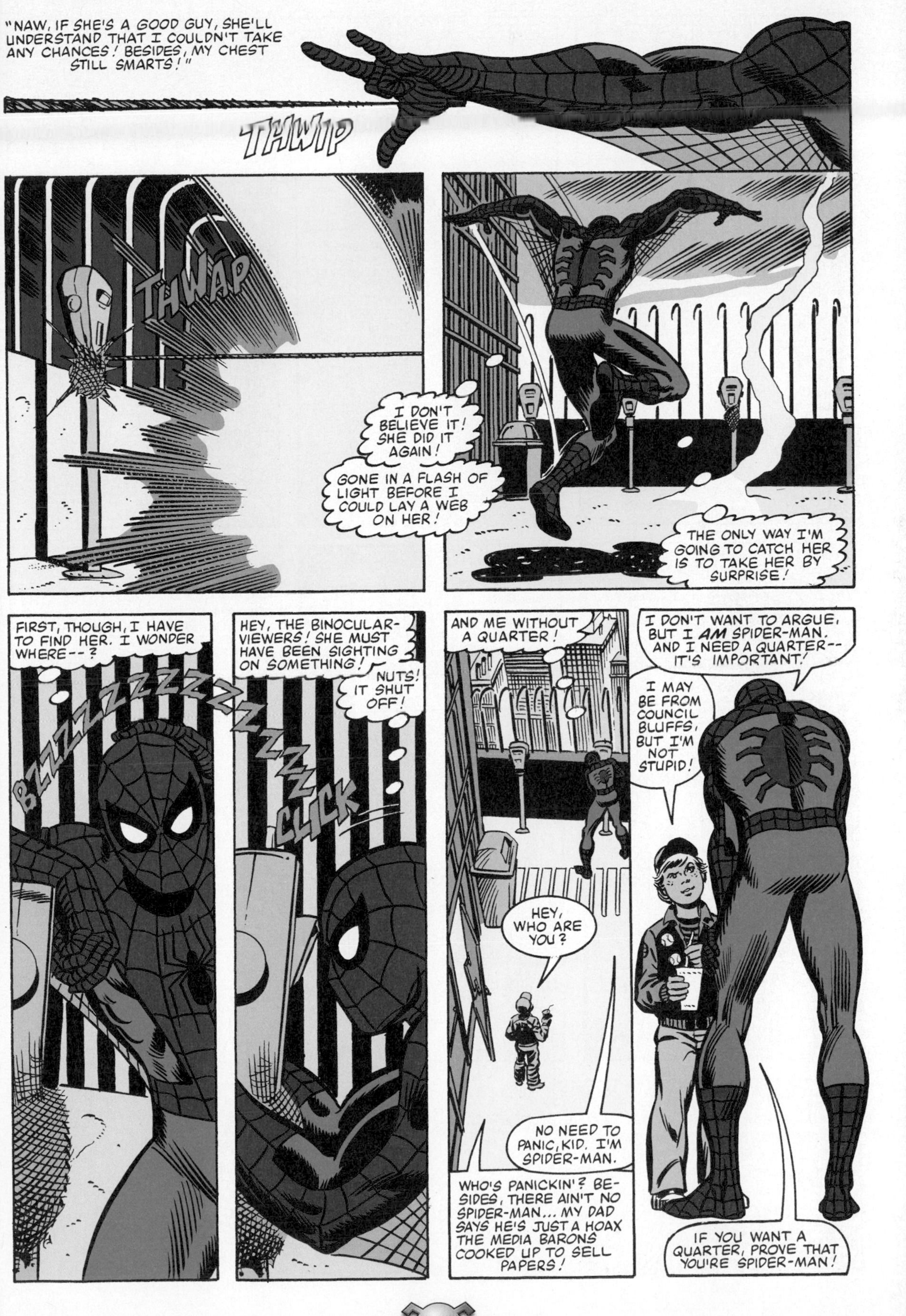
"NAW, IF SHE'S A GOOD GUY, SHE'LL UNDERSTAND THAT I COULDN'T TAKE ANY CHANCES! BESIDES, MY CHEST STILL SMARTS!"
THWIP
THWAP
I DON'T BELIEVE IT! SHE DID IT AGAIN!
GONE IN A FLASH OF LIGHT BEFORE I COULD LAY A WEB ON HER!
THE ONLY WAY I'M GOING TO CATCH HER IS TO TAKE HER BY SURPRISE!
FIRST, THOUGH, I HAVE TO FIND HER. I WONDER WHERE--?
BZZZZZZZZZZZZZZZZ
HEY, THE BINOCULAR-VIEWERS! SHE MUST HAVE BEEN SIGHTING ON SOMETHING!
NUTS! IT SHUT OFF!
CLICK
AND ME WITHOUT A QUARTER!
HEY, WHO ARE YOU?
NO NEED TO PANIC, KID. I'M SPIDER-MAN.
WHO'S PANICKIN'? BESIDES, THERE AIN'T NO SPIDER-MAN... MY DAD SAYS HE'S JUST A HOAX THE MEDIA BARONS COOKED UP TO SELL PAPERS!
I DON'T WANT TO ARGUE, BUT I AM SPIDER-MAN. AND I NEED A QUARTER-- IT'S IMPORTANT!
I MAY BE FROM COUNCIL BLUFFS, BUT I'M NOT STUPID!
IF YOU WANT A QUARTER, PROVE THAT YOU'RE SPIDER-MAN!

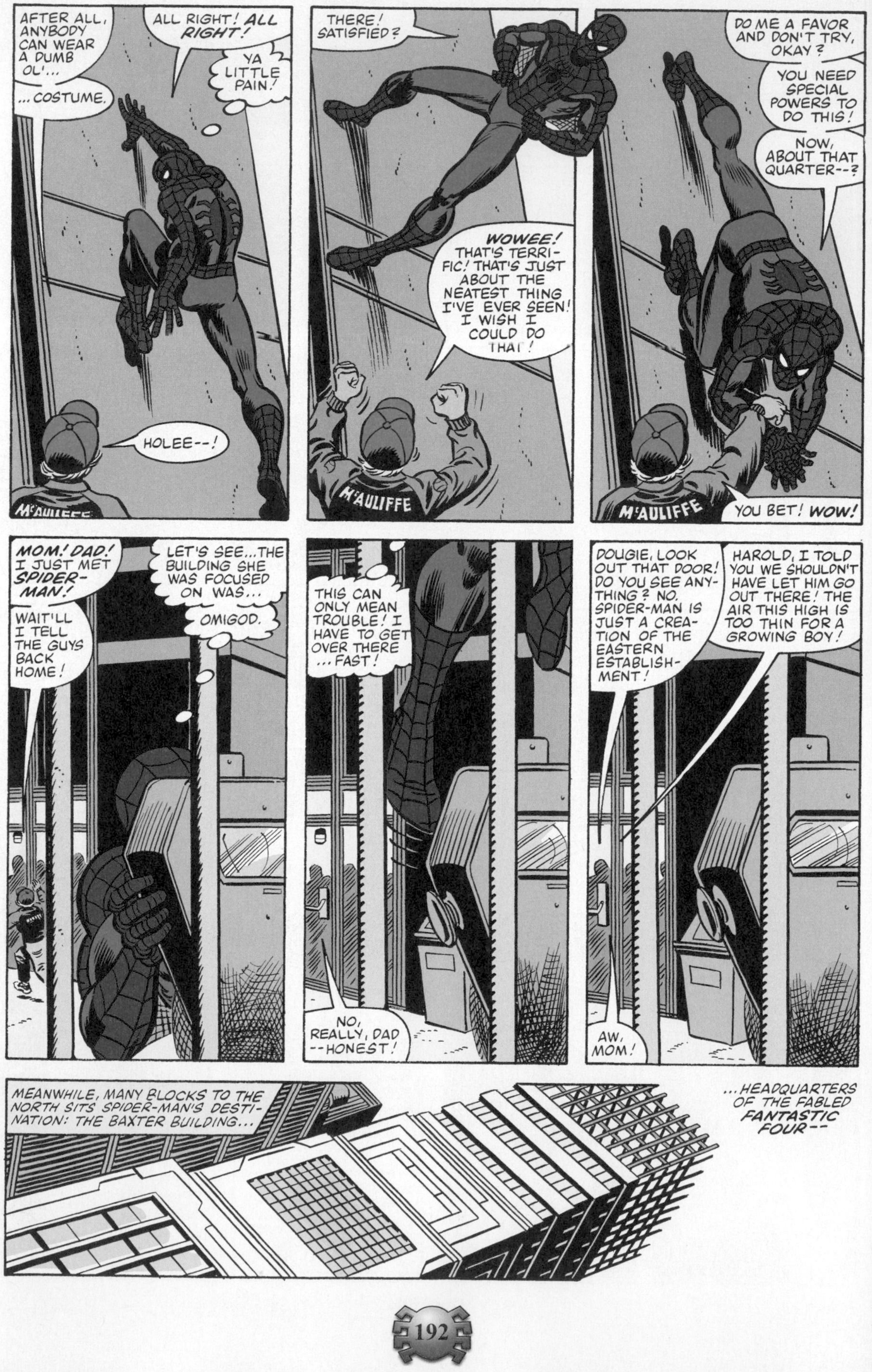
AFTER ALL, ANYBODY CAN WEAR A DUMB OL'...
...COSTUME.
ALL RIGHT! ALL RIGHT!
YA LITTLE PAIN!
HOLEE--!
M^cAULIFFE
THERE! SATISFIED?
WOWEE! THAT'S TERRIFIC! THAT'S JUST ABOUT THE NEATEST THING I'VE EVER SEEN! I WISH I COULD DO THAT!
M^cAULIFFE
DO ME A FAVOR AND DON'T TRY, OKAY?
YOU NEED SPECIAL POWERS TO DO THIS!
NOW, ABOUT THAT QUARTER--?
YOU BET! WOW!
M^cAULIFFE
MOM! DAD! I JUST MET SPIDER-MAN!
WAIT'LL I TELL THE GUYS BACK HOME!
LET'S SEE...THE BUILDING SHE WAS FOCUSED ON WAS...
OMIGOD.
THIS CAN ONLY MEAN TROUBLE! I HAVE TO GET OVER THERE ...FAST!
NO, REALLY, DAD --HONEST!
DOUGIE, LOOK OUT THAT DOOR! DO YOU SEE ANYTHING? NO. SPIDER-MAN IS JUST A CREATION OF THE EASTERN ESTABLISHMENT!
HAROLD, I TOLD YOU WE SHOULDN'T HAVE LET HIM GO OUT THERE! THE AIR THIS HIGH IS TOO THIN FOR A GROWING BOY!
AW, MOM!
MEANWHILE, MANY BLOCKS TO THE NORTH SITS SPIDER-MAN'S DESTINATION: THE BAXTER BUILDING...
...HEADQUARTERS OF THE FABLED FANTASTIC FOUR--

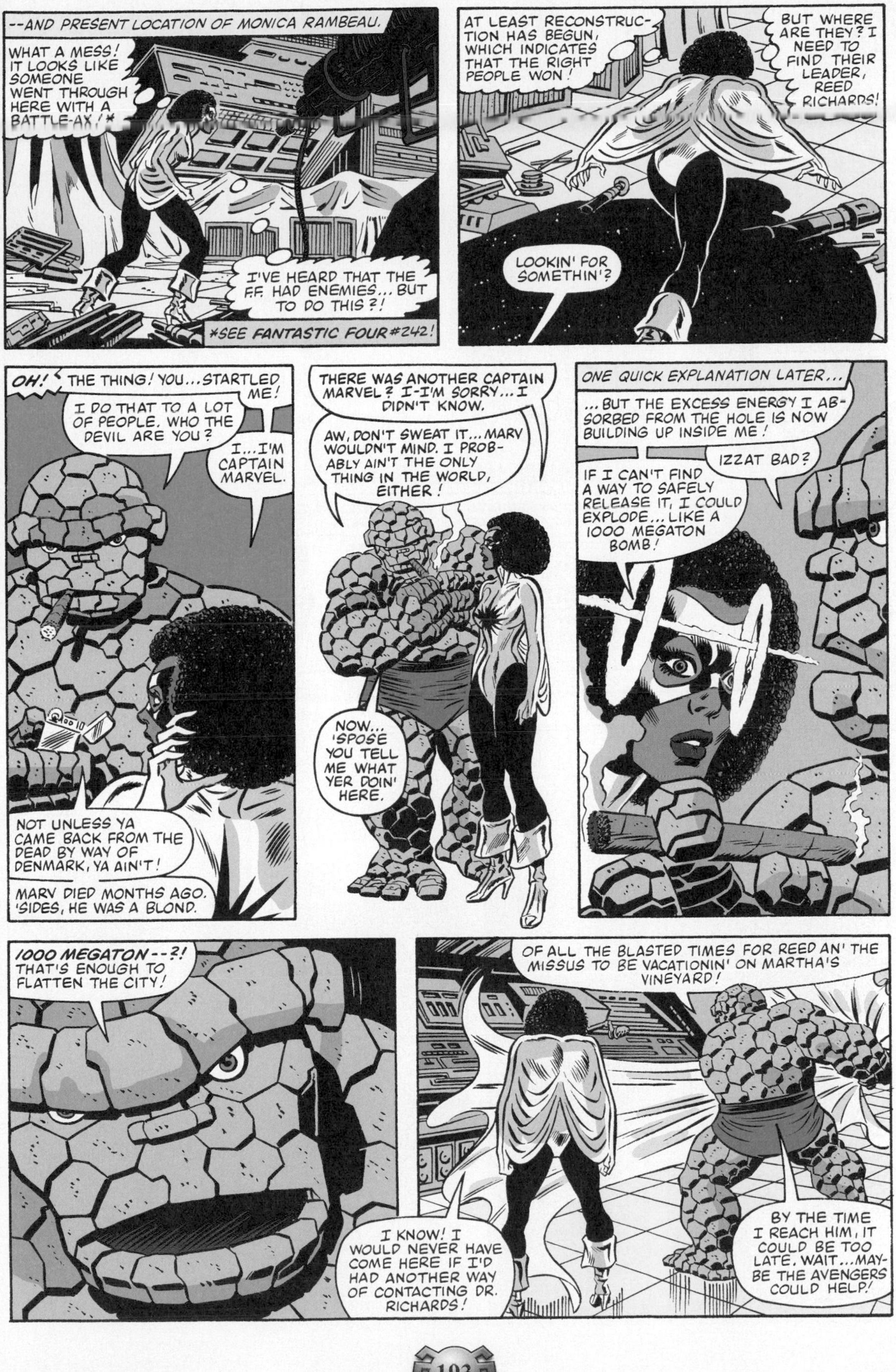
--AND PRESENT LOCATION OF MONICA RAMBEAU.
WHAT A MESS! IT LOOKS LIKE SOMEONE WENT THROUGH HERE WITH A BATTLE-AX!*
I'VE HEARD THAT THE F.F. HAD ENEMIES... BUT TO DO THIS?!
*SEE FANTASTIC FOUR #242!
AT LEAST RECONSTRUCTION HAS BEGUN, WHICH INDICATES THAT THE RIGHT PEOPLE WON!
BUT WHERE ARE THEY? I NEED TO FIND THEIR LEADER, REED RICHARDS!
LOOKIN' FOR SOMETHIN'?
OH! THE THING! YOU... STARTLED ME!
I DO THAT TO A LOT OF PEOPLE. WHO THE DEVIL ARE YOU?
I...I'M CAPTAIN MARVEL.
NOT UNLESS YA CAME BACK FROM THE DEAD BY WAY OF DENMARK, YA AIN'T!
MARV DIED MONTHS AGO. 'SIDES, HE WAS A BLOND.
THERE WAS ANOTHER CAPTAIN MARVEL? I-I'M SORRY... I DIDN'T KNOW.
AW, DON'T SWEAT IT... MARV WOULDN'T MIND. I PROBABLY AIN'T THE ONLY THING IN THE WORLD, EITHER!
NOW... 'SPOSE YOU TELL ME WHAT YER DOIN' HERE.
ONE QUICK EXPLANATION LATER...
...BUT THE EXCESS ENERGY I ABSORBED FROM THE HOLE IS NOW BUILDING UP INSIDE ME!
IZZAT BAD?
IF I CAN'T FIND A WAY TO SAFELY RELEASE IT, I COULD EXPLODE... LIKE A 1000 MEGATON BOMB!
1000 MEGATON--?! THAT'S ENOUGH TO FLATTEN THE CITY!
I KNOW! I WOULD NEVER HAVE COME HERE IF I'D HAD ANOTHER WAY OF CONTACTING DR. RICHARDS!
OF ALL THE BLASTED TIMES FOR REED AN' THE MISSUS TO BE VACATIONIN' ON MARTHA'S VINEYARD!
BY THE TIME I REACH HIM, IT COULD BE TOO LATE. WAIT... MAYBE THE AVENGERS COULD HELP!

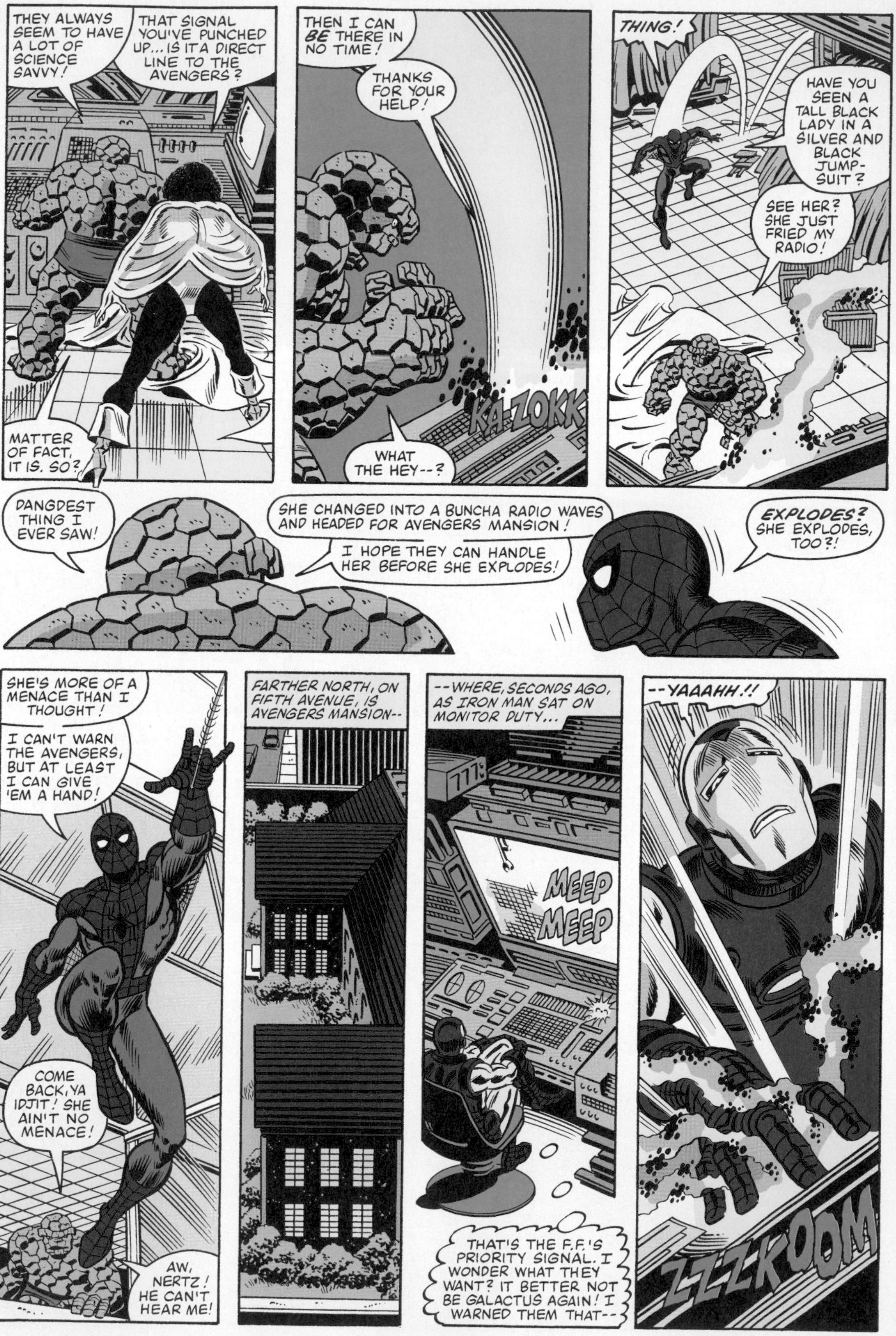
THEY ALWAYS SEEM TO HAVE A LOT OF SCIENCE SAVVY!
THAT SIGNAL YOU'VE PUNCHED UP... IS IT A DIRECT LINE TO THE AVENGERS?
MATTER OF FACT, IT IS. SO?
THEN I CAN BE THERE IN NO TIME!
THANKS FOR YOUR HELP!
KA-ZOKK
WHAT THE HEY--?
THING!
HAVE YOU SEEN A TALL BLACK LADY IN A SILVER AND BLACK JUMP-SUIT?
SEE HER? SHE JUST FRIED MY RADIO!
DANGDEST THING I EVER SAW!
SHE CHANGED INTO A BUNCHA RADIO WAVES AND HEADED FOR AVENGERS MANSION!
I HOPE THEY CAN HANDLE HER BEFORE SHE EXPLODES!
EXPLODES? SHE EXPLODES, TOO?!
SHE'S MORE OF A MENACE THAN I THOUGHT!
I CAN'T WARN THE AVENGERS, BUT AT LEAST I CAN GIVE 'EM A HAND!
COME BACK, YA IDJIT! SHE AIN'T NO MENACE!
AW, NERTZ! HE CAN'T HEAR ME!
FARTHER NORTH, ON FIFTH AVENUE, IS AVENGERS MANSION--
--WHERE, SECONDS AGO, AS IRON MAN SAT ON MONITOR DUTY...
MEEP MEEP
THAT'S THE F.F.'S PRIORITY SIGNAL. I WONDER WHAT THEY WANT? IT BETTER NOT BE GALACTUS AGAIN! I WARNED THEM THAT--
--YAAAHH!!
ZZZKOOM

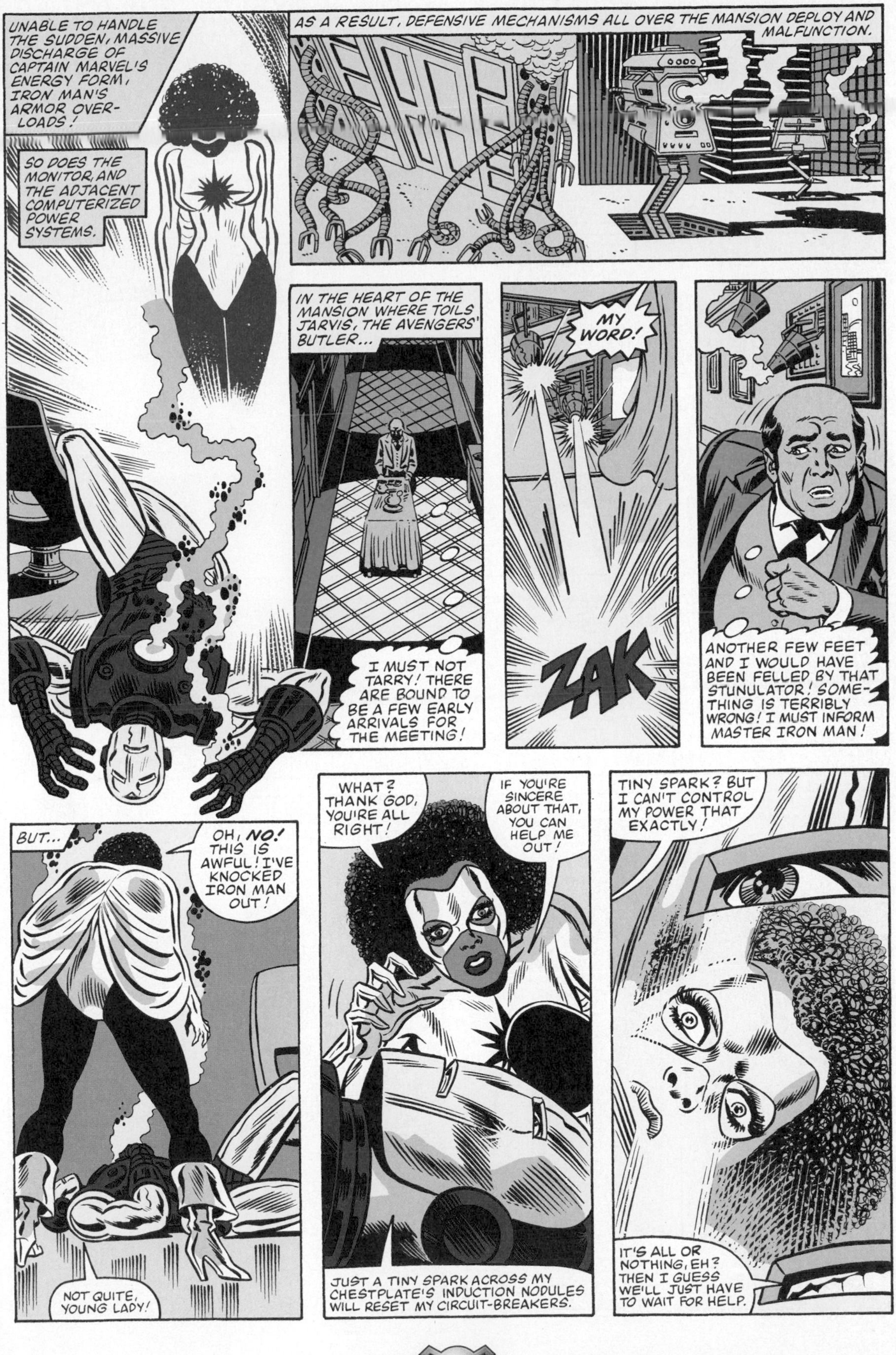

UNABLE TO HANDLE THE SUDDEN, MASSIVE DISCHARGE OF CAPTAIN MARVEL'S ENERGY FORM, IRON MAN'S ARMOR OVER-LOADS!
SO DOES THE MONITOR, AND THE ADJACENT COMPUTERIZED POWER SYSTEMS.
AS A RESULT, DEFENSIVE MECHANISMS ALL OVER THE MANSION DEPLOY AND MALFUNCTION.
IN THE HEART OF THE MANSION WHERE TOILS JARVIS, THE AVENGERS' BUTLER...
I MUST NOT TARRY! THERE ARE BOUND TO BE A FEW EARLY ARRIVALS FOR THE MEETING!
MY WORD!
ZAK
ANOTHER FEW FEET AND I WOULD HAVE BEEN FELLED BY THAT STUNULATOR! SOMETHING IS TERRIBLY WRONG! I MUST INFORM MASTER IRON MAN!
BUT...
OH, NO! THIS IS AWFUL! I'VE KNOCKED IRON MAN OUT!
NOT QUITE, YOUNG LADY!
WHAT? THANK GOD, YOU'RE ALL RIGHT!
IF YOU'RE SINCERE ABOUT THAT, YOU CAN HELP ME OUT!
JUST A TINY SPARK ACROSS MY CHESTPLATE'S INDUCTION NODULES WILL RESET MY CIRCUIT-BREAKERS.
TINY SPARK? BUT I CAN'T CONTROL MY POWER THAT EXACTLY!
IT'S ALL OR NOTHING, EH? THEN I GUESS WE'LL JUST HAVE TO WAIT FOR HELP.

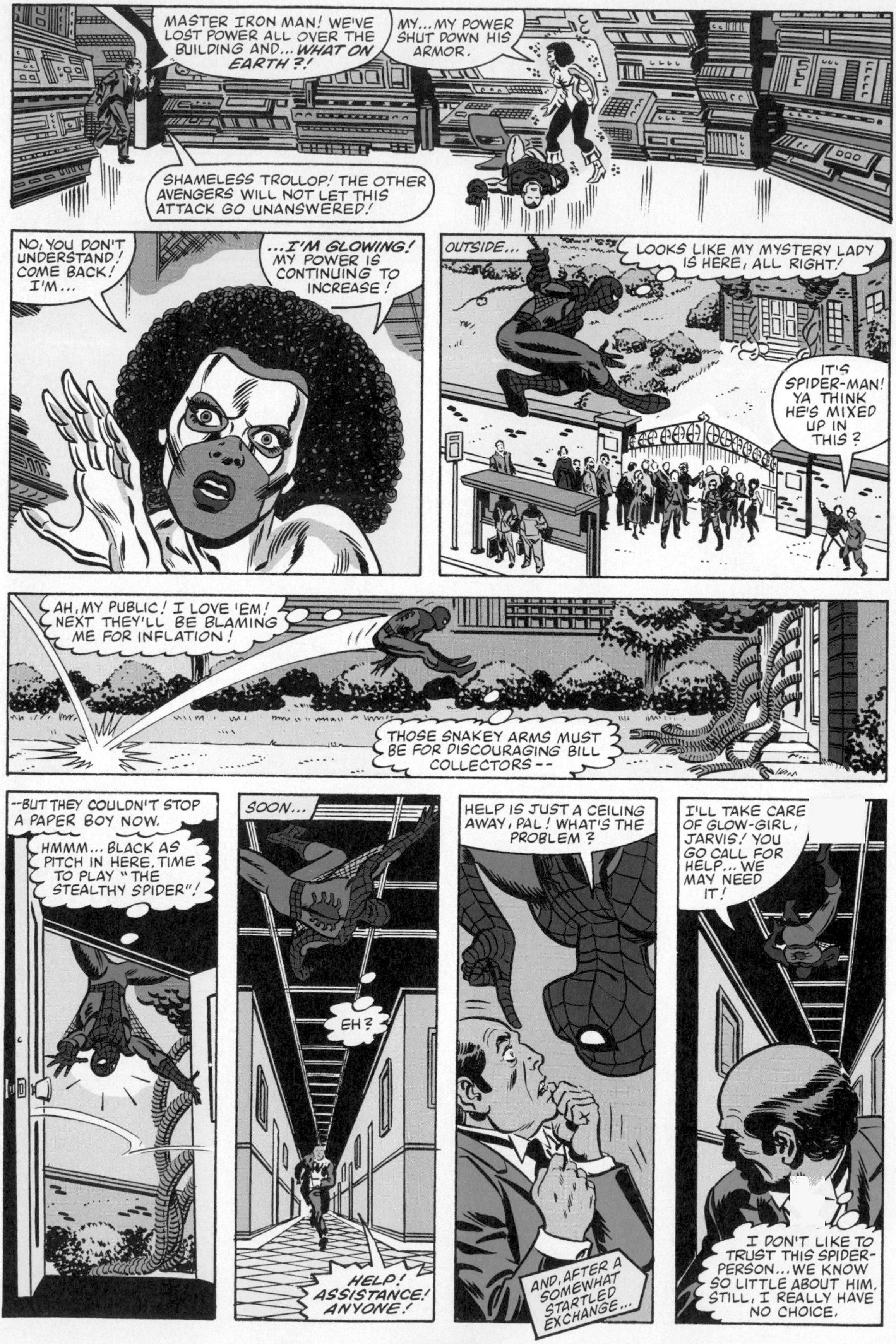
MASTER IRON MAN! WE'VE LOST POWER ALL OVER THE BUILDING AND... WHAT ON EARTH?!
MY... MY POWER SHUT DOWN HIS ARMOR.
SHAMELESS TROLLOP! THE OTHER AVENGERS WILL NOT LET THIS ATTACK GO UNANSWERED!
NO, YOU DON'T UNDERSTAND! COME BACK! I'M...
...I'M GLOWING! MY POWER IS CONTINUING TO INCREASE!
OUTSIDE...
LOOKS LIKE MY MYSTERY LADY IS HERE, ALL RIGHT!
IT'S SPIDER-MAN! YA THINK HE'S MIXED UP IN THIS?
AH, MY PUBLIC! I LOVE 'EM! NEXT THEY'LL BE BLAMING ME FOR INFLATION!
THOSE SNAKEY ARMS MUST BE FOR DISCOURAGING BILL COLLECTORS--
--BUT THEY COULDN'T STOP A PAPER BOY NOW.
HMMM... BLACK AS PITCH IN HERE. TIME TO PLAY "THE STEALTHY SPIDER"!
SOON...
EH?
HELP! ASSISTANCE! ANYONE!
HELP IS JUST A CEILING AWAY, PAL! WHAT'S THE PROBLEM?
AND, AFTER A SOMEWHAT STARTLED EXCHANGE...
I'LL TAKE CARE OF GLOW-GIRL, JARVIS! YOU GO CALL FOR HELP... WE MAY NEED IT!
I DON'T LIKE TO TRUST THIS SPIDER-PERSON... WE KNOW SO LITTLE ABOUT HIM. STILL, I REALLY HAVE NO CHOICE.

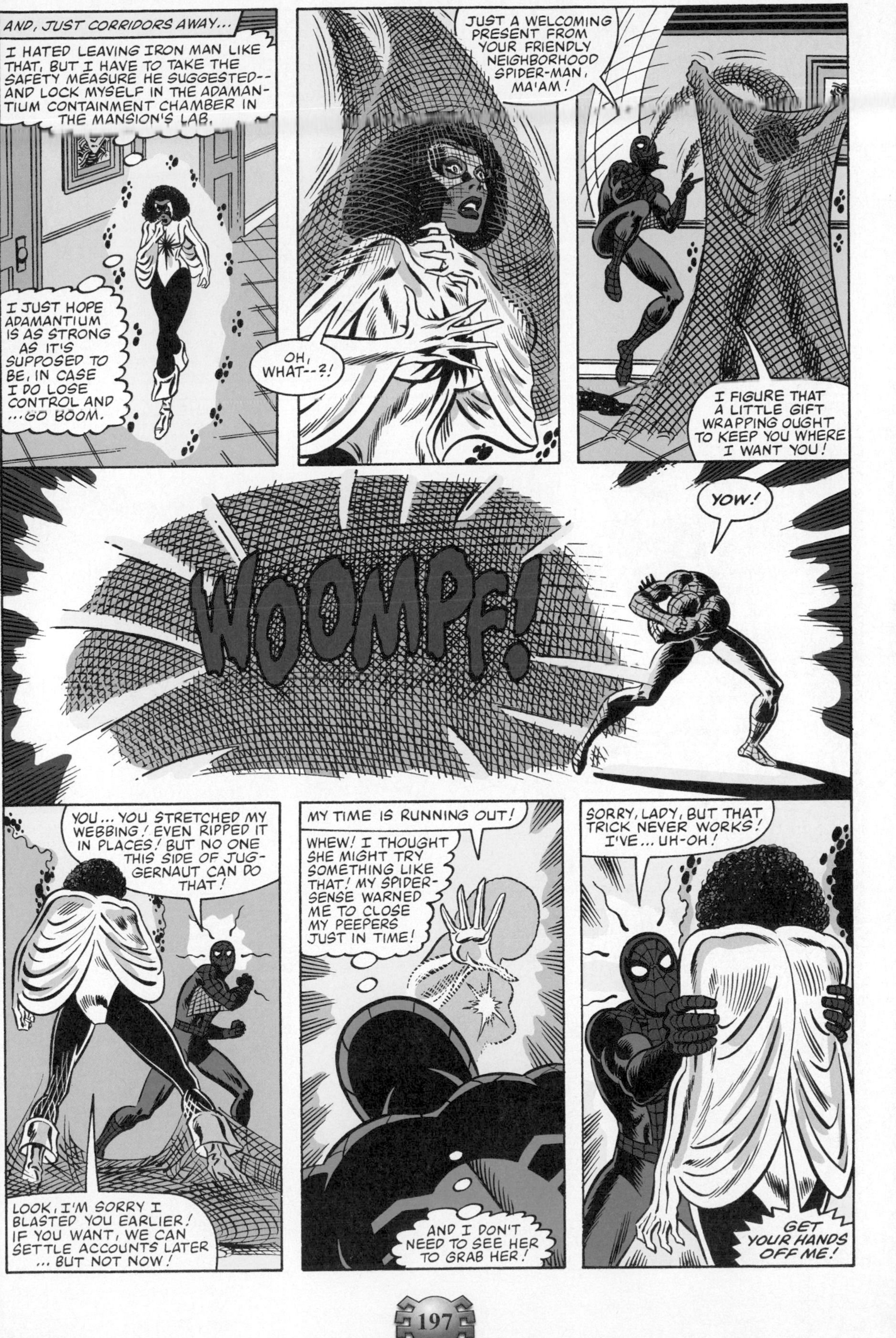
AND, JUST CORRIDORS AWAY...
I HATED LEAVING IRON MAN LIKE THAT, BUT I HAVE TO TAKE THE SAFETY MEASURE HE SUGGESTED-- AND LOCK MYSELF IN THE ADAMANTIUM CONTAINMENT CHAMBER IN THE MANSION'S LAB.
I JUST HOPE ADAMANTIUM IS AS STRONG AS IT'S SUPPOSED TO BE, IN CASE I DO LOSE CONTROL AND ...GO BOOM.
JUST A WELCOMING PRESENT FROM YOUR FRIENDLY NEIGHBORHOOD SPIDER-MAN, MA'AM!
OH, WHAT--?!
I FIGURE THAT A LITTLE GIFT WRAPPING OUGHT TO KEEP YOU WHERE I WANT YOU!
WOOMPF!
YOW!
YOU... YOU STRETCHED MY WEBBING! EVEN RIPPED IT IN PLACES! BUT NO ONE THIS SIDE OF JUGGERNAUT CAN DO THAT!
LOOK, I'M SORRY I BLASTED YOU EARLIER! IF YOU WANT, WE CAN SETTLE ACCOUNTS LATER ... BUT NOT NOW!
MY TIME IS RUNNING OUT!
WHEW! I THOUGHT SHE MIGHT TRY SOMETHING LIKE THAT! MY SPIDER-SENSE WARNED ME TO CLOSE MY PEEPERS JUST IN TIME!
AND I DON'T NEED TO SEE HER TO GRAB HER!
SORRY, LADY, BUT THAT TRICK NEVER WORKS! I'VE... UH-OH!
GET YOUR HANDS OFF ME!

YEESH! SHE'S PLAYING HARDBALL!

IF NOT FOR THAT OL' SPIDER-SENSE WARNING, I'D HAVE HAD TWO HANDS FULL OF ELECTRICITY. BUT SHE SEEMS TO BE USING HER ENERGY-STUFF SPARINGLY. ONCE SHE COOLS DOWN--

--I'LL MAKE MY MOVE!

SORRY, TOOTS, BUT I CAN MOVE PRETTY FAST TOO!

SPIDER-MAN-- *NO!*

SMEK

YOU YOUNG *FOOL!*

IRON MAN?! BUT I THOUGHT THIS LADY HAD--!

AN ACCIDENT! THE WASP GOT ME GOING AGAIN!

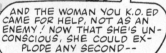

AND THE WOMAN YOU K.O.ED CAME FOR HELP, NOT AS AN ENEMY! NOW THAT SHE'S UNCONSCIOUS, SHE COULD EXPLODE ANY SECOND--

"--UNLESS WE CAN LEACH OFF HER EXCESS POWER. IF YOU WANT TO MAKE AMENDS, GET ME 12 FEET OF HIGH-INDUCTION FLEX-CABLE FROM BEHIND THAT CEILING PANEL--"

--AND COIL IT AROUND HER...GENTLY!

IRON MAN, WHAT ARE YOU--?

I'M OVERRIDING MY ARMOR'S MICROCIRCUIT-BREAKERS, WASP. THE ONLY THING AT HAND THAT CAN HANDLE HER KIND OF POWER IS *ME!*

SPIDER-MAN, THAT WEBBING OF YOURS IS A NON-CONDUCTOR, ISN'T IT?

I READ YOU, SHELL-HEAD!

NOT JUST THE POWER JUNCTURE! I WANT YOU TO COVER ME--

--RIGHT OUT TO THE WRISTS!

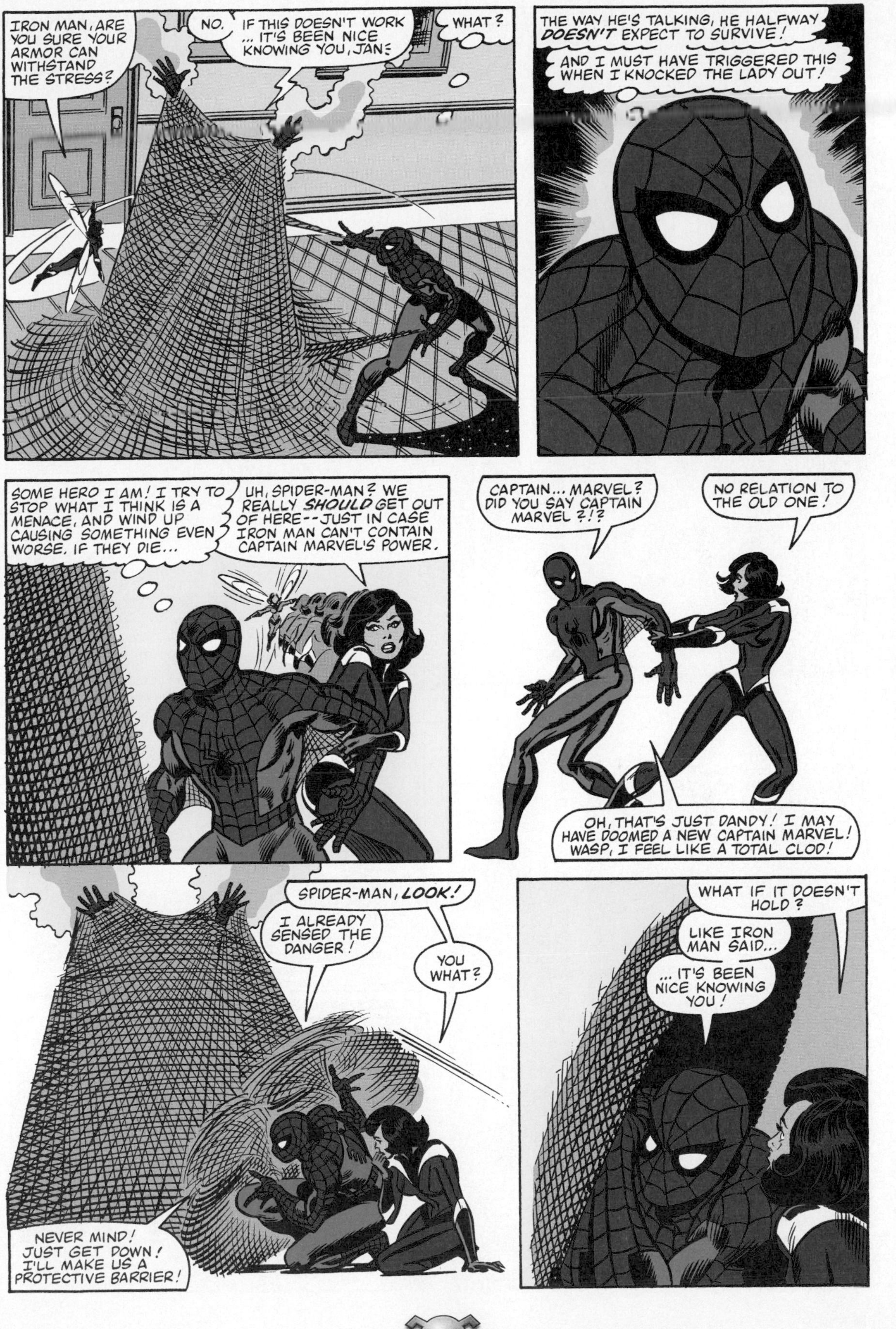
IRON MAN, ARE YOU SURE YOUR ARMOR CAN WITHSTAND THE STRESS?
NO.
IF THIS DOESN'T WORK ... IT'S BEEN NICE KNOWING YOU, JAN!
WHAT?
THE WAY HE'S TALKING, HE HALFWAY DOESN'T EXPECT TO SURVIVE!
AND I MUST HAVE TRIGGERED THIS WHEN I KNOCKED THE LADY OUT!
SOME HERO I AM! I TRY TO STOP WHAT I THINK IS A MENACE, AND WIND UP CAUSING SOMETHING EVEN WORSE. IF THEY DIE...
UH, SPIDER-MAN? WE REALLY SHOULD GET OUT OF HERE--JUST IN CASE IRON MAN CAN'T CONTAIN CAPTAIN MARVEL'S POWER.
CAPTAIN... MARVEL? DID YOU SAY CAPTAIN MARVEL?!?
NO RELATION TO THE OLD ONE!
OH, THAT'S JUST DANDY! I MAY HAVE DOOMED A NEW CAPTAIN MARVEL! WASP, I FEEL LIKE A TOTAL CLOD!
SPIDER-MAN, LOOK!
I ALREADY SENSED THE DANGER!
YOU WHAT?
NEVER MIND! JUST GET DOWN! I'LL MAKE US A PROTECTIVE BARRIER!
WHAT IF IT DOESN'T HOLD?
LIKE IRON MAN SAID...
... IT'S BEEN NICE KNOWING YOU!

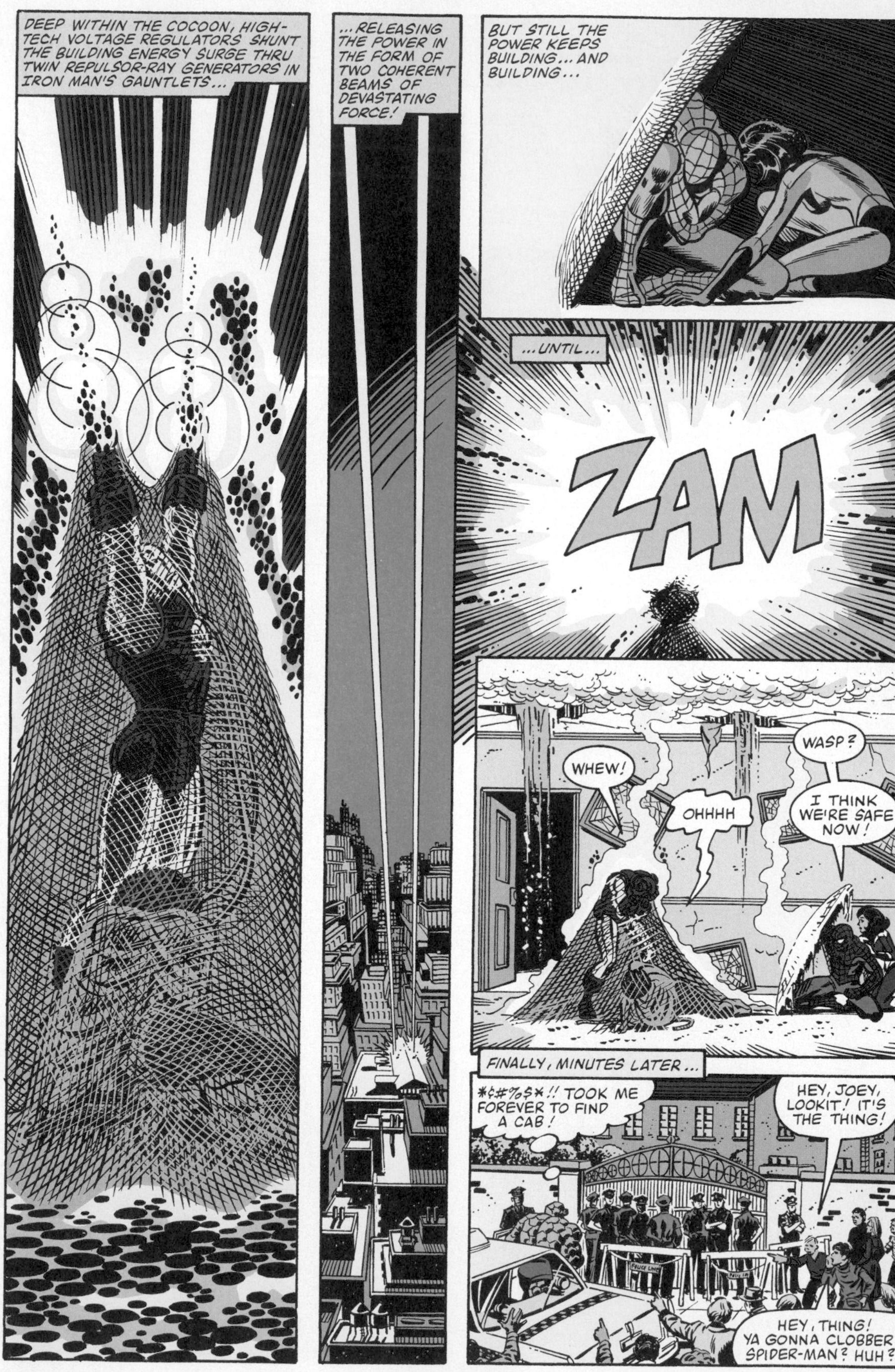
DEEP WITHIN THE COCOON, HIGH-TECH VOLTAGE REGULATORS SHUNT THE BUILDING ENERGY SURGE THRU TWIN REPULSOR-RAY GENERATORS IN IRON MAN'S GAUNTLETS...
...RELEASING THE POWER IN THE FORM OF TWO COHERENT BEAMS OF DEVASTATING FORCE!
BUT STILL THE POWER KEEPS BUILDING... AND BUILDING...
...UNTIL...
ZAM
WHEW!
OHHHH
WASP?
I THINK WE'RE SAFE NOW!
FINALLY, MINUTES LATER...
¢#%$!! TOOK ME FOREVER TO FIND A CAB!
HEY, JOEY, LOOKIT! IT'S THE THING!
HEY, THING! YA GONNA CLOBBER SPIDER-MAN? HUH?

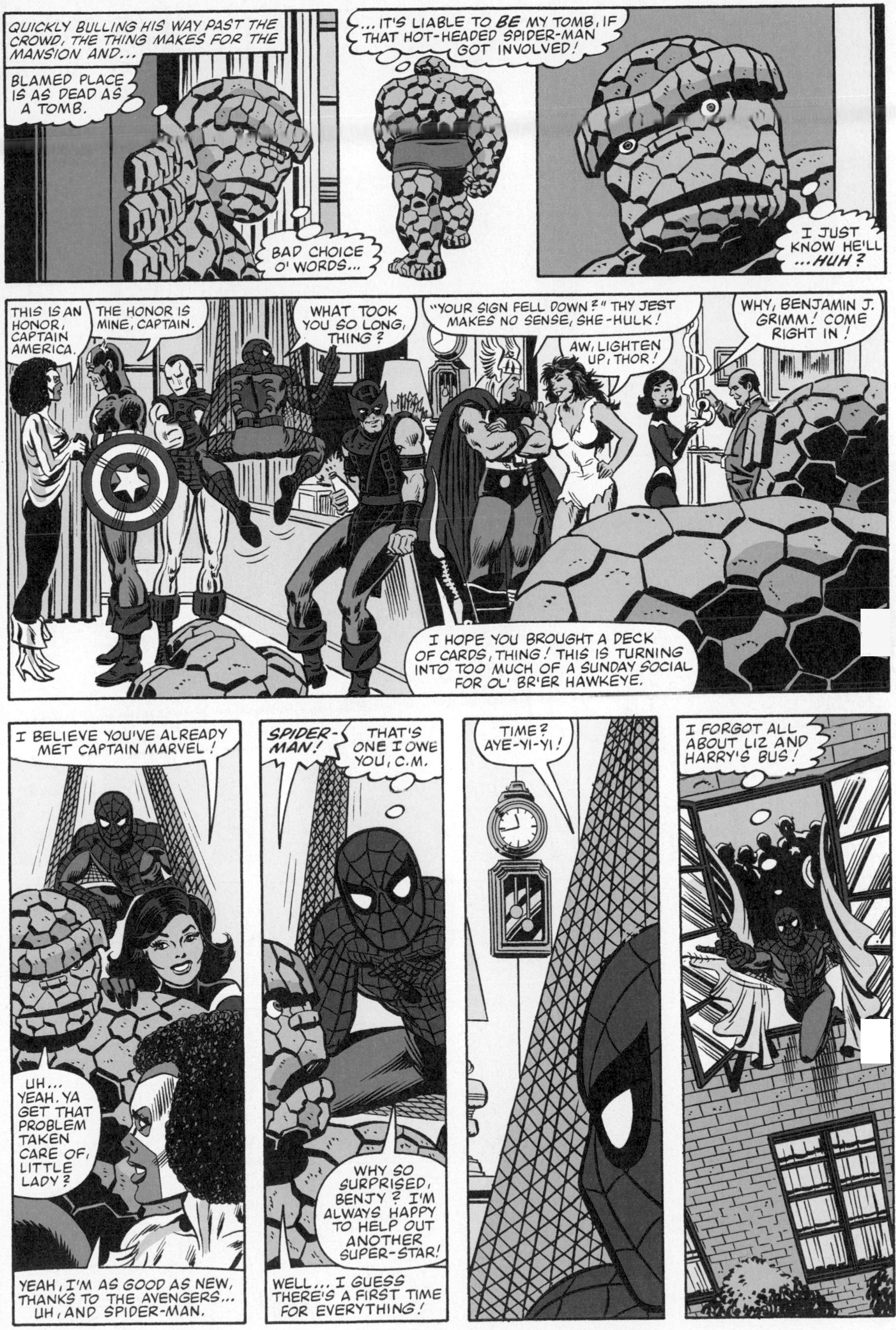
QUICKLY BULLING HIS WAY PAST THE CROWD, THE THING MAKES FOR THE MANSION AND...
BLAMED PLACE IS AS DEAD AS A TOMB.
BAD CHOICE O' WORDS...
...IT'S LIABLE TO BE MY TOMB, IF THAT HOT-HEADED SPIDER-MAN GOT INVOLVED!
I JUST KNOW HE'LL ...HUH?
THIS IS AN HONOR, CAPTAIN AMERICA.
THE HONOR IS MINE, CAPTAIN.
WHAT TOOK YOU SO LONG, THING?
"YOUR SIGN FELL DOWN?" THY JEST MAKES NO SENSE, SHE-HULK!
AW, LIGHTEN UP, THOR!
WHY, BENJAMIN J. GRIMM! COME RIGHT IN!
I HOPE YOU BROUGHT A DECK OF CARDS, THING! THIS IS TURNING INTO TOO MUCH OF A SUNDAY SOCIAL FOR OL' BR'ER HAWKEYE.
I BELIEVE YOU'VE ALREADY MET CAPTAIN MARVEL!
UH... YEAH, YA GET THAT PROBLEM TAKEN CARE OF, LITTLE LADY?
YEAH, I'M AS GOOD AS NEW, THANKS TO THE AVENGERS... UH, AND SPIDER-MAN.
SPIDER-MAN!
THAT'S ONE I OWE YOU, C.M.
WHY SO SURPRISED, BENJY? I'M ALWAYS HAPPY TO HELP OUT ANOTHER SUPER-STAR!
WELL... I GUESS THERE'S A FIRST TIME FOR EVERYTHING!
TIME? AYE-YI-YI!
I FORGOT ALL ABOUT LIZ AND HARRY'S BUS!

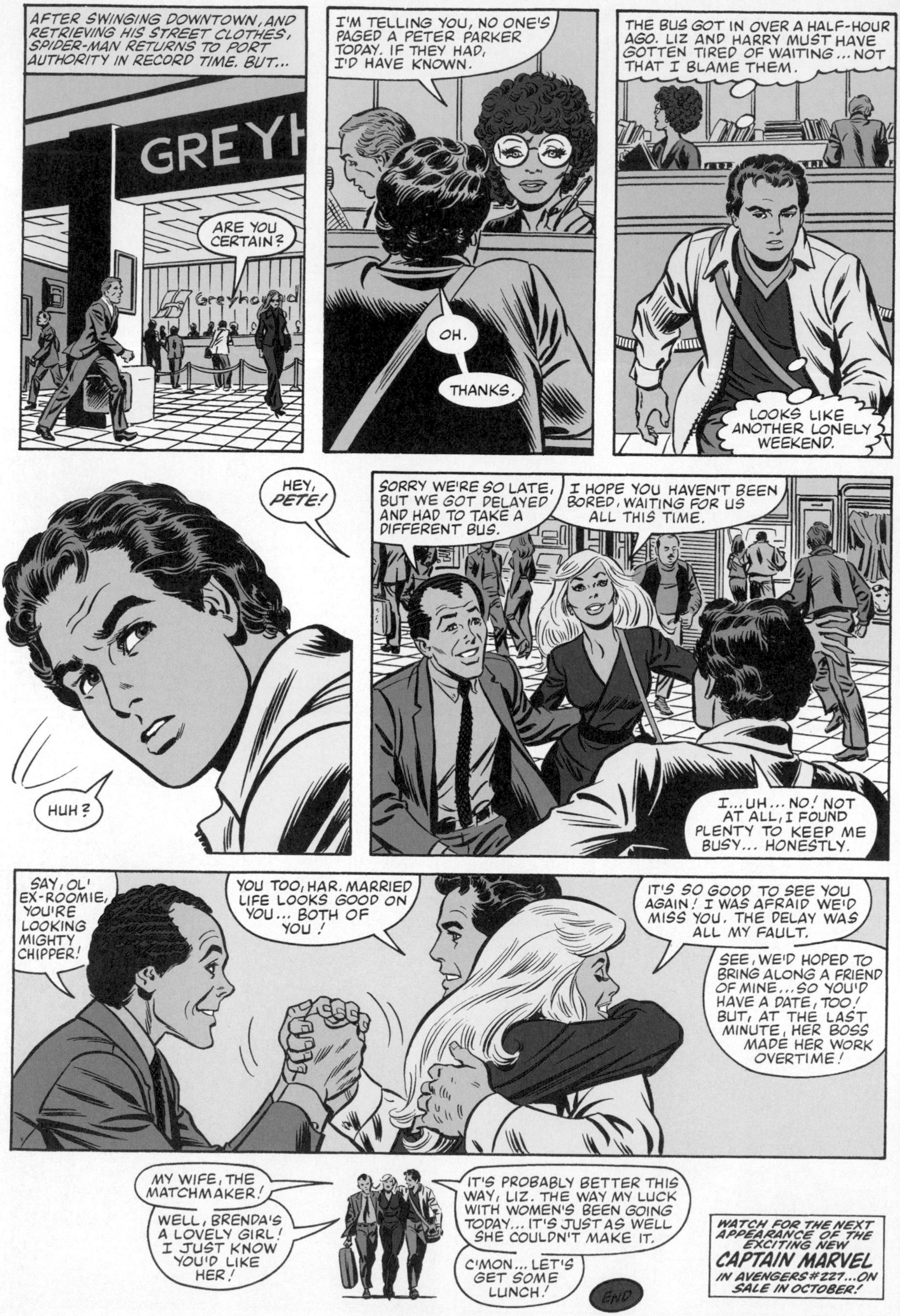
AFTER SWINGING DOWNTOWN, AND RETRIEVING HIS STREET CLOTHES, SPIDER-MAN RETURNS TO PORT AUTHORITY IN RECORD TIME. BUT...
GREYH
Greyhound
ARE YOU CERTAIN?
I'M TELLING YOU, NO ONE'S PAGED A PETER PARKER TODAY. IF THEY HAD, I'D HAVE KNOWN.
OH.
THANKS.
THE BUS GOT IN OVER A HALF-HOUR AGO. LIZ AND HARRY MUST HAVE GOTTEN TIRED OF WAITING... NOT THAT I BLAME THEM.
LOOKS LIKE ANOTHER LONELY WEEKEND.
HEY, PETE!
HUH?
SORRY WE'RE SO LATE, BUT WE GOT DELAYED AND HAD TO TAKE A DIFFERENT BUS.
I HOPE YOU HAVEN'T BEEN BORED, WAITING FOR US ALL THIS TIME.
I... UH... NO! NOT AT ALL, I FOUND PLENTY TO KEEP ME BUSY... HONESTLY.
SAY, OL' EX-ROOMIE, YOU'RE LOOKING MIGHTY CHIPPER!
YOU TOO, HAR. MARRIED LIFE LOOKS GOOD ON YOU... BOTH OF YOU!
IT'S SO GOOD TO SEE YOU AGAIN! I WAS AFRAID WE'D MISS YOU. THE DELAY WAS ALL MY FAULT.
SEE, WE'D HOPED TO BRING ALONG A FRIEND OF MINE... SO YOU'D HAVE A DATE, TOO! BUT, AT THE LAST MINUTE, HER BOSS MADE HER WORK OVERTIME!
MY WIFE, THE MATCHMAKER!
WELL, BRENDA'S A LOVELY GIRL! I JUST KNOW YOU'D LIKE HER!
IT'S PROBABLY BETTER THIS WAY, LIZ. THE WAY MY LUCK WITH WOMEN'S BEEN GOING TODAY... IT'S JUST AS WELL SHE COULDN'T MAKE IT.
C'MON... LET'S GET SOME LUNCH!
END
WATCH FOR THE NEXT APPEARANCE OF THE EXCITING NEW CAPTAIN MARVEL IN AVENGERS #227... ON SALE IN OCTOBER!

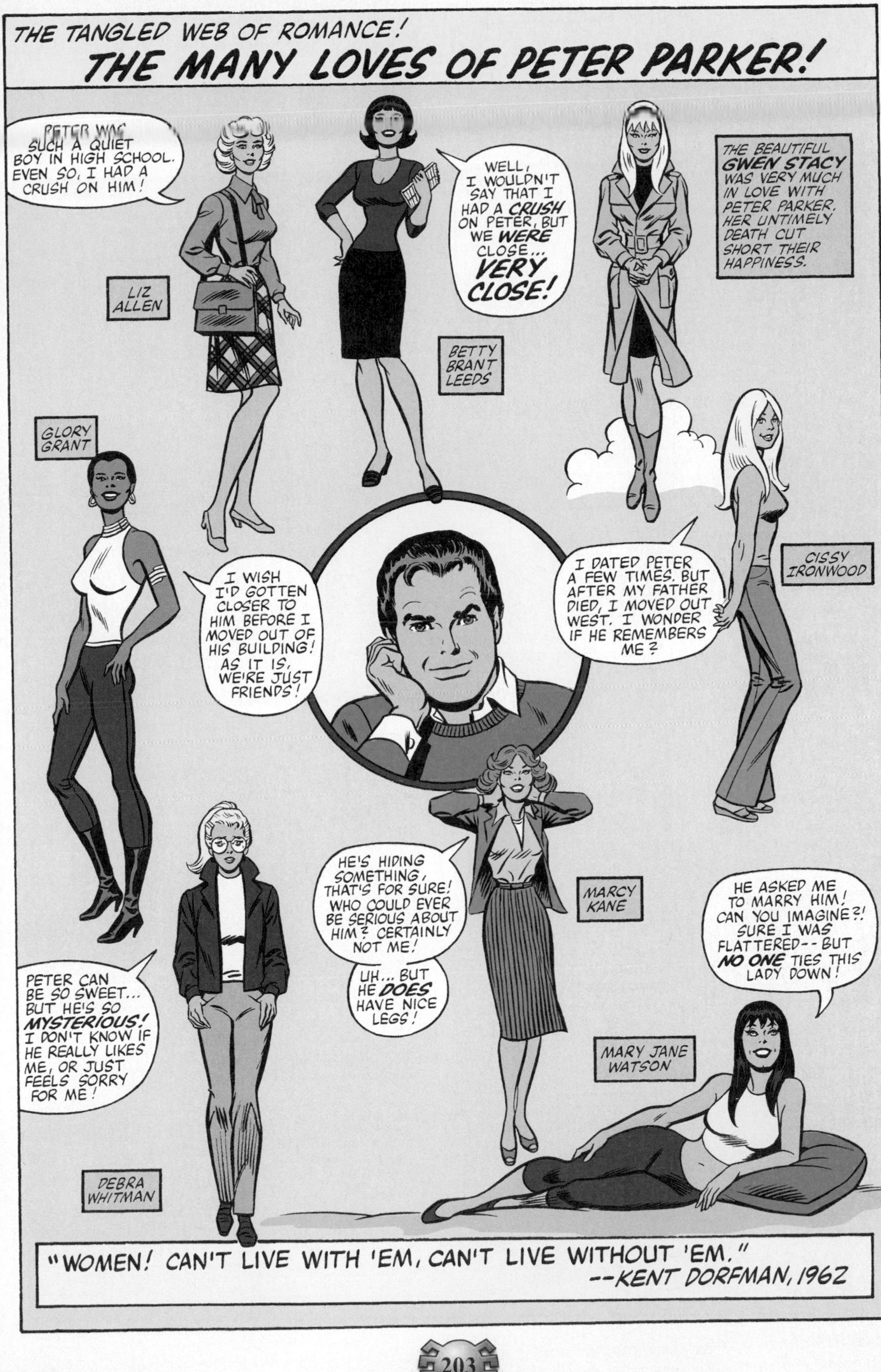
THE TANGLED WEB OF ROMANCE!
THE MANY LOVES OF PETER PARKER!
PETER WAS SUCH A QUIET BOY IN HIGH SCHOOL. EVEN SO, I HAD A CRUSH ON HIM!
LIZ ALLEN
WELL, I WOULDN'T SAY THAT I HAD A CRUSH ON PETER, BUT WE WERE CLOSE... VERY CLOSE!
BETTY BRANT LEEDS
THE BEAUTIFUL GWEN STACY WAS VERY MUCH IN LOVE WITH PETER PARKER. HER UNTIMELY DEATH CUT SHORT THEIR HAPPINESS.
GLORY GRANT
I WISH I'D GOTTEN CLOSER TO HIM BEFORE I MOVED OUT OF HIS BUILDING! AS IT IS, WE'RE JUST FRIENDS!
I DATED PETER A FEW TIMES. BUT AFTER MY FATHER DIED, I MOVED OUT WEST. I WONDER IF HE REMEMBERS ME?
CISSY IRONWOOD
HE'S HIDING SOMETHING, THAT'S FOR SURE! WHO COULD EVER BE SERIOUS ABOUT HIM? CERTAINLY NOT ME!
UH... BUT HE DOES HAVE NICE LEGS!
MARCY KANE
HE ASKED ME TO MARRY HIM! CAN YOU IMAGINE?! SURE I WAS FLATTERED-- BUT NO ONE TIES THIS LADY DOWN!
PETER CAN BE SO SWEET... BUT HE'S SO MYSTERIOUS! I DON'T KNOW IF HE REALLY LIKES ME, OR JUST FEELS SORRY FOR ME!
MARY JANE WATSON
DEBRA WHITMAN
"WOMEN! CAN'T LIVE WITH 'EM, CAN'T LIVE WITHOUT 'EM."
--KENT DORFMAN, 1962

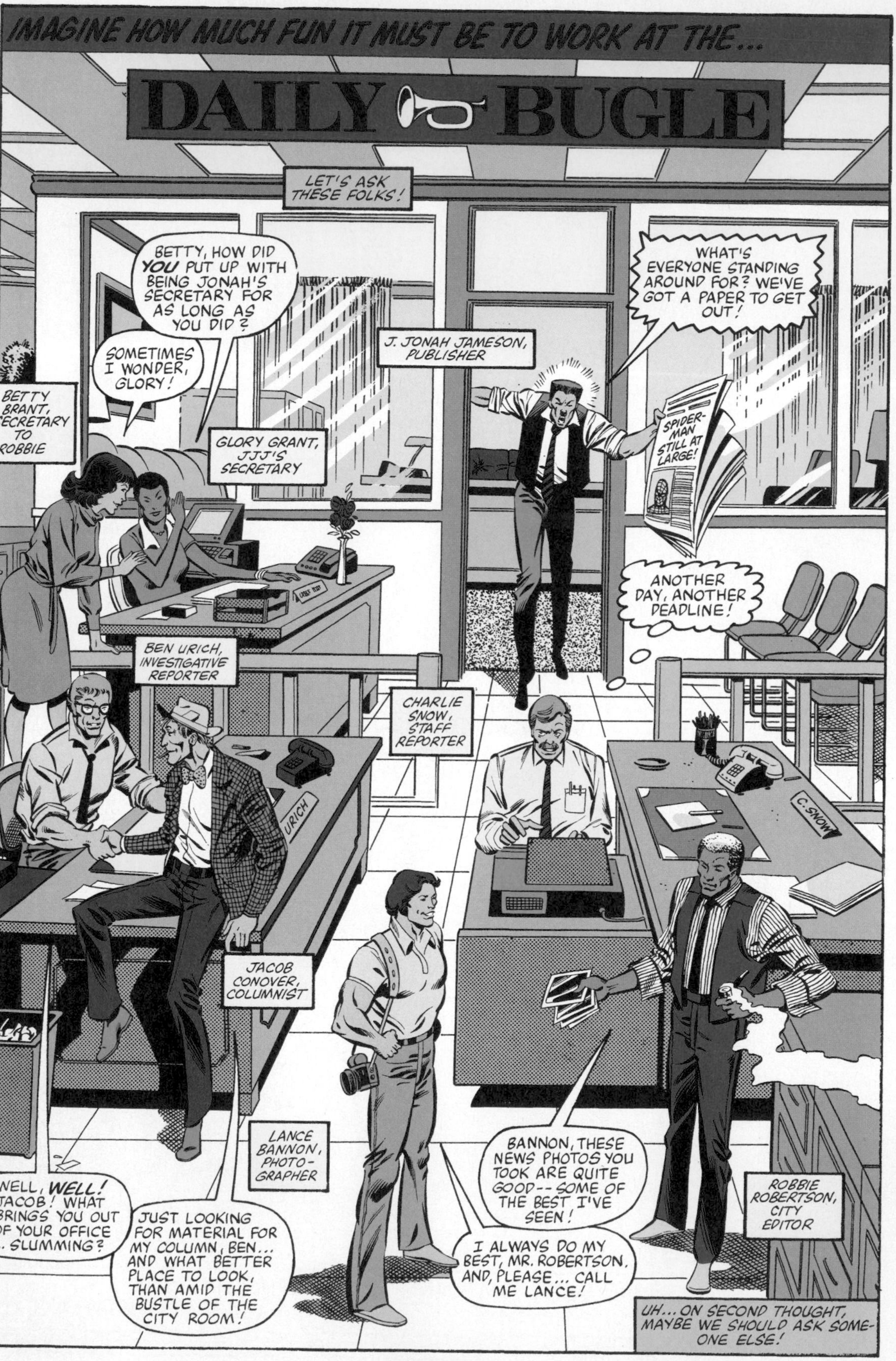
IMAGINE HOW MUCH FUN IT MUST BE TO WORK AT THE...
DAILY BUGLE
LET'S ASK THESE FOLKS!
BETTY, HOW DID YOU PUT UP WITH BEING JONAH'S SECRETARY FOR AS LONG AS YOU DID?
SOMETIMES I WONDER, GLORY!
BETTY BRANT, SECRETARY TO ROBBIE
GLORY GRANT, JJJ'S SECRETARY
J. JONAH JAMESON, PUBLISHER
WHAT'S EVERYONE STANDING AROUND FOR? WE'VE GOT A PAPER TO GET OUT!
SPIDER-MAN STILL AT LARGE!
ANOTHER DAY, ANOTHER DEADLINE!
BEN URICH, INVESTIGATIVE REPORTER
CHARLIE SNOW, STAFF REPORTER
URICH
C. SNOW
JACOB CONOVER, COLUMNIST
LANCE BANNON, PHOTO-GRAPHER
WELL, WELL! JACOB! WHAT BRINGS YOU OUT OF YOUR OFFICE ... SLUMMING?
JUST LOOKING FOR MATERIAL FOR MY COLUMN, BEN... AND WHAT BETTER PLACE TO LOOK, THAN AMID THE BUSTLE OF THE CITY ROOM!
BANNON, THESE NEWS PHOTOS YOU TOOK ARE QUITE GOOD-- SOME OF THE BEST I'VE SEEN!
I ALWAYS DO MY BEST, MR. ROBERTSON, AND, PLEASE... CALL ME LANCE!
ROBBIE ROBERTSON, CITY EDITOR
UH... ON SECOND THOUGHT, MAYBE WE SHOULD ASK SOME-ONE ELSE!

***THE MARVEL GUIDE TO COLLECTING COMICS*, BOUND INSIDE *AMAZING SPIDER-MAN #234*, WAS A 16-PAGE INSERT CONTAINING BASIC INFORMATION ABOUT COMIC BOOKS—INCLUDING TIPS ON GRADING, COLLECTIBILITY AND STORAGE. COVER ART BY WALTER SIMONSON.**

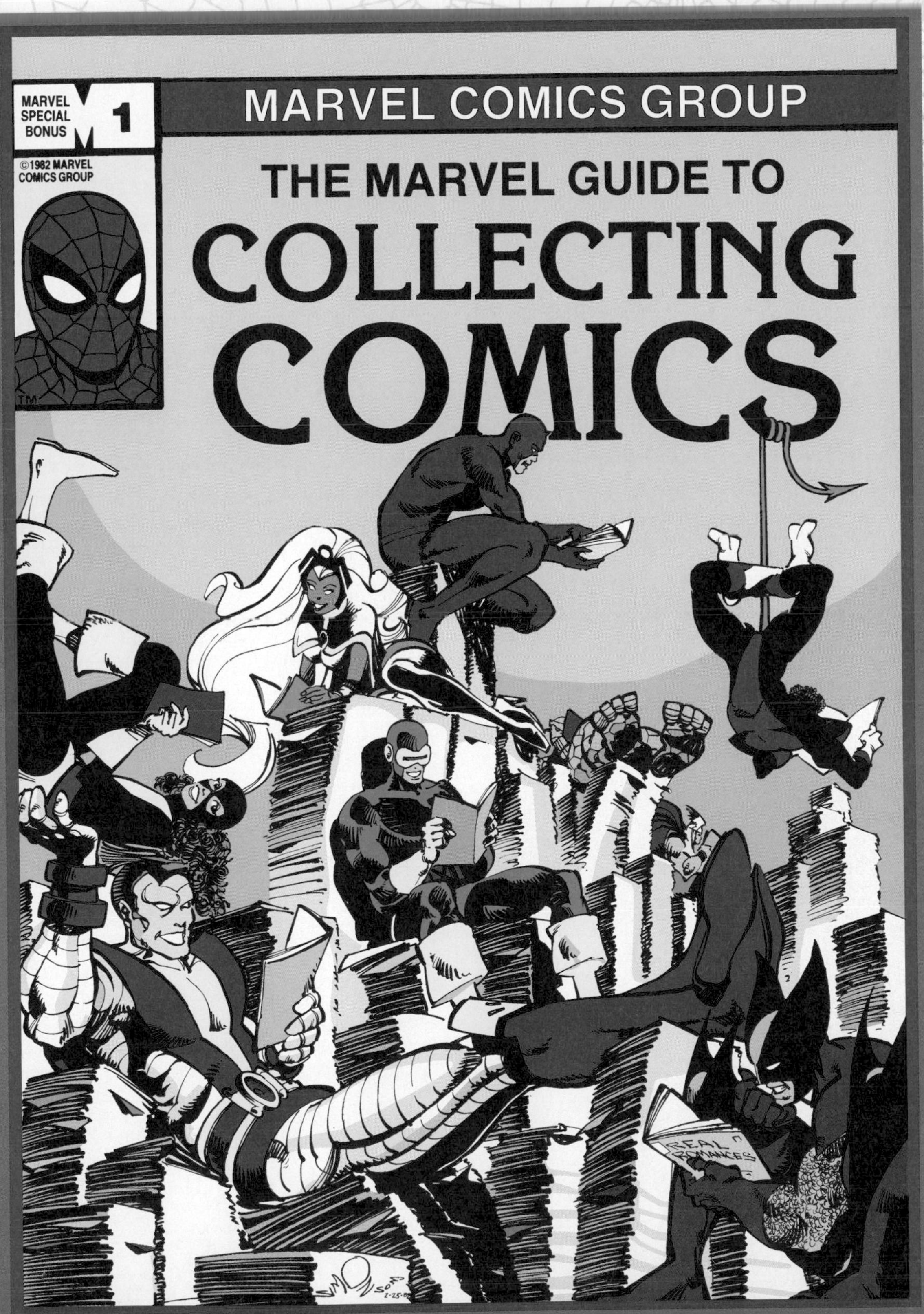

MARVEL SPECIAL BONUS
1
©1982 MARVEL COMICS GROUP
MARVEL COMICS GROUP
THE MARVEL GUIDE TO
COLLECTING COMICS
REAL ROMANCES

***SPIDER-MAN MEGAZINE* #4 REPRINTED *AMAZING SPIDER-MAN* #231-232, AS WELL AS *MARVEL TEAM-UP* #4 AND *AMAZING SPIDER-MAN* #19. COVER ART BY STUART IMMONEN, KARL STORY & JUNG CHOI.**

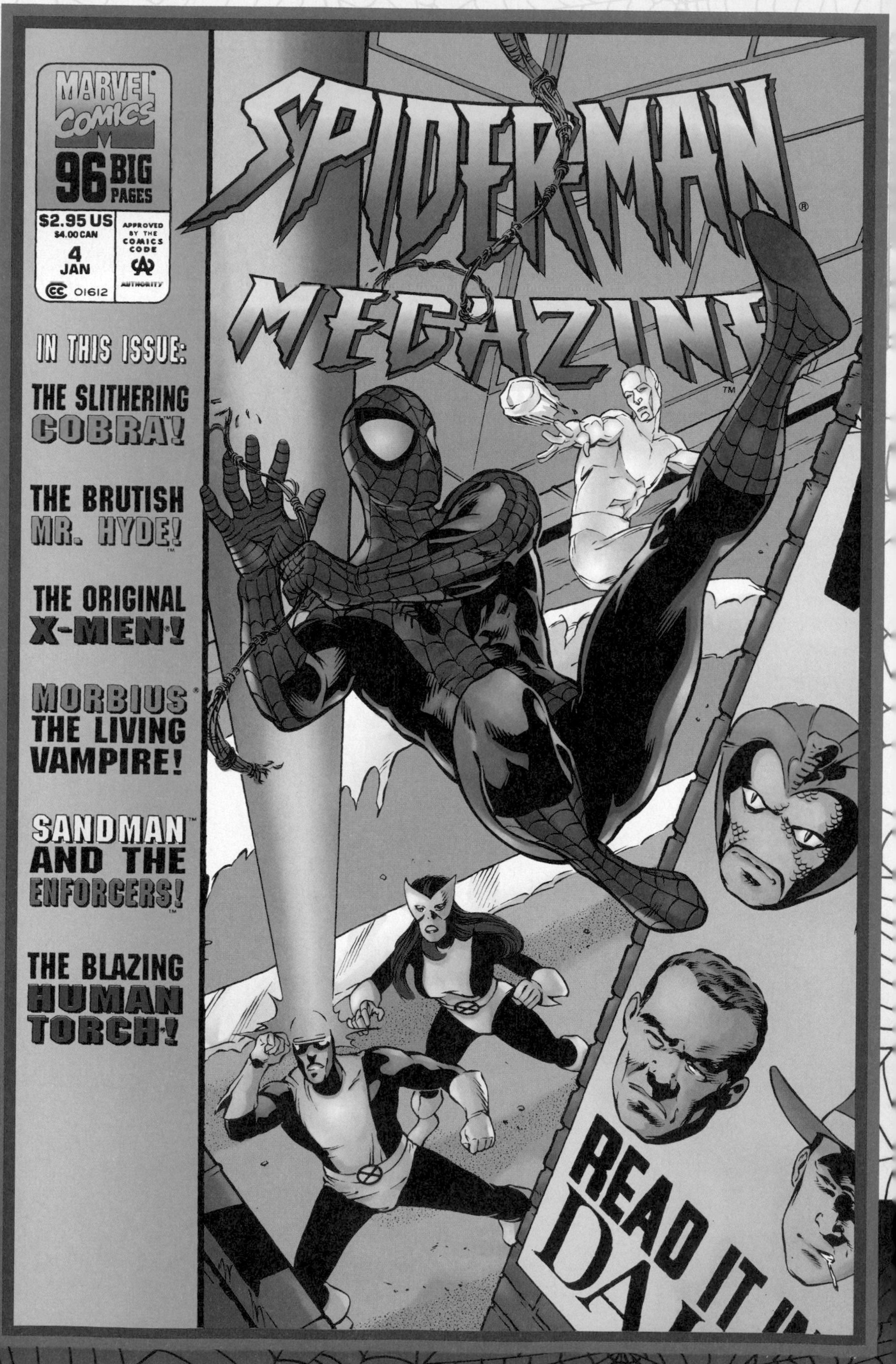
MARVEL COMICS
96 BIG PAGES
$2.95 US
$4.00 CAN
4
JAN
APPROVED BY THE COMICS CODE AUTHORITY
01612
SPIDER-MAN
MEGAZINE
IN THIS ISSUE:
THE SLITHERING COBRA!
THE BRUTISH MR. HYDE!
THE ORIGINAL X-MEN!
MORBIUS THE LIVING VAMPIRE!
SANDMAN AND THE ENFORCERS!
THE BLAZING HUMAN TORCH!
READ IT IN
DAI

***SPIDER-MAN MEGAZINE* #5 REPRINTED *AMAZING SPIDER-MAN* #233-234, AS WELL AS *MARVEL TEAM-UP* #5 AND *AMAZING SPIDER-MAN* #20. COVER ART BY KIRK JARVINEN, JASON MOORE & JUNG CHOI.**

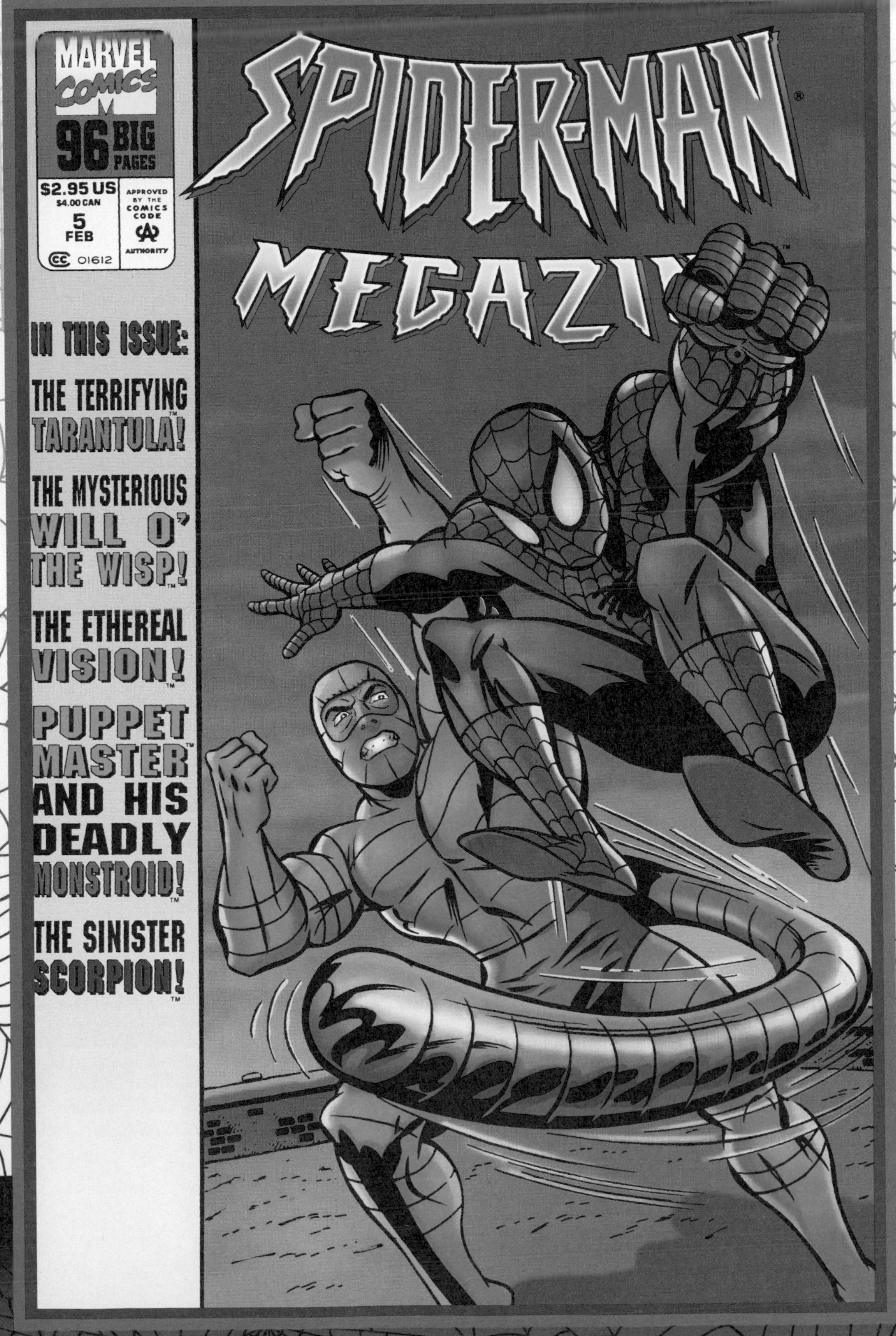
MARVEL COMICS
96 BIG PAGES
$2.95 US
$4.00 CAN
5
FEB
APPROVED BY THE COMICS CODE AUTHORITY
01612
SPIDER-MAN®
MEGAZINE™
IN THIS ISSUE:
THE TERRIFYING TARANTULA!™
THE MYSTERIOUS WILL O' THE WISP!™
THE ETHEREAL VISION!™
PUPPET MASTER™ AND HIS DEADLY MONSTROID!™
THE SINISTER SCORPION!™

***SPIDER-MAN MEGAZINE* #6 REPRINTED *AMAZING SPIDER-MAN* #235-236, AS WELL AS *MARVEL TEAM-UP* #6 AND *AMAZING SPIDER-MAN* #21. COVER ART BY MARK BUCKINGHAM & JUNG CHOI.**

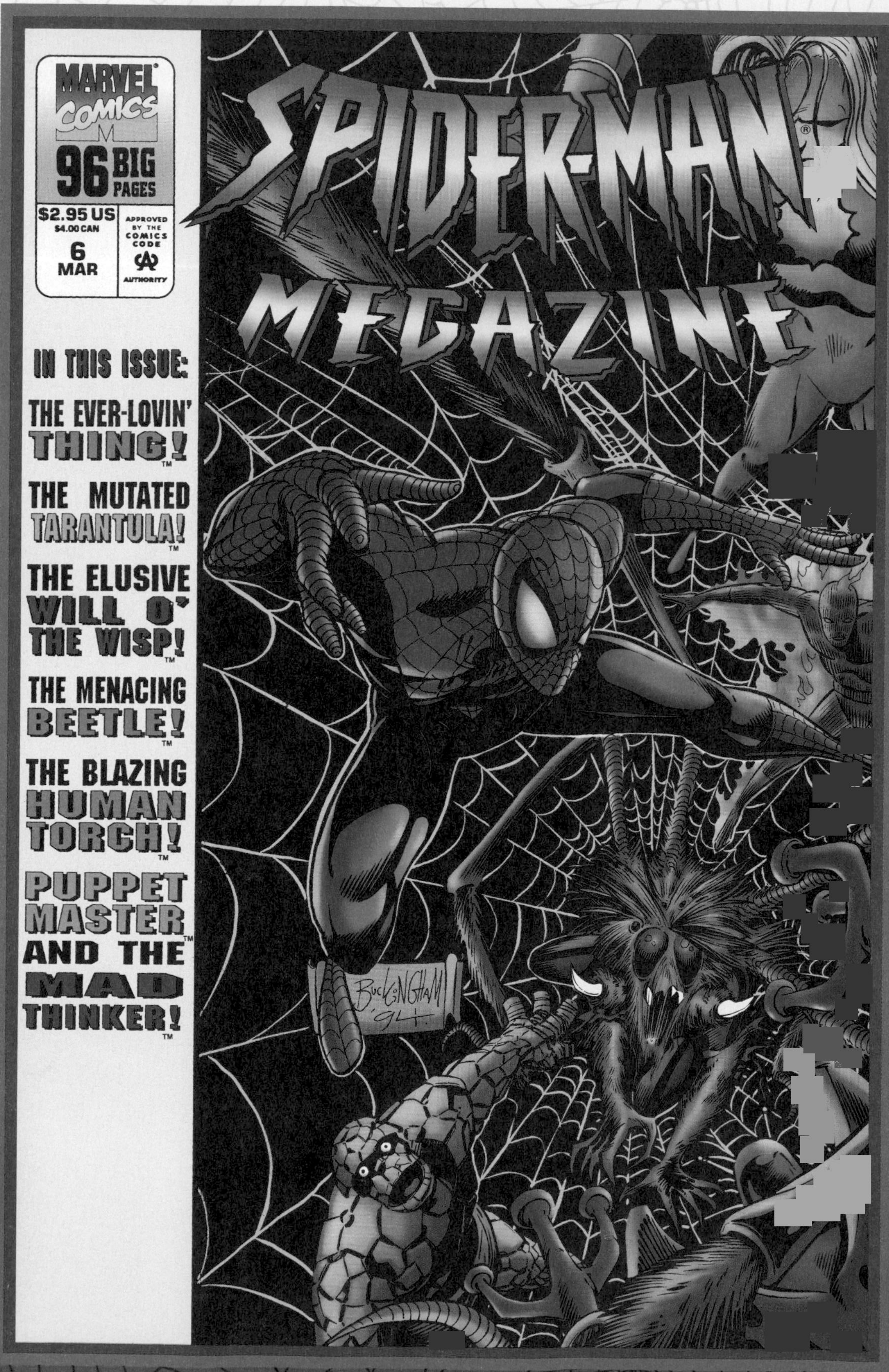
MARVEL COMICS
96 BIG PAGES
$2.95 US
$4.00 CAN
6
MAR
APPROVED BY THE COMICS CODE AUTHORITY
SPIDER-MAN
MEGAZINE
IN THIS ISSUE:
THE EVER-LOVIN' THING!
THE MUTATED TARANTULA!
THE ELUSIVE WILL O' THE WISP!
THE MENACING BEETLE!
THE BLAZING HUMAN TORCH!
PUPPET MASTER AND THE MAD THINKER!
BUCKINGHAM '94

OFFICIAL HANDBOOK OF THE MARVEL UNIVERSE #2 PROFILE – ART BY JOHN ROMITA JR., JOSEF RUBINSTEIN

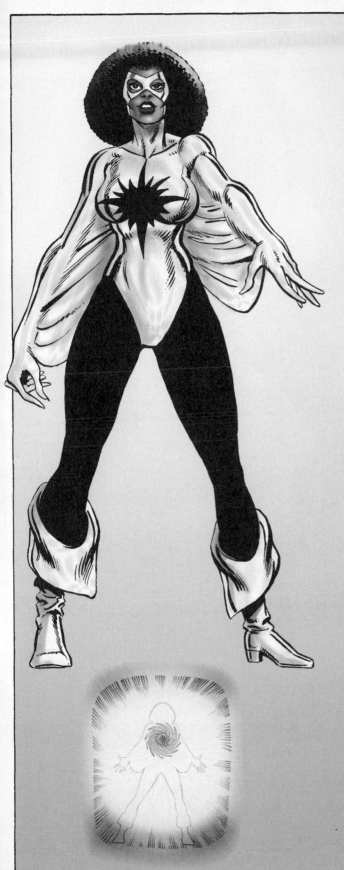

CAPTAIN MARVEL

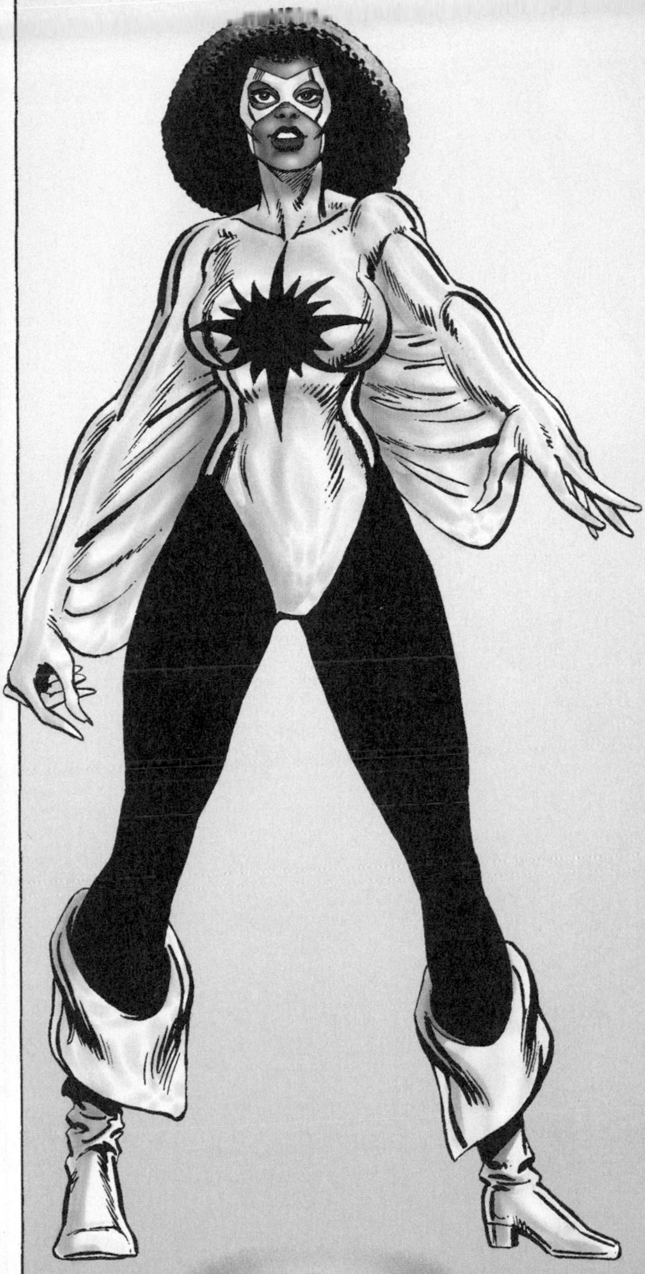

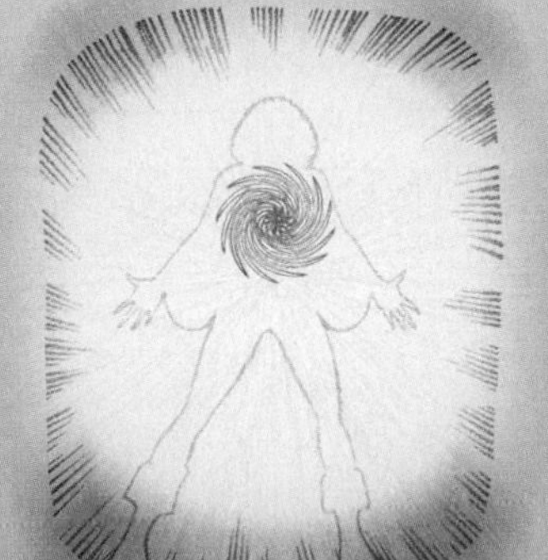

Real Name: Monica Rambeau
Occupation: Ex-lieutenant in New Orleans police, assigned to harbor patrol.
Legal status: American citizen with no criminal record
Identity: Secret
Place of birth: New Orleans, Louisiana
Marital status: Single
Known relatives: None
Group affiliation: Avengers (active member)
Base of operations: New Orleans, Louisiana
First appearance: AMAZING SPIDER-MAN ANNUAL #16
Origin: While working with funds obtained from a South American dictator, physicist Andre LeClare discovered a means to draw natural energies from alternate dimensions. Learning that the dictator intended to use his discovery to make a weapon, LeClare went to harbor patroller Monica Rambeau, the daughter of an old friend. Rambeau accompanied LeClare to the dictator's base and in an attempt to destroy the energy-weapon, she was bombarded by its extradimensional energies. Rambeau soon discovered that she had gained the power to convert her physical form into pure energy. With her newfound power, she leaped into the growing dimensional breech caused by the weapon's wreckage and sealed it by absorbing its rampant energies. She was dubbed "Captain Marvel" by the media.
Height: 5' 10"
Weight: 130 lbs
Eyes: Brown
Hair: Black
Powers: Captain Marvel has the ability to transform her body into any form of electromagnetic energy, from radio waves to x-rays, and every wavelength in between. She accomplishes this transformation by mentally shunting the matter of her body into the other dimension (from which she draws her power) and replacing it with a discrete parcel of that dimension's energy. Her mind remains in this dimension to control the energy-parcel that has taken the place of her body. At present there does not seem to be a limit to the amount of time Captain Marvel can remain in an energy-form. By assuming a given energy-form, she assumes all of the properties of that energy. For instance, if she assumes a body of light, she is able to travel at the speed of light. If she assumes a body of radio waves, she is able to pass through solid objects. Any of her energy-forms permit her to fly.

Besides being able to totally exchange her matter for energy, Captain Marvel is also able to create a partial interface with the dimension she derives her powers from, and divert small amounts of various energies for employment as force-beams. She is, at present, able to wield a force with a maximum explosive power equivalent to 300 tons of TNT.

TARANTULA

Real name: Anton Miguel Rodriguez
Occupation: Revolutionary terrorist, later government operative, later professional criminal
Identity: Publicly known
Legal status: Citizen of an unidentified South American country with an international crime record
Other aliases: Mr. Valdez
Place of birth: An unidentified South American country
Place of death: New York City
Marital status: Unrevealed, presumed single
Known relatives: None
Group affiliation: Former ally of Lightmaster, Kraven the Hunter, the Jackal, Senor Suerte II, and the Brand Corporation
Base of operations: An unnamed South American country, later New York City and Miami Beach
First appearance: AMAZING SPIDER-MAN #134
Final appearance: AMAZING SPIDER-MAN #236
Origin: AMAZING SPIDER-MAN #135
History: Anton Miguel Rodriguez was a member of a small revolutionary band that opposed the dictatorship of an unidentified South American country. Rodriguez and his associates were terrorists who blew up supply trains, kidnapped politicians and held them for ransom, and then killed them if the ransom was not paid. Rodriguez was particularly bloodthirsty, however, and his fellow revolutionaries expelled him from their organization shortly after he murdered a guard without cause during a robbery.

Rodriguez then went over to the other side and joined the army of the repressive dictatorship. The government created the costumed identity of the Tarantula for Rodriguez, intending him to serve as their country's counterpart to the United States' Captain America (see *Captain America*). The Tarantula was sent to hunt down his former revolutionary comrades, a mission that gave him great pleasure.

But the Tarantula could still not restrain his love of violence and killing. During the interrogation of a captured revolutionary, the Tarantula murdered a guard who would not let him beat the prisoner as much as he wanted. As a result, the Tarantula was forced to flee the country.

After a series of unrevealed exploits, the Tarantula arrived in New York City and began familiarizing himself with the city's criminal underworld. He hired accomplices and afterwards hijacked a Hudson River dayliner, a boat that went on tours up the Hudson River, in order to rob the passengers and hold them for ransom. The costumed crimefighters known as Spider-Man and the Punisher disrupted the Tarantula's plan, and the Tarantula and his accomplices escaped (see *Punisher, Spider-Man*). Subsequently, the Punisher defeated the Tarantula's accomplices, and Spider-Man captured the Tarantula himself.

Months later, the Tarantula escaped prison with the help of his new ally, the Jackal, who sought vengeance on Spider-Man (see *Deceased: Jackal*). Spider-Man defeated the Tarantula in battle only to be captured by the Jackal. Presumably the Tarantula escaped capture on this occasion. he Jackal died shortly afterwards.

Later, the Tarantula was hired by Lightmaster to commit various kidnappings and murders; Lightmaster also hired Kraven the

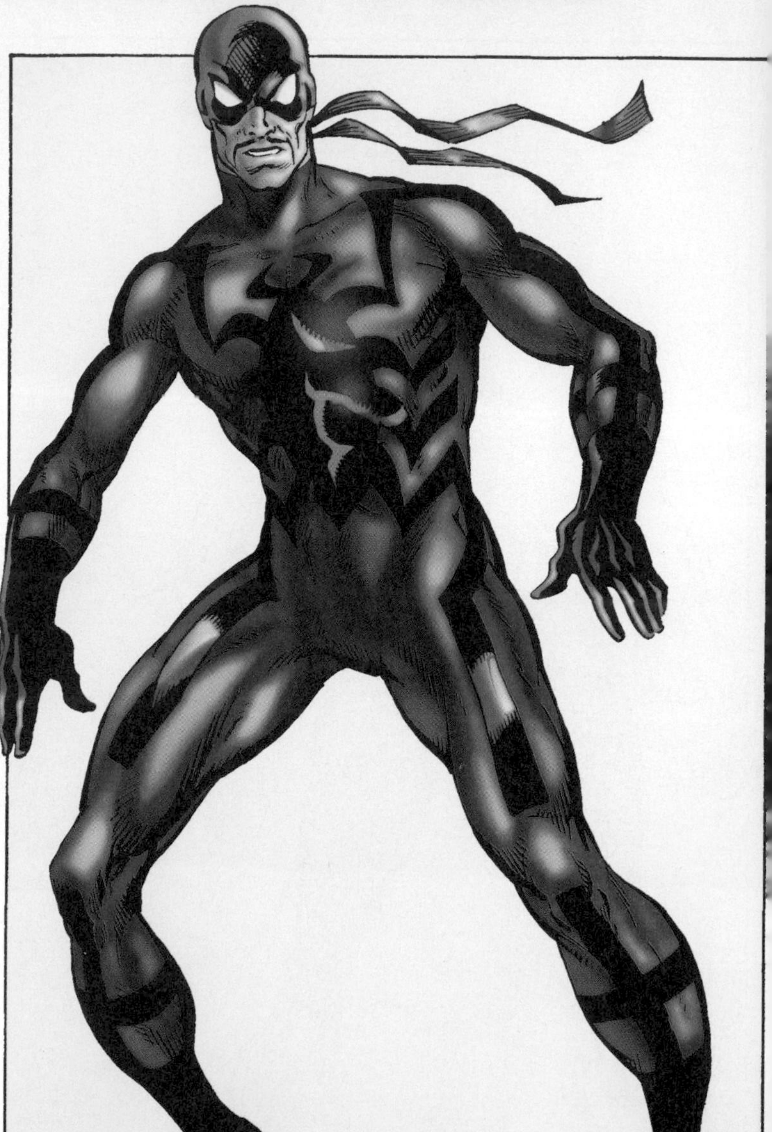

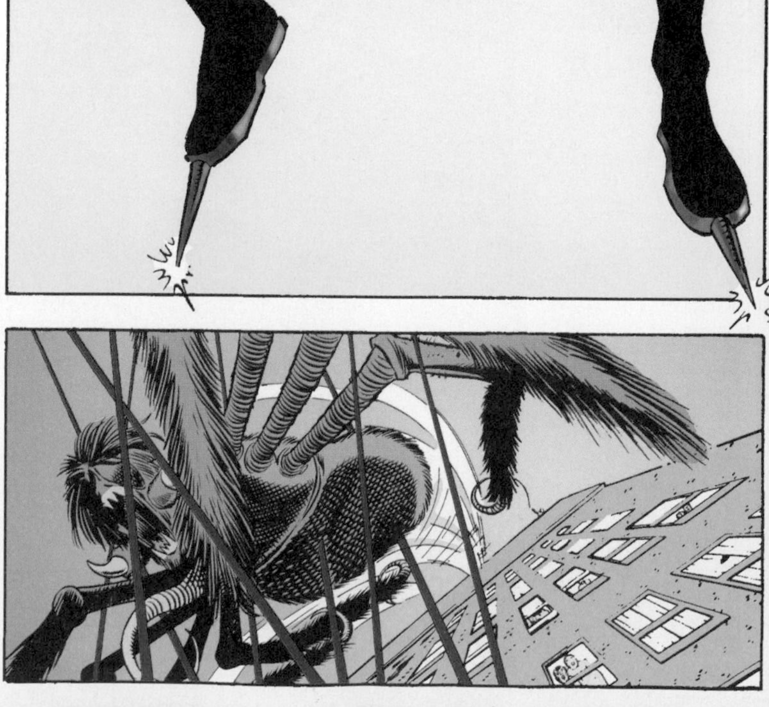

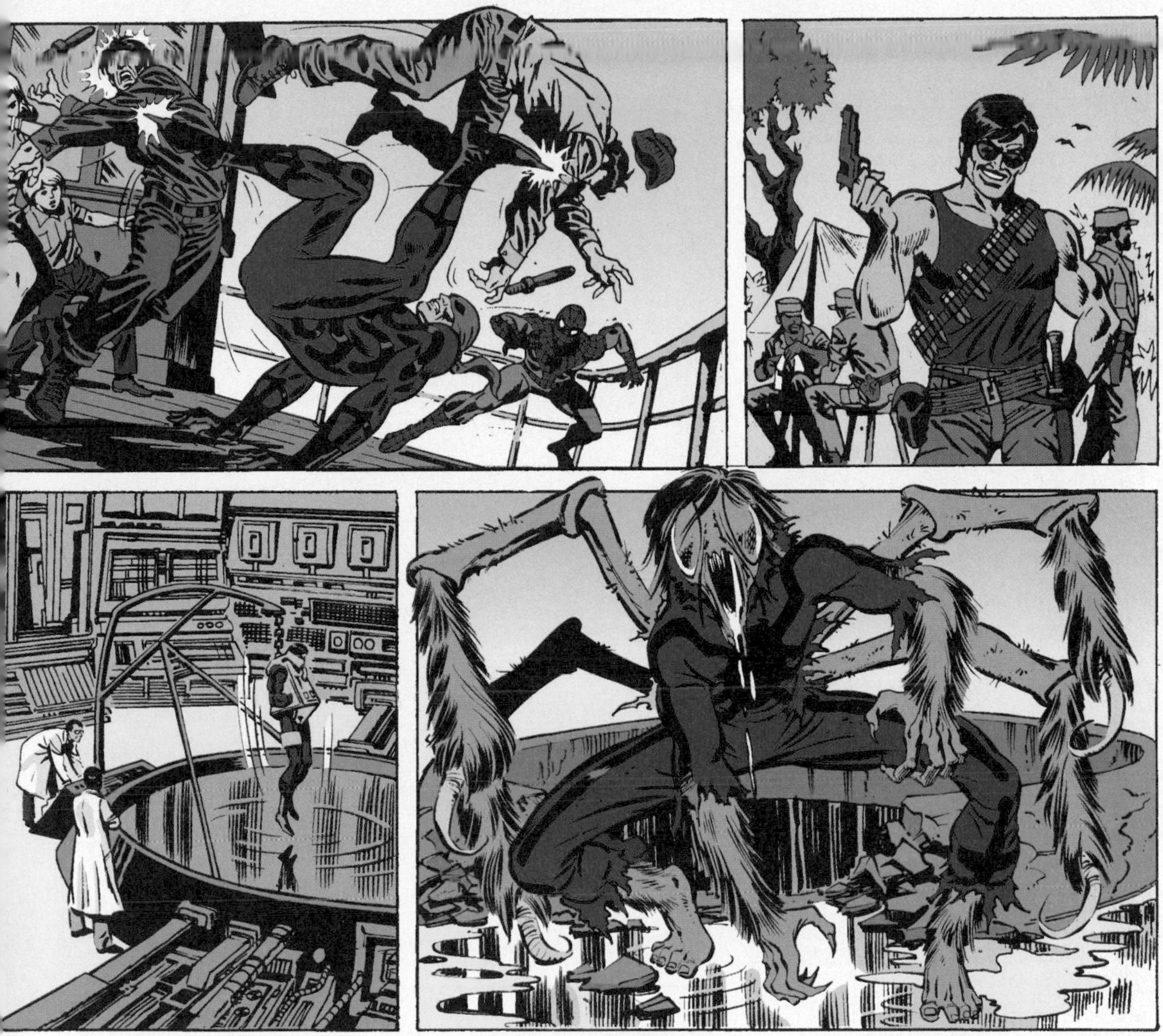

Hunter to assist the Tarantula (see *Kraven the Hunter, Lightmaster*). Again, the Tarantula ran afoul of Spider-Man, who thwarted Lightmaster's schemes.

Months later, the Tarantula and his new partner, the second Senor Suerte, tried to steal the powerful weapons called the "mad-bombs" and use them for the purpose of extortion, but were defeated by Captain America (see *Appendix: Senor Suerte II*).

Somehow regaining his freedom once more, Rodriguez kept a low profile in the Miami beach area and engaged in smuggling activities. He was finally hired by a representative of the Brand Corporation, a subsidiary of Roxxon Oil, to silence an informer known as "Nose" Norton (see *Roxxon Oil*). Again the Tarantula clashed with Spider-Man and failed in his assignment.

Then, however, Brand representatives offered to bestow superhuman powers similar to Spider-Man's upon the Tarantula if he would afterwards help them to kill Spider-Man. The Tarantula agreed, went to Brand's laboratories in Queens, New York, and there was injected with a mutagenic serum and placed within an electrolyte bath while wearing a life support harness.

But then the being known as Will o'the Wisp, who held Brand responsible for his own transformation into an inhuman creature, began wreaking havoc on the machinery in the laboratory, causing power discharges that radically affected the ongoing mutagenic process that the Tarantula was undergoing (see *Will o'the Wisp*). As a result, the Tarantula transformed into an eight-limbed being that resembled a humanoid spider, possessing superhuman strength. Spider-Man himself, who had arrived on the scene, and Will o'the Wisp both battled the transformed Tarantula, and the latter two fell into Jamaica bay.

But both the Tarantula and Will o'the Wisp survived this plunge, and the Tarantula continued to mutate. Finally, the Tarantula and Spider-Man met in battle atop a New York City building. By now the Tarantula looked like an enormous spider with no trace of human appearance at all. His mind was becoming increasingly primitive and he could only speak in broken phrases. Horrified at what he had become, and seeing policemen massed on the sidewalk and street below, the Tarantula committed suicide by hurling himself from the roof of the building. He was dead from police gunfire before he landed on the street below.

Note: The physical characteristics listed below apply to the Tarantula's human form.

Height: 6′ 1″
Weight: 185 lbs
Eyes: Brown
Hair: Black
Strength level: In human form the Tarantula possessed the normal human strength of a man of his age, height, and build who engaged in intensive regular exercise. As a giant spider the Tarantula had superhuman strength and could lift (press) 10 tons (were his limbs capable of lifting objects).
Known superhuman powers: In human form the Tarantula had no superhuman powers. As a giant spider he possessed superhuman strength and could spin webbing as a real spider can.
Other abilities: The Tarantula, in human form, was a brilliant athlete with great agility, especially in leaping. He was an excellent hand-to-hand combatant.
Weapons: The Tarantula wore gloves that contained retractable blades and boots that contained retractable, razor sharp points. These blades and points were anointed with drugs that rendered a victim whom the Tarantula stabbed with them unconscious. ■

AMAZING SPIDER-MAN #235, PAGE 2
ART BY JOHN ROMITA JR. & FRANK GIACOIA

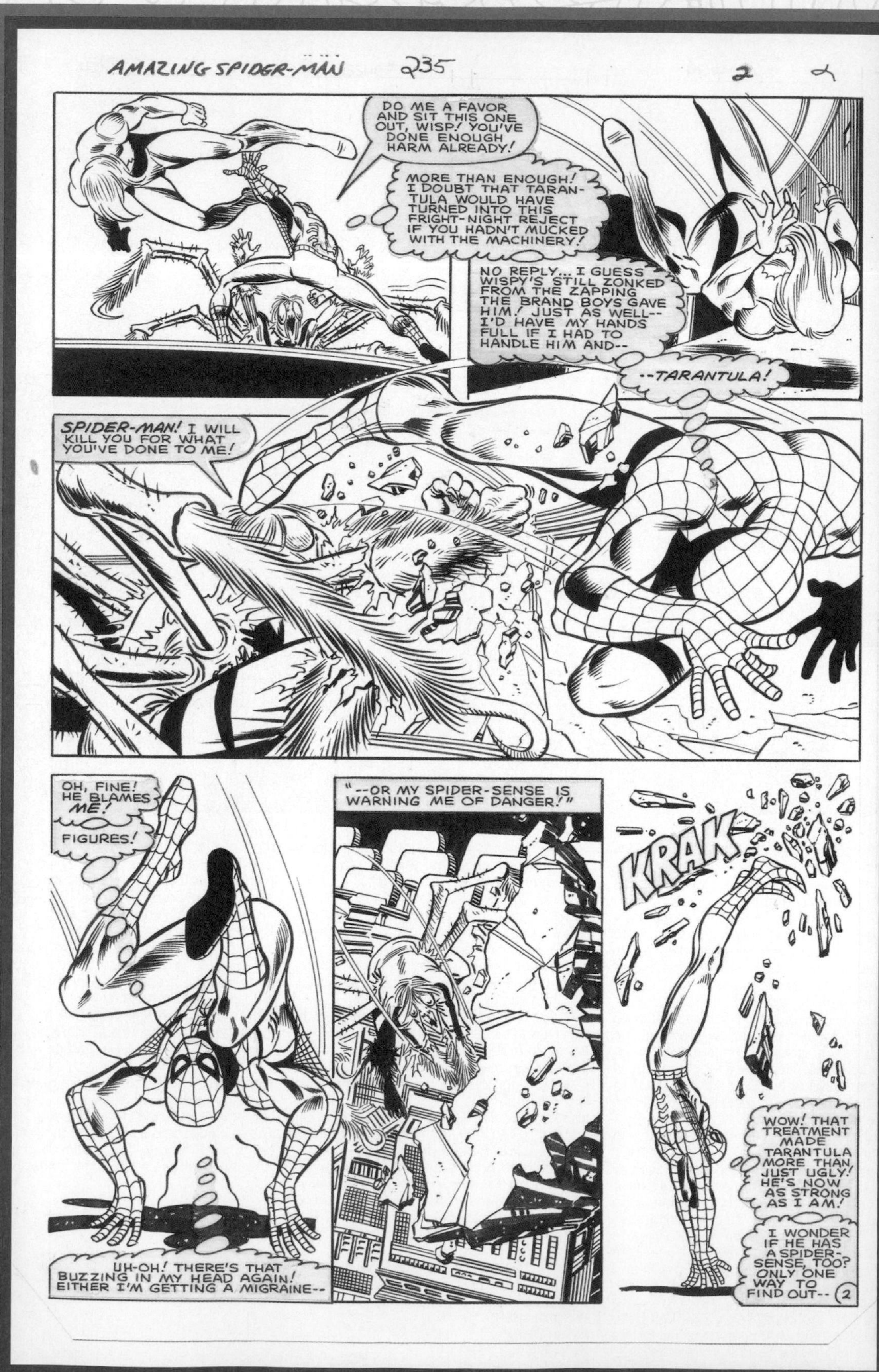
AMAZING SPIDER-MAN 235 2
DO ME A FAVOR AND SIT THIS ONE OUT, WISP! YOU'VE DONE ENOUGH HARM ALREADY!
MORE THAN ENOUGH! I DOUBT THAT TARANTULA WOULD HAVE TURNED INTO THIS FRIGHT-NIGHT REJECT IF YOU HADN'T MUCKED WITH THE MACHINERY!
NO REPLY... I GUESS WISPY'S STILL ZONKED FROM THE ZAPPING THE BRAND BOYS GAVE HIM! JUST AS WELL-- I'D HAVE MY HANDS FULL IF I HAD TO HANDLE HIM AND--
--TARANTULA!
SPIDER-MAN! I WILL KILL YOU FOR WHAT YOU'VE DONE TO ME!
OH, FINE! HE BLAMES ME!
FIGURES!
UH-OH! THERE'S THAT BUZZING IN MY HEAD AGAIN! EITHER I'M GETTING A MIGRAINE--
"--OR MY SPIDER-SENSE IS WARNING ME OF DANGER!"
KRAK
WOW! THAT TREATMENT MADE TARANTULA MORE THAN JUST UGLY! HE'S NOW AS STRONG AS I AM!
I WONDER IF HE HAS A SPIDER-SENSE, TOO? ONLY ONE WAY TO FIND OUT--
2

AMAZING SPIDER-MAN ANNUAL #16, PAGE 33
ART BY JOHN ROMITA JR. & JOHN ROMITA SR.

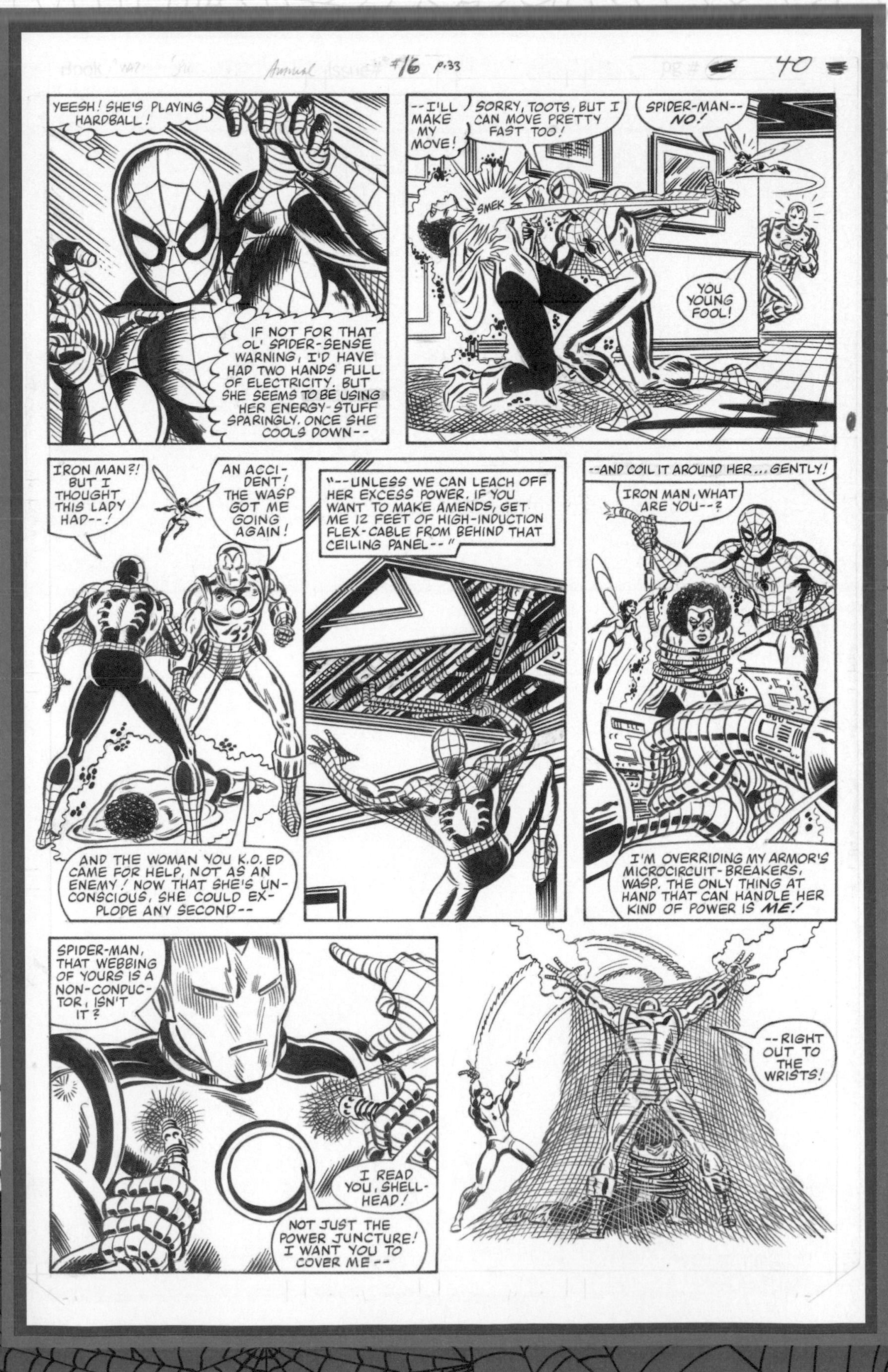
Annual #16 p.33
40
YEESH! SHE'S PLAYING HARDBALL!
IF NOT FOR THAT OL' SPIDER-SENSE WARNING, I'D HAVE HAD TWO HANDS FULL OF ELECTRICITY. BUT SHE SEEMS TO BE USING HER ENERGY-STUFF SPARINGLY. ONCE SHE COOLS DOWN--
--I'LL MAKE MY MOVE!
SORRY, TOOTS, BUT I CAN MOVE PRETTY FAST TOO!
SPIDER-MAN-- NO!
SMEK
YOU YOUNG FOOL!
IRON MAN?! BUT I THOUGHT THIS LADY HAD--!
AN ACCIDENT! THE WASP GOT ME GOING AGAIN!
AND THE WOMAN YOU K.O.ED CAME FOR HELP, NOT AS AN ENEMY! NOW THAT SHE'S UNCONSCIOUS, SHE COULD EXPLODE ANY SECOND--
"--UNLESS WE CAN LEACH OFF HER EXCESS POWER. IF YOU WANT TO MAKE AMENDS, GET ME 12 FEET OF HIGH-INDUCTION FLEX-CABLE FROM BEHIND THAT CEILING PANEL--"
--AND COIL IT AROUND HER... GENTLY!
IRON MAN, WHAT ARE YOU--?
I'M OVERRIDING MY ARMOR'S MICROCIRCUIT-BREAKERS, WASP. THE ONLY THING AT HAND THAT CAN HANDLE HER KIND OF POWER IS ME!
SPIDER-MAN, THAT WEBBING OF YOURS IS A NON-CONDUCTOR, ISN'T IT?
I READ YOU, SHELL-HEAD!
NOT JUST THE POWER JUNCTURE! I WANT YOU TO COVER ME--
--RIGHT OUT TO THE WRISTS!

AMAZING SPIDER-MAN #234 COVER COLOR GUIDE – ART BY JOHN ROMITA JR. & AL MILGROM

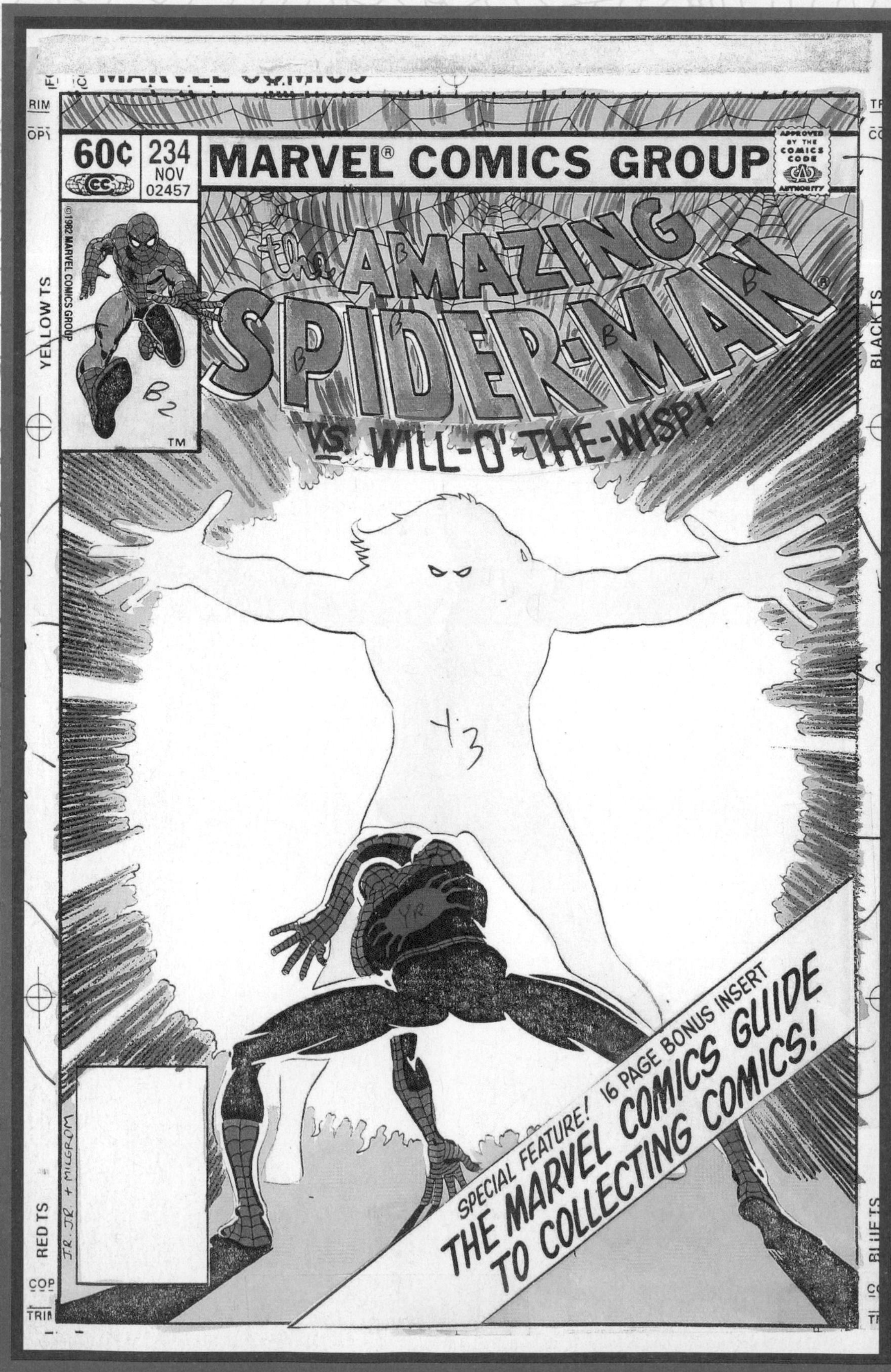
60¢
234
NOV
02457
MARVEL® COMICS GROUP
APPROVED BY THE COMICS CODE AUTHORITY
© 1982 MARVEL COMICS GROUP
the AMAZING SPIDER-MAN®
VS. WILL-O'-THE-WISP!
SPECIAL FEATURE! 16 PAGE BONUS INSERT
THE MARVEL COMICS GUIDE TO COLLECTING COMICS!
JR. JR. + MILGROM
YELLOW TS
BLACK TS
RED TS
BLUE TS

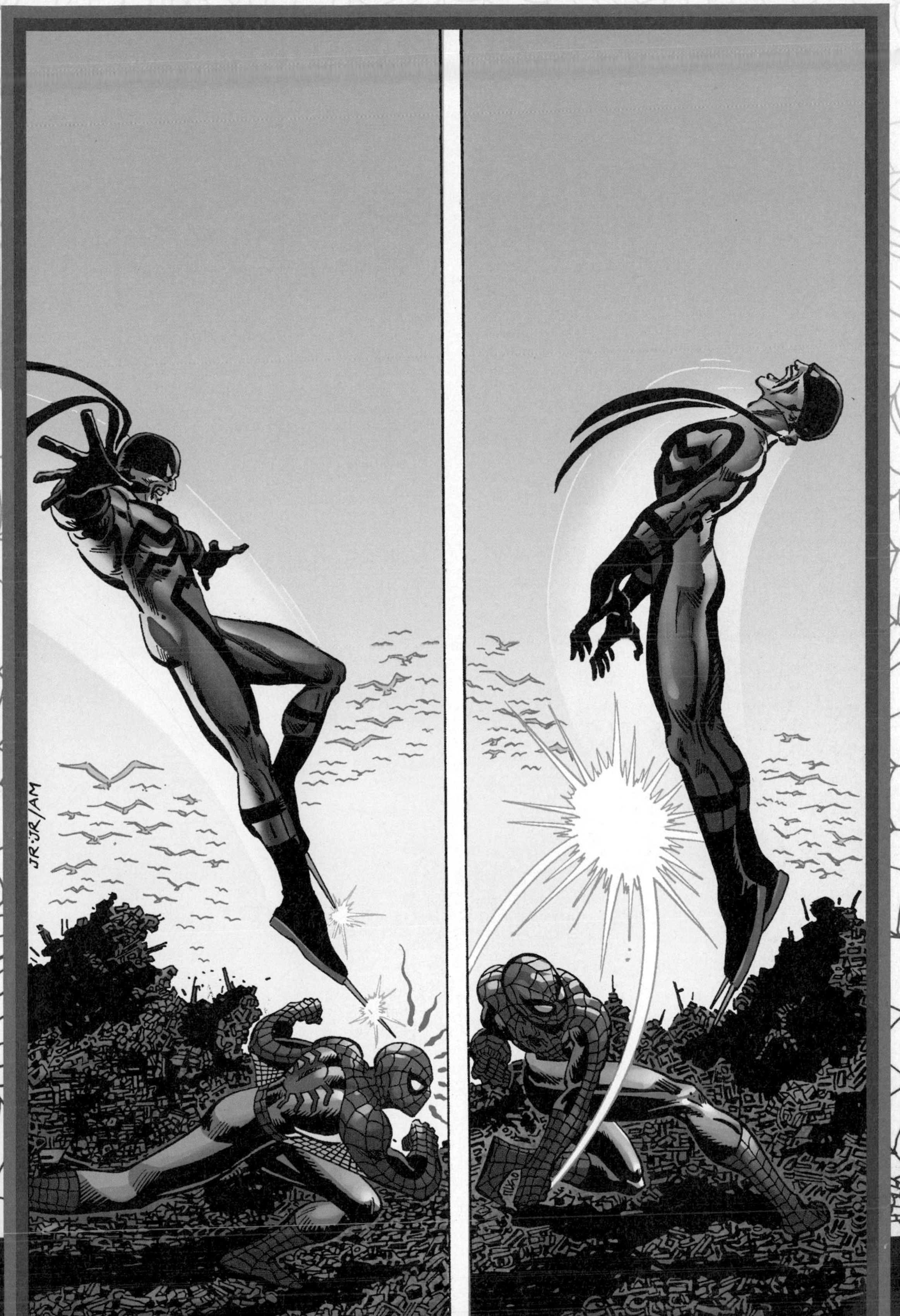
JR JR/AM

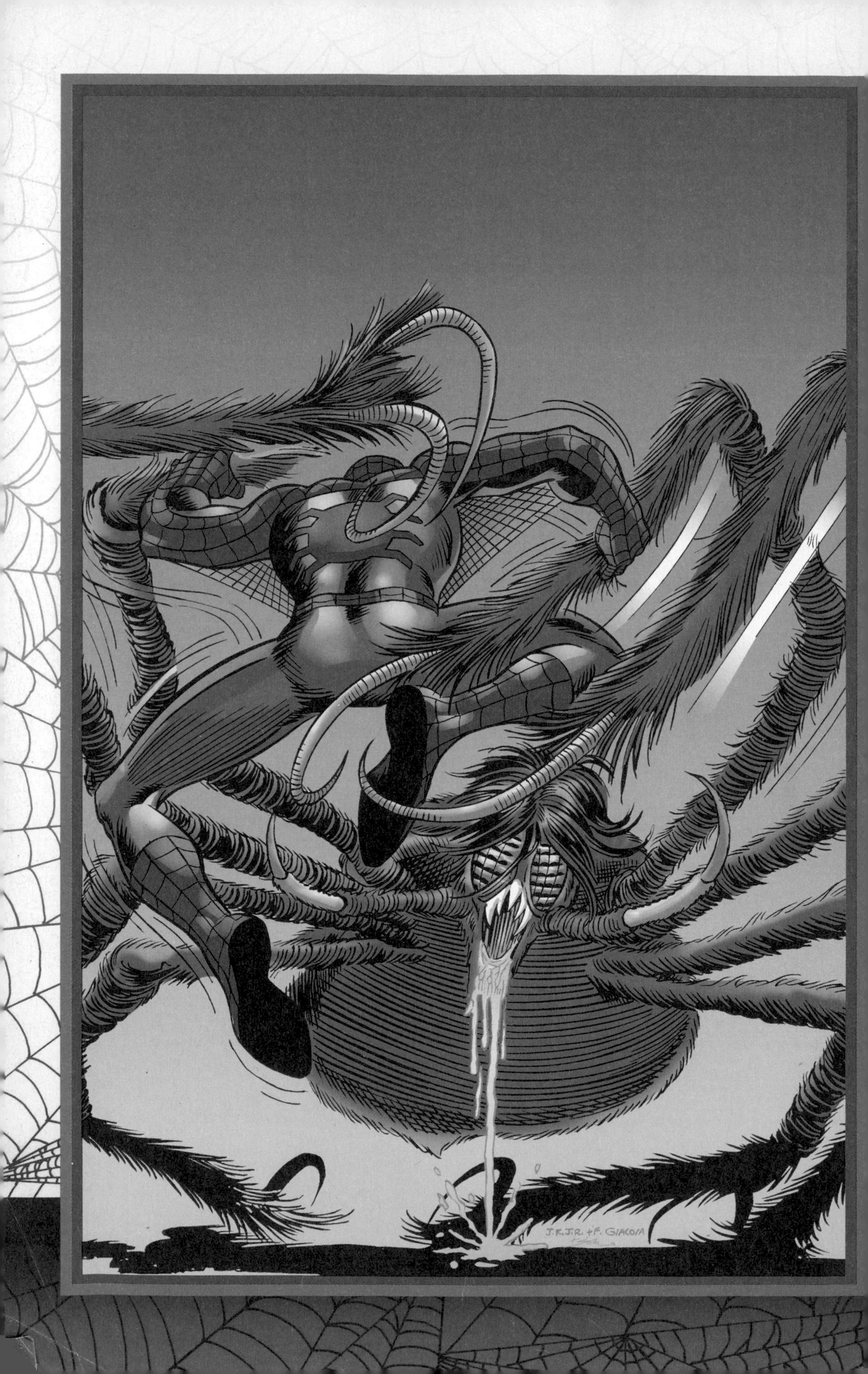
J.R.J.R. + F. GIACOIA